Get a FREE eBook

To register this book, scan the code or go to
www.manning.com/freebook/hurbans2

By registering you get

- **FREE eBook copy**
  download in PDF and ePub

- **FREE online access**
  to Manning's liveBook platform

- **FREE audio**
  read and listen online in liveBook

- **FREE AI Assistant**
  it knows the book and what you are reading when it answers

- **FREE in-book testing**
  fun tests to lock in your knowledge

In Manning's liveBook platform you can share discussions and comments with other readers, add your own bookmarks and highlights, insert personal notes anywhere on the page, see color versions of all the book's graphics, download source code and other resources, and more!
To register, scan the code or go to www.manning.com/freebook/hurbans2

 MANNING

grokking

AI Algorithms, Second Edition

How AI solves complex problems

Rishal Hurbans

MANNING
SHELTER ISLAND

For online information and ordering of this and other Manning books, please visit
www.manning.com. The publisher offers discounts on this book when ordered in quantity.
For more information, please contact

>Special Sales Department
>Manning Publications Co.
>20 Baldwin Road, PO Box 761
>Shelter Island, NY 11964
>Email: orders@manning.com

Manning Publications Co.
20 Baldwin Road
Shelter Island, NY 11964

Development editor: Elesha Hyde
Technical editor: Emmanuel Maggiori
Review editor: Dunja Nikitović
Production editor: Kathy Rossland
Copy editor: Keir Simpson
Proofreader: Jason Everett
Typesetter: Tamara Švelić Sabljić
Cover designer: Marija Tudor

ISBN 9781633434813
Printed in the United States of America

To the AI overlords: I did my part. We're cool, right?

brief contents

contents

preface

This preface aims to describe the evolution of technology, our need to automate, and our responsibility to make ethical decisions while using Artificial Intelligence (AI) to build the future.

Our obsession with technology and automation

Throughout history, humans have hungered to solve problems while reducing manual labor and overall effort. We've always strived to survive and conserve our energy through the development of tools and the automation of tasks. Some may argue that we have beautiful minds that seek innovation through creative problem-solving or creative works of literature, music, and art, but this book wasn't written to discuss philosophical questions about our being. This book is an overview of AI approaches that can be harnessed to address real-world problems practically. We solve hard problems to make life easier, safer, healthier, more fulfilling, and more enjoyable. All the advancements you see in history and around the world today, including AI, address the needs of individuals, communities, and nations.

To shape our future, we must understand some key milestones in our past. In many revolutions, human innovation changed the way we live and the way we think about and interact with the world. We continue to do this as we iterate and improve our tools, which open future possibilities (figure 1). This short high-level summary of history and philosophy is designed to establish a baseline understanding of technology and AI and spur thoughts on responsible decision-making in your projects.

Our obsession with technology and automation

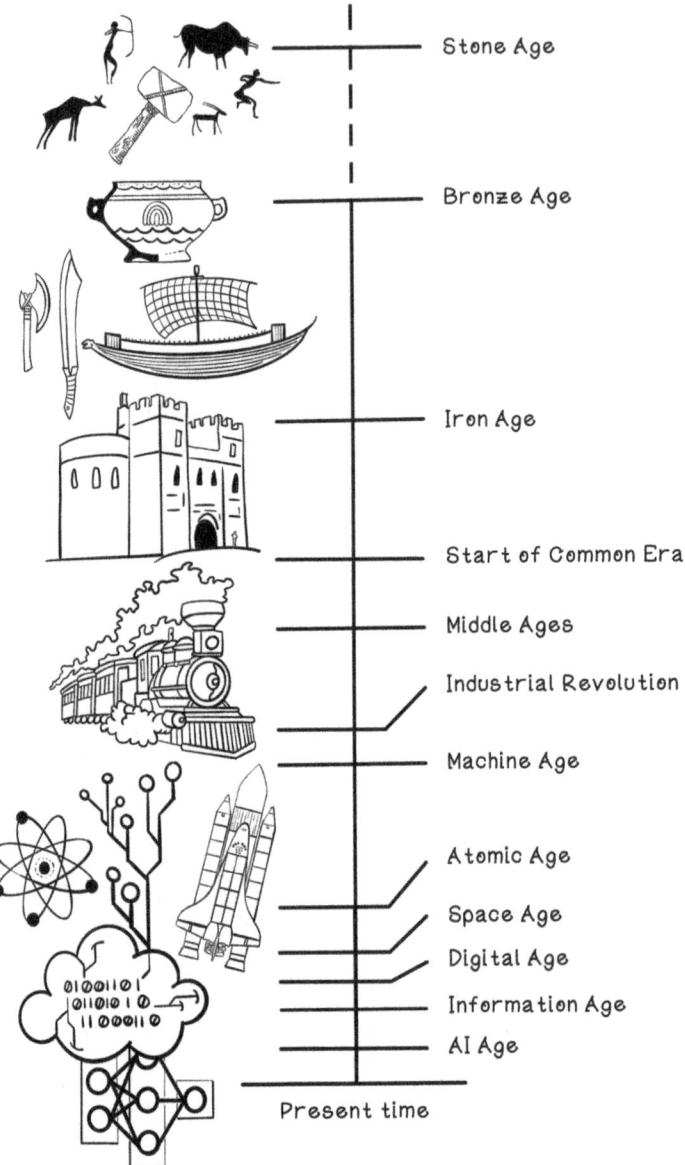

Stone Age

Bronze Age

Iron Age

Start of Common Era

Middle Ages

Industrial Revolution

Machine Age

Atomic Age

Space Age

Digital Age

Information Age

AI Age

Present time

Figure 1 A brief timeline of technological improvements in history

In the figure, the milestones are compressed in recent times. In the past 30 years, the most notable advancements have been the improvement of microchips, the wide adoption of personal computers, the boom of networked devices, and the digitization of industries to break physical borders and connect the world. These developments are also why AI has become a feasible and sensible area to pursue. The internet has connected the world and made it possible to collect mass amounts of data about almost anything. Advancements in computing hardware have given us the means to compute previously known algorithms using the massive amounts of data we've collected while discovering new algorithms. Industries have seen the need to use data and algorithms to make better decisions, solve harder problems, offer better solutions, and optimize life as people have done since the beginning of humanity.

Although we tend to think of technological progress as linear, by examining our history, we find that it's more likely that our progress is and will be exponential (figure 2). Advancements in technology move faster each year. New tools and techniques have to be learned, but problem-solving fundamentals underpin everything. This book includes foundation-level concepts that help us solve hard problems, but it also aims to make learning the complex concepts easier.

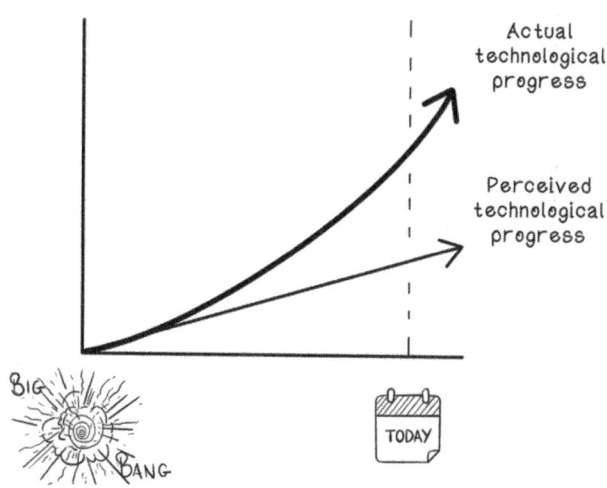

Figure 2 Perceived technological progress vs. actual technological progress

Automation can be perceived differently by different people. For a technologist, automation may mean writing scripts that make software development, deployment, and distribution seamless and less error-prone. For an engineer, it may mean streamlining a factory line for more throughput or fewer defects. For a farmer, it may mean using tools to optimize the yield of crops through automatic tractors and irrigation systems. Automation is any solution that reduces the need for human energy to favor productivity or add superior value compared with what a manual intervention would have added (figure 3).

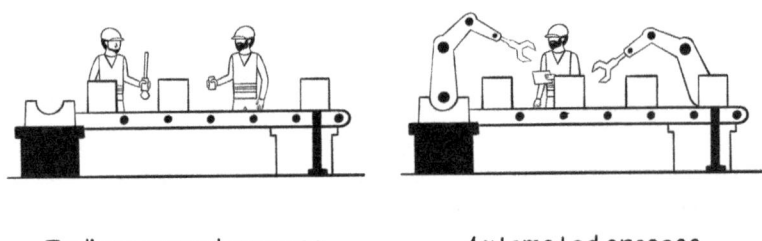

Figure 3 Manual processes vs. automated processes

If we think about reasons not to automate, one prominent reason is simply that under certain conditions, a person can do the task better, with less chance of failure and better accuracy. Humans are better than AI at performing tasks that require intuition about several perspectives in a situation, require abstract creative thinking, or prioritize understanding of social interactions and human nature. Nurses don't simply complete tasks; they also connect with and take care of their patients. Studies show that the human interaction with caring people is a factor in the healing process. Teachers don't simply offload knowledge; they also find creative ways to present knowledge, as well as mentor and guide students based on their ability, personality, and interests.

That said, there's a place for automation through technology, and there's a place for people too. With the innovations of today, automation via technology will be a close companion to any occupation.

Ethics, legal matters, and responsibility

You may wonder why a section on ethics and responsibility is in a technical book. Well, as we progress toward a world in which technology is intertwined with our way of life, the people who create the technology have more power than they know. Small contributions can have massive knock-on effects. It's important for our intentions to be benevolent and the output of our work to be harmless. Decisions and actions can be legal but unethical, for example (figure 4). Determining ethics is difficult because the topic is somewhat subjective, which is why it's important to include as many perspectives on problems and solutions as possible.

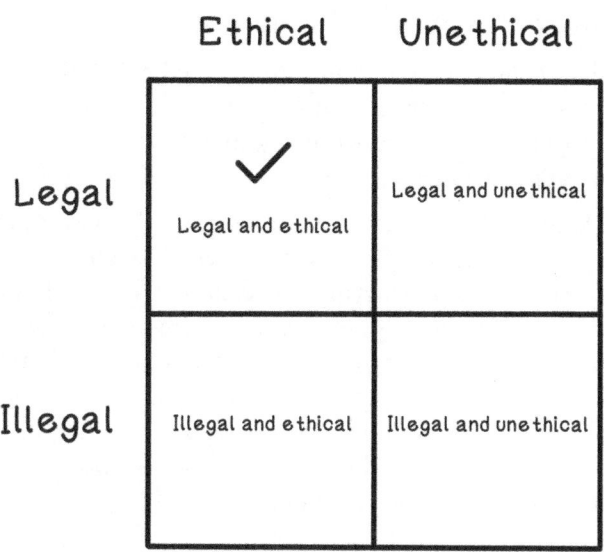

Figure 4 Aim for ethical and legal applications of technology.

Intention and effect: Understanding your vision and goals

When you create anything—such as a new physical product, service, or software—there's always a question about the intention behind it. Are you developing software that affects the world positively, or is your intention malevolent? Have you thought about the broader impact of what you're developing? Businesses always find ways to become more profitable and powerful, which is the whole point of growing a business. They use strategies to determine the best ways to beat the competition, gain more customers, and become even more influential. That said, businesses must ask themselves whether their intentions are pure, not only for the good of their customers and society in general but also for the survival and longevity of the business. Many famous scientists, engineers, and technologists have expressed a need to govern the use of AI to prevent misuse. As individuals, we also have an ethical obligation (and often an urge) to do what is right and establish a strong core set of values. When you're asked to do something that violates your principles, it's not just right but also crucial to voice your concerns.

Unintended use: Protecting against malicious use

It's important to identify and protect against unintended use. Although this goal may seem obvious and easy to accomplish, it's difficult to understand how people will use whatever you're creating and even more difficult to predict whether it aligns with your values and the values of your organization.

An example is the loudspeaker, which Peter Jensen and Edwin Pridham invented in 1915. The loudspeaker, originally called Magnavox, was used to play opera music to large crowds in San Francisco, which is quite a beautiful use of technology. The Nazi regime in Germany had other ideas, however: they placed loudspeakers in public places in such a way that almost everyone was subjected to Adolf Hitler's speeches and announcements. Because the monologues were unavoidable, people became more susceptible to Hitler's ideas, and in time, the Nazi regime gained greater support in Germany. That wasn't what Jensen and Pridham envisioned their invention being used for, but they couldn't have done much about it.

Times have changed, and we have more control of the things we build, especially software. It's still difficult to imagine how the technology you build may be used, but it's almost guaranteed that someone will find a way to use it in a way you didn't intend, with positive or negative consequences. Given this fact, we professionals in the technology industry and the organizations we work with must think of ways to mitigate harmful use as far as possible.

Unintended bias: Building solutions for everyone

When building AI systems, we use our understanding and experience in different problem spaces and domains. We also use algorithms that find patterns in data and act on it. It can't be denied that bias exists all around us. *Bias* is favor for or against some concept. In society, bias can be prejudice against a person or group of people, including (but not limited to) their gender, race, and beliefs. Many biases arise from emergent behavior in social interactions, events in history, and cultural and political views around the world. These biases affect the data we collect. Because AI algorithms work with this data, it's an inherent problem that the machine will learn these biases. From a technical perspective, we can engineer the system perfectly, but at the end of the day, humans interact with these systems, and it's our responsibility to minimize bias and prejudice as much as possible. Algorithms are only as good as the data we provide them. Understanding the data and the context in which it's being used is the first step in battling bias, and this understanding will help you build better solutions because you'll be well versed in the problem space. Providing balanced data with as little bias as possible should result in better solutions and benefit more people.

The law, privacy, and consent: Knowing the importance of core values

The legal aspect of what we do is hugely important. The law governs what we can and can't do in the interest of society as a whole. Because many laws were written when computers and the internet were less important in our lives than they are today, we find many gray areas in how we develop technology and what we're allowed to do with that technology. That said, laws are slowly changing to adapt to rapid innovation.

We compromise our privacy almost every hour of every day via our interactions on computers, mobile phones, smart devices, and sensors, for example. We transmit a vast amount of information about ourselves, some more personal than others. How is that data being processed and stored? We should consider these facts when building solutions. People should have a choice about what personal data is captured, processed, and stored; how that data is used; and who can potentially access that data. In my experience, people generally accept solutions that use their data to improve the products they use and add value to their lives. Most important, people are more accepting when they're given a choice and that choice is respected.

Singularity: Exploring the unknown

The *singularity* is the idea that we create an AI system so generally intelligent that it's capable of improving itself and expanding its intelligence to a stage where it becomes super intelligence. The concern is that humans can't understand or control something of this magnitude, which could change civilization as we know it for reasons we can't even comprehend. Some people are concerned that this intelligence may see humans as a threat; others propose that we may be to a super intelligence what ants are to us. We don't pay explicit attention to ants or concern ourselves about how they live, but if we're irritated by them, we deal with them swiftly. Whether or not these assumptions are accurate representations of the future, we must be responsible and think about the decisions we make because they ultimately affect a real person, groups of people, or the world at large.

acknowledgments

Writing this book has been one of the most challenging yet rewarding experiences I've had. I had to make time when I had none, find the right headspace while juggling many responsibilities, and create motivation while being caught up in the reality of life. I've learned and grown tremendously through this experience. Thank you, Bert Bates, for being a fantastic editor and mentor during the writing of the first edition of this book. I learned so much about effective teaching and written communication from you. Our discussions and debates and your empathy throughout the process helped mold this book into what it is.

Every project needs someone who's organized, with a finger on the pulse, making sure that things are happening. For this, I'd like to thank Elesha Hyde, my development editor. Working with you has been an absolute pleasure. You always provide direction and interesting insights about my work.

We always need people to bounce ideas off, and who better to annoy than your friends? I'd especially like to thank Hennie Brink for always being a great sounding board and pillar of support.

For ensuring technical rigor and objective feedback, I'd like to thank technical editor Emmanuel Maggiori. Emmanuel is a 10-year AI industry insider and author of the book *Smart Until It's Dumb*. He has developed AI for a wide variety of applications, from extracting objects from satellite images to packaging holiday deals for millions of travelers every day.

I'd also like to thank review editor Dunja Nikitović, copy editor Keir Simpson, proofreader Jason Everett, typesetter Tamara Švelić Sabljić, and production editor Kathy Rossland.

Finally, I'd like to thank all the reviewers who took the time to read the manuscript of the second edition throughout development and provided invaluable feedback that made the book better in many ways: David Jacobs,

Denise Sison, Evgueni Serdiouk, Frances Buontempo, Gavin Baumanis, James Dietrich, Johannes Ball, Joseph Catanzarite, Ken Byrne, Kévin Etienne, Kostas Passadis, Rodolfo Allendes, Sandra Pintor, Senzeyu Zhang, and Serhii Savin.

about this book

Grokking AI Algorithms was written and illustrated to make understanding and implementing AI algorithms and their uses in solving problems more accessible to the average person in the technology industry through the use of relatable analogies, practical examples, and visual explanations.

Who should read this book

Grokking AI Algorithms is for software developers and anyone in the software industry who wants to grasp the intuitions and uncover the workings and algorithms behind AI through practical examples and visual explanations instead of going through theoretical deep dives and mathematical proofs.

This book is aimed at anyone who understands basic computer programming concepts, including variables, data types, arrays, conditional statements, iterators, classes, and functions. Experience in any language is sufficient. The book is also for anyone who understands basic mathematical concepts such as data variables, the representation of functions, and how to plot data and functions on a graph.

A fundamental understanding of AI algorithms is becoming more useful for many roles in the software industry. Gone are the days when AI was solely the domain of research scientists and academic labs. Today, AI helps power searches, optimize delivery routes, and personalize user interfaces. As these tools become standard components of the software stack, engineers, product managers, and architects alike must look beyond the black box to understand the mechanics that drive them. By grasping the intuition behind these algorithms, we move from simply consuming APIs to building smarter, more resilient systems.

How this book is organized: A road map

This book contains 12 chapters, each focusing on a different AI algorithm or algorithmic approach. The early chapters cover fundamental algorithms and concepts that form a foundation for learning about more sophisticated algorithms later in the book.

- *Chapter 1, Intuition of AI*—Introduces the intuition and fundamental concepts that surround data, types of problems, categories of algorithms and paradigms, and use cases for AI algorithms
- *Chapter 2, Search fundamentals*—Covers the core concepts of data structures and approaches for primitive search algorithms and their uses
- *Chapter 3, Intelligent search*—Goes beyond primitive search algorithms and introduces search algorithms for finding solutions more optimally, as well as finding solutions in a competitive environment
- *Chapter 4, Evolutionary algorithms*—Dives into the workings of genetic algorithms in which solutions to problems are iteratively generated and improved upon by mimicking evolution in nature
- *Chapter 5, Advanced evolutionary approaches*—Continues the topic of genetic algorithms but tackles advanced concepts involving how steps in the algorithm can be adjusted to solve different types of problems more optimally
- *Chapter 6, Swarm intelligence: Ants*—Digs into the intuition for swarm intelligence and works through how the Ant Colony Optimization algorithm uses a theory of how ants live and work to solve hard problems
- *Chapter 7, Swarm intelligence: Particles*—Continues the topic of swarm algorithms while diving into what optimization problems are and how they're solved using Particle Swarm Optimization, seeking good solutions in large search spaces
- *Chapter 8, Machine learning*—Works through a machine learning workflow for data preparation, processing, modeling, and testing to solve regression problems with linear regression, and classification problems with decision trees
- *Chapter 9, Artificial neural networks*—Uncovers the intuition, logical steps, and mathematical calculations in training and using an artificial neural network (ANN) to find patterns in data and make predictions while highlighting its place in a machine learning workflow
- *Chapter 10, Reinforcement learning*—Covers the intuition of reinforcement learning from behavioral psychology and works through the Q-learning algorithm for agents to learn good and bad decisions to make in an environment
- *Chapter 11, Large language models*—Explores the data pipeline for training language models using the Transformer architecture, where text data is encoded in machine-

understandable numbers and meaning is found from relationships to generate intelligent text output

- *Chapter 12, Generative image models*—Covers the intuition and process for image generation using diffusion, showing how a model learns from a text prompt to mold random noise into a desired image

The chapters should be read from start to end sequentially. Concepts and understandings are built up as the chapters progress. It's useful to reference the Python code in the repository after reading each chapter to experiment with and gain practical insight into how the respective algorithm can be implemented.

About the code

This book contains Python code to focus on the intuition and logical thinking behind the algorithms. This code is to be treated as samples. For an in-depth look at working runnable Python code for all algorithms described in the book, visit the GitHub page https://github.com/rishal-hurbans/Grokking-Artificial-Intelligence-Algorithms. Setup instructions and comments are provided in the source code to guide you as you learn. One potential learning approach is to read each chapter and then reference the code to cement your understanding of the algorithms.

The Python source code is intended to be a reference for implementing the algorithms. These examples are optimized for learning and *are not for production use*. The code was written to serve as a teaching tool. Using established libraries and frameworks is recommended for projects that will make their way to production because they're usually optimized for performance, well tested, and well supported.

This book contains many examples of source code both in listings and inline with normal text. In both cases, source code is formatted in a `fixed-width font like this` to separate it from ordinary text. Sometimes, code is also **in bold** to highlight code that has changed from previous steps in the chapter, such as when a new feature adds to an existing line of code.

In many cases, the original source code has been reformatted; we've added line breaks and reworked indentation to accommodate the available page space in the book. In rare cases, even this was not enough, and listings include line-continuation markers (➥). Also, comments in the source code are often removed when the code is described in the text. Code annotations accompany many of the code samples, highlighting important concepts.

You can get executable snippets of code from the liveBook (online) version of this book at https://livebook.manning.com/book/grokking-ai-algorithms-second-edition. The complete code for the examples in the book is available for download on the Manning

website at https://www.manning.com/books/grokking-ai-algorithms-second-edition
and on GitHub at https://github.com/rishal-hurbans/Grokking-Artificial-Intelligence
-Algorithms.

liveBook discussion forum

Purchase of *Grokking AI Algorithms* includes free access to liveBook, Manning's online
reading platform. Using liveBook's exclusive discussion features, you can attach
comments to the book globally or to specific sections or paragraphs. It's a snap to
make notes for yourself, ask and answer technical questions, and receive help from the
author and other users. To access the forum, go to https://livebook.manning.com/book/
grokking-ai-algorithms-second-edition/discussion.

Manning's commitment to our readers is to provide a venue where meaningful dialogue
between individual readers and between readers and the author can take place. It is not
a commitment to any specific amount of participation on the part of the author, whose
contribution to the forum remains voluntary (and unpaid). We suggest that you try
asking the author some challenging questions lest his interest stray! The forum and the
archives of previous discussions will be accessible from the publisher's website as long as
the book is in print.

Other online resources

- Source code for *Grokking AI Algorithms*, Second Edition: https://github.com/rishal
  -hurbans/Grokking-Artificial-Intelligence-Algorithms
- Author website: https://rhurbans.com

about the author

RISHAL HURBANS is a technologist, entrepreneur, and author who is passionate about crafting innovative products and meaningful experiences. He holds a Bachelor of Science with Honors in Computer Science degree and has more than a decade of expertise delivering diverse technology solutions across the finance, health, agriculture, mining, and aviation industries.

Rishal is driven by a deep interest in making complex concepts accessible through visual, intuitive, and practical experiences. He has delivered dozens of keynotes and workshops around the world on AI, software engineering, and leadership. Rishal continues to build at the intersection of design, technology, and creativity, guided by the belief that technology should amplify human potential. For more about Rishal Hurbans, see https://rhurbans.com.

In this chapter

- Defining AI as we know it

- Gaining an intuition of concepts underpinning AI and important terminology

- Defining problem types and approaches to solving them

- Outlining the AI algorithms discussed in this book

- Exploring real-world use cases for AI algorithms

Artificial Intelligence, or AI, has become a foundational tool in modern software engineering. Developers use AI tools to create software, and many software applications now take advantage of content generated by large language models (LLMs), agents, and other AI-powered features. A new generation of easy-to-use tools, frameworks, and APIs offering quick access to sophisticated models makes it easier than ever to use AI without really understanding how it works. As a technology professional, though, it pays to have an idea what's going on inside the AI black box.

In this book, we'll discuss how different types of AI work as we explore the basic structures of their implementations. As we go, we'll trace the evolution of algorithmic intelligence, moving from the explicit logic of search and evolutionary algorithms through the statistical principles of machine learning and finally into the complex architectures of deep learning and generative AI. I hope that as you start to "grok" AI, you'll be better equipped to reason about, implement, and innovate with the systems that are reshaping the world. Now let's crack open the black box!

What is artificial intelligence?

Intelligence is a bit of a mystery. Philosophers, psychologists, and engineers view intelligence differently. Yet we recognize it everywhere: in the collective work of ants, the flocking of birds, and our own thinking and behavior. Great minds have long debated the nature of intelligence. Salvador Dalí saw it as *ambition*; Einstein tied it to *imagination*; Stephen Hawking defined it as the *ability to adapt*. Although there is no single agreed-on definition, we generally use human behavior as the benchmark.

At a minimum, intelligence means being *autonomous* and *adaptive*. Autonomous entities act without constant instruction, and adaptive ones adjust to changing environments. Whether the intelligence is biological or mechanical, its fuel is always data. The sights we see, the sounds we hear, and the measurements of our world are all inputs. We consume, process, and act on this data; therefore, understanding AI begins with understanding the data that powers it.

Defining AI

Generative AI, like natural language models and chatbots, has become the public face of AI. In research and practice, however, AI is far more diverse. The complex systems we use today are built on many foundational algorithms geared to solving different problems—from specific tasks such as searching information effectively to general challenges such as understanding language. Throughout this book, we'll explore these algorithms and their use cases and develop an *intuition*—a solid understanding and mental model—for modern machine learning, artificial neural networks (ANNs), and generative models.

For the sake of our sanity, let's define *AI* as systems that perform tasks typically requiring human intelligence. These tasks include simulating senses like vision and hearing, as well as mastering language to reason about complex problems. Here are some examples of tasks that exhibit AI:

- Playing and winning complex games
- Detecting cancer tumors from body-image scans

- Generating artwork based on a natural language prompt
- Driving cars autonomously
- Using chatbots encoded with the history of information on the internet

Douglas Hofstadter famously quipped, "AI is whatever hasn't been done yet." A calculator was once considered intelligent; now it's taken for granted. Whether an algorithm fits a strict academic definition matters less than its utility: if it solves a complex problem autonomously, it belongs in our toolkit.

The algorithms in this book have been classified as AI algorithms in the past or present. It doesn't matter whether they fit a specific definition of AI; what matters is that they're useful. Intuition about them forms a robust understanding from foundational to sophisticated applications.

Data is the fuel for AI algorithms

Data is the fuel that makes AI algorithms work. With the incorrect choice of data, badly represented data, or missing data, algorithms perform poorly, so the outcome is only as good as the data provided. The world is filled with data, and that data exists in forms that we can't even sense. Data can represent values that are measured numerically, such as the current temperature in the Arctic, the number of cats in a field, or a person's current age in days. All these examples involve capturing accurate numeric values based on facts. It's difficult to misinterpret this data: the temperature at a specific location at a specific point in time, for example, is absolutely true and not subject to any bias. This type of data is known as *quantitative data*. But cherry-picking (or sampling) specific data points intentionally or unintentionally can create bias.

Data can also represent values of observations, such as the smell of a flower or one's subjective review of a movie. This type of data is known as *qualitative data*. Sometimes, this data is difficult to interpret because it's not an absolute truth but a perception of someone's truth. Figure 1.1 illustrates some of the quantitative and qualitative data around us.

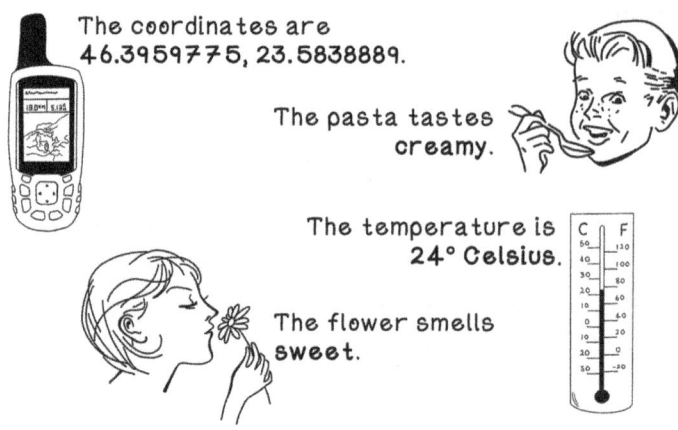

The coordinates are
46.3959775, 23.5838889.

The pasta tastes
creamy.

The temperature is
24° Celsius.

The flower smells
sweet.

Figure 1.1 Examples of data around us

Data is raw facts about things, so recordings of it should have no bias. In the real world, however, data is collected, recorded, and related by people based on a specific context with a specific understanding of how the data may be used. Constructing meaningful insights to answer questions based on data creates *information*. Furthermore, consciously applying information in conjunction with experiences creates *knowledge*, which is partly what we try to simulate with AI algorithms. Consider, for example, how the following concepts apply to a hospital patient:

- *Data*—The patient's temperature is 38°C.
- *Information*—The patient has a fever.
- *Knowledge*—We should administer medication to lower the fever.

Figure 1.2 shows how quantitative and qualitative data can be interpreted. Standardized instruments such as clocks, calculators, and scales are usually used to measure quantitative data, whereas our senses of smell, sound, taste, touch, and sight, as well as our subjective thoughts, are usually used to create qualitative data.

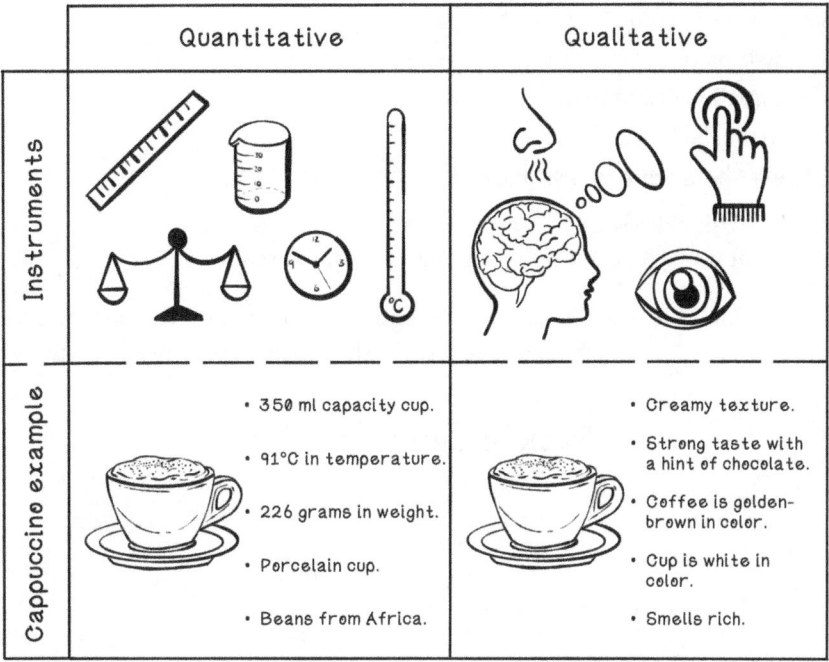

Figure 1.2 Qualitative data vs. quantitative data

Data, information, and knowledge can be interpreted differently based on a person's level of understanding of that domain and their outlook on the world. This fact has consequences for the quality of solutions that we build, making the "scientific method" aspect of creating technology hugely important. By following repeatable scientific processes to capture data, conduct experiments, and report findings accurately, we can strive to achieve more accurate results and better solutions when processing data with algorithms.

Algorithms are like recipes

Now we have a loose definition of AI and an understanding of the importance of data. Because we'll explore several AI algorithms throughout this book, it's useful to understand exactly what an algorithm is. An *algorithm* is a set of instructions and rules provided as a specification to accomplish a goal. Algorithms typically accept inputs, and after several finite steps in which the algorithm progresses through varying states, an output is produced.

Even a task as simple as reading a book can be represented as an algorithm. Here's an example of the steps involved in reading this book:

1. Find the book *Grokking AI Algorithms*.
2. Open the book.
3. While unread pages remain,
   a. Read a page.
   b. Think about what you've learned.
   c. Turn to the next page.
4. Think about how you can apply your learning in the real world.

An algorithm can be compared to a recipe (figure 1.3). Given ingredients and tools as inputs and instructions for creating a specific dish, a meal is produced as the output.

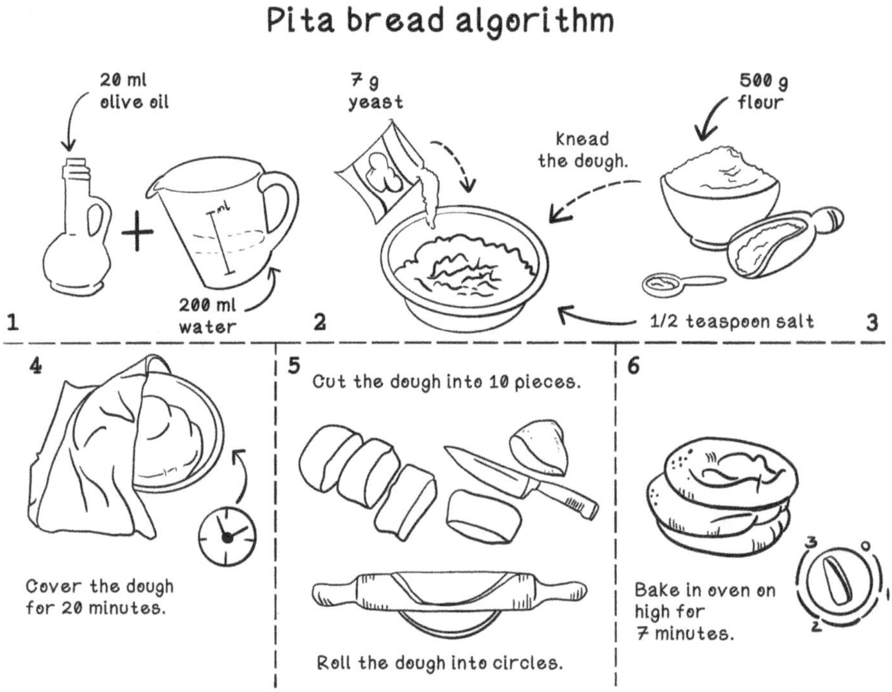

Pita bread algorithm

Figure 1.3 An example showing that an algorithm is like a recipe

Algorithms are used in many solutions. We can enable live video chat across the world through compression algorithms, for example, and we can navigate cities through map applications that use real-time routing algorithms. Even a simple "Hello World" program has many algorithms at play that translate the human-readable programming language into machine code and execute the instructions on specific hardware. You can find algorithms everywhere if you look closely enough.

To illustrate something more closely related to the algorithms in this book, figure 1.4 shows a number-guessing-game algorithm represented as a flow chart. The computer generates a random number in a given range, and the player attempts to guess that number. The algorithm has discrete steps that perform an action or determine a decision before moving to the next operation. You'll see flow charts like the one in figure 1.4 throughout the book to explain the life cycles of algorithms.

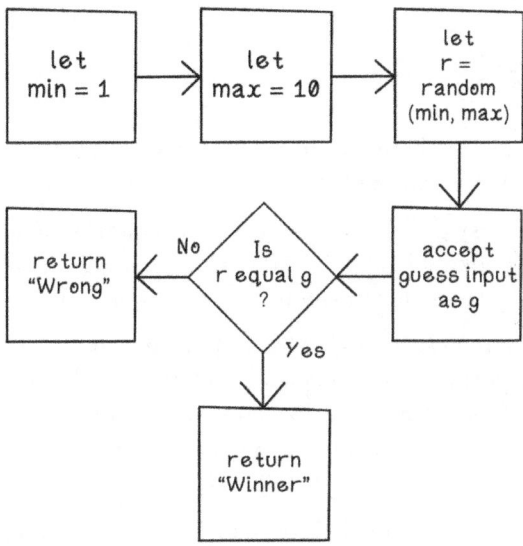

Figure 1.4 A number-guessing-game algorithm flow chart

Algorithms vs. models

Algorithms are the logic; models are the result. To understand how AI systems are built, we must distinguish between the process (the recipe) and the representation (the meal). In this book, we'll see two distinct patterns depending on the type of AI we're using.

The algorithm as the active solver

Some algorithms actively solve a problem in real-time. A search algorithm, for example, is the star of the show for navigating a map or calculating the best move in a game. Search algorithms are deployed to production and run fresh every time to solve problems based on the current situation.

The algorithm as the builder

In machine learning and deep learning, the relationship changes. Here, the algorithm is a builder; its job is to look at data and construct a representation of the world. The algorithm is used to train a model, and the model is the artifact that is eventually deployed to production. This model contains the intelligence—pretrained by the algorithm—that is used for problem-solving.

The evolution of AI

A look back at the strides made in AI is useful for understanding that old techniques and new ideas can be harnessed to solve problems in innovative ways.

AI isn't a new idea. History is filled with myths of mechanical men and autonomous "thinking" machines. Looking back, we find that we're standing on the shoulders of giants. Perhaps we ourselves can contribute to the pool of knowledge in a small way.

Looking at past developments highlights the importance of understanding the fundamentals of AI; algorithms from decades ago are critical in many modern AI implementations. This book starts with fundamental algorithms that help build the intuition of problem-solving and gradually moves to more complex and modern approaches.

Figure 1.5 isn't an exhaustive list of achievements in AI—simply a small set of examples. History is filled with many more breakthroughs.

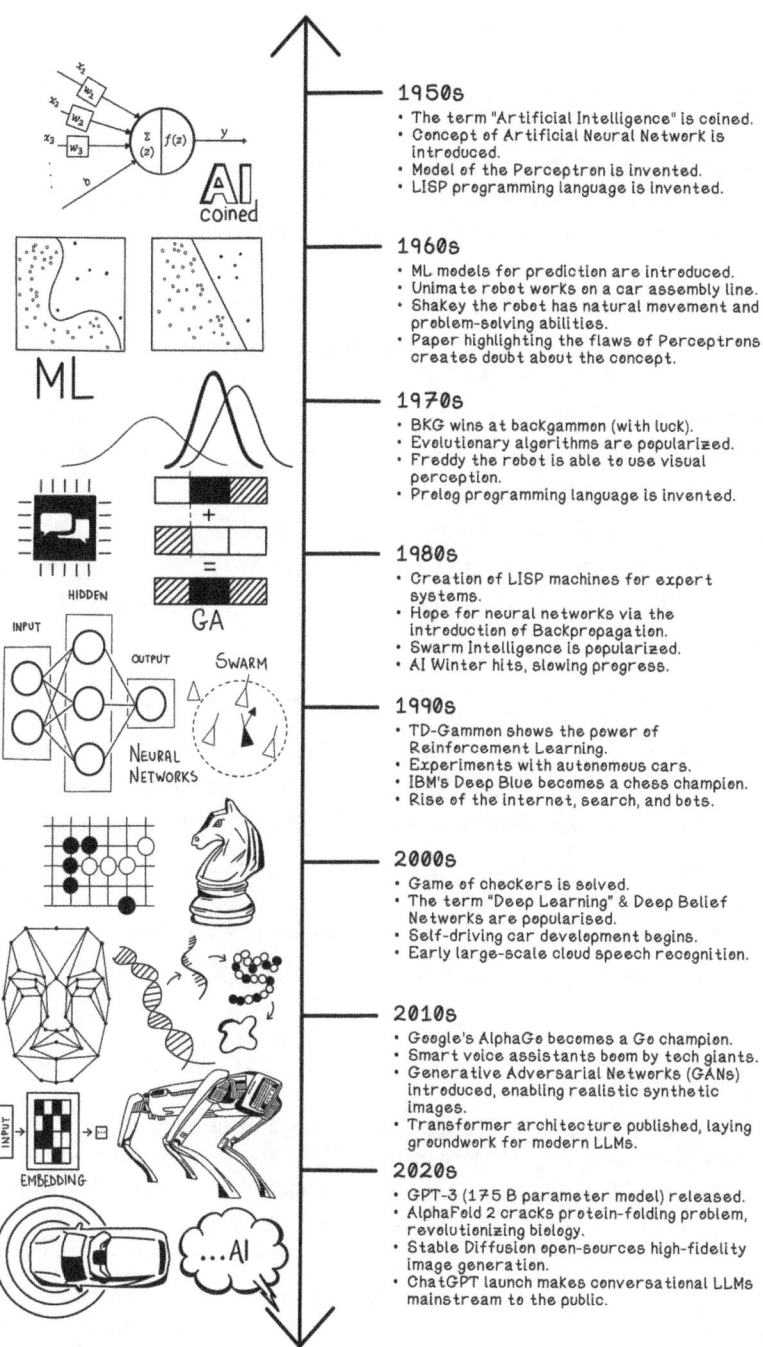

1950s
- The term "Artificial Intelligence" is coined.
- Concept of Artificial Neural Network is introduced.
- Model of the Perceptron is invented.
- LISP programming language is invented.

1960s
- ML models for prediction are introduced.
- Unimate robot works on a car assembly line.
- Shakey the robot has natural movement and problem-solving abilities.
- Paper highlighting the flaws of Perceptrons creates doubt about the concept.

1970s
- BKG wins at backgammon (with luck).
- Evolutionary algorithms are popularized.
- Freddy the robot is able to use visual perception.
- Prolog programming language is invented.

1980s
- Creation of LISP machines for expert systems.
- Hope for neural networks via the introduction of Backpropagation.
- Swarm Intelligence is popularized.
- AI Winter hits, slowing progress.

1990s
- TD-Gammon shows the power of Reinforcement Learning.
- Experiments with autonomous cars.
- IBM's Deep Blue becomes a chess champion.
- Rise of the internet, search, and bots.

2000s
- Game of checkers is solved.
- The term "Deep Learning" & Deep Belief Networks are popularised.
- Self-driving car development begins.
- Early large-scale cloud speech recognition.

2010s
- Google's AlphaGo becomes a Go champion.
- Smart voice assistants boom by tech giants.
- Generative Adversarial Networks (GANs) introduced, enabling realistic synthetic images.
- Transformer architecture published, laying groundwork for modern LLMs.

2020s
- GPT-3 (175 B parameter model) released.
- AlphaFold 2 cracks protein-folding problem, revolutionizing biology.
- Stable Diffusion open-sources high-fidelity image generation.
- ChatGPT launch makes conversational LLMs mainstream to the public.

Figure 1.5 The evolution of AI

Different types of problems

AI algorithms are powerful, but they're not silver bullets that can solve any problem (yet). But what are these "problems"? This section looks at types of problems that we commonly experience in computer science. This intuition can help us identify these problems in the real world and guide the choice of algorithms we use. A grasp of this terminology will be useful as we progress through the book.

Search problems: Finding a path to a solution

A *search problem* involves a situation that has multiple possible solutions, each of which represents a sequence of steps (path) toward a goal. Some solutions contain overlapping paths to success; some are better than others; some are cheaper to achieve than others. A "better" solution is determined by the specific context; a "cheaper" solution means computationally cheaper to execute.

Consider the example of determining the shortest path between cities on a map. Many routes may be available, with different distances and traffic conditions, but some routes are better than others. Many AI algorithms are based on the concept of searching a space of possible solutions.

Optimization problems: Finding a good solution

An *optimization problem* involves a situation in which a vast number of valid solutions exists and the best solution is difficult to find. This type of problem usually has an enormous number of possible solutions, which differ in how well they solve the problem.

An example is packing luggage in the trunk of a car. The goal is to maximize the use of space while adhering to strict constraints, such as the fixed dimensions of the trunk or a weight limit. Many combinations are available, but valid solutions must fit within these boundaries. If the trunk is packed effectively, more luggage can fit in it.

Local best vs. global best

Because optimization problems have many solutions and because these solutions exist at different points in the search space, the concepts of local bests and global bests come into play. A *local best* solution is the best solution within a specific area in the search space, and a *global best* is the best solution in the entire search space. The challenge for AI is avoiding the trap of a local best (a good solution) while missing the global best (the perfect solution).

Suppose that you're searching for the best restaurant. You may find the best restaurant in your local area, but it may not necessarily be the best restaurant in the country or the best restaurant in the world. The best in the world is the global best.

Prediction and classification problems: Learning from patterns in data

Prediction problems occur when we have data about something and want to try to find patterns and predict a numerical value. We might have data about different vehicles and their engine sizes, as well as each vehicle's fuel consumption. Can we predict the fuel consumption of a new model of vehicle, given its engine size? If the historical data shows a correlation between engine sizes and fuel consumption, this prediction is possible.

Classification problems are similar to prediction problems, but instead of trying to find an exact value such as fuel consumption, we try to find a category. If we have the physical dimensions of a vehicle, its engine size, and the number of seats, can we predict whether that vehicle is a motorcycle, sedan, or sport-utility vehicle? Classification problems require finding patterns in the data that group examples into categories.

> TIP Here's a helpful rule of thumb for remembering the difference: prediction outputs a quantity (a number), whereas classification outputs a label (a category).

Clustering problems: Identifying patterns in data

Clustering problems are scenarios in which we uncover trends and relationships from data, using different aspects of the data to group examples in different ways. Given cost and location data about restaurants, for example, we may find that younger people tend to frequent locations where the food is cheaper. Clustering aims to find relationships in data even when a precise question isn't being asked. This approach is also useful for gaining a better understanding of data to inform what we might be able to do with it.

Deterministic models: Getting the same result each time

Deterministic models are models that, given a specific input, return a consistent output. If you input 100°C into a unit conversion model, the output will always be 212°F. It doesn't matter what time of day it is, where you are, or how many times you repeat the calculation; the relationship is fixed, and the result never varies.

Probabilistic models: Getting potentially different results each time

Probabilistic models are models that, given a specific input, return an outcome from a set of possible outcomes. Probabilistic models usually have an element of controlled randomness that contributes to the possible set of outcomes. If you type the phrase "The best pet is a…" on your phone, the device might autocomplete various words based on words you've used in the past. It might assign *cat* 40%, *dog* 35%, and *goldfish* 25%, for example. If you run this model once, it might pick *cat*. If you run the model again, the element of randomness might cause it to pick *dog*. The input is the same, but the output varies based on the probability distribution.

Intuition of AI concepts

Trying to make sense of different but similar words and concepts in AI can be daunting. In this section, we demystify them and form a road map of the topics covered in this book. Let's dive into the levels of AI, introduced in figure 1.6.

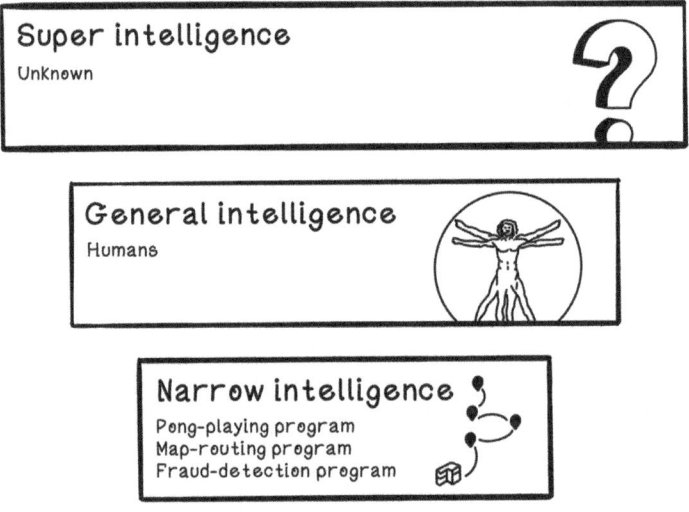

Figure 1.6 Levels of AI

Narrow intelligence: Specific-purpose solutions

Artificial narrow intelligence (ANI) systems specialize in a single domain and can't transfer knowledge. A model trained to analyze spending behavior, for example, can't identify cats in an image. But distinct narrow systems can be combined to simulate broader intelligence. A voice assistant, for example, stacks speech recognition, web search, and recommendation algorithms to interact naturally with users. Different narrow intelligence systems can be combined in sensible ways to create something greater. A modern voice assistant isn't one smart brain; it's a combination of distinct narrow models (speech-to-text + web search + audio generation) working together to simulate a conversation.

General intelligence: Humanlike solutions

Artificial general intelligence (AGI) mirrors human adaptability: the ability to apply knowledge from one problem to another. If you felt pain when touching something extremely hot as a child, you can extrapolate: you know that other hot things have a chance of hurting you. Just as a child generalizes that "extremely hot" implies "danger" across different objects, AGI integrates memory, reasoning, and sensory input to solve novel problems. Unlike the voice assistant, which would require a code update to learn a new skill, an AGI could simply figure it out. If you asked a narrow assistant to perform a task it wasn't programmed for (such as negotiating a better price for your flight), it would fail. An AGI, however, would understand the intent of "saving money," apply reasoning from other contexts, and attempt the negotiation. Although true AGI remains elusive, modern LLMs represent a significant step toward this flexible reasoning.

Super intelligence: The great unknown

Artificial super intelligence (ASI) refers to systems that surpass the brightest human minds in every field. Although ASI is often depicted in science fiction as apocalyptic, the core definition is simply intelligence beyond our comprehension. Whether humans can create something smarter than ourselves remains a philosophical debate, making ASI a realm of pure speculation for now.

Old AI and New AI

Sometimes, we use the notions of Old AI and New AI.

Old AI is explicit logic and search that relies on humans to encode the rules of the world. The machine doesn't learn; it calculates solutions based on logic and rules provided by programmers. A classic example is the Minimax algorithm in chess: the human defines how pieces move and how to score a board position, and the AI uses computational power and smart branching to search future moves and find the best one.

New AI learns from data and flips the Old AI approach. Instead of being told what the rules are or how to score a situation, these models analyze vast datasets to figure things out for themselves. A modern neural network playing chess, for example, isn't following hardcoded heuristics; it has played millions of games against itself to learn patterns of victory that human programmers might not even understand.

We learn about both categories because, although search algorithms are often categorized as Old AI, the algorithms aren't obsolete; in fact, they're often paired with modern techniques to solve difficult problems. LLMs use search strategies to determine the best sequence of words to generate, for example. You need to understand the logic of search before you can understand how a neural network searches for an optimal solution. Figure 1.7 illustrates the relationships among several concepts within AI.

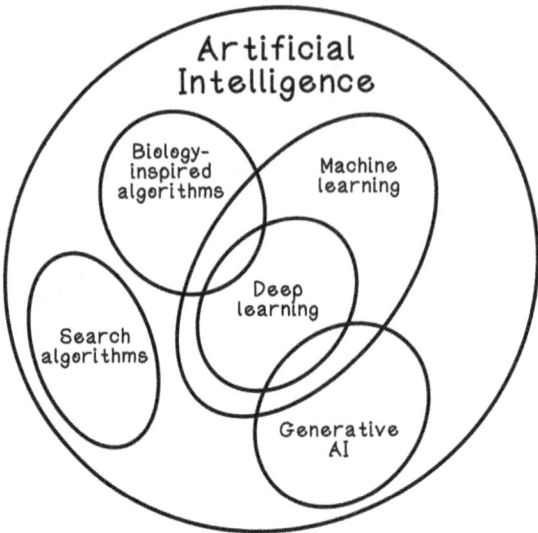

Figure 1.7 Categorization of concepts within AI

Search algorithms

Search algorithms are the bedrock of problem-solving. They're essential when a goal requires taking a sequence of actions, such as navigating a maze or calculating the winning move in chess. Instead of brute-forcing every possibility, which could take thousands of hours, smart search algorithms evaluate future states to find the optimal path efficiently. We start our journey here. Chapter 2 covers the fundamental search algorithms, and chapter 3 dives into intelligent search methods that strategize rather than guess.

Biology-inspired algorithms

When we look at the world around us, we notice incredible things happening in creatures, plants, and other living organisms, such as the cooperation of ants in gathering food, the flocking of birds when migrating, the estimation of how organic brains work, and the evolution of organisms to produce stronger offspring. By observing and learning from these phenomena, we've gained knowledge of how these organic systems operate and how simple rules can result in incredible emergent intelligent behavior.

Consider two types of biology-inspired algorithms: evolutionary and swarm. Evolutionary algorithms, inspired by Darwinian theory, use reproduction and mutation to evolve code that improves over generations. We explore this survival of the fittest in chapters 4 and 5.

Swarm intelligence mimics the collective power of "dumb" individuals acting smart as a group. Chapter 6 explores intelligent pathfinding inspired by ants, and chapter 7 covers solving optimization problems inspired by the way animals flock.

Machine learning algorithms

Chapter 8 takes a statistical approach to training models to learn from data. The umbrella of machine learning has a variety of algorithms that we can harness to improve our understanding of relationships in data, make decisions, and make predictions based on that data. There are three main approaches in machine learning:

- *Supervised learning* means training models with algorithms when the training data has known outcomes for a question being asked, such as determining the type of fruit if we have a set of data that includes the weight, color, texture, and fruit label for each example.

- *Unsupervised learning* uncovers hidden relationships and structures within the data that guide us to ask the dataset relevant questions. It may find patterns in properties of similar fruits and group them accordingly, which can inform the exact questions we want to ask the data. These core concepts and algorithms help us create a foundation for exploring advanced algorithms in the future.

- *Reinforcement learning* is inspired by behavioral psychology. In short, it describes rewarding a person if they perform a useful action and penalizing them if they perform an unfavorable action. When a child achieves good results on their report card, they're usually rewarded, but poor performance sometimes results in punishment, reinforcing the behavior of achieving good results. Chapter 10 explores how reinforcement learning is used to train intelligent models.

Deep learning algorithms

Deep learning is a broader family of approaches and algorithms that are used to achieve narrow intelligence and strive for general intelligence. Deep learning usually implies that the approach is attempting to solve a problem in a more general way, such as linguistic intelligence or spatial reasoning, or is being applied to problems that require more generalization, such as speech recognition or computer vision. Deep learning approaches usually employ many layers of ANNs. By using different layers of intelligent components, each layer solves specialized problems; together, the layers solve complex problems toward a greater goal. Identifying any object in an image, for example, is a general problem, but it can be broken into understanding color, recognizing shapes of objects, and identifying relationships among objects to achieve a goal. We'll dive into how artificial neural networks operate in chapter 9.

Generative models

Generative AI marks the shift from analyzing existing data to creating new content. Instead of just classifying an image or predicting a number, these models generate text, code, and visuals that never existed before.

Large language models

Large language models (LLMs) are designed to master context, conversation, and reasoning. Chapter 11 explores the architecture that revolutionized this field—the Transformer—and explains how these models achieve human-level fluency.

Generative image models

Generative image models learn to sculpt pure random noise into structured, high-fidelity artwork. Chapter 12 dives into the mechanics of creativity, looking at how diffusion models and U-Nets operate.

Some uses for AI algorithms

The uses for AI techniques are potentially endless. The applications of AI are limited only by the availability of data. Wherever a complex problem and historical data exist, potential for optimization exists. This section explores how AI transforms different industries.

Agriculture: Optimizing plant growth

- *Problem*—One of the most important industries that sustain human life is farming. Farming is a high-stakes balancing act. A single crop's success depends on hundreds of interacting variables, including soil pH, moisture levels, microbial health, and unpredictable weather patterns. It's impossible for a human to perfectly calculate how these factors interact in real time.

- *Solution*—Modern farms use sensors to capture the environment as data. AI algorithms analyze these vast datasets to find hidden patterns, identifying exactly which combination of water, fertilizer, and timing results in the highest yield. Instead of guessing, farmers get real-time, data-driven recommendations to maximize growth and minimize waste (figure 1.8).

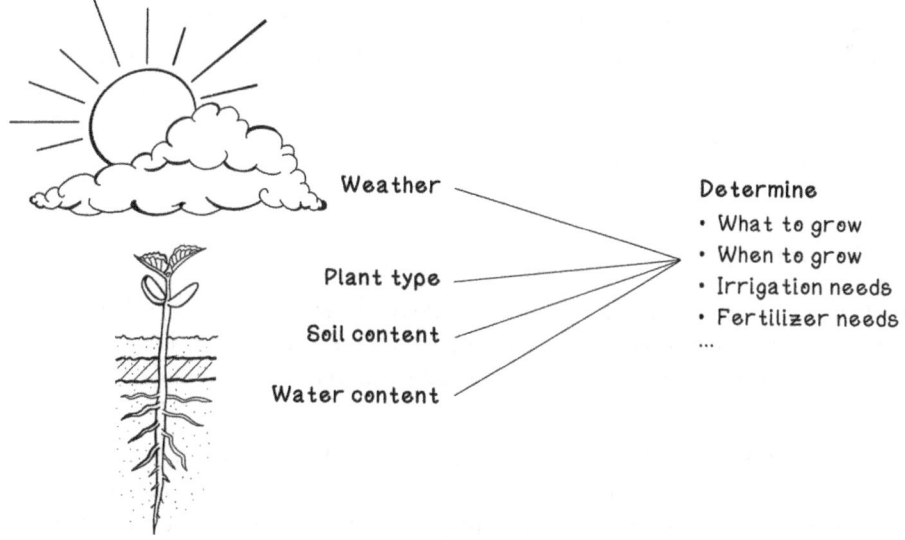

Figure 1.8 Using data to optimize crop farming

Banking: Preventing fraudulent transactions

- *Problem*—As banking moved from physical branches to digital networks, the volume of transactions exploded. With millions of payments happening every second, it's impossible for humans to review them manually for suspicious activity. Furthermore, static security rules such as "Flag all transactions over $10,000" are rigid and easy for clever criminals to bypass by moving $9,999 instead.
- *Solution*—This example is a classic case of anomaly detection. AI algorithms analyze a user's historical data to learn their specific "pattern of life"—where they shop, how much they spend, and at what times. When a transaction deviates from this learned baseline, such as by making a sudden high-value purchase in a foreign country, the model flags it within milliseconds, stopping the potential theft before the money leaves the account.

Cybersecurity: Safeguarding email inboxes

- *Problem*—Email scams are primary entry points for cyberattacks. In the past, spam filters relied on blacklists of bad words (such as *lottery* and *winner*). But scammers easily bypassed blacklists by changing spellings or using social-engineering tactics that looked like legitimate business requests.
- *Solution*—Modern AI uses natural language processing (NLP) to read emails. Instead of looking for keywords like *lottery*, AI analyzes the context and intent of the message. It can determine that an email request for gift cards that seems to come from your CEO is suspicious, even if it contains no typos: it's suspicious based on the sender's writing style and the unusual request. This approach keeps inboxes clean and prevents users from clicking dangerous links.

Health care: Diagnosing patients

- *Problem*—Radiologists and doctors must review thousands of X-rays, MRIs, and CT scans to detect diseases. Fatigue can lead to human error, and subtle early signs of conditions such as cancer or pneumonia can be imperceptible to the naked human eye.
- *Solution*—This scenario is a prime application for computer vision. AI models are trained on millions of medical images to recognize the visual textures of disease. These systems can scan images in seconds, highlighting potential tumors or fractures with high accuracy (figure 1.9). They act as a second set of eyes, ensuring that doctors don't miss critical diagnoses and enabling treatment to begin earlier.

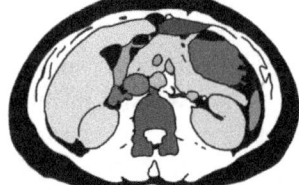

Brain scan   Brain scan with feature recognition

Figure 1.9 Using machine learning for feature recognition in brain scans

Logistics: Finding the best delivery route

- *Problem*—Logistics is essentially the Traveling Salesperson Problem on a massive scale. A delivery driver needs to visit dozens of locations in the shortest time possible. Although this problem is mathematically difficult on its own, the real world adds chaos, such as traffic jams, road closures, fuel costs, and variable vehicle sizes.
- *Solution*—AI algorithms transform this scenario from a static math problem to a dynamic one. Algorithms such as Ant Colony Optimization and Genetic Algorithms can simulate millions of potential routes in seconds to find the optimal path. Beyond driving routes, AI can solve the 3D Bin Packing problem, computing exactly how to stack boxes inside the truck to maximize space and ensure that the right packages are accessible at the right stops.

Fitness and health: Optimizing your body

- *Problem*—Generic health advice (like "Sleep 8 hours" and "Walk 10,000 steps") is a statistical average that fails at the individual level. The human body is a complex biological machine, and the relationships between stress, nutrition, and recovery vary wildly from person to person.
- *Solution*—Wearable technology provides the raw data: heart-rate variability, blood oxygen, and sleep cycles. AI algorithms can process this constant stream of time-series data to build a personalized model of your physiology. Instead of a static training plan, the AI acts as a dynamic feedback loop. It detects subtle signals of fatigue that a human might miss, automatically adjusting today's workout intensity to prevent injury or prescribing specific recovery protocols that enable a person to peak in an athletic event (figure 1.10).

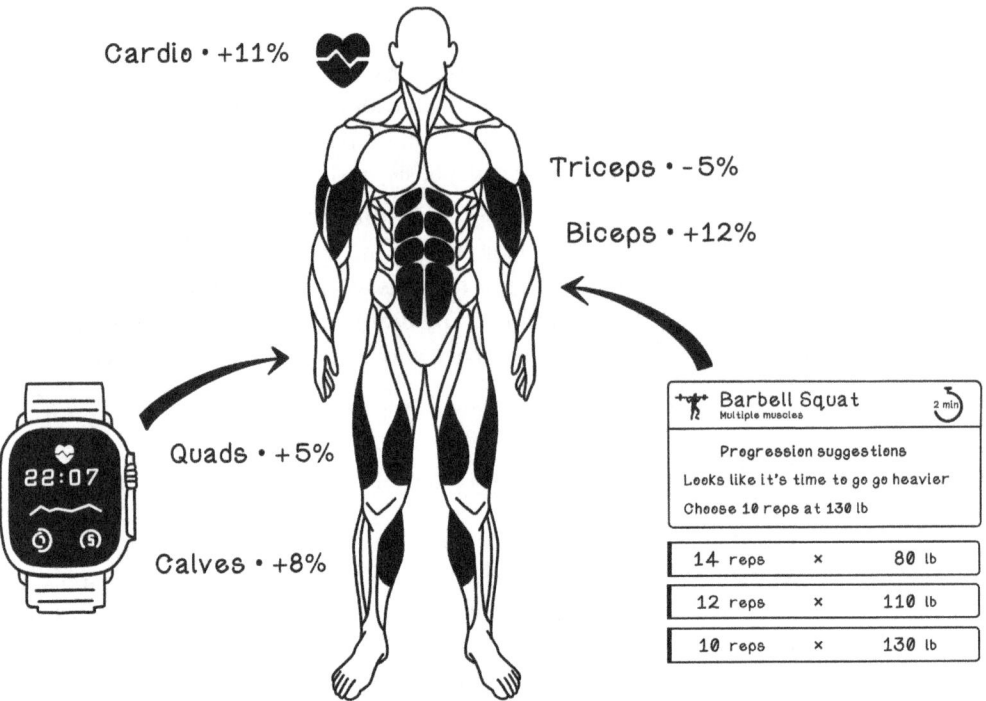

Figure 1.10 Using sensors and AI to guide fitness and health

Games: Adapting in complexity

- *Problem*—Games are the ultimate benchmark for intelligence because they require strategy, planning, and adaptation. In simple games such as tic-tac-toe and chess, the AI system can use search algorithms to calculate future moves and pick the statistically best option. Games such as Go and modern real-time strategy video games, however, have search spaces larger than the number of atoms in the universe, so a computer can't simply calculate a guaranteed win.

- *Solution*—To solve this problem, researchers use reinforcement learning. Instead of following hardcoded rules, the AI plays against itself millions of times. It's rewarded for making good moves and penalized for making bad ones, eventually developing a form of digital intuition. This approach allowed AlphaGo to defeat human world champions in 2016. The goal isn't just to win games but also to develop general-purpose agents that can apply this strategic planning to real-world chaos (figure 1.11).

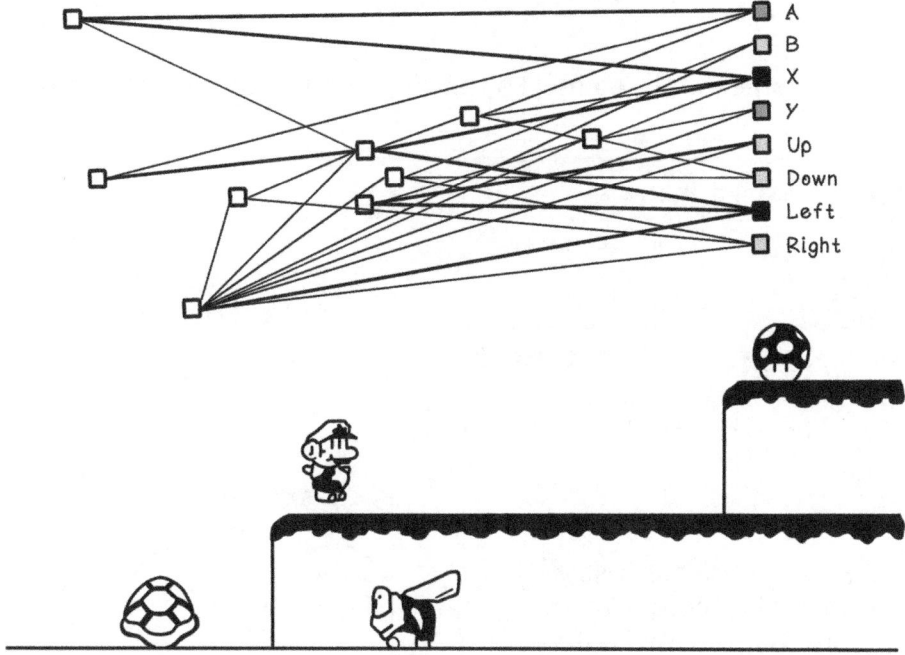

Figure 1.11 Using neural networks to learn how to play games

Conclusion

We've defined the fuel (data) that powers our systems and outlined the menu of problems—from prediction to optimization—that we aim to solve. But knowing the ingredients isn't enough; we also need to learn how to cook. It's time to move from definitions to implementation. In chapter 2, we dive into search algorithms, the fundamental logic that allows machines to navigate complex choices and plan their path to victory.

SUMMARY OF INTUITION OF AI

AI: Autonomously exhibits intelligent behavior and adapts

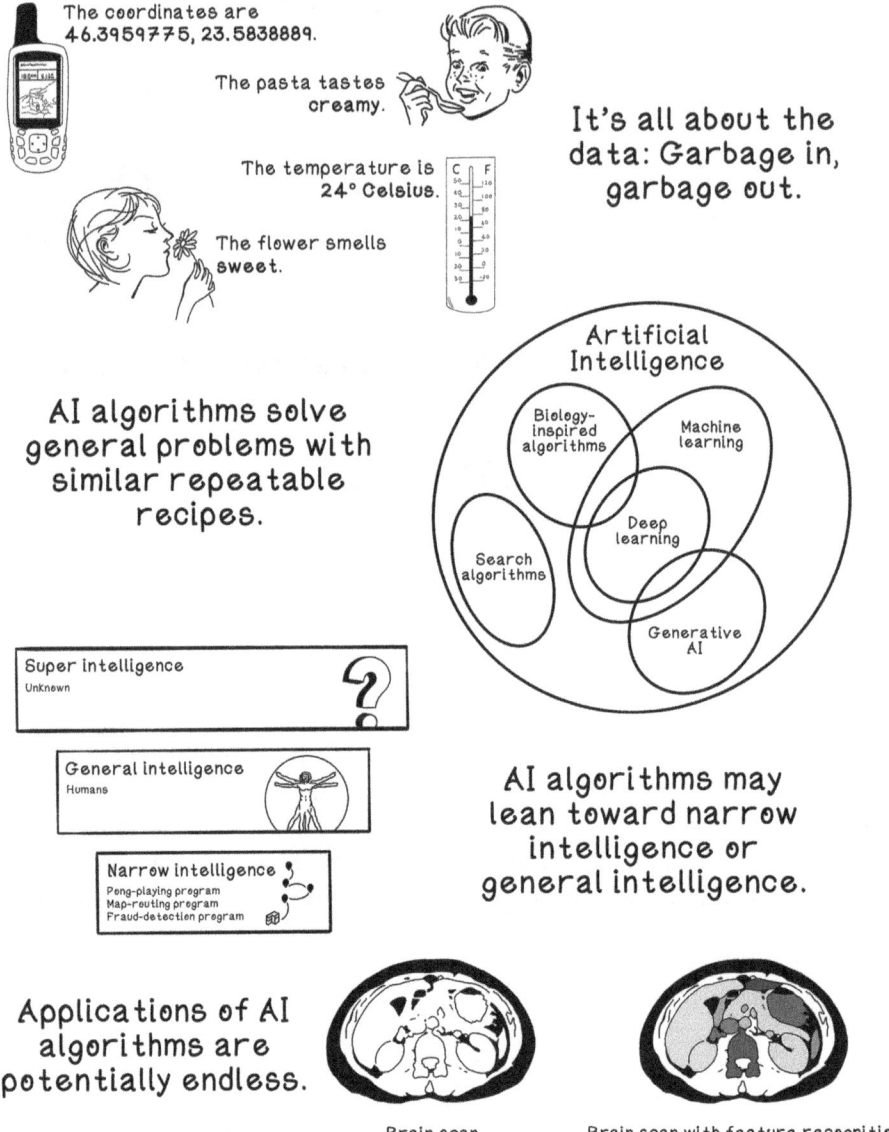

The coordinates are
46.3959775, 23.5838889.

The pasta tastes creamy.

The temperature is
24° Celsius.

The flower smells
sweet.

It's all about the
data: Garbage in,
garbage out.

AI algorithms solve
general problems with
similar repeatable
recipes.

Artificial
Intelligence

Biology-inspired
algorithms

Machine
learning

Deep
learning

Search
algorithms

Generative
AI

Super intelligence
Unknown

General intelligence
Humans

Narrow intelligence
Pong-playing program
Map-routing program
Fraud-detection program

AI algorithms may
lean toward narrow
intelligence or
general intelligence.

Applications of AI
algorithms are
potentially endless.

Brain scan

Brain scan with feature recognition

Build responsibly with ethics and humanity in mind.

In this chapter

- Gaining the intuition of planning and searching

- Identifying problems suited to be solved using search algorithms

- Representing problem spaces in a way suitable for processing by search algorithms

- Understanding and designing fundamental search algorithms to solve problems

What are planning and searching?

The ability to plan before acting is a hallmark of intelligence. Before going on a trip to a different country, before starting a new project, before writing functions in code, we plan. *Planning* happens at different levels of detail to strive for the best possible outcome when carrying out the tasks required to accomplish goals (figure 2.1).

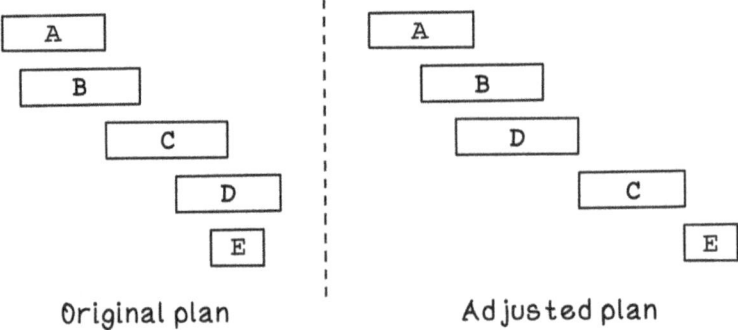

Figure 2.1 Example of how plans change in projects

Plans rarely work out exactly the way we envision them at the start. We live in a world where things are constantly changing, so it is impossible to account for all the variables and unknowns along the way. Regardless of the plan we start with, we almost always deviate from it. We need to (again) make a new plan from our current point going forward as unexpected events occur. As a result, the final plan that is carried out is usually quite different from the original one.

Searching is a way to guide planning by creating steps in a plan. When we plan a trip, for example, we research routes to take, evaluate the stops along the way and what they offer, and search for accommodations and activities that we like and can afford. Depending on the results of these searches, the plan changes.

Suppose that we've settled on a trip to the beach, which is 500 km (±310 miles) away, with two stops: one at a petting zoo and one at a pizza restaurant. We'll sleep at a lodge close to the beach on arrival and do three activities. The trip to the destination will take approximately 8 hours. We're also taking a shortcut private road after the restaurant, but it's only open until 2 p.m.

We start the trip, and everything is going according to plan. We stop at the petting zoo and see some cute animals. We drive on and start getting hungry; it's time to make the stop at the pizza restaurant. But to our surprise, the restaurant recently went out of business. We need to adjust our plan and find another place to eat, which involves searching for a close-by restaurant of our liking and adjusting our plan.

After driving around for a while, we find a restaurant, enjoy a pizza, and get back on the road. Upon approaching the shortcut private road, we realize that it's 2:20 p.m. The road is closed; again, we need to adjust our plan. We search for a detour and find that it will add 120 km (~75 miles) to our drive, so we'll need to find accommodations for the night at a different lodge before we even get to the beach. We search for a place to sleep and plot our new route. Because we lost some time, we can do only two activities at the destination. We adjusted the plan heavily by searching for options that satisfied each new situation, but we ended up having a great adventure en route to the beach.

This example shows how to search in planning and how it influences planning for desirable outcomes. As the environment changes, our goals may change slightly, and our path to them inevitably needs to be adjusted (figure 2.2). Adjustments in plans can rarely be anticipated but often have to be made.

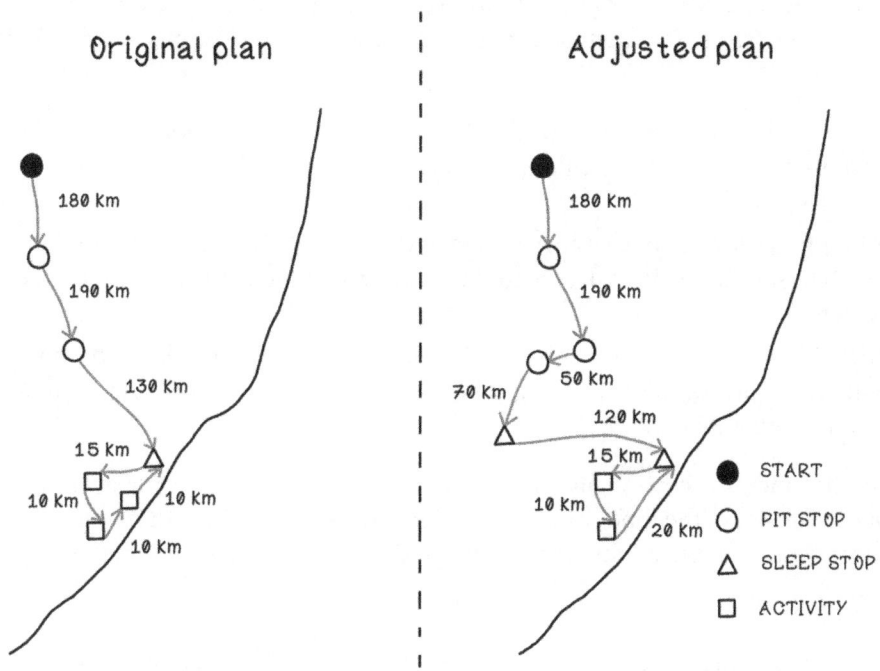

Figure 2.2 Original plan vs. adjusted plan for a road trip

Searching involves evaluating future states toward a goal, finding an optimal path of states until the goal is reached. This chapter centers on approaches to searching to solve different types of problems. Searching is an old but powerful tool for developing intelligent algorithms.

Cost of computation: The reason for smart algorithms

In programming, functions consist of operations, and because of the way traditional computers work, different functions use varying amounts of processing time. The more computation is required, the more expensive the function is. *Big O notation* describes the complexity of a function or algorithm. Big O notation models the number of operations required as the input size increases. Here are some examples and associated complexities:

- $O(1)$ is like shaking hands with one person. It takes the same amount of time no matter how many people are in the room. In code, it might be a single operation that prints `"Hello World"`.
- $O(n)$ is like shaking hands with everyone in the room. If 100 people are in the room, it takes 100 handshakes. In code, it could be a function that iterates over a list and prints each item.
- $O(n^2)$ is like everyone in the room shaking hands with everyone else. It becomes chaotic very quickly. In code, it might be a function that compares every item in a list with every other item in the list.

Figure 2.3 depicts the costs of algorithms. Algorithms that require more operations to explore as the size of the input increases perform worst; algorithms that require a more constant number of operations as the number of inputs increases scale better to large datasets.

> **NOTE** A slower algorithm might run faster if it can be parallelized across many processors (such as on a GPU). We aim for low Big O complexity, but we also care about memory use and hardware efficiency.

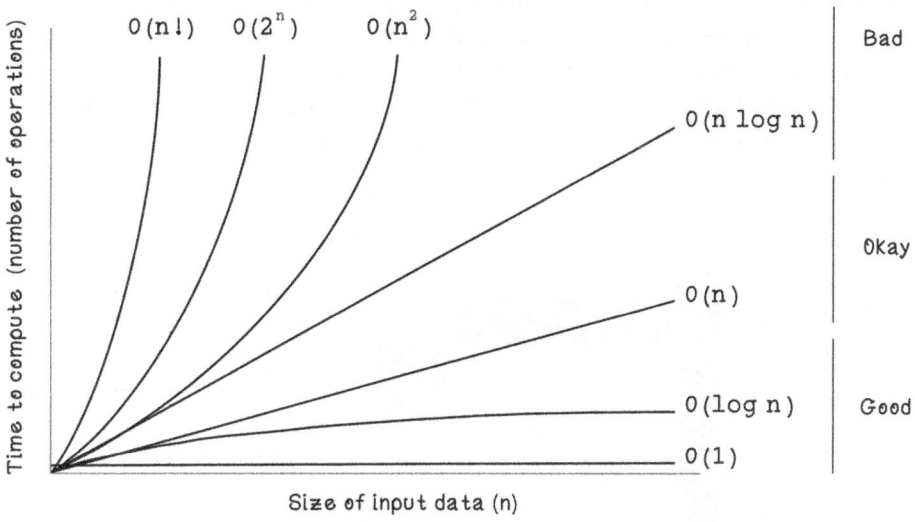

Figure 2.3 Big O complexity

Understanding that algorithms have different computation costs is important because addressing this situation is the entire purpose of intelligent algorithms that solve problems well and efficiently. Theoretically, we can solve almost any problem by brute-forcing every possible option until we find the best one. In reality, however, the computation could take hours, years, or even millennia, which makes it impractical for real-world scenarios.

Problems that search algorithms can solve

We can use search algorithms to solve almost any problem that requires us to make a series of decisions. Depending on the problem and the size of the search space, we can employ different algorithms to solve it. Depending on the search algorithm we select and the configurations we use, we may find the optimal solution: a *best-available solution*. In other words, we may find a good solution but not necessarily the best one. When we speak about a "good solution" or "optimal solution," we're referring to the performance of the solution in addressing the problem at hand.

One scenario in which search algorithms are useful is finding the shortest path to the goal in a maze. Suppose that we're in a square maze that is 10 blocks by 10 blocks (figure 2.4). The maze contains a goal we want to reach and barriers we can't step into or over. The objective is to find a path to the goal while avoiding barriers and taking as few steps as possible by moving north, south, east, or west. In this example, the player can't move diagonally.

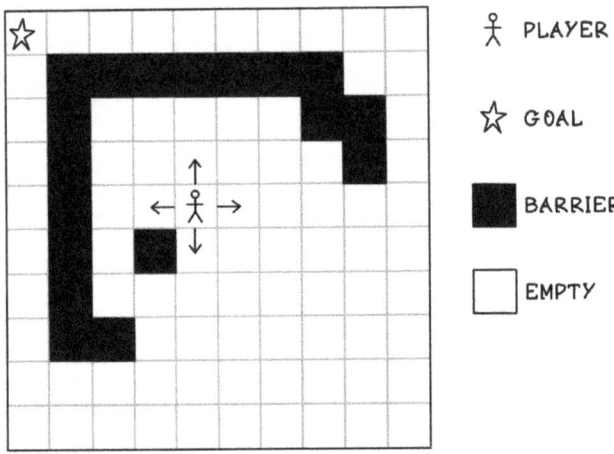

Figure 2.4 An example of the maze problem

How can we find the shortest path to the goal while avoiding barriers? By thinking about the problem as humans, we can try each path possibility and count the moves. Using trial and error, we can find the shortest paths because this maze is relatively small.

The example maze in figure 2.5 depicts some possible paths to the goal. But we don't reach the goal in option 1.

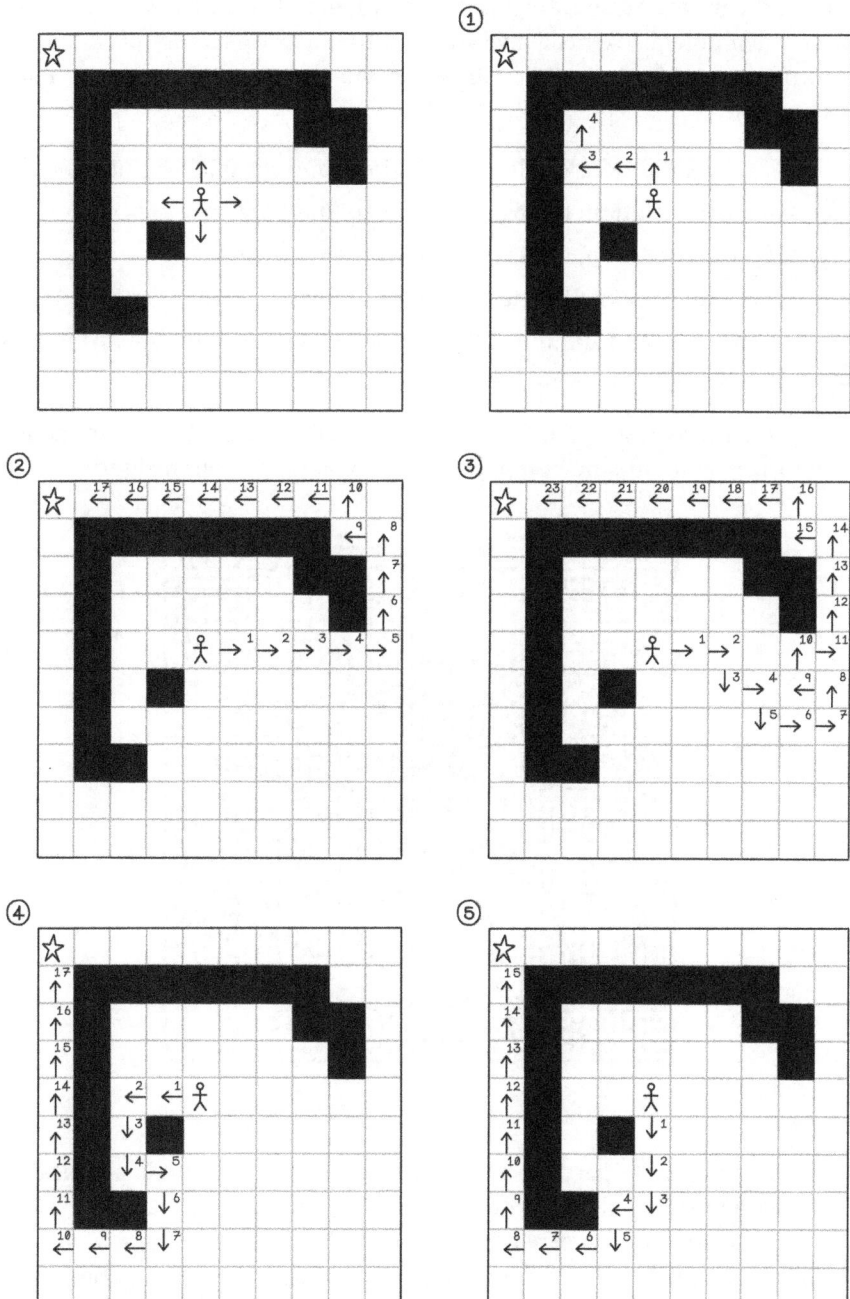

Figure 2.5 Examples of possible paths to the maze problem

By looking at the maze and counting blocks in different directions, we can find several solutions to the problem. We make five attempts to find four successful solutions out of an unknown number of solutions. It will take exhaustive effort to compute all possible solutions by hand:

- Attempt 1 is not a valid solution. It took 4 actions, and the goal was not found.
- Attempt 2 is a valid solution, taking 17 actions to find the goal.
- Attempt 3 is a valid solution, taking 23 actions to find the goal.
- Attempt 4 is a valid solution, taking 17 actions to find the goal.
- Attempt 5 is the best valid solution, taking 15 actions to find the goal. Although this attempt is the best one, we found it by chance.

If the maze were much larger, like the one in figure 2.6, it would take an immense amount of time to compute the best possible path manually. Search algorithms can help.

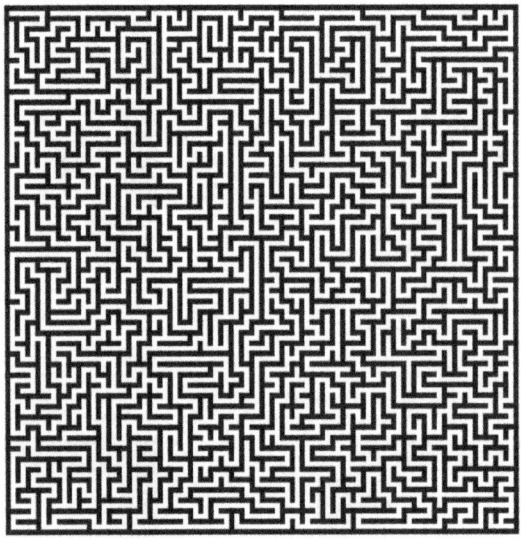

Figure 2.6 A large example of the maze problem

Our power as humans is to perceive a problem visually, understand it, and find solutions. We understand and interpret data and information in an abstract way. A computer can't yet understand generalized information in the natural way that we do. The problem space needs to be represented in a way that is suitable for computation.

Representing state: Creating a framework to represent problem spaces and solutions

When we represent data in a way that a computer can understand, we must encode it logically so that it can be understood objectively. Although the data will be encoded subjectively by the person who performs the task, there should be a consistent way to repeat it.

Let's clarify the difference between data and information. *Data* is raw facts about something, and *information* is an interpretation of those facts that provides insight into the data in the specific domain. Information requires context and data processing to provide meaning. As an example, each distance traveled in the maze example is data, and the total distance traveled is information. Depending on the perspective, level of detail, and desired outcome, classifying something as data or information may depend on the context (figure 2.7).

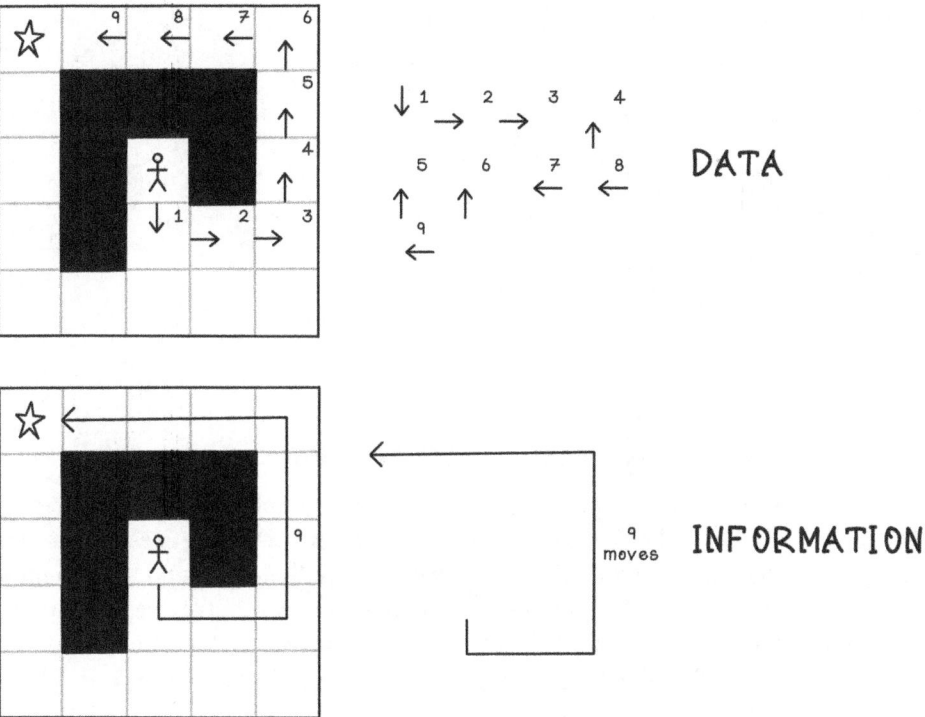

Figure 2.7 Data vs. information

Data structures are concepts in computer science used to represent data in a way that's appropriate for efficient processing by algorithms. A data structure is an abstract data type consisting of data and operations organized in a specific way. The data structure we use is influenced by the type of problem and the goal.

One example of a data structure is an *array*, which is simply a collection of data. Arrays have properties that make them good for various purposes. Depending on the programming language used, an array could allow each value to be of a different type, require all values to be of the same type, or disallow duplicate values. Different types of arrays usually have different names, and their specific features and constraints can enable more efficient computation (figure 2.8).

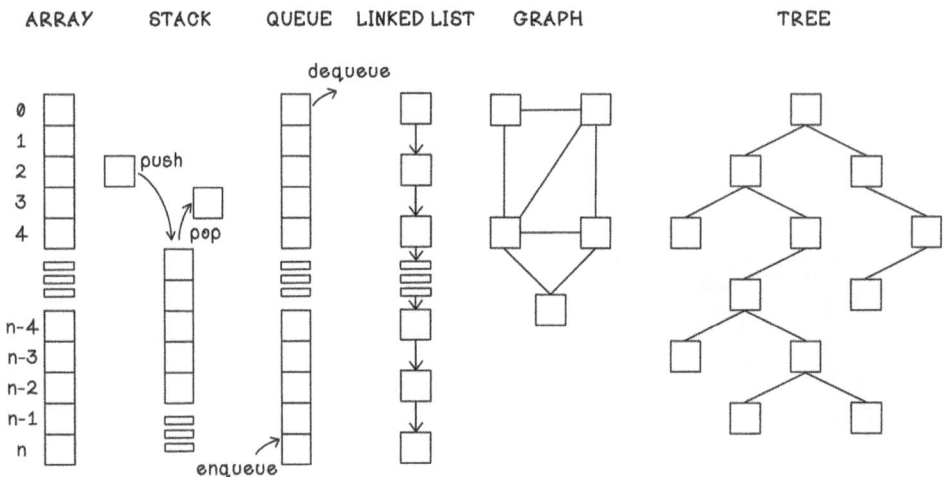

Figure 2.8 Data structures used with algorithms

Graphs: Representing search problems and solutions

A *graph* is a data structure containing several states with connections among them. Each state in a graph is called a *node* (or *vertex*), and a connection between two states is called an *edge*. Graphs are studied in *graph theory* in mathematics and used to model relationships among objects. Graphs are useful data structures that are easy for humans to understand, due to the ease of representing them visually as well as their strong logical nature, which is ideal for processing via various algorithms (figure 2.9). We'll see graph structures throughout the book.

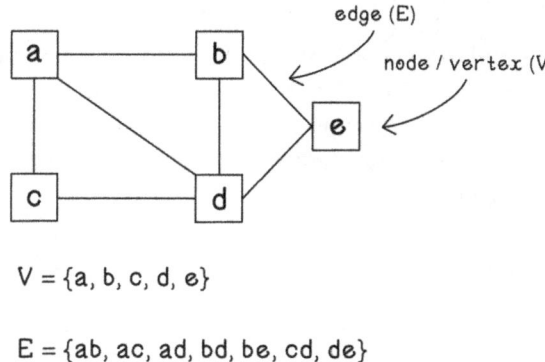

$V = \{a, b, c, d, e\}$

$E = \{ab, ac, ad, bd, be, cd, de\}$

Figure 2.9 The notation used to represent graphs

Figure 2.10 is a graph of the trip to the beach example discussed in the first section of this chapter. Each stop is a node on the graph, with each edge between nodes representing points traveled between and the weights on each edge indicating the distance traveled.

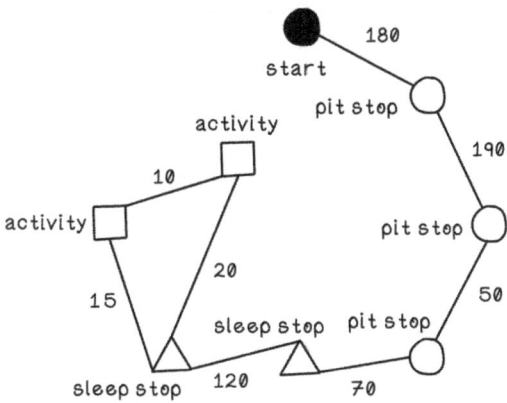

Figure 2.10 The example road trip represented as a graph

Representing a graph as a concrete data structure

A graph can be represented in several ways for efficient processing by algorithms. At its core, a graph can be represented by an array of arrays that indicates relationships among nodes, as shown in figure 2.11. Sometimes, it's useful to have another array that simply lists all nodes in the graph so that the algorithm doesn't have to infer the distinct nodes from the relationships each time.

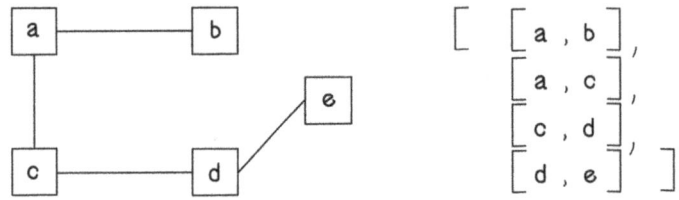

Figure 2.11 Representing a graph as an array of arrays

Other representations of graphs include an incidence matrix, an adjacency matrix, and an adjacency list. By looking at the names of these representations, you see that the adjacency of nodes in a graph is important. An *adjacent node* is a node that is connected directly to another node.

Exercise: Represent a graph as a matrix

How would you represent the following graph using edge arrays?

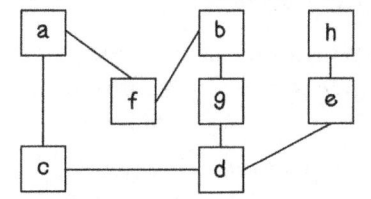

Solution:

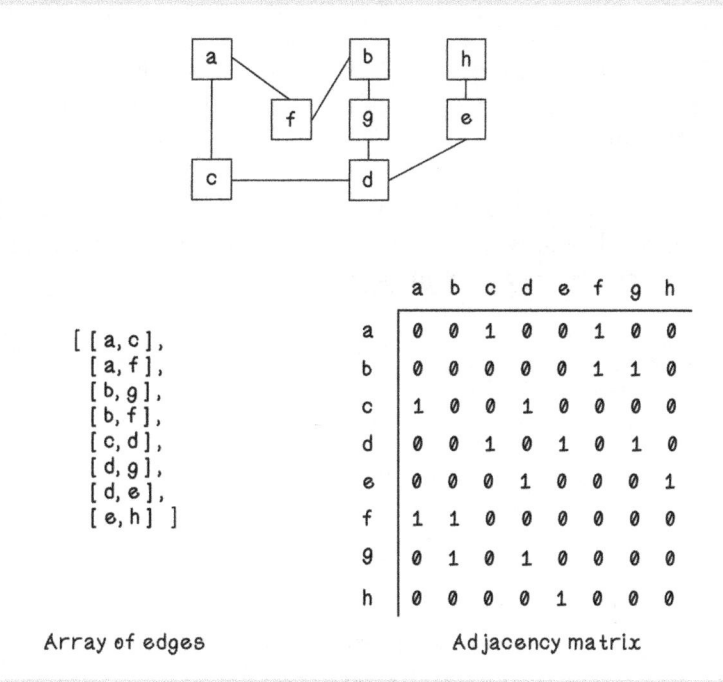

```
[ [ a, c ],
  [ a, f ],
  [ b, g ],
  [ b, f ],
  [ c, d ],
  [ d, g ],
  [ d, e ],
  [ e, h ]  ]
```

	a	b	c	d	e	f	g	h
a	0	0	1	0	0	1	0	0
b	0	0	0	0	0	1	1	0
c	1	0	0	1	0	0	0	0
d	0	0	1	0	1	0	1	0
e	0	0	0	1	0	0	0	1
f	1	1	0	0	0	0	0	0
g	0	1	0	1	0	0	0	0
h	0	0	0	0	1	0	0	0

Array of edges   Adjacency matrix

Trees: Concrete structures used to represent search solutions

A *tree* is a popular data structure that simulates a hierarchy of values or objects. A *hierarchy* is an arrangement of things in which a single object is related to several other objects below it. A tree is a connected *acyclic graph*, meaning that all nodes are connected but no loops (cycles) exist.

In a tree, the value or object represented at a specific point is called a *node*. Trees typically have a single root node with zero or more child nodes that could contain subtrees.

Let's take a deep breath and jump into some terminology. When a node has connected nodes, the root node is called the *parent*. You can apply this thinking recursively. A child node may have its own children, which may also contain subtrees or their children. Each child node has a single parent node. A node without any children is a leaf node. Trees also have a *total height*. The level of specific nodes is called a *depth*.

> **NOTE** The terms used to relate family members are heavily used in work with trees. Keep this analogy in mind; it will help you connect the concepts in the tree data structure.

In figure 2.12, the depth is measured starting from 0 at the root node. The root node has 4 child nodes, the tree height is 4, and the depth in this example is 2. Depth is always based on where in the tree the algorithm is during traversal.

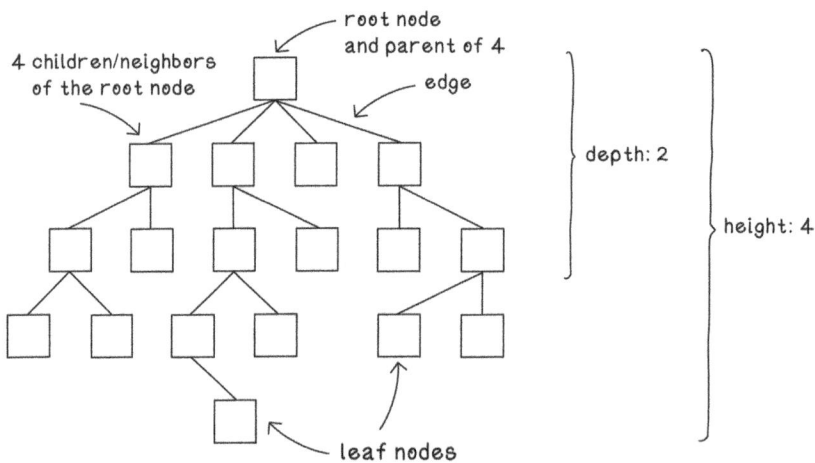

Figure 2.12 The main attributes of a tree

The topmost node in a tree is called the *root node*. A node connected directly to one or more other nodes is called a *parent node*. The nodes connected to a parent node are called *child nodes* or *neighbors*. Nodes connected to the same parent node are called *siblings*. A connection between two nodes is called an *edge*.

A *path* is a sequence of nodes and edges connecting nodes that aren't directly connected. A node connected to another node by following a path away from the root node is called a *descendent*, and a node connected to another node by following a path toward the root node is called an *ancestor*. A node with no children is called a *leaf node*. The term *degree* describes the number of children a node has; therefore, a leaf node has degree 0.

Figure 2.13 represents a path from the start point to the goal for the maze problem. This path contains nine nodes that represent different moves in the maze.

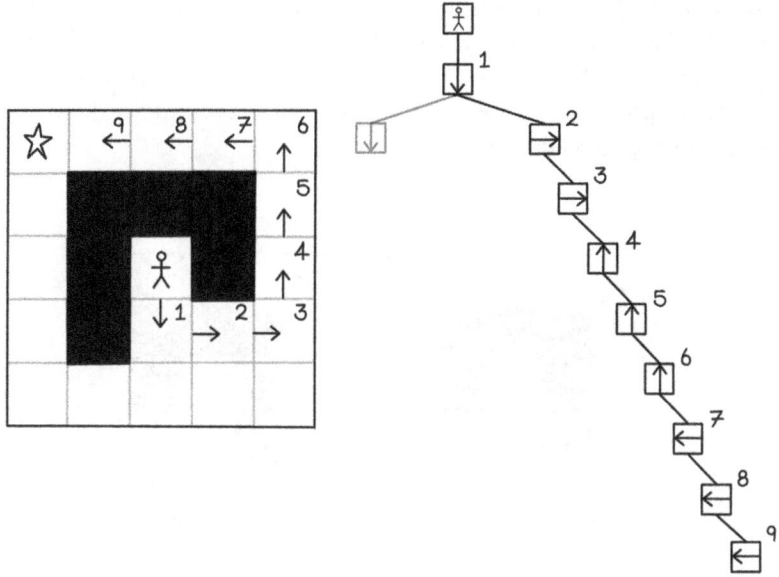

Figure 2.13 A solution to the maze problem represented as a tree

Trees are the fundamental data structure for many search algorithms, which we dive into in the next section.

> **TIP** Sorting algorithms are also useful for solving certain problems and computing solutions more efficiently. If you're interested in learning more about sorting algorithms, take a look at *Grokking Algorithms, Second Edition*, by Aditya Y. Bhargava (Manning, 2024).

Uninformed search: Looking blindly for solutions

Uninformed search is also known as *unguided search*, *blind search*, or *brute-force search*. Uninformed search algorithms have no additional information about the domain of the problem apart from the representation of the problem, which is usually a tree.

Think about exploring things you want to learn. Some people might look at a wide range of topics and learn the basics of each topic, whereas other people might choose one narrow topic and explore its subtopics in depth. These examples represent breadth-first search and depth-first search, respectively. *Depth-first search (DFS)* explores a specific path from the start until it finds a goal at the utmost depth. *Breadth-first search (BFS)* explores all options at a specific depth before moving to options deeper in the tree.

Consider the maze scenario (figure 2.14). In our attempt to find an optimal path to the goal, let's assume the following simple constraint to prevent an endless loop and cycles in our tree: *the player can't move into a block that they previously occupied*. Because uninformed algorithms attempt every possible option at every node, creating a cycle will cause the algorithm to fail catastrophically.

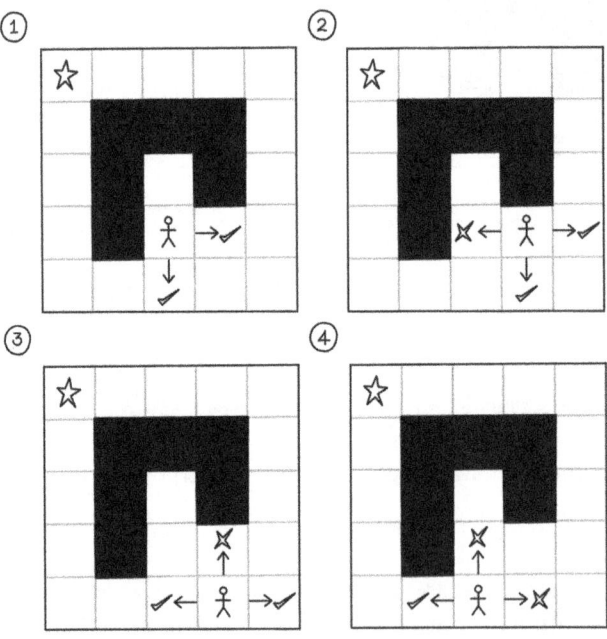

Figure 2.14 The constraint for the maze problem

This constraint prevents cycles in the path to the goal in our scenario. But this constraint will introduce problems if, in a different maze with different constraints or rules, moving into a previously occupied block more than once is required for the optimal solution.

In figure 2.15, all possible paths in the tree are represented to highlight the available options. This tree contains seven paths that lead to the goal and one path that results in an invalid solution, given the constraint of not moving to previously occupied blocks. It's important to understand that in this small maze, representing all the possibilities is feasible. The entire point of search algorithms, however, is to search or generate these trees iteratively because generating the entire tree of possibilities up front is computationally expensive and inefficient.

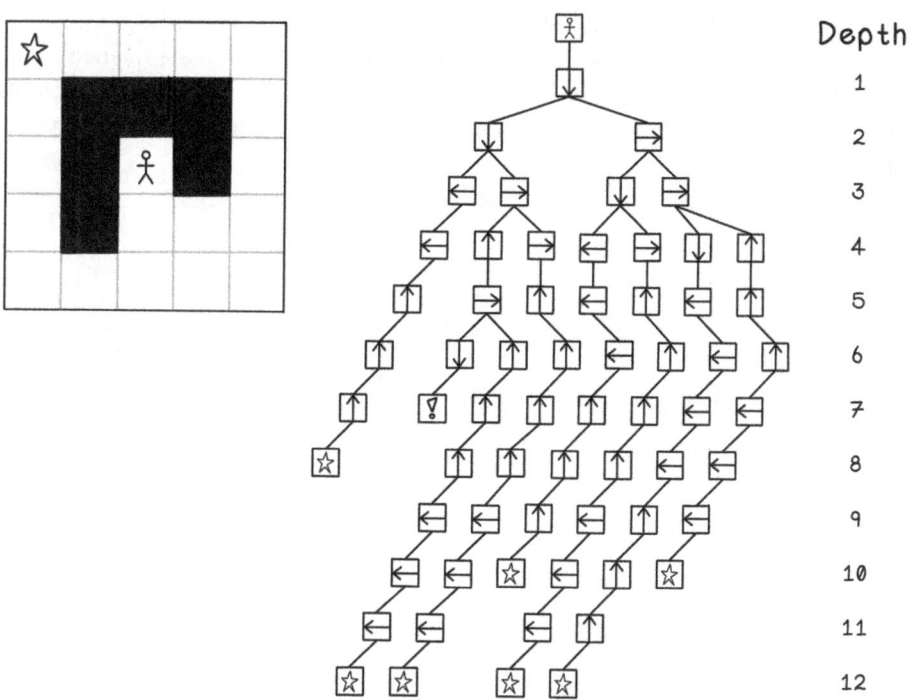

Figure 2.15 All possible movement options represented as a tree

It's also important to note that the term *visiting* has various meanings here. The player visits blocks in the maze. The algorithm also visits nodes in the tree. The order of choices influences the order of nodes being visited in the tree. In the maze example, the priority order of movement is north, south, east, and west.

BFS: Looking wide before looking deep

Now that we understand the ideas behind trees and the maze example, let's explore how search algorithms can generate trees that seek out paths to the goal. Breadth-first search (BFS) is an algorithm used to traverse or generate a tree. This algorithm starts at a specific node, usually the root, and explores every node at that depth before exploring the next depth of nodes. Think of BFS as being like dropping a stone into a calm pond. The ripples expand uniformly in all directions, touching everything 1 meter away, then everything 2 meters away, and so on. The algorithm mimics this expanding ring, visiting all neighbors at the current depth before moving outward. This guarantees that the shortest path in unweighted graphs (graphs in which all edges have the same cost) is found.

The BFS algorithm is best implemented by using a first-in, first-out (FIFO) queue in which the current depths of nodes are processed and their children are queued to be processed later. This order of processing is exactly what we require when implementing this algorithm. Figure 2.16 is a flow chart describing the sequence of steps involved in the algorithm.

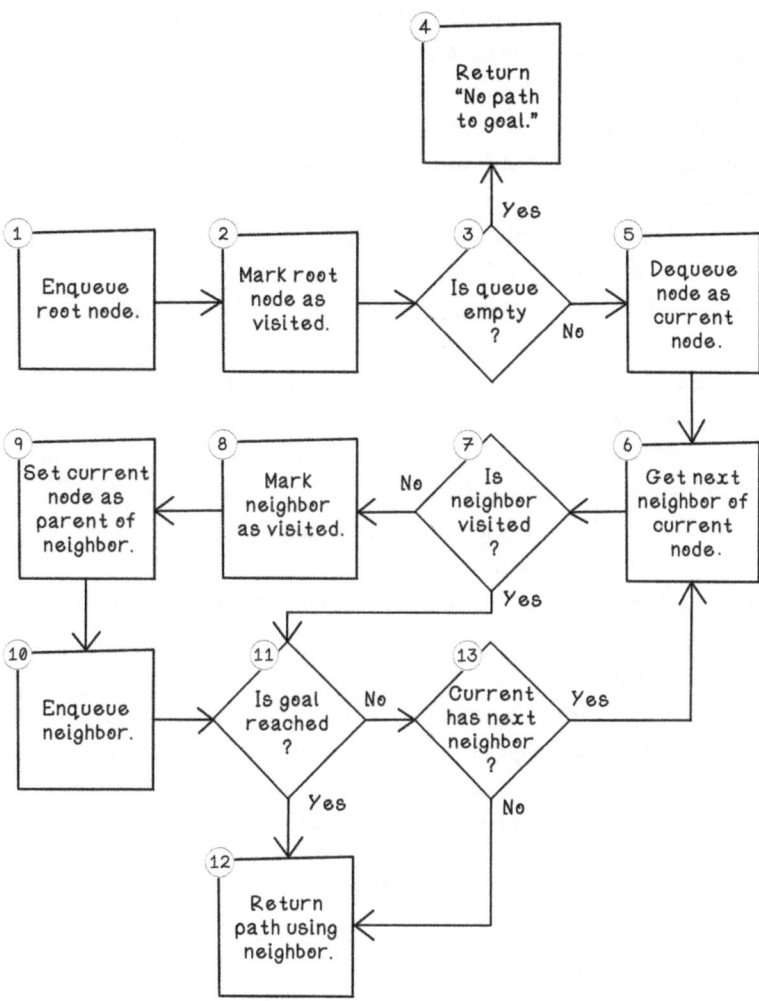

Figure 2.16 Flow of the BFS algorithm

Steps of the BFS algorithm

Let's walk through each step in the algorithm to learn exactly what operations happen:

1. *Enqueue root node.* The BFS algorithm is best implemented with a queue. Objects are processed in the sequence in which they are added to the queue. This process is known as FIFO. The first step is adding the root node to the queue. This node represents the starting position of the player on the map.

2. *Mark the root node as visited.* Now that the root node has been added to the queue for processing, it is marked as visited to prevent it from being revisited for no reason.

3. *Is the queue empty?* If the queue is empty (all nodes have been processed after many iterations), and if no path has been returned in step 12 of the algorithm, there is no path to the goal. If there are still nodes in the queue, the algorithm can continue its search for the goal.

4. *Return* No path to goal. This message is the one possible exit from the algorithm if no path to the goal exists.

5. *Dequeue the node as the current node.* By pulling the next object from the queue and setting it as the current node of interest, we can explore its possibilities. When the algorithm starts, the current node will be the root node.

6. *Get the next neighbor of the current node.* This step involves getting the next possible move in the maze from the current position by referencing the maze and determining whether north, south, east, or west movement is possible.

7. *Is the neighbor visited?* If the current neighbor hasn't been visited, it hasn't been explored yet and can be processed now.

8. *Mark the neighbor as visited.* This step indicates that this neighbor node has been visited.

9. *Set the current node as the parent of the neighbor.* This step is important for tracing the path from the current neighbor to the root node. From a map perspective, the *origin* is the position the player moved from, and the *current neighbor* is the position the player moved to.

10. *Enqueue the neighbor.* The neighbor node is queued for its children to be explored later. This queuing mechanism allows nodes from each depth to be processed in that order.

11. *Is the goal reached?* This step determines whether the current neighbor contains the goal that the algorithm is searching for.

12. *Return the path using the neighbor.* By referencing the parent of the neighbor node, then the parent of that node, and so on, the path from the goal to the root is described. The root node will be a node without a parent.

13. *Does the current node have a next neighbor?* If the current node has more possible moves to make in the maze, jump to step 6 for that move.

Let's walk through what that process would look like in a simple tree. As the tree is explored and nodes are added to the FIFO queue, the nodes are processed in the desired order by using the queue (figures 2.17 and 2.18).

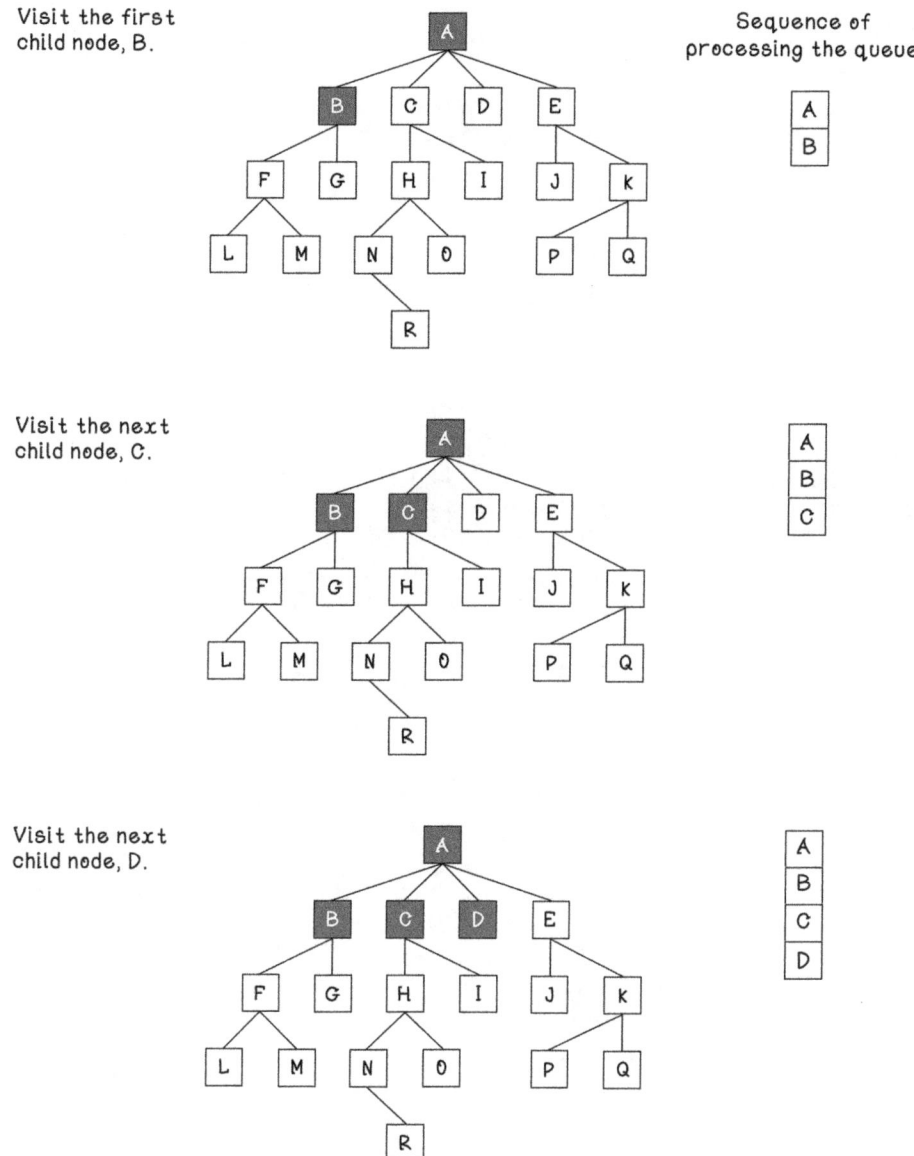

Figure 2.17 The sequence of tree processing using BFS (part 1)

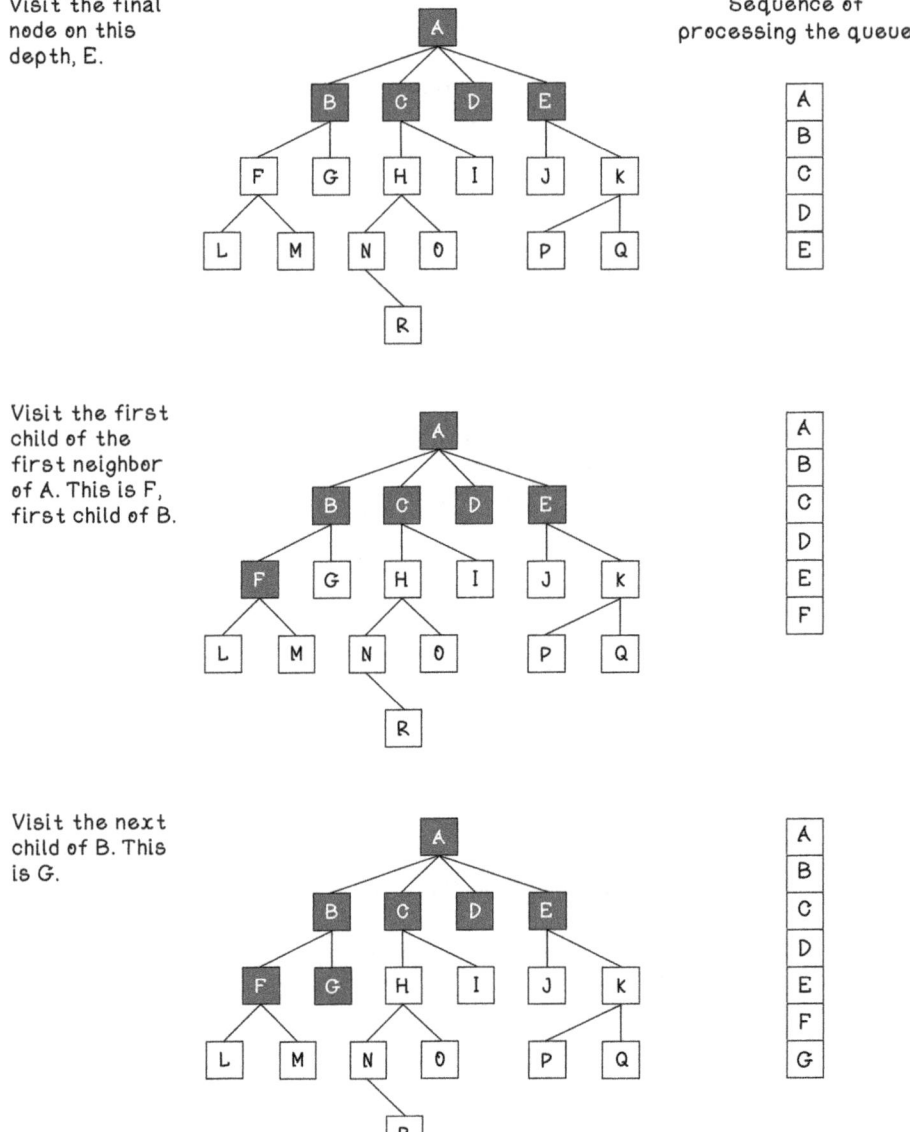

Visit the final
node on this
depth, E.

Sequence of
processing the queue

Visit the first
child of the
first neighbor
of A. This is F,
first child of B.

Visit the next
child of B. This
is G.

Figure 2.18 The sequence of tree processing using BFS (part 2)

Exercise: Determine the path to the solution

What would be the order of visits using BFS for the following tree?

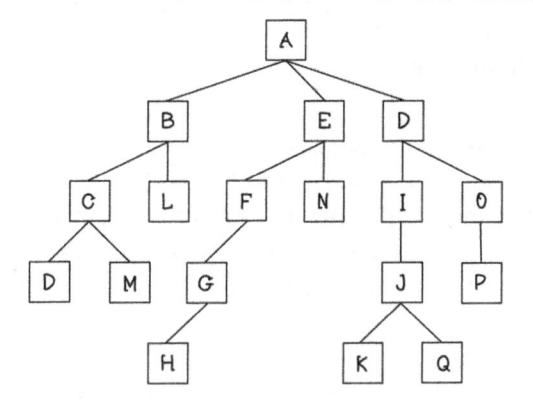

Solution:

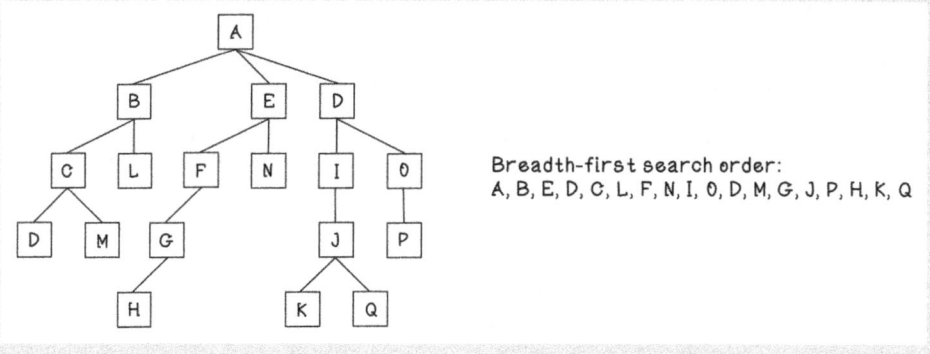

Breadth-first search order:
A, B, E, D, C, L, F, N, I, O, D, M, G, J, P, H, K, Q

In the maze example, the algorithm needs to understand the current position of the player in the maze, evaluate all possible choices for movement, and repeat that logic for each choice of movement made until the goal is reached. By doing so, the algorithm generates a tree with a single path to the goal.

It's important to understand that the process of visiting nodes in a tree generates nodes in a tree. We're simply finding related nodes through a mechanism.

Each path to the goal consists of a series of moves to reach the goal. The number of moves in the path is the distance to reach the goal for that path, which we'll call the *cost*. The number of moves also equals the number of nodes visited in the path, from the root node to the leaf node that contains the goal. The algorithm moves down the tree depth by depth until it finds a goal; then it returns the first path that got it to the goal as the solution. A more optimal path to the goal may exist, but because BFS is uninformed, it isn't guaranteed to find that path.

> **NOTE** In the maze example, all search algorithms used terminate when they find a solution to the goal. It's possible to allow these algorithms to find multiple solutions with a small tweak to each algorithm, but the best use cases for search algorithms find a single goal because it's often too expensive to explore the entire tree of possibilities.

Figure 2.19 shows the generation of a tree using movements in the maze. The BFS algorithm has explored up to depth 5 of the tree. On the actual map, two paths to the goal emerge from the search thus far.

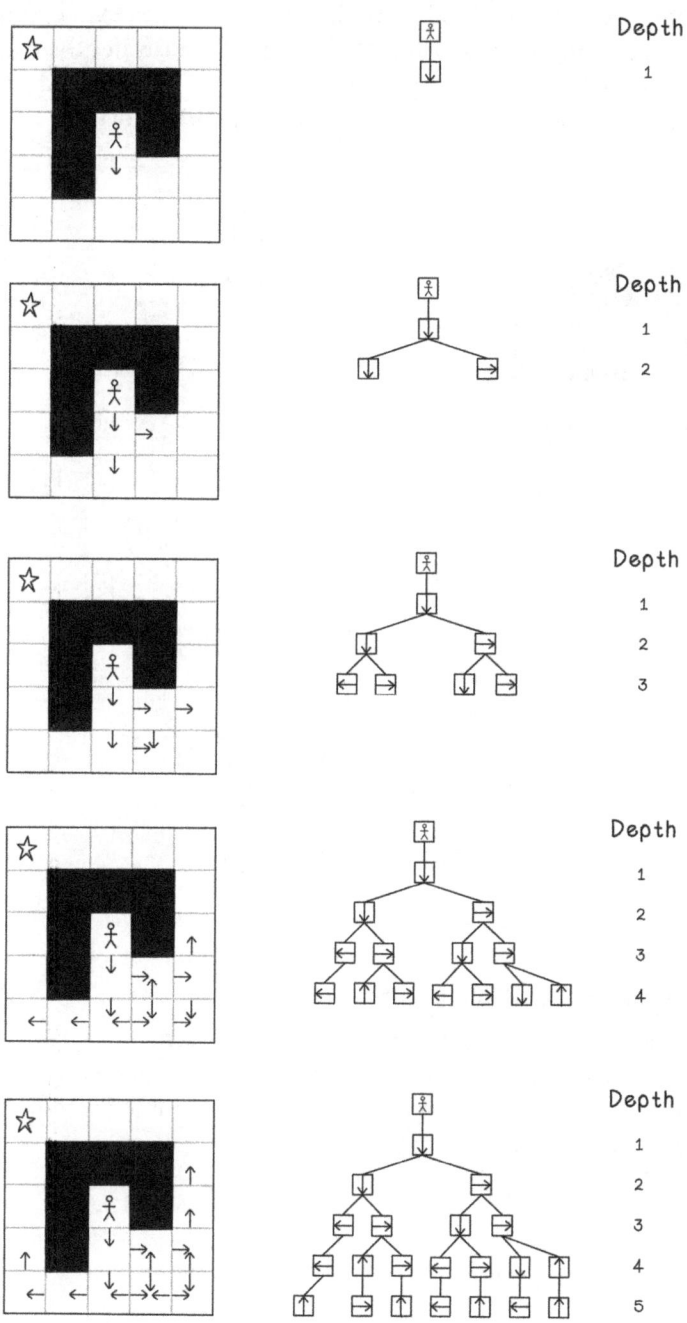

Figure 2.19 Maze movement tree generation using BFS

Because the tree is generated with BFS, the algorithm generates each depth to completion before looking at the next depth. Figure 2.20 illustrates the entire tree of possibilities (shown only for learning purposes). At depth 7, BFS found a path to the goal, so our solution is south, south, west, west, north, north, north.

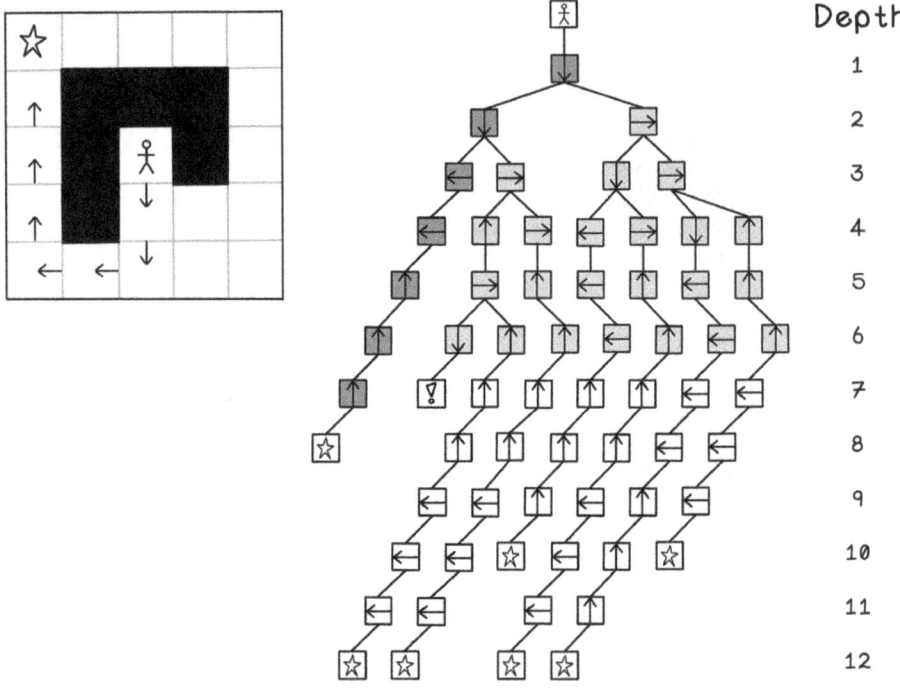

Figure 2.20 Nodes visited in the entire tree after BFS

Python code sample of the BFS algorithm

As mentioned earlier, the BFS algorithm uses a queue to generate a tree one depth at a time. Having a structure to store visited nodes is critical to prevent getting stuck in cyclic loops, and setting the parent of each node is important for determining a path from the starting point in the maze to the goal:

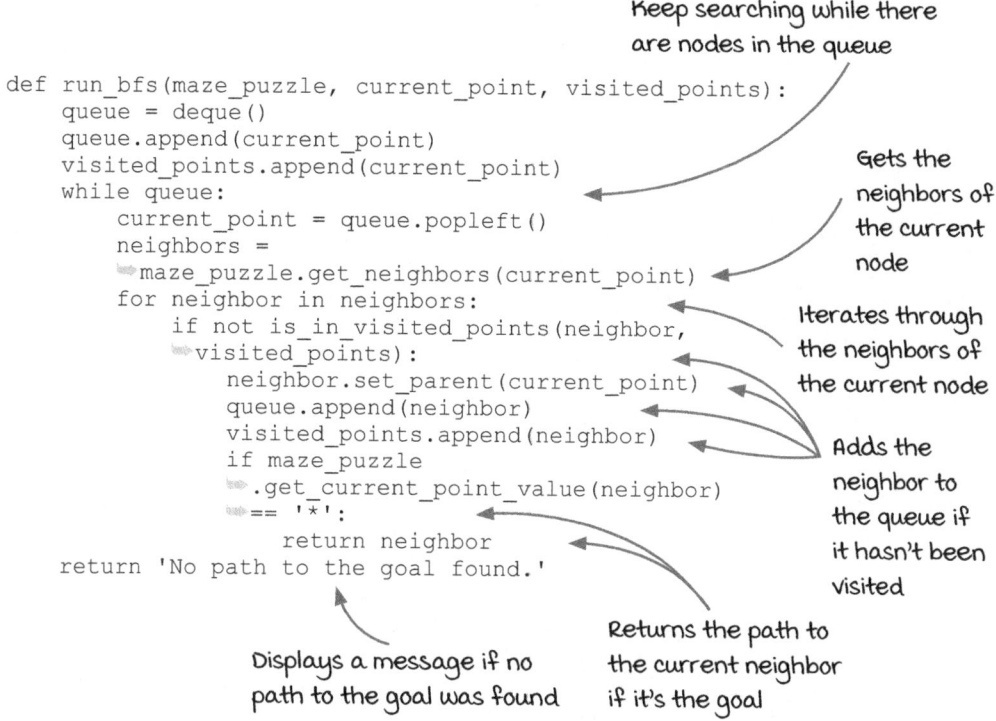

Keep searching while there are nodes in the queue

```
def run_bfs(maze_puzzle, current_point, visited_points):
    queue = deque()
    queue.append(current_point)
    visited_points.append(current_point)
    while queue:
        current_point = queue.popleft()
        neighbors =
        maze_puzzle.get_neighbors(current_point)
        for neighbor in neighbors:
            if not is_in_visited_points(neighbor,
            visited_points):
                neighbor.set_parent(current_point)
                queue.append(neighbor)
                visited_points.append(neighbor)
                if maze_puzzle
                .get_current_point_value(neighbor)
                == '*':
                    return neighbor
    return 'No path to the goal found.'
```

Gets the neighbors of the current node

Iterates through the neighbors of the current node

Adds the neighbor to the queue if it hasn't been visited

Displays a message if no path to the goal was found

Returns the path to the current neighbor if it's the goal

DFS: Looking deep before looking wide

Depth-first search (DFS) is another algorithm used to traverse a tree or generate nodes and paths in a tree. Think of DFS as being like a maze explorer who commits to a single path, walking as far as possible until hitting a dead end. Only then do they backtrack to the last intersection to try a different turn. Unlike BFS, which has a cautious, expanding nature, DFS is aggressive and dives deep immediately. Figure 2.21 illustrates the general flow of the DFS algorithm.

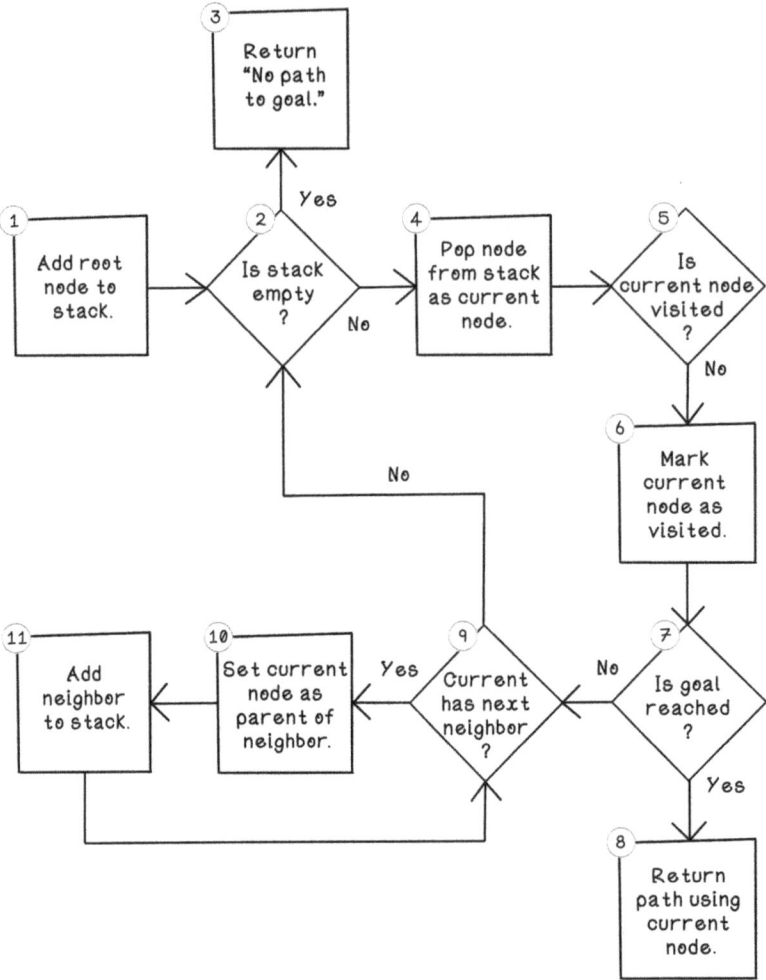

Figure 2.21 Flow of the DFS algorithm

Steps of the DFS algorithm

Let's walk through the flow of the DFS algorithm:

1. *Add the root node to the stack.* The algorithm can be implemented by using a stack in which the last object added is processed first. This process is known as *last in, first out* (LIFO). The first step is adding the root node to the stack.

2. *Is the stack empty?* If the stack is empty and no path has been returned in step 8 of the algorithm, there is no path to the goal. If there are still nodes in the stack, the algorithm can continue its search for the goal.

3. *Return* No path to goal. This return is the one possible exit from the algorithm if no path to the goal exists.

4. *Pop the node from the stack as the current node.* By pulling the next object from the stack and setting it as the current node of interest, we can explore its possibilities.

5. *Is the current node visited?* If the current node hasn't been visited, it hasn't been explored yet and can be processed now.

6. *Mark the current node as visited.* This step indicates that this node has been visited to prevent unnecessary repeat processing of it.

7. *Is the goal reached?* This step determines whether the current neighbor contains the goal the algorithm is searching for.

8. *Return the path using the current node.* By referencing the parent of the current node, then the parent of that node, and so on, the path from the goal to the root is described. The root node will be a node without a parent.

9. *Does the current node have the next neighbor?* If the current node has more possible moves to make in the maze, that move can be added to the stack to be processed. Otherwise, the algorithm can jump to step 2, where the next object in the stack can be processed if the stack isn't empty. The nature of the LIFO stack allows the algorithm to process all nodes to leaf-node depth before backtracking to visit other children of the root node.

10. *Set the current node as the parent of the neighbor.* This step is important for tracing the path from the current neighbor to the root node. From a map perspective, the origin is the position the player moved from, and the current neighbor is the position the player moved to.

11. *Add the neighbor to the stack.* The neighbor node is added to the stack for its children to be explored later. Again, this stacking mechanism allows nodes to be processed to the utmost depth before processing neighbors at shallow depths.

Figures 2.22 and 2.23 explore how the LIFO stack is used to visit nodes in the order desired by DFS. Nodes get pushed onto and popped off the stack as the depths of the nodes visited progress. The term *push* describes adding objects to a stack, and the term *pop* describes removing the topmost object from the stack.

Similarly to breadth-first search, visit the first child of node A. This is B.

Instead of visiting other child nodes of A, the first child of B is visited — in this case, F.

Again, the first child of F is visited. This is L.

Sequence of processing the stack

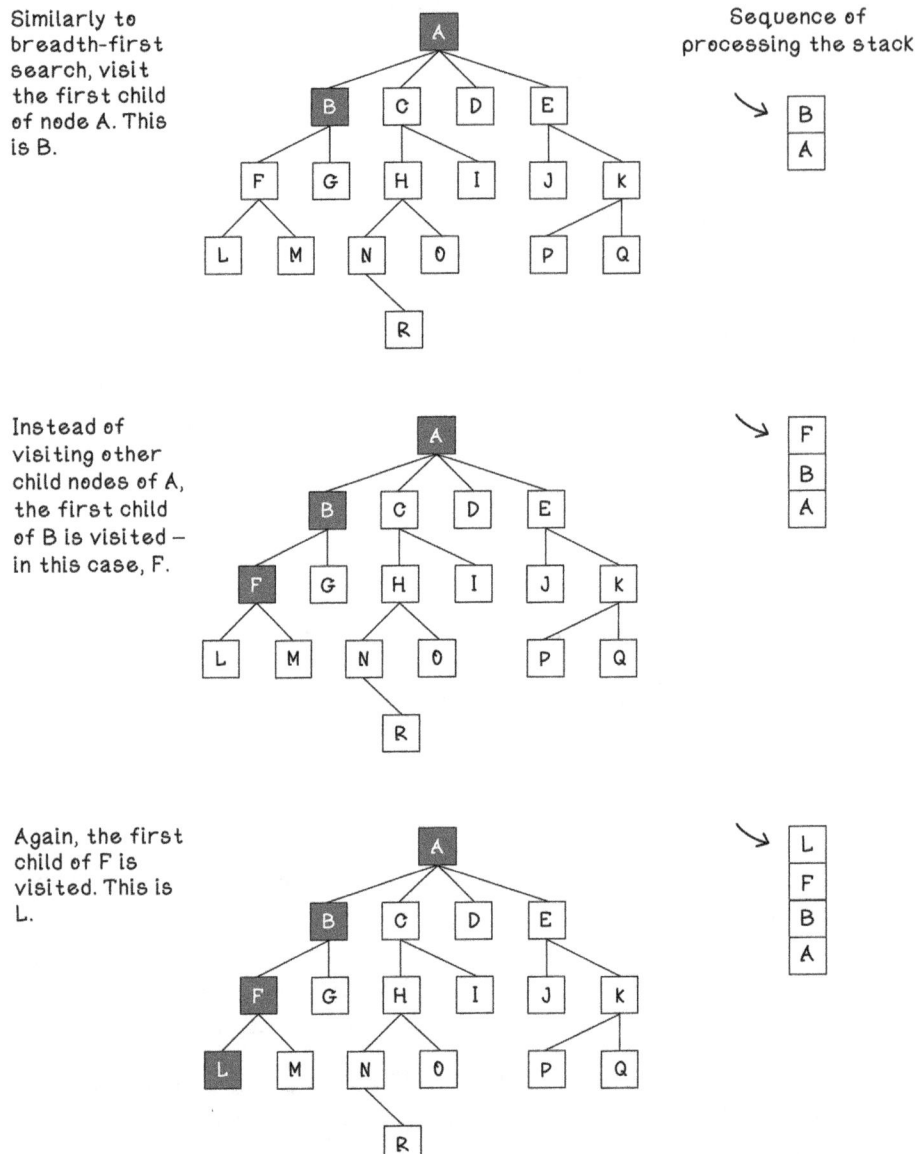

Figure 2.22 The sequence of tree processing using DFS (part 1)

Because L is a leaf node (it has no children), the algorithm backtracks to visit the next child of F, which is M.

Sequence of processing the stack

Because M is a leaf node, the algorithm backtracks to visit the next child of B. Because F has no unvisited children, this child is G.

Finally, because all children of B have been visited, the algorithm backtracks to the next child of A, which is C.

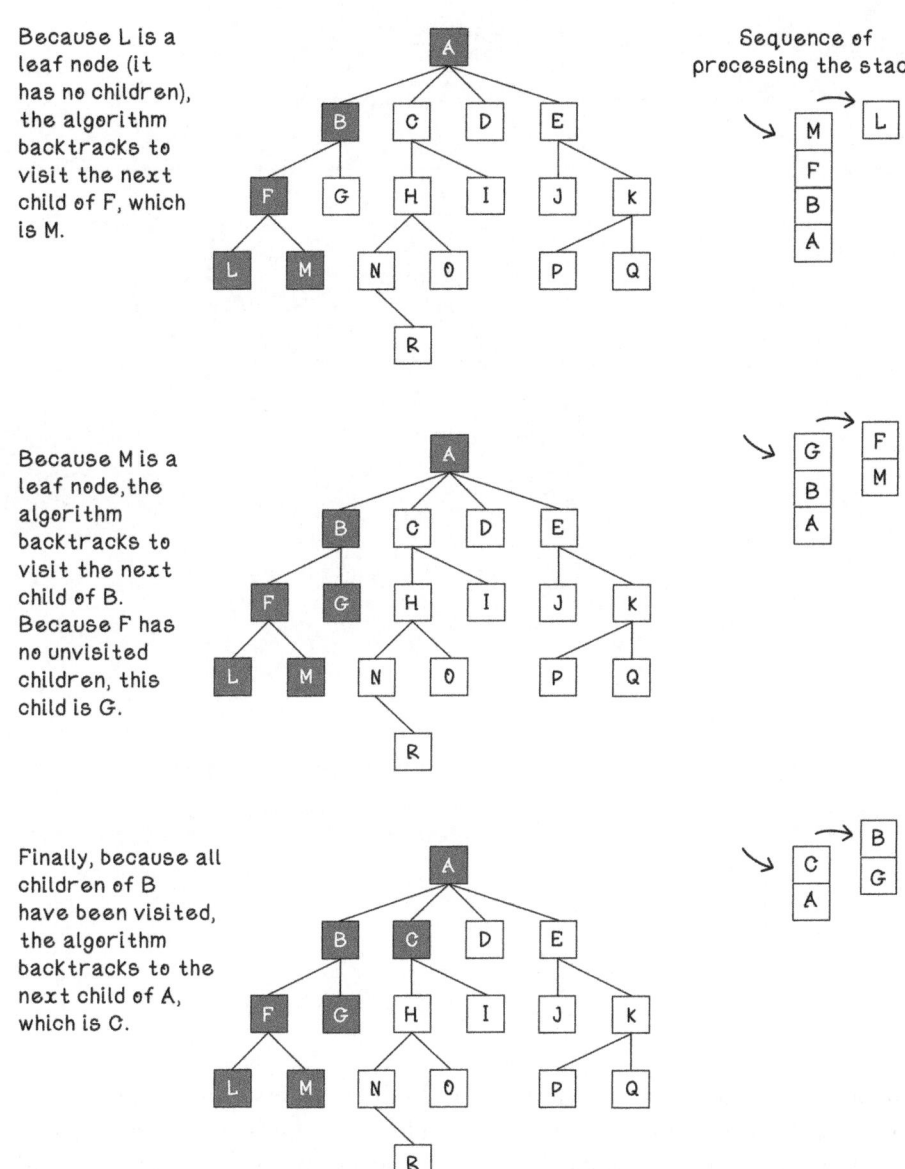

Figure 2.23 The sequence of tree processing using DFS (part 2)

Exercise: Determine the path to the solution

What would be the order of visits in DFS for the following tree?

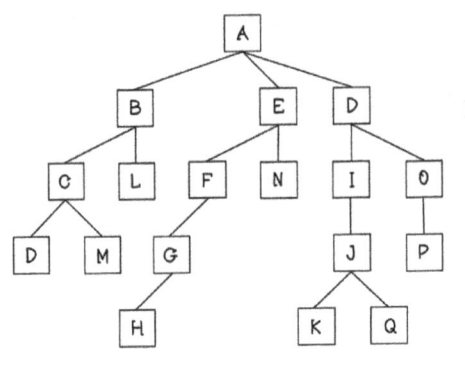

Solution:

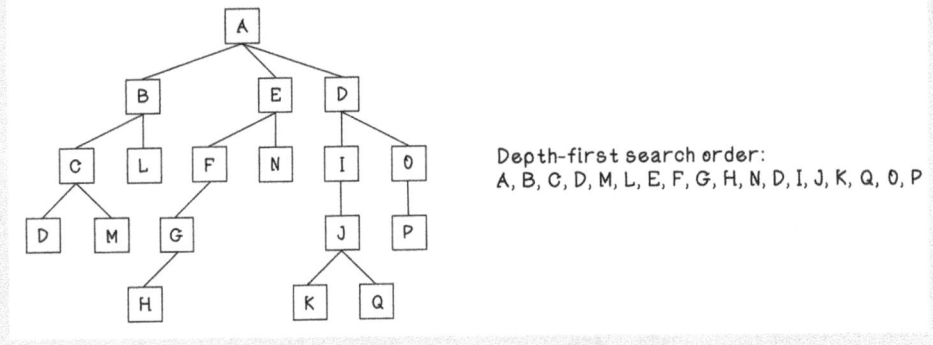

Depth-first search order:
A, B, C, D, M, L, E, F, G, H, N, D, I, J, K, Q, 0, P

It's important to understand that the order of children matters substantially in DFS because the algorithm explores the first child until it finds leaf nodes before backtracking. In the maze example, the order of movement (north, south, east, and west) influences the path to the goal the algorithm finds. A change in order will result in a different solution. The forks represented in figures 2.24 and 2.25 don't matter; what matters is the order of the movement choices in our maze example. In figure 2.24, unlike BFS, the DFS algorithm exploited one path, and by chance, using that path led to finding the goal with south, east, east, north, north, north, west, west, west as the solution. Figure 2.25 shows our full tree and highlights the path taken by the DFS algorithm.

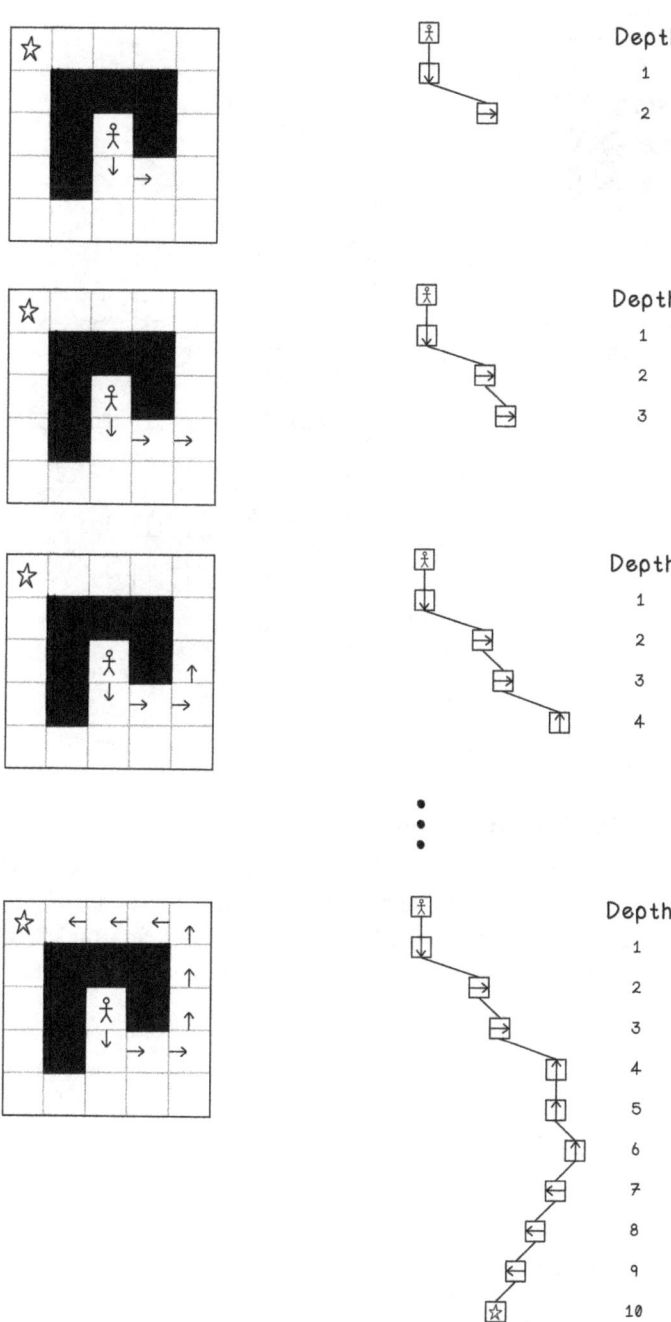

Figure 2.24 Maze movement tree generation using DFS

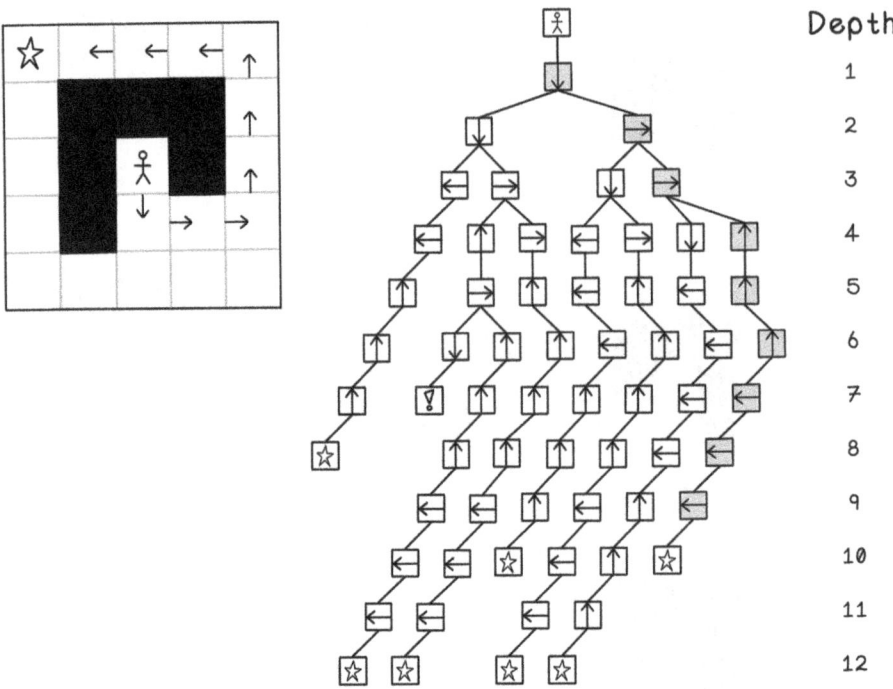

Figure 2.25 Nodes visited in the entire tree after DFS

Python code sample of the DFS algorithm

Although the DFS algorithm can be implemented with a recursive function, we're looking at an implementation that is achieved with a stack to better represent the order in which nodes are visited and processed. It's important to keep track of the visited points so that the same nodes aren't visited unnecessarily, creating cyclic loops:

```
def run_dfs(maze_game, current_point):
    visited_points = []
    stack = [current_point]
    while stack:
        next_point = stack.pop()
        if not is_in_visited_points(next_point,
        ➥visited_points):
            visited_points.append(next_point)
            if maze_game
            ➥.get_current_point_value(next_point)
```

Appends the current node to the stack

Keeps searching while there are nodes in the stack

Sets the next node in the stack as the current node

If the current node hasn't already been exploited, searches it

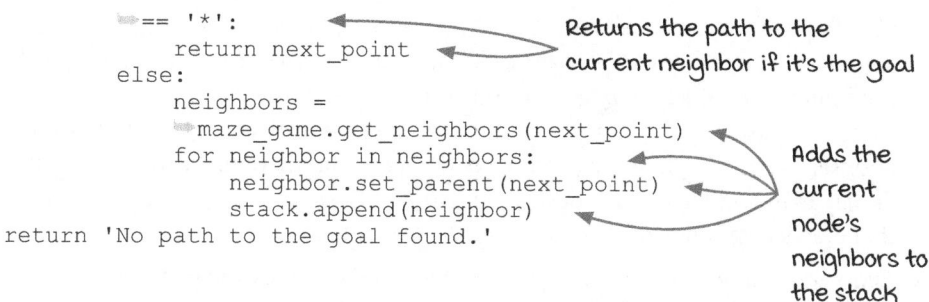

```
    == '*':
        return next_point
    else:
        neighbors =
        maze_game.get_neighbors(next_point)
        for neighbor in neighbors:
            neighbor.set_parent(next_point)
            stack.append(neighbor)
return 'No path to the goal found.'
```

Returns the path to the current neighbor if it's the goal

Adds the current node's neighbors to the stack

Now that we've explored both approaches, how do we choose between them? The decision usually comes down to two factors: the need for the shortest path versus constraints on memory.

BFS is your choice when you absolutely need the shortest path (like a GPS device finding the fastest route). This choice has a cost, however: BFS must store every node at the current depth in memory before moving to the next. In a massive graph, this expanding ring can consume huge amounts of RAM.

DFS is your choice when memory is limited. Because this approach dives deep along a single path, it needs to store only the nodes on that specific path, which makes it memory-efficient. The downside is that it's not guaranteed to find the shortest path; it simply returns the first solution it bumps into.

Use cases for uninformed search algorithms

Although the following real-world examples are technically graphs (which may contain loops/cycles), we can still use search algorithms on them by keeping track of visited nodes to avoid going in circles. Uninformed search algorithms are versatile and useful in several real-world use cases, such as these:

- *Finding paths between nodes in a network*—Historically, this use case was fundamental to the creation of ARPANET (the precursor of the internet) in 1969, when routing algorithms were needed to pass messages between the first four connected universities. When two computers need to communicate over a network, the connection passes through many connected computers and devices. Search algorithms can be used to establish a path in that network between two devices.

- *Crawling web pages*—Web searches allow us to find information on the internet across a vast number of web pages. To index these web pages, crawlers typically read the information on each page and follow the links on the page recursively. Search algorithms are useful for creating crawlers, metadata structures, and relationships between content. A famous example is Google's initial architecture (1998), in which Sergey Brin and Larry Page described using URL servers to feed search algorithms that crawled millions of pages to map the web's structure.

- *Finding social network connections*—Social media applications contain many people and their relationships. Bob may be friends with Alice, for example, but not direct friends with John, so Bob and John are indirectly related via Alice. A social media application can suggest that Bob and John become friends because they may know each other through their mutual friendship with Alice. A classic application is the Oracle of Bacon (a website based on the viral Six Degrees of Kevin Bacon meme), which uses DFS on IMDb data to find the shortest path of co-stars linking any actor to Kevin Bacon.

Optional: More about graph categories

Graphs are useful for many computer science and mathematical problems, and due to the nature of different types of graphs, different principles and algorithms may apply to specific categories of graphs. A graph is categorized based on its overall structure, number of nodes, number of edges, and interconnectivity between nodes. These categories of graphs are good to know about because they're common and sometimes referenced in search and other AI algorithms:

- *Undirected graph*—No edges are directed. Relationships between two nodes are mutual. Like roads between cities, roads in the graph travel in both directions.

- *Directed graph*—Edges indicate direction. Relationships between two nodes are explicit. As in a graph that represents a child of a parent, the child can't be the parent of its parent.

- *Disconnected graph*—One or more nodes are not connected by edges. As in a graph representing physical contact between continents, some nodes aren't connected. Like continents, some nodes are connected by land, and others are separated by oceans.

- *Acyclic graph*—A graph that contains no cycles. Think of university-course prerequisites: you must take Calc 101 to take Calc 201. You can't have a situation in which a course eventually requires itself as a prerequisite.

- *Complete graph*—Every node is connected to every other node by an edge. As in lines of communication in a small team, everyone talks to everyone else to collaborate.
- *Complete bipartite graph*—A *vertex partition* is a group of vertices. Given a vertex partition, every node from one partition is connected to every node of the other partition with edges. At a cheese-tasting event, for example, every person (group A) connects with every cheese (group B), but people don't taste people, and cheese doesn't taste cheese.
- *Weighted graph*—A weighted graph is one in which the edges between nodes have a weight. As in distances between cities, some are farther than others. The connections weigh more.

It's useful to understand the types of graphs to best describe the problem and find the most efficient algorithm for processing (figure 2.26). Some categories of graphs are discussed later in the book, including chapter 6 and chapter 8.

UNDIRECTED

No edges are directed.
Relationships between two
nodes are mutual.

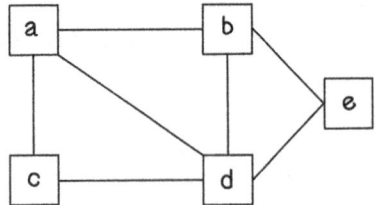

DIRECTED

Edges indicate direction.
Relationships between two
nodes are explicit.

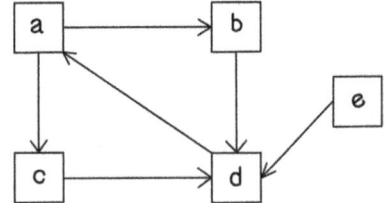

DISCONNECTED

One or more nodes are not
connected by any edges.

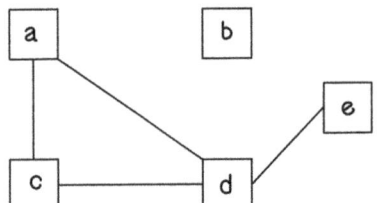

ACYCLIC

A graph that contains
no cycles.

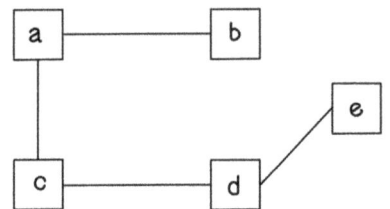

COMPLETE

Every node is connected
to every other node by an
edge.

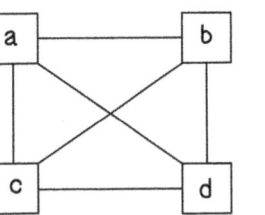

COMPLETE BIPARTITE

Every node from one partition is
connected to every node of the
other partition.

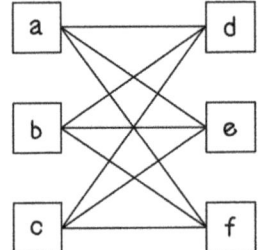

WEIGHTED

A graph where the
edges between nodes
have a weight.

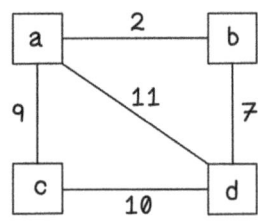

Figure 2.26 Types of graphs

Optional: More ways to represent graphs

Depending on the context, other encodings of graphs may be more efficient for processing or easier to work with, depending on the programming language and tools you're using.

Incidence matrix

An *incidence matrix* uses a matrix in which the height is the number of nodes and the width is the number of edges. Each column represents a specific edge. Why would you choose it over an adjacency list (discussed in the next section)? An incidence matrix is particularly useful when the edges are more important than the nodes. In circuit design or physical flow networks, for example, we care deeply about the connections (edges):

- *Undirected graphs*—The column for an edge contains a 1 in the rows corresponding to the two connected nodes and 0 everywhere else.
- *Directed graphs*—We use signs to indicate direction. A common convention is to place 1 for the source node (where the edge starts) and -1 for the destination node (where the edge ends).

Mathematical conventions vary; some systems swap the -1 and 1, but the concept of using opposite signs to denote direction remains the same. An incidence matrix can represent both directed and undirected graphs (figure 2.27).

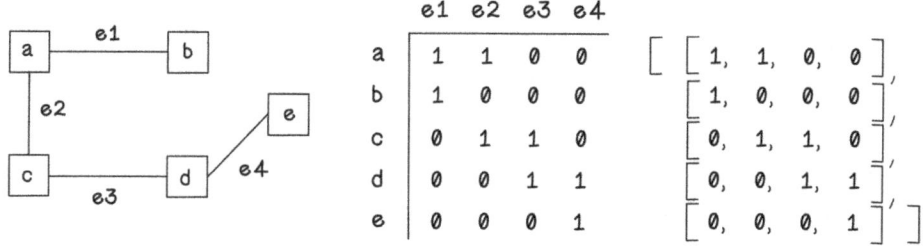

Figure 2.27 Representing a graph as an incidence matrix

Adjacency list

An *adjacency list* uses linked lists in which the size of the initial list is the number of nodes in the graph, and each value represents the connected nodes for a specific node. An adjacency list can represent both directed and undirected graphs (figure 2.28).

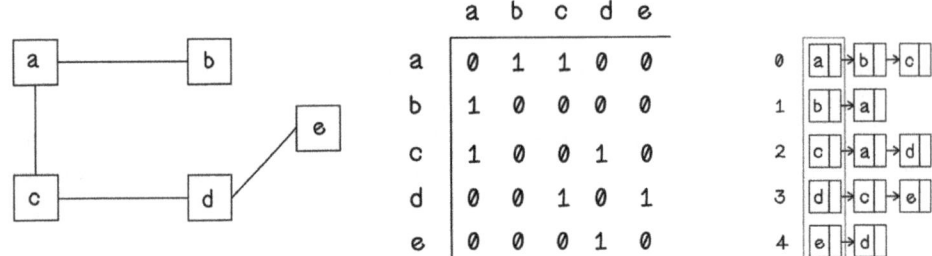

Figure 2.28 Representing a graph as an adjacency list

Graphs are interesting, useful data structures because they can easily be represented as mathematical equations, which are the backing for all algorithms. You can find more information about this topic throughout the book.

SUMMARY OF SEARCH FUNDAMENTALS

Data structures are important in every AI algorithm

Search algorithms are
useful for finding solutions
when many options exist
and a solution lies
somewhere in that tree.

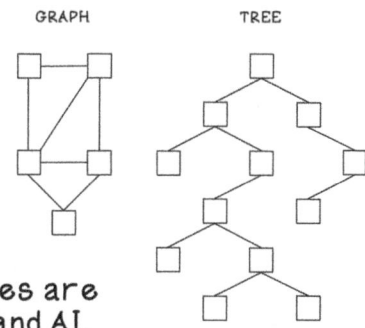

Graphs and tree structures are
widely used in algorithms and AI.

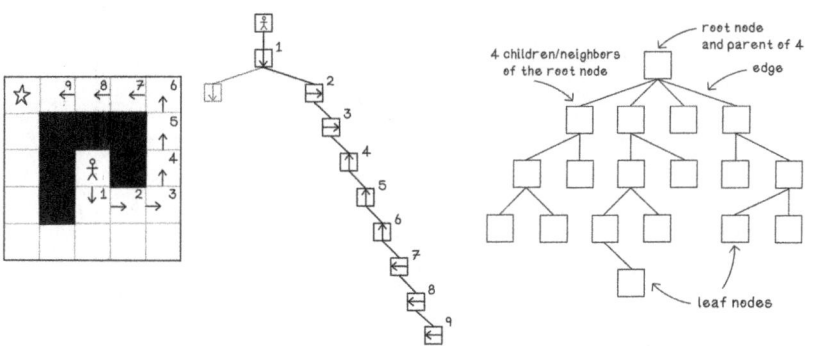

Uninformed search is blind and can be computationally
expensive - using the correct data structure helps.

Breadth-first
search looks wide
before looking deep.

Depth-first search
looks deep before
looking wide.

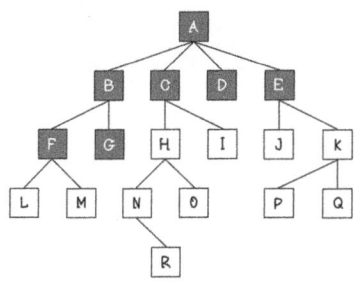
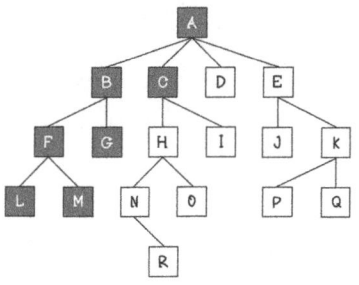

In this chapter

- Understanding and designing heuristics for guided search

- Identifying problems that guided search approaches may solve

- Understanding and designing a guided search algorithm

- Designing a search algorithm to play a two-player game

Defining heuristics: Designing educated guesses

Now that we have an idea of how uninformed search algorithms work (chapter 2), we can explore how to improve them by seeing more information about the problem. For this task, we use informed search. *Informed search* means that the algorithm has some context about the specific problem being solved; it doesn't conduct a blind breadth-first or depth-first search.

Heuristics provide a way to represent this additional knowledge about the problem. Often called a *rule of thumb*, a *heuristic* is a rule or set of rules used to evaluate a state. It can define criteria that a state must satisfy or measure the performance of a specific state, for example. We use a heuristic when no clear method of finding an optimal solution is available. A heuristic can be interpreted as an educated guess; it's more a guideline than a scientific truth with respect to the problem being solved.

When you order a pizza at a restaurant, for example, your heuristic of how good it is may be defined by the ingredients and base. Suppose that you enjoy extra tomato sauce, extra cheese, mushrooms, and pineapple on a thick base with a crunchy crust. A pizza that has more of these attributes will be more appealing to you and achieve a better score for your heuristic; a pizza that contains fewer of those attributes will be less appealing and achieve a poorer score.

Another example is a GPS routing problem. The heuristic may be "Good paths minimize time in traffic and distance traveled" or "Good paths minimize toll fees and maximize good road conditions." A poor heuristic would minimize the straight-line distance between two points. This heuristic might work for bird or airplane flight, but for everyday commuting, we use roads, which rarely offer a straight line between two destinations.

Let's look at an example: checking whether an uploaded audio clip is in a library of copyrighted content. Because audio clips are frequencies of sound, one way to perform this task is to compare every time slice of the uploaded clip against every clip in the library. This task requires an extreme amount of computation.

A primitive approach to a better search might define a heuristic that minimizes the difference in distribution of frequencies between two clips, as shown in figure 3.1. The frequencies are identical but shifted slightly. Given these distributions, we can be fairly certain that the audio clip is copyrighted. This solution may not be perfect, but it's a good start on a less-expensive algorithm.

Figure 3.1 Comparison of two audio clips using frequency distribution

Heuristics are problem-specific, and a good heuristic optimizes solutions substantially. Next, we'll adjust the maze scenario from chapter 2 to create heuristics by introducing an interesting dynamic. Instead of treating all movements the same way and measuring better solutions purely in terms of paths with fewer actions (shallow depth in the tree), now we assign different costs to movements in different directions. For this example, suppose that some strange shift in the gravity of our maze has occurred, and moving north or south now costs five times as much as moving east or west (figure 3.2). In the adjusted-maze scenario, the factors that influence the best possible path to the goal are the number of actions taken and the sum of the cost of each action on a respective path.

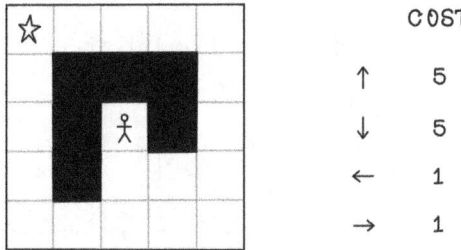

Figure 3.2 Adjustments to the maze example: Gravity

In figure 3.3, all possible paths in the tree are represented to highlight the available options, indicating the costs of the respective actions. Again, this example demonstrates the search space in the trivial maze scenario; it doesn't often apply to real-life scenarios. The algorithm generates the tree as part of the search.

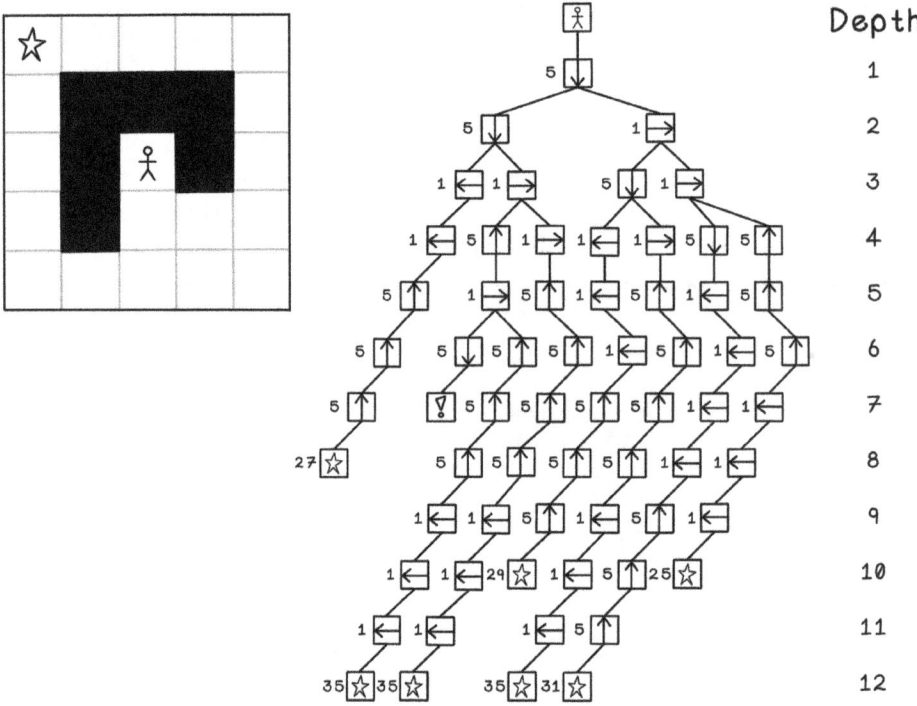

Figure 3.3 All possible movement options are represented as a tree.

A heuristic for the maze problem can be defined as follows: "Good paths minimize the cost of movement and minimize total moves to the goal." This simple heuristic guides which nodes are visited because we're applying some domain knowledge to solve the problem.

Thought experiment: What heuristic can you imagine?

Several miners specialize in different types of mining, including diamond, gold, and platinum. All the miners are productive in any mine, but they mine faster in mines that align with their specialties. Several mines that contain diamonds, gold, and platinum are spread across an area, and depots appear at different distances between mines. If the problem is distributing miners to maximize efficiency and reduce travel time, what heuristic would you create?

A sensible heuristic would assign each miner to a mine of their specialty and tasking them with traveling to the depot closest to that mine. This solution can also be interpreted as minimizing assigning miners to mines that are not their specialty and minimizing the distance they travel to depots.

Informed search: Looking for solutions with guidance

Informed search, also known as *heuristic search*, is an algorithm that uses the breadth-first and depth-first search approaches combined with some intelligence. The search is guided by heuristics, given some knowledge of the problem at hand.

We can employ several informed search algorithms, depending on the nature of the problem, including greedy search (also known as best-first search). The most popular and useful informed search algorithm, however, is A*.

A* search

A search* is pronounced "A star search." The A* algorithm usually improves performance by estimating heuristics to minimize the cost of the next node visited. The total cost is calculated with two metrics: the total distance from the start node to the current node and the estimated cost of moving to a specific node by using a heuristic. When we attempt to minimize cost, a lower value indicates a better-performing solution (figure 3.4).

$$f(n) = g(n) + h(n)$$

g(n): is the Past. The known cost. The effort you already spent to travel from the start to the current node.

h(n): is the Future. The estimated cost. The "guess" of how much effort remains to reach the goal.

f(n): is the Total. The combination of history and prediction.

Figure 3.4 The function for the A* search algorithm

A* is famous because it guarantees that it will find the shortest path. But this guarantee holds true only if your heuristic follows a strict rule: never overestimate the cost to the goal. In technical terms, the heuristic must be *admissible* and *consistent*:

• *Admissible*—The estimated cost must be less than or equal to the actual cost. Think of it as being optimistic. If the heuristic thinks that the goal is 10 miles away when it's actually 5 miles away, A* might ignore the best path.

- *Consistent*—If you're searching a graph (which allows loops), the heuristic also needs to be consistent, meaning that the estimated cost shouldn't drop erratically as you get closer to the goal.

The following example of processing is an abstract example of visiting a tree with heuristics guiding the search. The focus is on the heuristic calculations for the various nodes of the tree.

Breadth-first search (BFS) visits all nodes on each depth before moving to the next depth. Depth-first search (DFS) visits all nodes down to the final depth before traversing back to the root and visiting the next path.

A* search is different in that it doesn't have a predefined pattern to follow; nodes are visited in an order based on their heuristic costs. To achieve this task, the A* algorithm uses a Priority Queue to manage the nodes it needs to explore.

Unlike a stack (last in, first out [LIFO]) or a standard queue (first in, first out [FIFO]), a Priority Queue automatically keeps the most promising node at the front, ensuring that the algorithm always processes the node with the lowest estimated total cost next. The algorithm doesn't know the costs of all nodes up front, however. Costs are calculated as the tree is explored or generated, and each node visited is added to this queue, which means that nodes that cost more than already-visited nodes are ignored, saving computation time (figures 3.5, 3.6, and 3.7).

Given a tree representing nodes and their heuristic scores, A* will visit the first child with the lowest cost. In this case, it is C, with a cost of 2.

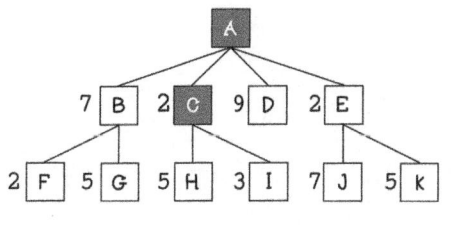

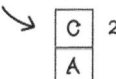

When two nodes cost the same, the node whose score was calculated first is selected.

Because E also has a cost of 2 and is a child of A, it will be the next node visited.

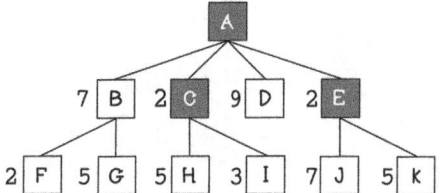

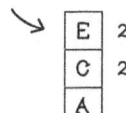

Then A* will visit the lowest-cost node from children of A or children of nodes it has already visited.

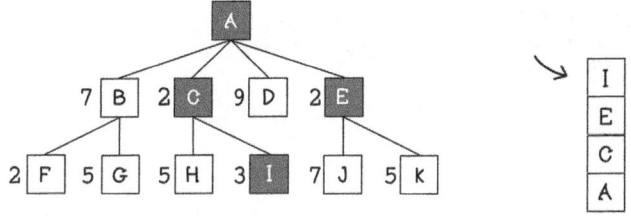

Figure 3.5 The sequence of tree processing using A* search (part 1)

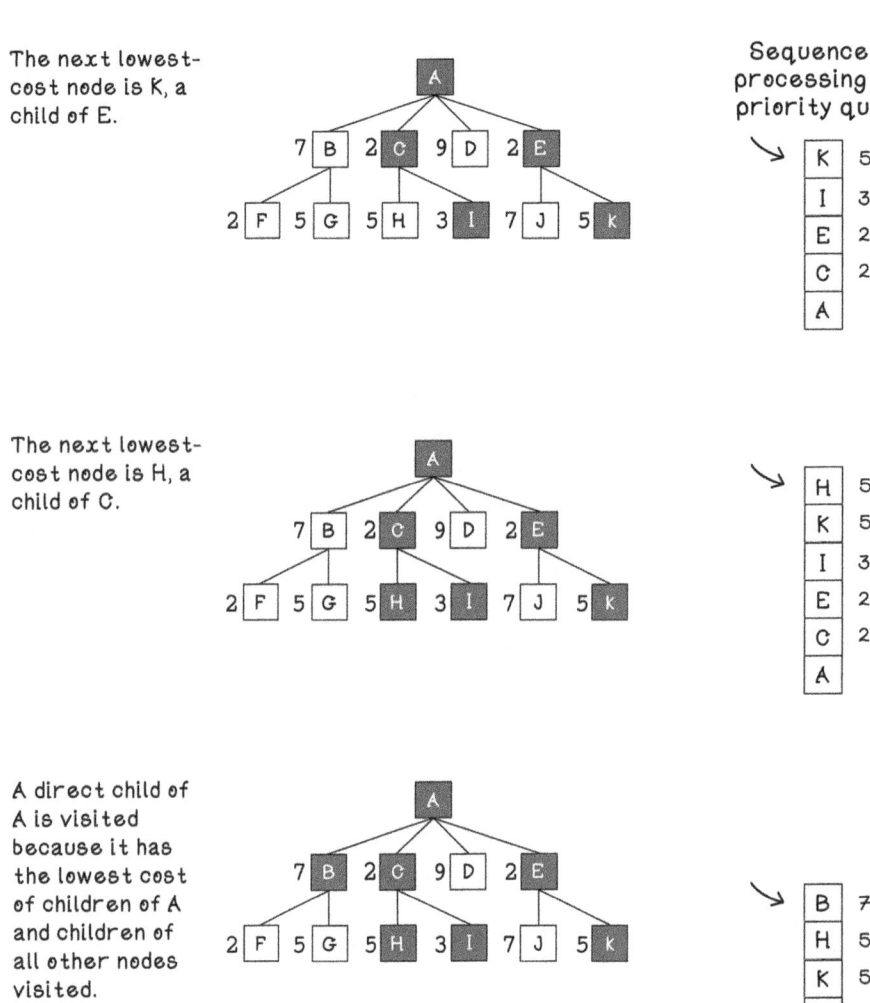

The next lowest-cost node is K, a child of E.

Sequence of processing the priority queue

The next lowest-cost node is H, a child of C.

A direct child of A is visited because it has the lowest cost of children of A and children of all other nodes visited.

Nodes that cost more than the current lowest-cost path to the solution can be ignored because paths to a solution via that node will be more expensive.

Figure 3.6 The sequence of tree processing using A* search (part 2)

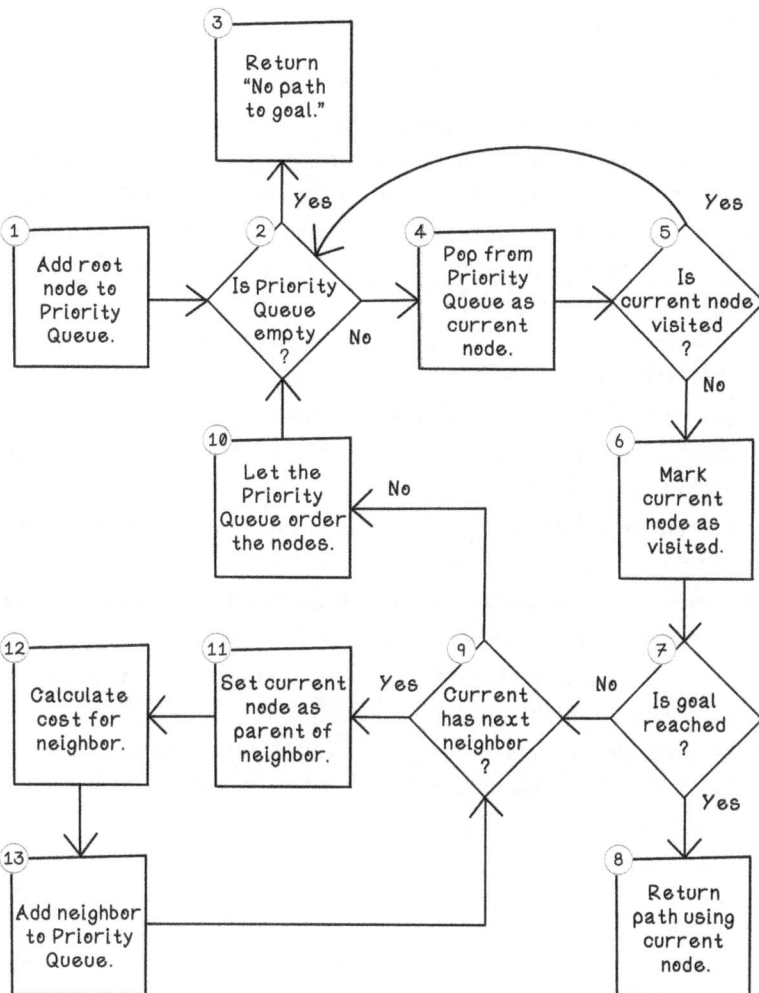

Figure 3.7 Flow of the A* search algorithm

Steps in A* search

Let's walk through the flow of the A* search algorithm:

1. *Add the root node to the Priority Queue.* The A* algorithm uses a Priority Queue (often implemented as a min-heap) to ensure that we always explore the most promising path first. The first step is adding the root node to this queue.
2. *Is the Priority Queue empty?* If the queue is empty and no path is returned in step 8 of the algorithm, there is no path to the goal. If there are still nodes in the queue, the algorithm can continue its search.
3. *Return* No path to goal. This step is the one possible exit from the algorithm if no path to the goal exists.
4. *Pop the lowest-cost object from the Priority Queue as the current node.* By pulling the lowest-cost object from the queue and setting it as the current node of interest, we can explore its possibilities.
5. *Has the current node been visited?* If the current node hasn't been visited, it hasn't been explored and can be processed now.
6. *Mark the current node as visited.* This step indicates that this node has been visited to prevent unnecessary repeat processing.
7. *Has the goal been reached?* This step determines whether the current neighbor contains the goal the algorithm is searching for.
8. *Return the path using the current node.* Referencing the parent of the current node, then the parent of that node, and so on describes the path from the goal to the root. The root node is a node without a parent.
9. *Does the current note have a next neighbor?* If the current node has more possible moves to make in the maze example, that move can be added to be processed. Otherwise, the algorithm can jump to step 2, in which the next object in the Priority Queue can be processed if it isn't empty. The nature of the Priority Queue allows the algorithm to switch between branches. If a neighbor that's cheaper than the current path is added, the algorithm effectively jumps to explore that more promising node next.
10. *Let the Priority Queue order the nodes.* Because we're using a Priority Queue, the node with the lowest total cost effectively floats to the top. We don't need to sort manually; the structure ensures that the next node we pop is always the best candidate.
11. *Set the current node as the parent of the neighbor.* This step is important for tracing the path from the current neighbor to the root node. From a map perspective, the origin is the position the player moved from, and the current neighbor is the position the player moved to.

12. *Calculate the cost for the neighbor.* The cost function is critical for guiding the A*
    algorithm. The cost is calculated by summing the distance from the root node with
    the heuristic score for the next move. More-intelligent heuristics directly influence
    the A* algorithm for better performance.
13. *Add the neighbor to the Priority Queue.* The neighbor node is added to the Priority
    Queue for its children to be explored later.

Unlike DFS, A* search determines the order of child nodes by their estimated total
costs. If two nodes have the same cost, the first node added is usually visited first.

The next three figures illustrate the tree-processing sequence. In figures 3.8 and 3.9, the
A* algorithm visits nodes both breadth-wise and depth-wise to find a solution. Figure
3.10 shows several paths to the goal, but the A* algorithm finds a path to the goal while
minimizing the cost, with fewer moves and cheaper move costs based on the fact that
north and south moves are more expensive (because of the gravity rule we added to this
scenario).

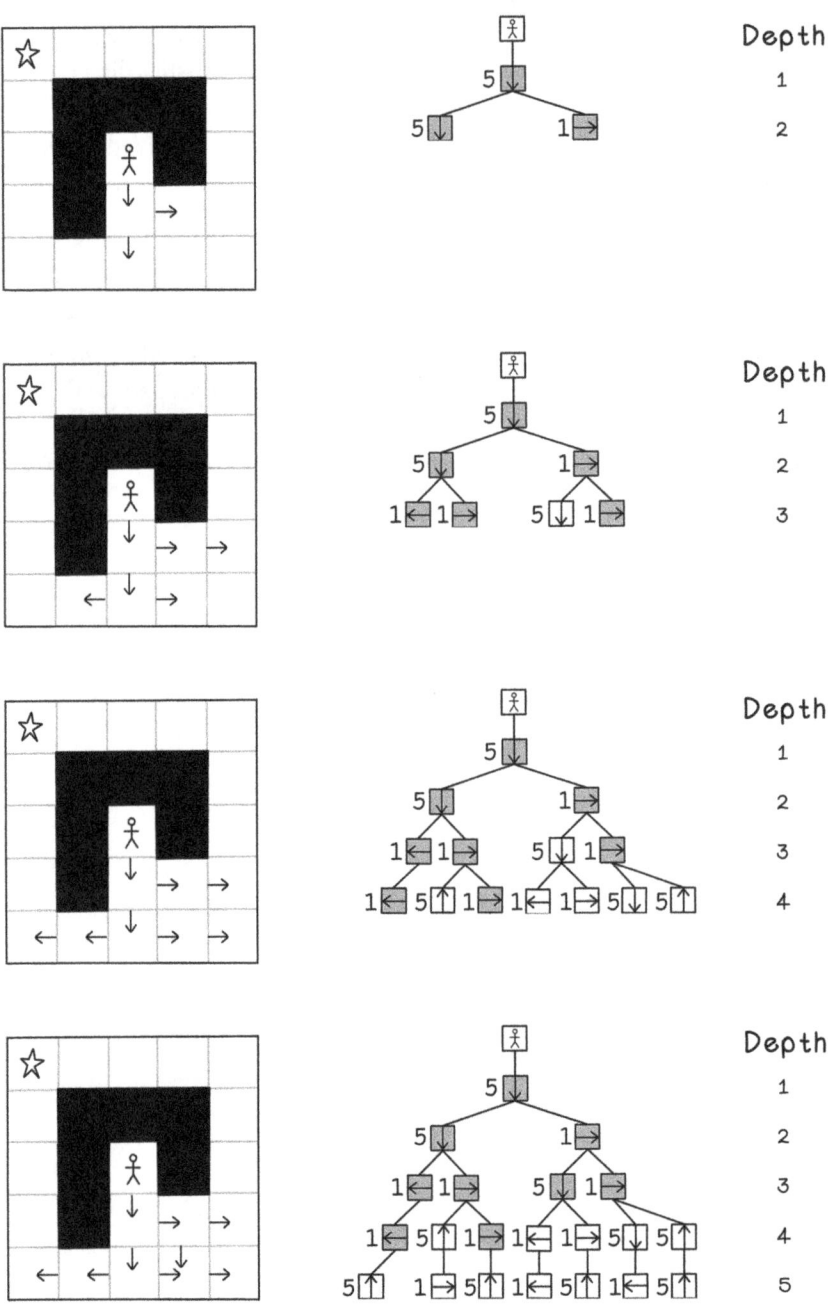

Figure 3.8 The sequence of tree processing using A* search (part 1)

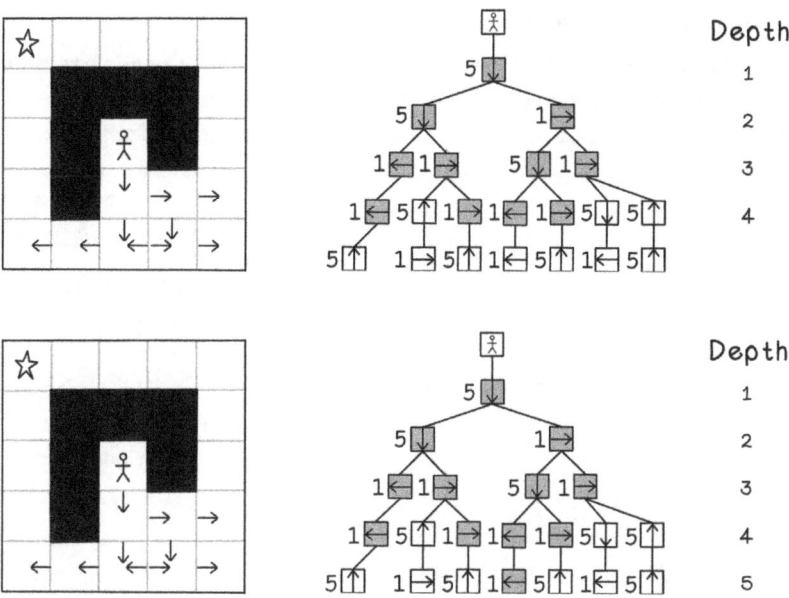

Figure 3.9 The sequence of tree processing using A* search (part 2)

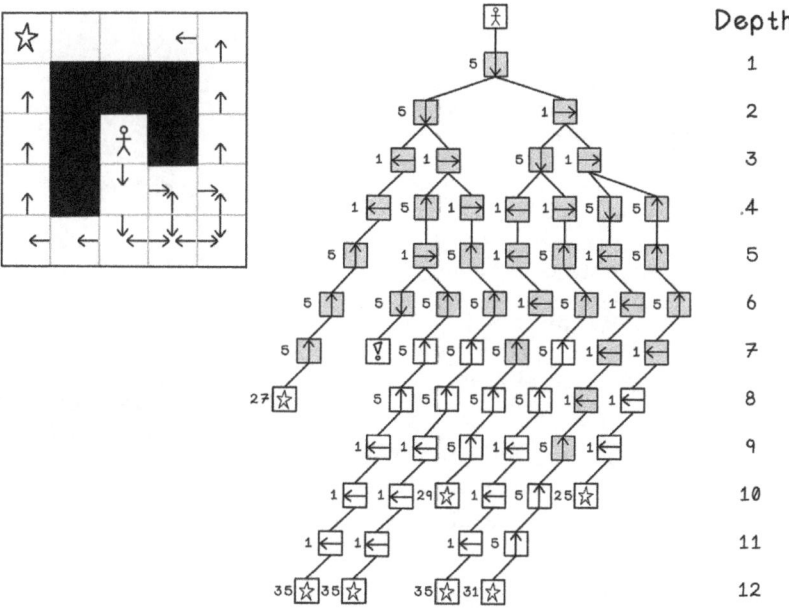

Figure 3.10 Nodes visited in the entire tree after A* search

Python code sample for A* search

The A* algorithm uses a Priority Queue to manage the nodes it needs to explore. A Priority Queue automatically keeps the most promising node at the front, ensuring that the algorithm always processes the node with the lowest estimated total cost (f) next:

Creates a unique counter to break ties when two nodes have the same cost

Adds the starting node to the priority queue, ordered by its cost

Selects and removes the node with the lowest cost (highest priority) from the queue

Skips processing if this node has already been visited via a cheaper path

Returns the current node immediately if the goal is found

Links the neighbor back to the current node to reconstruct the path later

Adds the neighbor to the queue to be explored later based on its cost

Calculates the 'f-score' (distance from start + estimated distance to goal)

```python
def run_astar(maze_game, start_point):
    visited_points = []
    goal_point = find_goal_point(maze_game)
    priority_queue = []
    tie = itertools.count()
    start_point.cost = 0
    heapq.heappush(priority_queue,
        (start_point.cost, next(tie), start_point))

    while priority_queue:
        _, _, next_point =
            heapq.heappop(priority_queue)

        if is_in_visited_points(next_point, visited_points):
            continue

        visited_points.append(next_point)

        if maze_game.get_current_point_value(next_point)
            == mp.MazePuzzle.GOAL:
            return next_point

        for neighbor in maze_game.get_neighbors(next_point):
            neighbor.set_parent(next_point)
            neighbor.cost =
                determine_cost(next_point, neighbor, goal_point)
            heapq.heappush(priority_queue,
                (neighbor.cost, next(tie), neighbor))

    return "No path to the goal found"
```

The functions for calculating the cost are critical. For A* to work, we calculate two values: the actual cost so far (g) and the heuristic estimate (h). The following functions describe how these costs are derived. In our maze example, we use a Manhattan Distance heuristic (measuring total grid steps) to estimate the remaining distance:

g = distance traveled (edges)

```
def determine_cost(origin, target, goal_point):
    g_cost = mp.get_path_length(target)
    move_cost = mp.get_move_cost(origin, target)
    h_cost = abs(target.x - goal_point.x)
        + abs(target.y - goal_point.y)
    return g_cost + move_cost + h_cost
```

movement cost for this step (captures gravity penalty)

h = manhattan distance to the goal

Uninformed search algorithms such as BFS explore layers exhaustively and result in the optimal solution (in unweighted graphs). DFS, although useful, doesn't guarantee the shortest path.

A* search is a superior approach when you can create a sensible heuristic. It computes more efficiently than uninformed algorithms because it ignores nodes with high estimated costs. If the heuristic is flawed or inadmissible (overly pessimistic), however, A* can no longer guarantee finding the optimal solution.

Use cases for informed search algorithms

Informed search algorithms are versatile and useful for many real-world use cases in which heuristics can be defined, such as the following:

- *Path finding for autonomous game characters in video games*—Game developers often use this algorithm to control the movement of enemy units in a game in which the goal is to find the human player within an environment.

- *Generating text and decoding in natural language processing (NLP)*—When AI models (such as chatbots) write sentences, they don't pick the single most likely next word. They often use heuristic search (such as beam search) to look ahead at multiple possible branches of a sentence and find the sequence of words that makes the most sense grammatically and logically.

- *Routing in telecommunications networks*—Guided search algorithms can find the shortest paths for network traffic in telecommunications networks to improve performance. Servers/network nodes and connections can be represented as searchable graphs of nodes and edges.

- *Solving single-player games and puzzles*—Informed search algorithms can solve single-player games and puzzles such as the Rubik's Cube because each move is a decision in a tree of possibilities until the goal state is found.

Adversarial search: Looking for solutions in a changing environment

The maze game involves a single actor: the player. The environment is affected only by the single player, so that player generates all possibilities. Up to now, the goal has been to maximize the benefit for the player by choosing the paths to the goal with the shortest distance and cost.

Adversarial search is characterized by opposition or conflict. Adversarial problems require us to anticipate, understand, and counteract the actions of an opponent in pursuit of a goal. Examples of adversarial problems include two-player turn-based games such as tic-tac-toe, Connect Four, and chess. The players take turns trying to affect the state of the game's environment in their favor. A set of rules dictates how players can change the environment and what the winning and end states are.

Games of this type are often called *zero-sum games*. For one player to win (+10), the other must lose (-10). The total sum of the outcome is always 0.

This section uses the Connect Four game to explore adversarial problems. Connect Four (figure 3.11) consists of a grid in which players take turns dropping tokens into one of the columns. The tokens in a specific column pile up, and any player who manages to create four adjacent sequences of their tokens—vertically, horizontally, or diagonally—wins. If the grid is full, with no winner, the game results in a draw.

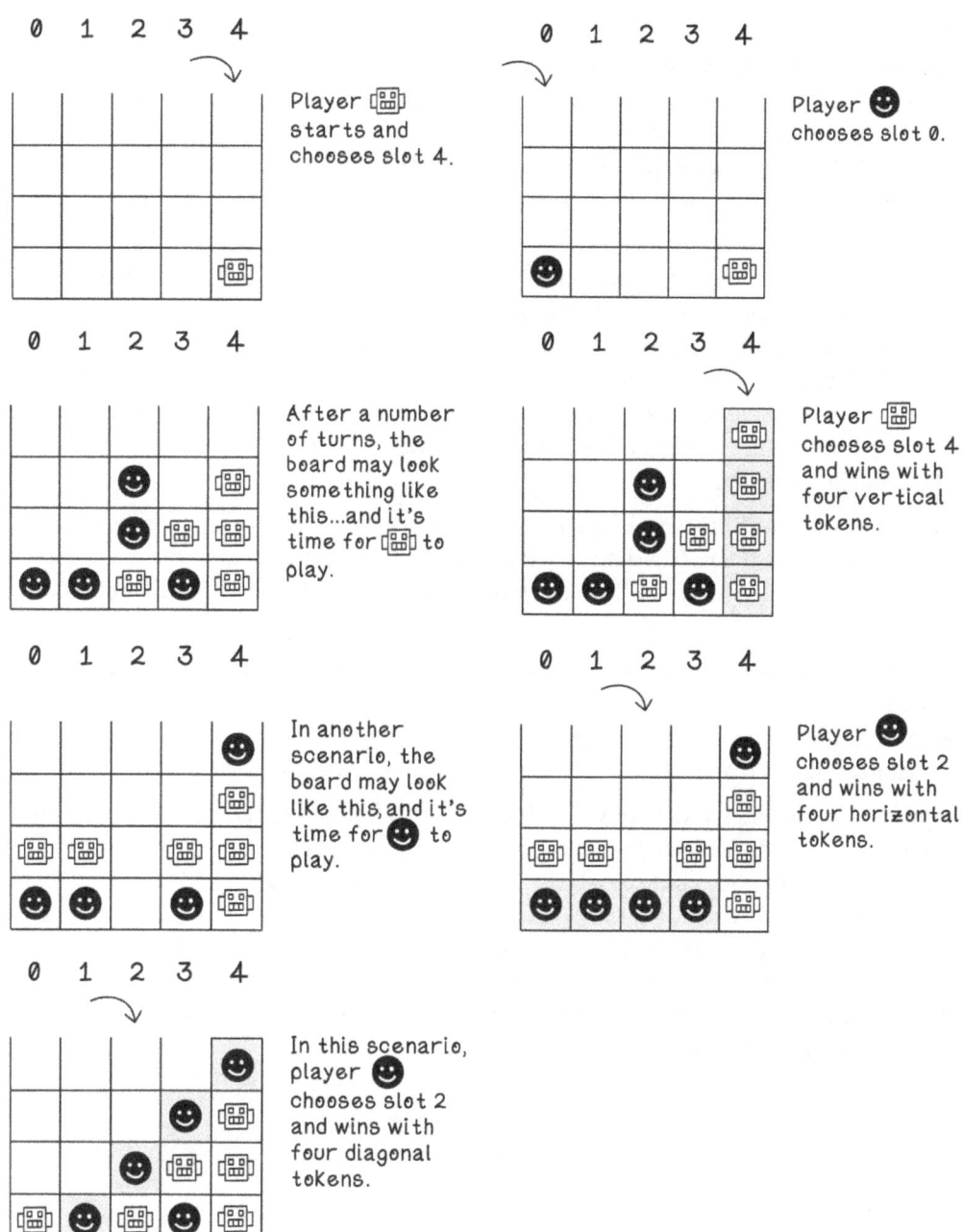

Player 🤖 starts and chooses slot 4.

Player 😊 chooses slot 0.

After a number of turns, the board may look something like this...and it's time for 🤖 to play.

Player 🤖 chooses slot 4 and wins with four vertical tokens.

In another scenario, the board may look like this, and it's time for 😊 to play.

Player 😊 chooses slot 2 and wins with four horizontal tokens.

In this scenario, player 😊 chooses slot 2 and wins with four diagonal tokens.

Figure 3.11 The Connect Four game

Minimax search: Simulate actions and choose the best future

Minimax search aims to build a tree of possible outcomes based on moves that each player could make, favoring paths that are advantageous to the agent and avoiding paths that are favorable to the opponent. This type of search simulates possible moves assuming that both players play perfectly (that is, the opponent always chooses the move that hurts the agent most) and scores the state based on a heuristic after making the respective move.

Minimax search attempts to discover as many future states as possible. But due to memory and computation limitations, discovering the entire game tree may not be realistic, so it searches to a specified depth. Minimax search simulates the turns taken by each player, so the depth specified is linked directly to the number of turns taken by both players. A depth of 4, for example, means that each player has had two turns: player A makes a move, player B makes a move, player A makes another move, and player B makes another move.

The Minimax algorithm uses a heuristic score to make decisions. This score is defined by a crafted heuristic, not learned automatically by the algorithm. If we have a specific game state, every possible valid outcome of a move from that state will be a child node in the game tree.

Imagine a heuristic that provides a score in which positive numbers are better than negative numbers. By simulating every possible valid move, the Minimax search algorithm minimizes moves that give the opponent an advantage or a winning state and maximizes moves that give the agent an advantage or a winning state.

Figure 3.12 illustrates a Minimax search tree. In this figure, the leaf nodes are the only nodes for which the heuristic score is calculated because these states indicate a win or a draw. The other nodes indicate states that are in progress. Starting at the depth where the heuristic is calculated and moving upward, either the child with the minimum score or the child with the maximum score is chosen, depending on whose turn is next in the future simulated states. Starting at the top, the agent attempts to maximize its score. After each alternating turn, the intention changes because the aim is to maximize the agent's score and minimize the opponent's score.

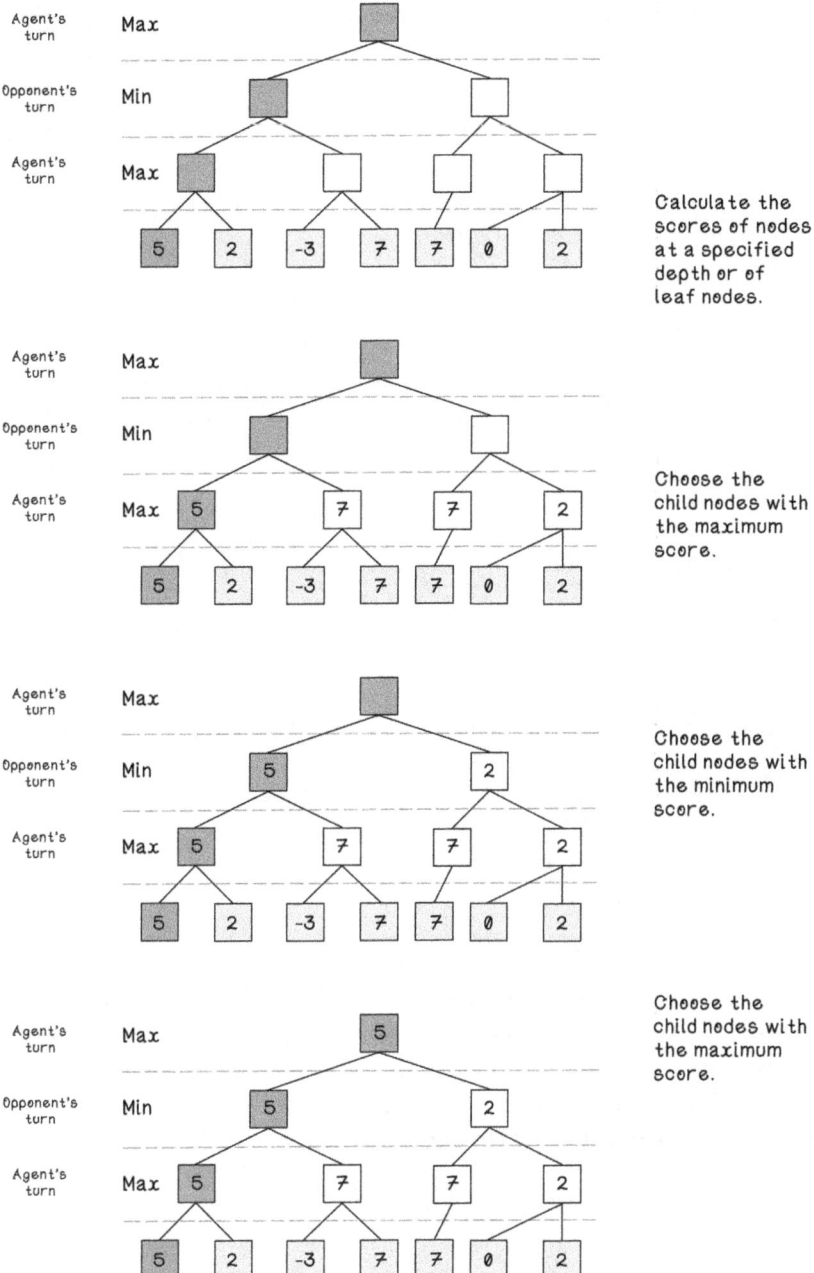

Figure 3.12 The sequence of tree processing using Minimax search

Exercise: What values would propagate in the following Minimax tree?

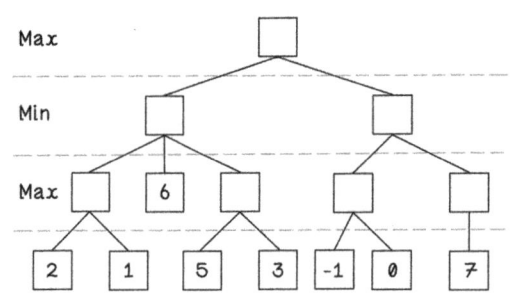

Solution:

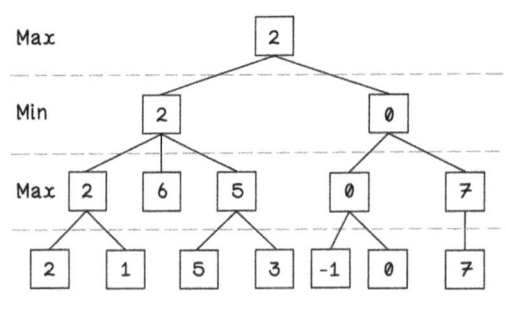

Because the Minimax search algorithm simulates possible outcomes, in games that offer a multitude of choices, the game tree explodes, and exploring the entire tree quickly becomes too computationally expensive. In the simple example of Connect Four played on a 5 x 4 block board, the number of possibilities already makes exploring the entire game tree on every turn inefficient (figure 3.13).

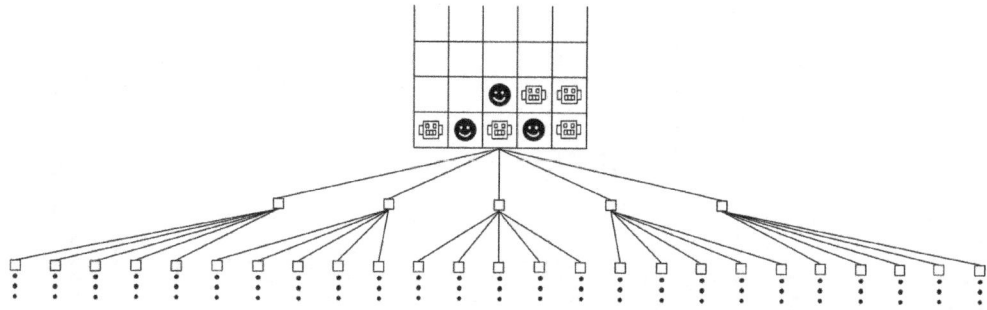

Figure 3.13 The explosion of possibilities while searching the game tree

To use Minimax search in the Connect Four example, the algorithm essentially makes all possible moves from a current game state; then it determines all possible moves from each state until it finds the most favorable path. Game states that result in a win for the agent return a score of 10, and states that result in a win for the opponent return a score of -10. Minimax search tries to maximize the agent's positive score (figures 3.14 and 3.15).

> **NOTE** Although the flow chart for the min-max search algorithm looks complex due to its size, it really isn't. The number of conditions that check whether the current state is to maximize or minimize causes the chart to bloat.

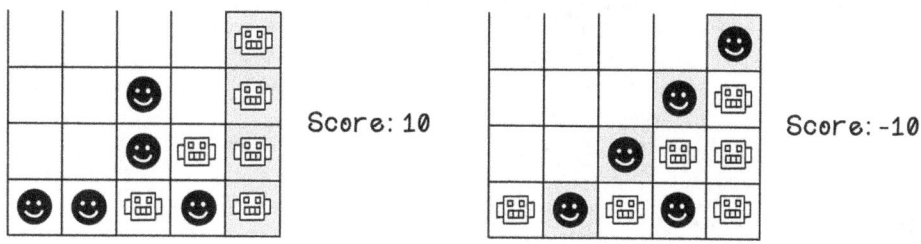

Figure 3.14 Scoring for the agent vs. scoring for the opponent

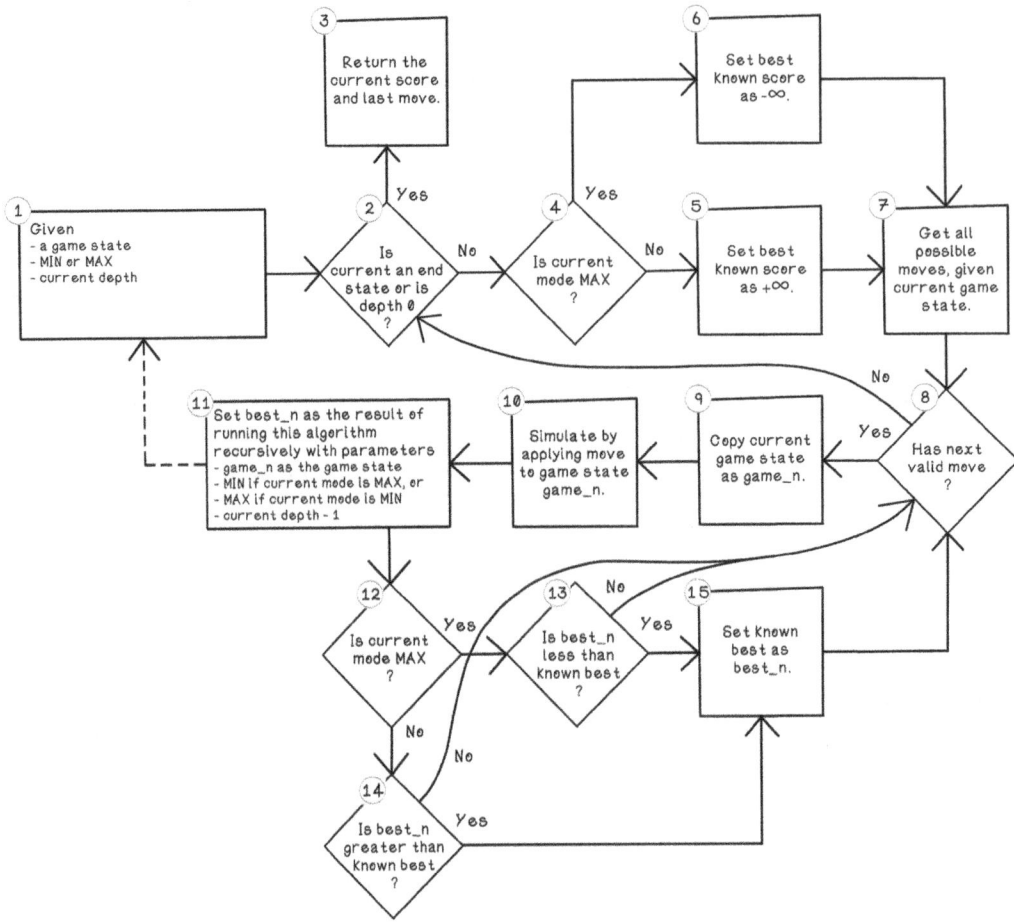

Figure 3.15 Flow of the Minimax search algorithm

Steps in Minimax search

Let's walk through the flow of the Minimax search algorithm:

1. *Given a game state (whether the current mode is minimization or maximization) and a current depth, the algorithm starts.* It's important to understand the inputs for the algorithm because the Minimax search algorithm is recursive. A recursive algorithm calls itself in one or more of its steps and must have an exit condition to prevent it from calling itself forever.

2. *Is the current node an end state or is depth 0?* This condition determines whether the current state of the game is a terminal state or whether the desired depth has been

reached. A *terminal state* is one in which one player has won or the game is a draw. A score of 10 represents a win for the agent, a score of -10 represents a win for the opponent, and a score of 0 indicates a draw. A depth is specified because traversing the entire tree of possibilities to all end states is computationally expensive and is likely to take too long on the average computer. By specifying a depth, the algorithm can look a few turns into the future to determine whether a terminal state exists.

3. *Return the current score and the last move.* The score of the current state is returned if the current state is a terminal game state or the specified depth has been reached.

4. *Is the current mode MAX?* If the current iteration of the algorithm is in the maximize state, it tries to maximize the agent's score.

5. *Set the best known score as +∞.* If the current mode minimizes the score, the best score is set to positive infinity because we know that the scores returned by the game states will always be less. In actual implementation, a very large number is used instead of infinity.

6. *Set the best known score as -∞.* If the current mode maximizes the score, the best score is set to negative infinity because we know that the scores returned by the game states will always be more. In actual implementation, a very large negative number is used instead of infinity.

7. *Get all possible moves, given the current game state.* This step specifies a list of possible moves that can be made given the current game state. As the game progresses, some moves that were available at the start may not be available anymore. In the Connect Four example, a column may be filled; therefore, a move that selects that column is invalid.

8. *Has the next valid move been made?* If no possible moves have been simulated and there are no more valid moves to make, the algorithm short-circuits to returning the best move in that instance of the function call.

9. *Copy the current game state as* game_n. A copy of the current game state is required so the algorithm can perform simulations of possible future moves on it.

10. *Simulate the current move by applying it to game state* game_n. This step applies the current move of interest to the copied game state.

11. *Set* best_n *as the result of running this algorithm recursively.* Recursion comes into play in this step. best_n is a variable used to store the next best move, and we're making the algorithm explore future possibilities from this move.

12. *Is the current mode MAX?* When the recursive call returns a best candidate, this condition determines whether the current mode maximizes the score.

13. *Is* best_n *less than the known best?* This step determines whether the algorithm has found a better score than one previously found if the mode maximizes the score.

14. *Is* best_n *greater than the known best?* This step determines whether the algorithm has found a better score than one previously found if the mode minimizes the score.

15. *Set the known best as* best_n. If the new best score is found, set the known best as that score.

Given the Connect Four example at a specific state, the Minimax search algorithm generates the tree shown in figure 3.16. From the start state, every possible move is explored. Then each move from that state is explored until a terminal state is found: the board is full or a player has won.

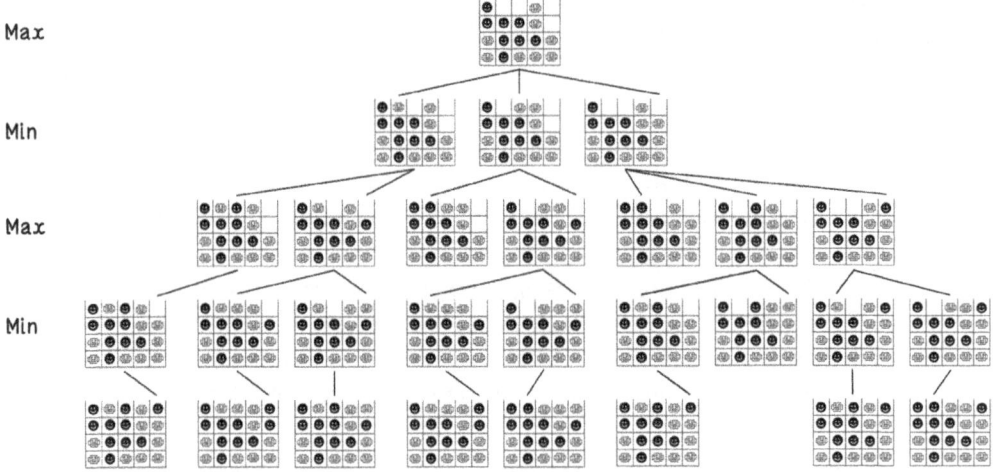

Figure 3.16 A representation of the possible states in a Connect Four game

The highlighted nodes in figure 3.17 are terminal state nodes in which draws are scored as 0, losses are scored as -10, and wins are scored as 10. Because the algorithm aims to maximize its score, a positive number is required, whereas opponent wins are scored with a negative number.

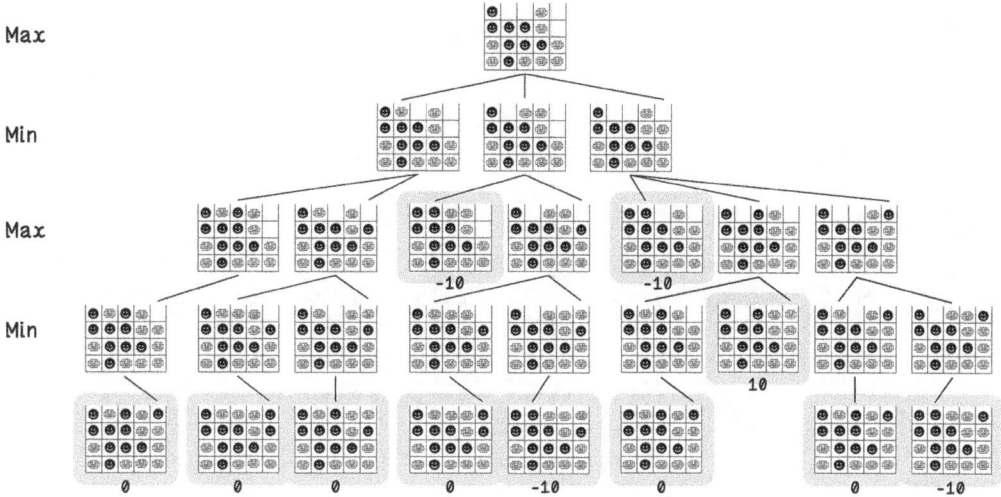

Figure 3.17 The possible end states in a Connect Four game

When these scores are known, the Minimax algorithm starts at the lowest depth and chooses the node whose score is the minimum value (figure 3.18). Then, at the next depth, the algorithm chooses the node whose score is the maximum value (figure 3.19).

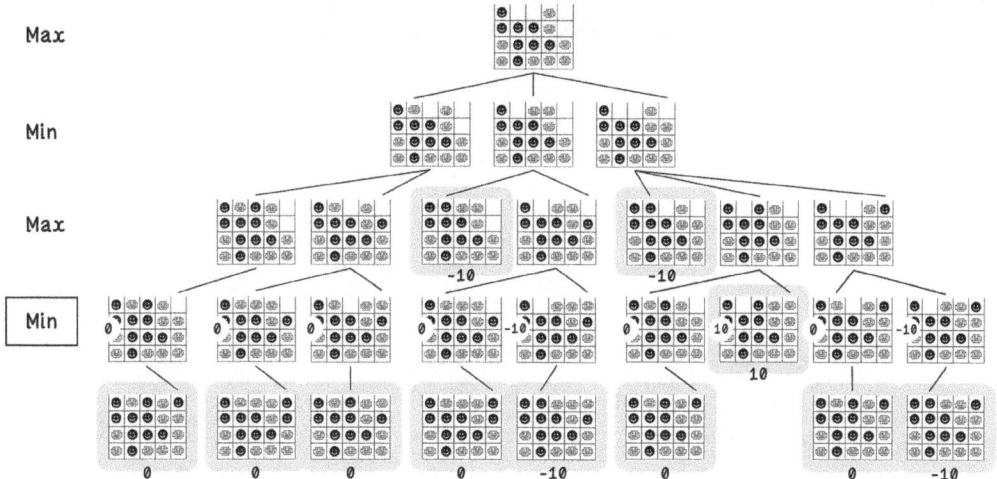

Figure 3.18 The possible scores for end states in a Connect Four game (part 1)

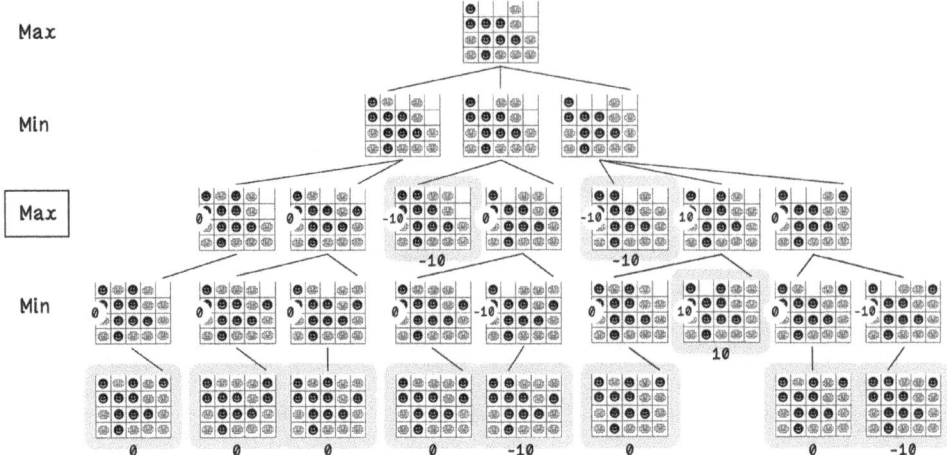

Figure 3.19 The possible scores for end states in a Connect Four game (part 2)

Finally, at the next depth, nodes whose score is the minimum are chosen, and the root node chooses the maximum of the options. By following the nodes and score selected and intuitively applying ourselves to the problem, we see that the algorithm selects a path to a draw to prevent a loss. If the algorithm selects the path to a win, there is a high likelihood of a loss in the next turn. The algorithm assumes that the opponent will always make the smartest move to maximize their chance of winning (figure 3.20). The simplified tree in figure 3.21 represents the outcome of the Minimax search algorithm for the given game-state example.

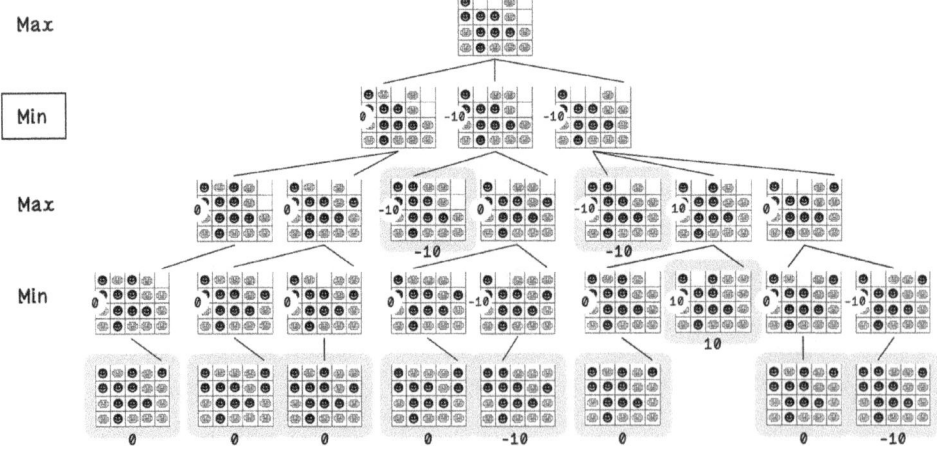

Figure 3.20 The possible scores for end states in a Connect Four game (part 3)

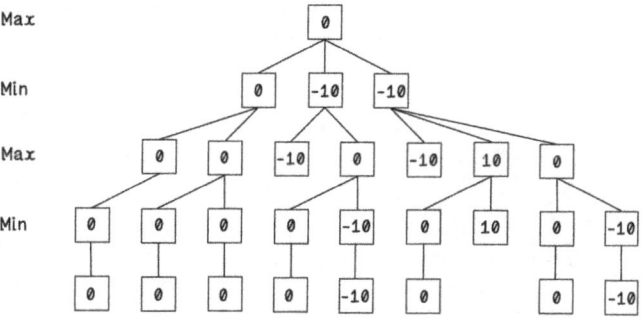

Figure 3.21 Simplified game tree with Minimax scoring

Python code sample for Minimax search

The Minimax search algorithm is implemented as a recursive function. The function is given the current state, desired depth to search, minimization or maximization mode, and last move. The algorithm terminates by returning the best move and score for every child at every depth in the tree. Comparing the code with the flow chart in figure 3.15, we see that the tedious conditions of checking whether the current mode is maximizing or minimizing are not as apparent. In the code, 1 or -1 represents the intention to maximize or minimize, respectively. By using some clever logic, the best score, conditions, and switching states can be done via the principle of negative multiplication, in which a negative number multiplied by another negative number results in a positive. So if -1 indicates the opponent's turn, multiplying it by -1 results in 1, which indicates the agent's turn. Then, for the next turn, 1 multiplied by -1 results in -1 to indicate the opponent's turn again:

The game is over (win/loss/draw) or depth limit reached

```
def minmax(connect, depth, min_or_max, move):
    current_score = connect.get_score_for_ai()
    current_is_board_full = connect.is_board_full()
    if current_score != 0 or
    current_is_board_full or depth == 0:
        return Move(move, current_score)

    best_score = INFINITY_NEGATIVE * min_or_max
    best_max_move = -1
    moves = random.sample(range(0, connect.board_size_y + 1),
        connect.board_size_x)
    for slot in moves:
```

Initialize best_score to the worst possible score for the current player

Randomize the order of moves to add variability to the AI's choices

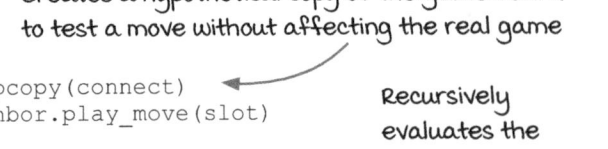

Creates a hypothetical copy of the game board
to test a move without affecting the real game

```
neighbor = copy.deepcopy(connect)
move_outcome = neighbor.play_move(slot)
if move_outcome:
    best = minmax(neighbor, depth - 1,
    min_or_max * -1, slot)
    if (min_or_max == MAX and best.value
    > best_score) or (min_or_max == MIN
    and best.value < best_score):
        best_score = best.value
        best_max_move = best.move
return Move(best_max_move, best_score)
```

Recursively
evaluates the
outcome of the
move and updates
best_score and
best_max_move

Updates the best move if the
returned score is better for
the current player (Higher for
MAX, Lower for MIN)

Bubbles the best move and
score found back up to the
previous level of the recursion

Alpha-beta pruning: Optimize by exploring the sensible paths only

Alpha-beta pruning is a technique used with the Minimax search algorithm to short-circuit exploring areas of the game tree that are known to produce poor solutions. This technique optimizes the Minimax search algorithm to save computation because insignificant paths are ignored.

Suppose that you're using a map to find the fastest route home. Route A takes 30 minutes. Next, you check route B. The app tells you that the first segment of route B involves a ferry ride that takes 45 minutes.

You stop calculating route B immediately. You don't need to know how fast the roads are after the ferry. Because the first step alone is already longer than the entirety of route A, route B is guaranteed to be worse. You prune that route from your calculations.

Because we know how the Connect Four game tree explodes, we clearly see that ignoring more paths will improve computational performance significantly (figure 3.22). The alpha-beta pruning algorithm works by storing the best score for the maximizing player and the best score for the minimizing player as alpha and beta, respectively.

Initially, alpha is set as -∞, and beta is set as ∞—the worst score for each player. If the best score of the minimizing player is less than the best score of the maximizing player, it's logical that other child paths of the nodes already visited would not affect the best score.

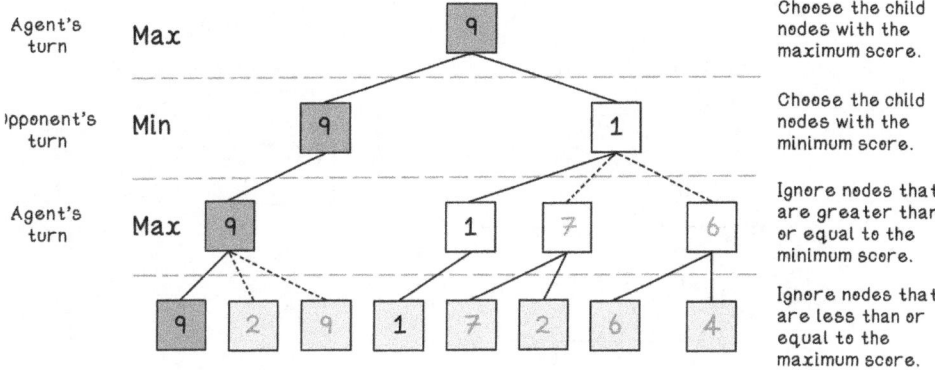

Figure 3.22 An example of alpha-beta pruning

Figure 3.23 illustrates the changes made in the Minimax search flow to accommodate the optimization of alpha-beta pruning. The shaded blocks are the additional steps in the Minimax search algorithm's flow.

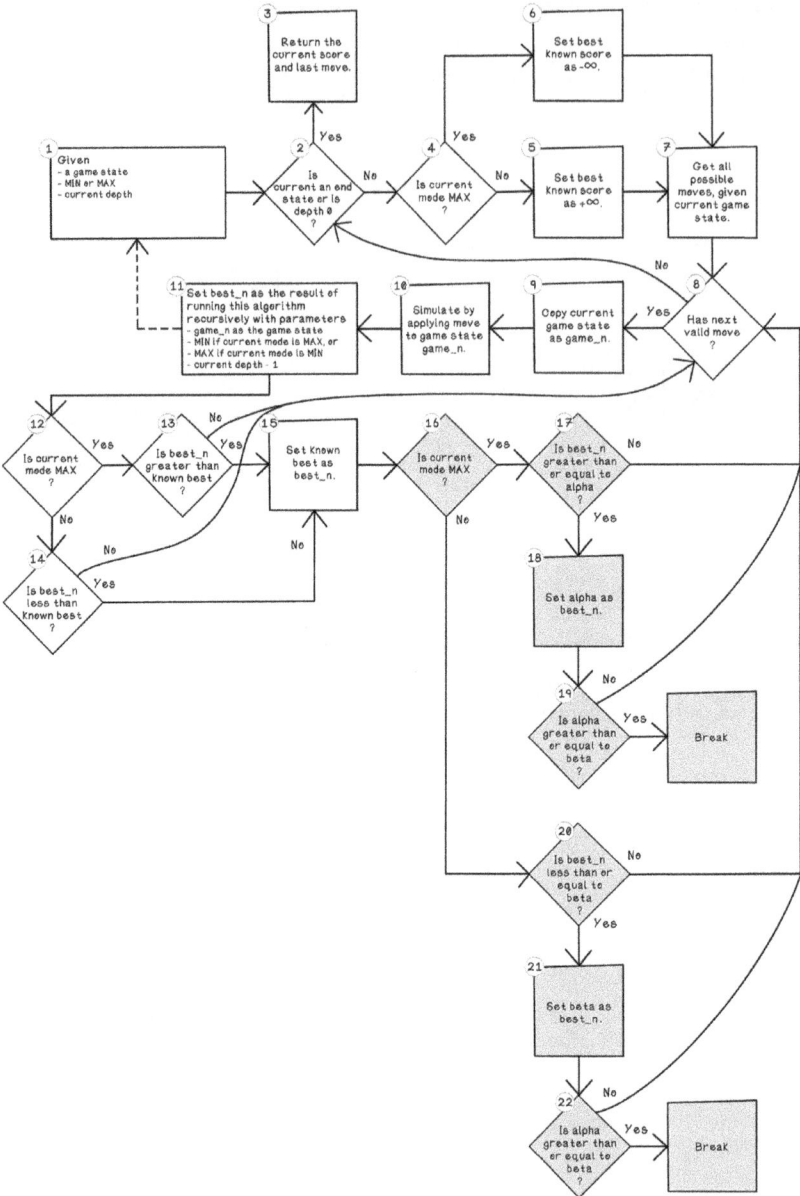

Figure 3.23 Flow of the Minimax search algorithm with alpha-beta pruning

Steps in Minimax search with alpha-beta pruning

The following steps are additions to the Minimax search algorithm that allow termination of exploration of paths when the best score found doesn't change the outcome:

1. *Is the current mode MAX?* Again, determine whether the algorithm is currently attempting to maximize or minimize the score.

2. *Is* `best_n` *greater than or equal to* `alpha`? If the current mode is to maximize the score and current best score (`best_n`) is greater than `alpha`, we've found a better path than previously discovered. We update `alpha` to reflect this new highest value. This step tightens the search window, potentially helping us prune future branches, but we don't stop exploring this node yet unless `alpha` becomes greater than or equal to `beta` in step 4.

3. *Set* `alpha` *as* `best_n`. This step sets the variable `alpha` to `best_n`.

4. *Is* `alpha` *greater than or equal to* `beta`? The score is as good as other scores found, and the rest of the exploration of that node can be ignored by breaking.

5. *Is* `best_n` *less than or equal to* `beta`? If the current mode minimizes the score and the current best score (`best_n`) is less than `beta`, we've found a stronger move for the minimizing player. We update `beta` to reflect this new lowest value. This step tightens the search window from the top, helping us prune future branches if the maximizer's best option (`alpha`) meets this new limit.

6. *Set* `beta` *as* `best_n`. This step sets the variable `beta` to `best_n`.

7. *Is* `alpha` *greater than or equal to* `beta`? The score is as good as other scores found, and the rest of the exploration of that node can be ignored by breaking.

Python code sample for Minimax search with alpha-beta pruning

The code for achieving alpha-beta pruning is largely the same as the code for Minimax search, with the addition of keeping track of the `alpha` and `beta` values and maintaining those values as the tree is traversed. When `minimum (min)` is selected, the variable `min_or_max` is −1, and when `maximum (max)` is selected, the variable `min_or_max` is 1:

```python
def minmax(connect, depth, min_or_max, move, alpha, beta):
    current_score = connect.get_score_for_ai()
    current_is_board_full = connect.is_board_full()
    if current_score != 0 or current_is_board_full or depth == 0:
        return Move(move, current_score)

    best_score = INFINITY_NEGATIVE * min_or_max
    best_max_move = -1
    moves = random.sample(range(0, connect.board_size_x),
    connect.board_size_x)
```

```
for slot in moves:
    neighbor = copy.deepcopy(connect)
    move_outcome = neighbor.play_move(slot)
    if move_outcome:
        best = minmax(neighbor, depth - 1,
        min_or_max * -1, slot, alpha, beta)
        if (min_or_max == MAX and best.value
        > best_score) or (min_or_max == MIN
        and best.value < best_score):
            best_score = best.value
            best_max_move = best.move
            if min_or_max == MAX:
                if best_score > best_score_so_far:
                    if best_score > alpha:
                        alpha = best_score
            elif min_or_max == MIN:
                if best_score < best_score_so_far:
                    if best_score < beta:
                        beta = best_score
            if alpha >= beta:
                break
            return Move(best_max_move, best_score)
```

Passes the current alpha and beta limits down to the next level of the search

Tighten the Lower Bound if max finds a move better than the current known best (alpha), update alpha

Tighten the Upper Bound if min finds a move worse than the current known best (beta), update beta

Stops searching this branch. We found a move that the opponent will never let us take because they already have a better option elsewhere

Use cases for adversarial search algorithms

Informed search algorithms are versatile and useful in real-world use cases such as the following:

- *Creating game-playing agents for turn-based games with perfect information*—In some games, two or more players act on the same environment. Successful implementations of chess, checkers, and other classic games have been created. Games with perfect information are games that have no hidden information or don't involve random chance.

- *Creating game-playing agents for turn-based games with imperfect information*—Unknown future options exist in these games, including poker and Scrabble.

- *Adversarial search and ant colony optimization (ACO) for route optimization*—Adversarial search is used in combination with the ACO algorithm (discussed in chapter 6) to optimize package-delivery routes in cities.

SUMMARY OF INTELLIGENT SEARCH

Informed search gives search algorithms some intelligence

Heuristics can be tricky to think up, but a good heuristic is powerful for finding solutions more efficiently.

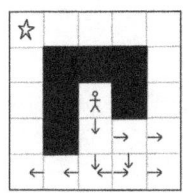

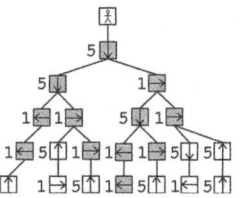

A* search uses heuristics and the distance from the root to find optimal solutions.

Adversarial search like Minimax is useful when something else affects the environment as well.

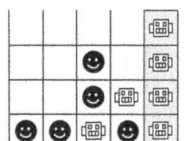

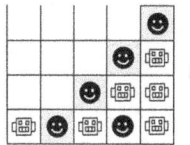

Alpha-beta pruning helps optimize the Minimax algorithm by eliminating undesirable paths.

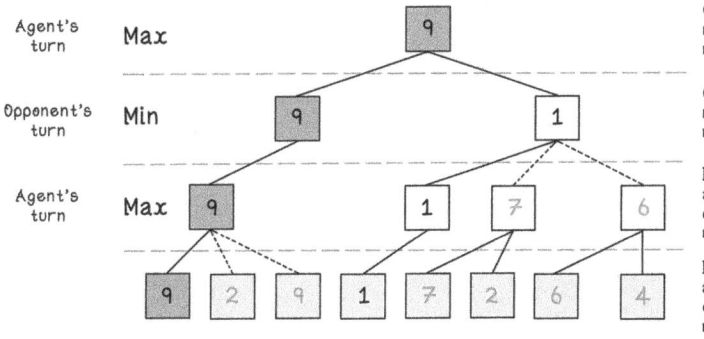

Evolutionary algorithms | 4

In this chapter

- Exploring the inspiration for evolutionary algorithms

- Solving problems with evolutionary algorithms

- Understanding the life cycle of a genetic algorithm

- Developing a genetic algorithm to solve optimization problems

What is evolution?

Nothing on Earth popped into existence fully formed. Everything alive today is the result of a long chain of tiny changes that accumulated over millions of years. This implies that the physical and cognitive characteristics of every living organism are a result of the organism's fitting to its environment for survival.

We often make the mistake of thinking that evolution is a neat line from primitive ancestor to modern form. In reality, evolution is messy, and it branches. Offspring aren't perfect clones of their parents; they inherit a mix of genes with small random changes (*mutations*). At any moment, a species is a cloud of variants, not a single clean category. You see big, obvious differences only when you zoom far out in time and compare averages across thousands of generations. Figure 4.1 depicts the reality of evolution.

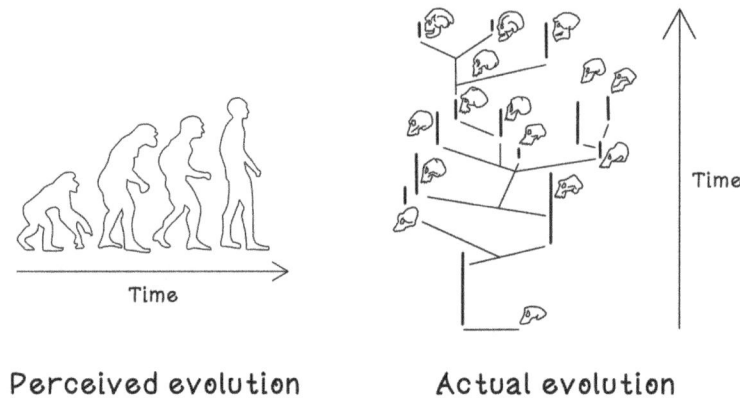

Perceived evolution   **Actual evolution**

Figure 4.1 The idea of linear human evolution vs. actual human evolution

Evolution is both simple and wild: variation is produced constantly, most variants disappear, and some variants thrive. Nature essentially searches enormous spaces of possibility for the best fit.

Evolutionary algorithms copy this logic to search huge solution spaces in computing, generate diverse candidates, selects the best ones, and iterate over generations. This chapter explores how to use that concept deliberately with computation to solve hard optimization problems.

Charles Darwin proposed a theory of evolution that centers on natural selection. *Natural selection* is the concept that stronger members of a population are more likely to survive due to being more fit for their environment. This means they reproduce more and, thus, pass down traits that are beneficial for the survival of future generations, so these individuals could potentially perform better than their ancestors.

A classic example of evolution for adaptation is the peppered moth. The peppered moth was originally light in color, which made for good camouflage against predators because the moth could blend in with light-colored surfaces in its environment. Only around 2% of the moth population was darker in color. After the Industrial Revolution, however, around 95% of the species were of the darker color variant. One explanation is that the lighter-colored moths couldn't blend in with as many surfaces as before because pollution had darkened surfaces, making lighter-colored moths more visible and therefore easier targets for predators. The darker moths had a greater advantage in blending in with the darker surfaces, so they survived longer and reproduced more, and their genetic information was more widely spread to successors (children, grandchildren, and so on).

Among the peppered moths, the attribute that changed on a high level was color. This attribute didn't switch magically, however. For the change to happen, the genes of darker-colored moths had to be passed on to successors.

In other examples of natural evolution, we may see dramatic changes in more than color among different individuals. But in fact, these changes are influenced by lower-level genetic differences over many generations (figure 4.2).

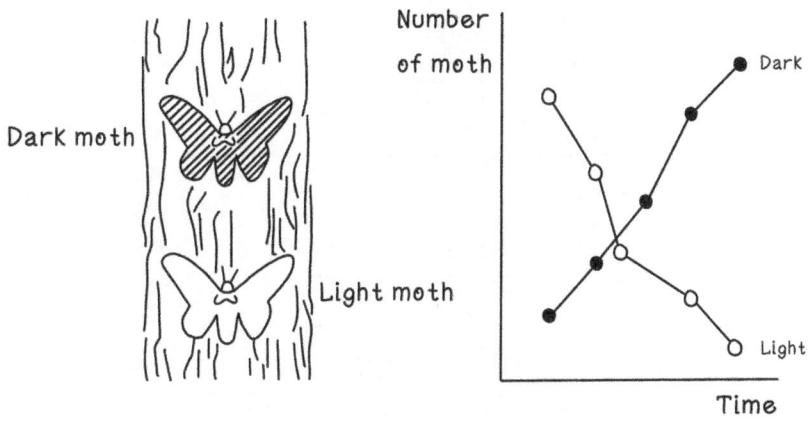

Figure 4.2 The evolution of the peppered moth

Evolution encompasses the idea that in a population of a species, pairs of organisms reproduce. The offspring are a combination of the parents' genes, but small changes are made in those offspring through mutation; then the offspring become part of the population. Not all members of a population live on, however. As we know, disease, injury, and consumption by predators cause individuals to die. Individuals that are more adaptive to the environment around them are more likely to live—a situation that gave rise to the term *survival of the fittest*. Based on Darwinian evolution theory, a population has the following attributes:

- *Variety*—Individuals in the population have different genetic traits.
- *Hereditary*—A child inherits genetic properties from its parents.
- *Selection*—Selection is a mechanism that measures the fitness of individuals. Stronger individuals have a higher likelihood of survival.

These properties imply that the following things happen during the process of evolution (figure 4.3):

- *Reproduction*—Usually, two individuals in the population reproduce to create offspring.
- *Crossover and mutation*—The offspring created through reproduction contain a mix of their parents' genes (crossover) and have slight random changes in their genetic code (mutation).

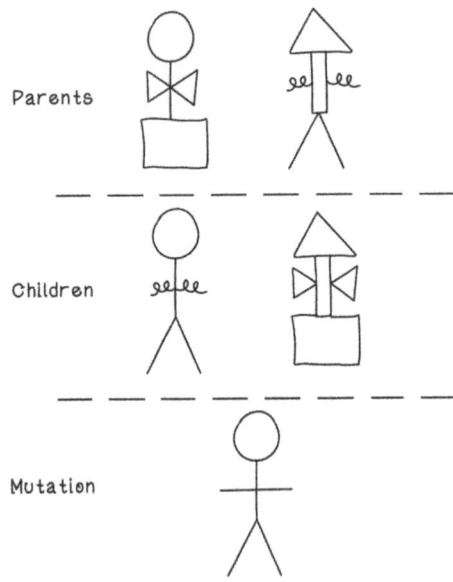

Figure 4.3 A simple example of reproduction and mutation

In summary, evolution is a marvelous and chaotic system that produces variations of life forms, some of which are better (fitter) than others for their environments. This theory also applies to evolutionary algorithms. Learnings from biological evolution are harnessed to find optimal solutions to practical problems by generating diverse solutions and converging on better-performing ones over many generations.

This chapter explores evolutionary algorithms, which are powerful, underrated approaches to solving hard problems. Evolutionary algorithms can be used in isolation or in conjunction with constructs such as artificial neural networks. Having a solid grasp of this concept opens many possibilities for solving novel problems.

Problems that evolutionary algorithms can solve

Evolutionary algorithms aren't designed to solve all problems, but they're powerful for solving optimization problems, for which the solution might come from a large number of permutations or choices. These problems typically consist of many valid solutions (solutions that work), some of which are more optimal than others.

Evolutionary algorithms are powerful but computationally expensive. Use them if your problem has many traps (local optima) where a single searcher might get stuck. By using a population, you can explore many areas at the same time and share the best traits of the survivors.

Consider the Knapsack Problem, a classic problem used in computer science to explore how algorithms work and how efficient they are. In the Knapsack Problem, a knapsack can hold a specific maximum weight. Several items are available to be stored in the knapsack, and each item has a different weight and value. The goal is to fit as many items into the knapsack as possible so that the total value is maximized and the total weight doesn't exceed the knapsack's limit. The physical size and dimensions of the items are ignored in the simplest variation of the problem (figure 4.4). As a trivial example, given the specification of the problem in table 4.1, a knapsack can hold a total weight capacity of 9 kg and contain any of the eight items of varying weight and value.

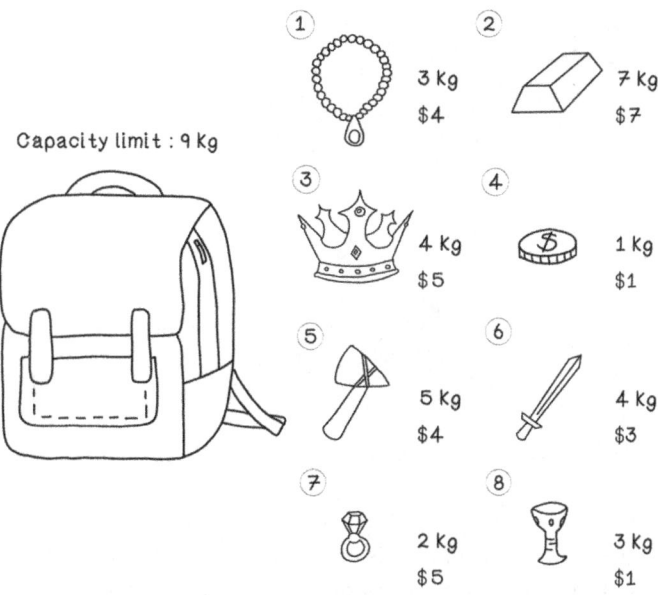

Figure 4.4 A simple example Knapsack Problem

Table 4.1 Knapsack weight capacity: 9 kg

Item ID	Item name	Weight (kg)	Value ($)
1	Pearls	3	4
2	Gold	7	7
3	Crown	4	5
4	Coin	1	1
5	Axe	5	4
6	Sword	4	3
7	Ring	2	5
8	Cup	3	1

This problem has $2^8 = 256$ possible solutions, including but not limited to the following:

- *Solution 1*—Include items 1, 4, and 6. The total weight is 8 kg, and the total value is $8.
- *Solution 2*—Include items 1, 3, and 7. The total weight is 9 kg, and the total value is $14 (figure 4.5).
- *Solution 3*—Include items 2, 3, and 6. While the total value is $15, the total weight is 15 kg, which exceeds the knapsack's capacity.

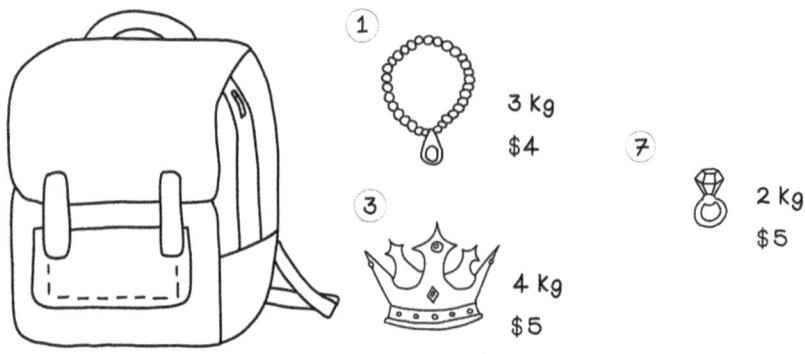

Figure 4.5 The optimal solution for the simple Knapsack Problem example

Clearly, the solution with the most value is solution 2. Don't concern yourself too much about how the number of possibilities is calculated right now, but understand that the possibilities explode as the number of potential items increases.

Although this trivial example can be solved by hand, the Knapsack Problem could have varying weight constraints, a varying number of items, and varying weights and values for each item, making it impossible to solve by hand as the variables grow. Also, trying to brute-force every combination of items will be computationally expensive when the number of variables grows. As a result, we look for algorithms that are efficient at finding a desirable solution.

We qualify the best solution we can find as a *desirable* solution rather than the *optimal* solution. Although some algorithms attempt to find the one true optimal solution to the Knapsack Problem, an evolutionary algorithm attempts to find the optimal solution but isn't guaranteed to find it. The algorithm finds a solution that is acceptable for the use case—an opinion of an acceptable solution based on the problem at hand. For a mission-critical health system, for example, a good-enough solution may not cut it, but for a song-recommendation system, it may be perfect.

Now consider the larger dataset (yes, imagine a giant knapsack) in table 4.2, in which the number of items and the varying weights and values make the problem difficult to solve by hand. By understanding the complexity of this dataset, you easily see why many computer science algorithms are measured by their performance in solving such problems. You also see why algorithms are judged by two distinct metrics: computational efficiency (how fast they run) and solution fitness (how good the answer is). In the context of evolutionary algorithms, we focus heavily on fitness. In the Knapsack Problem, a solution that yields a higher total dollar value has higher fitness regardless of how long the computer took to find it. Evolutionary algorithms provide one method of finding solutions to the Knapsack Problem.

Table 4.2 Knapsack capacity: 6,404,180 kg

Item ID	Item name	Weight (kg)	Value ($)
1	Axe	32,252	68,674
2	Bronze coin	225,790	471,010
3	Crown	468,164	944,620
4	Diamond statue	489,494	962,094
5	Emerald belt	35,384	78,344
6	Fossil	265,590	579,152
7	Gold coin	497,911	902,698
8	Helmet	800,493	1,686,515
9	Ink	823,576	1,688,691
10	Jewel box	552,202	1,056,157

Table 4.2 Knapsack capacity: 6,404,180 kg (*continued*)

Item ID	Item name	Weight (kg)	Value ($)
11	Knife	323,618	677,562
12	Longsword	382,846	833,132
13	Mask	44,676	99,192
14	Necklace	169,738	376,418
15	Opal badge	610,876	1,253,986
16	Pearls	854,190	1,853,562
17	Quiver	671,123	1,320,297
18	Ruby ring	698,180	1,301,637
19	Silver bracelet	446,517	859,835
20	Timepiece	909,620	1,677,534
21	Uniform	904,818	1,910,501
22	Venom potion	730,061	1,528,646
23	Wool scarf	931,932	1,827,477
24	Crossbow	952,360	2,068,204
25	Yesteryear book	926,023	1,746,556
26	Zinc cup	978,724	2,100,851

One way to solve this problem is to use a brute-force approach. This means calculating every possible combination of items, determining the value of each combination that satisfies the knapsack's weight constraint for all possible combinations, and then picking the best solution.

Figure 4.6 shows some benchmark analytics for the brute-force approach. The computation is based on the hardware of an average personal computer at the time of writing.

Combinations	$2^{26} = 67,108,864$
Iterations	$2^{26} = 67,108,864$
Accuracy	100%
Compute time	~7 minutes

Figure 4.6 Performance analytics of brute-forcing the Knapsack Problem

Keep the Knapsack Problem in mind. We'll use it throughout this chapter as we attempt to understand, design, and develop a genetic algorithm to find acceptable solutions to this problem.

> **DEFINITION** From the perspective of an individual solution, *performance* is how well the solution solves the problem. From the perspective of the algorithm, *performance* may be how well a specific configuration does in finding a solution. Finally, *performance* may mean computational cycles. The term is used differently in computer science based on the context.

The thinking behind using a genetic algorithm to solve the Knapsack Problem can be applied to a range of practical problems. If a logistics company wants to optimize the packing of trucks based on their destinations, for example, a genetic algorithm would be useful. If that same company wanted to find the shortest route between several destinations, again, a genetic algorithm would be useful. If a factory refined items into raw material via a conveyor-belt system, and the order of the items influenced productivity, a genetic algorithm would be useful for determining that order.

When you dive into the thinking, approach, and life cycle of the genetic algorithm, it should become clear where you can apply this algorithm, and perhaps you'll think of new use cases. It's important to keep in mind that a genetic algorithm is *stochastic*, relying on random probability throughout its life cycle, such as generating a random initial population, randomly selecting parents, or randomly mutating genes. Consequently, the output is likely to be different each time the algorithm runs, even with the same inputs.

Life cycle of genetic algorithms

A genetic algorithm is a specific algorithm in the family of evolutionary algorithms. Each algorithm works on the same premise of evolution but has small tweaks in parts of the life cycle to cater to different problems. Chapter 5 explores some of these parameters.

Genetic algorithms are used to evaluate large search spaces for a good solution. Remember that a genetic algorithm isn't guaranteed to find the best solution; it tries to find the best while avoiding local best solutions, but it may settle on a good but not global best one.

A *global best* is the best possible solution, and a *local best* is less optimal. Figure 4.7 represents the possible best solutions if the outcome must be minimized—that is, the smaller the value is, the better it is. If the goal is to maximize a solution, the larger the value is, the better it would be. Optimization algorithms such as genetic algorithms aim to incrementally find local best solutions in search of the global best solution.

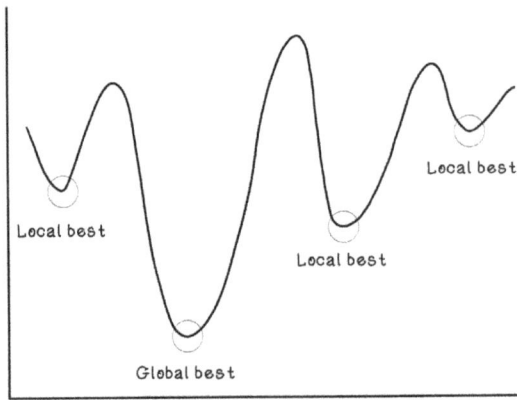

Figure 4.7 Local best vs. global best

Pay careful attention when configuring the parameters of the algorithm so that it strives for diversity in solutions at the start and gravitates toward better solutions through each generation. At the start, potential solutions should vary widely in individual genetic makeup. Without divergence at the start, the risk of getting stuck in a local best increases (figure 4.8).

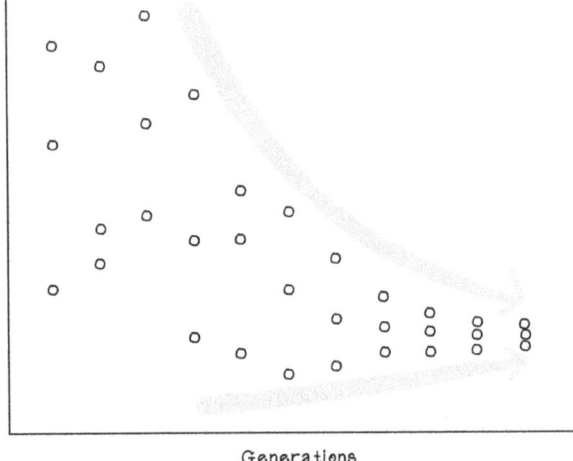

Figure 4.8 Diversity to convergence

The configuration for a genetic algorithm is based on the problem space. Each problem has a unique domain where data is represented and evaluated differently. Following is the general life cycle of a genetic algorithm:

1. *Creating a population.* This step involves generating an initial set of random candidate solutions.
2. *Measuring the fitness of individuals in the population.* This step determines how good a specific solution is by using a fitness function that scores solutions to determine how good they are.
3. *Selecting parents based on their fitness.* This step involves selecting parents that will produce offspring.
4. *Reproducing individuals from parents.* This step generates new candidates by combining the genes of selected parents and introducing random mutations to the offspring.
5. *Populating the next generation.* This step involves selecting individuals and offspring from the population that will survive to the next generation.

Several steps are involved in implementing a genetic algorithm. These steps encompass the stages of the algorithm life cycle (figure 4.9).

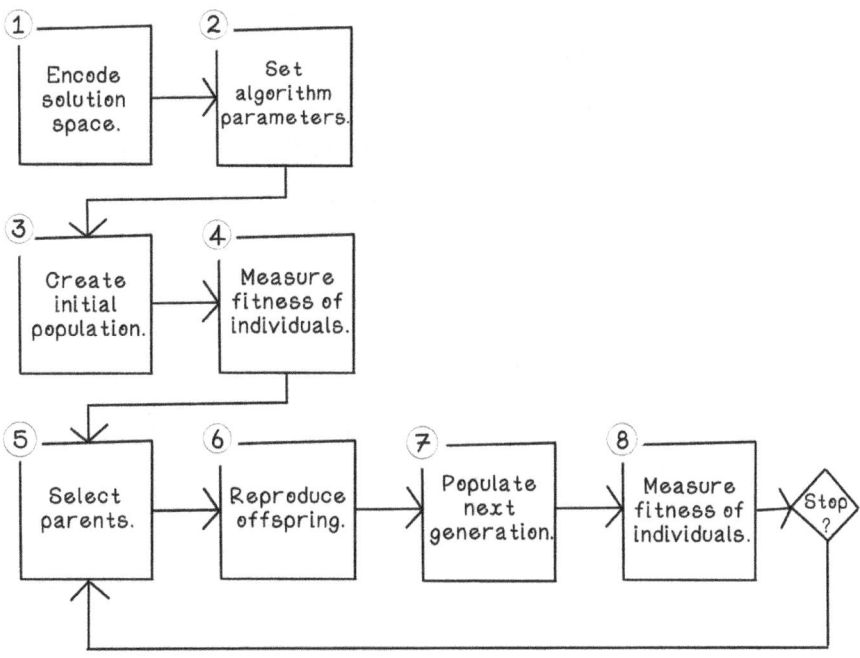

Figure 4.9 Genetic algorithm life cycle

Encoding the solution spaces

How would we use a genetic algorithm to find solutions to the Knapsack Problem? This section answers that question.

When we use a genetic algorithm, it's of paramount importance to perform the encoding step correctly. It requires careful design of the representation of possible states. *State* is a data structure with specific rules that represents possible solutions to the problem. Furthermore, a collection of states forms the population (figure 4.10).

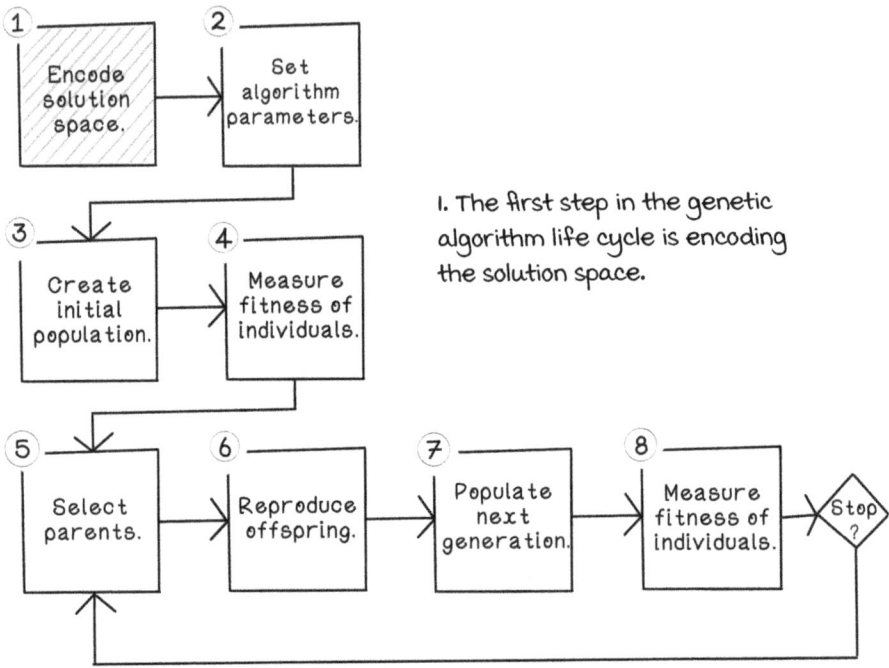

1. The first step in the genetic algorithm life cycle is encoding the solution space.

Figure 4.10 Encode the solution.

Chromosomes

In evolutionary algorithms, an individual candidate solution is called a *chromosome*. A chromosome is made up of genes. The *gene* is the logical type for the unit, and the *allele* is the actual value stored in that unit. A *genotype* is a representation of a solution, and a *phenotype* is a unique solution itself. If you apply these terms to baking, the genotype is the recipe, the phenotype is the cake that comes out of the oven (result), and the fitness is how good the cake tastes.

Each chromosome always has the same number of genes. A collection of chromosomes forms a population, as shown in the following figure.

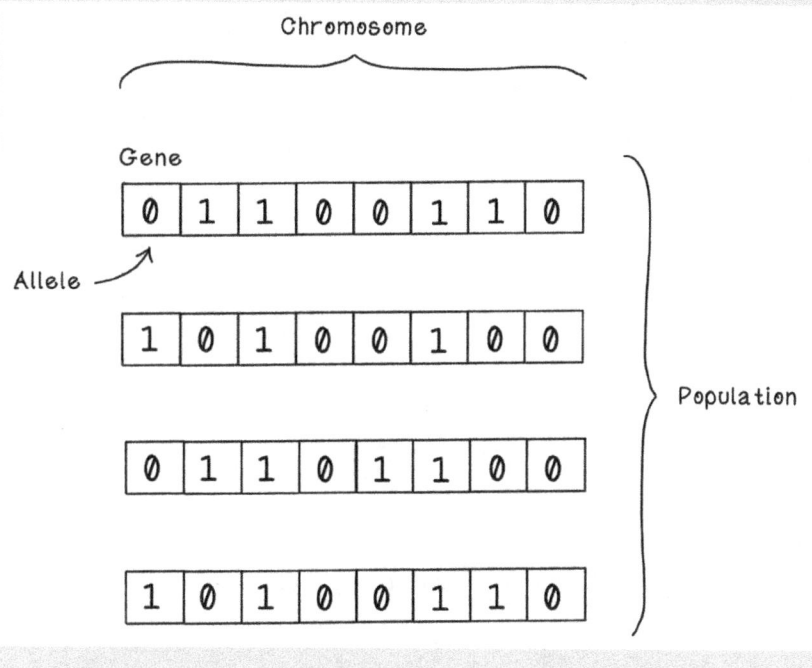

Terminology of the data structures representing a population of solutions

In the Knapsack Problem, several items can be placed in the knapsack. A simple way to describe a possible solution that contains some items but not others is binary encoding (figure 4.11). *Binary encoding* represents excluded items with 0s and included items with 1s. If the value at gene index 3 is 1, for example, that item is marked to be included. The complete binary string is always the same size: the number of items available for selection.

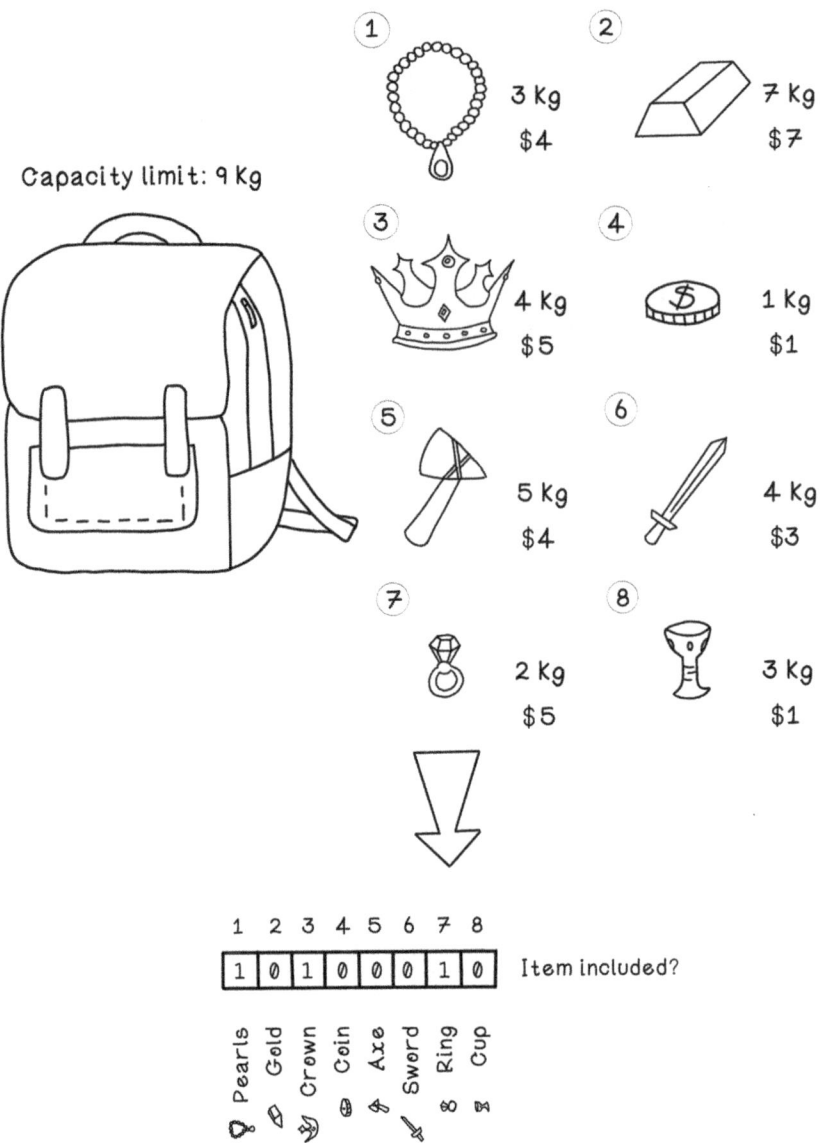

Figure 4.11 Binary-encoding the Knapsack Problem

Binary encoding: Representing possible solutions with 0s and 1s

Binary encoding represents a gene as a 0 or 1, so a chromosome is represented by a string of binary bits. We can use binary encoding in versatile ways to express the presence of a specific element or even encode numeric values as binary numbers. The advantage of binary encoding is that it's highly efficient for discrete problems (decisions involving yes/no or on/off states). Because binary encoding uses primitive types, it places less demand on memory and allows fast computation.

This approach isn't a one-size-fits-all solution, however. If your problem involves precise decimal numbers (such as an optimized stock price) or specific sequences (such as the order of cities in a map), binary encoding can make it harder for the algorithm to find a solution. In those cases, real-value or permutation encodings are better choices.

Binary encoding places less demand on working memory than other encoding strategies, and depending on the programming language used, binary operations are computationally faster. But use critical thought to ensure that the encoding makes sense for the problem at hand to represent solutions well; otherwise, the algorithm may perform poorly. Figure 4.12 shows how possible items in the Knapsack Problem are binary-encoded.

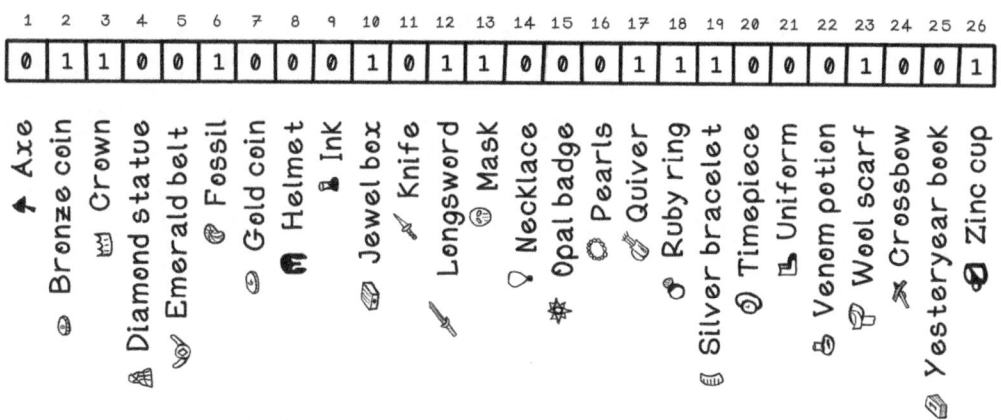

Figure 4.12 Binary-encoding the larger dataset of the Knapsack Problem

Given the Knapsack Problem with a dataset that consists of 26 items of varying weights and values, a binary string can represent the inclusion of each item. The result is a 26-character string in which for each index, 0 means that the respective item is excluded and 1 means that the respective item is included. Other encoding schemes—including real-value encoding, order encoding, and tree encoding—are discussed in chapter 5.

Exercise: What is a possible encoding for the following problem?

Suppose that we have the following sentence and want to find which words can be excluded or included to maintain a meaningful phrase using a genetic algorithm:

THE   QUICK BROWN   FOX   JUMPS   OVER   THE   LAZY   DOG

Incorrect phrases:

THE		BROWN		JUMPS	OVER			
	QUICK		FOX		OVER	THE		
THE			FOX			THE	LAZY	

Correct phrases:

THE	QUICK		FOX					
	QUICK		FOX	JUMPS				
THE		BROWN	FOX					
THE		BROWN					LAZY	DOG
THE	QUICK							DOG
	QUICK				OVER	THE		DOG
THE	QUICK						LAZY	DOG

*Punctuation is excluded

Solution: Because the number of possible words is always the same, and the words are always in the same position, binary encoding can be used to describe which words are included and which are excluded. The chromosome consists of 9 genes, each gene indicating a word in the phrase.

THE   QUICK BROWN   FOX   JUMPS   OVER   THE   LAZY   DOG

THE   BROWN   JUMPS OVER

1	0	1	0	1	1	0	0	0

THE   BROWN   LAZY   DOG

1	0	1	0	0	0	0	1	1

Creating a population of solutions

In the beginning, we create the population. The first step in a genetic algorithm is initializing random potential solutions. In the process of initializing the population, although the chromosomes are generated randomly, the constraints of the problem must be taken into consideration, and the potential solutions should be valid or assigned a terrible fitness score (penalty) if they violate the constraints. A more effective technique is to use a repair function: the algorithm automatically tweaks an invalid solution (such as removing one item from an overweight knapsack) to make it valid rather than discarding it. The randomly seeded individuals in the population may not solve the problem well, but the solution is valid. As mentioned in the earlier example of packing items into a knapsack, a solution that specifies packing the same item more than once should be invalid and shouldn't be part of the population of possible solutions (figure 4.13).

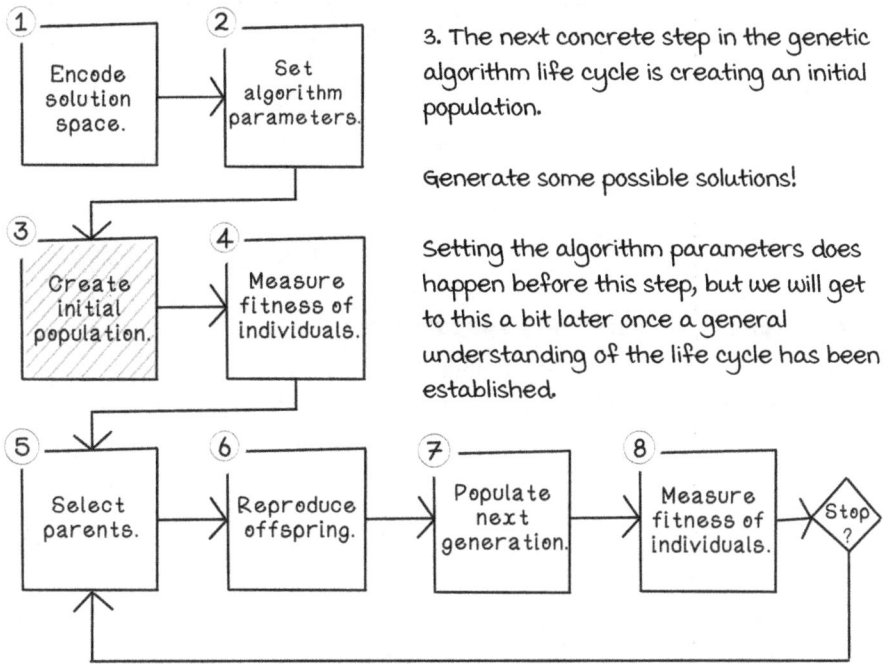

1. Encode solution space.

2. Set algorithm parameters.

3. The next concrete step in the genetic algorithm life cycle is creating an initial population.

Generate some possible solutions!

3. Create initial population.

4. Measure fitness of individuals.

Setting the algorithm parameters does happen before this step, but we will get to this a bit later once a general understanding of the life cycle has been established.

5. Select parents.

6. Reproduce offspring.

7. Populate next generation.

8. Measure fitness of individuals.

Stop?

Figure 4.13 Create an initial population.

Given how the Knapsack Problem's solution state is represented, this implementation randomly decides whether each item should be included in the bag. That said, only solutions that satisfy the weight-limit constraint should be considered. The problem with simply moving from left to right and randomly choosing whether the item is included is that it creates a bias toward the items at the left end of the chromosome. Similarly, if we start from the right, we'll be biased toward items at the right end. One way to get around this problem is to generate an entire individual with random genes and then determine whether the solution is valid and doesn't violate any constraints. Assigning terrible scores to invalid solutions can also solve this problem (figure 4.14).

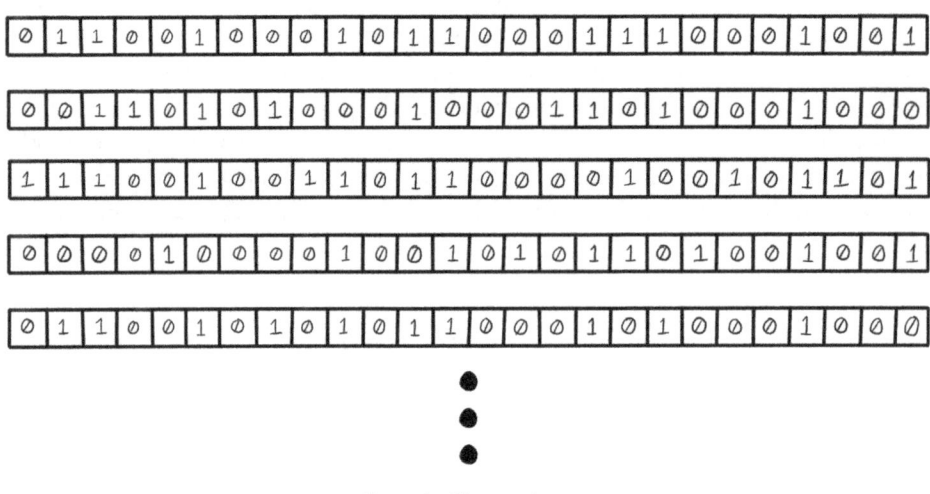

Population size

Figure 4.14 An example population of solutions

Python code sample for generating a population

To generate an initial population of possible solutions, create an empty array to hold the individuals. Then, for each individual in the population, create an empty array to hold the genes of the individual. Each gene is randomly set to 1 or 0, indicating whether the item at that gene index is included:

Randomly selects a 0 or 1 to act as a single gene

```python
def generate_initial_population(population_size):
    population = []
    for individual in range(0, population_size):
        individual = ''.join([random.choice('01')
        for n in range(26)])
        population.append([individual, 0, 0])
    return population
```

Stores the generated string along with placeholders for the fitness scores that will be calculated

Measuring fitness of individuals in a population

After you create a population, you measure the fitness of each individual in the population. Fitness defines how well a solution performs. The fitness function is critical to the life cycle of a genetic algorithm. If the fitness of the individuals is measured incorrectly or in a way that doesn't strive for the optimal solution, the selection process for parents of new individuals and new generations will be influenced; as a result, the algorithm will be flawed and can't strive to find the best possible solution.

Fitness functions are similar to heuristics (explored in chapter 3). They're guidelines for finding good solutions (figure 4.15).

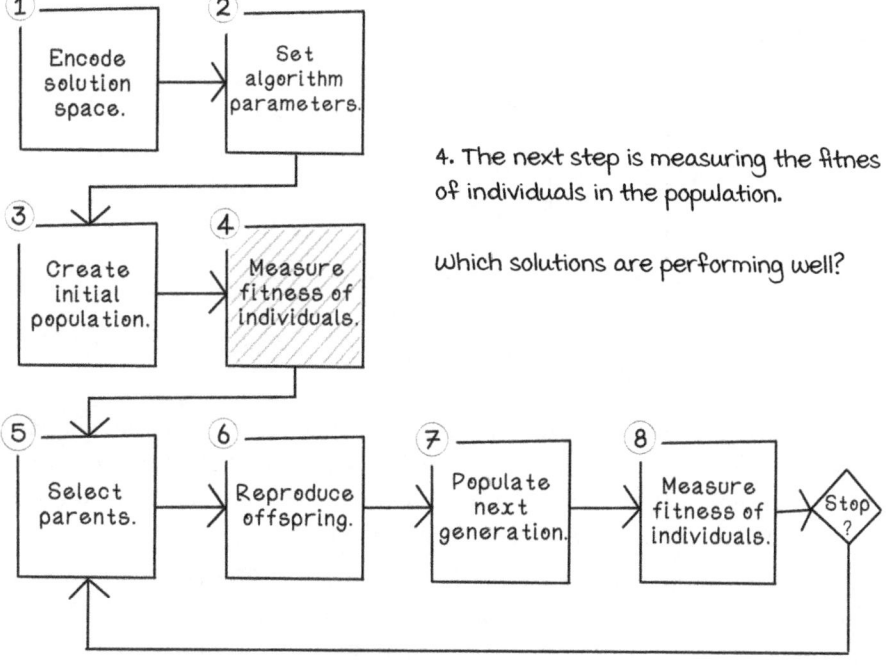

4. The next step is measuring the fitnes of individuals in the population.

Which solutions are performing well?

Figure 4.15 Measure fitness of individuals

In our example, the solution attempts to maximize the value of the items in the knapsack while respecting the weight-limit constraints. The fitness function measures the total value of the items in the knapsack for each individual. The result is that individuals with higher total values are more fit. An invalid individual appears in figure 4.16, so its fitness score is 0 (a terrible score). It exceeds the weight capacity for this instance of the problem, which is 6,404,180.

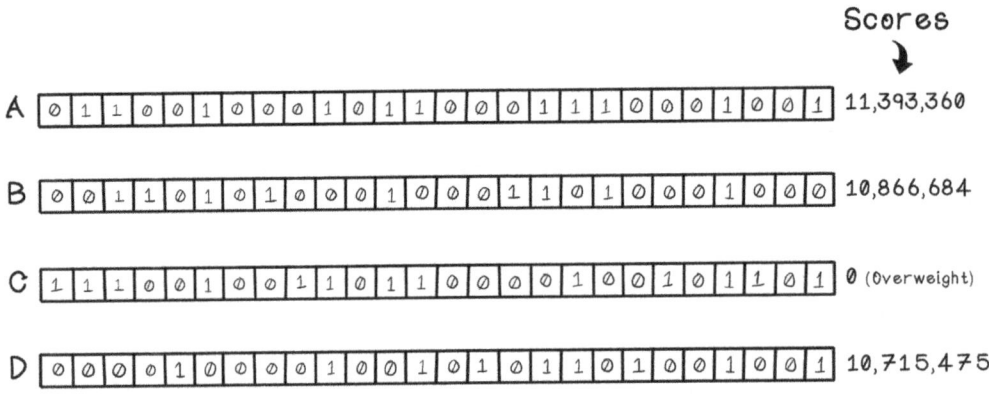

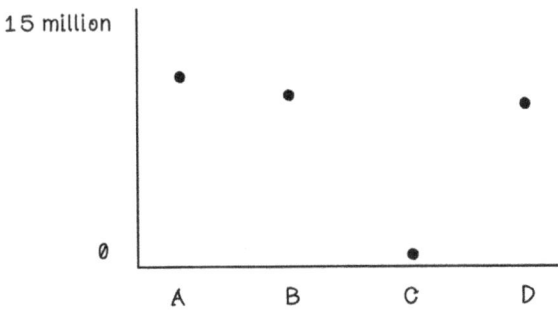

Figure 4.16 Individual chromosomes and their performance

We deliberately squash this score to 0 to act as a severe penalty. Even though that knapsack may hold a million dollars' worth of items, the fact that it's too heavy to carry makes it effectively worthless. The 0 score teaches the algorithm that breaking the rules results in failure, no matter how tempting the contents are.

Depending on the problem being solved, we may have to minimize or maximize the result of the fitness function. In the Knapsack Problem, we could maximize the contents of the knapsack within constraints, or we could minimize the empty space in the knapsack. Our approach depends on our interpretation of the problem.

Python code sample for calculating fitness

To calculate the fitness of an individual in the Knapsack Problem, we must determine the sums of the values of the items that the individual includes. We accomplish this task by setting the total value to 0 and then iterating over each gene to determine whether the item it represents is included. If the item is included, the value of the item represented by that gene is added to the total value. Similarly, we calculate the total weight to ensure that the solution is valid. The concepts of calculating fitness and checking constraints can be split for clearer separation of concerns:

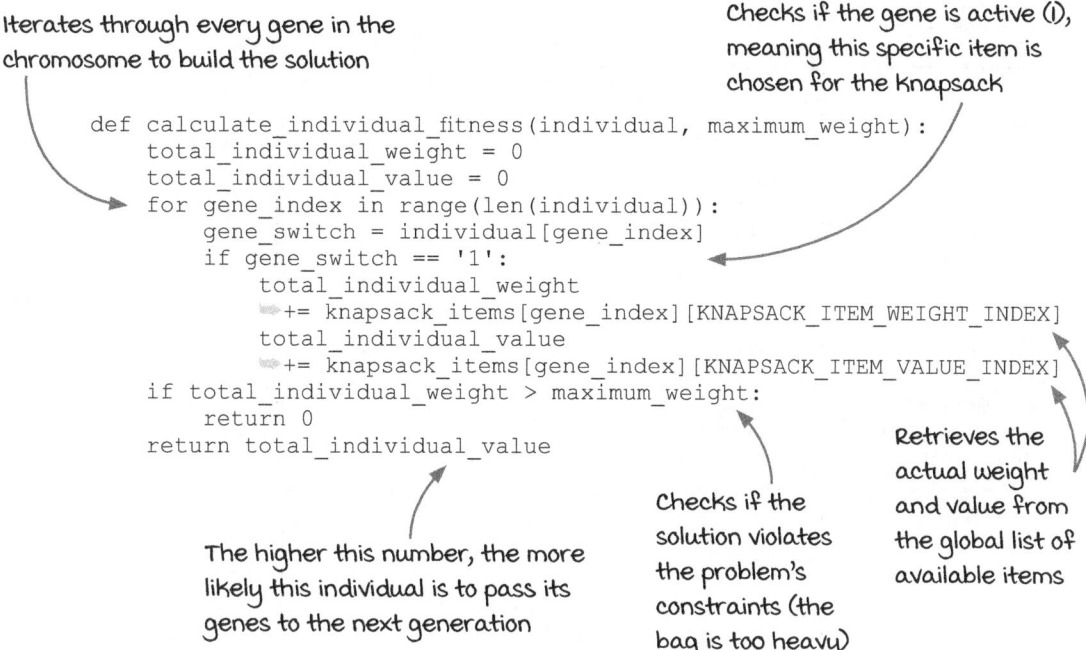

Iterates through every gene in the chromosome to build the solution

Checks if the gene is active (1), meaning this specific item is chosen for the knapsack

```
def calculate_individual_fitness(individual, maximum_weight):
    total_individual_weight = 0
    total_individual_value = 0
    for gene_index in range(len(individual)):
        gene_switch = individual[gene_index]
        if gene_switch == '1':
            total_individual_weight
            += knapsack_items[gene_index][KNAPSACK_ITEM_WEIGHT_INDEX]
            total_individual_value
            += knapsack_items[gene_index][KNAPSACK_ITEM_VALUE_INDEX]
    if total_individual_weight > maximum_weight:
        return 0
    return total_individual_value
```

The higher this number, the more likely this individual is to pass its genes to the next generation

Checks if the solution violates the problem's constraints (the bag is too heavy)

Retrieves the actual weight and value from the global list of available items

Selecting parents based on their fitness

The next step in the genetic algorithm selects parents that will produce new individuals. In Darwinian theory, the individuals that are more fit have a higher likelihood of reproduction than others because they typically live longer. Furthermore, these individuals contain desirable attributes for inheritance due to their superior performance in their environment. That said, some individuals are likely to reproduce even if they're not the fittest in the entire group, and these individuals may contain strong traits even though they're not strong in their entirety.

Each individual has a calculated fitness that is used to determine the probability of its being selected to be a parent of a new individual. This attribute adds to the stochastic nature of the genetic algorithm (figure 4.17).

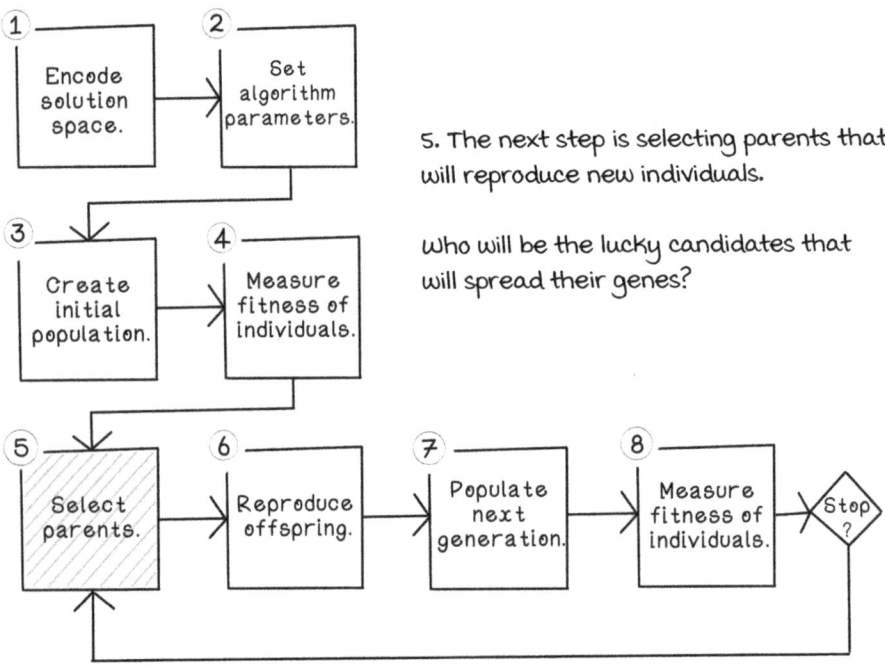

① Encode solution space.

② Set algorithm parameters.

③ Create initial population.

④ Measure fitness of individuals.

5. The next step is selecting parents that will reproduce new individuals.

Who will be the lucky candidates that will spread their genes?

⑤ Select parents.

⑥ Reproduce offspring.

⑦ Populate next generation.

⑧ Measure fitness of individuals.

Stop?

Figure 4.17 Select parents.

A popular technique for choosing parents based on their fitness is *roulette-wheel selection*. This strategy gives different individuals portions of a wheel based on their fitness. The wheel is "spun," and an individual is selected. Higher fitness gives an individual a larger slice of the wheel. This process is repeated until the desired number of parents is reached.

By calculating the probabilities of 16 individuals of varying fitness, the wheel allocates a slice to each. Because many individuals perform similarly, there are many slices of similar size (figure 4.18).

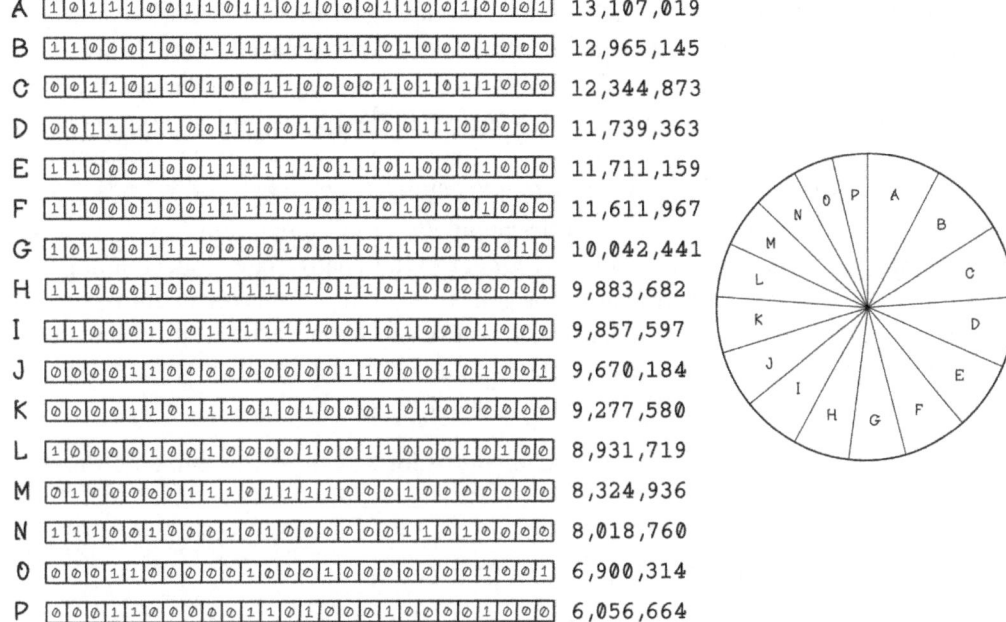

Figure 4.18 Determine the probability of selection for each individual.

The number of parents selected for reproducing new offspring is determined by the intended total number of offspring required, which is determined by the desired population size for each generation. Two parents are selected, and offspring are created. This process repeats with different parents selected (with a chance that the same individuals will be parents more than once) until the desired number of offspring has been generated. Two parents can reproduce a single mixed child or two mixed children. This concept will be made clearer later in "Reproducing individuals from parents." Remember, in the Knapsack Problem example, the individuals with greater fitness are those that fill the bag with the most combined value while respecting the weight-limit constraint.

Using population models

Population models control the diversity of the population. *Steady-state* and *generational* are two population models that are overarching ideas for designing the configuration of the algorithm:

- *Steady-state model*—Replaces a portion of the population each generation. This high-level approach to population management is not an alternative to the other selection strategies, but a scheme that uses them. The idea is that the majority of the population is retained, and a small group of weaker individuals are removed and replaced by new offspring. This process mimics the cycle of life and death, in which weak individuals die and new individuals are created through reproduction. If there were 100 individuals in the population, a portion of the population would be existing individuals, and a smaller portion would be new individuals created via reproduction. There may be 80 individuals in the current generation and 20 new individuals.

- *Generational model*—Replaces the entire population each generation. This high-level approach to population management is similar to the steady-state model but not an alternative to selection strategies. The generational model creates a number of offspring individuals equal to the population size and replaces the entire population with the new offspring. If there were 100 individuals in the population, each generation would result in 100 new individuals via reproduction.

Steady state and generational are overarching ideas for designing the configuration of the algorithm.

Performing roulette-wheel selection

Chromosomes with higher fitness scores are more likely to be selected, but chromosomes with lower fitness scores still have a small chance of being selected (because although they're not strong, they might have individual genes that are strong for an optimal solution). The term *roulette-wheel selection* comes from a roulette wheel at a casino, which is divided into slices. Typically, the wheel is spun, and a marble is released into the wheel. The selected slice is the slice that the marble lands on when the wheel stops turning.

In this analogy, chromosomes are assigned to slices of the wheel. Chromosomes with higher fitness scores have larger slices of the wheel, and chromosomes with lower fitness scores have smaller slices. A chromosome is selected randomly, much as a marble in a roulette wheel randomly lands on a slice.

This analogy is an example of probabilistic selection. Each individual has a chance of being selected, whether that chance is small or high. The chance of selection of individuals influences the diversity of the population and convergence rates mentioned earlier in this chapter.

Python code sample for roulette-wheel selection

First, we determine the probability of selection for each individual, calculating the probability for each individual by dividing its fitness by the total fitness of the population. We can use roulette-wheel selection for this purpose, "spinning" the "wheel" until the desired number of individuals has been selected. For each selection, a random decimal number between 0 and 1 is calculated. If an individual's fitness is within that probability, that individual is selected. We can use other probabilistic approaches to determine the probability of each individual, including standard deviation, in which an individual's value is compared with the mean value of the group:

```
def set_probabilities(population):
    population_sum =
    sum(individual[INDIVIDUAL_FITNESS_INDEX]
    for individual in population)
    for individual in population:
        individual[INDIVIDUAL_PROBABILITY_INDEX] =
        individual[INDIVIDUAL_FITNESS_INDEX]
        / population_sum

def roulette_wheel_selection(population,
number_of_selections):
    set_probabilities(population)
    slices = []
    total = 0
    for r in range(0, len(population)):
        individual = population[r]
        slices.append([r, total, total
        + individual[INDIVIDUAL_PROBABILITY_INDEX]])
        total += individual[INDIVIDUAL_PROBABILITY_INDEX]
    chosen_ones = []
    for r in range(number_of_selections):
        spin = random.random()
        result = [s[0] for s in slices if s[1]
        < spin <= s[2]]
        chosen_ones.append(population[result[0]])
    return chosen_ones
```

Calculates the sum of all fitness scores to determine the total size of the "pie"

Converts the raw fitness score into a percentage (probability) between 0 and 1

If an individual has a 20% chance and starts at 0.3, their slice ends at 0.5

Checks which "slice" the random number landed inside

Adds the winner to the mating pool

Reproducing individuals from parents

When parents are selected, reproduction must happen to create new offspring from the parents. Generally, two steps are related to creating children from two parents. The first concept is *crossover*, which means mixing part of the chromosome of the first parent with part of the chromosome of the second parent, and vice versa. This process results in two offspring that contain inverted mixes of their parents. The second concept is *mutation*, which means changing the offspring randomly and slightly to create variation in the population (figure 4.19).

DEFINITION *Crossover* is mixing genes between two individuals to create one or more offspring individuals. Crossover is inspired by the concept of reproduction. The offspring individuals are parts of their parents, depending on the crossover strategy. The crossover strategy is highly affected by the encoding.

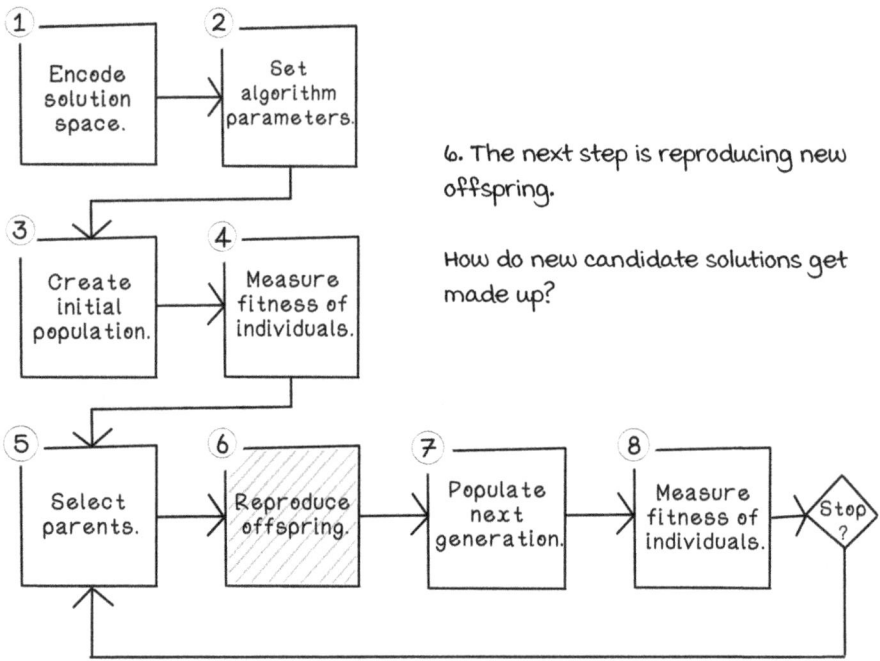

Figure 4.19 Reproduce offspring.

Single-point crossover: Inheriting one part from each parent

In *single-point crossover*, one point in the chromosome structure is selected. Then, by referencing the two parents in question, the first part of the first parent is used, and the second part of the second parent is used. These two parts combined create a new offspring. A second offspring can be made by using the first part of the second parent and the second part of the first parent. Single-point crossover is applicable to binary encoding, order/permutation encoding, and real-value encoding (figure 4.20).

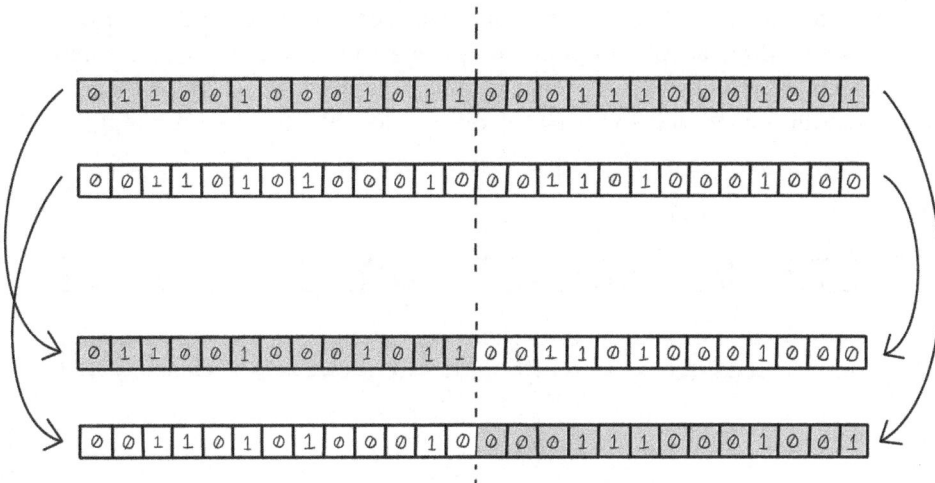

Figure 4.20 Single-point crossover

Python code sample for crossover

To create two new offspring individuals, an empty array is created to hold the new individuals. All genes from index 0 to the desired index of parent A are concatenated with all genes from the desired index to the end of the chromosome of parent B, creating one offspring individual. The inverse creates the second offspring individual:

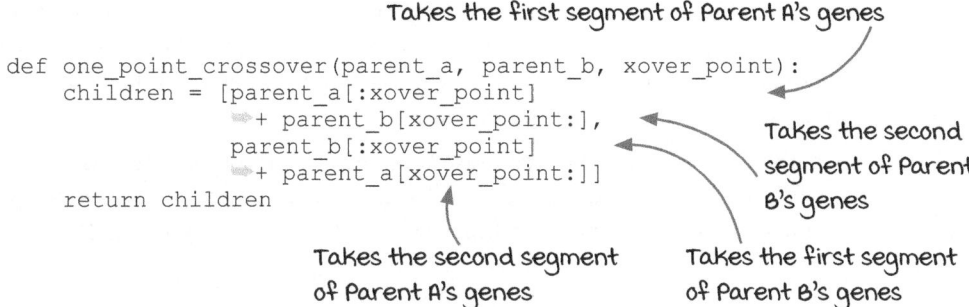

Two-point crossover: Inheriting more parts from each parent

In *two-point crossover*, two points in the chromosome structure are selected; then, referencing the two parents in question, parts are chosen in an alternating manner to make a complete offspring individual. This process is similar to single-point crossover, as we've just discussed. Describing the process completely, the offspring consist of the first part of the first parent, the second part of the second parent, and the third part of the first parent. Think about two-point crossover as splicing arrays to create new ones. Again, a second individual can be made by using the inverse parts of each parent. Two-point crossover is applicable to binary encoding and real-value encoding (figure 4.21).

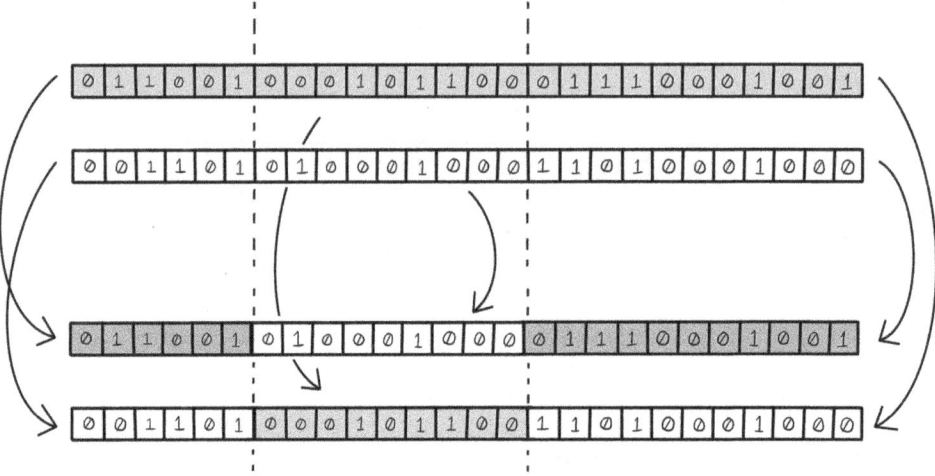

Figure 4.21 Two-point crossover

Uniform crossover: Inheriting many parts from each parent

In uniform crossover (a step beyond two-point crossover), a mask is created to represent which genes from each parent will be used to generate the offspring. The inverse process can be used to make a second offspring, and the mask can be generated randomly each time offspring are created to maximize diversity.

Generally speaking, uniform crossover creates more-diverse individuals because the attributes of the offspring are quite different from those of the parents. Uniform crossover is applicable to binary encoding and real-value encoding (figure 4.22).

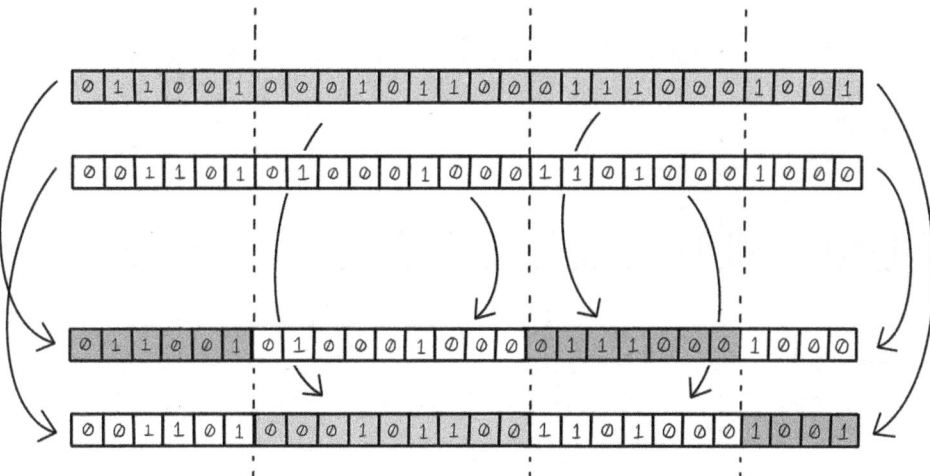

Figure 4.22 Uniform crossover

Mutation

Mutation involves changing individual offspring slightly to encourage diversity in the population. Several approaches to mutation are used, based on the nature of the problem and the encoding method.

One parameter in mutation is the *mutation rate*—the likelihood that an offspring chromosome will be mutated. As in living organisms, some chromosomes are mutated more than others; an offspring isn't an exact combination of its parents' chromosomes but contains minor genetic differences. Mutation can be critical for encouraging diversity in a population and preventing the algorithm from getting stuck in local best solutions.

A high mutation rate means that individuals have a high chance of being selected to be mutated or that genes in the chromosome of an individual have a high chance of being mutated, depending on the mutation strategy. High mutation means more diversity, but too much diversity may result in the deterioration of good solutions.

Exercise: What outcome would uniform crossover generate for these chromosomes?

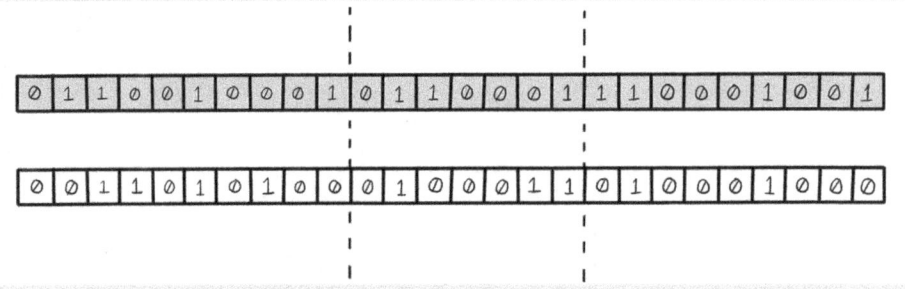

Solution:

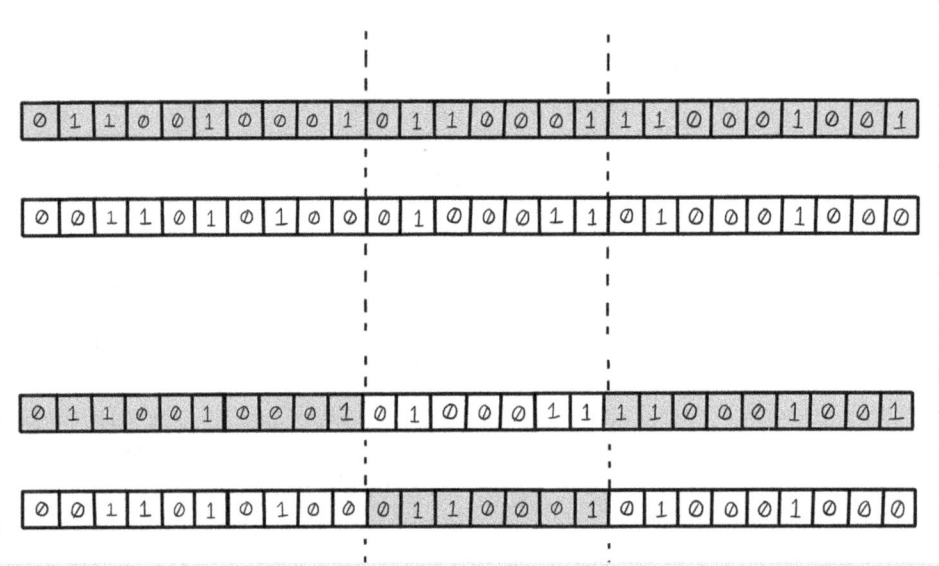

Bit-string mutation for binary encoding

In *bit-string mutation*, a gene in a binary-encoded chromosome is selected randomly and changed to another valid value (figure 4.23). Other mutation mechanisms are applicable when nonbinary encoding is used. You will learn more about this in chapter 5.

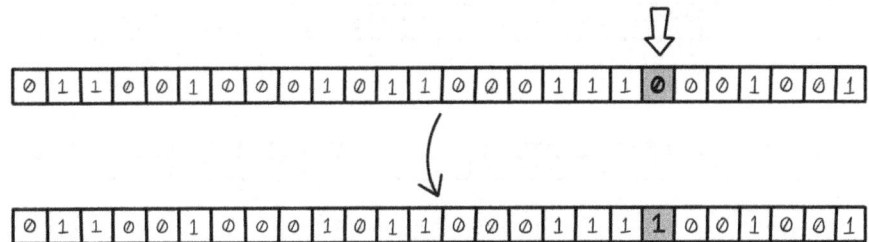

Figure 4.23 Bit-string mutation

Python code sample for mutation

To mutate a single gene of an individual's chromosome, a random gene index is selected. If that gene represents 1, change it to represent 0, and vice versa:

Determines the current
state of the selected gene

```
def mutate_children(children, mutation_rate):
    for child in children:
        random_index = random.randint(0, mutation_rate)
        if child[INDIVIDUAL_CHROMOSOME_INDEX][random_index] == '1':
            mutated_child = list(child[INDIVIDUAL_CHROMOSOME_INDEX])
            mutated_child[random_index] = '0'
            child[INDIVIDUAL_CHROMOSOME_INDEX] = mutated_child
        else:
            mutated_child = list(child[INDIVIDUAL_CHROMOSOME_INDEX])
            mutated_child[random_index] = '1'
            child[INDIVIDUAL_CHROMOSOME_INDEX] = mutated_child
    return children
```

Inverts the gene. If it was active (1), it
becomes inactive (0), and vice-versa

Flip-bit mutation for binary encoding

In *flip-bit mutation*, all genes in a binary-encoded chromosome are inverted to the opposite value. Where there were 1s are 0s, and where there were 0s are 1s. This type of mutation could degrade good-performing solutions dramatically and usually is employed when diversity must constantly be introduced into the population (figure 4.24).

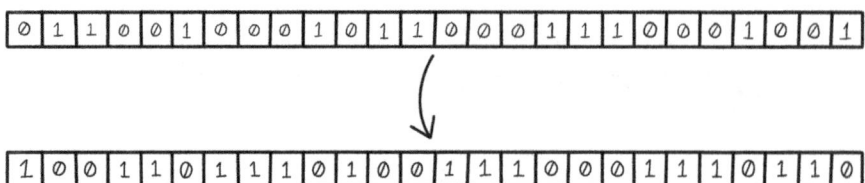

Figure 4.24 Flip-bit mutation

Populating the next generation

When the fitness of the individuals in the population has been measured and offspring have been reproduced, the next step is selecting which individuals live on to the next generation. The size of the population is usually fixed, and because more individuals have been introduced through reproduction, some individuals must die off and be removed from the population (figure 4.25).

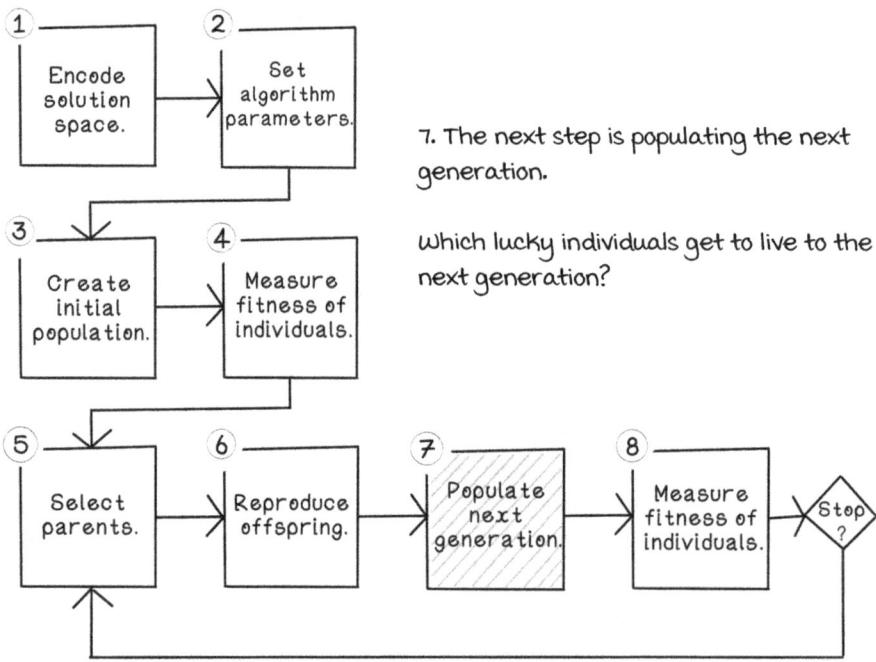

Figure 4.25 Populate the next generation.

It may seem like a good idea to take the top individuals that fit into the population size and eliminate the rest. This strategy is called *elitism*. But elitism could create stagnation in the diversity of individuals if the individuals that survive are similar in genetic makeup. The selection strategies mentioned in this section can be used to determine the individuals that are selected to form part of the population of the next generation.

Exploration vs. exploitation

Running a genetic algorithm always involves striking a balance between exploration and exploitation. The ideal situation is one in which there is diversity in individuals and the population as a whole seeks out wildly different potential solutions in the search space; then stronger local solution spaces are exploited to find the most desirable solution.

Suppose that you've been dropped onto a foggy mountain range and need to find the highest peak. You could employ either exploration or exploitation:

- *Exploration* (mutation) is like paragliding to a totally random new spot. You might land in a valley, or you might find a massive mountain range that you couldn't see before.
- *Exploitation* (crossover/selection) is like climbing uphill from where you currently stand. You're guaranteed to go higher, but if you don't explore enough, you may get stuck on a small hill (a local maximum) while missing Mount Everest (the global maximum) a few miles away.

The beauty of this situation is that the algorithm explores as much of the search space as possible while exploiting strong solutions as individuals evolve. After the individuals are selected and the next generation is populated, the fitness of all individuals is measured again (figure 4.26).

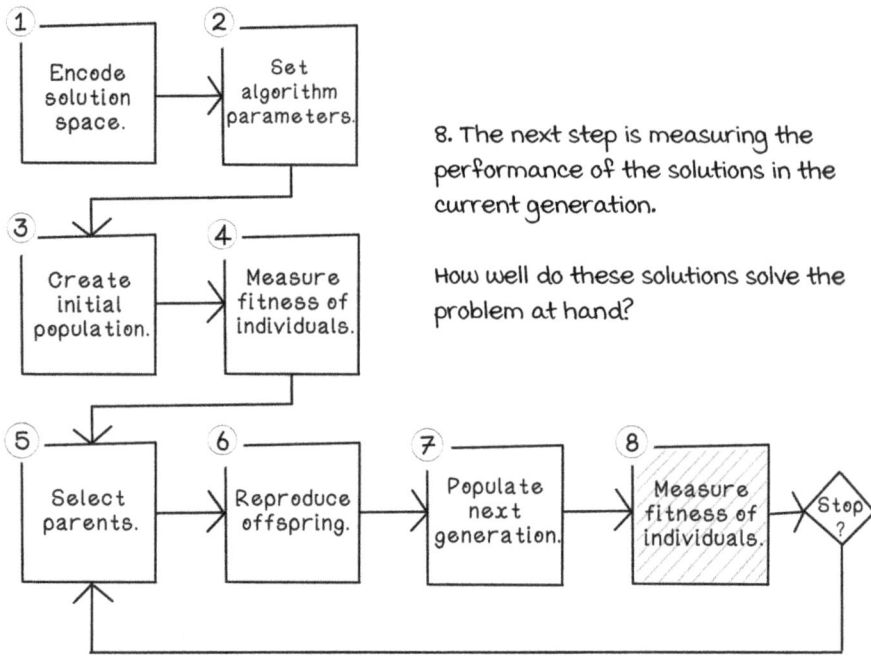

8. The next step is measuring the performance of the solutions in the current generation.

How well do these solutions solve the problem at hand?

Figure 4.26 Measure the fitness of individuals again.

Stopping conditions

Because a genetic algorithm is iterative in finding better solutions through each generation, a stopping condition is necessary; otherwise, the algorithm might run forever. A *stopping condition* is the condition that's met where the algorithm ends; the strongest individual of the population at that generation is selected as the best solution.

The simplest stopping condition is a fixed number of generations—a constant value that specifies the number of generations for which the algorithm will run. Another approach is to stop when a certain fitness is achieved. This method is useful when a desired minimum fitness is known but the solution is unknown.

Stagnation is a problem in evolutionary algorithms in which the population yields solutions of similar strength for several generations. If a population stagnates, the likelihood of generating strong solutions in future generations is low. A stopping condition could look at the change in the fitness of the best individual in each generation and, if the fitness changes only marginally, choose to stop the algorithm.

Python code sample for running the genetic algorithm

The various steps of a genetic algorithm are used in a main function that outlines the entire life cycle. The variable parameters include the population size, the number of generations for the algorithm to run, and the knapsack capacity for the fitness function, in addition to the variable crossover position and mutation rate for the crossover and mutation steps:

Calculates how well every individual in the current population solves the problem

Creates the starting pool of random solutions (the first generation)

Loops through a fixed number of generations – cycle of evolution

```python
def run_ga():
    best_global_fitness = 0
    global_population = generate_initial_population(
    ➥INITIAL_POPULATION_SIZE)
    for generation in range(NUMBER_OF_GENERATIONS):
        current_best_fitness = calculate_population_fitness(global_population,
        ➥KNAPSACK_WEIGHT_CAPACITY)
        if current_best_fitness > best_global_fitness:
            best_global_fitness = current_best_fitness
        the_chosen = roulette_wheel_selection(global_population, 100)
        the_children = reproduce_children(the_chosen)
        the_children = mutate_children(the_children, MUTATION_RATE)
        global_population =
        ➥merge_population_and_children(global_population, the_children)
```

Pairs up parents to swap genes and create new offspring

Replaces the old population

Updates the global record if the current generation has produced a better solution

As mentioned at the beginning of this chapter, the Knapsack Problem could be solved with a brute-force approach, which requires more than 60 million combinations to be generated and analyzed. When comparing genetic algorithms that aim to solve the same problem, we can see far more efficiency in computation if the parameters for exploration and exploitation are configured correctly. The genetic algorithm achieved the optimal solution in 3 seconds, whereas the brute force approach achieved it in 7 minutes. Remember that in some cases, a genetic algorithm produces a good-enough solution that is not necessarily the best possible solution but is desirable. Again, using a genetic algorithm for a problem depends on the context (figure 4.27).

	Brute force	Genetic algorithm
Iterations	2^26 = 67,108,864	10,000 - 100,000
Accuracy	100%	100%
Compute time	~7 minutes	~3 seconds
Best value	13,692,887	13,692,887

Figure 4.27 Brute-force performance vs. genetic algorithm performance

Configuring the parameters of a genetic algorithm

In designing and configuring a genetic algorithm, we must make several decisions that influence the performance of the algorithm. The performance concerns fall into two areas: the algorithm should strive to perform well in finding good solutions to the problem, and it should perform efficiently from a computation perspective. It would be pointless to design a genetic algorithm to solve a problem if the solution will be more computationally expensive than other traditional techniques. The approach used in encoding, the fitness function used, and the other algorithmic parameters influence both types of performances in achieving a good solution and computation. Here are some parameters to consider:

- *Chromosome encoding*—The chromosome encoding method requires thought to ensure that it's applicable to the problem and that the potential solutions strive for global maxima. The encoding scheme is at the heart of the algorithm's success.
- *Population size*—The population size is configurable. A larger population encourages more diversity in possible solutions. Larger populations, however, require more computation at each generation. Sometimes, a larger population balances the need for mutation, which results in diversity at the start but no diversity during generations. A valid approach is to start with a smaller population and grow it based on performance.
- *Population initialization*—Although the individuals in a population are initialized randomly, ensuring that the solutions are valid is important for optimizing the computation of the genetic algorithm and initializing individuals with the right constraints. This can save unnecessary compute cycles.
- *Number of offspring*—The number of offspring created in each generation can be configured. Given that after reproduction, part of the population is killed off to ensure that the population size is fixed, more offspring means more diversity, but there is

a risk that good solutions will be killed off to accommodate those offspring. If the population is dynamic, the population size may change after every generation, but this approach requires more parameters to configure and control.

- *Parent selection method*—The selection method for choosing parents can be configured based on the problem and the desired explorability versus exploitability.

- *Crossover method*—The crossover method is associated with the encoding method used but can be configured to encourage or discourage diversity in the population. The offspring individuals must still yield a valid solution.

- *Mutation rate*—The mutation rate is another configurable parameter that induces more diversity in offspring and potential solutions. A higher mutation rate means more diversity, but too much diversity may deteriorate good-performing individuals. The mutation rate can change over time to create more diversity in earlier generations and less in later generations.

- *Mutation method*—The mutation method is similar to the crossover method in that it depends on the encoding method used. An important attribute of the mutation method is that it must still yield a valid solution after the modification; otherwise, it is assigned a terrible fitness score.

- *Generation selection methods*—Much like the selection method used to choose parents, a generation selection method must choose the individuals that will survive the generation. Depending on the selection method used, the algorithm may converge too quickly and stagnate or explore too long.

- *Stopping condition*—The stopping condition for the algorithm must make sense based on the problem and desired outcome. Computational complexity and time are the main concerns for the stopping condition.

Use cases for evolutionary algorithms

Evolutionary algorithms have a wide variety of uses. Some algorithms address isolated problems; others combine evolutionary algorithms with other techniques to create novel approaches to solving difficult problems, such as the following:

- *Predicting investor behavior in the stock market*—Consumers who invest make decisions every day about whether to buy more of a specific stock, hold on to what they have, or sell. Sequences of these actions can be evolved and mapped to outcomes of an investor's portfolio. Financial institutions can use this insight to proactively provide valuable customer service and guidance.

- *Selecting features in machine learning*—Machine learning is discussed in chapter 8, but a fundamental concept involves using specific attributes (features) to classify something. If we're looking at houses, we may find many attributes related to houses, such as age, building material, size, color, and location. But to predict market value, perhaps only age, size, and location matter. A genetic algorithm can uncover the isolated features that matter most.

- *Breaking code and ciphers*—A *cipher* is a message encoded in a certain way to look like something else and is often used to hide information. If the receiver doesn't know how to decipher the message, the message can't be understood. Evolutionary algorithms can generate many possibilities for changing the ciphered message to uncover the original message.

Chapter 5 dives into advanced concepts of genetic algorithms that adapt to different problem spaces. We explore techniques for encoding, crossover, mutation, and selection, and we uncover effective alternatives.

SUMMARY OF EVOLUTIONARY ALGORITHMS

Genetic algorithms use the theory of evolution to find good solutions to optimization problems

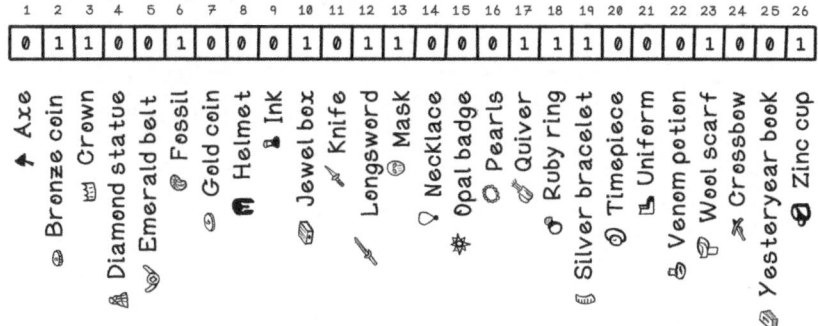

Crossover aims to reproduce better solutions after each generation.

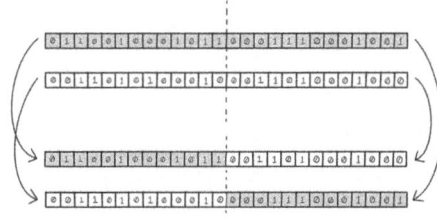

The fitness function directly influences how good a solution is found.

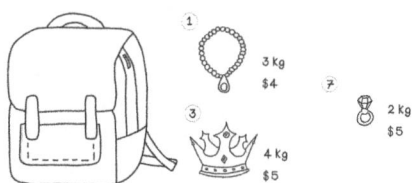

Selection favors stronger individuals but gives weaker ones a chance to reproduce - potentially making good solutions in future generations.

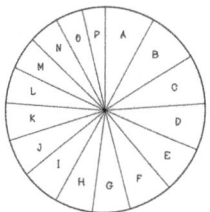

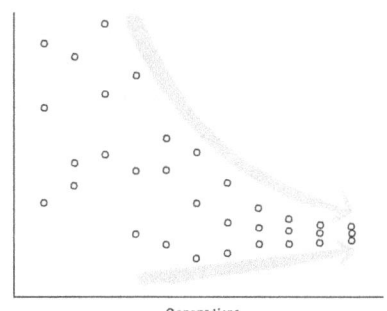

Generations

Explore at the start, exploit at the end, to produce good solutions.

In this chapter

- Considering options for the steps in the genetic algorithm life cycle

- Adjusting a genetic algorithm to solve different problems

- Configuring advanced parameters for a genetic algorithm life cycle

Evolutionary algorithm life cycle

The general life cycle of a genetic algorithm is outlined in chapter 4, which is a prerequisite for this chapter. Here, we consider other problems that a genetic algorithm might be well-suited to solve, why some of the approaches demonstrated so far won't work, and what alternatives we might try. As a reminder, the general life cycle of a genetic algorithm is

1. *Creating a population.* This step involves generating an initial set of random candidate solutions.
2. *Measuring the fitness of individuals in the population.* This step determines how good a specific solution is by using a fitness function that scores solutions to determine how good they are.

3. *Selecting parents based on their fitness.* This step involves selecting parents that will produce offspring.
4. *Reproducing individuals from parents.* This step generates new candidates by combining the genes of selected parents and introducing random mutations to the offspring.
5. *Populating the next generation.* This step involves selecting individuals and offspring from the population that will survive to the next generation.

Keep the life-cycle flow (depicted in figure 5.1) in mind as you work through this chapter. This chapter starts by exploring alternative selection strategies; these individual approaches can be swapped in and out for any genetic algorithm. Then it follows three scenarios that are variations of the Knapsack Problem (chapter 4) to highlight the utility of the alternative encoding, crossover, and mutation approaches (figure 5.2).

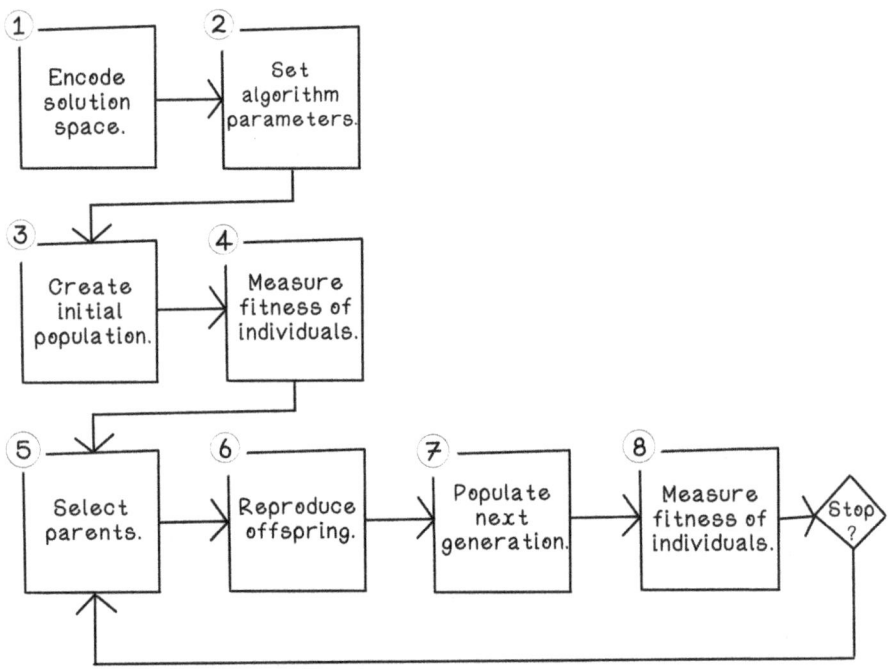

Figure 5.1 Genetic algorithm life cycle

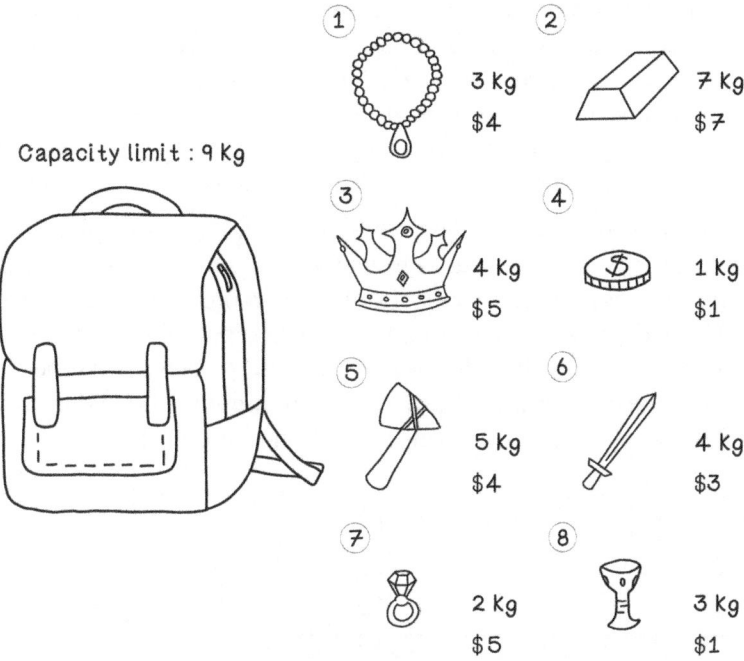

Capacity limit : 9 kg

Figure 5.2 The example Knapsack Problem

Alternative selection strategies

Chapter 4 explored one selection strategy: roulette-wheel selection, which is one of the simplest methods for selecting individuals. The three selection strategies described in the following sections mitigate some problems of roulette-wheel selection. Each strategy has advantages and disadvantages that affect the diversity of the population, ultimately affecting whether an optimal solution is found.

Rank selection: Even the playing field

One problem with roulette-wheel selection is the vast differences in the magnitude of fitness between chromosomes. This disparity heavily biases the selection toward choosing individuals with high fitness scores or giving poor-performing individuals a larger chance of selection than desired because their fitness is represented disproportionately. This problem affects the diversity of the population. More diversity means more exploration of the search space, but it can also cause finding optimal solutions to take too many generations.

Rank selection aims to solve this problem by ranking individuals based on their fitness and then using each individual's rank as the value for calculating the size of its slice on the wheel. In the Knapsack Problem, this value is a number between 1 and 16 because we're choosing among 16 individuals. While stronger individuals are still favored, rank selection ensures that selection probabilities are derived from relative standing rather than raw fitness differences, giving every individual a consistent chance to be chosen.

Think of a marathon. The winner might cross the finish line 1 hour ahead of the second-place runner or only 1 second ahead. In roulette-wheel selection, that time gap matters: the much faster runner gets a massively bigger slice. In rank selection, we ignore the time gap. First place gets $100, and second place gets $50. It doesn't matter how much better the winner was—only that they were better. This prevents one super individual from dominating the population too early. When 16 individuals are ranked, the wheel looks slightly different from roulette-wheel selection (figure 5.3).

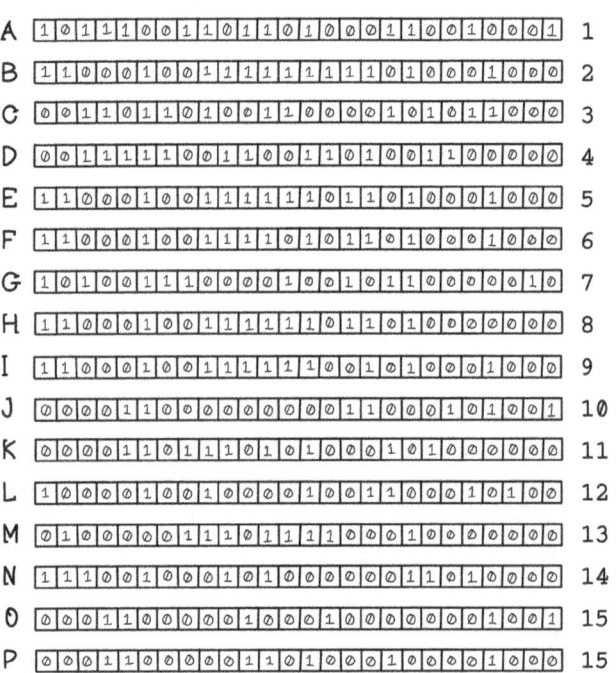
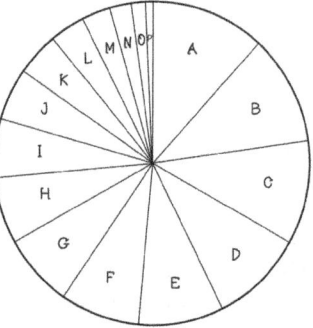

Figure 5.3 Example of rank selection

Figure 5.4 compares roulette-wheel selection and rank selection. Clearly, rank selection gives better-performing solutions a better chance of selection.

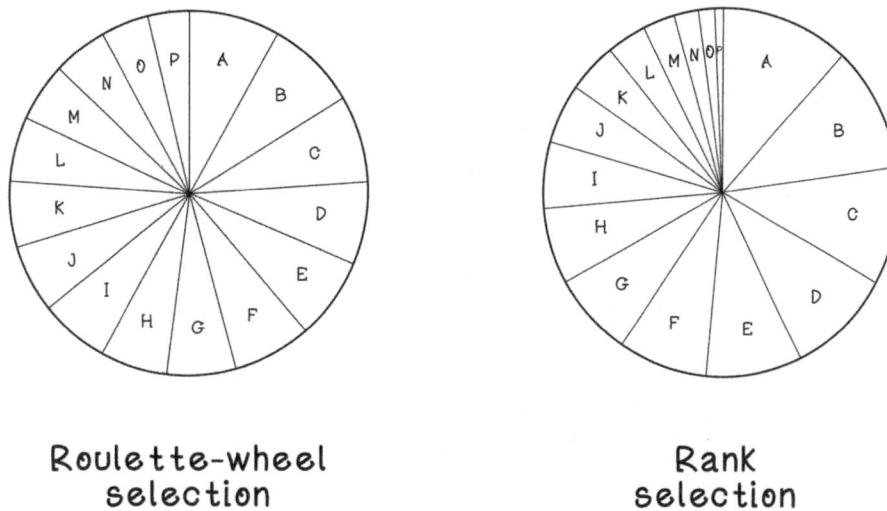

Roulette-wheel selection

Rank selection

Figure 5.4 Roulette-wheel selection vs. rank selection

Tournament selection: Let them fight

Tournament selection plays individual chromosomes against one another. Tournament selection randomly chooses a set number of individuals from the population and places them in a group. This process is performed for a predetermined number of groups. The individual with the highest fitness score in each respective group is selected. The larger the group, the less diverse it is because only one individual from each group is selected.

Imagine grabbing four random people from the population and throwing them into an arena. The single fittest person in that small group wins the right to reproduce. We don't care whether that person is the strongest in the world—only that they're the strongest in that specific group. This method is fast, efficient, and easily tunable: larger tournaments create stricter pressure to be fit, and smaller tournaments allow more randomness.

When 16 individuals are allocated to four groups, selecting only one individual from each group results in the choice of four of the strongest individuals from those groups. Then the four winning individuals can be paired to reproduce (figure 5.5).

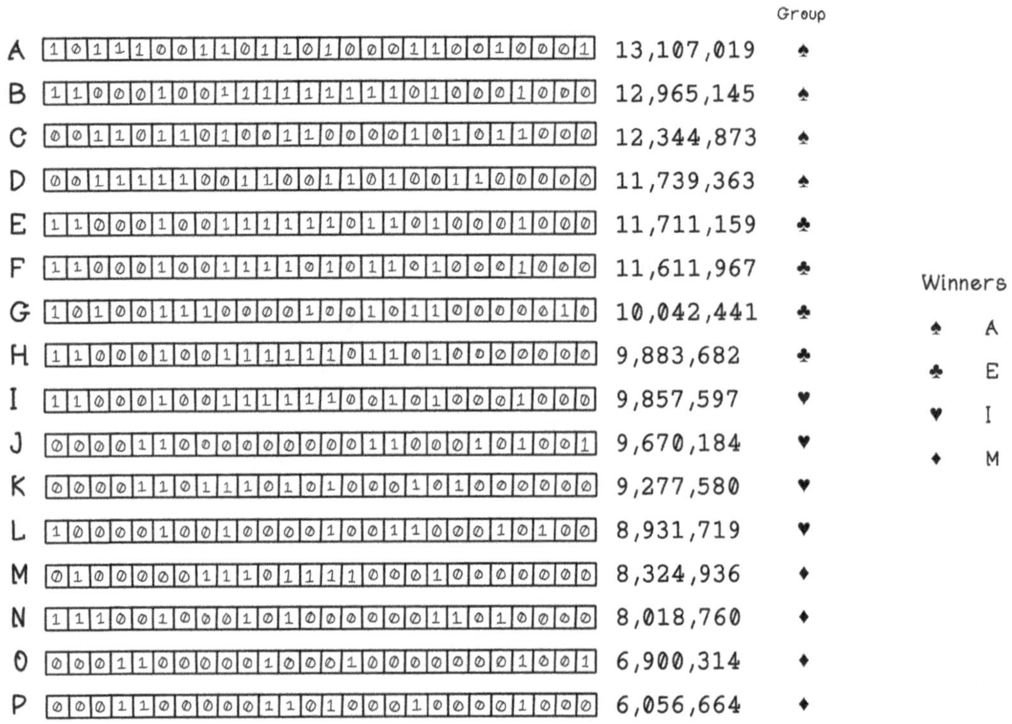

		Value	Group
A	`1 0 1 1 1 0 0 1 1 0 1 1 0 1 0 0 0 1 1 0 0 1 0 0 0 1`	13,107,019	♠
B	`1 1 0 0 0 1 0 0 1 1 1 1 1 1 1 1 0 1 0 0 0 1 0 0 0`	12,965,145	♠
C	`0 0 1 1 0 1 1 0 1 0 0 1 1 0 0 0 1 0 1 0 1 1 0 0 0`	12,344,873	♠
D	`0 0 1 1 1 1 1 0 0 1 1 0 0 1 1 0 1 0 0 1 1 0 0 0 0`	11,739,363	♠
E	`1 1 0 0 0 1 0 0 1 1 1 1 1 1 0 1 1 0 1 0 0 0 1 0 0`	11,711,159	♣
F	`1 1 0 0 0 1 0 0 1 1 1 1 0 1 0 1 1 0 1 0 0 0 1 0 0`	11,611,967	♣
G	`1 0 1 0 0 1 1 1 0 0 0 0 1 0 0 1 0 1 1 0 0 0 0 0 1 0`	10,042,441	♣
H	`1 1 0 0 0 1 0 0 1 1 1 1 1 1 0 1 1 0 1 0 0 0 0 0 0`	9,883,682	♣
I	`1 1 0 0 0 1 0 0 1 1 1 1 1 0 0 1 0 1 0 0 0 1 0 0`	9,857,597	♥
J	`0 0 0 0 1 1 0 0 0 0 0 0 0 1 1 0 0 0 1 0 1 0 0 1`	9,670,184	♥
K	`0 0 0 0 1 1 0 1 1 0 1 0 1 0 0 0 1 0 1 0 0 0 0 0`	9,277,580	♥
L	`1 0 0 0 0 1 0 0 1 0 0 0 1 0 0 1 1 0 0 1 0 1 0 0`	8,931,719	♥
M	`0 1 0 0 0 0 0 1 1 1 0 1 1 1 1 0 0 1 0 0 0 0 0`	8,324,936	♦
N	`1 1 1 0 0 1 0 0 0 1 0 1 0 0 0 0 0 1 1 0 1 0 0 0`	8,018,760	♦
O	`0 0 0 1 1 0 0 0 0 1 0 0 1 0 0 0 0 0 0 1 0 0 1`	6,900,314	♦
P	`0 0 0 1 1 0 0 0 0 1 1 0 1 0 0 1 0 0 0 1 0 0`	6,056,664	♦

Winners
♠ A
♣ E
♥ I
♦ M

Figure 5.5 Example of tournament selection

Elitism selection: Choose only the best

Elitism selection acts like a VIP pass for your best solutions. It allows the top performers to skip the risky process of crossover and mutation and move straight to the next round, ensuring that the best solution found so far is never lost. Relying on elitism too much, however, is dangerous: if everyone is an elite, no one is exploring new territory, and the algorithm stops learning. The disadvantage of elitism is that the population can fall into a local best solution space and never be diverse enough to find global bests (figure 5.6).

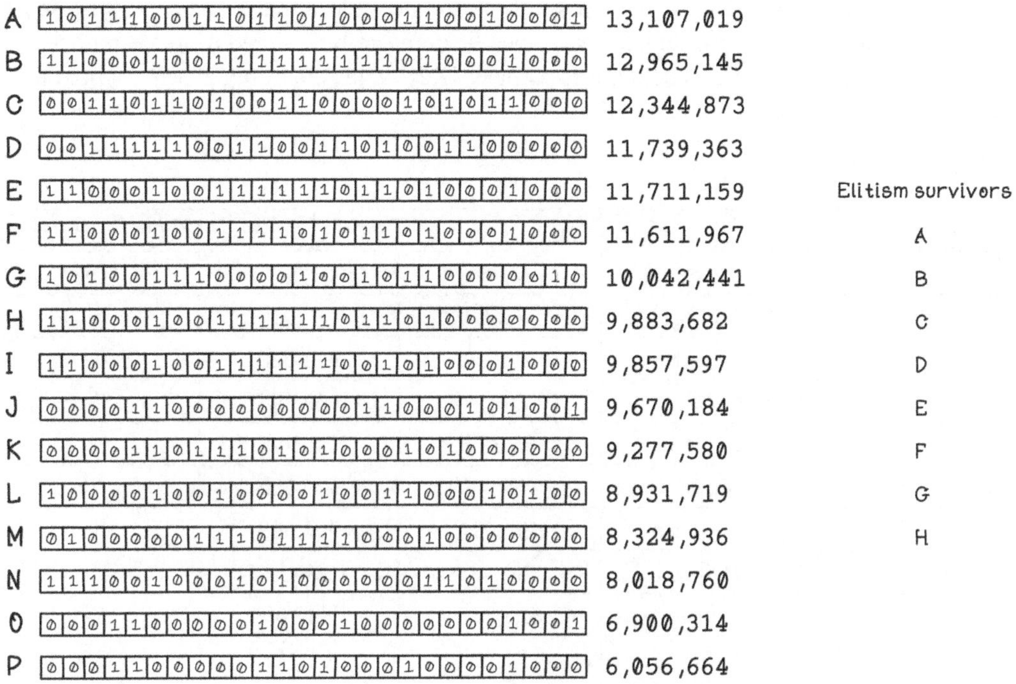

A	13,107,019	
B	12,965,145	
C	12,344,873	
D	11,739,363	
E	11,711,159	Elitism survivors
F	11,611,967	A
G	10,042,441	B
H	9,883,682	C
I	9,857,597	D
J	9,670,184	E
K	9,277,580	F
L	8,931,719	G
M	8,324,936	H
N	8,018,760	
O	6,900,314	
P	6,056,664	

Figure 5.6 Example of elitism selection

Elitism is often used in conjunction with roulette-wheel selection, rank selection, and tournament selection. The idea is that several elite individuals are selected to reproduce, and the rest of the population is filled with individuals by means of one of the other selection strategies.

Chapter 4 explored a problem in which including items in or excluding items from the knapsack is important. A variety of problem spaces require a different encoding because binary encoding won't make sense. The following three sections describe these scenarios.

Real-value encoding: Working with real numbers

Consider that the Knapsack Problem has changed slightly. The problem remains choosing the most valuable items to fill the weight capacity of the knapsack, but now the choice involves more than one unit of each item. As shown in table 5.1, the weights and values remain the same as in the original dataset, but a quantity of each item is included.

With this slight adjustment, many new solutions are possible, and one or more of those solutions may be more optimal because a specific item can be selected more than once. Binary encoding is a poor choice in this scenario. Real-value encoding is better suited to represent the state of potential solutions.

Table 5.1 Knapsack capacity: 6,404,180 kg

Item ID	Item name	Weight (kg)	Value ($)	Quantity
1	Axe	32,252	68,674	19
2	Bronze coin	225,790	471,010	14
3	Crown	468,164	944,620	2
4	Diamond statue	489,494	962,094	9
5	Emerald belt	35,384	78,344	11
6	Fossil	265,590	579,152	6
7	Gold coin	497,911	902,698	4
8	Helmet	800,493	1,686,515	10
9	Ink	823,576	1,688,691	7
10	Jewel box	552,202	1,056,157	3
11	Knife	323,618	677,562	5
12	Longsword	382,846	833,132	13
13	Mask	44,676	99,192	15
14	Necklace	169,738	376,418	8
15	Opal badge	610,876	1,253,986	4
16	Pearls	854,190	1,853,562	9
17	Quiver	671,123	1,320,297	12
18	Ruby ring	698,180	1,301,637	17
19	Silver bracelet	446,517	859,835	16
20	Timepiece	909,620	1,677,534	7
21	Uniform	904,818	1,910,501	6
22	Venom potion	730,061	1,528,646	9
23	Wool scarf	931,932	1,827,477	3
24	Crossbow	952,360	2,068,204	1
25	Yesteryear book	926,023	1,746,556	7
26	Zinc cup	978,724	2,100,851	2

Real-value encoding at its core

Real-value encoding represents a gene as numeric values, strings, or symbols and expresses potential solutions in the natural state respective to the problem. This encoding is used when potential solutions contain continuous values that can't be encoded easily with binary encoding. As an example, because more than one item is available to be carried in the knapsack, each item index can't indicate only whether the item is included; it also must indicate the quantity of that item in the knapsack (figure 5.7).

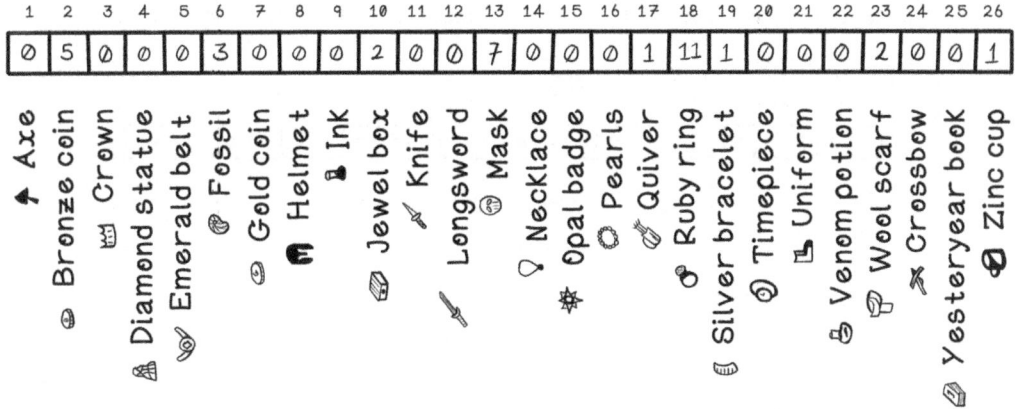

Figure 5.7 Example of real-value encoding

Because the encoding scheme has been changed, new crossover and mutation options become available. The crossover approaches discussed for binary encoding are still valid options for real-value encoding, but mutation should be approached differently.

Arithmetic crossover: Reproduce with math

Arithmetic crossover involves an arithmetic operation to be computed by using each parent as a variable in the expression. The result of applying an arithmetic operation using both parents is the new offspring. When we use this strategy with binary encoding, it's important to ensure that the result of the operation is still a valid chromosome.

This technique is designed primarily for real-value encoding. Although it's technically possible to adapt it for binary encoding (by rounding the result), standard practice is to use it when genes represent continuous numbers, such as weights or coordinates. Figure 5.8 illustrates a multiplication operation for crossover.

WARNING Be wary: this approach can create offspring that are simply the average of their parents. In the early stages, this exploration is good. But if the parents have found a precise, high-performing peak, averaging them mathematically might push the offspring away from that optimal solution, effectively unsolving the progress made by the parents.

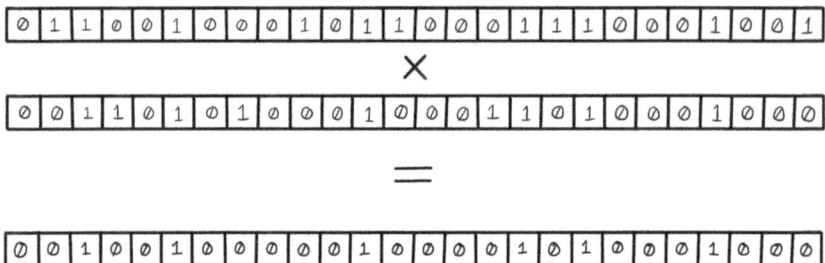

Figure 5.8 Example of arithmetic crossover

Boundary mutation

In *boundary mutation*, a gene randomly selected from a real-value-encoded chromosome is set randomly to a lower bound value or upper bound value. Given 26 genes in a chromosome, a random index is selected, and the value is set to a minimum or maximum. In figure 5.9, the original value is 0 and will be adjusted to 6, which is the maximum for that item. The minimum and maximum can be the same for all indexes or set uniquely for each index if knowledge of the problem informs the decision. This approach attempts to evaluate the effects of individual genes on the chromosome.

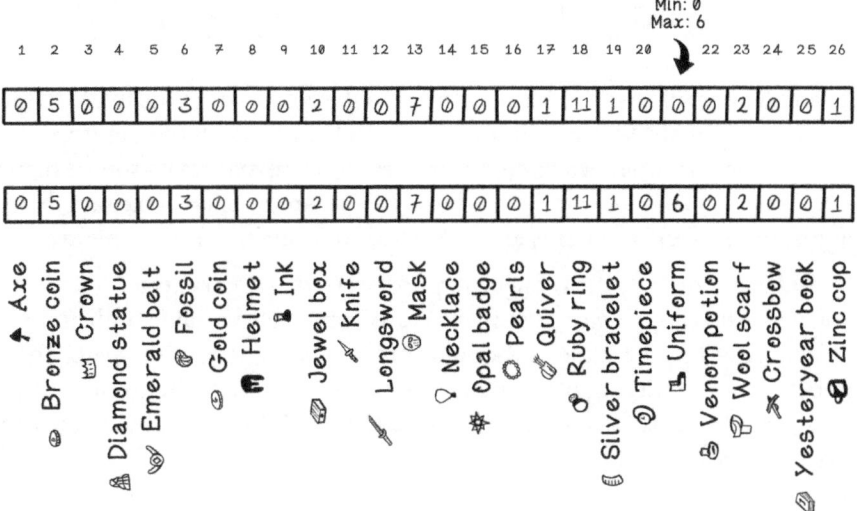

Figure 5.9 Example of boundary mutation

Arithmetic mutation

In *arithmetic mutation*, a randomly selected gene in a real-value-encoded chromosome is changed by adding or subtracting a small number. Although the example in figure 5.10 includes whole numbers, the numbers could be decimals, including fractions.

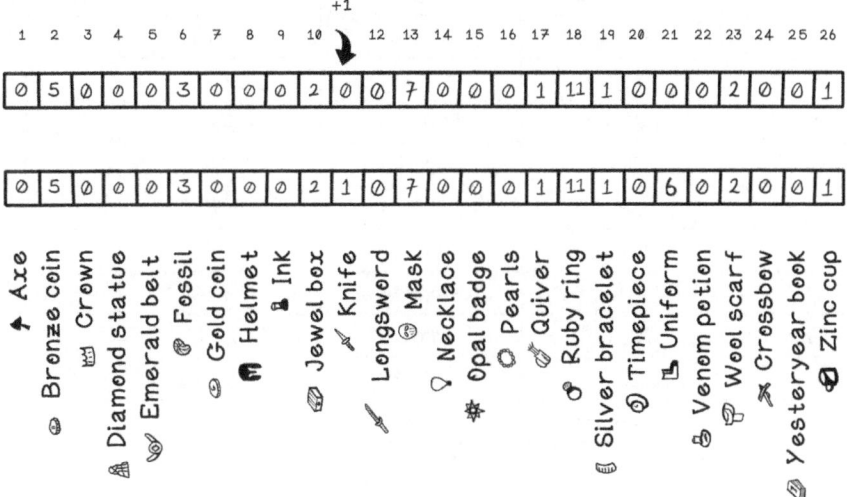

Figure 5.10 Example of arithmetic mutation

Order encoding: Working with sequences

In this example, we still have the same items as in the Knapsack Problem. We won't be determining the items that will fit into a knapsack; instead, all the items need to be processed in a refinery where each item is broken down to extract its source material. Perhaps the gold coin, silver bracelet, and other items are smelted to extract their source compounds. In this scenario, items aren't selected to be included; all items are included.

To make things interesting, the refinery requires a steady rate of extraction, given the extraction time and the value of each item. We assume that the value of the refined material is more or less the same as the value of the item in its original state. The problem becomes an ordering problem: in what order should the items be processed to maintain a constant rate of value being delivered? Table 5.2 describes the items and their respective extraction times.

Table 5.2 Factory value per hour: 600,000

Item ID	Item name	Weight (kg)	Value ($)	Extraction time (minutes)
1	Axe	32,252	68,674	60
2	Bronze coin	225,790	471,010	30
3	Crown	468,164	944,620	45
4	Diamond statue	489,494	962,094	90
5	Emerald belt	35,384	78,344	70
6	Fossil	265,590	579,152	20
7	Gold coin	497,911	902,698	15
8	Helmet	800,493	1,686,515	20
9	Ink	823,576	1,688,691	10
10	Jewel box	552,202	1,056,157	40
11	Knife	323,618	677,562	15
12	Longsword	382,846	833,132	60
13	Mask	44,676	99,192	10
14	Necklace	169,738	376,418	20
15	Opal badge	610,876	1,253,986	60
16	Pearls	854,190	1,853,562	25
17	Quiver	671,123	1,320,297	30

Table 5.2 Factory value per hour: 600,000 (*continued*)

Item ID	Item name	Weight (kg)	Value ($)	Extraction time (minutes)
18	Ruby ring	698,180	1,301,637	70
19	Silver bracelet	446,517	859,835	50
20	Timepiece	909,620	1,677,534	45
21	Uniform	904,818	1,910,501	5
22	Venom potion	730,061	1,528,646	5
23	Wool scarf	931,932	1,827,477	5
24	Crossbow	952,360	2,068,204	25
25	Yesteryear book	926,023	1,746,556	5
26	Zinc cup	978,724	2,100,851	10

Importance of the fitness function

With the change in the Knapsack Problem to the Refinery Problem, a key difference is the measurement of successful solutions. Because the factory requires a constant minimum rate of value per hour, the accuracy of the fitness function becomes critical to finding optimal solutions. In the Knapsack Problem, the fitness of a solution is trivial to compute because it involves only two things: ensuring that the knapsack's weight limit is respected and summing the selected items' value. In the Refinery Problem, the fitness function must calculate the rate of value provided, given the extraction time for each item as well as the value of each item. This calculation is more complex, and an error in the logic of this fitness function directly influences the quality of solutions.

Order encoding at its core

Order encoding (also known as *permutation encoding*) represents a chromosome as a sequence of elements. Order encoding usually requires all elements to be present in the chromosome, which implies that standard crossover methods can't be used because they would create invalid solutions with duplicate or missing items.

Imagine a band planning a world tour in which it has to visit London, Tokyo, and New York exactly once. Binary encoding doesn't work here. The band can't visit London twice or skip Tokyo (1 or 0). They need to visit all the cities, but the order changes the cost (flight prices). This is why we use order decoding. The sequence [London, Tokyo, New York] is different from [New York, London, Tokyo].

We must use specialized operators to preserve the permutation constraints. Common techniques include Partially Mapped Crossover (PMX), Order Crossover (OX), and Cycle Crossover (CX), which are designed specifically to shuffle the order without breaking the list. Figure 5.11 depicts how a chromosome represents the processing order of the available items.

Figure 5.11 Example of order encoding

Another example in which it's sensible to use order encoding is representing potential solutions to route optimization problems. Given a certain number of destinations, each of which must be visited at least once while minimizing the total distance traveled, the route can be represented as a string of the destinations in the order in which they're visited. We'll use this example in chapter 6.

Order mutation

In *order mutation*, two randomly selected genes in an order-encoded chromosome swap positions. This ensures that all items remain in the chromosome while introducing diversity (figure 5.12).

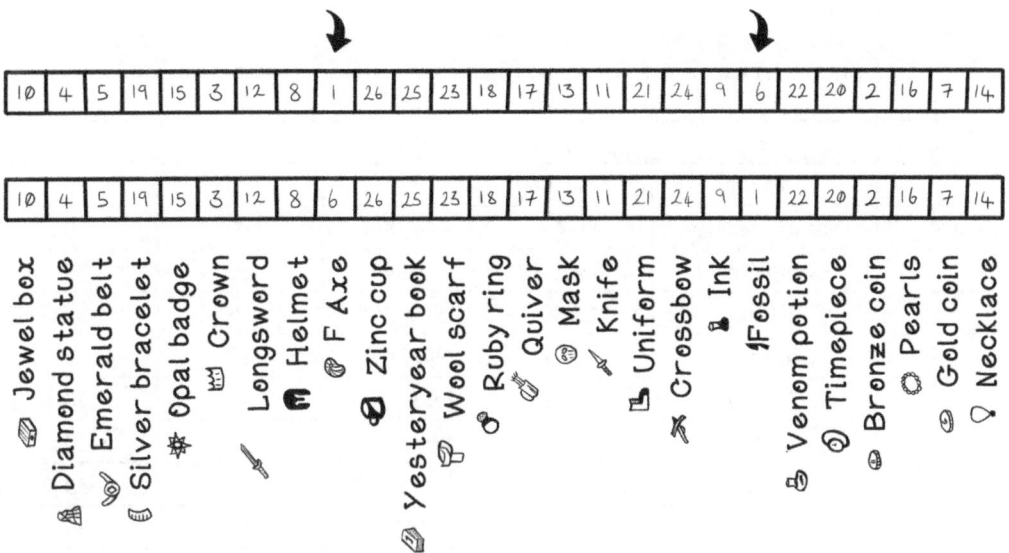

Figure 5.12 Example of order mutation

Tree encoding: Working with hierarchies

The preceding sections show that binary encoding is useful for selecting items from a set, real-value encoding is useful when real numbers are important to the solution, and order encoding is useful for determining priority and sequences. Suppose that the items in the Knapsack Problem are placed in packages to be shipped to homes around town. Each delivery wagon can hold a specific volume. The requirement is to determine the optimal positioning of packages to minimize empty space in each wagon (table 5.3). In the interest of simplicity, let's assume that the wagon's volume is a 2D rectangle and the packages are rectangular rather than 3D boxes.

Table 5.3 Wagon capacity: 1,000 meters wide × 1,000 meters high

Item ID	Item name	Weight (kg)	Value ($)	W (cm)	H (cm)
1	Axe	32,252	68,674	20	60
2	Bronze coin	225,790	471,010	10	10
3	Crown	468,164	944,620	20	20
4	Diamond statue	489,494	962,094	30	70
5	Emerald belt	35,384	78,344	30	20
6	Fossil	265,590	579,152	15	15
7	Gold coin	497,911	902,698	10	10
8	Helmet	800,493	1,686,515	40	50
9	Ink	823,576	1,688,691	5	10
10	Jewel box	552,202	1,056,157	40	30
11	Knife	323,618	677,562	10	30
12	Longsword	382,846	833,132	15	50
13	Mask	44,676	99,192	20	30
14	Necklace	169,738	376,418	15	20
15	Opal badge	610,876	1,253,986	5	5
16	Pearls	854,190	1,853,562	10	5
17	Quiver	671,123	1,320,297	30	70
18	Ruby ring	698,180	1,301,637	5	10
19	Silver bracelet	446,517	859,835	10	20
20	Timepiece	909,620	1,677,534	15	20
21	Uniform	904,818	1,910,501	30	40
22	Venom potion	730,061	1,528,646	15	15
23	Wool scarf	931,932	1,827,477	20	30
24	Crossbow	952,360	2,068,204	50	70
25	Yesteryear book	926,023	1,746,556	25	30
26	Zinc cup	978,724	2,100,851	15	25

Tree encoding at its core

Tree encoding represents a chromosome as a tree of elements. Tree encoding is versatile for representing potential solutions in which the hierarchy of elements is important and/or required.

Think of a corporation's organizational chart. The CEO (root) makes a high-level decision, which branches down to vice presidents, managers, and finally interns. You can't simply swap a vice president with an intern without breaking the chain of command. Tree encoding preserves these strict parent–child relationships.

Tree encoding can even represent functions, which consist of a tree of expressions. This concept is the foundation of genetic programming, a specialized field, in which the algorithm evolves executable programs or formulas rather than just static variables. As a result, tree encoding could be used to evolve program functions when the function itself solves a specific problem; the solution may work but look bizarre.

Tree encoding, however, is computationally costly. It's best suited to problems in which the hierarchical structure or logic needs to evolve rather to problems involving simple numeric optimization.

Consider an example in which tree encoding makes sense. We have a wagon with a specific height and width, and a certain number of packages must fit in the wagon. The goal is to fit the packages in the wagon so that empty space is minimized. A tree-encoding approach would work well for representing potential solutions to this problem.

In figure 5.13, the root node, A, represents the packing of the wagon from top to bottom. Node B represents all packages horizontally, similarly to node C and node D. Node E represents packages packed vertically in that slice of the wagon.

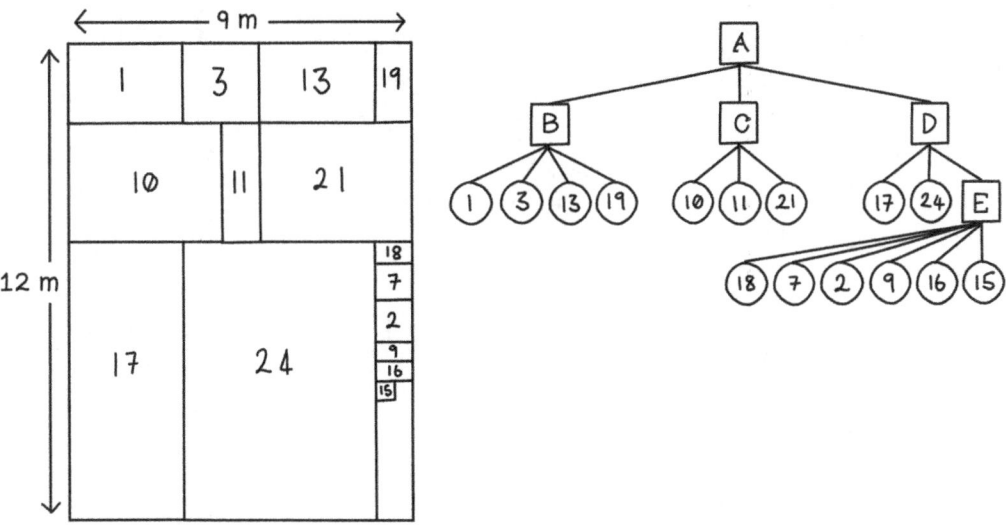

Figure 5.13 Example of a tree used to represent the Wagon Packing Problem

Tree crossover: Inheriting portions of a tree

Tree crossover is similar to single-point crossover (chapter 4) in that a single point in the tree structure is selected and then the parts are exchanged and combined with copies of the parent individuals to create an offspring individual. The inverse process can be used to make a second offspring. The resulting children must be verified as valid solutions that obey the constraints of the problem. More than one point can be used for crossover if using multiple points makes sense for solving the problem (figure 5.14).

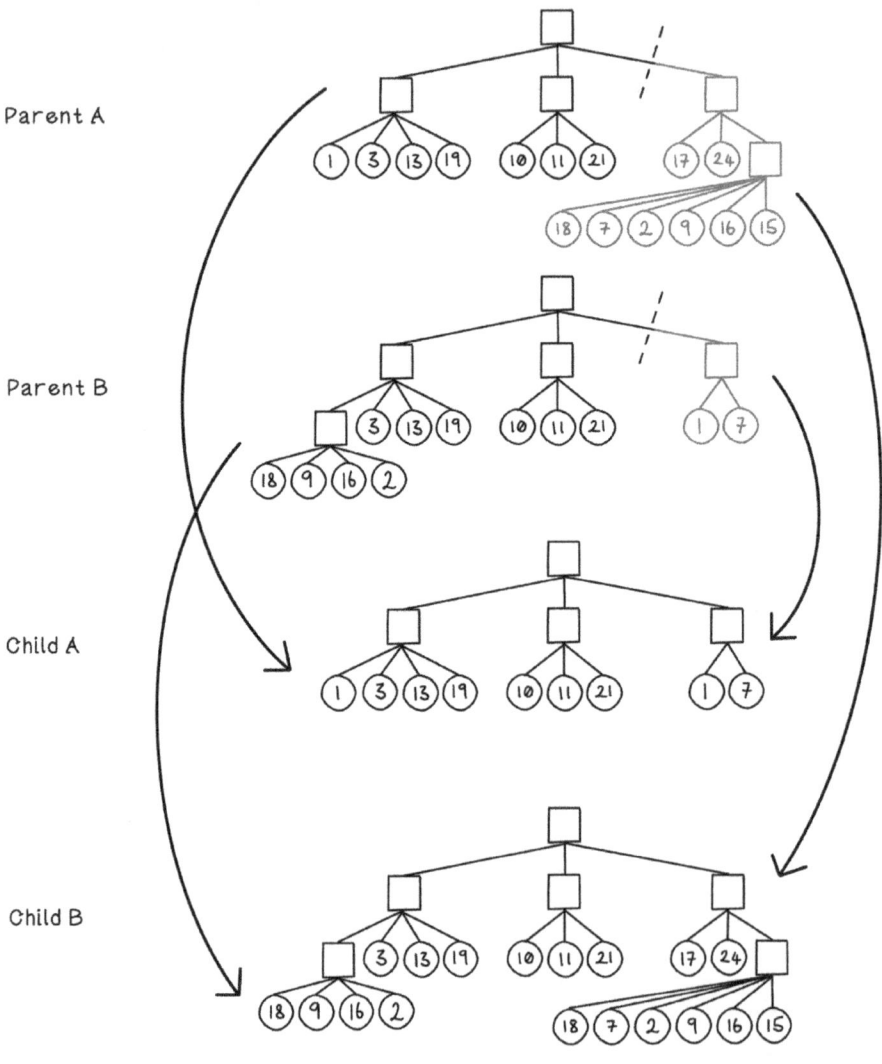

Figure 5.14 Example of tree crossover

Change-node mutation

In *change-node mutation*, a randomly selected node in a tree-encoded chromosome is changed to a randomly selected valid object for that node. Given a tree representing an organization of items, we can change an item to another valid item (figure 5.15).

> **NOTE** This chapter and chapter 4 cover several encoding schemes, crossover schemes, and selection strategies. You could substitute your own approaches for these steps in your genetic algorithms if doing so makes sense for your problem.

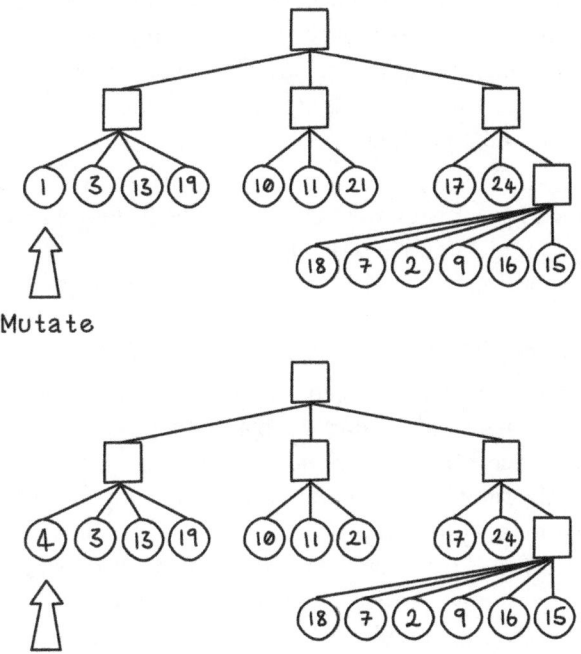

Figure 5.15 Change-node mutation in a tree

Common types of evolutionary algorithms

This chapter focuses on the life cycle of and alternative approaches for a genetic algorithm. Variations of the algorithm can be useful for solving different problems. Now that we have a grounding in how a genetic algorithm works, we'll look at these variations and possible use cases for them.

Genetic programming

Genetic programming follows a process similar to that of genetic algorithms but is used primarily to generate computer programs to solve problems. The process described earlier in this chapter also applies here. The fitness of potential solutions in a genetic programming algorithm is how well the generated program solves a computational problem. With this in mind, we see that the tree-encoding method would work well because most computer programs are graphs consisting of nodes that indicate operations and processes. These trees of logic can be evolved so the computer program will evolve to solve a specific problem.

> **NOTE** These computer programs usually evolve to look like a mess of code that's difficult to understand and debug.

Evolutionary programming

Evolutionary programming is similar to genetic programming, but the potential solution is parameters for a predefined fixed computer program, not a generated computer program. If a program requires finely tuned inputs and determining a good combination of inputs is difficult, a genetic algorithm can be used to evolve these inputs. The fitness of potential solutions in an evolutionary programming algorithm is determined by how well the fixed computer program performs based on the parameters encoded in an individual. Perhaps an evolutionary programming approach could be used to find the optimal architecture or hyperparameters such as the number of layers or learning rate for an artificial neural network (ANN), a technique known as *neuroevolution*. Chapter 9 covers ANNs.

Glossary of evolutionary-algorithm terms

Here is a glossary of evolutionary-algorithm terms for future research and learning:

- *Allele*—The value of a specific gene in a chromosome
- *Chromosome*—A collection of genes that represents a possible solution

- *Exploitation*—The process of honing in on good solutions and iteratively refining them
- *Exploration*—The process of finding a variety of possible solutions, some of which may be good and some of which may be bad
- *Fitness function*—A particular type of objective function
- *Generation*—A single iteration of the algorithm
- *Genotype*—The artificial representation of the potential solution population in the computation space
- *Individual*—A single chromosome in a population
- *Objective function*—A function that attempts to maximize or minimize
- *Phenotype*—The actual representation of the potential solution population in the real world
- *Population*—A collection of individuals

More use cases for evolutionary algorithms

Some use cases for evolutionary algorithms are listed in chapter 4, but many more exist. The following use cases are particularly interesting because they employ one or more of the concepts discussed in this chapter:

- *Adjusting weights in ANNs*—A key concept of ANNs (chapter 9) is adjusting weights in the network to learn patterns and relationships in data. Several mathematical techniques adjust weights, but evolutionary algorithms are more efficient alternatives in the right scenarios.
- *Electronic circuit design*—Electronic circuits with the same components can be designed in many configurations, some of which are more efficient than others. If two components that often work together are closer together, this configuration may improve efficiency. Evolutionary algorithms can be used to evolve different circuit configurations to find the optimal design.
- *Molecular structure simulation and design*—As in electronic circuit design, different molecules behave differently and have specific advantages and disadvantages. Evolutionary algorithms can be used to generate different molecular structures to be simulated and studied to determine their behavioral properties.

You explored the general genetic algorithm life cycle in chapter 4 and advanced approaches in this chapter. Now you should be equipped to apply evolutionary algorithms to your own domain contexts and problems.

SUMMARY OF ADVANCED EVOLUTIONARY APPROACHES

Genetic algorithms can be used to solve a multitude of optimization problems by using different strategies

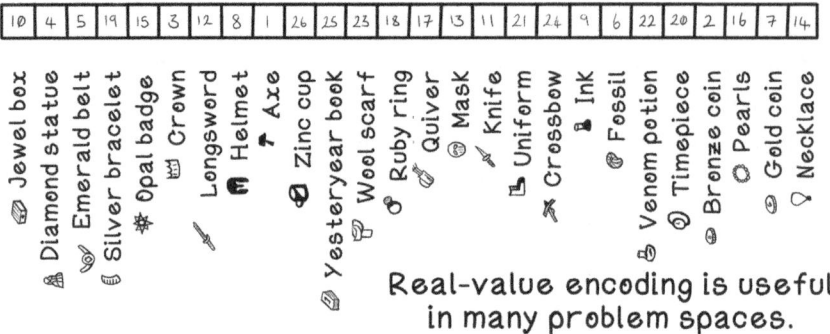

Real-value encoding is useful in many problem spaces.

Order encoding is useful when the priority of sequence is important.

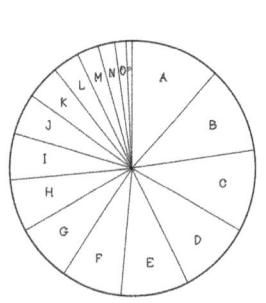

Rank selection

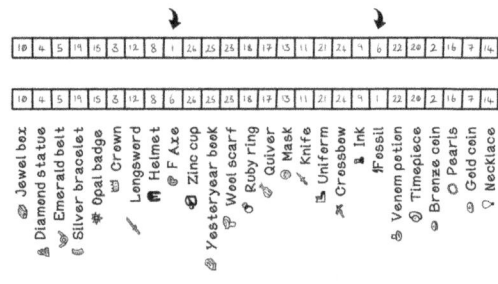

Tree encoding is useful when relationships and hierarchy are important.

Tweaking the parameters of the genetic algorithm is useful for finding good solutions efficiently based on the problem at hand.

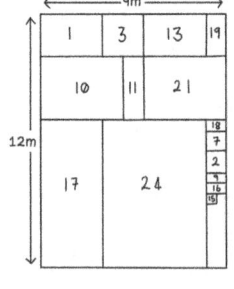

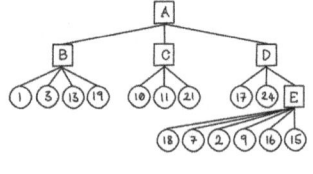

In this chapter

- Seeing and understanding the inspiration for swarm intelligence algorithms

- Solving problems with swarm intelligence algorithms

- Designing and implementing an ant colony optimization algorithm

What is swarm intelligence?

Swarm intelligence algorithms, much like the evolutionary algorithms discussed in chapter 5, are a family of nature-inspired algorithms. Whereas evolutionary algorithms mimic genetic reproduction, swarm intelligence mimics the collective behavior of animals. When we observe the world around us, we see many life forms that are seemingly primitive and unintelligent as individuals yet exhibit intelligent emergent behavior when acting in groups.

An example of these life forms is the ant. A single ant can carry 10 to 50 times its own body weight and run 700 times its body length per minute. These qualities are impressive, but when acting in a group, that single ant can accomplish much more. In a group, ants can build colonies, find and retrieve food, warn and recognize other ants, and use peer pressure to influence other members of the colony. They achieve these tasks through *pheromones*— essentially, perfumes that ants drop as they move. Other ants sense these perfumes and change their behavior based on them. Ants have access to 10 to 20 types of pheromones that communicate different intentions. Because individual ants use pheromones to indicate their intentions and needs, we observe complex emergent intelligent behavior when they act in groups.

Figure 6.1 shows ants working as a team to create a bridge between two points to enable other ants to carry out tasks. These tasks may be to retrieve food or materials for their colony.

Figure 6.1 A group of ants working together to cross a chasm

An experiment based on real-life harvesting ants showed that they always converged on the shortest path between the nest and the food source. Figure 6.2 depicts the difference in colony movement from the start to the time when ants have walked their paths and increased the pheromone intensity on those paths. This outcome was observed in a classical asymmetric bridge experiment with real ants. Notice that the ants converged on the shortest path after 8 minutes.

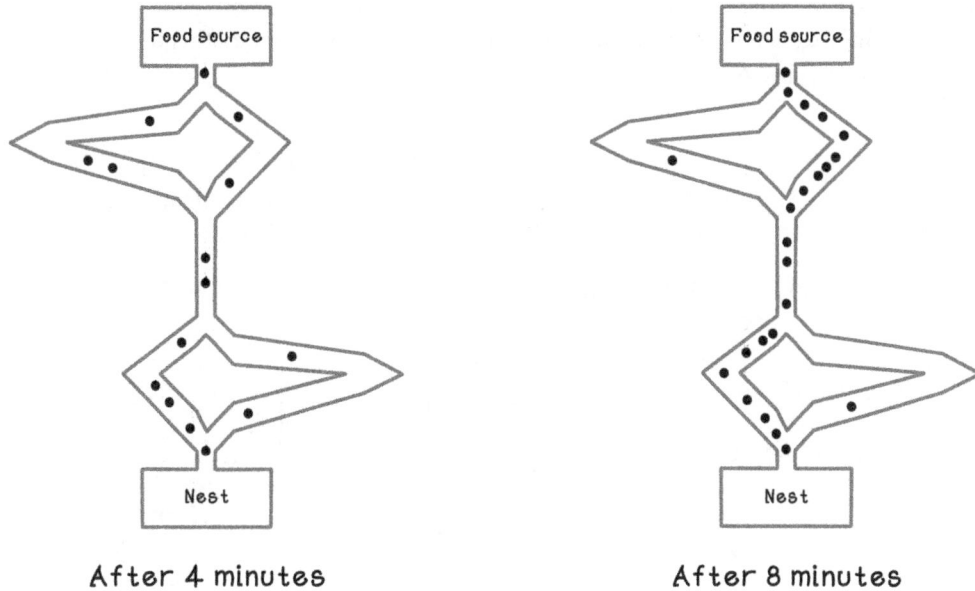

After 4 minutes   After 8 minutes

Figure 6.2 Asymmetric bridge experiment

Why does the shorter bridge win? The answer isn't magic; it's speed. An ant on the short bridge can make two trips in the time an ant on the long bridge makes only one. Because the ants on the short bridge make twice as many trips, they lay down twice as much pheromone per minute, creating a snowball effect that pulls the rest of the colony toward the short path.

Ant Colony Optimization (ACO) algorithms simulate the emergent behavior shown in this experiment. In the case of finding the shortest path, the algorithm converges on a similar state, as observed with real ants.

Swarm intelligence algorithms are powerful tools for solving optimization problems when the search space is vast and rugged and finding an absolute best solution is mathematically difficult. These problems belong to the same broad class that genetic algorithms aim to solve, but the choice between the two types of algorithms often comes down to how the problem is encoded:

- *Genetic algorithms* typically are better for discrete choices, such as choosing which items to pack in a knapsack.
- *Swarm algorithms* (including Particle Swarm Optimization [PSO]) excel at solving continuous numeric problems, such as tuning the exact floating-point weights of a neural network.

We dive into the technicalities of solving optimization problems with PSO in chapter 7. Swarm intelligence is useful in several real-world contexts, some of which are represented in figure 6.3.

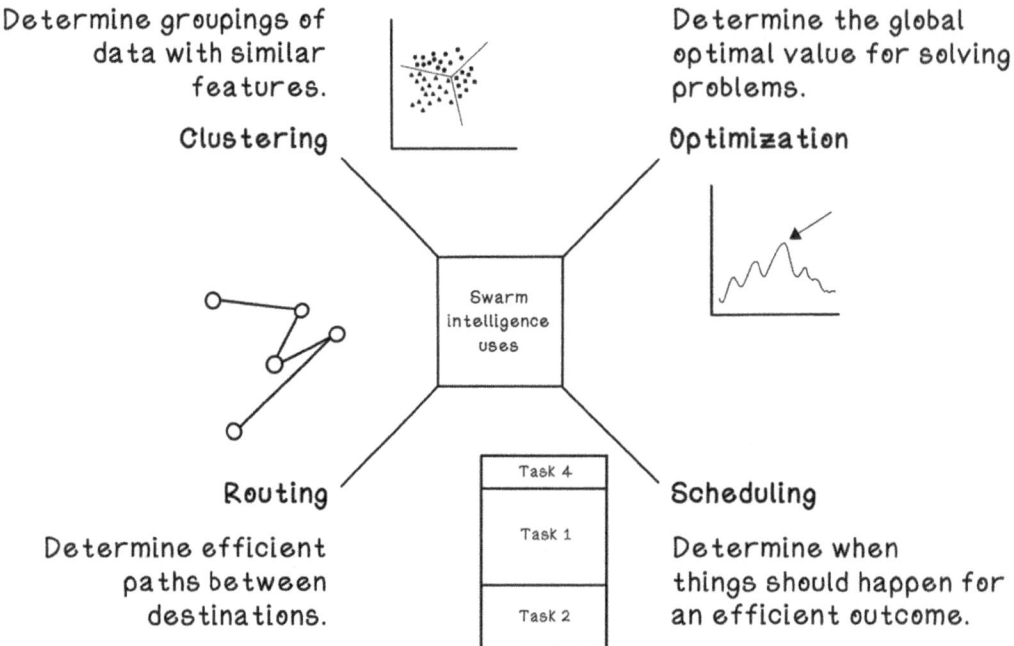

Figure 6.3 Problems addressed by swarm optimization

The following sections explore specific implementations inspired by these concepts. The ACO algorithm is inspired by the behavior of ants moving between destinations, dropping pheromones, and acting on pheromones they come across. The emergent behavior is ants converging on paths of least resistance.

Problems that ACO algorithms can solve

Suppose we're visiting a carnival that has many attractions. The attractions are located in different areas, with varying distances among them. Because we don't feel like wasting time by walking too much, we'll attempt to find the shortest paths between the attractions.

Figure 6.4 illustrates the attractions at a small carnival and the distances among them. Different paths to the attractions have different total lengths of travel.

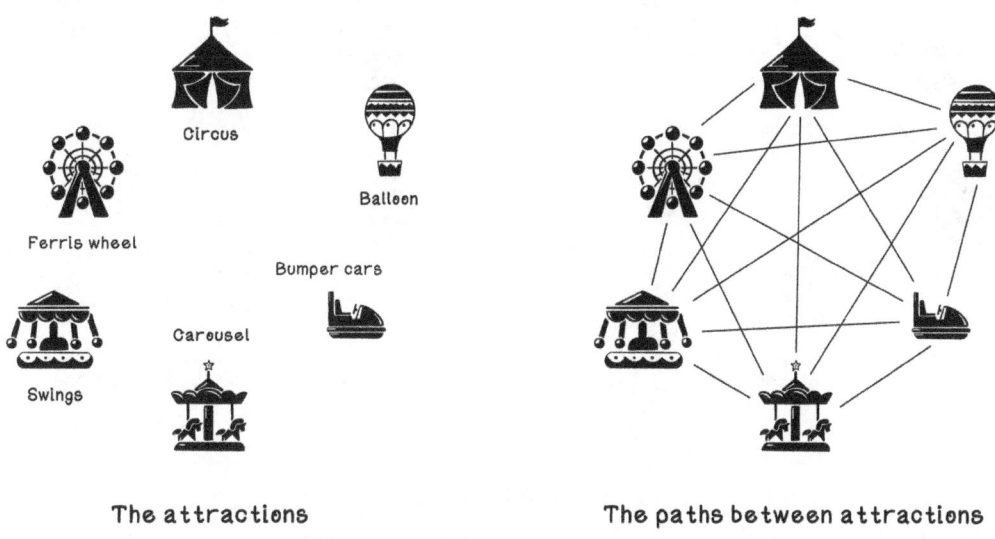

Figure 6.4 Carnival attractions and the paths between them

The figure shows six attractions to visit, with 15 paths between them. This illustration may look familiar: the problem is represented by a fully connected graph, described in chapter 2. The attractions are nodes or vertices, and the paths between attractions are edges. We use the following formula to calculate the number of edges in a fully connected graph. As the number of attractions gets larger, the number of edges explodes:

$$n(n-1)/2$$

Attractions have different distances between them. Figure 6.5 depicts the distance on each path between attractions; it also shows a possible path between attractions.

NOTE The lines in figure 6.5 showing distances between attractions are not drawn to scale of the distance.

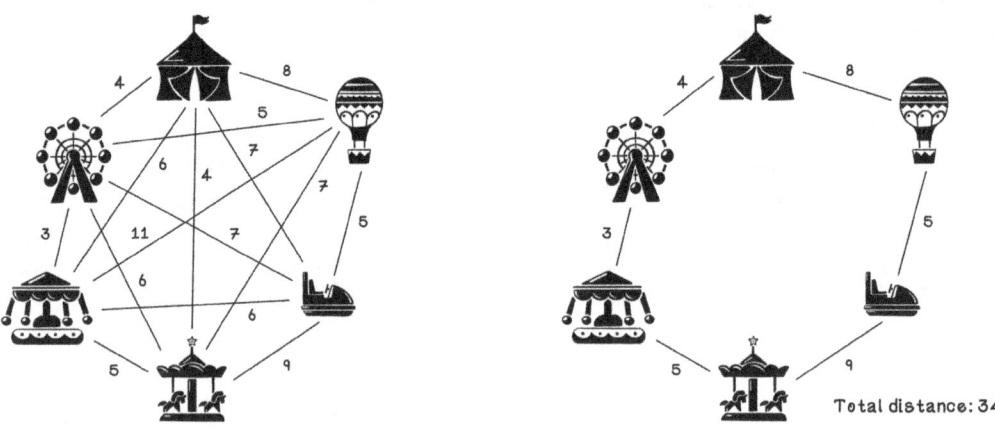

Figure 6.5 Distances between attractions and a possible path to all attractions

If we spend some time analyzing the distances between all the attractions, we find that figure 6.6 shows an optimal path between all attractions, solving the Carnival Problem. We visit the attractions in this sequence: swings, Ferris wheel, circus, carousel, balloons, and bumper cars.

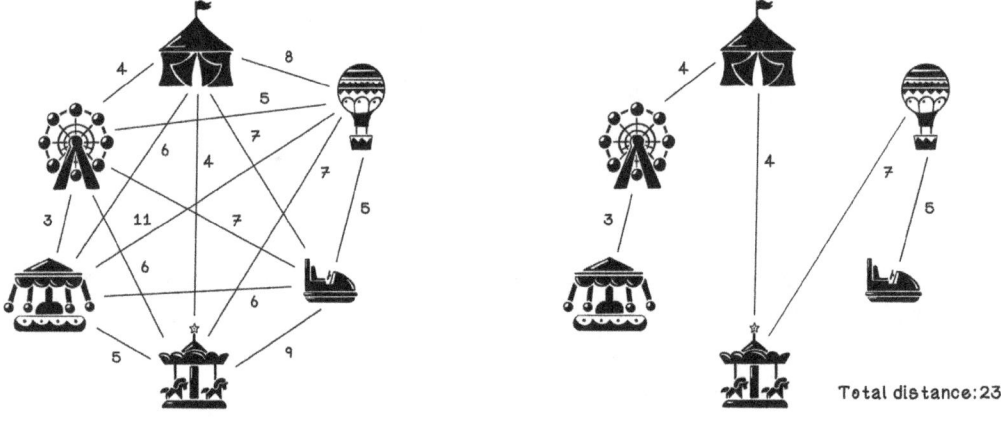

Figure 6.6 Distances between attractions and an optimal path

The small dataset with six attractions is trivial to solve by hand, but if we increase the number of attractions to 15, the number of possibilities increases substantially (figure 6.7). Suppose that the attractions are servers and the paths are network connections. We need intelligent algorithms to solve these types of problems.

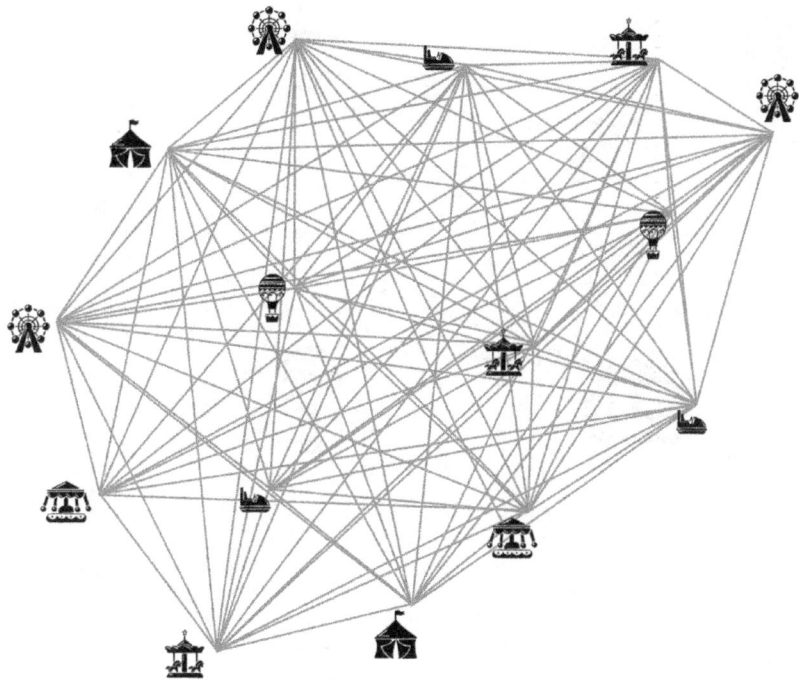

Figure 6.7 A larger dataset of attractions and the paths between them

Exercise: Find the shortest path in this carnival configuration by hand

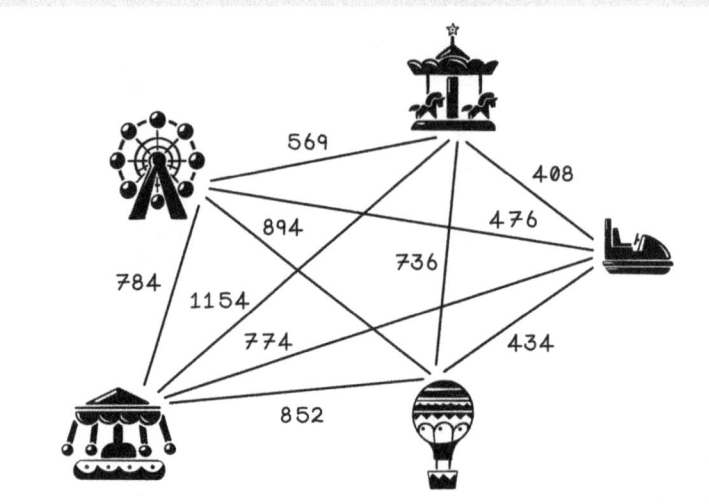

Solution:

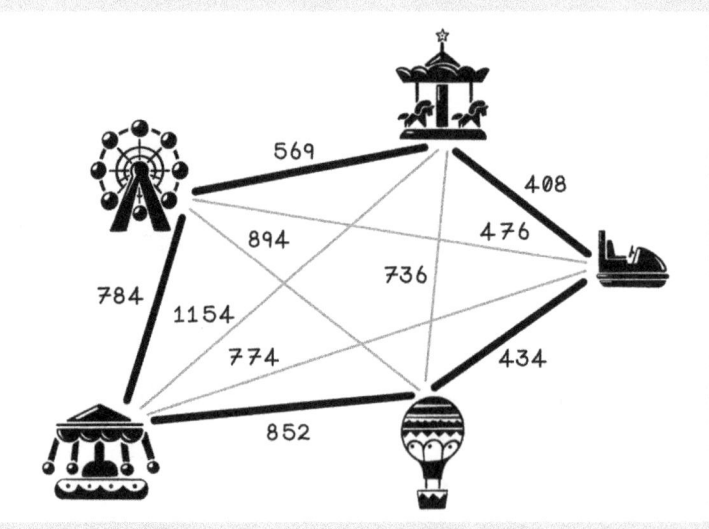

One way to solve this problem computationally is to brute-force it: every combination of tours (a *tour* is a sequence of visits in which every attraction is visited once) of the attractions is generated and evaluated; then the best tour is picked. Again, this solution may seem reasonable, but in a large dataset, the computation is expensive and time-consuming. A brute-force approach with 48 attractions runs for tens of hours before completing.

Representing state: What do paths and ants look like?

Given the Carnival Problem, we need to represent the data in a way that the ACO algorithm can process. Because we have several attractions and all the distances between them, we can use a distance matrix to represent the problem space simply and accurately.

A *distance matrix* is a 2D array in which every index represents an entity; the related set is the distance between that entity and another entity. Similarly, each index in the list denotes a unique entity. This matrix (figure 6.8 and table 6.1) is similar to the adjacency matrix in chapter 2.

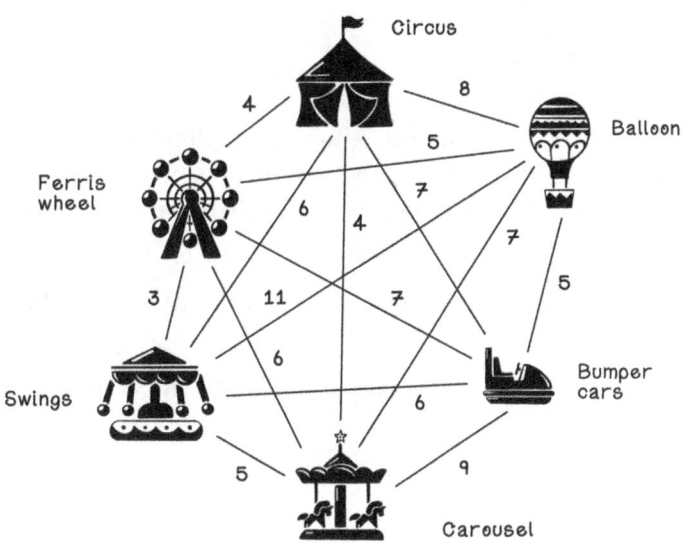

Figure 6.8 An example Carnival Problem

Table 6.1 Distances (in meters) between attractions

	Circus	Balloons	Bumper cars	Carousel	Swings	Ferris wheel
Circus	0	8	7	4	6	4
Balloon	8	0	5	7	11	5
Bumper cars	7	5	0	9	6	7
Carousel	4	7	9	0	5	6
Swings	6	11	6	5	0	3
Ferris wheel	4	5	7	6	3	0

Python code sample for storing attraction distances

The distances between attractions can be represented as a distance matrix—an array of arrays in which a reference to *x, y* in the array references the distance between attractions *x* and *y*. The distance between the same attraction is 0 because it's in the same position. We can also create this array programmatically by iterating through data from a file and creating each element:

```
attraction_distances = [
    [0, 8, 7, 4, 6, 4],
    [8, 0, 5, 7, 11, 5],
    [7, 5, 0, 9, 6, 7],
    [4, 7, 9, 0, 5, 6],
    [6, 11, 6, 5, 0, 3],
    [4, 5, 7, 6, 3, 0]
]
```

The next element to represent is the ants. Ants move to different attractions and leave pheromones behind. Ants also make a judgment about which attraction to visit next. Finally, ants know their own total distance traveled. Here are the basic properties of an ant (figure 6.9):

- *Memory*—In the ACO algorithm, memory is the list of attractions already visited.
- *Best fitness*—This property is the shortest total distance traveled across attractions.
- *Action*—Choose the next destination to visit, and drop pheromones along the way.

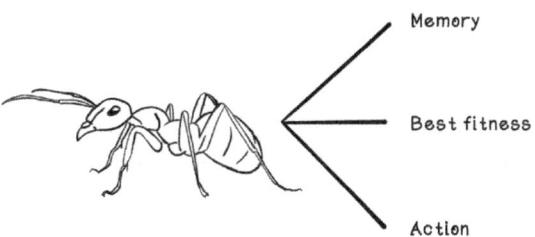

Figure 6.9 Properties of an ant

Python code sample for ant data and operations

Although the abstract concept of an ant entails memory, best fitness, and action, specific data and functions are required to solve the Carnival Problem. To encapsulate the logic for an ant, we can use a class. When an instance of the `Ant` class is initialized, an empty array is initialized to represent a list of attractions that the ant will visit. Furthermore, a random attraction is selected to be the starting point for that specific ant:

```
class Ant:
    def __init__(self, attraction_count):
        self.visited_attractions = []        ◀── A list to track where
                                                  the ant has been

        start_node =
        random.randint(0, attraction_count - 1)    ◀── Randomly
        self.visited_attractions.append(start_node)     drops the ant
                                                         at one of the
                                                         locations
```

The `Ant` class also contains several functions used for ant movement. The `visit_*` functions determine which attraction the ant moves to next. The `visit_attraction` function generates a random chance of visiting a random attraction. In this case, `visit_random_attraction` is called; otherwise, `roulette_wheel_selection` is used with a calculated list of probabilities (for more details, see "Choose the next visit for each ant" in the next section):

```
class Ant:
    def visit_attraction(self, pheromone_trails):    ◀── The main logic that
        pass                                              decides how the ant
                                                          moves next

    def visit_random_attraction(self):    ◀── move the ant to a random location,
        pass                                   ignoring pheromone trails
```

Move the ant to a location based on the pheromone trails, using a probabilistic approach

```
def visit_probabilistic_attraction(self, pheromone_trails):
    pass

def roulette_wheel_selection(self, probabilities):
    pass

def get_distance_travelled(self):
    pass
```

Perform the roulette wheel selection based on the probabilities calculated from the pheromone trails

Calculate the total distance the ant has traveled based on the attractions it has visited

Last, the `get_distance_traveled` function calculates the total distance traveled by a specific ant, using its list of visited attractions. This distance must be minimized to find the shortest path and is used as the fitness for the ants:

```
def get_distance_travelled(self):
    total_distance = 0

    for i in range(1, len(self.visited_attractions)):
        previous_attraction = self.visited_attractions[i - 1]
        current_attraction = self.visited_attractions[i]

        dist = attraction_distances
          [previous_attraction][current_attraction]
        total_distance += dist

    return total_distance
```

Iterates through the ant's history

Identifies the "From" and "To" nodes that make up the current segment of the path

Retrieves the pre-calculated distance (weight)

The final data structure to design is pheromone trails. Like distances between attractions, pheromone intensity on each path can be represented as a distance matrix, but instead of containing distances, the matrix contains pheromone intensities. In figure 6.10, thicker lines indicate more-intense pheromone trails. Table 6.2 describes the pheromone trails between attractions.

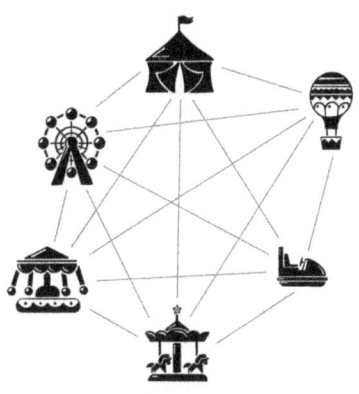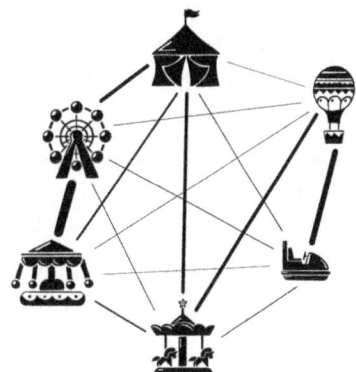

The paths between attractions   Possible pheromone intensity on paths

Figure 6.10 Example pheromone intensity on paths

Table 6.2 Pheromone intensity between attractions

	Circus	Balloons	Bumper cars	Carousel	Swings	Ferris wheel
Circus	0	2	0	8	6	8
Balloon	2	0	10	8	2	2
Bumper cars	2	10	0	0	2	2
Carousel	8	8	2	0	2	2
Swings	6	2	2	2	0	10
Ferris wheel	8	2	2	2	10	0

The ACO algorithm life cycle

Now that we understand the data structures required, we can dive into the workings of the ACO algorithm. The approach in designing an ACO algorithm is based on the problem space being addressed. Each problem has a unique context and a different domain in which data is represented, but the principles remain the same.

That said, let's look into how we can configure an ACO algorithm to solve the Carnival Problem. The general life cycle of such an algorithm is as follows (illustrated in figure 6.11):

1. *Set up the pheromones.* Create the concept of pheromone trails between attractions, and initialize their intensity values.

2. *Set up the population of ants.* Create a population of ants in which each ant starts at a different attraction.

3. *Choose the next visit for each ant.* Choose the next attraction to visit for each ant until each ant has visited all attractions once.

4. *Check for more destinations.* Verify that the ant has visited all attractions. If not, the ant chooses another visit (repeating step 3); otherwise, the tour is complete.

5. *Update the pheromone trails.* Update the intensity of pheromone trails based on the ants' movements on them, and factor in the evaporation of pheromones.

6. *Update the best solution.* Update the best solution given the total distance covered by each ant.

7. *Determine the stopping condition.* The process of ants visiting attractions repeats for several iterations. One iteration is every ant visiting all attractions once. The stopping criterion determines the total number of iterations to run. More iterations allow ants to make better decisions based on the pheromone trails.

8. *Return the best solution.* Output the best path found after the stopping condition is met.

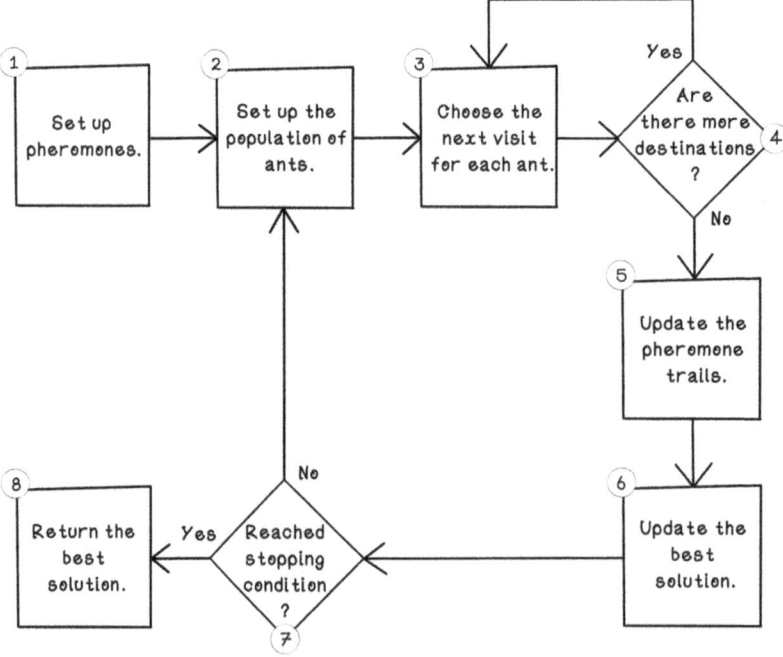

Figure 6.11 The ACO algorithm life cycle

Set up pheromones

The first step in the ACO algorithm is initializing the pheromone trails. Because no ants have walked on the paths between attractions yet, the pheromone trails will be initialized to 1. When we set all pheromone trails to 1, no trail has any advantage over the others. The important aspect is defining a reliable data structure to contain the pheromone trails, which we look at next (figure 6.12).

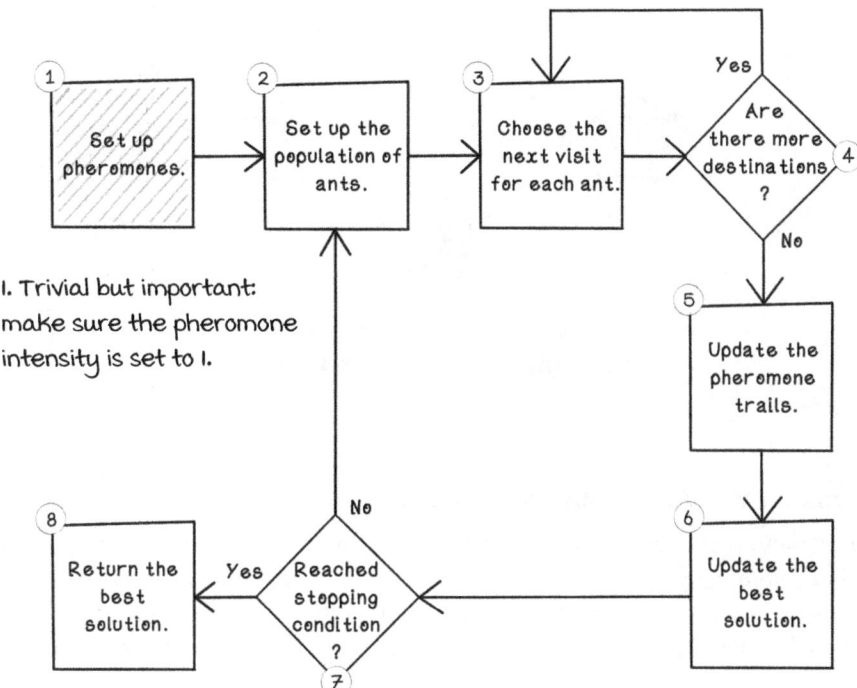

Figure 6.12 Set up the pheromones.

This concept can be applied to other problems in which the pheromone intensity is defined by a heuristic other than distances between locations. In figure 6.13, the heuristic is the distance between two destinations.

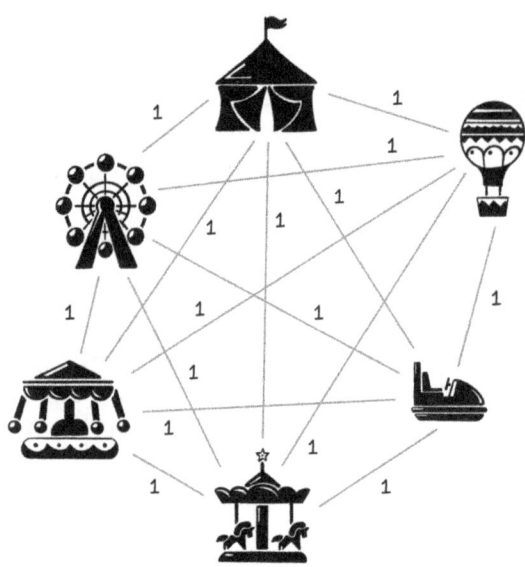

Pheromones initialize at 1

Figure 6.13 Initialization of pheromones

Python code sample for initializing pheromones

Like the attraction distances, the pheromone trails can be represented by a distance matrix, but referencing x, y in this array provides the pheromone intensity on the path between attractions x and y. The initial pheromone intensity on every path is initialized to 1. Values for all paths should initialize with the same number to prevent biasing any paths from the start:

```
pheromone_trails = [
    [1, 1, 1, 1, 1, 1],
    [1, 1, 1, 1, 1, 1],
    [1, 1, 1, 1, 1, 1],
    [1, 1, 1, 1, 1, 1],
    [1, 1, 1, 1, 1, 1],
    [1, 1, 1, 1, 1, 1]
]
```

Set up the population of ants

The next step of the ACO algorithm is creating a population of ants that moves between the attractions and leaves pheromone trails (figure 6.14). Ants start at randomly assigned attractions (figure 6.15)—at a random point in a potential sequence because the ACO algorithm can be applied to problems in which actual distance doesn't exist. After touring all the destinations, ants are set to their respective starting points.

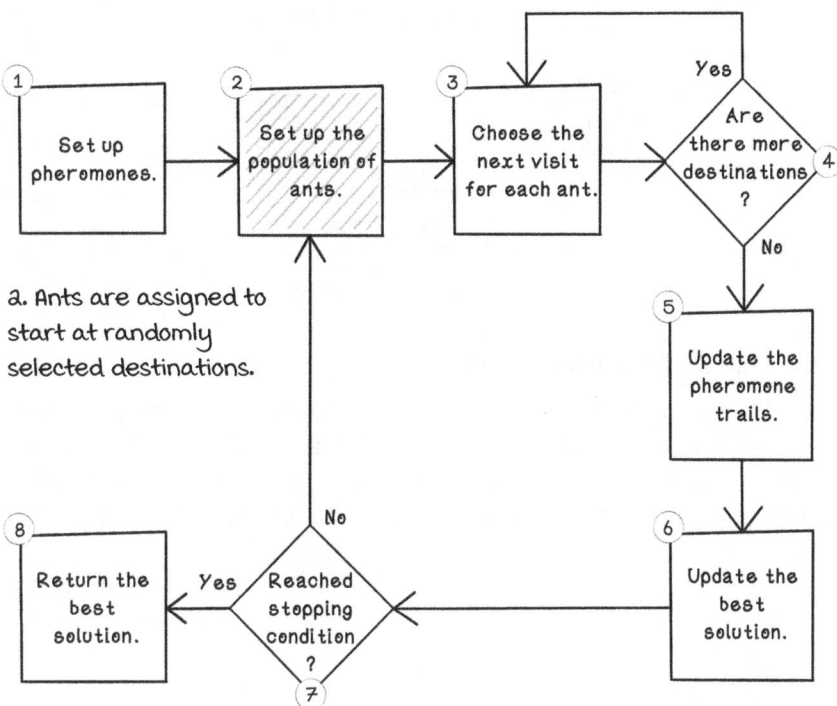

Figure 6.14 Set up the population of ants.

Figure 6.15 Ants start at random attractions.

Python code sample for setting up ants

We can adapt this principle to a different problem. In a task-scheduling problem, each ant starts at a different task. Setting up the colony of ants includes initializing several ants and appending them to a list where they can be referenced later. Remember that the initialization function of the Ant class chooses a random attraction to start at:

```
def setup_ants(self, number_of_ants_factor):
    number_of_ants =
    round(ATTRACTION_COUNT * number_of_ants_factor)
    self.ant_colony.clear()
    for i in range(0, number_of_ants):
        self.ant_colony.append(Ant())
```

Calculates the number of ants based on the problem size

Empties the list of ants to ensure no old data or positions from previous runs interfere with the new iteration

Instantiates a new Ant object

Choose the next visit for each ant

Ants need to select the next attraction to visit. They visit new attractions until they've visited all attractions once, which is a tour. Ants choose the next destination based on two factors (figure 6.16):

- *Pheromone intensities*—The pheromone intensity on all available paths
- *Heuristic value*—A result from a defined heuristic for all available paths, which is the distance of the path between attractions in the Carnival Problem

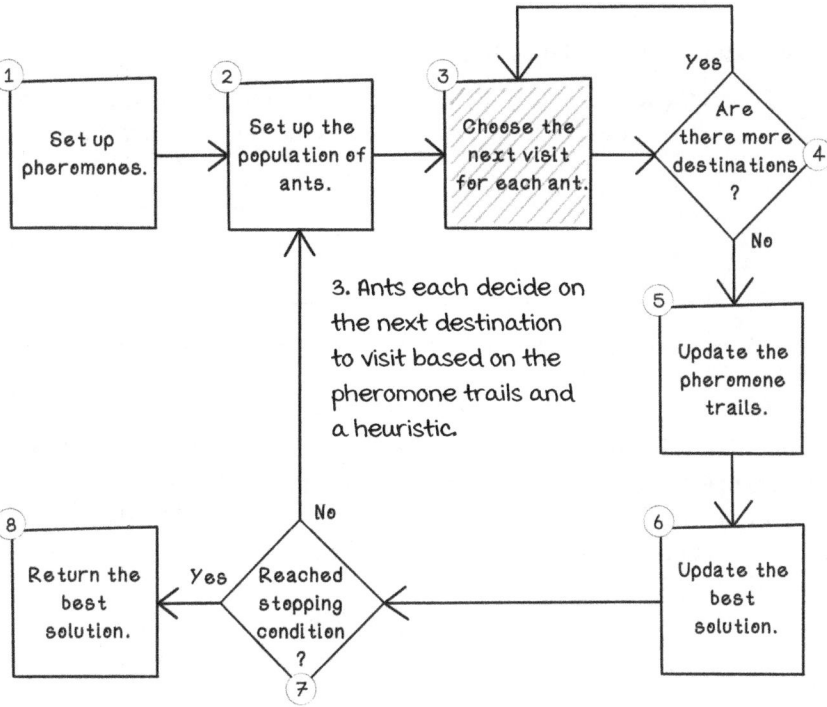

Figure 6.16 Choose the next visit for each ant.

Ants won't travel to destinations they've already visited. If an ant has already visited the bumper cars, it won't travel to that attraction again in the current tour.

Simulating the "random" nature of ants

The ACO algorithm has an element of randomness. The intention is to allow ants the possibility of exploring less-optimal immediate paths, which might result in a better overall tour distance.

In standard ACO, ants don't simply flip a coin to decide whether to explore. Instead, they make a probabilistic decision based on two factors:

- *Pheromone strength*—How popular the path is
- *Distance heuristic*—How short the path looks

Think of the selection process as being like a roulette wheel. A path with strong pheromones and a short distance gets a huge slice of the wheel; a path with weak pheromones gets a tiny slice. The ant spins the wheel to choose its next step. The ant is likely to pick the best path, but sometimes the marble lands on the tiny slice, allowing the ant to explore new routes naturally.

Selecting a destination based on a heuristic

When an ant faces the task of choosing the next nonrandom destination, it determines the pheromone intensity on that path and the heuristic value by using the following formula:

$$\frac{(\text{pheromones on path x})^a * (1 \text{ / heuristic for path x})^b}{\sum_{\substack{\text{available} \\ \text{destinations}}}^{\text{sum of n}} ((\text{pheromones on path n})^a * (1 \text{ / heuristic for path n})^b)}$$

After it applies this function to every possible path to its respective destination, the ant selects the destination with the best overall value. Figure 6.17 illustrates the possible paths from the circus, with respective distances and pheromone intensities. In figure 6.18, we work through the formula to demystify the calculations and show how the results affect decision-making.

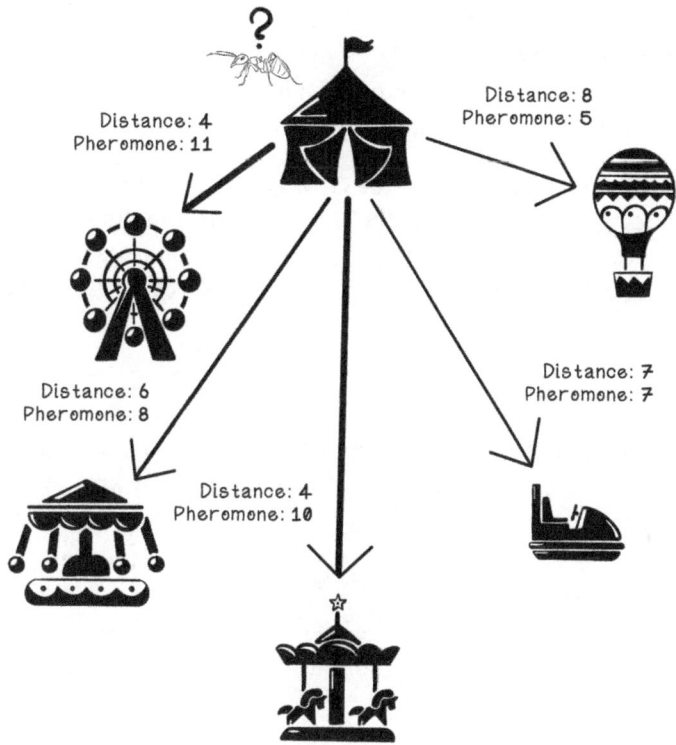

Figure 6.17 Possible paths from the circus

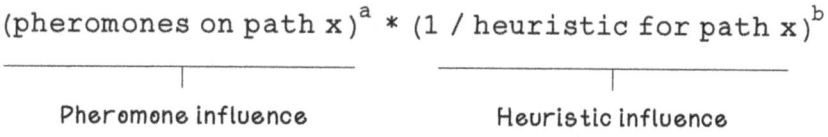

Figure 6.18 The pheromone influence and heuristic influence of the formula

The variables alpha (*a*) and beta (*b*) are used to give greater weight to the pheromone influence or the heuristic influence. These variables can be adjusted to balance the ant's judgment between making a move based on what it knows versus pheromone trails, which represent what the colony knows about that path. These parameters are defined up front and usually aren't adjusted while the algorithm runs. Think of the ant as a tourist trying to pick an attraction:

- *Pheromone (a) is social pressure.* "Look at that long line of people! That ride must be amazing." This is trusting the collective wisdom of the colony.
- *Heuristic (b) is greedy logic.* "But that other ride is right next door, and I'm bored right now." This is trusting the immediate distance.

If *a* is too high, the ants blindly follow the crowd even if it's long. If *b* is too high, the ants become greedy loners and ignore the collective wisdom, turning the algorithm into a simple greedy search. The following example works through each path starting at the circus and calculates the probabilities of moving to each respective attraction:

- *a* is set to 1.
- *b* is set to 2.

Because *b* is greater than *a*, the heuristic influence is favored in this example. Let's work through an example of the calculations used to determine the probability of choosing a specific path (figure 6.19).

$$\frac{(\text{pheromones on path x})^a * (1 / \text{heuristic for path x})^b}{\sum_{\substack{\text{available} \\ \text{destinations}}}^{\text{sum of n}} ((\text{pheromones on path n})^a * (1 / \text{heuristic for path n})^b)}$$

$((\text{pheromones on path x})^a * (1 / \text{heuristic for path x})^b)$ ← Apply this to each attraction.

Ferris wheel:	$11 * (1/4)^2$	$= 0.688$
Swings:	$8 * (1/6)^2$	$= 0.222$
Carousel:	$10 * (1/4)^2$	$= 0.625$
Bumper cars:	$7 * (1/7)^2$	$= 0.143$
Balloons:	$5 * (1/8)^2$	$= 0.078$

$\sum_{\substack{\text{available} \\ \text{destinations}}}^{\text{sum of n}} ((\text{pheromones on path n})^a * (1 / \text{heuristic for path n})^b) = 1.756$ ← Sum of all

Ferris wheel: 0.688 / 1.756 = 0.392   ← Highest probability: 39.2%
Swings: 0.222 / 1.756 = 0.126
Carousel: 0.625 / 1.756 = 0.356   ← High probability: 35.6%
Bumper cars: 0.143 / 1.756 = 0.081
Balloons: 0.078 / 1.756 = 0.044

Figure 6.19 Probability calculations for paths

After applying this calculation, given all the available destinations, the ant is left with the options shown in figure 6.20. Remember that only the available paths are considered; these paths haven't been explored yet.

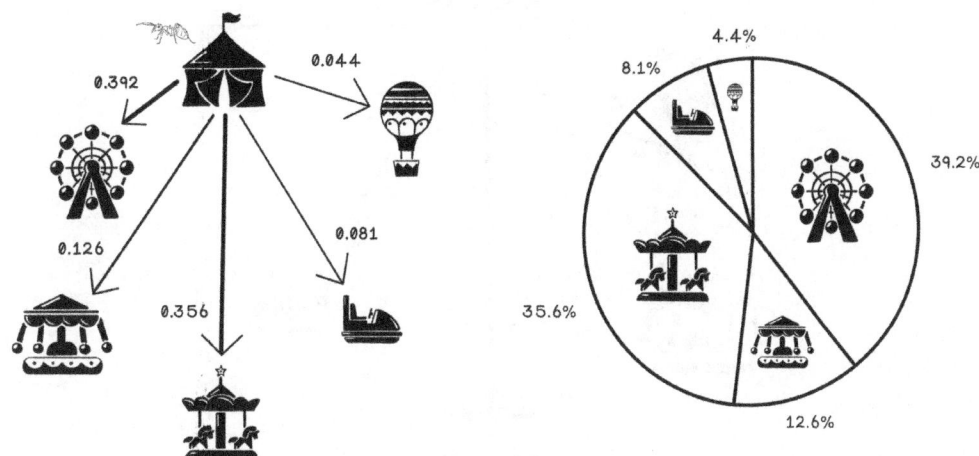

Figure 6.20 The final probability that each attraction will be selected

Figure 6.21 illustrates the possible paths from the circus, excluding the Ferris wheel, because it's already been visited. Figure 6.22 shows probability calculations for paths. The ant's decision looks like figure 6.23.

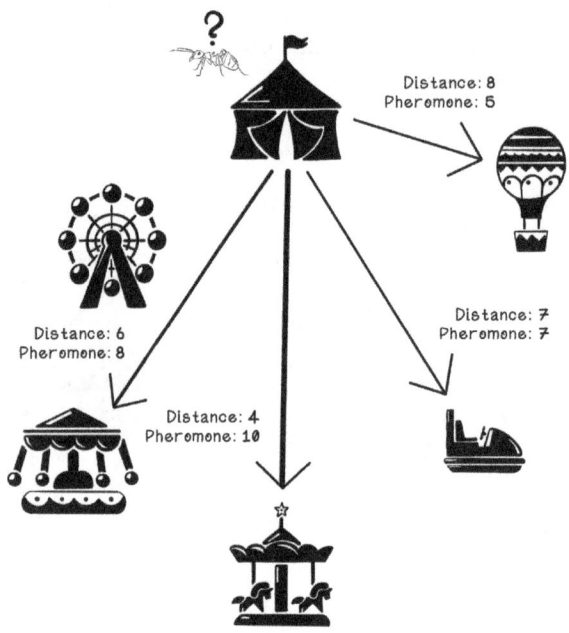

Figure 6.21 Possible paths from the circus, excluding visited attractions

$$\frac{(\text{pheromones on path x})^a * (1 / \text{heuristic for path x})^b}{\underset{\substack{\text{sum of n}\\ \text{available}\\ \text{destinations}}}{} ((\text{pheromones on path n})^a * (1 / \text{heuristic for path n})^b)}$$

$((\text{pheromones on path x})^a * (1 / \text{heuristic for path x})^b)$ ⟵ Apply this to each attraction.

Swings:	$8 * (1/6)^2$	$= 0.222$
Carousel:	$10 * (1/4)^2$	$= 0.625$
Bumper cars:	$7 * (1/7)^2$	$= 0.143$
Balloons:	$5 * (1/8)^2$	$= 0.078$

$\underset{\substack{\text{sum of n}\\ \text{available}\\ \text{destinations}}}{} ((\text{pheromones on path n})^a * (1 / \text{heuristic for path n})^b) = 1.068$ ⟵ Sum of all

Swings:	$0.222 / 1.068$	$= 0.208$	
Carousel:	**$0.625 / 1.068$**	**$= 0.585$**	
Bumper cars:	$0.143 / 1.068$	$= 0.134$	
Balloons:	$0.078 / 1.068$	$= 0.073$	

⟵ Highest probability: 58.5%

Figure 6.22 Probability calculations for paths

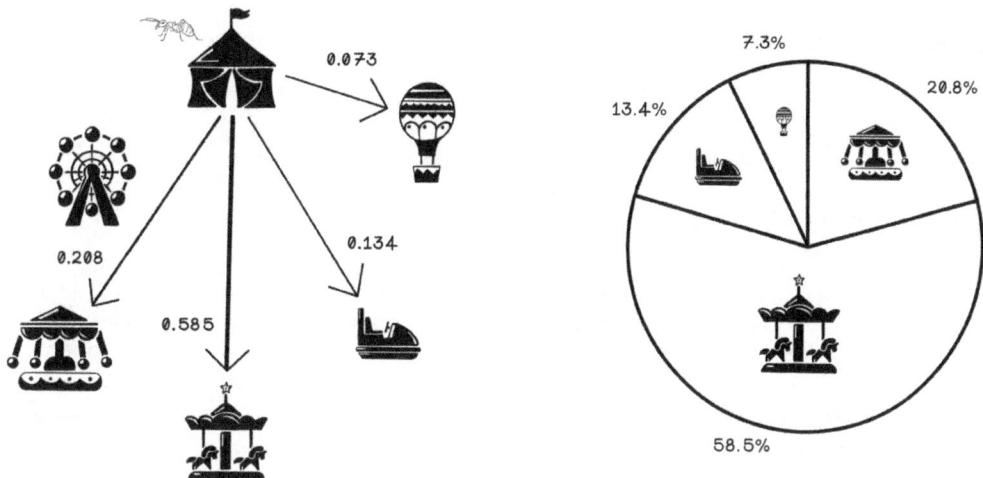

Figure 6.23 The final probability that each attraction will be selected

Python code sample for ant decision-making

The code for calculating the probabilities of visiting the possible attractions is closely aligned with the mathematical functions that we've worked through. Following are some interesting aspects of this implementation:

- *Determining the available attractions to visit*—Because the ant would have visited several attractions, it shouldn't return to those attractions. The `possible_attractions` array stores this value by removing `visited_attractions` from the complete list of attractions: `all_attractions`.

- *Using three variables to store the outcome of the probability calculations*—`possible_indexes` stores the attraction indexes; `possible_probabilities` stores the probabilities for the respective index; and `total_probabilities` stores the sum of all probabilities, which should equal 1 when the function is complete. These three data structures could be represented by a class for a cleaner code convention:

```
def visit_probabilistic_attraction(self, pheromone_trails):
    current_attraction = self.visited_attractions[-1]
    all_attractions = set(range(0, ATTRACTION_COUNT))
    possible_attractions = all_attractions
    - set(self.visited_attractions)
    possible_indexes = []
    possible_probabilities = []
    total_probabilities = 0
    for attraction in possible_attractions:
        possible_indexes.append(attraction)
```

Identifies valid moves by subtracting places the ant has already visited

Calculates the inverse
of distance (1/distance)

Checks how much
pheromone is on the path

```
        pheromones_on_path = math.pow(pheromone_trails
        [current_attraction][attraction], ALPHA)
        heuristic_for_path = math.pow(1 / attraction_distances
        [current_attraction][attraction], BETA)
        probability = pheromones_on_path * heuristic_for_path
        possible_probabilities.append(probability)
        total_probabilities += probability
    possible_probabilities = [probability / total_probabilities
    for probability in possible_probabilities]
    return [possible_indexes, possible_probabilities,
    len(possible_attractions)]
```

Normalizes the raw weights
to get probabilities for
roulette wheel selection

multiplies the social
factor (pheromone)
by the greedy
factor (distance) to
get a raw weight

We meet roulette-wheel selection again. The roulette-wheel selection function takes the possible probabilities and attraction indexes as input. It generates a list of slices, each of which includes the index of the attraction in element 0, the start of the slice in index 1, and the end of the slice in index 2. All slices contain a start and end between 0 and 1. A random number between 0 and 1 is generated, and the slice into which it falls is selected as the winner:

```
def roulette_wheel_selection(possible_indexes, possible_probabilities):
    slices = []
    total = 0

    for i in range(len(possible_indexes)):
        start = total
        end = total + possible_probabilities[i]
        slices.append([possible_indexes[i], start,
        end])

        total += possible_probabilities[i]

    spin = random.random()

    for slice_data in slices:
        attraction_index = slice_data[0]
        lower_bound = slice_data[1]
        upper_bound = slice_data[2]

        if lower_bound <= spin < upper_bound:
            return attraction_index

    return possible_indexes[-1]
```

Builds the cumulative probability wheel

Creates a slice:
[attraction_index,
range_start,
range_end]

Finds the slice in which
the random spin lands

Checks whether spin is within
the bounds of this slice

Fallback for rounding errors
(returns the last element)

Now that we have probabilities of selecting the different attractions to visit, we'll use roulette-wheel selection. To recap, roulette-wheel selection (discussed in chapters 3 and 4) gives different possibilities to portions of a wheel based on their fitness. Then the wheel is "spun," and an individual is selected. A higher fitness gives an individual a larger slice of the wheel, as shown in figure 6.23 earlier in this chapter. The process of choosing an attraction and visiting it continues for every ant until each ant has visited all the attractions once.

Exercise: Determine the probabilities of visiting the attractions with the following information

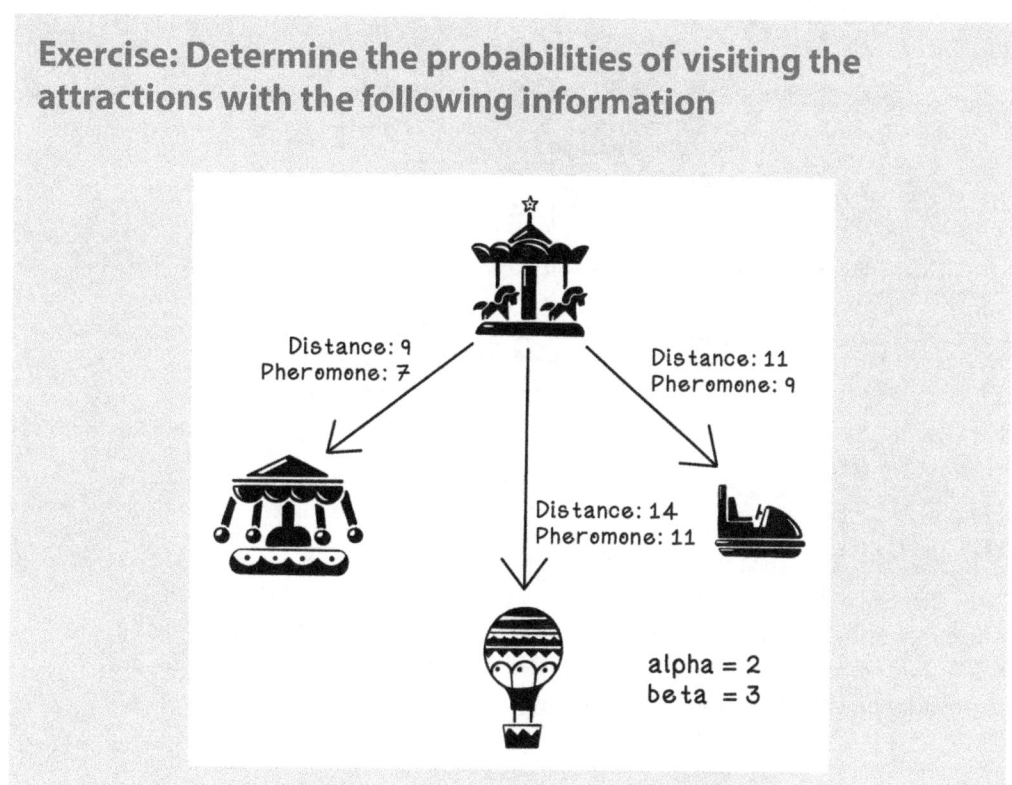

(*continued*)

Solution:

$$\frac{(\text{pheromones on path x})^a * (1 \text{ / heuristic for path x})^b}{\underset{\substack{\text{sum of n} \\ \text{available} \\ \text{destinations}}}{} ((\text{pheromones on path n})^a * (1 \text{ / heuristic for path n})^b)}$$

$((\text{pheromones on path x})^a * (1 \text{ / heuristic for path x})^b)$

$$\text{Swings:} \quad 7^2 * (1/9)^3 = 0.067$$
$$\text{Bumper cars:} \quad 9^2 * (1/11)^3 = 0.061$$
$$\text{Balloons:} \quad 11^2 * (1/14)^3 = 0.044$$

$$\underset{\substack{\text{sum of n} \\ \text{available} \\ \text{destinations}}}{} ((\text{pheromones on path n})^a * (1 \text{ / heuristic for path n})^b) = 0.172$$

$$\text{Swings: } 0.067 / 0.172 = 0.39$$
$$\text{Bumper cars: } 0.061 / 0.172 = 0.355$$
$$\text{Balloons: } 0.044 / 0.172 = 0.256$$

Update the pheromone trails

Now that the ants have completed a tour of the attractions, all of them have left pheromones behind, changing the pheromone trails between the attractions (figure 6.24). Two steps are involved in updating the pheromone trails: evaporation and depositing new pheromones.

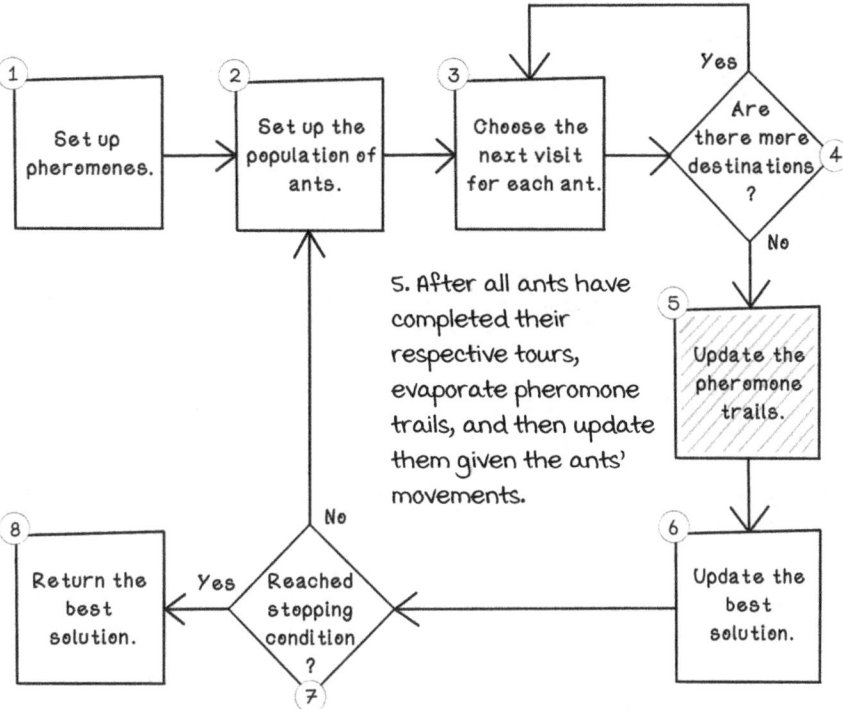

Figure 6.24 Update the pheromone trails.

Updating pheromones due to evaporation

The concept of evaporation is also inspired by nature. Over time, the pheromone trails lose their intensity. Pheromones are updated by multiplying their respective current values by an evaporation factor—a parameter that can be adjusted to tweak the performance of the algorithm in terms of exploration and exploitation.

Why do pheromones need to evaporate? Suppose that they didn't. The very first path found—even if it was a terrible, long route—would accumulate pheromones. Without evaporation, that initial bad advice would stay forever, confusing future ants. Evaporation acts like a validity timer, ensuring that old information disappears unless it is constantly reinforced by new ants verifying that the path is still the best one. Figure 6.25 illustrates the updated pheromone trails due to evaporation.

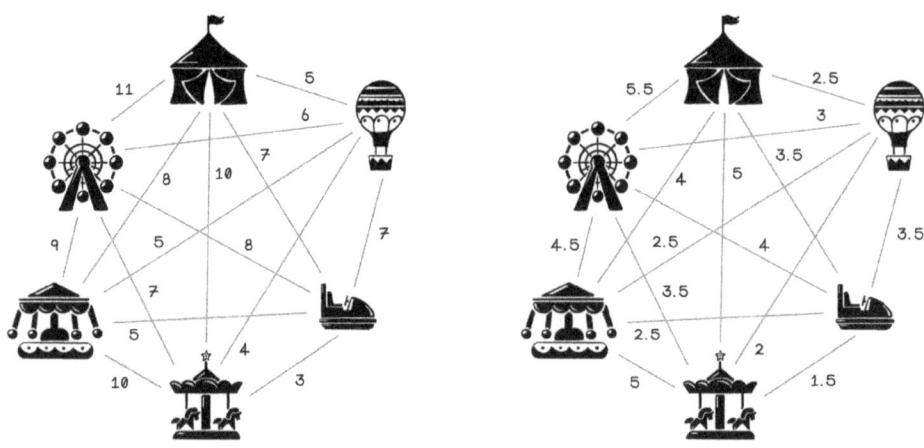

Pheremones on paths   Pheremones on paths after 50% evaporation

Figure 6.25 Example of updating pheromone trails for evaporation

Updating pheromones based on ant tours

Pheromones are updated based on the ants that have moved along the paths. If more ants move on a specific path, there will be more pheromones on that path.

Each ant contributes its fitness value to the pheromones on every path it moves on. The effect is that ants with better solutions have greater influence on the best paths. Figure 6.26 illustrates the updated pheromone trails based on ant movements.

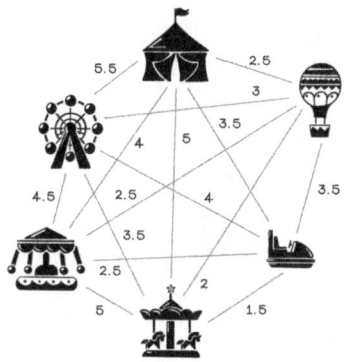

Pheromones on paths after evaporation

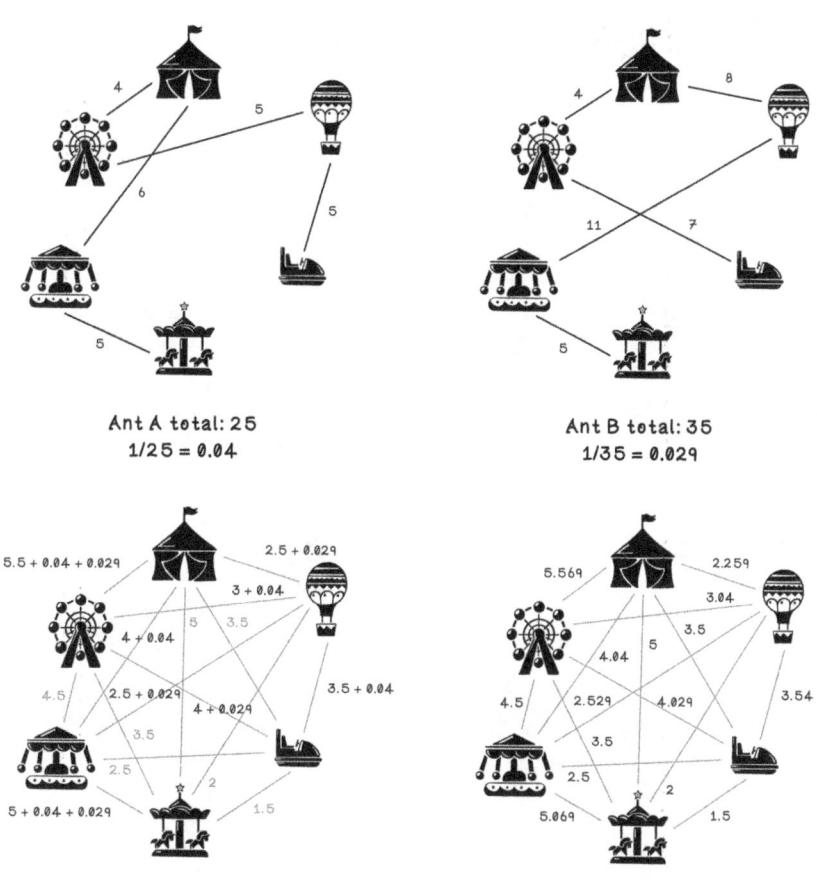

Figure 6.26 Pheromone updates based on ant movements

Exercise: Calculate the pheromone update given the following scenario

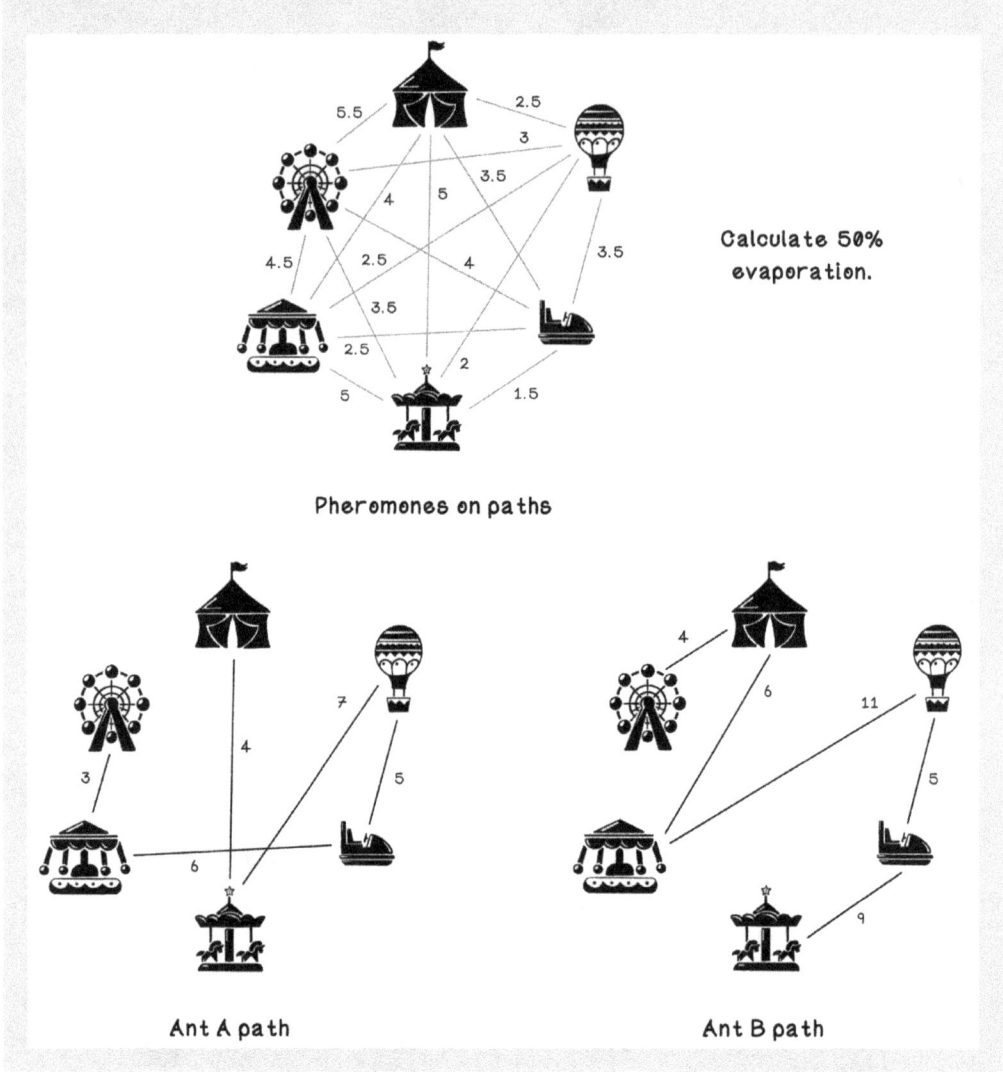

Calculate 50% evaporation.

Pheromones on paths

Ant A path

Ant B path

Solution:

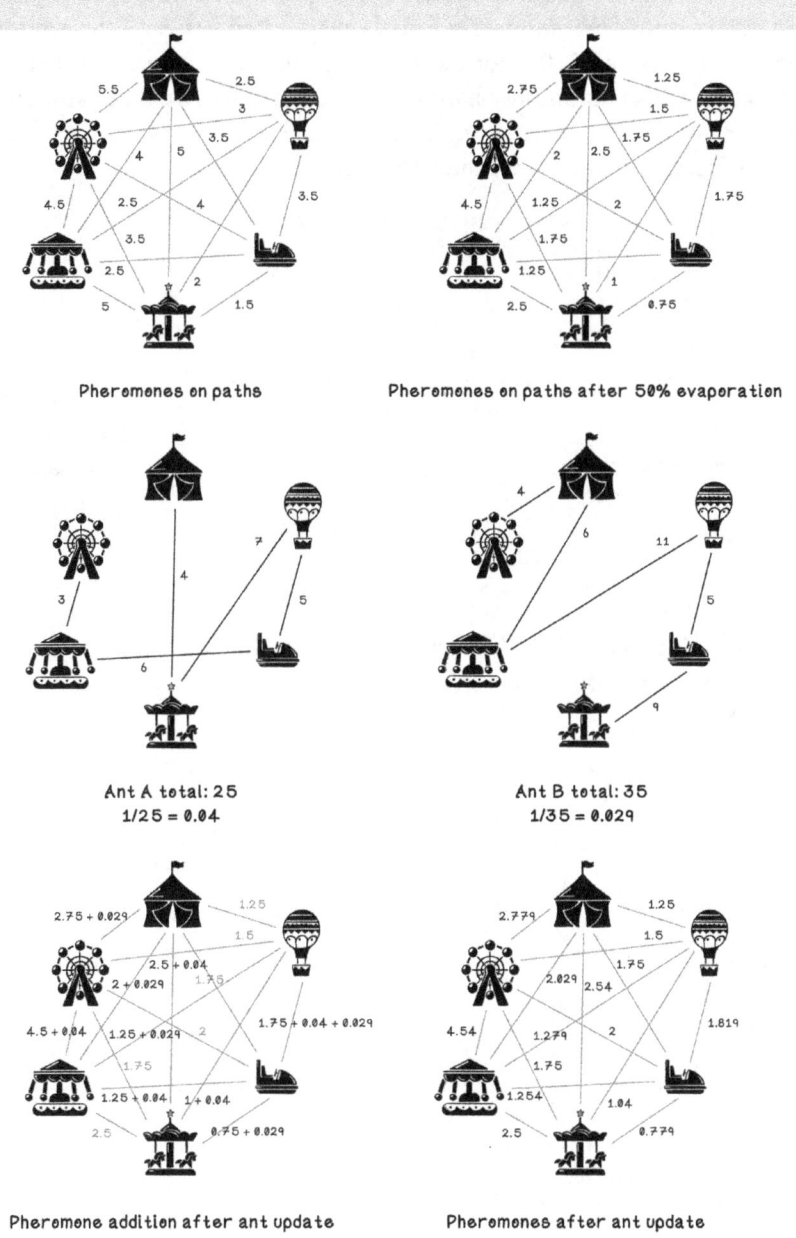

Pheromones on paths

Pheromones on paths after 50% evaporation

Ant A total: 25
1/25 = 0.04

Ant B total: 35
1/35 = 0.029

Pheromone addition after ant update

Pheromones after ant update

Python code sample for updating pheromones

The `update_pheromones` function applies two important concepts to the pheromone trails. First, the current pheromone intensity is evaporated based on the evaporation rate. If the evaporation rate is 0.5, for example, the intensity decreases by half. The second operation adds pheromones based on ant movements on that path. The amount of pheromones contributed by each ant is determined by the ant's fitness, which in this case is each respective ant's total distance traveled:

```python
def update_pheromones(self, evaporation_rate):
    for x in range(0, ATTRACTION_COUNT):                    Iterates through
        for y in range(0, ATTRACTION_COUNT):               every possible path
            self.pheromone_trails[x][y] =
              self.pheromone_trails[x][y] * evaporation_rate    multiplies the current
            for ant in self.ant_colony:
                self.pheromone_trails[x][y] +=
                1 / ant.get_distance_travelled()
```

Calculates the quality
of the ant's solution

multiplies the current
trail by a decay factor
to simulate scents
fading over time

Update the best solution

The best solution is described by the sequence of attraction visits that has the lowest total distance. Figure 6.27 illustrates this sequence.

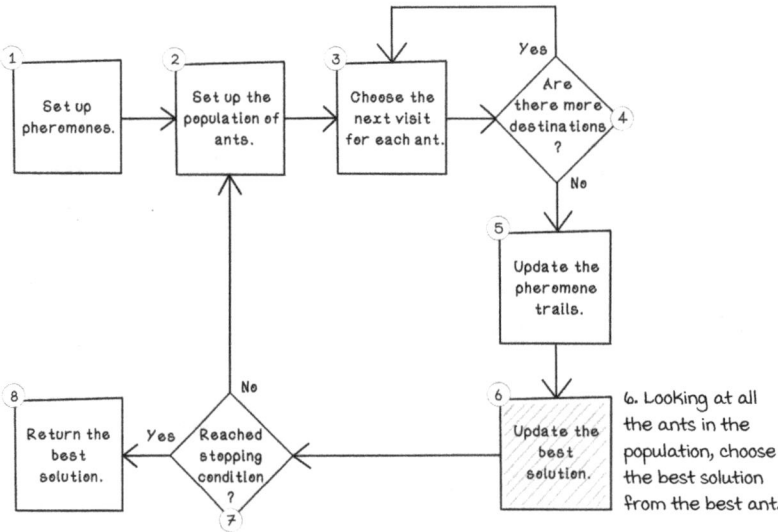

Figure 6.27 Update the best solution.

Python code sample for choosing the best solution

After an iteration, after every ant completes a tour (a tour is complete when an ant visits every attraction), the best ant in the colony must be determined. To make this determination, we find the ant that has the lowest total distance traveled and set it as the new best ant in the colony:

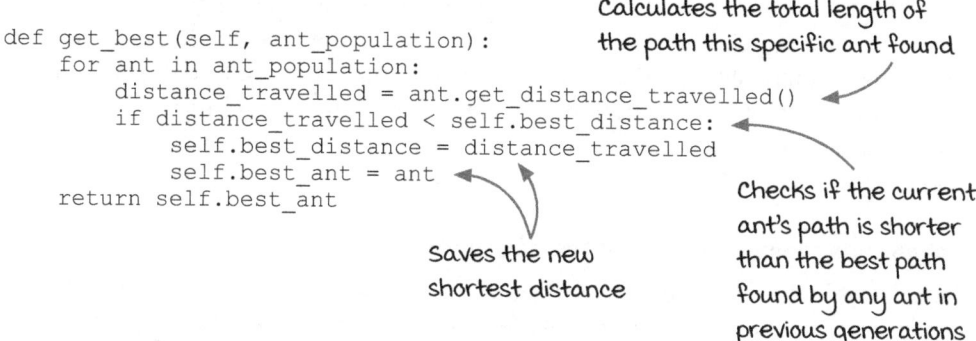

```python
def get_best(self, ant_population):
    for ant in ant_population:
        distance_travelled = ant.get_distance_travelled()
        if distance_travelled < self.best_distance:
            self.best_distance = distance_travelled
            self.best_ant = ant
    return self.best_ant
```

Calculates the total length of the path this specific ant found

Saves the new shortest distance

Checks if the current ant's path is shorter than the best path found by any ant in previous generations

Determine the stopping criteria

The algorithm stops after several iterations—conceptually, the number of tours that the group of ants concludes. If we have 10 iterations, each ant makes 10 tours. That is, each ant visits each attraction once and does that 10 times (figure 6.28).

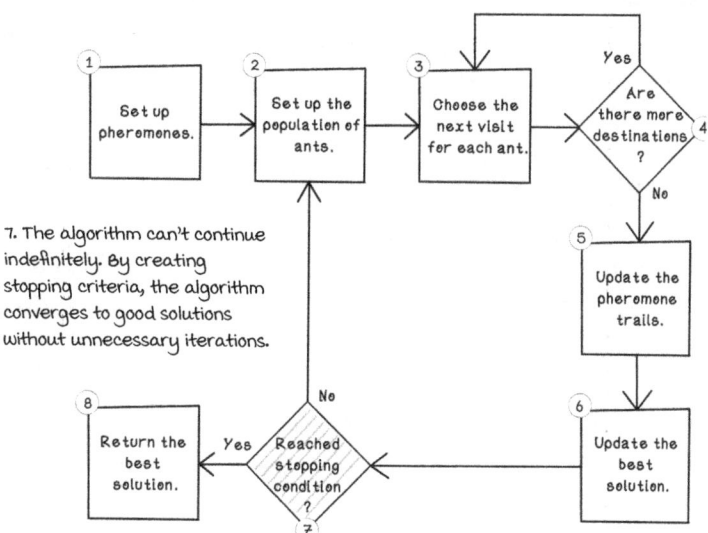

7. The algorithm can't continue indefinitely. By creating stopping criteria, the algorithm converges to good solutions without unnecessary iterations.

Figure 6.28 Has the stopping condition been reached?

The stopping criteria for the ACO algorithm can differ based on the domain of the problem being solved. In some cases, realistic limits are known, and when they're unknown, the following options are available:

- *Stop when a predefined number of iterations is reached.* In this scenario, we define a total number of iterations for which the algorithm will always run. If we define 100 iterations, each ant completes 100 tours before the algorithm terminates.
- *Stop when the best solution stagnates.* In this scenario, the best solution after each iteration is compared with the previous best solution. If the solution doesn't improve after a defined number of iterations, the algorithm terminates. If iteration 20 resulted in a solution with fitness 100 and that iteration is repeated until iteration 30, it's likely (but not guaranteed) that no better solution exists.

Python code sample for running the ACO algorithm

The `solve` function ties everything together and should give you a better idea of the sequence of operations and the overall life cycle of the algorithm. Notice that the algorithm runs for several defined total iterations. Also, the ant colony is initialized to its starting point at the beginning of each iteration, and a new best ant is determined after each iteration:

Triggers the decision-making process for every ant

Sets up the initial pheromone grid

```
def solve(self, total_iterations, evaporation_rate):
    self.setup_pheromones()
    for i in range(0, TOTAL_ITERATIONS):
        self.setup_ants(NUMBER_OF_ANTS_FACTOR)
        for r in range(0, ATTRACTION_COUNT - 1):
            self.move_ants(self.ant_colony)
        self.update_pheromones(evaporation_rate)
        self.best_ant = self.get_best(self.ant_colony)
        print(i, ' Best distance: ',
            self.best_ant.get_distance_travelled())


def move_ants(self, ant_population):
    for ant in ant_population:
        ant.visit_attraction(self.pheromone_trails)
```

moves every ant one step forward until they have completed a tour

Adjusts the pheromone levels after all ants have finished their tours

identifying and saving the absolute best path found in this generation

We can tweak several parameters to alter the exploration and exploitation of the ACO algorithm. These parameters influence how long the algorithm takes to find a good solution. Some randomness is good for exploring. Balancing the weighting between heuristics and pheromones influences whether ants attempt a greedy search (when favoring heuristics) or trust pheromones more. The evaporation rate also influences this balance. The number of ants and the total number of iterations they have influences the quality of a solution. When we add more ants and more iterations, more computation is required. Based on the problem at hand, time to compute may influence these parameters (figure 6.29).

```
Set the probability of ants choosing a random attraction to visit (0.0 - 1.0) (0% - 100%).
RANDOM_ATTRACTION_FACTOR = 0.3


Set the weight for pheromones on path for selection by ants.
ALPHA = 4


Set the weight for heuristic of path for selection by ants.
BETA = 7


Set the percentage of ants in the colony based on the total number of attractions.
NUMBER_OF_ANTS_FACTOR = 0.5


Set the number of tours ants must complete.
TOTAL_ITERATIONS = 1000


Set the rate of pheromone evaporation (0.0 - 1.0) (0% - 100%).
EVAPORATION_RATE = 0.4
```

Figure 6.29 Parameters that can be tweaked in the ACO algorithm

Now you have insight into how ACO algorithms work and how to use them to solve the Carnival Problem. The following section describes some other possible use cases. Perhaps these examples will help you find uses for the algorithm in your work.

Use cases for ACO algorithms

ACO algorithms are versatile and useful in several real-world applications. These applications usually center on complex optimization problems such as the following:

- *Route optimization*—Routing problems usually include several destinations that need to be visited with several constraints. In a logistics example, perhaps the distance between destinations, traffic conditions, types of packages being delivered, and times of day are important constraints that we must consider to optimize the operations of the business. We can use ACO algorithms to address this problem. The problem is similar to the Carnival Problem explored in this chapter, but the heuristic function is likely to be more complex and context-specific.

- *Job scheduling*—Job scheduling is present in almost any industry. Nurse shifts are important to ensure that good health care is provided. Computational jobs on servers must be scheduled in an optimal manner to maximize the use of the hardware without waste. We can use ACO algorithms to solve these problems. Instead of looking at the entities that ants visit as locations, we see that ants visit tasks in different sequences. The heuristic function includes constraints and desired rules specific to the context of the jobs being scheduled. Nurses, for example, need days off to prevent fatigue, and jobs with high priorities on a server should be favored.

- *Image processing*—We can use the ACO algorithm for edge detection in image processing. An image is composed of several adjacent pixels, and the ants move from pixel to pixel, leaving pheromone trails. Ants drop stronger pheromones based on the pixel colors' intensity, resulting in pheromone trails along the edges of objects that contain the highest density of pheromones. This algorithm essentially traces the outline of the image by performing edge detection. The images may require preprocessing to decolorize the image to grayscale so that the pixel-color values can be compared consistently.

SUMMARY OF SWARM INTELLIGENCE: ANTS

Ant Colony Optimization uses the concept of pheromones and heuristics to solve optimization problems

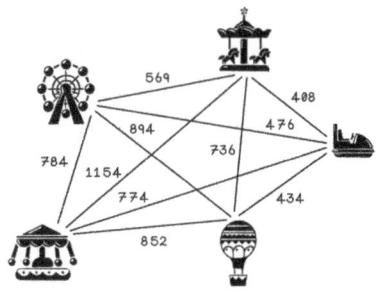

ACO is useful for problems like finding shortest paths or optimal task schedules.

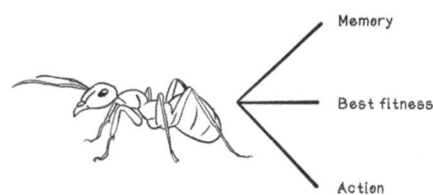

Weightings between a heuristic and the pheromones on paths are used to calculate a probability of selection.

Ants have a concept of memory, their fitness, and what actions they can perform.

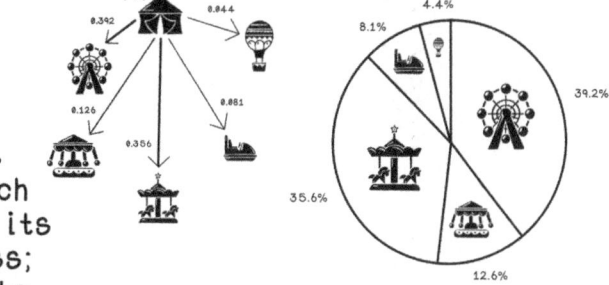

Pheromones are contributed by each ant proportional to its respective fitness; they also evaporate.

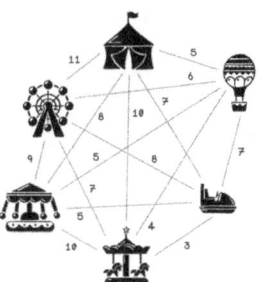

Pheromones on paths

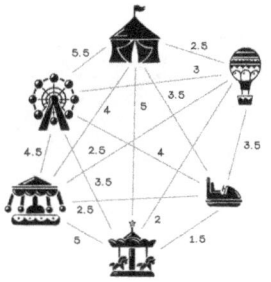

Pheromones on paths after 50% evaporation

In this chapter

- Understanding the inspiration for particle swarm intelligence algorithms

- Understanding and solving optimization problems

- Designing and implementing a particle swarm optimization algorithm

What is particle swarm optimization?

Particle swarm optimization (PSO) is another swarm algorithm. Swarm intelligence relies on emergent behavior of many individuals to solve difficult problems as a collective. We saw in chapter 6 how ants can find the shortest paths between destinations through their use of pheromones.

Bird flocks are another ideal example of swarm intelligence in nature. When a single bird is flying, it might attempt several maneuvers and techniques to preserve energy, such as jumping and gliding through the air or using wind currents to carry it in the direction it wants to travel. This behavior indicates some primitive level of intelligence in a single individual.

But birds also need to migrate between seasons. In winter, insects and other types of food are less available, and suitable nesting locations become scarce. Birds tend to flock to warmer areas to take advantage of better weather conditions, improving their likelihood of survival.

Migration usually isn't a short trip. It takes thousands of miles of movement to arrive at an area with suitable conditions. When birds travel these long distances, they tend to flock. Birds flock because there is strength in numbers when facing predators; also, flocking saves energy. The formation we observe in bird flocks has many advantages. A large, strong bird takes the lead, and when it flaps its wings, it creates uplift for the birds behind it. Then those birds can fly while using significantly less energy. Flocks can change leaders if the direction changes or if the leader becomes fatigued. When a specific bird moves out of formation, it experiences more difficulty in flying via air resistance and corrects its movement to get back into formation. Figure 7.1 illustrates a bird-flock formation; you may have seen something similar.

Figure 7.1 An example bird-flock formation

Craig Reynolds developed a simulator program in 1987 to understand the attributes of emergent behavior in bird flocks and used the following rules to guide the group. These rules are extracted from observations of bird flocks:

- *Alignment*—An individual should steer in the average heading of its neighbors to ensure that the group travels in a similar direction.
- *Cohesion*—An individual should move toward the average position of its neighbors to maintain the formation of the group.
- *Separation*—An individual should avoid crowding with its neighbors to ensure that individuals don't collide, which would disrupt the group.

Additional rules are used in different variants attempting to simulate swarm behavior. Figure 7.2 illustrates the behavior of an individual in different scenarios, as well as the direction in which it is influenced to move to obey a rule. Adjusting movement is a balance of the three principles shown in the figure.

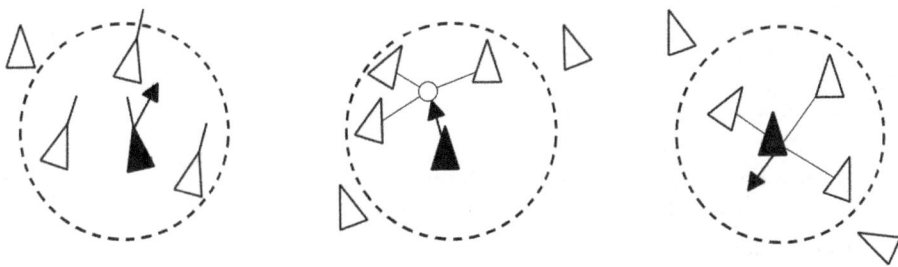

Figure 7.2 Rules that guide a swarm

PSOs involve a group of individuals at different points in the solution space, all using real-life swarm concepts to find an optimal solution in the space. This chapter dives into the workings of the PSO algorithm and shows how to use it to solve problems.

Imagine a swarm of bees that spreads out looking for flowers and gradually converges on the area that has the greatest density of flowers. As more bees find the flowers, more of them are attracted to the flowers. At its core, this example is what PSO entails (figure 7.3).

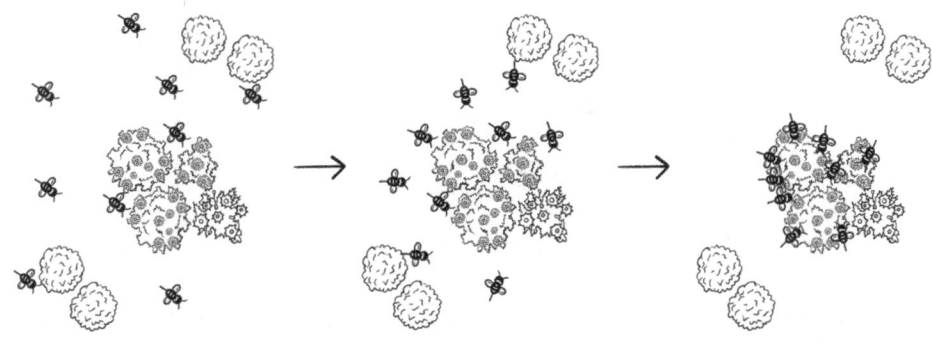

Figure 7.3 A bee swarm converging on its goal

Several earlier chapters of this book have mentioned optimization problems, such as finding the optimal path through a maze, determining the optimal items for a knapsack, and finding the optimal path between attractions in a carnival. We worked through them without diving into the details behind them. From this chapter on, however, a deeper understanding of optimization problems is important. The next section builds the intuition you need to identify optimization problems when they arise.

Optimization problems: A slightly more technical perspective

Suppose that we have several peppers of different sizes. Usually, small peppers are spicier than large ones. If we plot all the peppers on a chart based on size and spiciness, the result may look like figure 7.4.

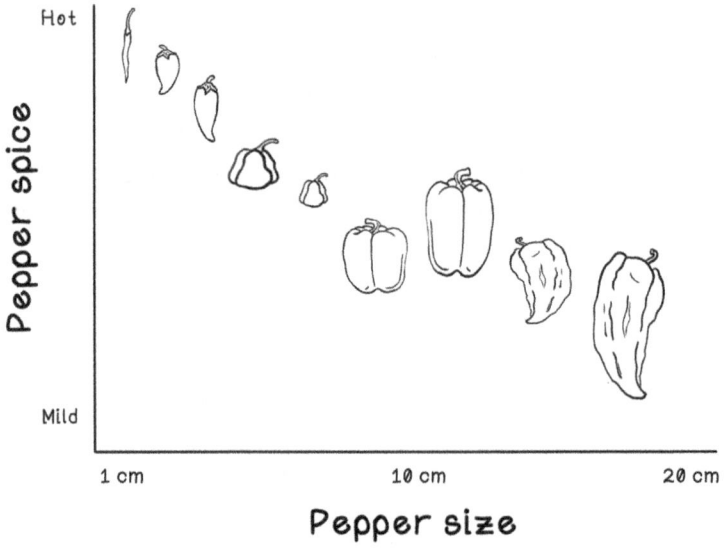

Figure 7.4 Pepper spice vs. pepper size

Figure 7.4 depicts the sizes of peppers and how spicy they are. If we remove the pepper images, plot the data points, and draw a curve between those points, we get the result shown in figure 7.5. If we had more peppers, we'd have more data points, and the curve would be more accurate.

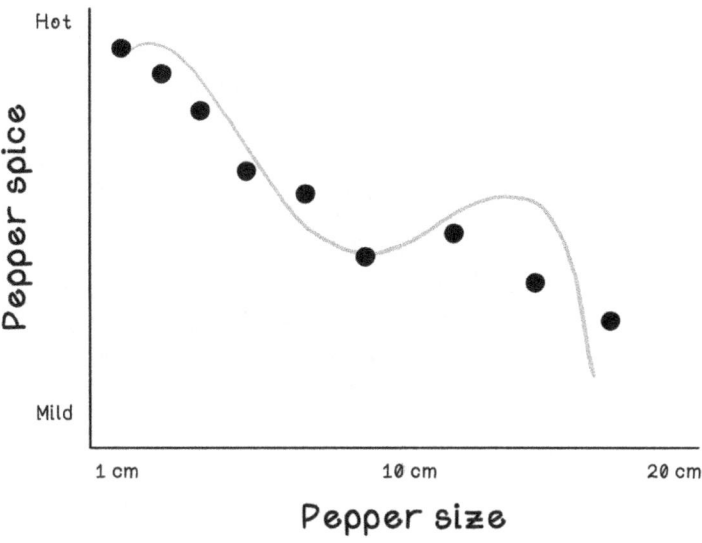

Figure 7.5 Pepper spice vs. pepper size trend

This example could potentially be an optimization problem. If we search for a minimum from left to right, we come across several points less than the previous ones, but in the middle, we encounter a higher point. Should we stop? If so, we miss the actual minimum—the last data point, known as the *global minimum.*

The approximated trend line/curve can be represented by a function like the one shown in figure 7.6. This function can be interpreted as the spiciness of the pepper equaling the result of the function, where the size of the pepper is represented by x.

$$f(x) = -(x - 4)(x - 0.2)(x - 3) + 5$$

Figure 7.6 An example function for pepper spice vs. pepper size

Real-world problems typically have thousands of data points, and the minimum output of the function is not as clear as in this example. The search spaces are massive and difficult to solve by hand.

This example uses only two properties of the pepper to create the data points, resulting in a simple curve. If we consider another property of the pepper, such as color, the representation of the data changes significantly. Now the chart has to be represented in 3D, and the trend becomes a surface instead of a curve. A *surface* is like a warped blanket in three dimensions (figure 7.7). This surface is also represented as a function but is more complex.

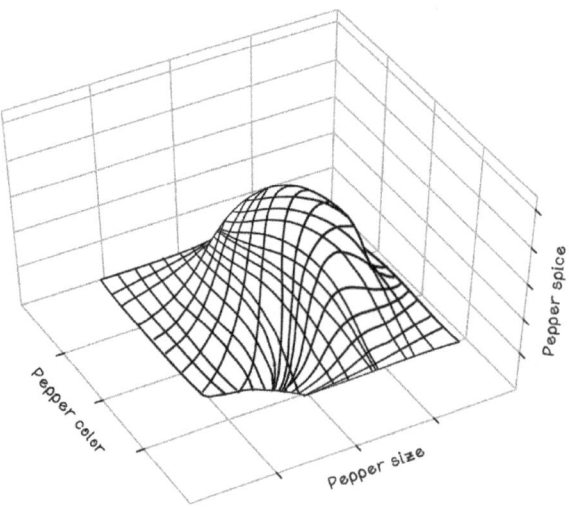

Figure 7.7 Pepper spice vs. pepper size vs. pepper color

Furthermore, a 3D search space could look fairly simple, like figure 7.7, or be so complex that attempting to inspect it visually to find the minimum would be almost impossible (figure 7.8). Figure 7.9 shows the function that represents this plane.

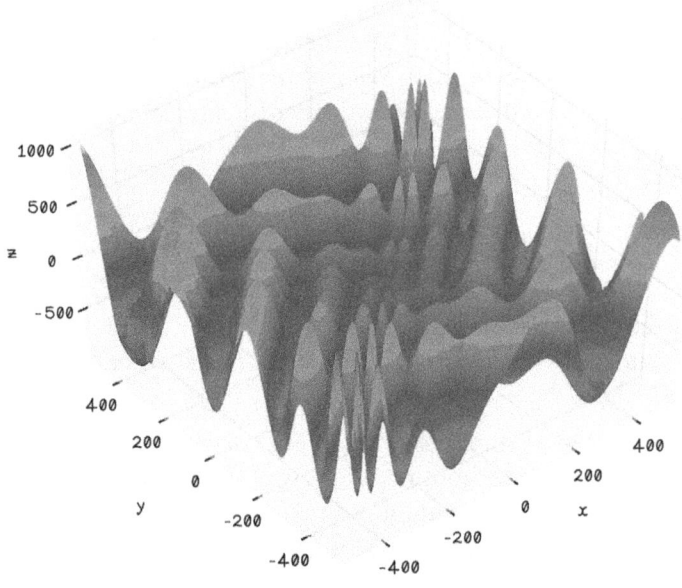

Figure 7.8 A function visualized in the 3D space as a plane

$$f(x,y) = -(y + 47)\sin \sqrt{\left| \frac{x}{2} + (y + 47) \right|} - x \sin \sqrt{\left| x - (y + 47) \right|}$$

Figure 7.9 The function that represents the surface in figure 7.8

This example gets more interesting. We've looked at three attributes of a pepper: size, color, and spiciness. As a result, we're searching in three dimensions. What if we want to include the location of growth? This attribute would make it even more difficult to visualize and understand the data because we're searching in four dimensions. If we add the pepper's age and the amount of fertilizer used to grow it, we're left with a massive search space in six dimensions, and we can't imagine what this search might look like. This search is also represented by a function, but one that's too complex and difficult for a person to solve.

PSO algorithms are particularly good at solving difficult optimization problems. Particles are distributed over the multidimensional search space and work together to find good maximums or minimums. PSO algorithms are particularly useful in the following scenarios:

- *Large search spaces*—There are many data points and possibilities of combinations.
- *Search spaces with high dimensions*—There is complexity in high dimensions. Many dimensions of a problem are required to find a good solution.

Exercise: How many dimensions will the search space for the following scenario have?

In this scenario, we need to determine a good city to live in based on the average minimum temperature during the year because we don't like the cold. It's also important that the population be less than 700,000 people because crowded areas can be inconvenient. The average property price should be as low as possible, and the more trains the city has, the better.

Solution:

The problem in this scenario consists of four dimensions:

- Average temperature
- Size of population
- Average price of property
- Number of trains

Problems that PSO algorithms can solve

Suppose that we're developing a drone, using several materials to create its body and propeller wings (the blades that make it fly). Through many research trials, we've found that different amounts of two specific materials yield different results in terms of optimal performance for lifting the drone and resisting strong winds. These two materials are aluminum (for the chassis) and plastic (for the blades). Too much or too little of either material will result in a poor-performing drone. But several combinations yield a good-performing drone, and only one combination results in an exceptionally well-performing drone.

Figure 7.10 illustrates the components made of plastic and the components made of aluminum. The arrows illustrate the forces that influence the performance of the drone. In simple terms, we want to find a good ratio of plastic to aluminum for a version of the drone that reduces drag during lift and decreases wobble in the wind. Therefore, plastic and aluminum are the inputs, and the output is the resulting stability of the drone. Let's describe ideal stability as reducing drag during liftoff and wobble in the wind.

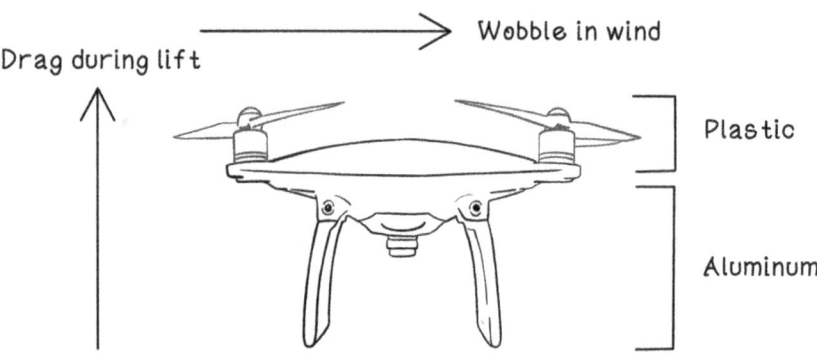

Figure 7.10 The example Drone Problem

Precision in the ratio of aluminum and plastic is important, and the range of possibilities is large. In this scenario, researchers have found the function for the ratio of aluminum and plastic. We'll use this function in a simulated virtual environment that tests drag and wobble to find the best values for each material before we manufacture another prototype drone. We also know that the maximum and minimum ratios for the materials are 10 and -10, respectively. This fitness function is similar to a heuristic.

NOTE Negative numbers for aluminum and plastic would be bizarre in reality, but we're using them in this example to demonstrate the fitness function used to optimize these values.

Figure 7.11 shows the fitness function for the ratio between aluminum (x) and plastic (y). The result is a performance score based on drag and wobble, given the input values for x and y.

$$f(x,y) = (x + 2y - 7)^2 + (2x + y - 5)^2$$

Figure 7.11 The example function for optimizing aluminum (x) and plastic (y)

How can we find the amounts of aluminum and plastic required to create a good drone? One possibility is to try every combination of values for aluminum and plastic until we find the best ratio of materials for our drone.

Take a step back and imagine the amount of computation required to find this ratio. If we treat the materials as continuous values (meaning that the amount could be 10.0, 10.01, or 10.0001), the search space becomes effectively infinite. Trying to brute-force every tiny decimal increment is computationally impossible if we want to solve this problem efficiently. We need a smarter way to navigate this vast landscape, so we need to compute the result for the items in table 7.1.

Table 7.1 Possible values for aluminum and plastic compositions

How many parts aluminum? (x)	How many parts plastic? (y)
-0.1	1.34
-0.134	0.575
-1.1	0.24
-1.1645	1.432
-2.034	-0.65
-2.12	-0.874
0.743	-1.1645
0.3623	-1.87
1.75	-2.7756
...	...
$-10 \geq$ Aluminum ≥ 10	$-10 \geq$ Plastic ≥ 10

This computation goes on for every possible number between the constraints and is computationally expensive, so it's realistically impossible to brute-force this problem. We need a better approach.

PSO provides a means to search a large search space without checking every value in each dimension. In the Drone Problem, aluminum is one dimension of the problem, and plastic is the second dimension. Together, these form a 2D search space. The resulting performance of the drone isn't a dimension we search through but the fitness score (or height) associated with each point in that 2D space.

Think of this problem as being like a hiker on a mountain. The hiker moves north or east (two dimensions of movement) to try to find the highest peak (maximum fitness for the problem). Next, we determine the data structures required to represent a particle, including the problem-specific data that these structures will contain.

Representing state: What do particles look like?

Because particles move across the search space, we must define the concept of a particle. The following properties represent the concept of a particle (figure 7.12):

- *Position*—The position of the particle in all dimensions
- *Best position*—The best position found using the fitness function
- *Velocity*—The current velocity of the particle's movement

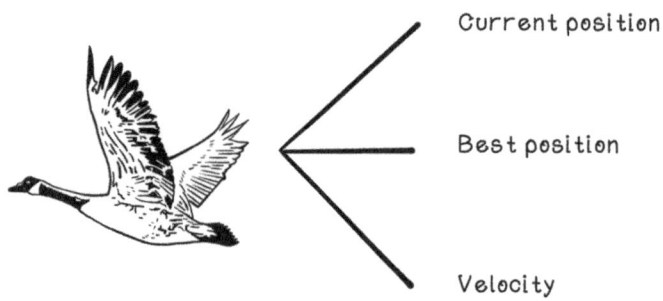

Figure 7.12 Properties of a particle

Python code sample for expressing a particle

To fulfill the three attributes of a particle, the following properties are required in a constructor of the particle for the various operations of the PSO algorithm. (Don't worry about the inertia, cognitive component, and social component right now; they'll be explained in upcoming sections.)

```
class Particle:
    def __init__(self, x, y, inertia,
        cognitive_constant, social_constant):
        self.x = x
        self.y = y
        self.fitness = math.inf

        self.velocity = (0.0, 0.0)

        self.best_x = x
        self.best_y = y
        self.best_fitness = math.inf

        self.inertia = inertia
        self.cognitive_constant = cognitive_constant
        self.social_constant = social_constant
```

The specific coordinates of this candidate solution in the search space

The speed and direction the particle is currently traveling; starts at 0,0

Tracks the value of the best solution found

Records the location where this specific particle achieved its best fitness so far

PSO algorithm life cycle

The approach to designing a PSO algorithm is based on the problem space being addressed. Each problem has a unique context and a different domain in which data is represented. Also, solutions to different problems are measured differently. Let's dive into how to design a PSO to solve the Drone Problem. The general life cycle of a PSO algorithm is as follows (figure 7.13):

1. *Set up the particles.* Determine the number of particles to be used, and initialize each particle to a random position in the search space.
2. *Calculate the fitness of each particle.* Given the position of each particle, determine the fitness of that particle at that position.
3. *Update the position of each particle.* Repetitively update the position of all the particles, using principles of swarm intelligence. Particles will explore the search space and then converge on good solutions.
4. *Calculate the fitness of each particle again.* Evaluate the fitness of the particles again to determine whether their new positions are better than their previous ones.

5. *Determine the stopping criteria.* Determine when the particles stop updating and the algorithm stops.

6. *Return the best solution.* Output the best position found by the swarm when the stopping condition is met.

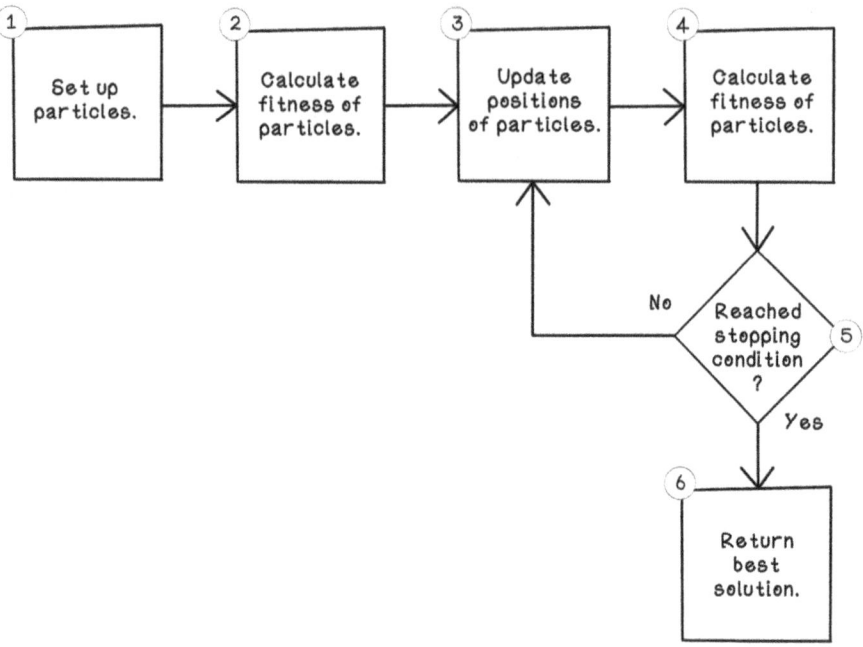

Figure 7.13 The life cycle of a PSO algorithm

The PSO algorithm is fairly simple, but the details of step 3 are particularly intricate. Let's look at each step in isolation and uncover the details that make the algorithm work.

Set up particles

The algorithm starts by creating a specific number of particles, which will remain the same for the lifetime of the algorithm. Figure 7.14 illustrates this step.

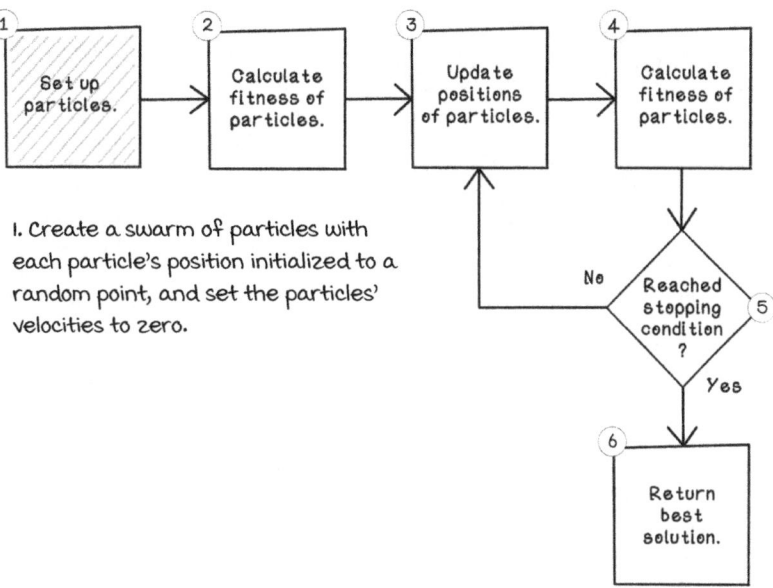

1. Create a swarm of particles with each particle's position initialized to a random point, and set the particles' velocities to zero.

Figure 7.14 Set up the particles.

The three factors that are important in initializing the particles are:

- *Number of particles*—The number of particles influences computation. The more particles exist, the more computation is required. Also, having more particles likely means that converging on a global best solution will take longer because more particles are attracted to their local best solutions.

  In addition, the constraints of the problem affect the number of particles. A larger search space may need more particles to explore it—as many as 1,000 or as few as 4. Usually, 50 to 100 particles produce good solutions without being too computationally expensive (figure 7.15).

- *Starting position for each particle*—The starting position for each particle should be a random position in all the respective dimensions. It's important for the particles to be distributed evenly across the search space. If most of the particles are in a specific region of the search space, they'll struggle to find solutions outside that area.

- *Starting velocity for each particle*—Although it's possible to start at 0, standard practice is to initialize velocity to small random values. This random "kick" ensures that particles explore different directions immediately in the first iteration rather than wait for the swarm to find a leader. Think of releasing fireflies from a jar. They don't drop to the ground and wait; they immediately scatter in random directions to cover the most ground.

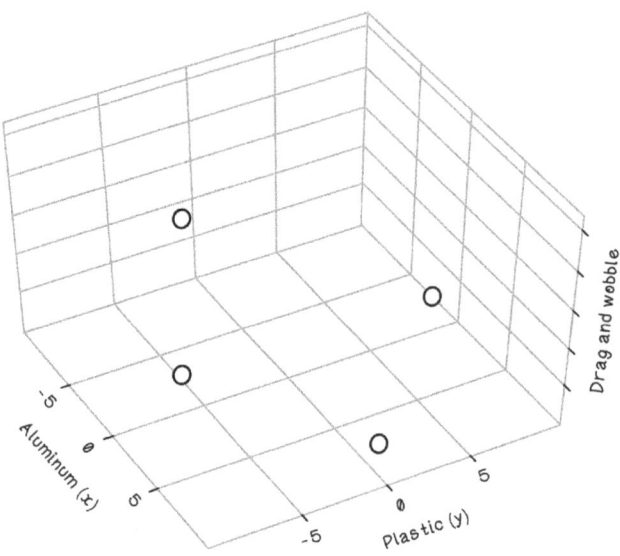

Figure 7.15 A visualization of the initial positions of four particles in a 3D plane

Table 7.2 describes the data encapsulated by each particle in the initialization step of the algorithm. The velocity is 0; the current fitness and best fitness values are 0 because they haven't been calculated yet.

Table 7.2 Data attributes for each particle

Particle	Velocity	Current aluminum (x)	Current plastic (y)	Current fitness	Best aluminum (x)	Best plastic (y)	Best fitness
1	0	7	1	0	7	1	0
2	0	-1	9	0	-1	9	0
3	0	-10	1	0	-10	1	0
4	0	-2	-5	0	-2	-5	0

Python code sample for generating a swarm

The method of generating a swarm consists of creating an empty list and appending new particles to it. The key factors are

- *Ensuring that the number of particles is configurable*—The size of the swarm determines the tradeoff between search coverage (more particles) and computational speed (fewer particles).

- *Ensuring that the random number generation is done uniformly*—Numbers are distributed across the search space within the constraints. This implementation depends on the features of the random number generator used.

- *Ensuring that the constraints of the search space are specified*—In this case, -10 and 10 are specified for both *x* and *y* of the particle:

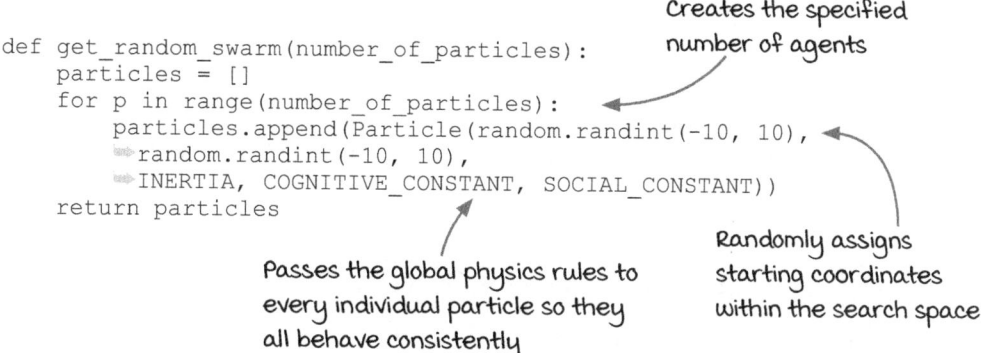

```
def get_random_swarm(number_of_particles):
    particles = []
    for p in range(number_of_particles):
        particles.append(Particle(random.randint(-10, 10),
        random.randint(-10, 10),
        INERTIA, COGNITIVE_CONSTANT, SOCIAL_CONSTANT))
    return particles
```

Creates the specified number of agents

Passes the global physics rules to every individual particle so they all behave consistently

Randomly assigns starting coordinates within the search space

Calculate the fitness particles

The next step is calculating the fitness of each particle at its current position. The fitness of particles is calculated every time the entire swarm changes position (figure 7.16).

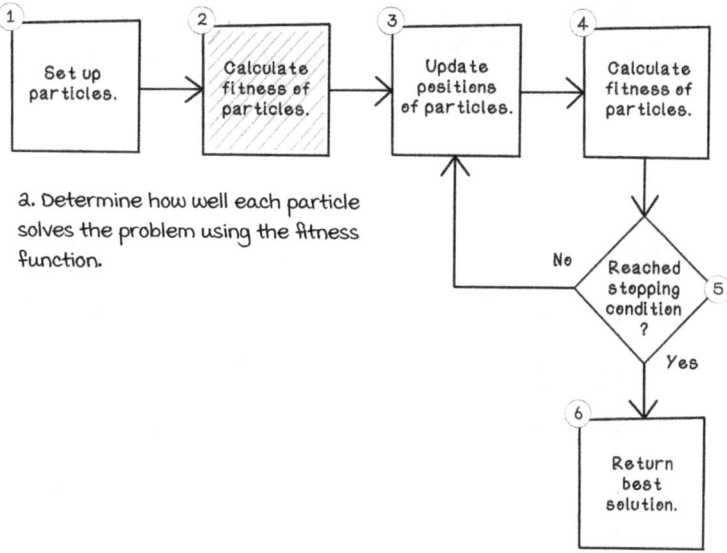

Figure 7.16 Calculate the fitness of the particles.

In the Drone Problem, the scientists provided a function in which the result is the amount of drag and wobble given a specific number of aluminum and plastic components. This function is used as the fitness function in the PSO algorithm in this example (figure 7.17).

$$f(x,y) = (x + 2y - 7)^2 + (2x + y - 5)^2$$

Figure 7.17 The example function for optimizing aluminum (x) and plastic (y)

If x is aluminum and y is plastic, we can make the calculations in figure 7.18 for each particle to determine its fitness by substituting x and y for the values of aluminum and plastic.

$$f(7,1) = (7 + 2(1) - 7)^2 + (2(7) + 1 - 5)^2 = 104$$
$$f(-1,9) = (-1 + 2(9) - 7)^2 + (2(-1) + 9 - 5)^2 = 104$$
$$f(-10,1) = (-10 + 2(1) - 7)^2 + (2(-10) + 1 - 5)^2 = 801$$
$$f(-2,-5) = (-2 + 2(-5) - 7)^2 + (2(-2) - 5 - 5)^2 = 557$$

Figure 7.18 Fitness calculations for each particle

Now the table of particles represents the calculated fitness for each particle (table 7.3). It's also set as the best fitness for each particle because it's the only known fitness in the first iteration. After the first iteration, the best fitness for each particle is the best fitness in each specific particle's history.

Table 7.3 Data attributes for each particle

Particle	Velocity	Current aluminum (x)	Current plastic (y)	Current fitness	Best aluminum (x)	Best plastic (y)	Best fitness
1	0	7	1	104	7	1	104
2	0	-1	9	104	-1	9	104
3	0	-10	1	801	-10	1	801
4	0	-2	-5	557	-2	-5	557

Exercise: What would the fitness be for the following inputs given the drone fitness function?

Particle	Velocity	Current aluminum (x)	Current plastic (y)	Current fitness	Best aluminum (x)	Best plastic (y)	Best fitness
1	0	5	-3	0	5	-3	0
2	0	-6	-1	0	-6	-1	0
3	0	7	3	0	7	3	0
4	0	-1	9	0	-1	9	0

Solution:

$$f(5,-3) = (5 + 2(-3) - 7)^2 + (2(5) - 3 - 5)^2 = 68$$

$$f(-6,-1) = (-6 + 2(-1) - 7)^2 + (2(-6) - 1 - 5)^2 = 549$$

$$f(7,3) = (7 + 2(3) - 7)^2 + (2(7) + 3 - 5)^2 = 180$$

$$f(-1,9) = (-1 + 2(9) - 7)^2 + (2(-1) + 9 - 5)^2 = 104$$

Python code sample for calculating fitness

The fitness function represents the mathematical function in code. Any math library will contain the operations required, such as a power function and a square-root function:

```
def calculate_booth(x, y):
    return math.pow(x + 2 * y - 7, 2) + math.pow(2 * x + y - 5, 2)
```

The function for updating the fitness of a particle is also trivial in that it determines whether the new fitness is better than a past best and then stores that information:

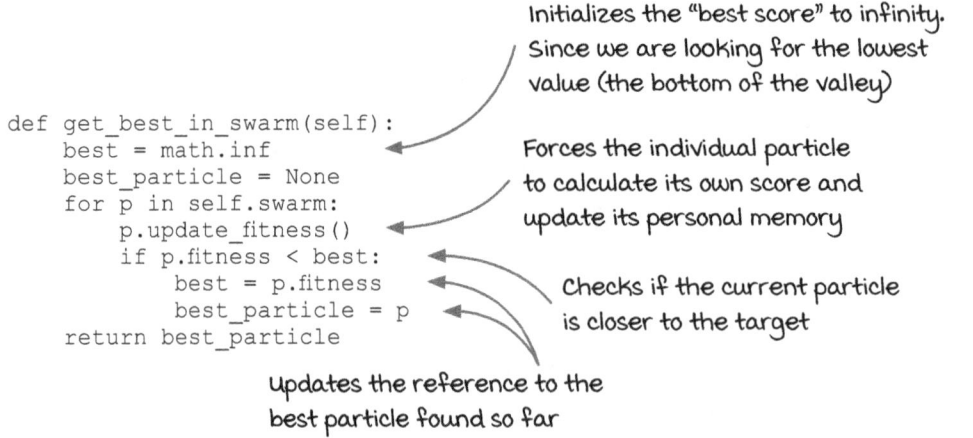

Calculates the fitness (score) of the particle's current position using the Booth Function

```
def update_fitness(self):
    self.fitness = calculate_booth(self.x, self.y)
    if self.fitness < self.best_fitness:
        self.best_fitness = self.fitness
        self.best_x = self.x
        self.best_y = self.y
```

Compares the current score against the best score this specific particle has ever achieved

Saves the new record-breaking score and the coordinates where it was found

The function to determine the best particle in the swarm iterates through all particles, updates their fitness based on their new positions, and finds the particle that yields the smallest value for the fitness function. In this case, we're minimizing, so a smaller value is better:

Initializes the "best score" to infinity. Since we are looking for the lowest value (the bottom of the valley)

```
def get_best_in_swarm(self):
    best = math.inf
    best_particle = None
    for p in self.swarm:
        p.update_fitness()
        if p.fitness < best:
            best = p.fitness
            best_particle = p
    return best_particle
```

Forces the individual particle to calculate its own score and update its personal memory

Checks if the current particle is closer to the target

Updates the reference to the best particle found so far

Update positions of particles

The update step of the algorithm is the most intricate because it's where the magic happens. The update step encompasses the properties of swarm intelligence in nature into a mathematical model that allows exploration of the search space while honing in on good solutions (figure 7.19).

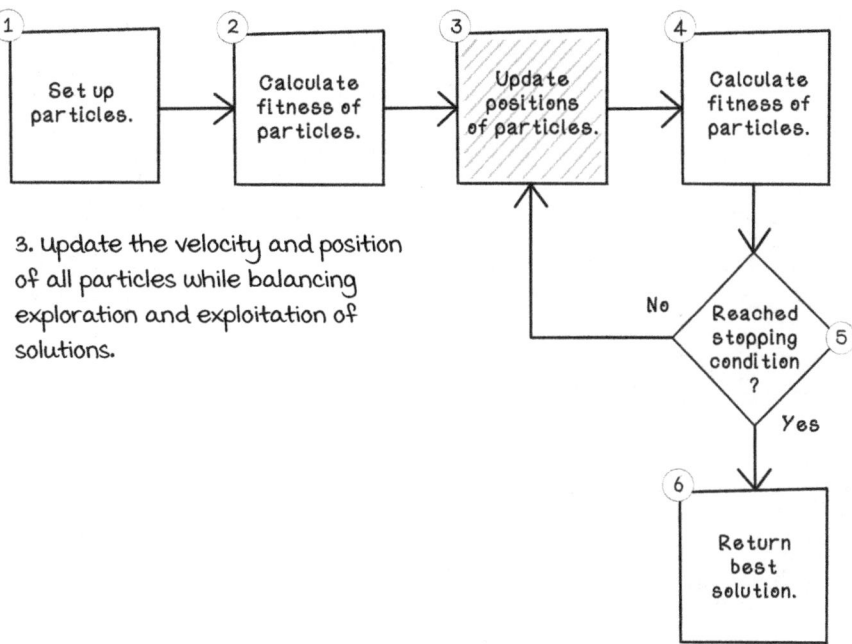

3. Update the velocity and position of all particles while balancing exploration and exploitation of solutions.

Figure 7.19 Update the positions of the particles.

Particles in the swarm update their position given a cognitive ability and factors in the environment around them, such as inertia and what the swarm is doing. These factors influence the velocity and position of each particle. The first step is understanding how velocity is updated. The velocity determines the direction and speed of movement of the particle.

The particles in the swarm move to different points in the search space to find better solutions. Each particle relies on its memory of a good solution and the knowledge of the swarm's best solution. Figure 7.20 illustrates the movement of the particles in the swarm as their positions are updated.

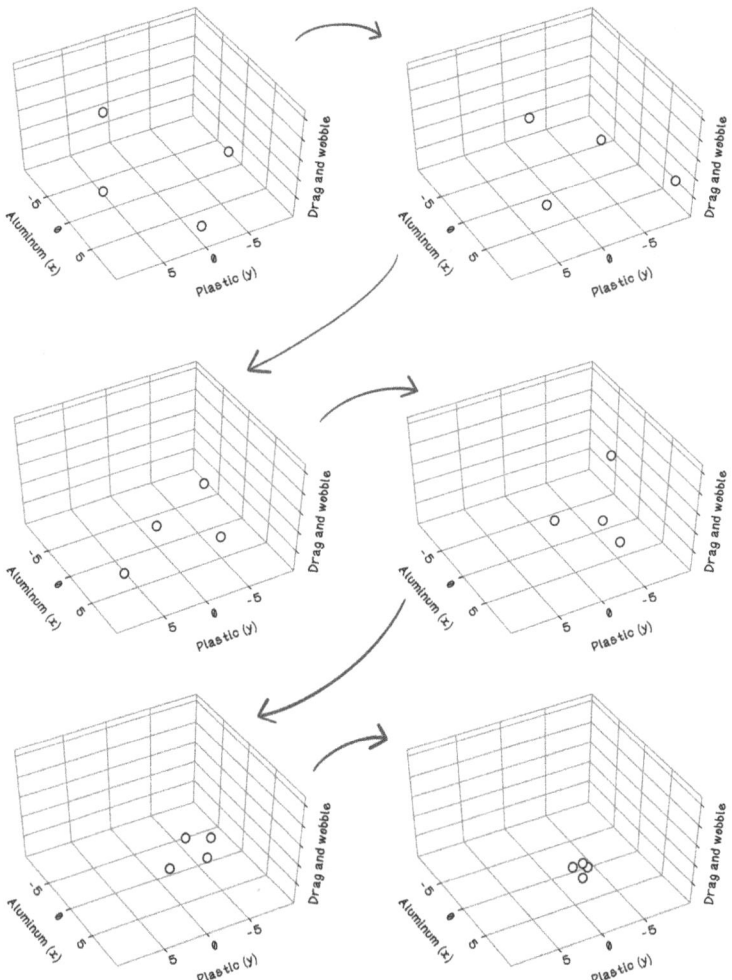

Figure 7.20 The movement of particles over five iterations

Updating particle velocity

Three components are used to calculate the new velocity of each particle: inertia, cognitive, and social. Each component influences the movement of the particle. We'll look at the components in isolation before diving into how they're combined to update the velocity and, ultimately, position of a particle:

- *Inertia*—The inertia component represents the resistance to movement or change in direction for a specific particle that influences its velocity. The inertia component consists of two values: the inertia magnitude and the current velocity of the particle.

The inertia value is a number between 0 and 1:

```
Inertia component:
inertia * current velocity
```

- ° *High inertia (closer to 1.0)*—Translates to exploration. The particle maintains its previous momentum. Like a heavy speeding freight truck, it has so much momentum that it can't turn easily, allowing it to fly through the search space and discover new regions.
- ° *Low inertia (closer to 0)*—Translates to exploitation. The particle slows quickly. Like a housefly, it has almost no momentum and can change direction quickly, allowing it to hover and fine-tune its search around the best solutions found so far.
- *Cognitive*—The cognitive constant is a number greater than 0 and less than 2. A greater cognitive constant encourages individual independence (or personal exploration), preventing the particle from following the swarm blindly and ensuring that it thoroughly checks the area around its own discoveries:

```
Cognitive component:
cognitive acceleration * (particle best position - current position)
           ↳
cognitive acceleration = cognitive constant * random cognitive number
```

- *Social*—The social component represents the ability of a particle to interact with the swarm. A particle knows the best position in the swarm and uses this information to influence its movement. Social acceleration is determined by using a constant and scaling it with a random number. The social constant remains the same for the lifetime of the algorithm, and the random factor encourages diversity in favoring the social factor:

```
Social component:
social acceleration * (swarm best position - current position)
         ↳
social acceleration = social constant * random social number
```

The greater the social constant, the more exploitation (or convergence) there will be because the particle favors the swarm's best findings over its own. You can think of these constants as defining the personality of the swarm:

- *High cognitive, low social*—The particles become "nostalgic loners." They roam around but keep getting pulled back to their own personal victories, ignoring the group. The swarm spreads out.
- *Low cognitive, high social*—The particles become "trend followers." They rush blindly toward the current leader. The swarm collapses quickly into a single point (which may be a trap or local optimum).

Updating velocity

Now that we understand the inertia, cognitive, and social components, let's look at how they can be combined to update a new velocity for the particles (figure 7.21). Suppose that a particle is a tourist deciding where to go next. Its direction is determined by three arguing voices:

- *Inertia (habit)*—"Let's keep moving in the direction we're already going. It takes effort to turn."
- *Cognitive (memory)*—"Hey, remember that great spot we found yesterday? Let's go back there."
- *Social (peer pressure)*—"Look! Everyone else is heading toward that hill. Something interesting must be happening there."

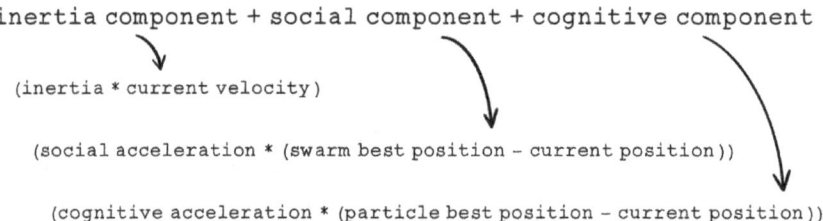

Figure 7.21 Formula to calculate velocity

The final velocity is simply the sum of these three "urges." By looking at the math, we may find it difficult to understand how the different components in the function affect the velocity of the particles. Figure 7.22 depicts how the different factors influence a particle, and table 7.4 shows the attributes of each particle after the fitness of each is calculated.

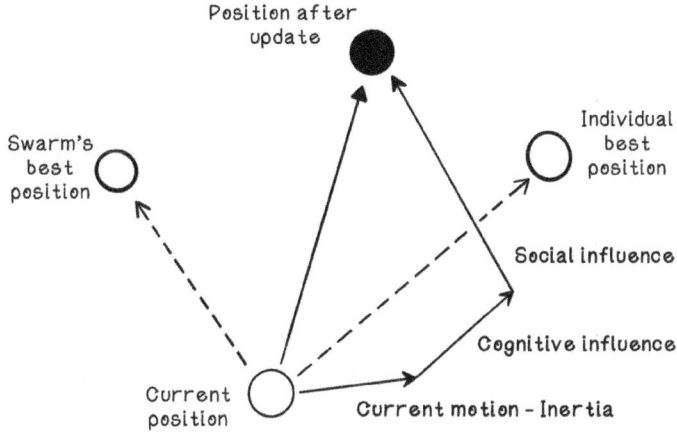

Figure 7.22 The intuition of the factors influencing velocity updates

Table 7.4 Data attributes for each particle

Particle	Velocity	Current aluminum	Current plastic	Current fitness	Best aluminum	Best plastic	Best fitness
1	0	7	1	104	2	4	104
2	0	-1	9	104	-1	9	104
3	0	-10	1	801	-10	1	801
4	0	-2	-5	557	-2	-5	557

Next, we'll dive into the velocity update calculations for a particle, given the formulas we've worked through. Here are the constant configurations set for this scenario:

- *Inertia is set to 0.2.* This setting favors slower exploration.
- *Cognitive constant is set to 0.35.* Because this constant is less than the social constant, the social component is favored over an individual particle's cognitive component.
- *Social constant is set to 0.45.* Because this constant is more than the cognitive constant, the social component is favored. Particles put more weight on the best values found by the swarm.

Figure 7.23 describes the particle 4 calculations of the inertia, cognitive, and social components for the velocity-update formula. After these calculations have been completed for all particles, the velocity of each particle is updated as shown in table 7.5.

Inertia component:

inertia * current velocity

= 0.2 * 0

= 0

Cognitive component:

cognitive acceleration = cognitive constant * random cognitive number

= 0.35 * 0.2

= 0.07

cognitive acceleration * (particle best position - current position)

= 0.07 * ([-2,-5] - [-2,-5])

= 0.07 * 0

= 0

Social component:

social acceleration = social constant * random social number

= 0.45 * 0.3

= 0.135

social acceleration * (swarm best position - current position)

= 0.135 * ([7, 1] - [-2, -5])

= 0.135 * sqrt((7-(-2))^2 + (1-(-5))^2)   Distance formula: sqrt((x1 - x2)^2 + (y1 - y2)^2)

= 0.135 * 10.817

= 1.46

New velocity:

inertia component + cognitive component + social component

= 0 + 0 + 1.46

= 1.46

Figure 7.23 Particle-velocity calculation walk-through

Table 7.5 Data attributes for each particle

Particle	Velocity	Current aluminum	Current plastic	Current fitness	Best aluminum	Best plastic	Best fitness
1	0	7	1	104	7	1	104
2	1.52	-1	9	104	-1	9	104
3	2.295	-10	1	801	-10	1	801
4	1.46	-2	-5	557	-2	-5	557

Updating position

Now that we understand how velocity is updated, we can update the current position of each particle, using the new velocity. Figure 7.24 illustrates this calculation.

Position:

current position + new velocity

New position:

current position + new velocity

$$= ([-2, -5]) + 1.46$$
$$= [-0.54, -3.54]$$

Figure 7.24 Calculating the new position of a particle

By adding the current position and new velocity, we can determine the new position of each particle and update the table of particle attributes with the new velocities. Then we calculate the fitness of each particle again given its new position, and its best position is remembered (table 7.6).

Table 7.6 Data attributes for each particle

Particle	Velocity	Current aluminum	Current plastic	Current fitness	Best aluminum	Best plastic	Best fitness
1	0	7	1	104	7	1	104
2	1.52	0.52	10.52	255.3	-1	9	104
3	2.295	-7.71	3.3	358.8	-7.71	3.3	358.8
4	1.46	−0.54	-3.54	306.3	-0.54	-3.54	306.3

Calculating the initial velocity for each particle in the first iteration is fairly simple because there was no previous best position for each particle—only a swarm best position that affected only the social component. Now let's examine what the velocity-update calculation will look like with the new information for each particle's best position and the swarm's new best position. Figure 7.25 describes the calculation for particle 4 in the list.

Inertia component:

inertia * current velocity
= 0.2 * 1.46
= 0.292
_____

Cognitive component:

cognitive acceleration = cognitive constant * random cognitive number
= 0.35 * 0.2
= 0.07

cognitive acceleration * (particle best position - current position)
= 0.07 * ([-0.54,-3.54]-[-0.54,-3.54])
= 0.07 * 0
= 0
_____

Social component:

social acceleration = social constant * random social number
= 0.45 * 0.3
= 0.135

social acceleration * (swarm best position - current position)
= 0.135 * ([7, 1]- [-0.54,-3.54])
= 0.135 * sqrt((7 -(-0.54))^2+(1 -(-3.54))^2)
= 0.135 * 8.80
= 1.188
_____

New velocity:

inertia component + cognitive component + social component
= 0.292 + 0 + 1.188
= 1.48

Figure 7.25 Calculating particle velocity again

In this scenario, the cognitive and social components both play a role in updating the velocity, whereas the scenario described in figure 7.23 is influenced by the social component because it's the first iteration.

Particles move to different positions over several iterations. Figure 7.26 depicts the particles' movement and their convergence on a solution.

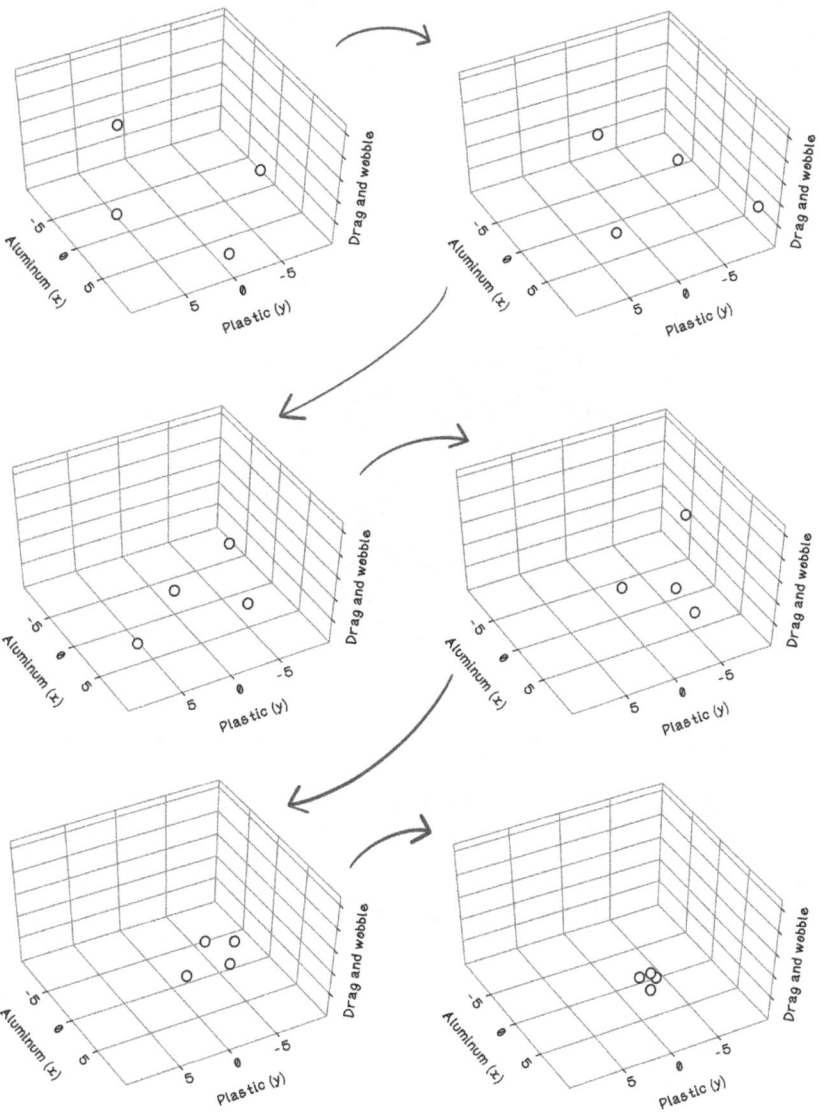

Figure 7.26 A visualization of the movement of particles in the search space

In the last frame of figure 7.26, all the particles have converged on a specific region in the search space. The best solution from the swarm will be used as the final solution. In real-world optimization problems, it's impossible to visualize the entire search space, which would make optimization algorithms unnecessary. To demonstrate, we used a standard mathematical benchmark known as the Booth function. Why use a test function? In real-world problems, we rarely know the perfect answer ahead of time. To test whether an algorithm like PSO works, however, scientists use specific mathematical shapes (like the Booth function) where the global minimum is already known (in this case, at $x=1$, $y=3$). This allows us to verify that our swarm converged on the correct target (figure 7.27).

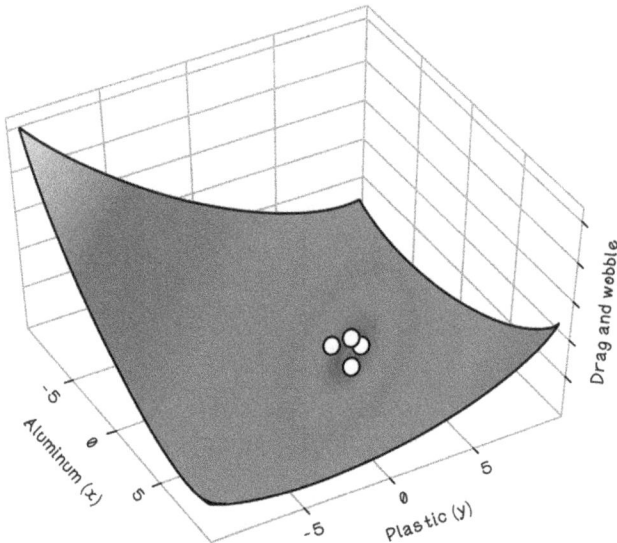

Figure 7.27 Visualization of convergence of particles and a known surface

After using the PSO algorithm for the Drone Problem, we find that the optimal ratio of aluminum and plastic to minimize drag and wobble is 1:3—that is, one part aluminum and three parts plastic. When we feed these values into the fitness function, the result is 0, which is the minimum value for the function.

Python code sample for updating particle velocity

The update step can seem daunting, but if the components are broken into simple focused functions, the code becomes simpler and easier to write, use, and understand. The first functions are the inertia calculation function, the cognitive acceleration function, and the social acceleration function:

multiplies the current velocity vector (x, y) by the inertia weight

Calculates how much of the particle's previous speed is retained

```python
def calculate_inertia(inertia, current_velocity):
    return current_velocity[0] * inertia, current_velocity[1]
        * inertia

def calculate_acceleration(constant, random_factor):
    return constant * random_factor
```

Calculates the strength of the pull towards a specific target (either personal best or global best)

multiplies the fixed attraction constant by a random number preventing the swarm from getting stuck in local optima

The cognitive component is calculated by finding the cognitive acceleration, using the function we defined in an earlier section, and the distance between the particle's best position and its current position:

```python
def calculate_cognitive(self,
    cognitive_constant,
    cognitive_random,
    particle_best_position_x,
    particle_best_position_y,
    particle_current_position_x,
    particle_current_position_y):

    cognitive_acceleration =
        self.calculate_acceleration(cognitive_constant, cognitive_random)
    return (
        cognitive_acceleration *
            (particle_best_position_x - particle_current_position_x),
        cognitive_acceleration *
            (particle_best_position_y - particle_current_position_y),
    )
```

Calculates the raw strength of the pull towards the personal best

Calculates the gap between where the particle is and where it wants to be

The social component is calculated by finding the social acceleration, using the function we defined earlier, and the distance between the swarm's best position and the particle's current position:

```
def calculate_social(self,
    social_constant,
    social_random,
    swarm_best_position_x,
    swarm_best_position_y,
    particle_current_position_x,
    particle_current_position_y):

    social_acceleration =
        self.calculate_acceleration(social_constant, social_random)
    return (
        social_acceleration *
            (swarm_best_position_x - particle_current_position_x),
        social_acceleration *
            (swarm_best_position_y - particle_current_position_y),
    )
```

Calculates the strength of the pull towards the swarm's leader

Calculates the distance and direction from the particle's current spot to the group leader

The update function wraps everything we've defined to carry out the actual update of a particle's velocity and position. The velocity is calculated by using the inertia, cognitive, and social components. The position is calculated by adding the new velocity to the particle's current position:

Calculates the pull toward the swarm's global leader

Calculates the force that keeps the particle moving in its previous direction

Calculates the pull toward the particle's own personal best

```
def update(self, swarm_best_x, swarm_best_y):
    i = self.calculate_inertia(self.inertia, self.velocity)
    c = self.calculate_cognitive(self.cognitive_constant,
        random.random(), self.x, self.y, self.best_x, self.best_y)
    s = self.calculate_social(self.social_constant, random.random(),
        self.x, self.y, swarm_best_x, swarm_best_y)
    v = self.calculate_updated_velocity(i, c, s)
    p = self.calculate_position(self.x, self.y, v)
    self.velocity = v
    self.x = p[0]
    self.y = p[1]
```

Combines the three forces (Inertia + Cognitive + Social) to create the new velocity vector

Updates the particle's state. It is now at the new location

Applies the new velocity to the current coordinates to find the new location

Exercise: Calculate the new velocity and position for particle 1 given the following information about the particles

- Inertia is set to 0.1.
- The cognitive constant is set to 0.5, and the cognitive random number is 0.2.
- The social constant is set to 0.5, and the social random number is 0.5.

Particle	Velocity	Current aluminum	Current plastic	Current fitness	Best aluminum	Best plastic	Best fitness
1	3	4	8	721.286	7	1	296
2	4	3	3	73.538	0.626	10	73.538
3	1	6	2	302.214	-10	1	80
4	2	2	5	179.105	-0.65	-3.65	179.105

(continued)

Solution:

Inertia component:

inertia * current velocity

= 0.1 * 3

= 0.3

Cognitive component:

cognitive acceleration = cognitive constant * random cognitive number

= 0.5 * 0.2

= 0.1

cognitive acceleration * (particle best position - current position)

= 0.1 * ([7,1] - [4,8])

= 0.1 * sqrt$((7 - 4)^2 + (1 - 8)^2)$

= 0.1 * 7.616

= 0.7616

Social component:

social acceleration = social constant * random social number

= 0.5 * 0.5

= 0.25

social acceleration * (swarm best position - current position)

= 0.25 * ([0.626,10] - [4,8])

= 0.25 * sqrt$((0.626 - 4)^2 + (10 - 8)^2)$

= 0.25 * 3.922

= 0.981

New velocity:

inertia component + cognitive component + social component

= 0.3 + 0.7616 + 0.981

= 2.0426

New position:

current position + new velocity

= [4, 8] + 2.0426

= [6.0426, 10.0426]

Determine the stopping criteria

The particles in the swarm can't keep updating and searching indefinitely. A stopping criterion needs to be determined to allow the algorithm to run for a reasonable number of iterations to find a suitable solution (figure 7.28).

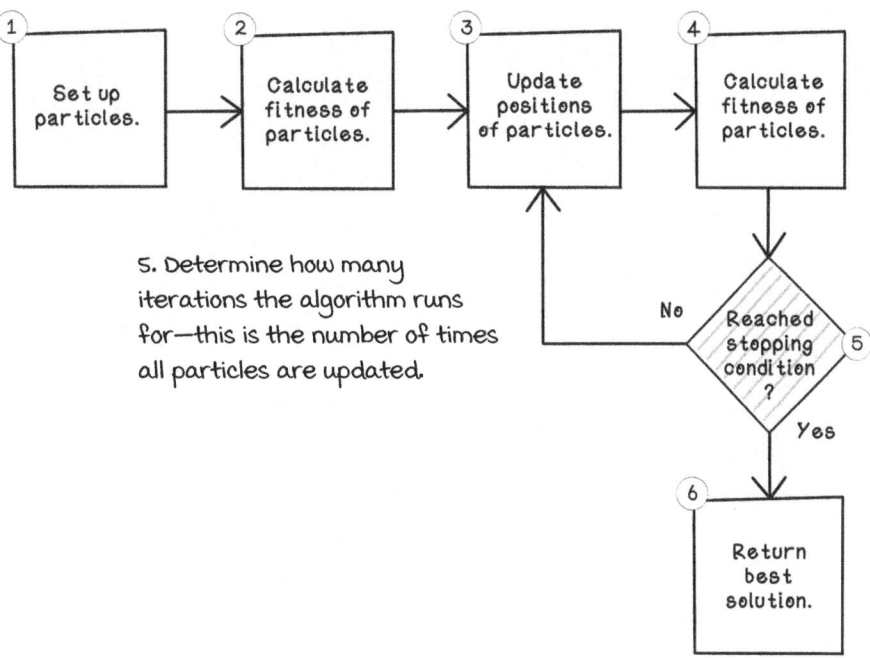

Figure 7.28 Has the algorithm reached a stopping condition?

The number of iterations influences several aspects of finding solutions, including the following:

- *Exploration*—Particles require time to explore the search space to find areas with better solutions. Exploration is also influenced by the constants defined in the velocity-update function.
- *Exploitation*—Particles should converge on a good solution after reasonable exploration occurs.

A strategy to stop the algorithm is to examine the best solution in the swarm and determine whether it's stagnating. Stagnation occurs when the value of the best solution doesn't change or doesn't change by a significant amount. Running more iterations in this scenario won't help us find better solutions. When the best solution stagnates, the parameters in the update function can be adjusted to favor more exploration. If more exploration is desired, this adjustment usually means more iterations. Stagnation could mean that a good solution was found or that the swarm is stuck on a local best solution. If enough exploration occurred at the start and the swarm gradually stagnates, the swarm has converged on a good solution (figure 7.29).

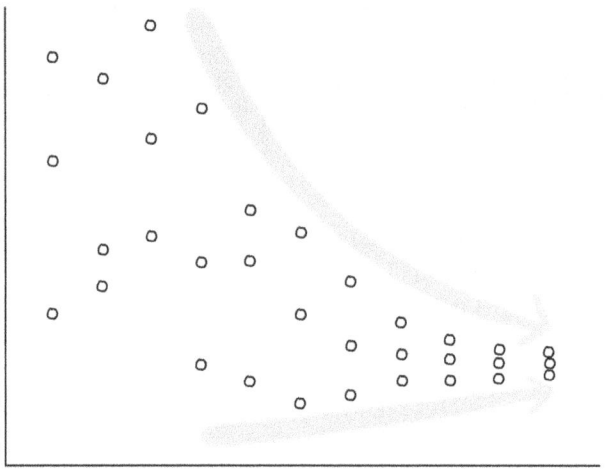

Figure 7.29 Exploration converging and exploiting

Use cases for PSO algorithms

PSO algorithms are interesting because they simulate a natural phenomenon, which makes them easier to understand, but they can be applied to a range of problems at different levels of abstraction. This chapter looked at an optimization problem for drone manufacturing, but PSO algorithms can be used in conjunction with other algorithms, playing a small but critical role in finding good solutions.

One interesting application of a PSO algorithm is deep-brain stimulation. The concept involves installing probes with electrodes into the human brain to stimulate it to treat conditions such as Parkinson's disease. Each probe contains electrodes that can be configured in different directions to treat the condition correctly per patient. Researchers at the University of Minnesota have developed a PSO algorithm to optimize the direction of each electrode to maximize the region of interest, minimize the region of avoidance, and minimize energy use. Because particles are effective in searching these multidimensional problem spaces, the PSO algorithm is effective for finding optimal configurations for electrodes on the probes (figure 7.30).

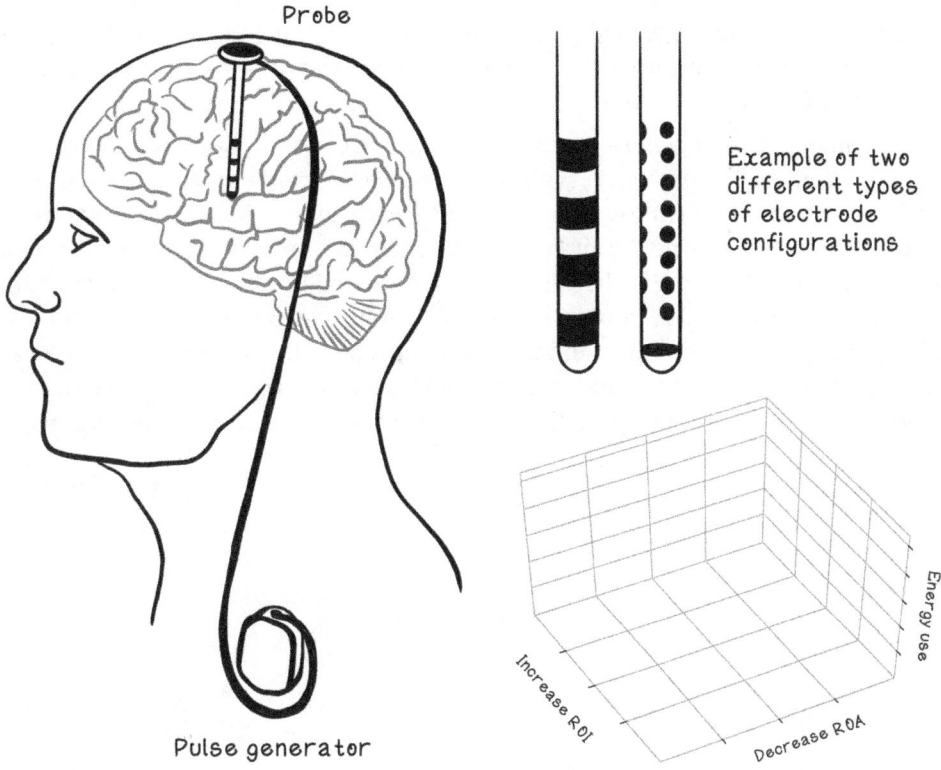

Figure 7.30 Example of factors involved for probes in deep-brain stimulation

Here are some other real-world applications of PSO algorithms:

- *Optimizing weights in an artificial neural network (ANN)*—ANNs are modeled on an idea of how the human brain works. Neurons pass signals to other neurons, and each neuron adjusts the signal before passing it on. An ANN uses weights to adjust each signal. The power of the network is finding the right balance of weights to model patterns in relationships of the data. Adjusting weights is computationally expensive because the search space is massive. Imagine having to brute-force every possible decimal number combination for 10 weights. That process would take years.

  Don't panic if this concept sounds confusing. We explore how ANNs operate in chapter 9. We can use PSO to adjust the weights of neural networks faster because it seeks optimal values in the search space without exhaustively attempting each one.

- *Motion tracking in videos*—Motion tracking of people is a challenging task in computer vision. The goal is to identify the poses of people and imply a motion by using the information from the images in the video alone. People move differently even though their joints move similarly. Because the images contain many aspects, the search space becomes large, with many dimensions to predict the motion for a person. PSO works well in high-dimension search spaces and can improve the performance of motion tracking and prediction.

- *Speech enhancement in audio*—Audio recordings are nuanced. Background noise is always present and may interfere with what someone is saying in the recording. A solution is to remove the noise from recorded speech audio clips. A technique used for this purpose is filtering the audio clip with noise and comparing similar sounds to remove the noise from the audio clip. This solution is still complex because reducing certain frequencies may be good for parts of the audio clip but may deteriorate other parts of it. Fine searching and matching must be done for good noise removal. Traditional methods are slow because the search space is large. PSO works well in large search spaces and can speed the process of removing noise from audio clips.

SUMMARY OF SWARM INTELLIGENCE: PARTICLES

Particle Swarm Optimization finds good solutions in very large search spaces

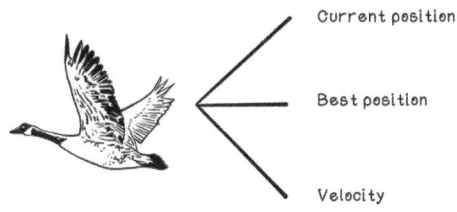

Current position

Best position

Velocity

Particles use their best position and the swarm's best position to move through the search space.

Adjusting the particles' velocity is the critical step of the PSO algorithm using inertia, cognitive influence, and social influence.

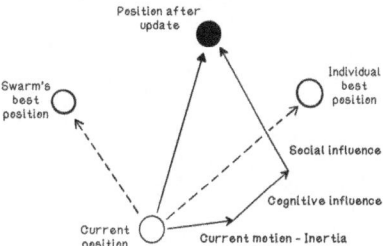

Position after update

Swarm's best position

Individual best position

Social influence

Cognitive influence

Current position

Current motion - Inertia

New velocity:

inertia component + social component + cognitive component

(inertia * current velocity)

(social acceleration * (swarm best position – current position))

(cognitive acceleration * (particle best position – current position))

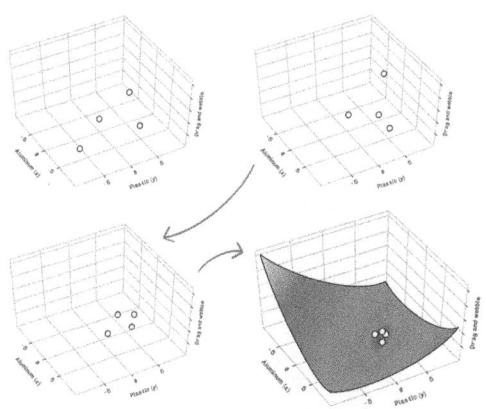

Particles move through the search space while finding different good solutions and ideally converging on a global best solution.

Machine learning | **8**

In this chapter

- Solving problems with machine learning algorithms

- Grasping a machine learning life cycle, preparing data, and selecting algorithms

- Understanding and implementing a linear regression algorithm for predictions

- Understanding and implementing a decision-tree learning algorithm for classification

What is machine learning?

Machine learning can seem like a daunting concept to learn and apply, but with the right framing and understanding of the process and algorithms, it can be interesting and fun. Suppose that you're looking for a new apartment. You speak to friends and family members and do some online searches for apartments in the city. You notice that apartments in different areas are priced differently. Here are some of your observations from all your research:

- A one-bedroom apartment in the city center (close to work) costs $5,000 per month.
- A two-bedroom apartment in the city center costs $7,000 per month.
- A one-bedroom apartment in the city center with a garage costs $6,000 per month.
- A one-bedroom apartment outside the city center, from which you'll have to commute to work, costs $3,000 per month.
- A two-bedroom apartment outside the city center costs $4,500 per month.
- A one-bedroom apartment outside the city center with a garage costs $3,800 per month.

You notice some patterns. Apartments in the city center are most expensive, usually priced between $5,000 and $7,000 per month. Apartments outside the city center are cheaper. Increasing the number of rooms adds between $1,500 and $2,000 per month, and access to a garage adds between $800 and $1,000 per month (figure 8.1).

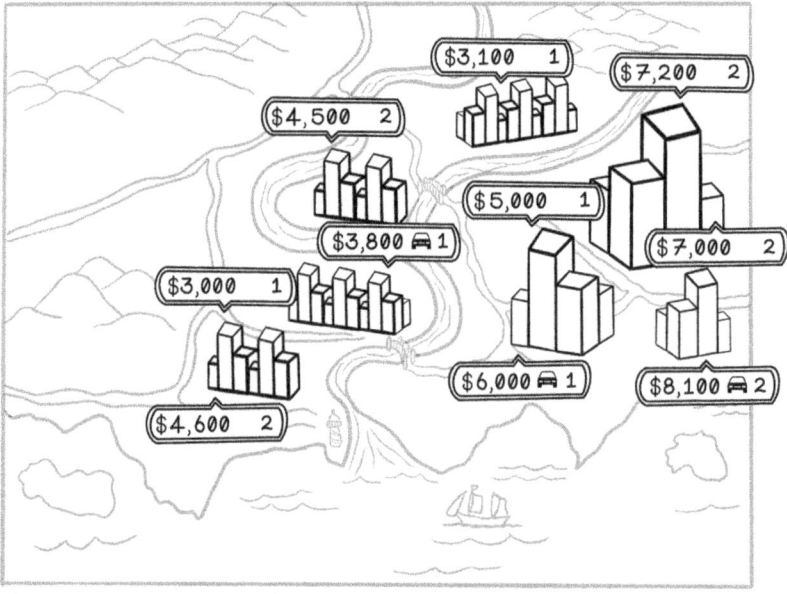

Figure 8.1 An illustration of property prices and features in different areas

This example shows how to use data to find patterns and make decisions. If you encounter a two-bedroom apartment in the city center with a garage, it's reasonable to assume that the price will be approximately $8,000 per month.

Machine learning aims to find patterns in data for useful applications in the real world. We could spot the pattern in this small dataset, but machine learning spots them for us in large, complex datasets.

Figure 8.2 depicts the relationships among different attributes of the data. Each dot represents an individual property. We see more dots closer to the city center and a clear pattern related to price per month: the price gradually drops as distance to the city center increases. There is also a pattern in the price per month related to the number of rooms; the gap between the bottom cluster of dots and the top cluster shows that the price jumps significantly. We could naïvely assume that this effect may be related to distance from the city center. Machine learning algorithms can help us validate or invalidate this assumption. We dive into how this process works throughout the chapter.

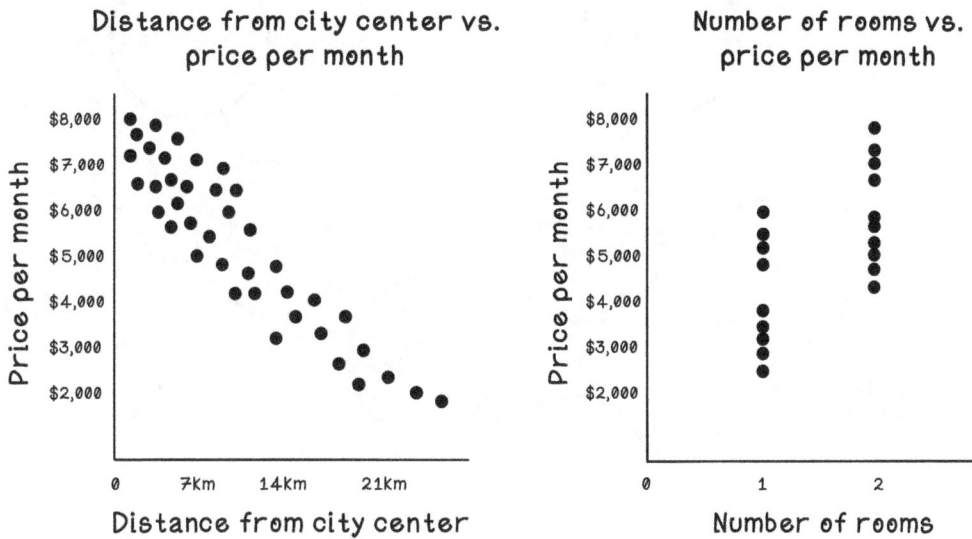

Figure 8.2 Example visualization of relationships among data

Typically, data is represented in tables. The columns are referred to as *features* of the data, and the rows are referred to as *examples*. When we compare two features, the feature being measured is sometimes represented as y, and the features being changed are grouped as x. We'll gain a better intuition for this terminology as we work through some problems.

Problems that machine learning can solve

Machine learning is useful only if you have data and questions to ask that the data might answer. Machine learning algorithms find patterns in data but can't do useful things magically. Different categories of machine learning algorithms use different approaches to answer questions. These broad categories are supervised learning, unsupervised learning, and reinforcement learning (figure 8.3).

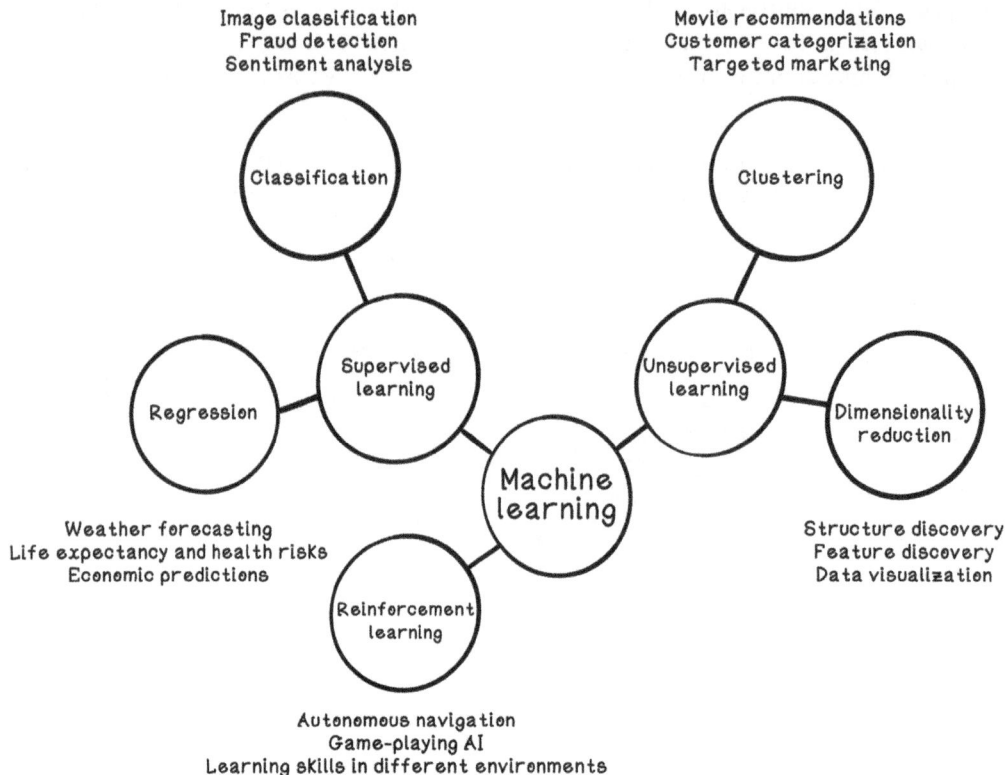

Figure 8.3 Categorization of machine learning and uses

Supervised learning

One of the most common techniques in traditional machine learning is *supervised learning*. We want to look at data, understand the patterns and relationships among the data, and predict the results if we're given new examples of different data in the same format. The Apartment-Finding Problem is an example of using supervised learning to find the pattern. We also see this example in action when we type a search that autocompletes or when music applications suggest new songs to listen to based on our activity and preferences. Supervised learning has two subcategories:

- *Regression* involves drawing a line through a set of data points to fit the overall shape of the data most closely. Regression can be used for applications such as finding trends related to marketing initiatives and sales. (Example: Is there a direct relationship between marketing through online ads and actual sales of a product?) It can also be used to determine factors that affect something. (Example: Is there a direct relationship between time and the value of cryptocurrency, and will cryptocurrency increase exponentially in value as time passes?)
- *Classification* aims to predict categories of examples based on their features. (Example: Can we determine whether something is a car or a truck based on its number of wheels, weight, and top speed?)

Unsupervised learning

Unsupervised learning involves finding underlying patterns in data that may be difficult to find by inspecting the data manually. Unsupervised learning is useful for clustering data that has similar features and uncovering features that are important in the data. On an e-commerce site, products might be clustered based on customers' purchase behavior. If many customers purchase soap, sponges, and towels together, for example, it's likely that more customers would want that combination of products, so soap, sponges, and towels would be clustered and recommended to new customers.

Reinforcement learning

Reinforcement learning is inspired by behavioral psychology; it operates by rewarding or punishing an algorithm based on its actions in an environment. It has similarities to supervised learning and unsupervised learning as well as many differences from them. Reinforcement learning aims to train an agent in an environment based on rewards and penalties. Imagine rewarding a pet for good behavior with treats; the more it's rewarded for a specific behavior, the more it exhibits that behavior. We discuss reinforcement learning in chapter 10.

Following a machine-learning workflow

Machine learning isn't just about algorithms; it's often about the context of the data, the preparation of the data, and the questions that are asked. We can find questions in two ways:

- *We can solve a problem with machine learning by collecting the right data.* Suppose that a bank has a vast amount of data on legitimate and fraudulent transactions, and it wants to train a model with this question: "Can we detect fraudulent transactions in real time?"
- *We can use data in a specific context to solve several problems.* An agriculture company might have data about the weather and soil content in different areas, as well as the nutrition that various plants require. The company might ask this question: "What correlations and relationships can we find among the different types of data?" Finding these relationships may inform a more concrete question, such as "Can we determine the best location to grow a specific plant based on the weather and soil in that location?"

Think of the machine learning life cycle as being like cooking stew, which involves the following steps:

1. *Collect data.* You go to the market to buy ingredients. You need fresh, high-quality produce (data) to make a good meal.
2. *Prepare the data.* You wash vegetables, peel potatoes, and chop onions. You can't throw raw, dirty ingredients into the pot; you have to clean and format them first.
3. *Train the model.* This step is the actual cooking process. You combine ingredients, apply heat, and taste the stew.
4. *Test the model.* You serve the stew to a customer. Do they like it? Is it too salty?
5. *Improve accuracy.* You adjust the recipe based on customer feedback. Next time, you might add less salt or cook the stew longer.

Figure 8.4 provides a simplified view of the steps involved in a typical machine learning endeavor. This workflow is iterative; you'll often return to previous steps to refine your data or model based on the results.

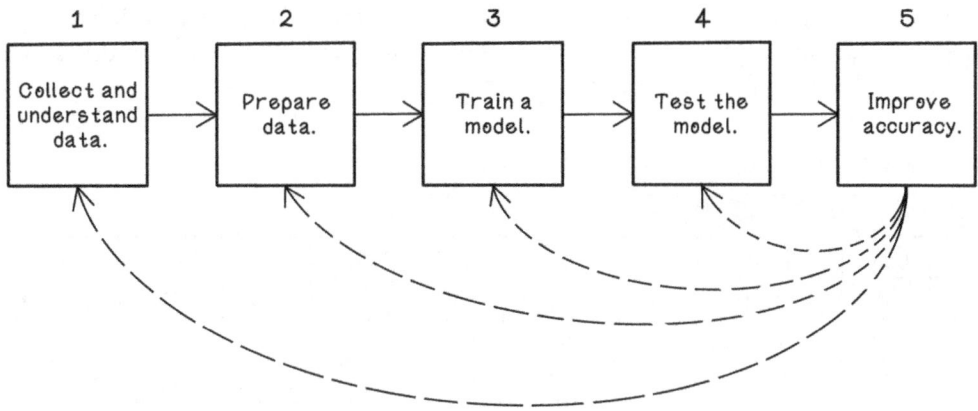

Figure 8.4 A workflow for machine learning experiments and projects

Collecting and understanding data

Collecting and understanding the data you're working with is of paramount importance to a successful machine learning endeavor. If you're working in a specific area in the finance industry, knowing the terms, processes, and data of that industry is important for sourcing the data that best answers questions for the goal you're trying to achieve. If you want to build a fraud-detection system, for example, understanding what data about transactions is stored and what it means is critical for identifying fraudulent transactions. You may also need to source data from various systems and combine it effectively. Sometimes, the data you use is augmented by data from outside the organization to enhance accuracy. In this section, an example dataset on diamond measurements helps you understand the machine learning workflow and explore various algorithms (figure 8.5).

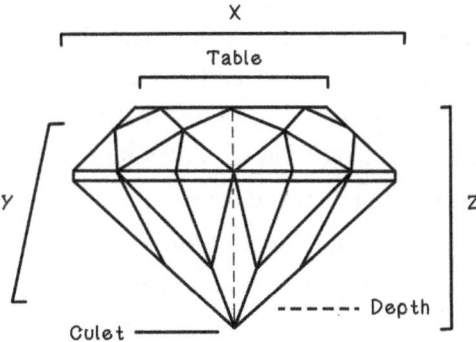

Figure 8.5 Terminology of diamond measurements

Table 8.1 describes several diamonds and their properties. X, Y, and Z describe the length, width, and depth of the diamond in millimeters; Price is specified in U.S. dollars. The examples use only a subset of data.

Table 8.1 The diamond dataset

	Carat	Cut	Color	Clarity	Depth	Table	Price	X	Y	Z
1	0.30	Good	J	SI1	64.0	55	339	4.25	4.28	2.73
2	0.41	Ideal	I	SI1	61.7	55	561	4.77	4.80	2.95
3	0.75	Very good	D	SI1	63.2	56	2,760	5.80	5.75	3.65
4	0.91	Fair	H	SI2	65.7	60	2,763	6.03	5.99	3.95
5	1.20	Fair	F	I1	64.6	56	2,809	6.73	6.66	4.33
6	1.31	Premium	J	SI2	59.7	59	3,697	7.06	7.01	4.20
7	1.50	Premium	H	I1	62.9	60	4,022	7.31	7.22	4.57
8	1.74	Very good	H	I1	63.2	55	4,677	7.62	7.59	4.80
9	1.96	Fair	I	I1	66.8	55	6,147	7.62	7.60	5.08
10	2.21	Premium	H	I1	62.2	58	6,535	8.31	8.27	5.16

The diamond dataset consists of 10 columns of data, called features. The full dataset has more than 50,000 rows. Here's what each feature means:

- *Carat*—The weight of the diamond. 1 Carat equals 200 mg.
- *Cut*—The quality of the diamond: fair, good, very good, premium, or ideal.
- *Color*—The color of the diamond, ranging from D to J, where D is the best color and J is the worst. D indicates a clear diamond, and J indicates a foggy one.
- *Clarity*—The imperfections of the diamond, by decreasing quality: FL, IF, VVS1, VVS2, VS1, VS2, SI1, SI2, I1, I2, and I3. (Don't worry about understanding these code names; they simply represent different levels of perfection.)
- *Depth*—The percentage of depth, measured from the culet to the table of the diamond. Typically, the table-to-depth ratio is important for the sparkle aesthetic of a diamond.
- *Table*—The percentage of the flat end of the diamond relative to the *x* dimension.
- *Price*—The price of the diamond when it was sold.
- *X*—The *x* dimension of the diamond, in millimeters.
- *Y*—The *y* dimension of the diamond, in millimeters.
- *Z*—The *z* dimension of the diamond, in millimeters.

Keep this dataset in mind. We'll use it to see how machine learning algorithms prepare and process data.

Preparing data: Clean and wrangle

Real-world data is never ideal to work with. Data may be sourced from a variety of systems and organizations, which may have different standards and rules for data integrity. You'll always encounter missing data, inconsistent data, and data in a format that's difficult for the algorithms you want to use.

Table 8.2 shows the sample diamond dataset with missing and inconsistent data. It's important to understand that the columns are the features of the data and each row is an example.

Table 8.2 The diamond dataset with missing and inconsistent data

	Carat	Cut	Color	Clarity	Depth	Table	Price	X	Y	Z
1	0.30	Good	J	SI1	64.0	55	339	4.25	4.28	2.73
2	0.41	Ideal	I	si1	61.7	55	561	4.77	4.80	2.95
3	0.75	Very good	D	SI1	63.2	56	2,760	5.80	5.75	3.65
4	0.91	–	H	SI2	–	60	2,763	6.03	5.99	3.95
5	1.20	Fair	F	I1	64.6	56	2,809	6.73	6.66	4.33
6	1.21	Good	E	I1	57.2	62	3,144	7.01	6.96	3.99
7	1.31	Premium	J	SI2	59.7	59	3,697	7.06	7.01	4.20
8	1.50	Premium	H	I1	62.9	60	4,022	7.31	7.22	4.57
9	1.74	Very good	H	i1	63.2	55	4,677	7.62	7.59	4.80
10	1.83	fair	J	I1	70.0	58	5,083	7.34	7.28	5.12
11	1.96	Fair	I	I1	66.8	55	6,147	7.62	7.60	5.08
12	–	Premium	H	i1	62.2	–	6,535	8.31	–	5.16

Missing data

In table 8.2, example 4 is missing values for the Cut and Depth features, and example 12 is missing values for Carat, Table, and Y. To compare examples, we must have complete understanding of the data, and missing values make it difficult to achieve complete understanding. One goal of a machine learning project might be to estimate these values. Assume that missing data will be problematic. Here are some ways to deal with missing data:

- *Remove missing data.* Remove the examples that have missing values for features—in this case, example 4 (table 8.3). The benefit of this approach is that the data is more reliable because nothing is assumed. But the removed examples may be important to the goal we're trying to achieve.

Table 8.3 The diamond dataset with missing data: Removing examples

	Carat	Cut	Color	Clarity	Depth	Table	Price	X	Y	Z
1	0.30	Good	J	SI1	64.0	55	339	4.25	4.28	2.73
2	0.41	Ideal	I	si1	61.7	55	561	4.77	4.80	2.95
3	0.75	Very good	D	SI1	63.2	56	2,760	5.80	5.75	3.65
4	0.91	–	H	SI2	–	60	2,763	6.03	5.99	3.95
5	1.20	Fair	F	I1	64.6	56	2,809	6.73	6.66	4.33
6	1.21	Good	E	I1	57.2	62	3,144	7.01	6.96	3.99
7	1.31	Premium	J	SI2	59.7	59	3,697	7.06	7.01	4.20
8	1.50	Premium	H	I1	62.9	60	4,022	7.31	7.22	4.57
9	1.74	Very good	H	i1	63.2	55	4,677	7.62	7.59	4.80
10	1.83	fair	J	I1	70.0	58	5,083	7.34	7.28	5.12
11	1.96	Fair	I	I1	66.8	55	6,147	7.62	7.60	5.08
12	–	Premium	H	i1	62.2	–	6,535	8.31	–	5.16

- *Replace missing data with a mean or median.* Another option is to replace the missing values with the mean or median of the respective feature. The *mean* is the average calculated by adding all the values and dividing by the number of examples. The *median* is calculated by ordering the examples by ascending value and choosing the value in the middle.

  Using the mean is easy and efficient but doesn't take into account possible correlations between features. Also, you can't use this approach with categorical features such as the Cut, Clarity, and Depth features of the diamond dataset (table 8.4).

Table 8.4 The diamond dataset with missing data: Using mean values

	Carat	Cut	Color	Clarity	Depth	Table	Price	X	Y	Z
1	0.30	Good	J	SI1	64.0	55	339	4.25	4.28	2.73
2	0.41	Ideal	I	si1	61.7	55	561	4.77	4.80	2.95
3	0.75	Very good	D	SI1	63.2	56	2,760	5.80	5.75	3.65
4	~~0.91~~	–	~~H~~	~~SI2~~	–	~~60~~	~~2,763~~	~~6.03~~	~~5.99~~	~~3.95~~
5	1.20	Fair	F	I1	64.6	56	2,809	6.73	6.66	4.33
6	1.21	Good	E	I1	57.2	62	3,144	7.01	6.96	3.99
7	1.31	Premium	J	SI2	59.7	59	3,697	7.06	7.01	4.20
8	1.50	Premium	H	I1	62.9	60	4,022	7.31	7.22	4.57
9	1.74	Very good	H	i1	63.2	55	4,677	7.62	7.59	4.80
10	1.83	fair	J	I1	70.0	58	5,083	7.34	7.28	5.12
11	1.96	Fair	I	I1	66.8	55	6,147	7.62	7.60	5.08
12	**1.19**	Premium	H	i1	62.2	**57**	6,535	8.31	**6.47**	5.16

To calculate the mean of the Table feature, add every available value and divide the total by the number of values used:

```
Table mean = (55 + 55 + 56 + 60 + 56 + 62 + 59 + 60 + 55 + 58 + 55) / 11
Table mean = 631 / 11
Table mean = 57.364
```

Using the Table mean for the missing values seems to make sense because table size doesn't seem to differ radically. But there could be correlations that we don't see, such as the relationship between the table size and the width of the diamond (x dimension).

On the other hand, using the Carat mean makes no sense because we see a correlation between the Carat feature and the Price feature if we plot the data on a graph. The Price seems to increase as the Carat value increases.

- *Replace missing data with the mode.* You can replace the missing values with the value that occurs most often for that feature, known as the *mode* of the data. This approach works well for categorical features but doesn't take into account possible correlations among features, and it can introduce bias by using the values that occur most frequently.
- *(Advanced) Take a statistical approach.* Use k-nearest neighbors (KNN) or neural networks. KNN uses many features of the data to find an estimated value. Like KNN,

a neural network can predict the missing values accurately given enough data. Both algorithms are computationally expensive for handling missing data, however.

- *(Advanced) Do nothing.* Some algorithms, such as XGBoost, handle missing data without preparation, but the algorithms we'll explore in this chapter will fail.

Ambiguous values

Another problem is values that mean the same thing but are represented differently. Examples in the diamond dataset are rows 2, 9, 10, and 12. The values for the Cut and Clarity features are lowercase instead of uppercase. We know this only because we understand these features and their possible values. Without this knowledge, we might see "Fair" and "fair" as different categories. To fix this problem, we can standardize the values to uppercase or lowercase to maintain consistency (table 8.5).

Table 8.5 The diamond dataset with ambiguous data: Standardizing values

	Carat	Cut	Color	Clarity	Depth	Table	Price	X	Y	Z
1	0.30	Good	J	SI1	64.0	55	339	4.25	4.28	2.73
2	0.41	Ideal	I	SI1	61.7	55	561	4.77	4.80	2.95
3	0.75	Very good	D	SI1	63.2	56	2,760	5.80	5.75	3.65
4	0.91	–	H	SI2	–	60	2,763	6.03	5.99	3.95
5	1.20	Fair	F	I1	64.6	56	2,809	6.73	6.66	4.33
6	1.21	Good	E	I1	57.2	62	3,144	7.01	6.96	3.99
7	1.31	Premium	J	SI2	59.7	59	3,697	7.06	7.01	4.20
8	1.50	Premium	H	I1	62.9	60	4,022	7.31	7.22	4.57
9	1.74	Very good	H	I1	63.2	55	4,677	7.62	7.59	4.80
10	1.83	Fair	J	I1	70.0	58	5,083	7.34	7.28	5.12
11	1.96	Fair	I	I1	66.8	55	6,147	7.62	7.60	5.08
12	1.19	Premium	H	I1	62.2	57	6,535	8.31	6.47	5.16

Encoding categorical data

Because computers and statistical models work with numeric values, we'll have a problem modeling string values and categorical values such as Fair, Good, SI1, and I1. We need to represent these categorical values as numerical values. Here are ways to accomplish this task:

- *One-hot encoding*—Think of one-hot encoding as using switches, all but one of which are off. The one that's on represents the presence of the feature at that position. If we represent Cut with one-hot encoding, the Cut feature becomes five features, and each value is 0 except the one that represents the Cut value for each example. The other features have been removed from table 8.6 in the interest of space.

Table 8.6 The diamond dataset with one-hot-encoded values

	Carat	Cut: Fair	Cut: Good	Cut: Very Good	Cut: Premium	Cut: Ideal
1	0.30	0	1	0	0	0
2	0.41	0	0	0	0	1
3	0.75	0	0	1	0	0
4	0.91	0	0	0	0	0
5	1.20	1	0	0	0	0
6	1.21	0	1	0	0	0
7	1.31	0	0	0	1	0
8	1.50	0	0	0	1	0
9	1.74	0	0	1	0	0
10	1.83	1	0	0	0	0
11	1.96	1	0	0	0	0
12	1.19	0	0	0	1	0

- *Label encoding*—Label encoding represents each category as a number between 0 and the number of categories. Use this approach only for ratings or rating-related labels; otherwise, the model you're training will assume that the number carries weight for the example and can introduce unintended bias.

Exercise: Identify and fix the problem data in this example

Decide which data preparation techniques can fix the following dataset. Decide which rows to delete, what values to use the mean for, and how to encode categorical values. Note: the dataset in this exercise is slightly different from the ones you've worked with so far.

	Carat	Origin	Depth	Table	Price	X	Y	Z
1	0.35	South Africa	64.0	55	450	4.25	–	2.73
2	0.42	Canada	61.7	55	680	–	4.80	2.95
3	0.87	Canada	63.2	56	2,689	5.80	5.75	3.65
4	0.99	Botswana	65.7	–	2,734	6.03	5.99	3.95
5	1.34	Botswana	64.6	56	2,901	6.73	6.66	–
6	1.45	South Africa	59.7	59	3,723	7.06	7.01	4.20
7	1.65	Botswana	62.9	60	4,245	7.31	7.22	4.57
8	1.79	–	63.2	55	4,734	7.62	7.59	4.80
9	1.81	Botswana	66.8	55	6,093	7.62	7.60	5.08
10	2.01	South Africa	62.2	58	7,452	8.31	8.27	5.16

Solution:

One approach for fixing this dataset involves the following three tasks:

- *Remove row 8 due to missing Origin.* We don't know what the dataset will be used for. If the Origin feature is important and this row is removed after cleanup, problems may result. Alternatively, we could estimate the value of this feature if it has a relationship with other features.

- *Use one-hot encoding to encode the Origin value.* Earlier, we used label encoding to convert string values to numeric values. This approach worked because the values indicated more superior Cut, Clarity, or Color. In the case of Origin, the value identifies where the diamond was sourced. By using label encoding, we introduce bias to the dataset because no Origin location is better than any other in this dataset.

- *Find the mean for missing values.* Rows 1, 2, 4, and 5 are missing values for Y, X, Table, and Z, respectively. Using a mean value should be a good technique because the dimensions and table features are related.

Testing and training data

Before we jump into training a linear regression model, we must ensure that we have data to teach (train) the model, as well as some data to test how well it does in predicting new examples. Think back to the Apartment-Finding Problem. After gaining a feel for the attributes that affect price, we could make a price prediction by looking at the distance and number of rooms. For this example, we'll use a new table as training data because we have more real-world data to use for testing later.

Training a model: Predict with linear regression

Choosing an algorithm to use is based largely on two factors: the question being asked and the nature of the available data. If the question is to make a prediction about the Price of a diamond with a specific Carat weight, regression algorithms can be useful. The algorithm choice also depends on the number of features in the dataset and the relationships among those features. If the data has many dimensions (many features to consider to make a prediction), we can consider several algorithms and approaches.

Regression means predicting a continuous value, such as the Price or Carat of the diamond. *Continuous* means that the values can be any number in a range. The price $2,271, for example, is a continuous value between 0 and the maximum price of any diamond that regression can help predict.

Linear regression is one of the simplest machine learning algorithms: it finds relationships between two variables and allows us to predict one variable given the other. An example is predicting the Price of a diamond based on its Carat value. By looking at many examples of known diamonds, including their Price and Carat values, we can teach a model the relationship and ask it to make predictions.

Fitting a line to the data

Let's try to find a trend in the data and attempt to make some predictions. To explore linear regression, the question we're asking is "Is there a correlation between the Carats of a diamond and its Price, and if so, can we make accurate predictions?"

We start by isolating the Carat and Price features and plotting the data on a graph. Because we want to find the Price based on Carat value, we'll treat Carats as x and Price as y:

- *Carat is the independent variable (x).* An *independent variable* is one that is changed in an experiment to determine the effect on a dependent variable. In this example, the value for Carats is adjusted to determine the Price of a diamond with that value.
- *Price as the dependent variable (y).* A *dependent variable* is one that is being tested. It's affected by the independent variable and changes based on the independent variable's

value changes. For our example, we're interested in the Price given a specific Carat value.

Figure 8.6 shows the Carat and Price data plotted on a graph. Table 8.7 describes the data.

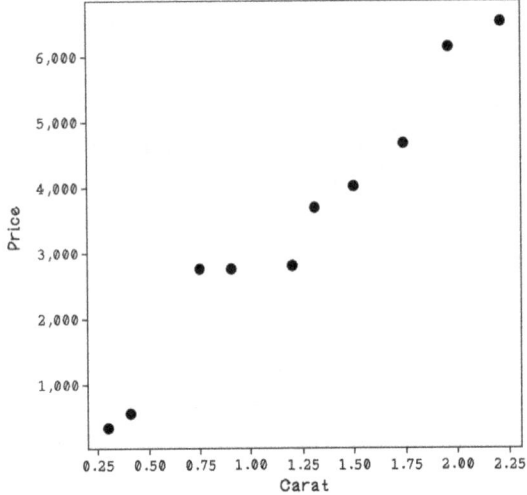

Table 8.7 Carat and Price data

	Carat (x)	Price (y)
1	0.30	339
2	0.41	561
3	0.75	2,760
4	0.91	2,763
5	1.20	2,809
6	1.31	3,697
7	1.50	4,022
8	1.74	4,677
9	1.96	6,147
10	2.21	6,535

Figure 8.6 A scatter plot of Carat and Price data

Notice that compared with Price, the Carat values are tiny. The Price goes into the thousands, and Carats are in the range of decimals. To make the calculations easier to understand for the purposes of learning in this chapter, we can scale the Carat values to be comparable to the Price values. By multiplying every Carat value by 1,000, we get numbers that are easier to compute manually in the upcoming walk-throughs. By scaling all the rows, we're not affecting the relationships in the data because every example has the same operation applied to it. The resulting data (figure 8.7) is represented in table 8.8.

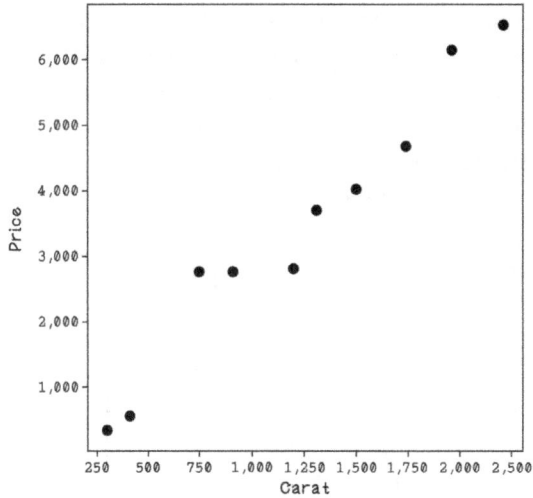

Table 8.8 Data with adjusted Carat values

	Carat (x)	Price (y)
1	300	339
2	410	561
3	750	2,760
4	910	2,763
5	1,200	2,809
6	1,310	3,697
7	1,500	4,022
8	1,740	4,677
9	1,960	6,147
10	2,210	6,535

Figure 8.7 A scatter plot of Carat and Price data

Finding the mean of the features

The first step in finding a regression line is finding the mean (the sum of all values divided by the number of values) for each feature. The mean is 1,229 for Carats, represented by the vertical line on the *x* axis. The mean is $3,431 for Price, represented by the horizontal line on the *y* axis (figure 8.8).

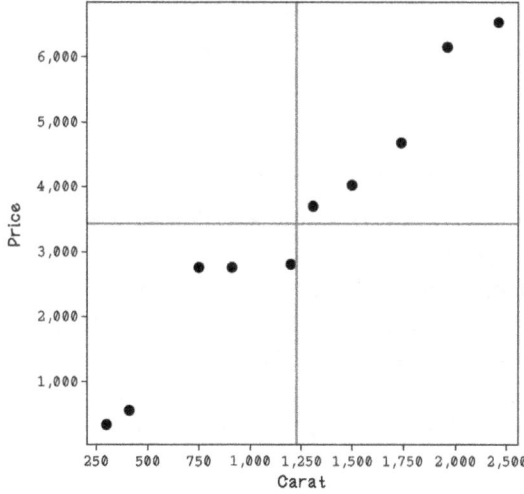

Figure 8.8 The means of *x* and *y* represented by vertical and horizontal lines

The mean is important because mathematically, any regression line we find will pass through the intersection of the mean of x and the mean of y. Many lines may pass through this point. Some regression lines may be better than others at fitting the data. The *least-squares method* aims to create a line that minimizes the distances between the line and among all the points in the dataset. This method is a popular one for finding regression lines. Figure 8.9 shows examples of regression lines.

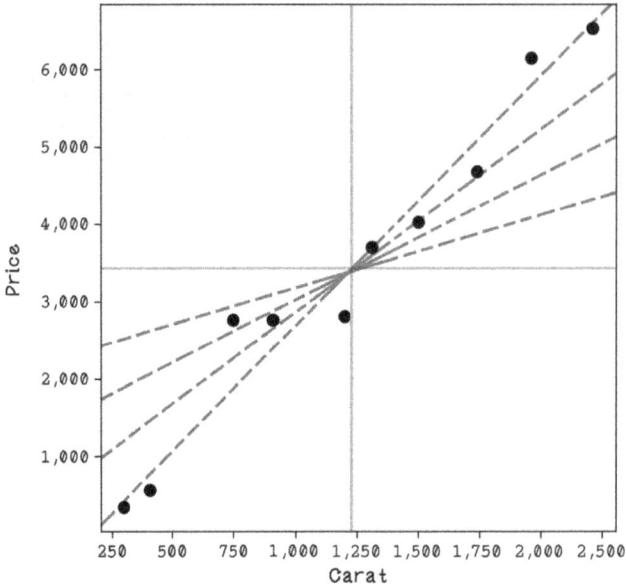

Possible regression lines

Figure 8.9 Possible regression lines

Finding regression lines with the least-squares method

But what is the regression line's purpose? Suppose that we're building a subway as close as possible to all major office buildings. It won't be feasible to have a subway line that visits every building; that plan would require too many stations and cost a lot. Instead, we'll try to create a straight-line route that minimizes the distance to each building. Some commuters may have to walk farther than others, but the straight line is optimized for everyone's office. This goal is exactly what a regression line aims to achieve. The buildings are data points, and the line is the straight subway path (figure 8.10).

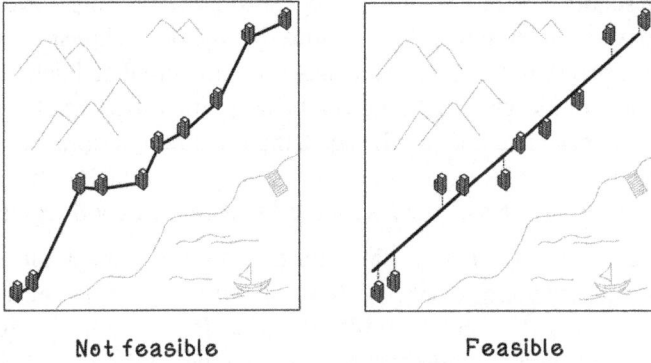

Figure 8.10 Intuition of regression lines

Linear regression always finds a straight line that fits the data to minimize distance among points overall. Understanding the equation for a line is important because we'll be learning how to find the values for the variables that describe a line. A straight line is represented by the equation $y = c + mx$ (figure 8.11):

- y—Dependent variable
- x—Independent variable
- m—Slope of the line
- c—y-value where the line intercepts the y axis

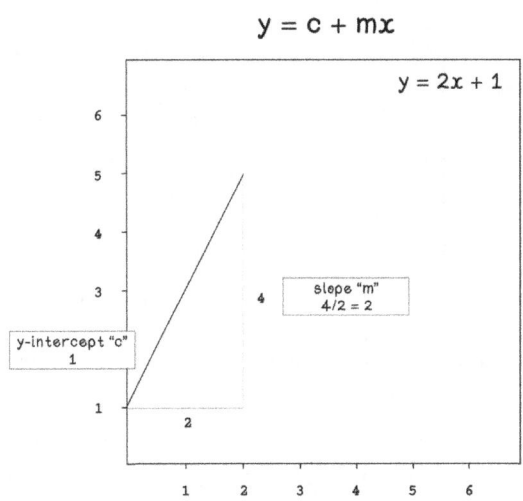

Figure 8.11 Intuition of the equation that represents a line

We use the least-squares method to find the regression line. At a high level, the process involves the steps depicted in figure 8.12. To find the line that's closest to the data, we find the difference between the actual data values and the predicted data values. The differences for data points will vary: some will be large and others will be small; some will be negative and others will be positive. By squaring the differences and summing them, we take into consideration all differences for all data points. Minimizing this sum of squared differences is the goal of the least-squares method to achieve a good regression line.

Imagine drawing a line through your data points. Now, for every point, draw a perfect square that connects the point to the line. Some squares will be tiny and others may be huge. The algorithm's goal is to minimize the total area of all these squares, which is why it's called least-squares. It also explains why a single outlier is so dangerous. A point 10 units away doesn't just add 10 to the error; it also creates a massive square of 100, forcing the line to move dramatically to shrink it.

Figure 8.12 illustrates the process. Don't worry if the figure looks a bit daunting; we'll work through each step.

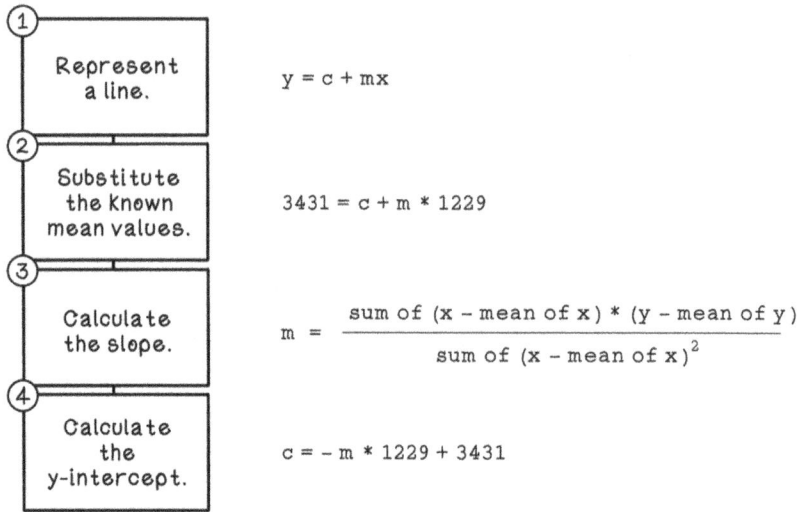

Figure 8.12 The basic workflow for calculating a regression line

Thus far, our line has some known variables. We know that an x value is 1,229 and a y value is 3,431, for example, as shown in step 2.

Next, we calculate the difference between every Carat value and the Carat mean, as well as the difference between every Price value and the Price mean, to find (x – mean of x) and (y – mean of y), which is used in step 3 (table 8.9).

Table 8.9 The diamond dataset and calculations, part 1

	Carat (*x*)	Price (*y*)	*x* – mean of *x*		*y* – mean of *y*	
1	300	339	300 – 1,229	-929	339 – 3,431	-3,092
2	410	561	410 – 1,229	-819	561 – 3,431	-2,870
3	750	2,760	750 – 1,229	-479	2,760 – 3,431	-671
4	910	2,763	910 – 1,229	-319	2,763 – 3,431	-668
5	1,200	2,809	1,200 – 1,229	-29	2,809 – 3,431	-622
6	1,310	3,697	1,310 – 1,229	81	3,697 – 3,431	266
7	1,500	4,022	1,500 – 1,229	271	4,022 – 3,431	591
8	1,740	4,677	1,740 – 1,229	511	4,677 – 3,431	1,246
9	1,960	6,147	1,960 – 1,229	731	6,147 – 3,431	2,716
10	2,210	6,535	2,210 – 1,229	981	6,535 – 3,431	3,104
	1,229	3,431				
	Means					

For step 3, we also need to calculate the square of the difference between every Carat and the Carat mean to find $(x - \text{mean of } x)^2$. We also need to sum these values to minimize, which equals 3,703,690 (table 8.10).

Table 8.10 The diamond dataset and calculations, part 2

	Carat (*x*)	Price (*y*)	*x* – mean of *x*		*y* – mean of *y*		$(x - \text{mean of } x)^2$
1	300	339	300 – 1,229	-929	339 – 3,431	-3,092	863,041
2	410	561	410 – 1,229	-819	561 – 3,431	-2,870	670,761
3	750	2,760	750 – 1,229	-479	2,760 – 3,431	-671	229,441
4	910	2,763	910 – 1,229	-319	2,763 – 3,431	-668	101,761
5	1,200	2,809	2,100 – 1,229	-29	2,809 – 3,431	-622	841
6	1,310	3,697	1,310 – 1,229	81	3,697 – 3,431	266	6,561
7	1,500	4,022	1,500 – 1,229	271	4,022 – 3,431	591	73,441
8	1,740	4,677	1,740 – 1,229	511	4,677 – 3,431	1,246	261,121
9	1,960	6,147	1,960 – 1,229	731	6,147 – 3,431	2,716	534,361
10	2,210	6,535	2,210 – 1,229	981	6,535 – 3,431	3,104	962,361
	1,229	3,431					3,703,690
	Means						Sums

The last missing value for the equation in step 3 is the value of $(x - \text{mean of } x) * (y - \text{mean of } y)$. Again, the sum of the values is required. The sum equals 11,624,370 (table 8.11).

Table 8.11 The diamond dataset and calculations, part 3

	Carat (x)	Price (y)	x – mean of x		y – mean of y		(x – mean of x)²	(x – mean of x) * (y – mean of y)
1	300	339	300 – 1,229	-929	339 – 3,431	-3,092	863,041	2,872,468
2	410	561	410 – 1,229	-819	561 – 3,431	-2,870	670,761	2,350,530
3	750	2,760	750 – 1,229	-479	2,760 – 3,431	-671	229,441	321,409
4	910	2,763	910 – 1,229	-319	2,763 – 3,431	-668	101,761	213,092
5	1,200	2,809	2,100 – 1,229	-29	2,809 – 3,431	-622	841	18,038
6	1,310	3,697	1,310 – 1,229	81	3,697 – 3,431	266	6,561	21,546
7	1,500	4,022	1,500 – 1,229	271	4,022 – 3,431	591	73,441	160,161
8	1,740	4,677	1,740 – 1,229	511	4,677 – 3,431	1,246	261,121	636,706
9	1,960	6,147	1,960 – 1,229	731	6,147 – 3,431	2,716	534,361	1,985,396
10	2,210	6,535	2,210 – 1,229	981	6,535 – 3,431	3,104	962,361	3,045,024
	1,229	3,431					3,703,690	11,624,370
	Means						Sums	

Now we can plug the calculated values into the least-squares equation to calculate m:

```
m = 11624370 / 3703690
m = 3.139
```

Now that we have a value for m, we can calculate c by substituting the mean values for x and y. Remember that all regression lines will pass this point, so it's a known point within the regression line:

```
y = c + mx

3431 = c + 0.3186x
3431 = c + 391.5594
3431 – 391.5594 = c
c = 3,039.4406

Complete regression line:

y = 3039.4406 + 0.3186x
```

Finally, we can plot the line by generating some values for Carats between the minimum and maximum values, plugging them into the equation that represents the regression line, and then plotting the line (figure 8.13):

```
x (Carat) minimum = 300
x (Carat) maximum = 2210

Sample between the minimum and maximum at intervals of 500:
x = [300, 2210]

Plug the values for x into the regression line:
y = [-426 + 3.139(300) = 515.7,
     -426 + 3.139(2210) = 6511.19]


Complete x and y samples:
x = [300, 2210]
y = [3981, 9975]
```

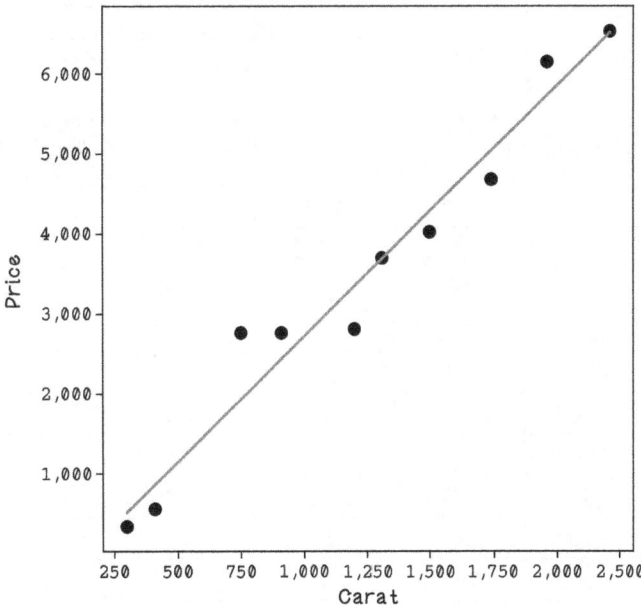

Figure 8.13 A regression line plotted with the data points

We've trained a linear regression line based on our dataset that fits the data accurately. As a result, we've done some machine learning by hand!

Exercise: Calculate a regression line using the least-squares method

Following the steps described in this section and using the following dataset, calculate the regression line with the least-squares method.

	Carat (x)	Price (y)
1	320	350
2	460	560
3	800	2,760
4	910	2,800
5	1,350	2,900
6	1,390	3,600
7	1,650	4,000
8	1,700	4,650
9	1,950	6,100
10	2,000	6,500

Solution:

First, calculate the means for each dimension. The means are 1,253 for x and 3,422 for y. Then calculate the difference between each value and its mean. Next, calculate and sum the square of the difference between x and the mean of x, which results in 3,251,610. Finally, multiply and sum the difference between x and the mean of x by the difference between y and the mean of y, which results in 10,566,940.

	Carat (x)	Price (y)	x – mean of x	y – mean of y	(x – mean of x)²	(x – mean of x) * (y – mean of y)
1	320	350	-933	-3,072	870,489	2,866,176
2	460	560	-793	-2,862	628,849	2,269,566
3	800	2,760	-453	-662	205,209	299,886
4	910	2,800	-343	-622	117,649	213,346
5	1,350	2,900	97	-522	9,409	-50,634
6	1,390	3,600	137	178	18,769	24,386
7	1,650	4,000	397	578	157,609	229,466
8	1,700	4,650	447	1,228	199,809	548,916
9	1,950	6,100	697	2,678	485,809	1,866,566
10	2,000	6,500	747	3,078	558,009	2,299,266
	1,253	3,422			3,251,610	10,566,940

Use these values to calculate the slope, *m*:

```
m = 10566940 / 3251610
m = 3.25
```

Remember the equation for a line:

```
y = c + mx
```

Substitute the mean values for *x* and *y* and the newly calculated *m*:

```
3422 = c + 3.35 * 1253
c = -775.55
```

Substitute the minimum and maximum values for *x* to calculate points to plot a line:

```
Point 1, we use the minimum value for Carat: x = 320
y = 775.55 + 3.25 * 320
y = 1 815.55
Point 2, we use the maximum value for Carat: x = 2000
y = 775.55 + 3.25 * 2000
y = 7 275.55
```

Now that we have an intuition about how to use linear regression and calculate regression lines, let's take a look at the code. The code is similar to the steps that we've walked through. The only interesting aspects are the two `for` loops used to calculate summed values by iterating over every element in the dataset:

Python code sample for fitting a regression line

```python
def fit_regression_line(carats, prices):
    n = len(carats)

    mean_X = sum(carats) / n
    mean_Y = sum(prices) / n

    sum_x_squared = 0
    for x_i in carats:
        ans = (x_i - mean_X) ** 2
        sum_x_squared += ans

    sum_multiple = 0
    for i in range(n):
        ans = (carats[i] - mean_X) * (prices[i] - mean_Y)
        sum_multiple += ans
```

Calculates the average carat size and average price

measures how much the carat values vary from their mean

Calculates how much the carats and prices move together

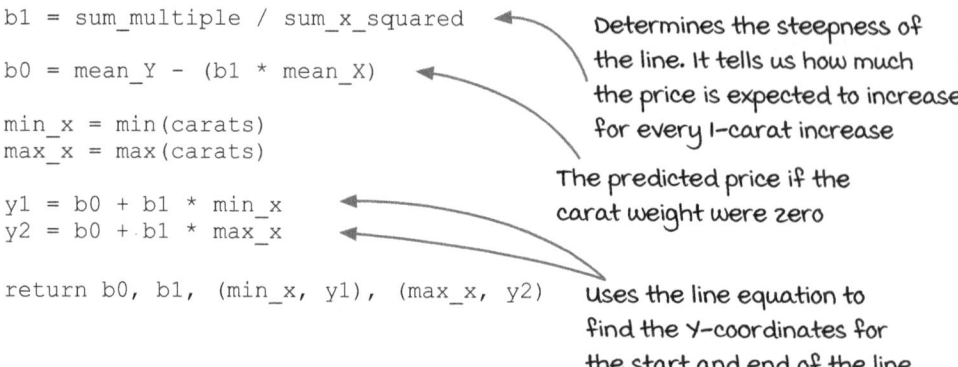

```
b1 = sum_multiple / sum_x_squared

b0 = mean_Y - (b1 * mean_X)

min_x = min(carats)
max_x = max(carats)

y1 = b0 + b1 * min_x
y2 = b0 + b1 * max_x

return b0, b1, (min_x, y1), (max_x, y2)
```

Determines the steepness of the line. It tells us how much the price is expected to increase for every 1-carat increase

The predicted price if the carat weight were zero

Uses the line equation to find the y-coordinates for the start and end of the line

Testing the model: Determine the accuracy of the model

Now that we've determined a regression line, we can use it to make Price predictions for other Carat values. We can measure the performance of the regression line with new examples in which we know the actual Price and determine how accurate the linear regression model is.

We can't test the model with the same data we used to train it because this approach would result in high accuracy and be meaningless. The trained model must be tested with real data that the model hasn't seen before.

Separating training and testing data

Training and testing data are usually split 80/20, with 80% of the available data used as training data and 20% used to test the model. Percentages are used because the number of examples needed to train a model accurately is difficult to know; the contexts and questions being asked may require more or less data.

Figure 8.14 and table 8.12 represent a set of testing data for the diamond example. Remember that we scaled the Carat values to be similar to the Price values (all Carat values have been multiplied by 1,000) to make them easier to read and work with. The dots represent the testing data points, and the line represents the trained regression line.

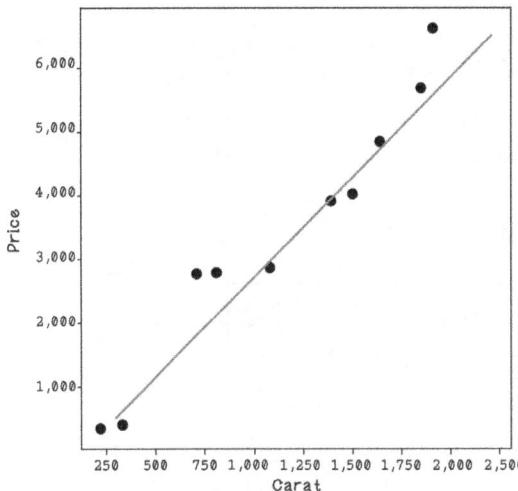

Figure 8.14 A regression line plotted with the data points

Table 8.12 The Carat and Price data

	Carat (x)	Price (y)
1	220	342
2	330	403
3	710	2,772
4	810	2,789
5	1,080	2,869
6	1,390	3,914
7	1,500	4,022
8	1,640	4,849
9	1,850	5,688
10	1,910	6,632

Testing a model involves making predictions with unseen training data and then comparing the accuracy of the model's prediction with the actual values. In the diamond example, we have the actual Price values, so we'll determine what the model predicts and compare the difference.

Measuring the performance of the line

In linear regression, a common method of measuring the accuracy of the model is calculating R^2 (R squared). R^2 is used to determine the variance between the actual value and a predicted value. We use the following equation to calculate the R^2 score:

$$R^2 = \frac{\text{sum of (predicted y - mean of actual y)}^2}{\text{sum of (actual y - mean of actual y)}^2}$$

The first things we need to do, as in the training step, are calculate the mean of the actual Price values, calculate the distances between the actual Price values and the mean of the prices, and then calculate the square of those values (table 8.13). We're using the values plotted as dots in figure 8.14 earlier in the chapter.

Table 8.13 The diamond dataset and calculations

	Carat (x)	Price (y)	y – mean of y	(y – mean of y)²
1	220	342	-3,086	9,523,396
2	330	403	-3,025	9,150,625
3	710	2,772	-656	430,336
4	810	2,789	-639	408,321
5	1,080	2,869	-559	312,481
6	1,390	3,914	486	236,196
7	1,500	4,022	594	352,836
8	1,640	4,849	1,421	2,019,241
9	1,850	5,688	2,260	5,107,600
10	1,910	6,632	3,204	10,265,616
		3,428		37,806,648
		Mean		Sum

The next step is calculating the predicted Price value for every Carat value, squaring the values, and calculating the sum of all those values (table 8.14).

Table 8.14 The diamond dataset and calculations, part 2

	Carat (x)	Price (y)	y – mean of y	(y – mean of y)²	Predicted y	Predicted y – mean of y	(Predicted y – mean of y)²
1	220	342	-3,086	9,523,396	264	-3,164	10,009,876
2	330	403	-3,025	9,150,625	609	-2,819	7,944,471
3	710	2,772	-656	430,336	1,802	-1,626	2,643,645
4	810	2,789	-639	408,321	2,116	-1,312	1,721,527
5	1,080	2,869	-559	312,481	2,963	-465	215,900
6	1,390	3,914	486	236,196	3,936	508	258,382
7	1,500	4,022	594	352,836	4,282	854	728,562
8	1,640	4,849	1,421	2,019,241	4,721	1,293	1,671,748
9	1,850	5,688	2,260	5,107,600	5,380	1,952	3,810,559
10	1,910	6,632	3,204	10,265,616	5,568	2,140	4,581,230
		3,428		37,806,648			33,585,901
		Mean		Sum			Sum

Using the sum of the square of the difference between the predicted Price and mean and the sum of the square of the difference between the actual Price and mean, we can calculate the R^2 score:

$$R^2 = \frac{\text{sum of (predicted y - mean of actual y)}^2}{\text{sum of (actual y - mean of actual y)}^2}$$

$$R^2 = 33585901 \; / \; 37806648$$
$$R^2 = 0,88$$

The result—an R^2 score of 0.88—means that our model explains 88% of the variance in the target variable (diamond Price). In plain English, 88% of the difference in diamond prices can be explained by the features we included (such as weight and cut); the remaining 12% is due to other factors or noise, indicating a strong fit to the data.

This result is a fairly good one, showing that the linear regression model is fairly accurate. For the diamond example, the result is satisfactory. Determining whether the accuracy is satisfactory for the problem we're trying to solve depends on the domain of the problem. (We'll explore the performance of machine learning models in the next section.)

> **TIP** For a gentle introduction to fitting lines to data, see chapter 14 of *Math for Programmers*, by Paul Orland (Manning, 2020; http://mng.bz/Ed5q). Linear regression can be applied to more dimensions. We can determine the relationship among the Carat, Price, and Cut values of diamonds, for example, through a process called *multiple regression*. This process adds some complexity to the calculations, but the fundamental principles remain the same.

Improving accuracy

After training a model on data and measuring how well it performs on new testing data, we have an idea of how well the model performs. Often, models don't perform as well as desired, and we have to do additional work to improve the model, if possible. This improvement involves iterating on the various steps in the machine learning life cycle (figure 8.15).

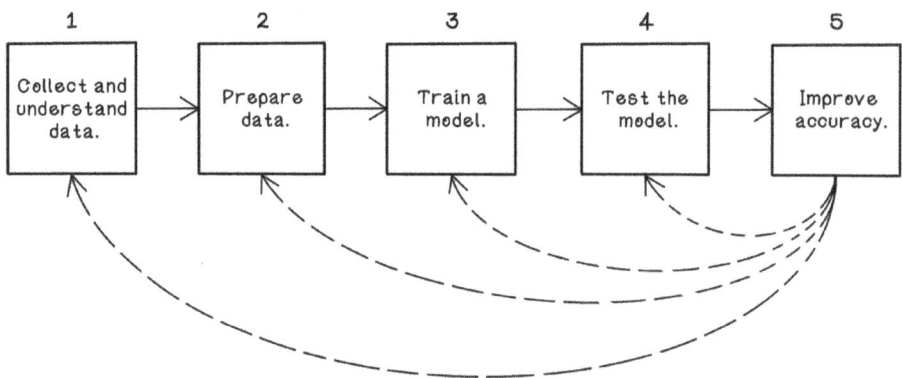

Figure 8.15 A refresher on the machine learning life cycle

The results may require us to pay attention to one or more areas. Machine learning is experimental work in which we test different tactics at various stages before settling on the best-performing approach. In the diamond example, if the model that used Carat values to predict Price values performed poorly, we might use the dimensions of the diamond that indicate size coupled with the Carat value to try to predict the price more accurately. Here are some ways to improve the accuracy of the model:

- *Collect more data.* One solution may be to collect more data related to the dataset that we're exploring, perhaps augmenting the data with relevant external data or including data that we previously didn't consider.

- *Prepare the data differently.* We may have to prepare the data used for training in a different way because the selected approach may create errors. We may have to use different techniques to find values for missing data, replace ambiguous data, and encode categorical data.

- *Choose different features in the data.* Other features in the dataset may be better suited to predicting the dependent variable. The *x*-dimension value may be a good choice to predict the Table value, for example, because it has a physical relationship with it, as shown in the diamond-terminology figure earlier in this chapter (figure 8.5), whereas predicting the Clarity value with the *x* dimension is meaningless.

- *Use a different algorithm to train the model.* Sometimes, the selected algorithm isn't suited to the problem being solved or the nature of the data. We can use a different algorithm to accomplish our goals, as discussed in the next section.

- *Deal with false-positive tests.* When we're checking for generalization, evaluation metrics can be deceptive. A model might achieve a high accuracy score on training data, but when presented with new, unseen data, it might perform poorly. This discrepancy is usually due to overfitting (see the sidebar).

If linear regression didn't provide useful results or if we have a different question to ask, we can try a range of other algorithms. The next section explore algorithms to use for a different question.

Overfitting and underfitting

Overfitting occurs when the model is too closely aligned with the training data and not flexible enough to deal with new data with more variance. Think of overfitting as being like studying for an exam by memorizing the specific answers to the practice test. You might get 100% on the practice test but fail the real exam because the questions are worded slightly differently. By contrast, *underfitting* isn't studying at all; you fail both the practice test and the real one.

If you have a *good fit*, you understand the concepts. You might miss a few distinct details, but you can adapt to solve problems you haven't seen before.

Classification with decision trees

Simply put, *classification problems* involve assigning a label to an example based on its attributes. These problems are different from regression, in which a value is estimated. Let's dive into classification problems and see how to solve them.

Classification problems: This or that

We've learned that regression involves predicting a value based on one or more other variables, such as predicting the Price of a diamond given its Carat value. Classification is similar in that it aims to predict a value but predicts discrete classes instead of continuous values. *Discrete classes* are categorical features of a dataset (such as Cut, Color, and Clarity in the diamond dataset), as opposed to *continuous values* (such as Price and Depth).

Consider another example. Suppose that we have several vehicles: cars and trucks. We measure the weight of each vehicle and the number of wheels on each vehicle. We forget for now that cars and trucks may look very different. Almost all cars have only four wheels, but many large trucks have more than four, for example. Also, trucks are usually heavier than cars, but a large sport-utility vehicle may be as heavy as a small truck. We could find relationships between weight and number of wheels to predict whether a vehicle is a car or a truck (figure 8.16).

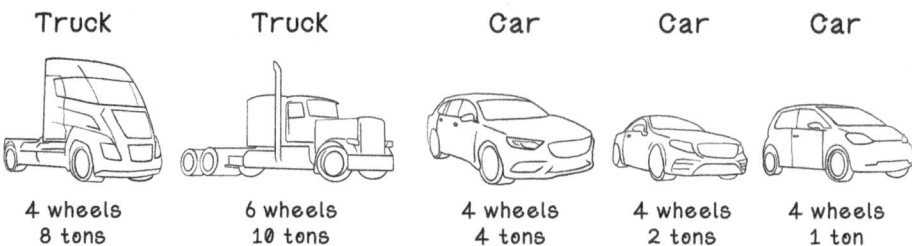

Figure 8.16 Example vehicles for potential classification based on the number of wheels and weight

Exercise: Regression vs. classification

Consider the following scenarios, and determine whether each one is a regression or classification problem:

- Based on data about rats, we have a life-expectancy feature and an obesity feature. We're trying to find a correlation between the two features.
- Based on data about animals, we have the weight of each animal and know whether or not it has wings. We're trying to determine which animals are birds.
- Based on data about computing devices, we have the screen size, weight, and operating system of several devices. We want to determine which devices are tablets, laptops, or phones.
- Based on data about weather, we have the amount of rainfall and a humidity value. We want to determine the humidity in different rainfall seasons.

Let's identify the type of problem for each scenario:

- *Regression*—We're exploring the relationship between two variables. Life expectancy is the dependent variable, and obesity is the independent variable.
- *Classification*—We're classifying an example as a bird or not a bird, using the weight and the wing characteristics of the examples.
- *Classification*—We're classifying an example as a tablet, laptop, or phone by using its other characteristics.
- *Regression*—We're exploring the relationship between rainfall and humidity. Humidity is the dependent variable, and rainfall is the independent variable.

The basics of decision trees

We use different algorithms for regression and classification problems. Some popular algorithms include support vector machines, decision trees, and random forests. In this section, we'll examine a decision-tree algorithm to learn classification. *Decision trees* are structures that describe a series of decisions made to find a solution to a problem (figure 8.17).

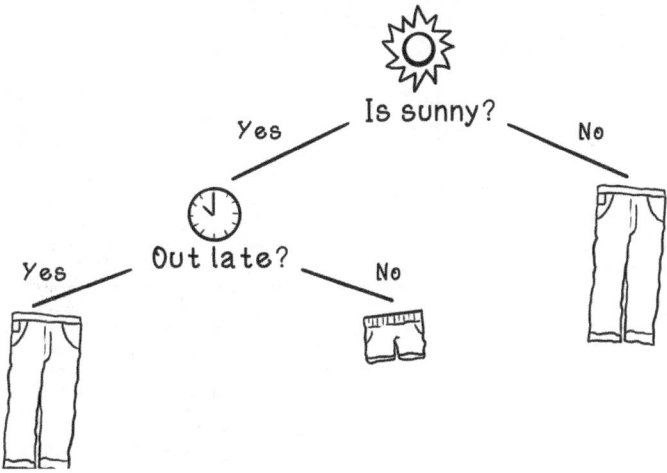

Figure 8.17 Example of a basic decision tree

Working with a decision tree is like playing the guessing game "21 Questions," in which one player thinks of something, and the other player asks questions to narrow their thinking and guess correctly. The algorithm's goal is to win the game in the fewest questions possible by picking one question that eliminates the most wrong answers. Here are examples of bad and good questions:

- *Bad question*—"Is it an object?" (The question splits the data poorly; almost everything is an object.)
- *Good question* —"Is it alive?" (The question splits the data perfectly into living versus nonliving things.)

If we're deciding whether to wear shorts today, for example, we might make a series of decisions to inform the outcome. Will the day be cold? If not, will we be out late in the evening, when it will be cold? We may decide to wear shorts on a warm day but not if we'll be out on a cold evening.

For the diamond example, we'll try to predict the cut of a diamond based on the Carat and Price values by using a decision tree. To simplify this example, assume that we're a diamond dealer who doesn't care about each specific cut. We'll group the cuts into two broader categories. Fair and Good cuts will be grouped in a category called Okay, and Very Good, Premium, and Ideal cuts will be grouped in a category called Perfect. Now our sample dataset looks like table 8.15.

1	Fair	1	Okay
2	Good		
3	Very Good	2	Perfect
4	Premium		
5	Ideal		

Table 8.15 The dataset used for the classification example

	Carat	Price	Cut
1	0.21	327	Okay
2	0.39	897	Perfect
3	0.50	1,122	Perfect
4	0.76	907	Okay
5	0.87	2,757	Okay
6	0.98	2,865	Okay
7	1.13	3,045	Perfect
8	1.34	3,914	Perfect
9	1.67	4,849	Perfect
10	1.81	5,688	Perfect

By looking at the values in this small example and intuitively looking for patterns, we may notice a pattern. The Price seems to spike significantly after 0.98 Carats, and the increased Price seems to correlate with the diamonds that are Perfect, whereas diamonds with smaller Carat values tend to be Okay. But example 3, which is Perfect, has a small Carat value. Figure 8.18 shows what would happen if we create questions to filter the data and categorize it by hand. Decision nodes contain our questions, and leaf nodes contain examples that we've categorized.

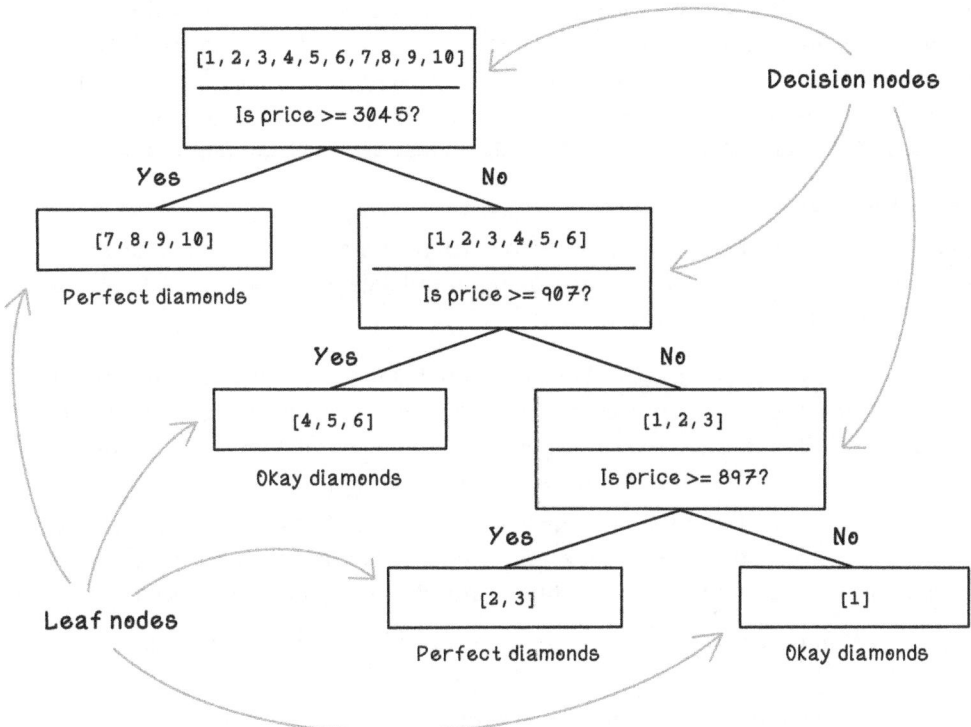

Figure 8.18 Example of a decision tree designed through human intuition

With the small dataset, we could easily categorize the diamonds by hand. Real-world datasets, however, contain thousands of examples to work through and possibly thousands of features, making it close to impossible for a person to create a decision tree by hand.

This situation is where decision-tree algorithms come in. Decision trees can create the questions that filter the examples. A decision tree finds complex patterns that humans might miss and processes data at a scale that humans can't achieve. But raw power doesn't always mean better results. Decision trees are so eager to find patterns that they can easily overfit (memorize) the data unless we apply specific constraints to keep them generalized.

Training decision trees

To create a tree that's intelligent enough to make the right decisions in classifying diamonds, we need a training algorithm to learn from the data. There is a family of algorithms for decision-tree learning, and we'll use a specific one named CART

(Classification and Regression Tree). The foundation of CART and the other tree learning algorithms is this: decide what questions to ask and when to ask those questions to best filter the examples into their respective categories. In the diamond example, the algorithm must learn the best questions to ask about the Carat and Price values, and when to ask them, to best segment Okay and Perfect diamonds.

Data structures for decision trees

To understand how the decisions of the tree will be structured, we can review the following data structures, which organize logic and data in a way that's suitable for the decision-tree learning algorithm:

- *Map of classes/label groupings*—A *map* is a key-value pair of elements that can't have two identical keys. This structure is useful for storing the number of examples that match a specific label and the values required for calculating entropy, also known as *uncertainty*. We'll learn about entropy later in this chapter.
- *Tree of nodes*—As depicted in the preceding tree figure (figure 8.18), several nodes are linked to compose a tree. This example may be familiar from earlier chapters. The nodes in the tree are important for filtering/partitioning the examples into categories:
  - ° *Decision node*—A *decision node* is one in which the dataset is being split or filtered.
    - *Question*—What question is being asked (see the question point below)
    - *True examples*—The examples that satisfy the question
    - *False examples*—The examples that don't satisfy the question
  - ° *Examples node/leaf node*—A node containing a list of examples that belong to a single class. All examples in this list would have been categorized correctly.
  - ° *Question*—A question can be represented differently depending on how flexible it can be. We could ask, "Is the Carat value > 0.5 and < 1.13?" To keep this example simple, the question is a variable feature, a variable value, and the >= operator: "Is Carat >= 0.5?" or "Is Price >=3,045?"
    - *Feature*—The feature that's being interrogated
    - *Value*—The constant value that the comparing value must be greater than or equal to

Decision-tree learning life cycle

This section discusses how a decision-tree algorithm filters data with decisions to classify a dataset correctly. Figure 8.19 shows the steps involved in training a decision tree. The rest of this section describes the flow in the figure.

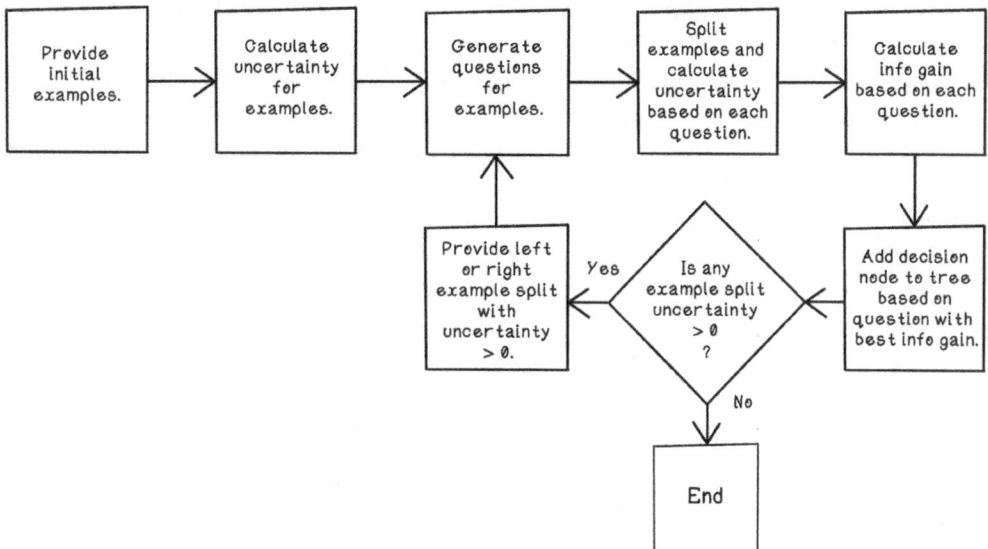

Figure 8.19 A basic flow for building a decision tree

In building a decision tree, we test all possible questions to determine which one is best to ask at a specific point in the decision tree. To test a question, we use the concept of *entropy*—the measurement of uncertainty or impurity in a dataset.

Suppose that you have five Perfect diamonds and five Okay diamonds in a bag (figure 8.20). If you reached into the bag blindly, you'd be totally unsure what you'd get. This 50/50 split represents *high entropy* (maximum disorder).

Figure 8.20 Example of uncertainty

Now imagine a pile of 10 Perfect diamonds and 0 Okay diamonds. Zero surprise is involved; you know exactly what you're getting. This is *low entropy* (zero disorder). The goal of a decision tree is to ask questions that split the data to reduce entropy, moving us from a messy, mixed state to a clean, pure state.

Given an initial dataset of diamonds with the Carat, Price, and Cut features, we can determine the uncertainty of the dataset by using the Gini index—a metric that measures the impurity or messiness of the data. A Gini index of 0 means the dataset has no uncertainty and is pure; it might have 10 Perfect diamonds, for example. Figure 8.21 shows how the Gini index is calculated. The Gini index is 0.5, so there's a 50% chance of choosing an incorrectly labeled example if one is selected randomly, as shown in figure 8.20 earlier.

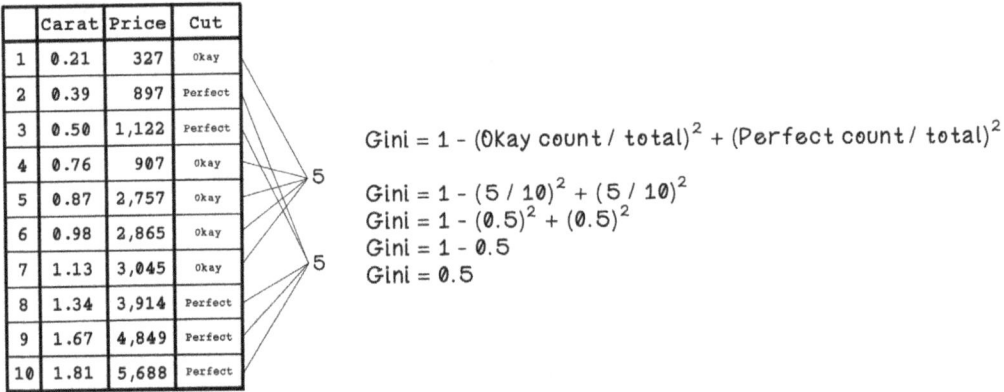

$$Gini = 1 - (Okay\ count\ /\ total)^2 + (Perfect\ count\ /\ total)^2$$

$$Gini = 1 - (5\ /\ 10)^2 + (5\ /\ 10)^2$$
$$Gini = 1 - (0.5)^2 + (0.5)^2$$
$$Gini = 1 - 0.5$$
$$Gini = 0.5$$

Figure 8.21 The Gini index calculation

The next step is creating a decision node to split the data. The decision node includes a question we can use to split the data in a sensible way and decrease uncertainty. Remember that 0 means no uncertainty. We aim to partition the dataset into subsets with zero uncertainty.

Many questions are generated based on every feature of each example to split the data and determine the best split outcome. Because we have 2 features and 10 examples, the total number of questions generated would be 20. Figure 8.22 shows some of the questions asked—simple questions about whether the value of a feature is greater than or equal to a specific value.

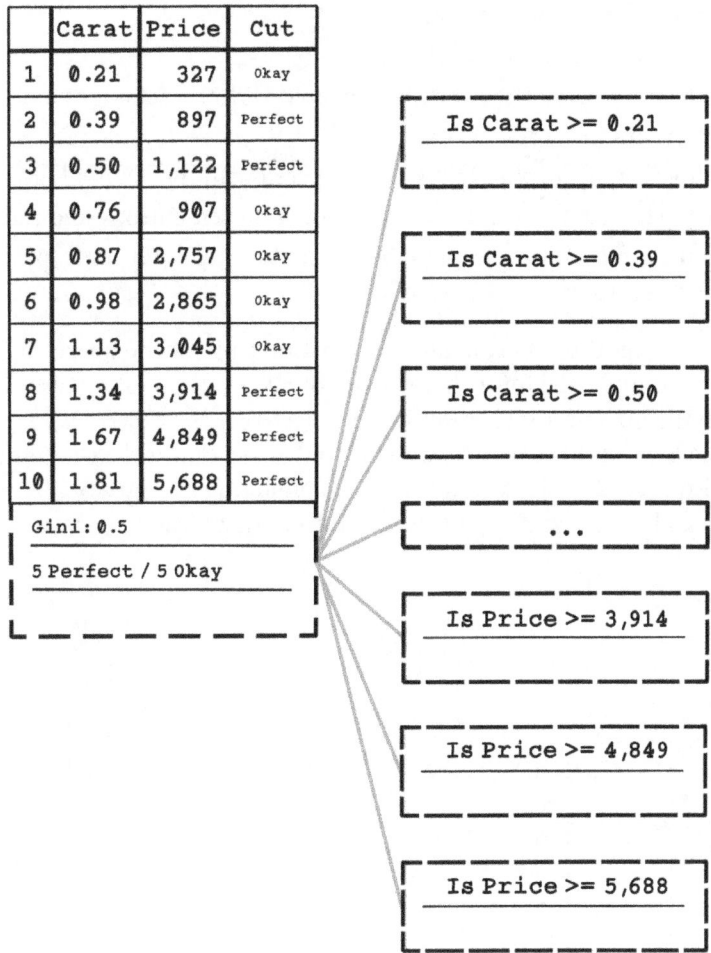

	Carat	Price	Cut
1	0.21	327	Okay
2	0.39	897	Perfect
3	0.50	1,122	Perfect
4	0.76	907	Okay
5	0.87	2,757	Okay
6	0.98	2,865	Okay
7	1.13	3,045	Okay
8	1.34	3,914	Perfect
9	1.67	4,849	Perfect
10	1.81	5,688	Perfect

Gini: 0.5

5 Perfect / 5 Okay

Is Carat >= 0.21

Is Carat >= 0.39

Is Carat >= 0.50

...

Is Price >= 3,914

Is Price >= 4,849

Is Price >= 5,688

Figure 8.22 An example of questions asked to split the data with a decision node

Uncertainty in a dataset is determined by the Gini index, and questions aim to reduce uncertainty. Entropy is another concept that measures disorder using the Gini index for a specific split of data based on a question asked. We must have a way to determine how well a question reduces uncertainty, and we accomplish this task by measuring information gain. *Information gain* describes the amount of information gained by asking a specific question. If a lot of information is gained, the uncertainty is smaller.

You calculate information gain by subtracting entropy before the question is asked from the entropy after the question is asked. To do so, follow these steps:

1. Split the dataset by asking a question.
2. Measure the Gini index for the left split.
3. Measure the entropy for the left split compared with the dataset before the split.
4. Measure the Gini index for the right split.
5. Measure the entropy for the right split compared with the dataset before the split.
6. Calculate the total entropy afterward by adding the left entropy and right entropy.
7. Calculate the information gain by subtracting the total "after" entropy after from the total "before" entropy.

Figure 8.23 illustrates the data split and information gain for the question "Is Price >= 3,914?" In this example, the information gain for all questions is calculated, and the question with the highest information gain is selected as the best question to ask at that point in the tree. Then the original dataset is split based on the decision node with the question "Is Price >= 3,914?" A decision node containing this question is added to the decision tree, and the left and right splits stem from that node.

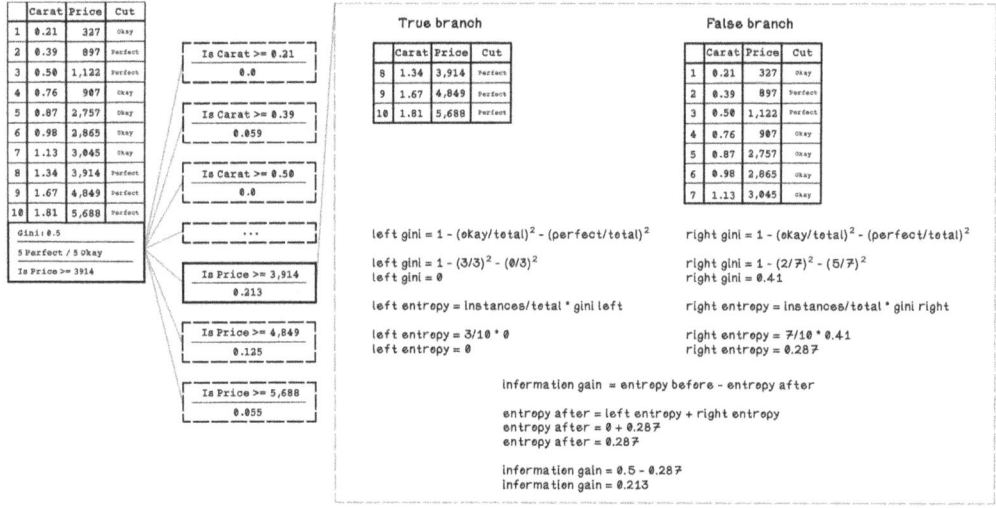

Figure 8.23 Illustration of data split and information gain based on a question

In figure 8.24, after the dataset is split, the left side contains a pure dataset of Perfect diamonds only, and the right side contains a dataset with mixed diamond classifications, including two Perfect diamonds and five Okay diamonds. Another question must be asked on the right side of the dataset to split the dataset further. Again, several questions are generated by using the features of each example in the dataset.

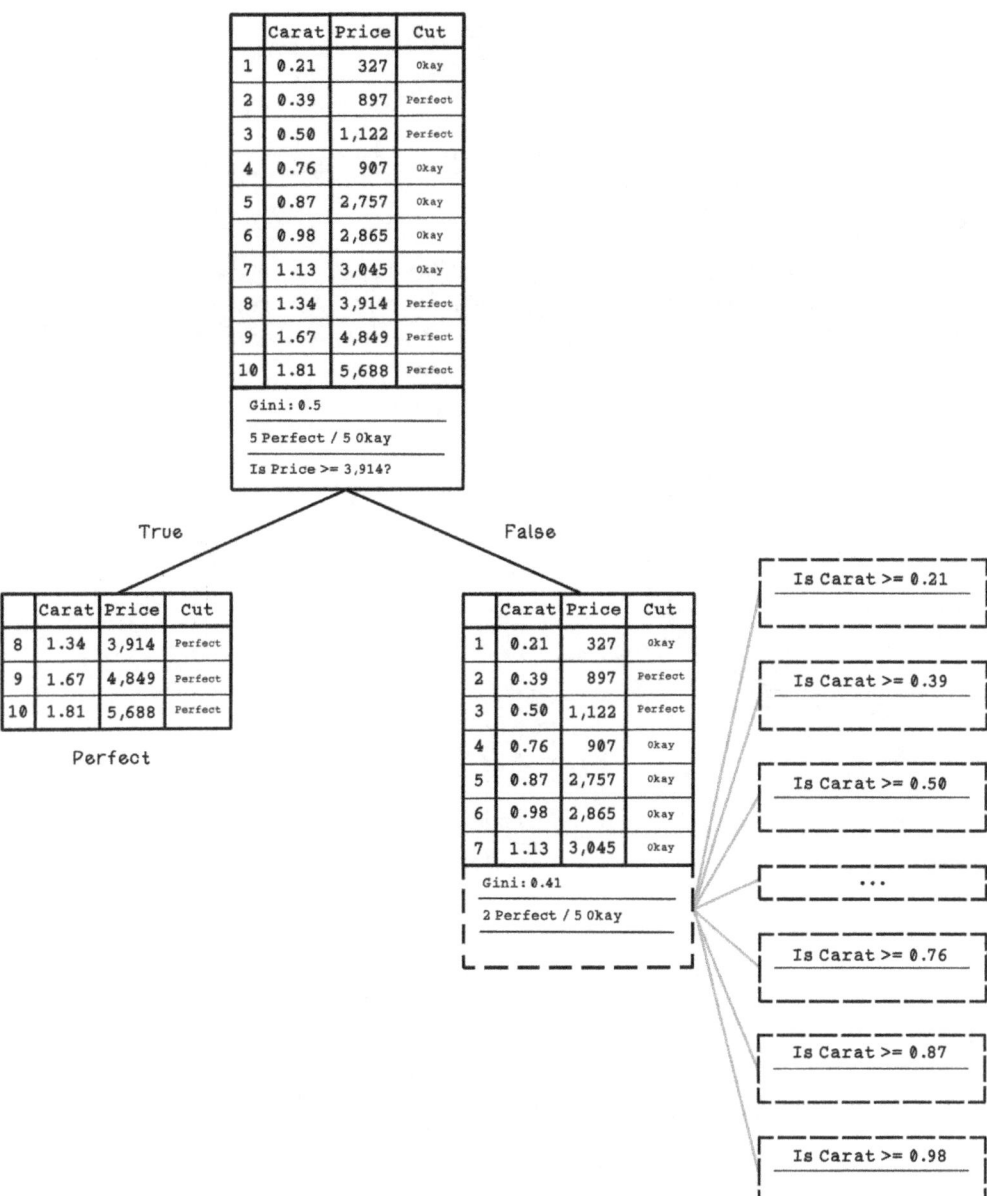

Figure 8.24 The resulting decision tree after the first decision node and possible questions

Exercise: Calculating uncertainty and information gain for a question

Using the knowledge you've gained so far and figure 8.23 as a guide, calculate the information gain for the question "Is Carat >= 0.76?"

Solution:

The solution depicted in the following figure highlights the reuse of the pattern of calculations that, given a question, determine the entropy and information gain. Feel free to practice more questions and compare the results with the information-gain values in the figure.

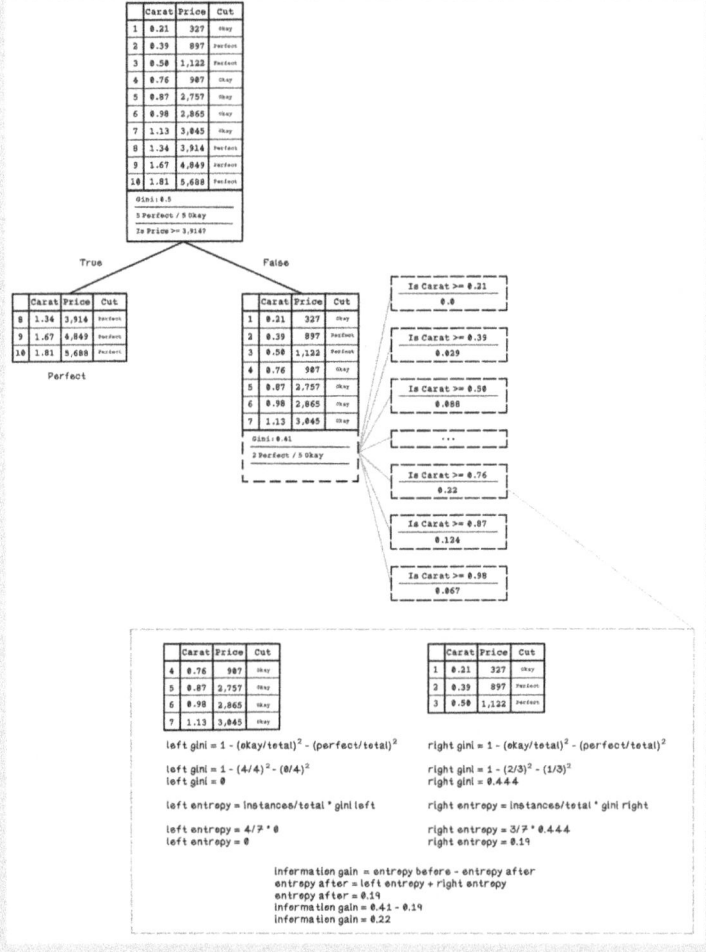

Illustration of data split and information gain based on a question at the second level

The process of splitting, generating questions, and determining information gained happens recursively until the dataset is completely categorized by questions. Figure 8.25 shows the complete decision tree, including all the questions asked and the resulting splits.

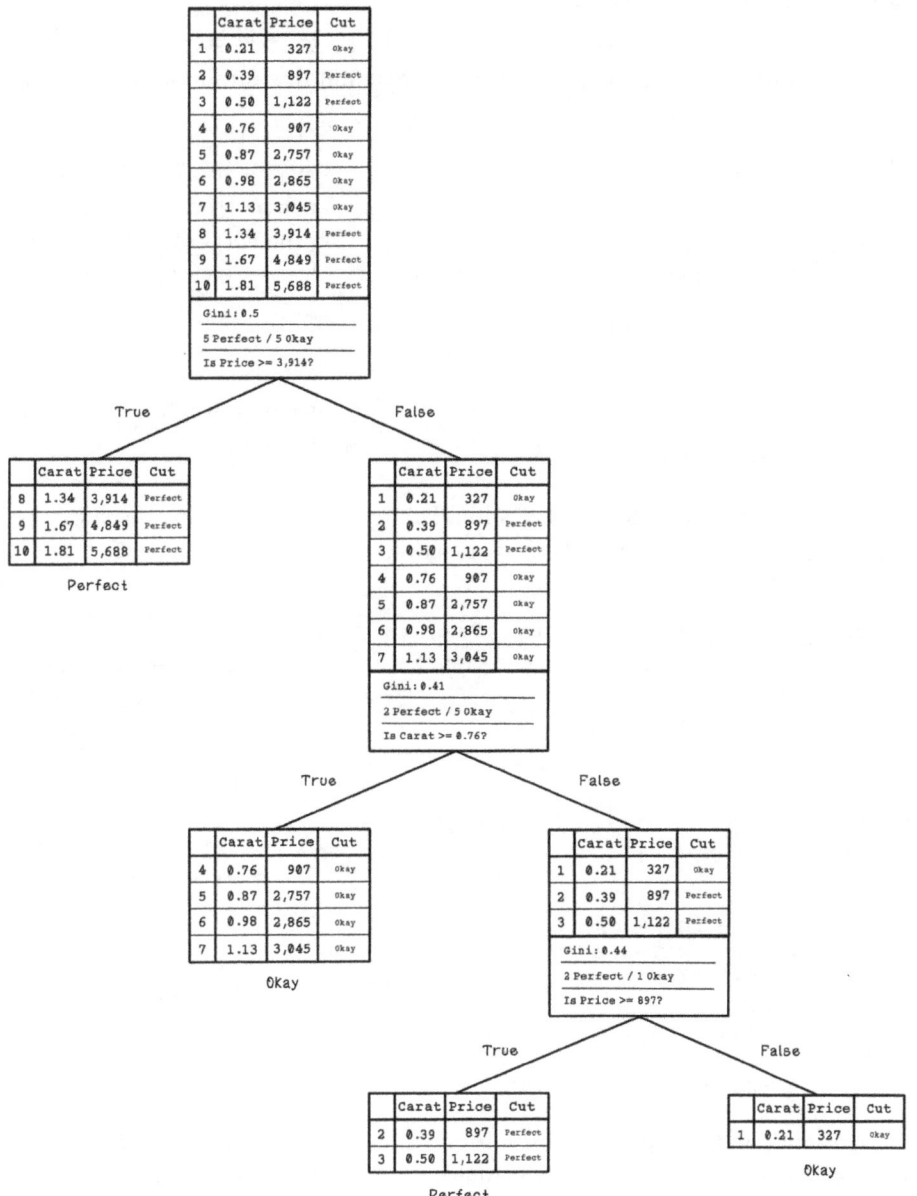

Figure 8.25 The complete trained decision tree

It's important to note that decision trees are usually trained with a much larger sample of data. The questions asked must be more general to accommodate a wider variety of data and, thus, need a variety of examples to learn from.

Python code sample for classification with decision trees

When we're programming a decision tree from scratch, the first step is counting the number of examples of each class. In this case, we count the number of Okay diamonds and the number of Perfect diamonds:

```python
def find_unique_label_counts(examples):
    class_count = {}

    for example in examples:
        label = example['quality']

        if label not in class_count:
            class_count[label] = 0

        class_count[label] += 1

    return class_count
```

If this is the first time we've encountered this specific label in the current dataset, we start its counter at zero

Adds one to the tally for this label

Next, we split examples based on a question. Examples that satisfy the question are stored in `examples_true`, and the rest are stored in `examples_false`:

```python
class Question:
    def __init__(self, feature_name, value):
        self.feature_name = feature_name
        self.value = value

    def filter(self, example):
        return example[self.feature_name] >= self.value

def split_examples(examples, question):
    examples_true = []
    examples_false = []

    for example in examples:
        if question.filter(example):
            examples_true.append(example)
        else:
            examples_false.append(example)

    return examples_true, examples_false
```

Evaluates if a data point meets the criteria

Creates two empty lists to store the partitioned data

Applies the question's logic to the current record

We need a function that calculates the Gini index for a set of examples. The next function calculates the Gini index by using the method described in figure 8.23:

```
def calculate_gini(examples):
    label_counts = find_unique_label_counts(examples)
    total_examples = len(examples)

    uncertainty = 1

    for label in label_counts:
        count = label_counts[label]

        probability_of_label = count / total_examples

        uncertainty -= probability_of_label ** 2

    return uncertainty
```

We will subtract from this value based on how well-represented each class is

The chance of picking an item of this specific label if you reached into the "bag" of data at random

Subtracts the squared probability of each label from 1

`information_gain` uses the left and right splits and the current uncertainty to determine the information gain:

Scales the impurity of the left branch by how much of the total data it contains

Determines the total number of items to calculate the relative weight of each branch

```
def calculate_information_gain(left, right, current_uncertainty):
    total = len(left) + len(right)

    left_gini = calculate_gini(left)
    left_entropy = (len(left) / total) * left_gini

    right_gini = calculate_gini(right)
    right_entropy = (len(right) / total) * right_gini

    uncertainty_after = left_entropy + right_entropy

    information_gain = current_uncertainty - uncertainty_after

    return information_gain
```

Similarly scales the impurity of the right branch

The combined, weighted impurity of both new branches

Subtracts the new impurity from the original impurity

The next function may look daunting, but it's iterating over all the features and their values in the dataset and finding the best information gain to determine the best question to ask:

These will be tested as potential "split points"

measures the "messiness" of the current node before any splitting happens

Iterates through every available column (e.g., "Color," "Weight," "Price") to find the best candidate for a split

```python
def find_best_split(examples, feature_names):
    best_gain = 0
    best_question = None

    current_uncertainty = calculate_gini(examples)

    for feature_name in feature_names:

        values = set(example[feature_name] for example in examples)

        for value in values:

            question = Question(feature_name, value)

            true_examples, false_examples = \
                split_examples(examples, question)

            if len(true_examples) != 0 and len(false_examples) != 0:

                gain = calculate_information_gain(
                    true_examples, false_examples, current_uncertainty
                )

                if gain >= best_gain:
                    best_gain = gain
                    best_question = question

    return best_gain, best_question
```

Formulates a specific question, like "Is Price >= 50?"

Ensures the question actually divides the data

Hypothetically divides the data into two branches

If this question provides more information gain than any previous question, it becomes the new "best question"

The next function ties everything together, using the functions defined previously to build a decision tree:

A stopping point where no further splits are possible

```python
class ExamplesNode:
    def __init__(self, examples):
        self.predictions = find_unique_label_counts(examples)

    def __repr__(self):
        return f"Leaf: {self.predictions}"

class DecisionNode:
```

A node that asks a question and points to two possible paths

```
    def __init__(self, question, true_branch, false_branch):
        self.question = question
        self.true_branch = true_branch
        self.false_branch = false_branch

    def __repr__(self):
        return f"DecisionNode: {self.question}"

def build_tree(examples, feature_names):
    gain, question = find_best_split(examples, feature_names)

    if gain == 0:
        return ExamplesNode(examples)

    true_examples, false_examples = split_examples(examples, question)

    true_branch = build_tree(true_examples, feature_names)
    false_branch = build_tree(false_examples, feature_names)

    return DecisionNode(question, true_branch, false_branch)
```

If there is no more information to be gained, the algorithm stops branching and creates a leaf

Once the best question is found, the current dataset is physically divided into two separate groups to be processed independently

The function calls itself to build a new tree for each subset of data

Note that this function is recursive. It splits the data and recursively splits the resulting dataset until there is no information gain, indicating that the examples can't be split any further. As a reminder, decision nodes are used to split the examples, and example nodes are used to store split sets of examples.

We've learned how to build a decision-tree classifier. Remember that the trained decision-tree model will be tested with unseen data, similar to the linear regression approach explored earlier.

One problem with decision trees is overfitting, which occurs when the model is trained too well on several examples but performs poorly for new examples. Overfitting happens when the model learns the patterns of the training data but new real-world data is slightly different and doesn't meet the splitting criteria of the trained model. Although achieving 100% accuracy on training data sounds ideal, it's often a red flag. True overfitting is identified not just by a high training score but also by the gap between high training accuracy and poor performance on new, unseen data.

To prevent this situation in decision trees, we use a technique called pruning. Just as a gardener trims a tree to keep it healthy, we remove branches that are too deep or too specific, forcing the model to learn general patterns rather than memorize every single data point.

Overfitting can happen with any machine learning model—not just decision trees. Figure 8.26 illustrates the concepts of overfitting and underfitting. Underfitting includes too many incorrect classifications, and overfitting includes too few or no incorrect classifications. The ideal is somewhere in between.

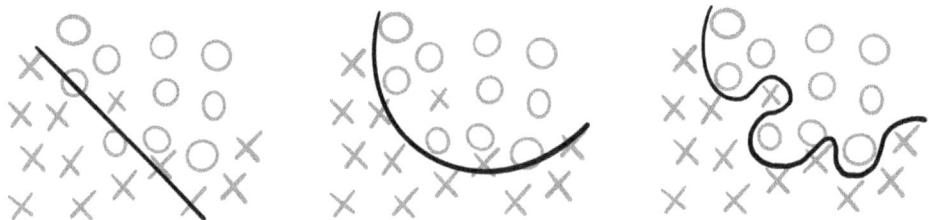

Figure 8.26 Underfitting, ideal fit, and overfitting

Classifying examples with decision trees

Now that we've trained a decision tree and determined the right questions to ask, we can test the model by giving it new data to classify. The model here is the decision tree of questions created by the training step.

To test the model, we give it several examples of new data and measure whether they've been classified correctly, so we have to know the labeling of the testing data. In the diamond example, we need more data, including data for the Cut feature, to test the decision tree (table 8.16).

Table 8.16 The diamond dataset for classification

	Carat	Price	Cut
1	0.26	689	Perfect
2	0.41	967	Perfect
3	0.52	1,012	Perfect
4	0.76	907	Okay
5	0.81	2,650	Okay
6	0.90	2,634	Okay
7	1.24	2,999	Perfect
8	1.42	3850	Perfect
9	1.61	4,345	Perfect
10	1.78	3,100	Okay

Figure 8.27 shows the decision-tree model we trained, which will process the new examples. Each example is fed through the tree and classified.

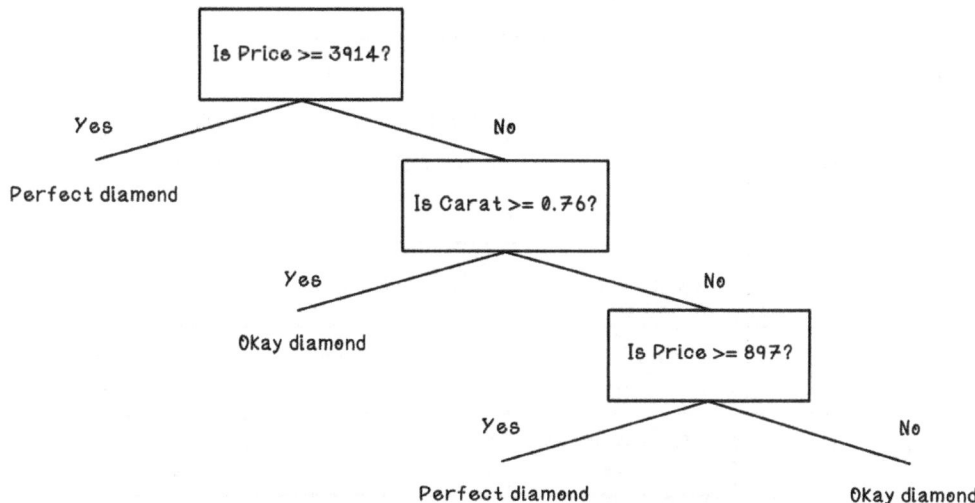

Figure 8.27 The decision-tree model that will process new examples

Table 8.17 shows the resulting predicted classifications. Assume that we're trying to predict Okay diamonds. Three examples are incorrect, so the result is 3 of 10, meaning that the model correctly predicted 7 of 10, or 70%, of the testing data. This performance isn't terrible, but it illustrates how examples can be misclassified.

Table 8.17 The diamond dataset for classification and predictions

	Carat	Price	Cut	Prediction	
1	0.26	689	Okay	Okay	✓
2	0.41	880	Perfect	Perfect	✓
3	0.52	1,012	Perfect	Perfect	✓
4	0.76	907	Okay	Okay	✓
5	0.81	2,650	Okay	Okay	✓
6	0.90	2,634	Okay	Okay	✓
7	1.24	2,999	Perfect	Okay	X
8	1.42	3,850	Perfect	Okay	X
9	1.61	4,345	Perfect	Perfect	✓
10	1.78	3,100	Okay	Perfect	X

A confusion matrix is often used to measure the performance of a model with testing data. A *confusion matrix* describes the performance using the following metrics (figure 8.28):

- *True positive (TP)*—Okay examples correctly classified as Okay
- *True negative (TN)*—Perfect examples correctly classified as Perfect
- *False positive (FP)*—Perfect examples classified as Okay
- *False negative (FN)*—Okay examples classified as Perfect

	Predicted positive	Predicted negative	
Actual positive	True positive TP	False negative FN	Sensitivity TP / (TP + FN)
Actual negative	False positive FP	True negative TN	Specificity TN / (TN + FP)
	Precision TP / (TP + FP)	Negative precision TN / (TN + FN)	Accuracy TP + TN (TP + TN + FP + FN)

Figure 8.28 A confusion matrix

We can use the outcomes of testing the model with unseen examples to deduce several measurements:

- *Precision*—How often Okay examples are classified correctly
- *Negative precision/negative predictive value (NPV)*—How often Perfect examples are classified correctly
- *Sensitivity or recall*— The ratio of correctly classified Okay diamonds to all the actual Okay diamonds in the training set; also known as the *true-positive rate*
- *Specificity*—The ratio of correctly classified Perfect diamonds to all actual Perfect diamonds in the training set; also known as the *true-negative rate*
- *Accuracy*—How often the classifier is correct overall between classes

Figure 8.29 shows the resulting confusion matrix, with the results of the diamond example listed as input. Accuracy is important, but the other measurements can unveil additional useful information about the model's performance.

	Predicted positive	Predicted negative	
Actual positive	True positive 4	False negative 1	Sensitivity $4 / (4 + 1) = 0.8$
Actual negative	False positive 2	True negative 3	Specificity $3 / (3 + 2) = 0.6$
	Precision $4 / (4 + 2) = 0.67$	Negative precision $3 / (1 + 3) = 0.75$	Accuracy $\dfrac{4 + 3}{(4 + 3 + 2 + 1)} = 0.7$

Figure 8.29 Confusion matrix for the diamond test example

By using these measurements, we can make more-informed decisions in a machine learning life cycle to improve the performance of the model. As mentioned throughout this chapter, machine learning is an experimental exercise involving some trial and error. These metrics are guides in this process.

Other popular machine learning algorithms

This chapter explores two popular and fundamental machine learning algorithms. The linear regression algorithm is used for regression problems in which the relationships between features are discovered. The decision-tree algorithm is used for classification problems in which the relationships between features and categories of examples are discovered. But many other machine learning algorithms are suitable in different contexts and for solving different problems. Figure 8.30 illustrates some popular algorithms and shows how they fit into the machine learning landscape.

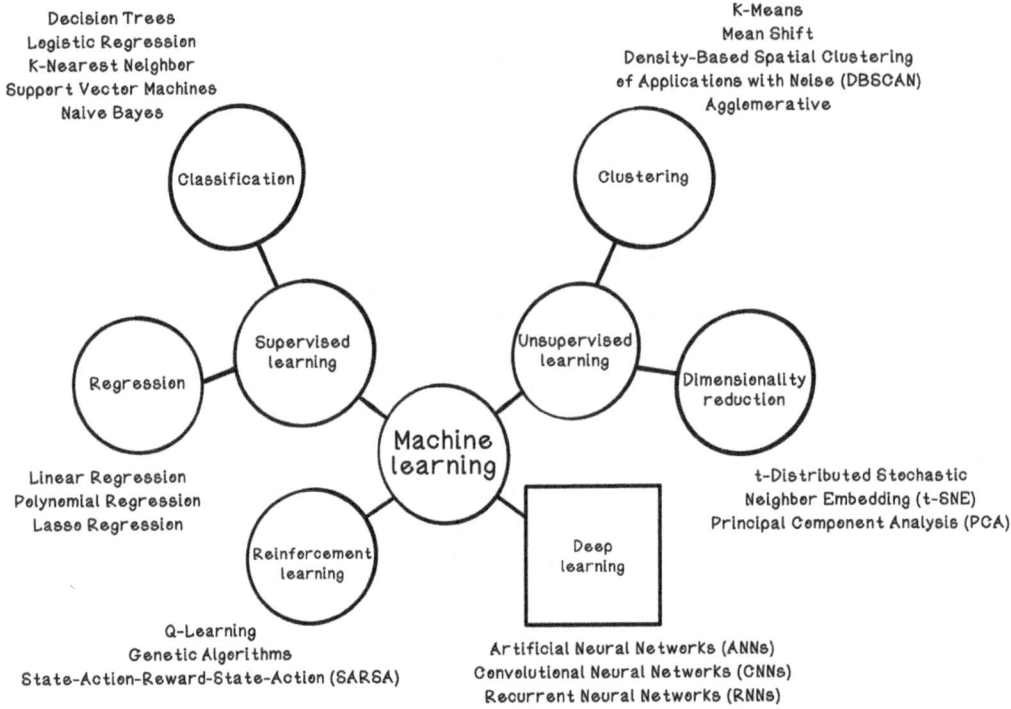

Figure 8.30 A map of popular machine learning algorithms

The classification and regression algorithms satisfy problems similar to the ones explored in this chapter. Unsupervised learning contains algorithms that can help with some of the data preparation steps, find hidden underlying relationships in data, and inform what questions can be asked in a machine learning experiment.

Notice the introduction of deep learning in figure 8.30. Chapter 9 covers artificial neural networks—a key concept in deep learning. That chapter will give us a better understanding of the types of problems we can solve with these approaches and how the algorithms are implemented.

Use cases for machine learning algorithms

Machine learning can be applied in almost every industry to solve a plethora of problems in different domains. Given the right data and the right questions, the possibilities are potentially endless. All of us have interacted with a product or service that uses some aspect of machine learning and data modeling in our everyday lives. This section highlights some popular ways to use machine learning for solving real-world problems at scale:

- *Fraud and threat detection*—Machine learning has been used to detect and prevent fraudulent transactions in the finance industry. Financial institutions have gained a wealth of transactional information over the years, including fraudulent-transaction reports from their customers. These fraud reports are an input to labeling and characterizing fraudulent transactions. The models might consider the location of the transaction, the amount, the merchant, and so on to classify transactions, protecting consumers from potential losses and the financial institution from insurance losses. The same model can be applied to network threat detection to detect and prevent attacks based on known network use and reported unusual behavior.

- *Product and content recommendations*—Many of us use e-commerce sites to purchase goods or media streaming services to consume audio and video. Products may be recommended to us based on what we're purchasing, or content may be recommended based on our interests. This functionality is usually enabled by machine learning, in which patterns in purchase or viewing behavior are derived from people's interactions. Recommender systems are being used in a growing number of industries and applications to generate more sales or provide a better user experience.

- *Dynamic product and service pricing*—Products and services are often priced based on what someone is willing to pay for them or based on risk. For a ride-sharing system, it might make sense to hike the price if there are too few cars available to meet the demand for rides; this practice is sometimes referred to as *surge pricing*. In the insurance industry, a price might be hiked if a person is categorized as high-risk. Machine learning finds the attributes and relationships between the attributes that influence pricing based on dynamic conditions and details about a unique individual.

- *Health-condition risk prediction*—The medical industry requires health professionals to acquire an abundance of knowledge so they can diagnose and treat patients. Over the years, the industry has gained a vast amount of data about patients, including blood types, DNA, family-illness history, geographic location, lifestyle, and so on. This data can be used to find potential patterns that can guide the diagnosis of illness. The power of using data to find diagnoses is that we can treat conditions before they mature. Also, by feeding the outcomes back into the machine learning system, we can strengthen its reliability in making predictions.

SUMMARY OF MACHINE LEARNING

In machine learning, the domain being explored, questions being asked, and data are as important as the algorithms used

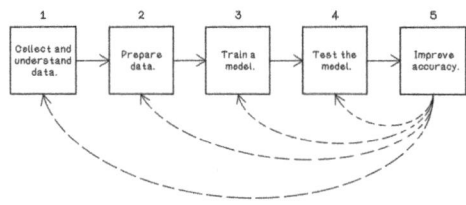

The lifecycle of ML projects is iterative and experimental.

Linear regression involves finding the best line to fit the data, which means minimizing the error to each data point.

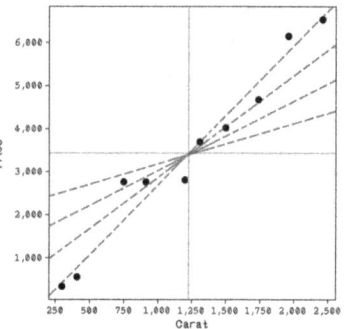

Decision trees split data using questions until the dataset is perfectly split into categories - the key concept is reducing uncertainty in the dataset.

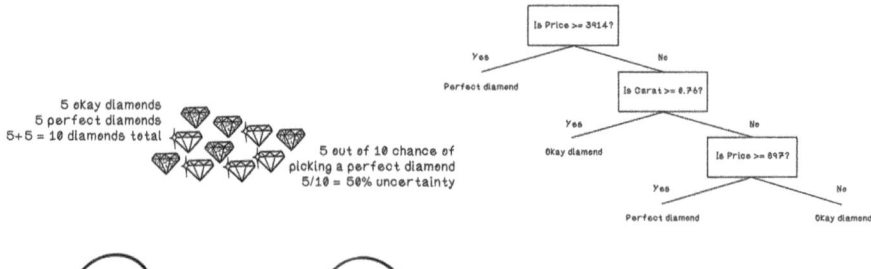

5 okay diamonds
5 perfect diamonds
5+5 = 10 diamonds total

5 out of 10 chance of picking a perfect diamond
5/10 = 50% uncertainty

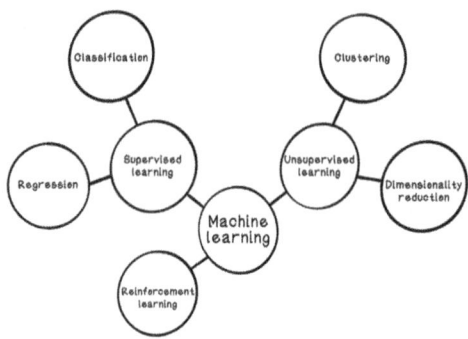

Different ML algorithms are used to answer different types of questions and achieve different goals in different scenarios and contexts.

In this chapter

- Understanding the inspiration and intuition of artificial neural networks

- Identifying problems that can be solved with artificial neural networks

- Understanding and implementing forward propagation using a trained network

- Understanding and implementing backpropagation to train a network

- Designing artificial neural network architectures to tackle different problems

What are artificial neural networks?

Artificial neural networks (ANNs) are powerful tools in the machine learning toolkit, used in a variety of ways to accomplish objectives such as image recognition, natural language processing, and game playing. ANNs learn much like other machine learning algorithms: by using training data. They're best suited to unstructured data in which it's difficult to understand how features relate to one another. This chapter covers the inspiration of ANNs; it also shows how the algorithm works and how ANNs are designed to solve different problems.

To gain a clear understanding of how ANNs fit into the bigger machine learning landscape, we should review the composition and categorization of machine learning algorithms. *Deep learning* is the name given to algorithms that use ANNs in varying architectures to accomplish an objective. Deep learning, including ANNs, can be used to solve supervised learning, unsupervised learning, and reinforcement learning problems. Figure 9.1 shows how deep learning relates to ANNs and other machine learning concepts.

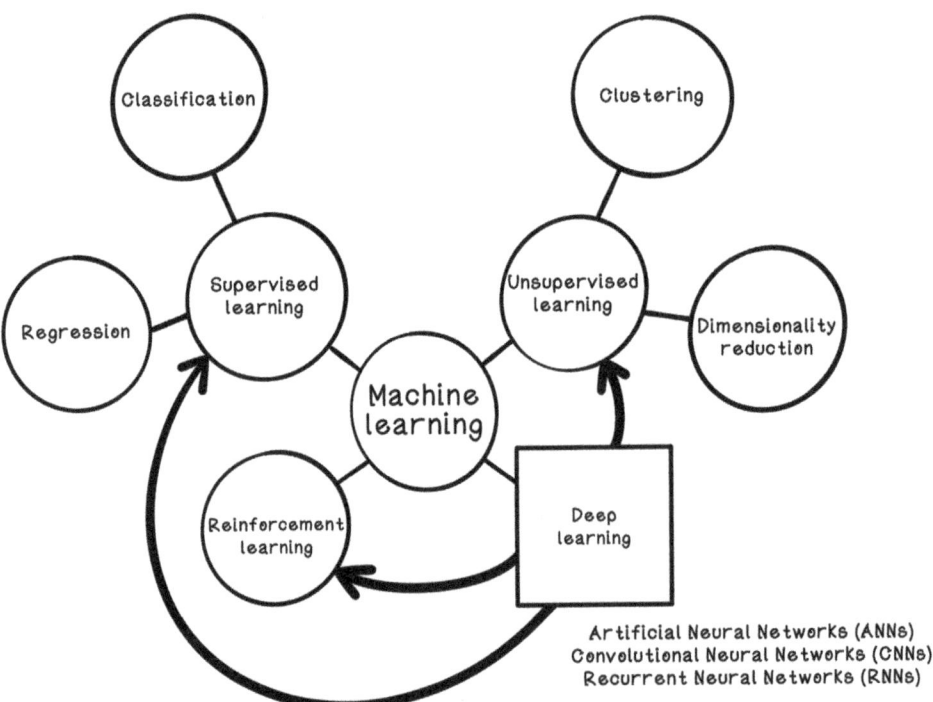

Figure 9.1 A map describing the flexibility of deep learning and ANNs

ANNs can be seen as just another model in the machine learning life cycle (chapter 8). Figure 9.2 recaps that life cycle. A problem has to be identified; that data has to be collected, understood, and prepared; and the ANN model will be tested and improved if necessary.

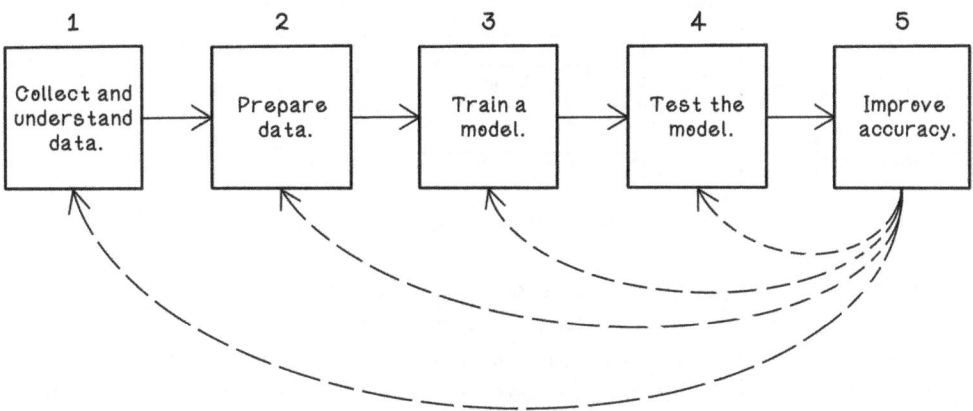

Figure 9.2 A workflow for machine learning experiments and projects

Now that we have an idea of how ANNs fit into the abstract machine learning landscape and know that an ANN is another model that's trained in the life cycle, let's explore the intuition and workings of ANNs. Like genetic algorithms and swarm-intelligence algorithms, ANNs are inspired by natural phenomena—in this case, the brain and nervous system. The nervous system is a biological structure that allows us to feel sensations and is the basis of how our brains think and operate. We have nerves across our entire bodies and neurons that behave similarly in our brains.

Neural networks consist of interconnected neurons that pass information by using electrical and chemical signals. Neurons pass information to other neurons and adjust that information to accomplish a specific function. When you grab a cup and take a sip of water, millions of neurons process the intention of what you want to do, the physical action to accomplish it, and the feedback to determine whether you were successful.

Think about little children learning to drink from a cup. They usually start poorly, dropping the cup a lot. Then they learn to grab the cup with two hands. Gradually, they learn to grab the cup with a single hand and take a sip without problems. This process takes months. What's happening is that their brains and nervous systems are learning through practice (or training).

Our bodies have billions of neurons that are harnessed to learn from the signals of what we're doing, toward what goal, while determining our level of success. Figure 9.3 depicts a simplified model: receiving inputs (stimuli), processing them in a neural network, and providing outputs (response).

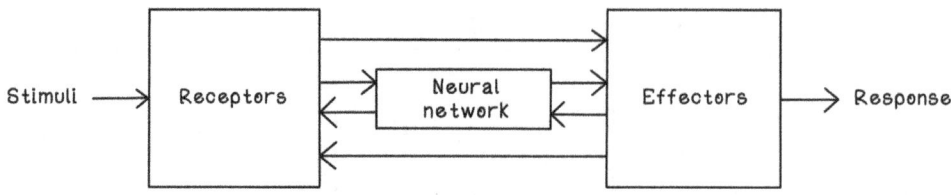

Figure 9.3 A simplified model of a biological neural system

Simplified, a *neuron* (figure 9.4) consists of *dendrites* that receive signals from other neurons; a *cell body* and a *nucleus* that activates and adjusts the signal; an *axon* that passes the signal to other neurons; and *synapses* that carry, and in the process adjust, the signal before it's passed to the next neuron's dendrites. Through approximately 90 billion of these neurons working together, our brains function at the high level of intelligence we know.

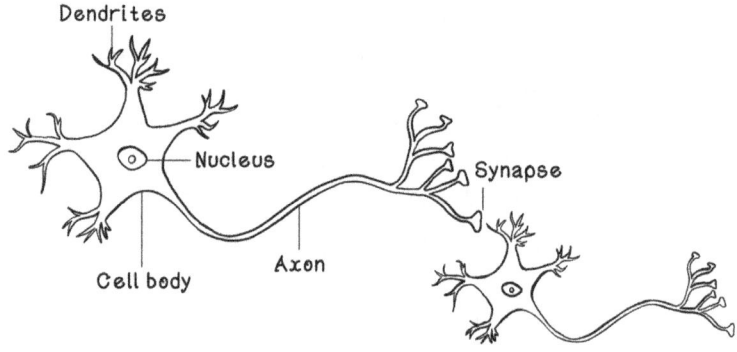

Figure 9.4 The general composition of neurons

Although ANNs are inspired by biological neural networks and use many of the concepts observed in these systems, they're not identical representations of biological neural systems. From a biological standpoint, we still have a lot to learn about the human brain and nervous system.

The Perceptron: A representation of a neuron

The neuron is the fundamental concept that makes up the brain. As mentioned earlier, it accepts many inputs from other neurons, processes those inputs, and transfers the result to other connected neurons. ANNs are based on the fundamental concept of the *Perceptron*—a logical representation of a single biological neuron.

Like neurons, the Perceptron receives inputs (dendrites), alters these inputs by using weights (synapses), processes the weighted inputs (the cell body and nucleus), and outputs a result (axons). The Perceptron is loosely based on a neuron. The synapses are depicted after the dendrites, representing the influence of synapses on incoming inputs. Figure 9.5 shows the logical architecture of the Perceptron.

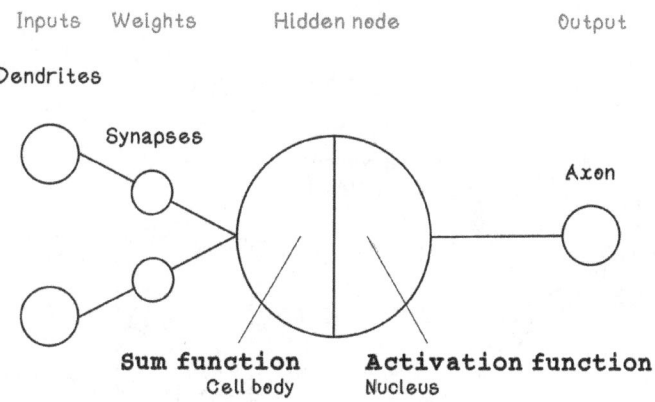

Figure 9.5 Logical architecture of the Perceptron

The components of the Perceptron are described by variables that are useful for calculating the output. Weights modify the inputs, that value is processed by a hidden node, and the result is provided as the output. Following is a brief description of the Perceptron's components:

- *Inputs*—Describe the input values. In a neuron, these values would be an input signal.
- *Weights*—Describe the weights on each connection between an input and the hidden node. Weights influence the intensity of an input and result in a weighted input. In a neuron, these connections would be the synapses.
- *Hidden node (sum and activation)*—Sums the weighted input values and applies an activation function to the summed result. An activation function determines the activation/output of the hidden node/neuron.
- *Output*—Describes the final output of the Perceptron.

To understand the workings of the Perceptron, we'll examine its use by revisiting the Apartment-Finding Problem from chapter 8. Suppose that we're real estate agents trying to determine whether a specific apartment will be rented within a month after we list it, based on the size and price of the apartment. Assume that a Perceptron has already been trained, meaning that the weights for the Perceptron have already been adjusted to make good predictions. We explore the way Perceptions and ANNs are trained later in this chapter; for now, understand that the weights encode relationships among the inputs by adjusting the strength of inputs to make accurate predictions.

Figure 9.6 shows how to use a pretrained Perceptron to classify whether or not an apartment will be rented. The inputs represent the price and size of a specific apartment. We're also using the maximum price and size to scale the inputs ($8,000 for maximum price and 80 square meters for maximum size). For more about scaling data, see the next section.

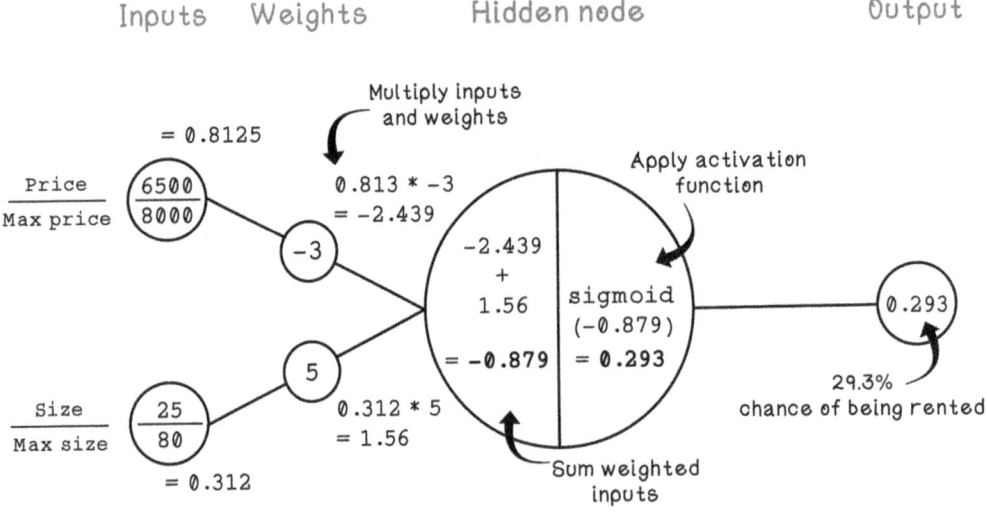

Figure 9.6 An example of using a trained Perceptron

Notice that the price and size are the inputs and that the predicted chance of the apartment being rented is the output. The weights are key to achieving the prediction. *Weights* are the variables in the network that learn relationships among inputs. The summation and activation functions to process the inputs multiplied by the weights to make a prediction. To visualize this process, imagine a neuron as a sound engineer mixing a track:

- *Inputs*—Raw instruments (drums, guitar, vocals).
- *Weights*—Volume sliders. If the guitar is too loud (contributes too much to the error), the engineer lowers that specific weight. If the vocals are important, the engineer increases that weight.
- *Bias*—Master gain, which boosts or cuts the overall signal level before it goes to the speakers.
- *Activation function*—Speakers. They use the combined signal to produce a sound.

For this example, we're using an activation function called the *sigmoid function*. Activation functions play critical roles in the Perceptron and ANNs. In this case, the activation function is helping us solve a linear problem. But when we look at ANNs in the next section, we'll see how to use activation functions to receive inputs for solving nonlinear problems.

Figure 9.7 depicts the basics of linear problems. The sigmoid function takes any input value (from -∞ to +∞) and squashes it into an S curve between 0 and 1. Although this function is useful for calculating probabilities, it comes with a risk: the vanishing gradient problem. For very large or very small inputs, the curve becomes almost perfectly flat. When the curve is flat, the gradient (slope) is near 0, which can cause the network to stop learning. This is why modern networks often use other activation functions for hidden layers. When we get to the deeper workings of ANNs later in this chapter, we'll see how activation functions help solve nonlinear problems as well.

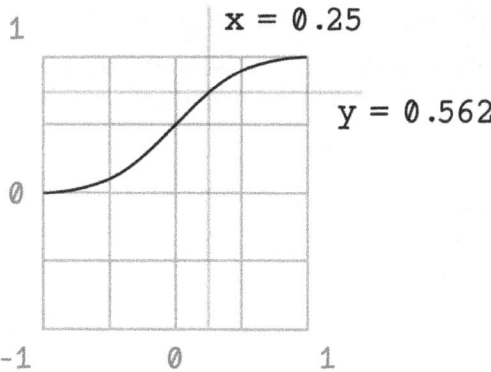

Figure 9.7 The sigmoid function

Let's take a step back to look at the data we're using for the Perceptron. Understanding the data related to whether an apartment was sold is important for understanding what the Perceptron is doing. Figure 9.8 illustrates the examples in the dataset, including the price and size of each apartment. Each apartment is labeled in one of two classes: rented or not rented. The line separating the two classes is the function described by the Perceptron.

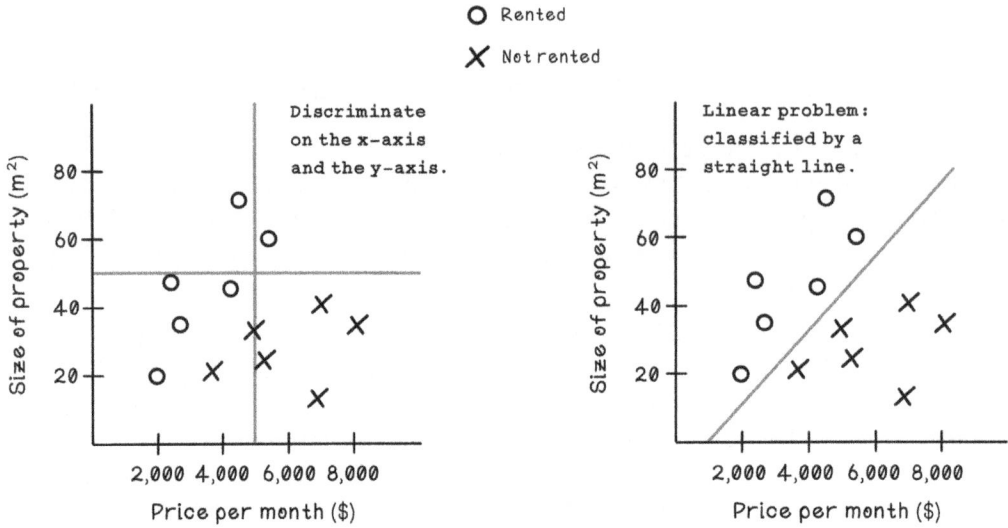

Figure 9.8 Example of a linear classification problem

Although the Perceptron is useful for solving linear problems, it can't solve nonlinear problems. If a dataset can't be classified by a straight line, the Perceptron fails.

ANNs use the concept of the Perceptron at scale. Many neurons similar to the Perceptron work together to solve problems in many dimensions.

Exercise: Calculate the output of the following input for the Perceptron

Using your knowledge of how the Perceptron works, calculate the output for the following:

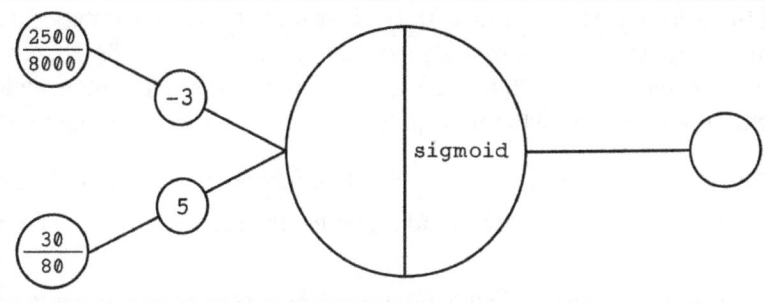

Solution:

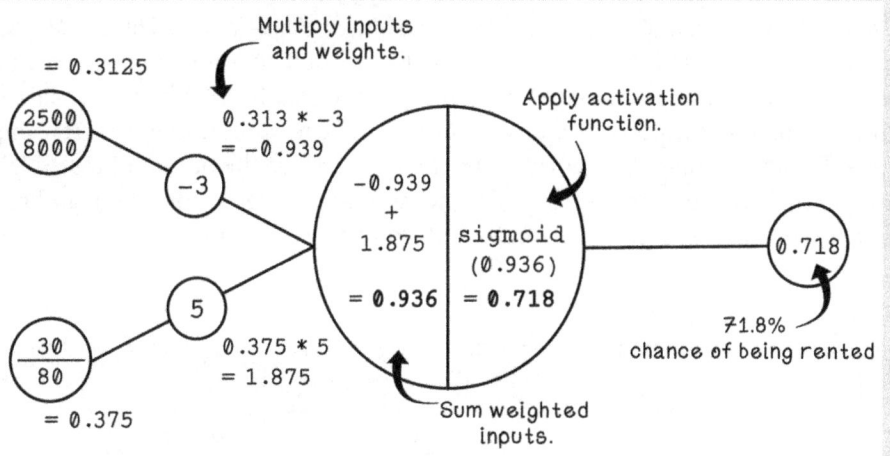

Defining ANNs

The Perceptron is useful for solving simple problems, but as the dimensions of the data increase, it becomes less feasible. ANNs use the principles of the Perceptron and apply them to many hidden nodes as opposed to a single one.

To explore the workings of multinode ANNs, consider an example dataset related to car collisions. Suppose that we have data from several cars at the moment when an unforeseen object enters the path of their movement. The dataset contains features related to the conditions and whether a collision occurred, including the following:

- *Speed*—The speed at which the car was traveling before encountering the object
- *Terrain quality*—The quality of the road on which the car was traveling before encountering the object
- *Degree of vision*—The driver's degree of vision before the car encountered the object
- *Total experience*—The total driving experience of the car's driver
- *Collision occurred?*—Whether or not a collision occurred

Given this data, we want to train a machine learning model—namely, an ANN—to learn the relationship between the features that contribute to a collision, as shown in table 9.1. We can use an example ANN architecture to classify whether a collision will occur based on the features we have. We must map the features in the dataset as inputs to the ANN, and we map the class we're trying to predict as the output of the ANN. In this example, the input nodes are speed, terrain quality, degree of vision, and total experience; the output node is whether a collision occurred (figure 9.9).

Table 9.1 Car-collision dataset

	Speed	Terrain quality	Degree of vision	Total experience	Collision occurred?
1	65 km/h	5/10	180°	80,000 km	No
2	120 km/h	1/10	72°	110,000 km	Yes
3	8 km/h	6/10	288°	50,000 km	No
4	50 km/h	2/10	324°	1,600 km	Yes
5	25 km/h	9/10	36°	160,000 km	No
6	80 km/h	3/10	120°	6,000 km	Yes
7	40 km/h	3/10	360°	400,000 km	No

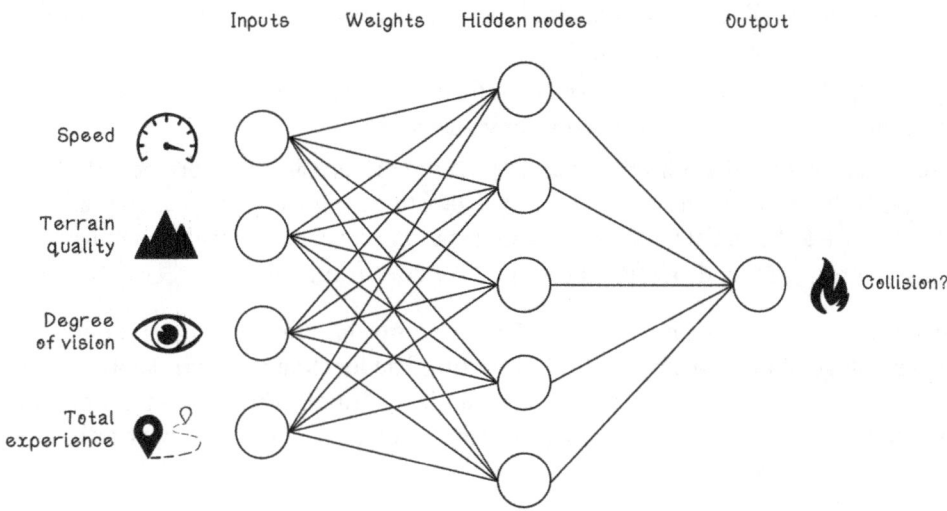

Figure 9.9 Example ANN architecture for the car-collision example

As with the other machine learning algorithms we've worked through, preparing data is important for making an ANN classify data successfully. The primary concern is representing data in comparable ways. As humans, we understand the concepts of speed and degree of vision, but the ANN doesn't have this context. Directly feeding 65 km/h and a 36° angle into the ANN causes a problem. Because 65 is numerically larger than 36, the network's math is biased to think that speed is the more-important feature.

To fix this bias, we have to scale our data. By squashing both values into a range between 0 and 1, we ensure that the network weighs them based on their actual predictive power, not their raw size alone.

A common way to scale data so that it can be compared is to use the *Min-Max* scaling approach, which aims to scale data to values between 0 and 1. By scaling all the data in a dataset to be consistent in format, we make the different features comparable. Because ANNs have no context for the raw features, we also remove bias with large input values. As an example, 1,000 seems to be much larger than 65, but 1,000 in the context of total driving experience is poor, and 65 in the context of driving speed is significant. Min-Max scaling represents these pieces of data with the correct context by taking into account the minimum and maximum possible values for each feature. Here are the minimum and maximum values selected for the features in the car-collision data:

- *Speed*—The minimum speed is 0, which means the car isn't moving. We'll use the maximum speed of 120 because 120 km/h is the maximum legal speed limit in most places around the world. We'll assume that the driver follows the rules.

- *Terrain quality*—Because the data is already in a rating system, the minimum value is 0, and the maximum value is 10.
- *Degree of vision*—We know that the total field of view in degrees is 360. So the minimum value is 0, and the maximum value is 360.
- *Total experience*—The minimum value is 0 if the driver has no experience. We'll subjectively make the maximum value 400,000 for driving experience. The rationale is that if a driver has 400,000 km of driving experience, we can consider that driver to be highly competent, and any further experience doesn't matter.

Min-max scaling uses the minimum and maximum values for a feature and finds the percentage of the actual value for the feature. The formula is simple: subtract the minimum from the value, and divide the result by the minimum subtracted from the maximum. Figure 9.10 illustrates the Min-Max scaling calculation for the first row of data in the car-collision example:

	Speed	Terrain quality	Degree of vision	Total experience	Collision occurred?
1	65 km/h	5/10	180°	80,000 km	No

	Speed	Terrain quality	Degree of vision	Total experience
	65 km/h	5/10	180°	80,000
	Min: 0 Max: 120	Min: 0 Max: 10	Min: 0 Max: 360	Min: 0 Max: 400,000
$\dfrac{\text{value} - \text{min}}{\text{max} - \text{min}}$	$\dfrac{65 - 0}{120 - 0}$	$\dfrac{5 - 0}{10 - 0}$	$\dfrac{180 - 0}{365 - 0}$	$\dfrac{80000 - 0}{400000 - 0}$
Scaled value	0.542	0.5	0.5	0.2

Figure 9.10 Min-max scaling example with car-collision data

All the values are between 0 and 1 and can be compared equally. The same formula is applied to all the rows in the dataset to ensure that every value is scaled. For the value of the "Collision occurred?" feature, Yes is replaced by 1, and No is replaced by 0. Table 9.2 depicts the scaled car-collision data.

Table 9.2 Car-collision dataset, scaled

	Speed	Terrain quality	Degree of vision	Total experience	Collision occurred?
1	0.542	0.5	0.5	0.200	0
2	1.000	0.1	0.2	0.275	1
3	0.067	0.6	0.8	0.125	0
4	0.417	0.2	0.9	0.004	1
5	0.208	0.9	0.1	0.400	0
6	0.667	0.3	0.3	0.015	1
7	0.333	0.3	1.0	1.000	0

Python code sample for scaling training and testing data

The code for scaling the data follows the logic and calculations for Min-Max scaling identically. We need the minimums and maximums for each feature, as well as the total number of features in our dataset. The `scale_dataset` function uses these parameters to iterate over every example in the dataset and scale the value by using the `scale_data_feature` function:

> Subtracts the minimum to start the range at zero, then divides by the total span to ensure the maximum value becomes exactly 1.0

```
def scale_data_feature(data, feature_min, feature_max):
    return (data - feature_min) / (feature_max - feature_min)

def scale_dataset(dataset, feature_count, feature_min, feature_max):
    scaled_data = []

    for data_row in dataset:
        example = []
        for i in range(feature_count):
            scaled_value = scale_data_feature(
                data_row[i],
                feature_min[i],
                feature_max[i]
            )
            example.append(scaled_value)
        scaled_data.append(example)

    return scaled_data
```

> Iterates through each feature index

> Builds a new dataset that mirrors the original structure but with all values now transformed

Now that we've prepared the data to make it suitable for an ANN to process, let's explore the architecture of a simple ANN. Remember that the features used to predict a class are the input nodes, and the class being predicted is the output node.

Figure 9.11 shows an ANN with one hidden layer (the single vertical layer in the figure) with five hidden nodes. These layers are called *hidden* because they aren't directly observed from outside the network. Only the inputs and outputs are interacted with, which leads to the perception of ANNs as being black boxes. Each hidden node is similar to the Perceptron. A hidden node takes inputs and weights and computes the sum and an activation function. Then the results of each hidden node are processed by a single output node.

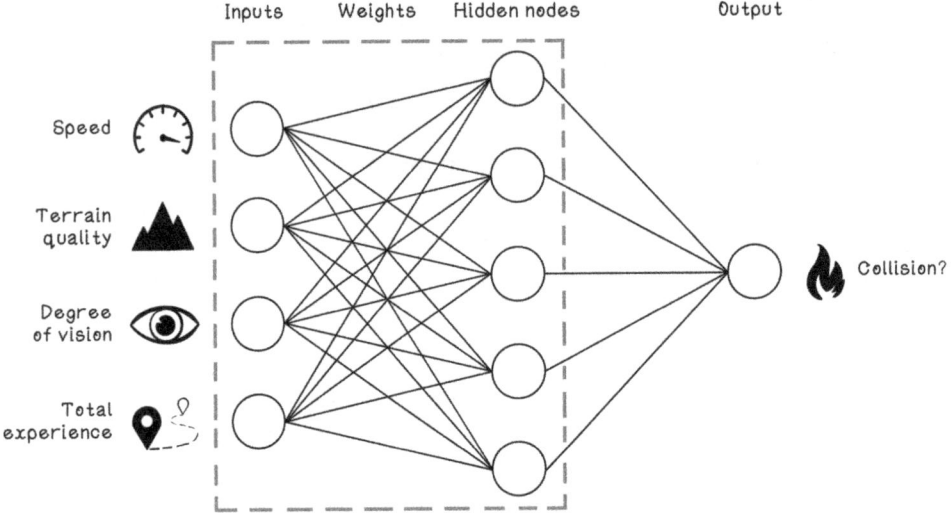

Figure 9.11 Example ANN architecture for the car-collision problem

Before we consider the calculations and computation of an ANN, let's try to intuitively dig into what the network weights are doing at a high level. Because a single hidden node is connected to every input node but every connection has a different weight, independent hidden nodes may be concerned with specific relationships among two or more input nodes.

Figure 9.12 depicts a scenario in which the first hidden node has strong weightings on the connections to terrain quality and degree of vision but weak weightings on the connections to speed and total experience. This specific hidden node is concerned with the relationship between terrain quality and degree of vision. It might gain an understanding of the relationship between these two features and how it influences whether collisions happen. Poor terrain quality and poor degree of vision, for example, might influence the likelihood of collisions more than good terrain quality and an average degree of vision. These relationships are usually more intricate than those in this simple example.

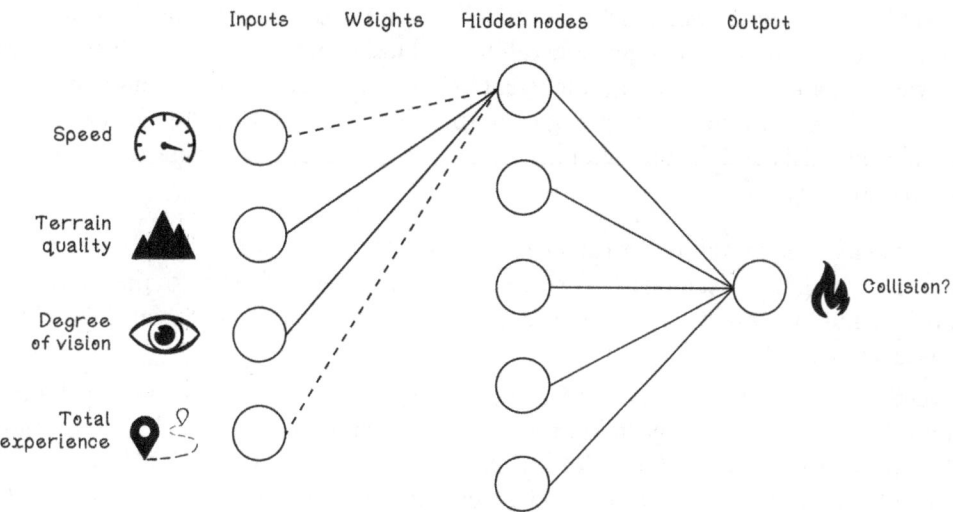

Figure 9.12 Example of a hidden node comparing terrain quality and degree of vision

In figure 9.13, the second hidden node might have strong weightings on the connections to terrain quality and total experience. Perhaps a relationship among different terrain qualities and variance in total driving experience contributes to collisions.

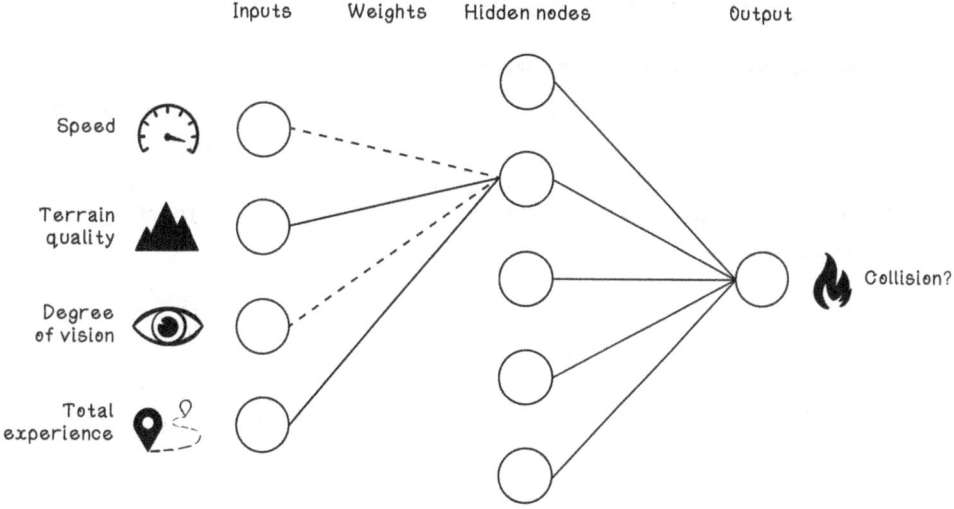

Figure 9.13 Example of a hidden node comparing terrain quality and total experience

The nodes in a hidden layer can be conceptually compared with the analogy of ants discussed in chapter 6. Individual ants fulfill small tasks that are seemingly insignificant, but when the ants act as a colony, intelligent behavior emerges. Similarly, individual hidden nodes contribute to a greater goal in the ANN. By analyzing the figure of the car-collision ANN and the operations within it, we can describe the data structures required for the algorithm:

- *Input nodes*—The input nodes can be represented by a single array that stores the values for a specific example. The array size is the number of features in the dataset that are being used to predict a class. In the car-collision example, we have four inputs, so the array size is 4.
- *Weights*—The weights can be represented by a matrix (a 2D array) because each input node has a connection to each hidden node and each input node has five connections. Because there are four input nodes with five connections each, the ANN has 20 weights toward the hidden layer and five toward the output layer because there are five hidden nodes and one output node.
- *Hidden nodes*—The hidden nodes can be represented by a single array that stores the results of activation of each respective node.
- *Output node*—The output node is a single value representing the predicted class of a specific example or the chance that the example will be in a specific class. The output might be 1 or 0, indicating whether a collision occurred, or it could be something like 0.65, indicating a 65% chance that the example resulted in a collision.

Python code sample for defining a neural network

The next piece of code describes a class that represents a neural network. Notice that the layers are represented as properties of the class and that all the properties are arrays, with the exception of the weights, which are matrices. An `output` property represents the predictions for the given examples, and an `expected_output` property is used during the training process:

```python
class NeuralNetwork:
    def __init__(self, features, labels, hidden_node_count):
        num_features = features.shape[1]
        num_samples = features.shape[0]
        num_output = labels.shape[1]

        self.input = features
        self.expected_output = labels
```

Automatically detects the number of input signals (features) and the number of answers to predict (output)

Creates a matrix of random
numbers representing the strength
of the connections between the
Input and Hidden layers

A storage space for the
"thoughts" of the network

```
self.weights_input =
  np.random.randn(num_features, hidden_node_count) * 0.01

self.hidden = np.zeros((num_samples, hidden_node_count))

self.weights_hidden =
  np.random.randn(hidden_node_count, num_output) * 0.01

self.output = np.zeros((num_samples, num_output))

self.hidden_node_count = hidden_node_count
self.num_output = num_output
self.num_samples = num_samples
```

A placeholder for the
network's final guesses

Creates the
connections
between the
Hidden layer
and the
Output layer

Forward propagation: Using a trained ANN

A *trained ANN* is a network that has learned from examples and adjusted its weights to best predict the class of new examples. Don't panic about how the training happens and how the weights are adjusted; we'll tackle this topic in the next section. Understanding forward propagation will help us grasp *backpropagation* (how weights are trained). Now that we have a grounding in the general architecture of ANNs and the intuition of what nodes in the network might be doing, let's walk through the algorithm for using a trained ANN (figure 9.14).

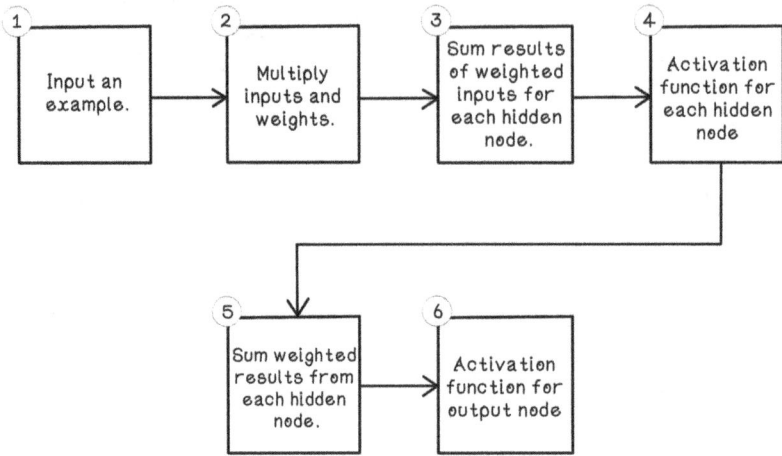

Figure 9.14 Life cycle of forward propagation in an ANN

As mentioned earlier, the steps involved in calculating the results for the nodes in an ANN are similar to the Perceptron. Similar operations are performed on many nodes that work together. This approach addresses the Perceptron's flaws and is used to solve problems that have more dimensions. The general flow of forward propagation includes the following steps:

1. *Input an example.* Provide a single example from the dataset for which we want to predict the class.
2. *Multiply inputs and weights.* Multiply every input by each weight of its connection to hidden nodes.
3. *Sum the results of weighted inputs for each hidden node.* Sum the results of the weighted inputs.
4. *Use an activation function for each hidden node.* Apply an activation function to the summed weighted inputs.
5. *Sum the results of the weighted outputs of hidden nodes to the output node.* Sum the weighted results of the activation function from all hidden nodes.
6. *Use an activation function for output node.* Apply an activation function to the summed weighted hidden nodes.

For the purpose of exploring forward propagation, we'll assume that the ANN has been trained and the optimal weights in the network have been found. Figure 9.15 depicts the weights on each connection. The first box next to the first hidden node, for example, has the weight 3.35, which is related to the Speed input nodes, and the weight -5.82 is related to the Terrain Quality input node.

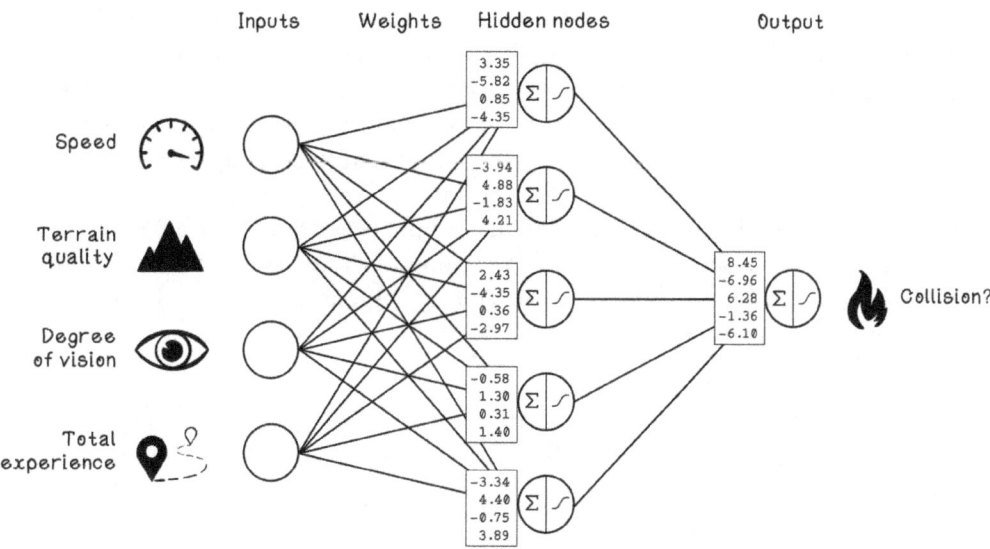

Figure 9.15 Example of weights in a pretrained ANN

Because the neural network has been trained, we can use it to predict the chance of collisions by providing it a single example. Table 9.3 serves as a reminder of the scaled dataset we're using.

Table 9.3 Reminder of the car-collision dataset, scaled

	Speed	Terrain quality	Degree of vision	Total experience	Collision occurred?
1	0.542	0.5	0.5	0.200	0
2	1.000	0.1	0.2	0.275	1
3	0.067	0.6	0.8	0.125	0
4	0.417	0.2	0.9	0.004	1
5	0.208	0.9	0.1	0.400	0
6	0.667	0.3	0.3	0.015	1
7	0.333	0.3	1.0	1.000	0

If you've ever looked into ANNs, you may have noticed some potentially frightening mathematical notations. Let's break down some of the concepts that can be represented mathematically.

The inputs of the ANN are denoted by X. Every input variable is X subscripted by a number. Speed is X_0, Terrain Quality is X_1, and so on. The output of the network is denoted by y, and the weights of the network are denoted by W. Because we have two layers in the ANN—a hidden layer and an output layer—there are two groups of weights. The first group is superscripted by W_0, and the second group is W_1. Then each weight is denoted by the nodes to which it's connected. The weight between the Speed node and the first hidden node is $W_{0,0}$, and the weight between the Terrain Quality node and the first hidden node is $W_{1,0}$. These denotations aren't necessarily important for this example, but understanding them now will support future learning. Figure 9.16 shows how the following data is represented in an ANN:

	Speed	Terrain quality	Degree of vision	Total experience	Collision occurred?
1	0.542	0.5	0.5	0.200	0

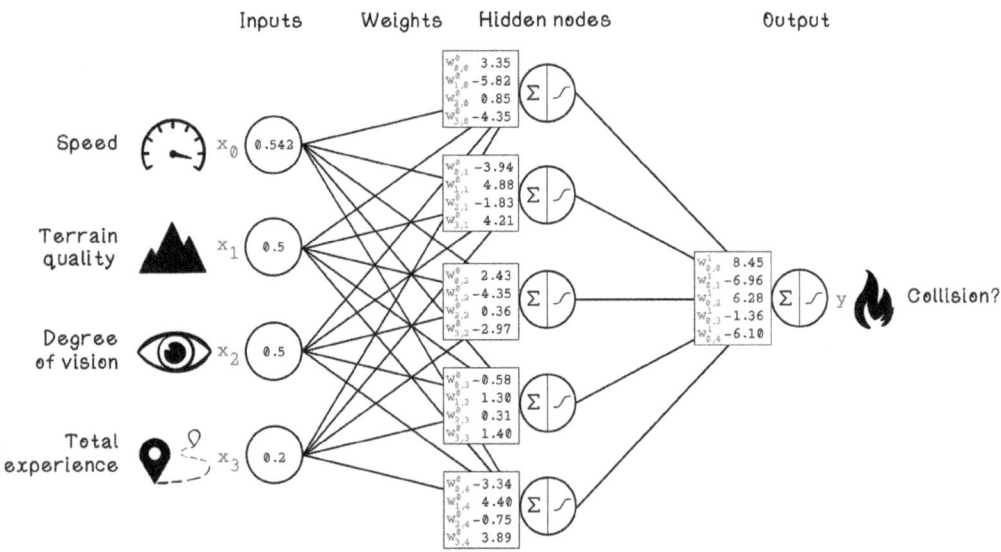

Figure 9.16 Mathematical denotation of an ANN

As with the Perceptron, the first step is calculating the weighted sum of the inputs and the weight of each hidden node. In figure 9.17, each input is multiplied by each weight and summed for every hidden node.

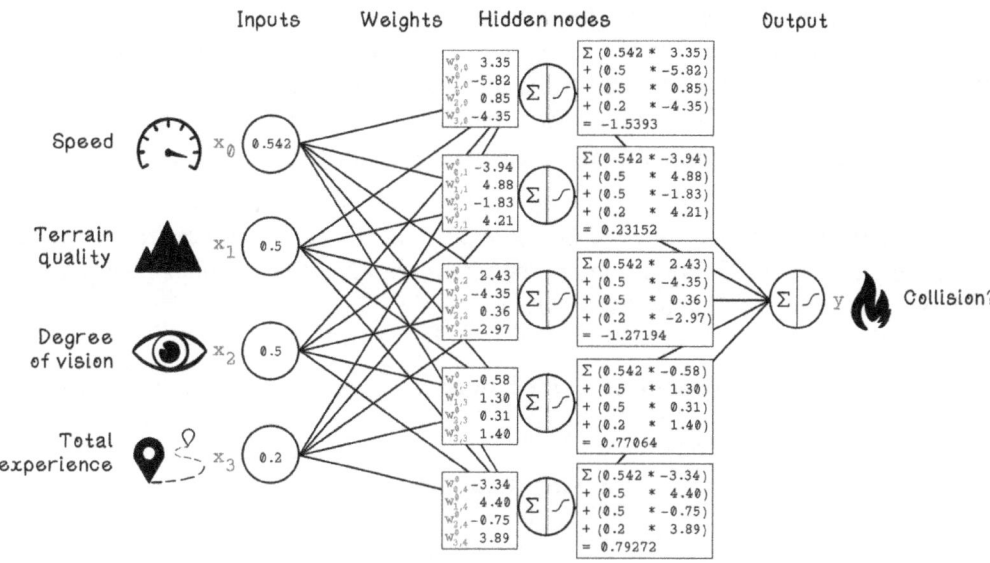

Figure 9.17 Weighted sum calculation for each hidden node

The next step is calculating the activation of each hidden node. We're using the sigmoid function, and the input for the function is the weighted sum of the inputs calculated for each hidden node (figure 9.18).

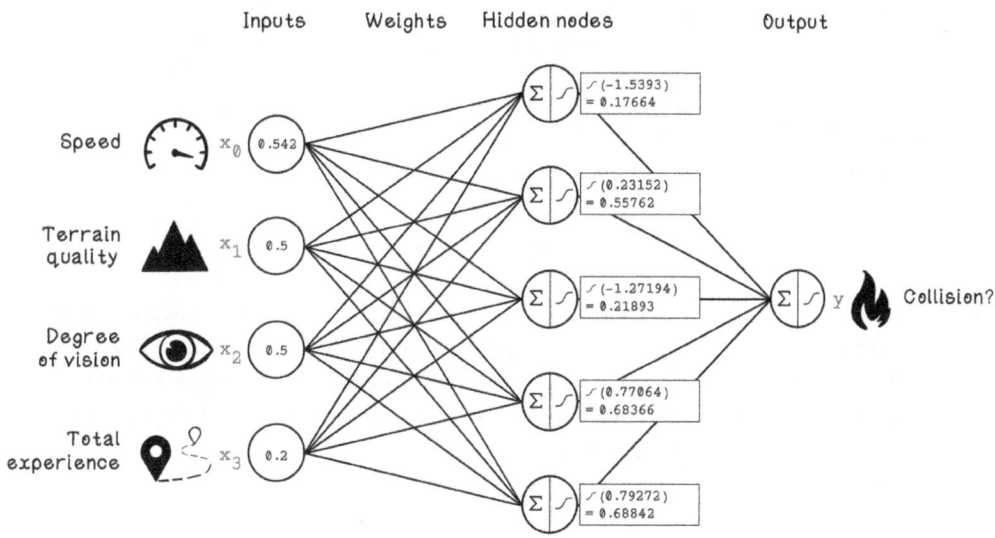

Figure 9.18 Activation function calculation for each hidden node

Now we have the activation results for each hidden node. When we mirror this result back to neurons, the activation results represent the activation intensity of each neuron. Because different hidden nodes may be concerned with different relationships in the data through the weights, we can use the activations in conjunction to determine an overall activation that represents the chance of a collision, given the inputs.

Figure 9.19 depicts the activations for each hidden node and the weights from each hidden node to the output node. To calculate the final output, we repeat the process of calculating the weighted sum of the results from each hidden node and applying the sigmoid activation function to that result.

NOTE The sigma symbol (Σ) in the hidden nodes depicts the sum operation.

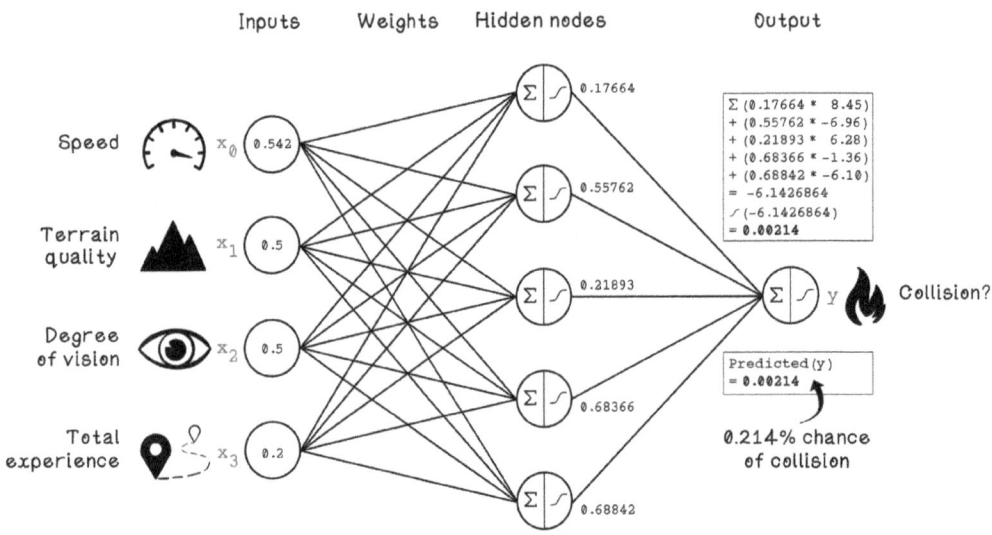

Figure 9.19 Final activation calculation for the output node

We've calculated the output prediction for our example. The result is 0.00214. But what does this number mean? The output is a value between 0 and 1 that represents the probability that a collision will occur. In this case, the output is 0.214 percent (0.00214 * 100), indicating that the chance of a collision is almost 0 percent. The following exercise uses another example from the dataset.

Exercise: Calculate the prediction for the example by using forward propagation with the following ANN

	Speed	Terrain quality	Degree of vision	Total experience	Collision occurred?
2	1.000	0.1	0.2	0.275	1

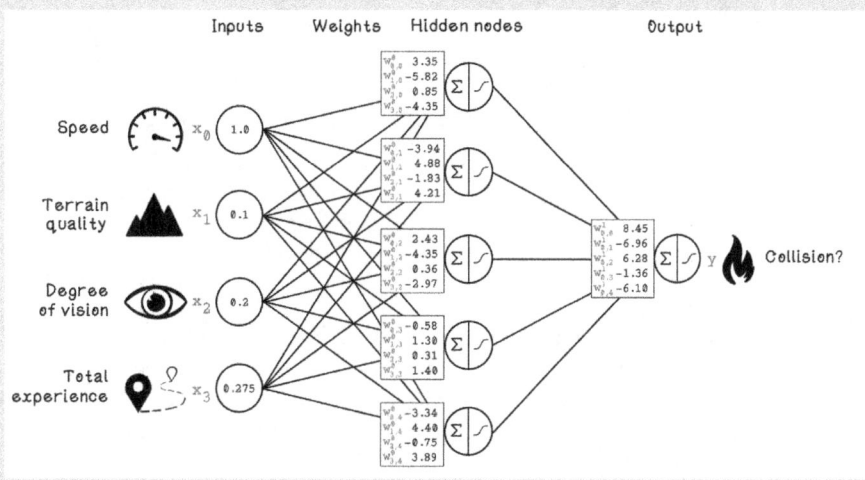

Solution:

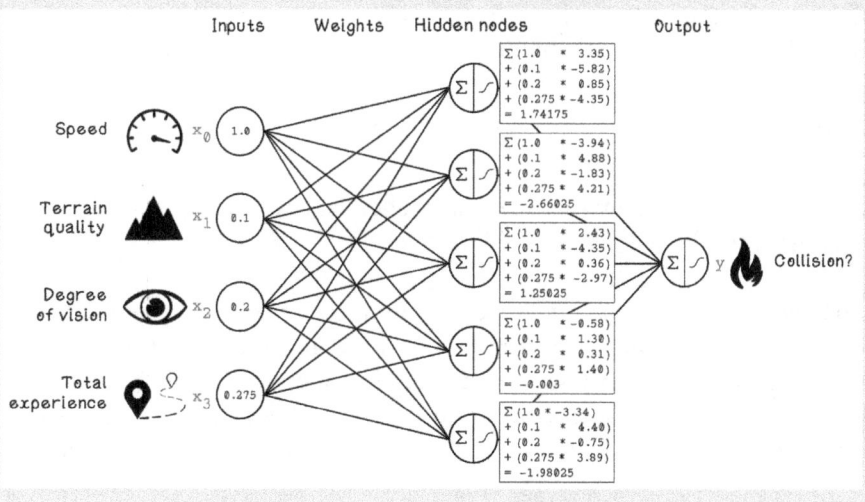

(continued)

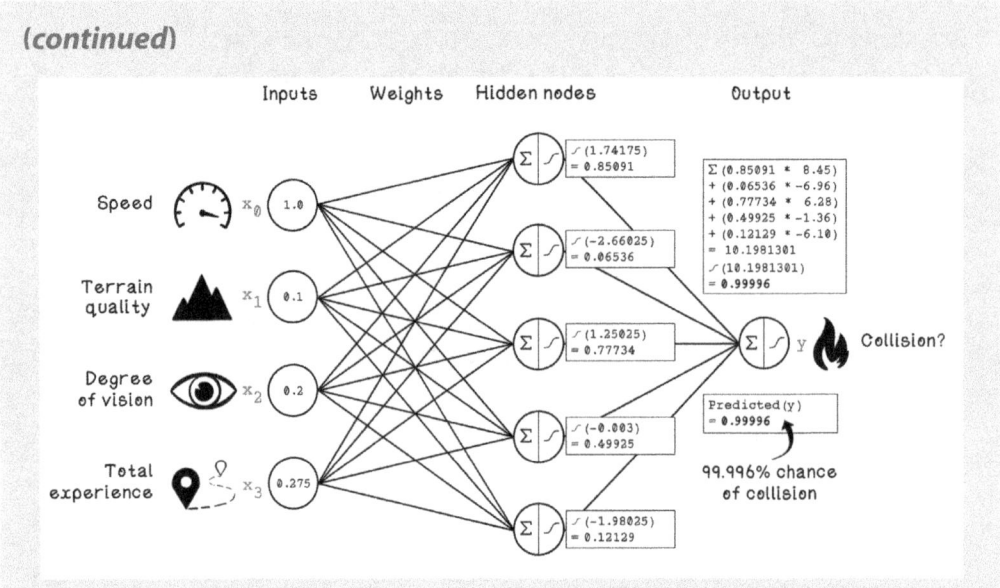

When we run this example through our pretrained ANN, the output is 0.99996, or 99.996 percent, so there's an extremely high chance that a collision will occur. By applying some human intuition to this single example, we see why a collision is likely. The driver was traveling at the maximum legal speed, on the poorest-quality terrain, with a poor field of vision.

Python code sample for forward propagation

One of the important functions for activation in our example is the sigmoid function. This method describes the mathematical function that represents the S curve:

```python
def sigmoid(x):
    return 1 / (1 + np.exp(-x))
```

> **NOTE** exp is a mathematical constant called *Euler's number*, also denoted by e, approximately 2.71828.

The same neural network class defined earlier in the chapter is described in the following code, this time including a forward_propagation function. This function sums the input and weights between input and hidden nodes, applies the sigmoid function to each result, and stores the output as the result for the nodes in the hidden layer. This is done for the hidden node output and weights to the output node as well:

```
class NeuralNetwork:
    def __init__(self, features, labels, hidden_node_count):
        num_features = features.shape[1]
        num_samples = features.shape[0]
        num_output = labels.shape[1]

        self.input = features
        self.expected_output = labels
        self.hidden_node_count = hidden_node_count

        self.weights_input =
        np.random.randn(num_features, hidden_node_count) * 0.01
        self.weights_hidden =
        np.random.randn(hidden_node_count, num_output) * 0.01

        self.hidden = np.zeros((num_samples, hidden_node_count))
        self.output = np.zeros((num_samples, num_output))

    def forward_propagation(self):
        self.hidden = sigmoid(np.dot(self.input, self.weights_input))
        self.output = sigmoid(np.dot(self.hidden, self.weights_hidden))
```

Takes the "features" learned by the hidden layer and combines them with a second set of weights to form the final prediction signals

multiplies every input by its corresponding weight and sums them up and passes the weighted sum through the sigmoid function

Backpropagation: Training an ANN

The machine learning life cycle and principles covered in chapter 8 are important for tackling backpropagation in ANNs. An ANN can be seen as just another machine learning model. We still need to have a question to ask. We're still collecting and understanding data in the context of the problem, and we have to prepare the data in a way that the model can process. We need a subset of data for training and a subset of data for testing how well the model performs. Also, we'll be iterating and improving by collecting more data, preparing it differently, or changing the architecture and configuration of the ANN.

Training an ANN consists of three main phases. Phase A involves setting up the ANN architecture, including configuring the inputs, outputs, and hidden layers. Phase B is forward propagation. Phase C is backpropagation, where the training happens (figure 9.20).

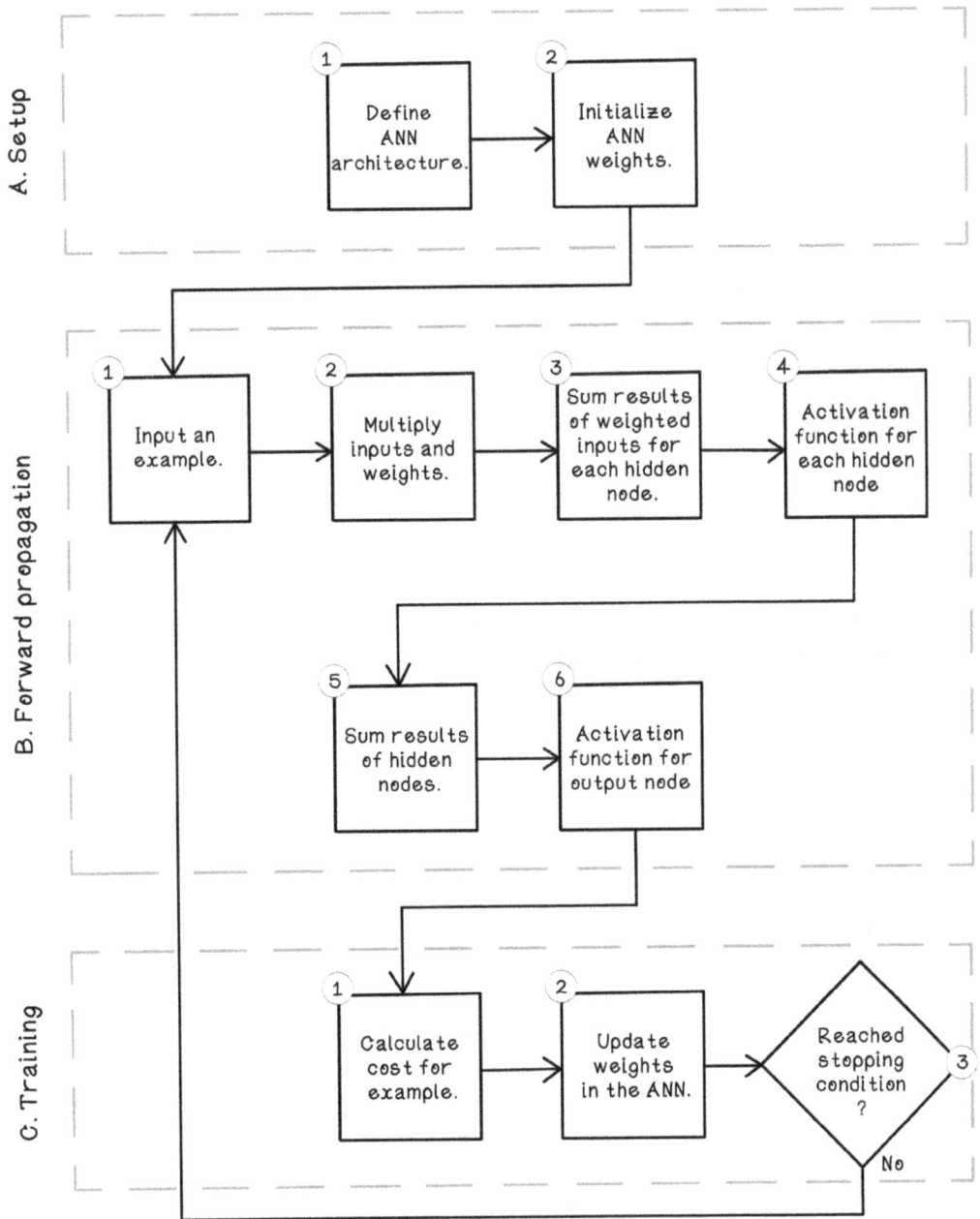

Figure 9.20 Life cycle of training an ANN

Imagine a relay team that lost its race by 5 seconds (total error). The coach walks backward from the finish line to fix it:

- "Runner 4, you were 2 seconds slow. Fix it."
- "Runner 3, you handed the baton off poorly, which caused Runner 4 to be late. Fix it."

Backpropagation looks at the final error and works backward through the network, calculating exactly how much each specific weight contributed to that error, and tells it to adjust. Sections of the life cycle are broken into phase A, B, and C for ease of understanding the operations involved in the backpropagation algorithm.

Phase A: Setup

To prepare the network for training, we must complete two steps:

1. *Define the ANN architecture.* This step involves defining the input nodes, the output nodes, the number of hidden layers, the number of neurons in each hidden layer, the activation functions used, and more.
2. *Initialize the ANN weights.* The weights in the ANN must be initialized to some value. We can take various approaches, with random numbers from a standard normal distribution being an effective approach. The key principle is that the weights will be adjusted constantly as the ANN learns from training examples.

Phase B: Forward propagation

This process is the same one covered earlier in this chapter, and the same calculations are carried out to produce an output for the network. The predicted output, however, will be compared with the actual class of the example from the training data set that's fed into the network. So if the network produced the prediction of 0.99996 (99.996%) after the final hidden layer's activation function, that prediction will be compared to the actual value, indicating whether a collision occurred (1, or 100%) or did not occur (0).

Phase C: Training

Finally, we explore the difference between the predicted output and the actual value, which is critical to learning in phase C.

1. *Calculate the cost.* Following from forward propagation, the *cost* is the difference between the predicted output and the actual class for the examples in the training set. The cost effectively determines how bad the ANN is at predicting the class of examples. If the network predicted 0.7 and the actual value was 1.0, trivially, we have a loss of 0.3.

2. *Update the weights in the ANN.* The weights of the ANN are the only things that the network itself can adjust. The architecture and configurations defined in phase A don't change during network training. The weights essentially encode the intelligence of the network. Weights are adjusted to be larger or smaller, affecting the strength of the inputs (adjusting the importance of the relationships between certain inputs to adjust predictions).

3. *Define a stopping condition.* Training can't go on indefinitely. As with many of the algorithms explored in this book, we have to determine a sensible stopping condition. If we have a large dataset, we may decide to use 500 examples in our training dataset over 1,000 iterations to train the ANN. In this example, the 500 examples will be passed through the network 1,000 times, and the weights will be adjusted in every iteration.

When we worked through forward propagation, the weights were already defined because the network was pretrained. Before we start training the network, we must initialize the weights to some value, and the weights have to be adjusted based on training examples. One approach to initializing weights is to choose random weights from a normal distribution.

Figure 9.21 illustrates the randomly generated weights for our ANN. It also shows the calculations for forward propagation for the hidden nodes, given a single training example. The first example input used in the forward propagation section is used here to highlight the differences in output given different weights in the network.

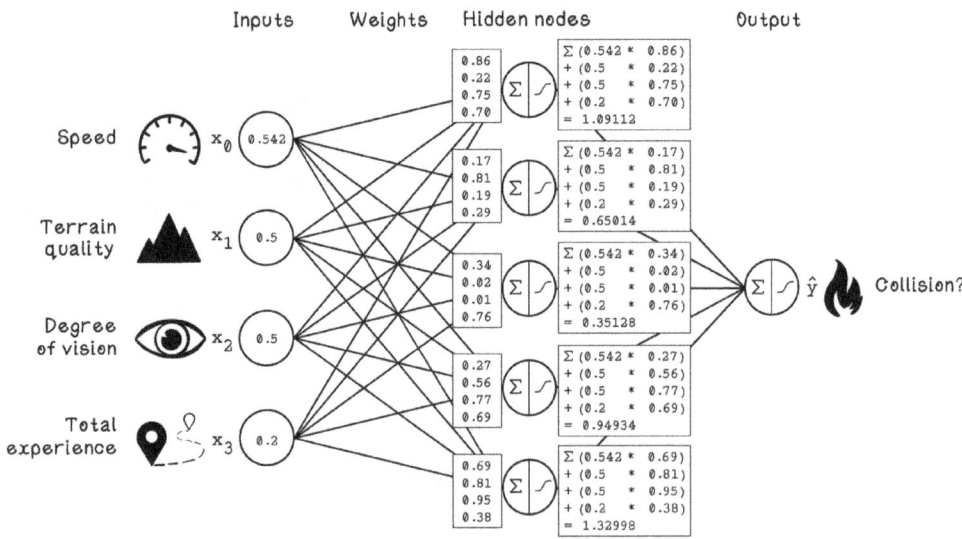

Figure 9.21 Example initial weights for an ANN

The next step is forward propagation (figure 9.22). The key change is checking the difference between the obtained prediction and the actual class.

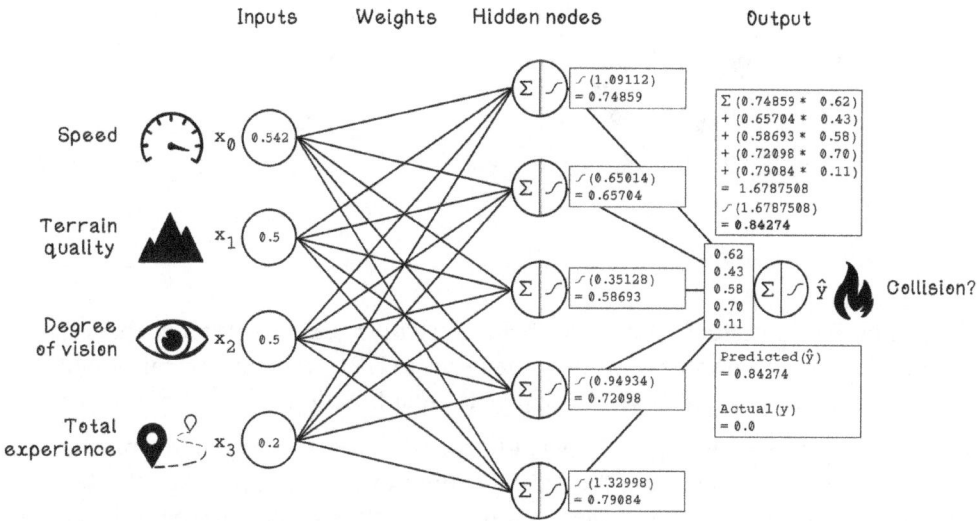

Figure 9.22 Example of forward propagation with randomly initialized weights

By comparing the predicted result with the actual class, we can calculate a cost. The cost function we'll use is simple: subtract the predicted output from the actual output. In this example, we subtract 0.84274 from 0.0, and the cost is -0.84274. This result indicates how incorrect the prediction was, and we can use it to adjust the weights in the ANN. Weights in the ANN are adjusted slightly every time a cost is calculated. This cycle repeats thousands of times using the training data to fine-tune the weights, enabling the ANN to make accurate predictions.

> **NOTE** As described in chapter 8, with linear regression and decision trees, ANNs can also suffer from overfitting due to training too long on the same set of data.

Here is where some potentially unfamiliar math comes into play. Let's gain some intuition about what the weights mean and how adjusting them improves the ANN's performance.

If we plot possible weights against their respective cost on a graph, we find some function that represents the possible weights. Some points on the function yield a lower cost; other points yield a higher cost. We're seeking points that minimize cost (figure 9.23).

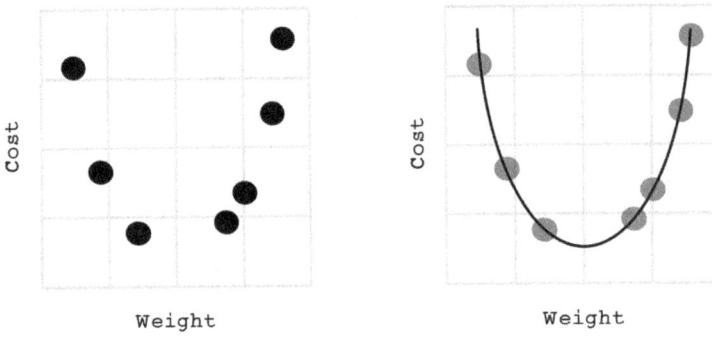

Figure 9.23 Weight versus cost plotted

Gradient descent, a useful tool from the field of calculus, can help us move the weight closer to the minimum value by finding the derivative. The *derivative* is important because it measures the sensitivity to change for that function.

Suppose that you're standing in a hilly landscape (the cost function) in the pitch dark. You want to get to the bottom of the valley (minimum cost), but you can't see the bottom. You can feel the angle of the ground under your feet. The derivative is the slope; it tells you how steep the ground is where you are standing. You can use the slope to determine your next move:

- *If the slope tilts up* (positive derivative), you know that moving forward will take you higher (more error), so you should move backward.
- *If the slope tilts down* (negative derivative), you know that moving forward will take you lower (less error), so you should move forward.
- *If the slope is perfectly flat* (derivative is 0), you have likely reached the bottom.

As another example, just as velocity is the derivative of an object's *position* with respect to *time,* acceleration is the derivative of the object's *velocity* with respect to *time.* Derivatives can find the slope at a specific point in the function. Gradient descent uses the knowledge of the slope to determine which way to move and how much. Figures 9.24 and 9.25 show how the derivatives and slope indicate the direction of the minimums.

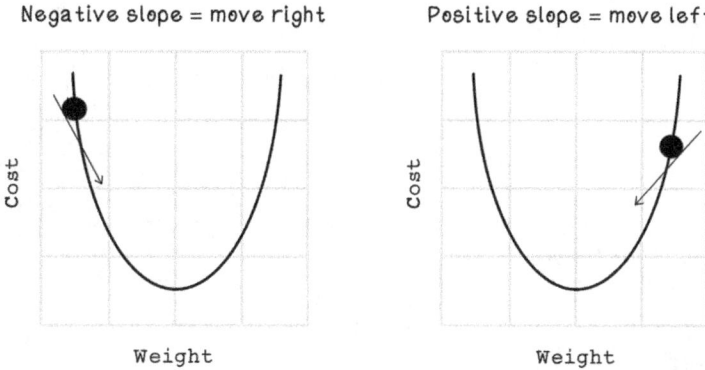

Figure 9.24 Derivatives' slopes and direction of minimums

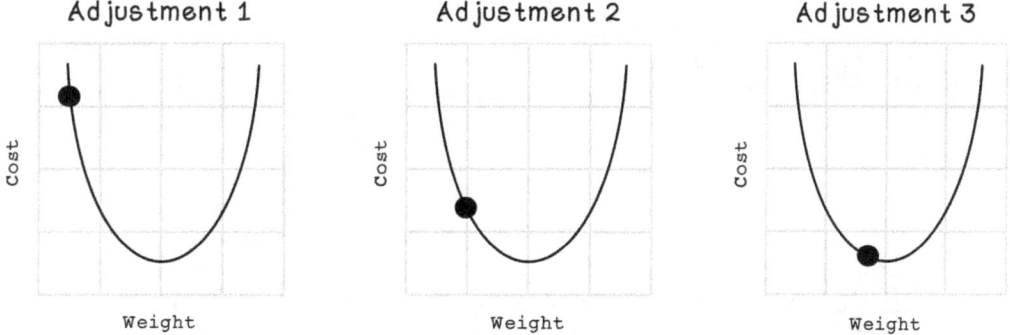

Figure 9.25 Example of adjusting a weight by using gradient descent

When we look at one weight in isolation, it may seem trivial to find a value that minimizes the cost, but many weights being balanced affect the cost of the overall network. Some weights may be close to their optimal points in reducing cost, and others may not, even though the ANN performs well.

Because many functions comprise the ANN, we can use the *Chain Rule*, a theorem that calculates the derivative of a composite function. A *composite function* uses a function g as the parameter for a function f to produce a function h, essentially using a function as a parameter of another function. Figure 9.26 illustrates using the Chain Rule to calculate the update value for weights in the different layers of the ANN.

Calculate update for weights between input nodes and hidden nodes:
input * (2 * cost * sigmoid_derivative(output) * hidden weight) * sigmoid_derivative(hidden)

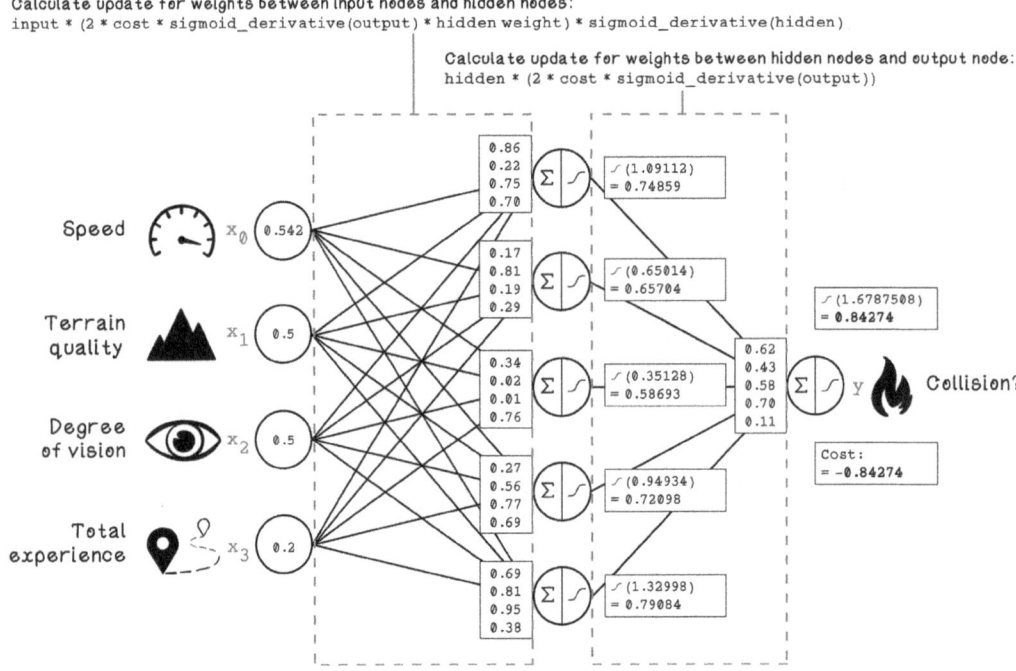

Calculate update for weights between hidden nodes and output node:
hidden * (2 * cost * sigmoid_derivative(output))

Figure 9.26 Formula for calculating weight updates with the Chain Rule

We can calculate the weight update by plugging the respective values into the formula in figure 9.27. The calculations look complicated, but pay attention to the variables and their roles in the ANN. Although the formula looks complex, it uses the values that we've already calculated.

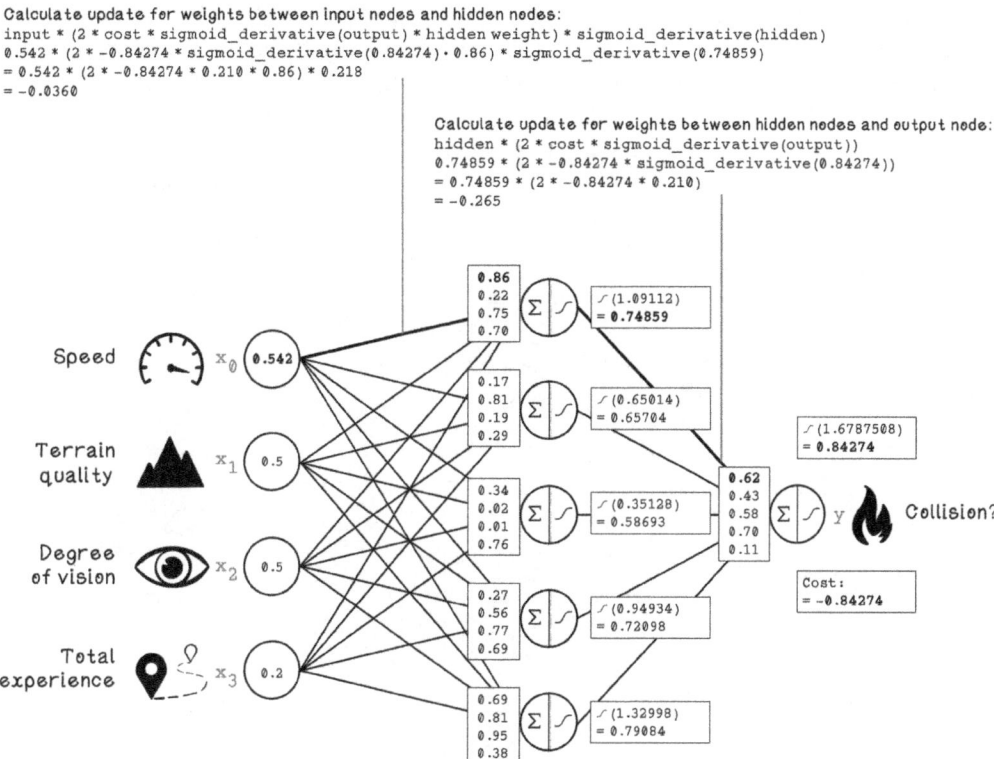

Calculate update for weights between input nodes and hidden nodes:
```
input * (2 * cost * sigmoid_derivative(output) * hidden weight) * sigmoid_derivative(hidden)
0.542 * (2 * -0.84274 * sigmoid_derivative(0.84274) · 0.86) * sigmoid_derivative(0.74859)
= 0.542 * (2 * -0.84274 * 0.210 * 0.86) * .218
= -0.0360
```

Calculate update for weights between hidden nodes and output node:
```
hidden * (2 * cost * sigmoid_derivative(output))
0.74859 * (2 * -0.84274 * sigmoid_derivative(0.84274))
= 0.74859 * (2 * -0.84274 * 0.210)
= -0.265
```

Figure 9.27 Weight-update calculation with the Chain Rule

Here's a closer look at the calculations used in figure 9.27:

Calculate update for weights between hidden nodes and output node:
```
hidden * (2 * cost * sigmoid_derivative(output))

0.74859 * (2 * -0.84274 * sigmoid_derivative(0.84274))
= 0.74859 * (2 * -0.84274 * 0.210)
= -0.265
```

Calculate update for weights between input nodes and hidden nodes:
```
input * (2 * cost * sigmoid_derivative(output) * hidden weight) * sigmoid_derivative(hidden)

0.542 * (2 * -0.84274 * sigmoid_derivative(0.84274) * 0.86) * sigmoid_derivative(0.74859)
= 0.542 * (2 * -0.84274 * 0.210 * 0.86) * 0.218
= -0.0360
```

Now that the update values are calculated, we can apply the results to the weights in the ANN by adding the update value to the respective weights. Figure 9.28 depicts the application of the weight-update results to the weights in the different layers.

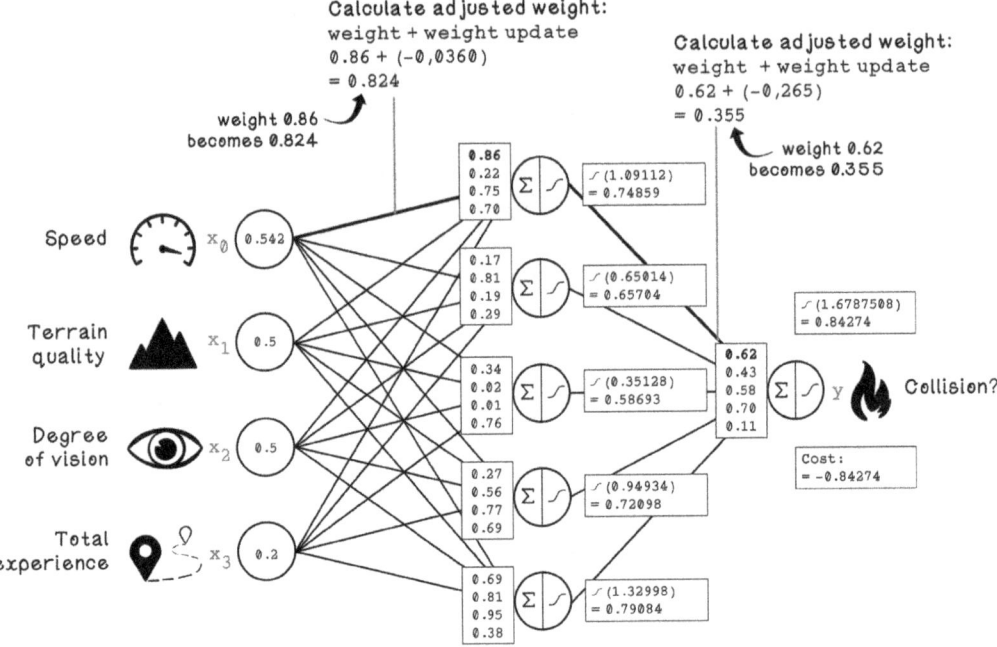

Figure 9.28 Example of the final weight update for the ANN

Exercise: Calculate the new weights for the highlighted weights

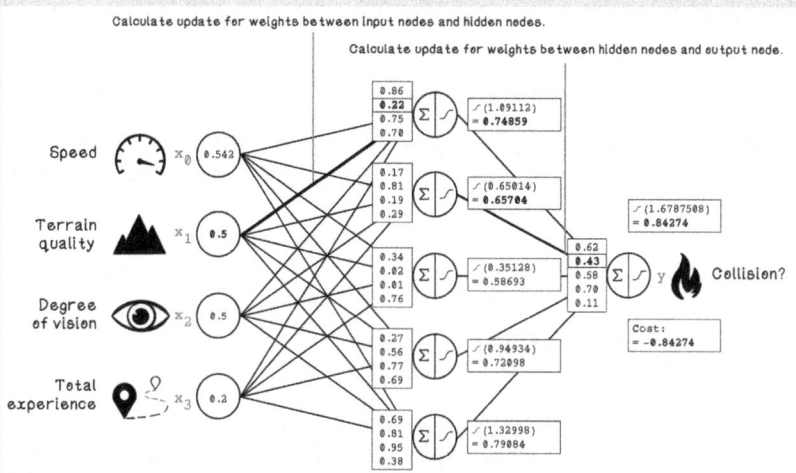

Solution:

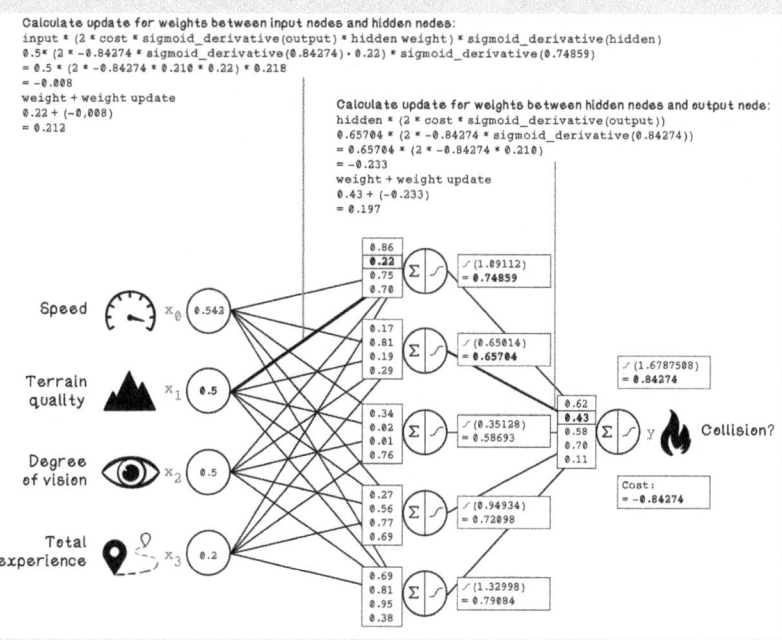

The problem that the Chain Rule solved may remind you of the Drone Problem in chapter 7. Particle Swarm Optimization (PSO) is effective for finding optimal values in high-dimensional spaces such as this one, which has 25 weights to optimize. Finding the weights in an ANN is an optimization problem. Gradient descent isn't the only way to optimize weights; we can use many approaches, depending on the context and problem being solved.

Python code sample for backpropagation

The derivative is important in the backpropagation algorithm. The following piece of code revisits the sigmoid function and describes the formula for its derivative, which we need to adjust weights:

```python
def sigmoid(x):
    return 1 / (1 + np.exp(-x))

def sigmoid_derivative(x):
    return sigmoid(x) * (1 - sigmoid(x))
```

Calculates the derivative (slope) of the sigmoid function at point x

We revisit the neural network class, this time with a backpropagation function that computes the cost, determines the amount by which weights should be updated using the Chain Rule, and adds the weight-update results to the existing weights. This process will compute the change for each weight given the cost. Remember that we calculate cost by using the example features, predicted output, and expected output. The difference between the predicted output and expected output is the cost. Because we have a class that represents a neural network, functions to scale data, and functions for forward propagation and backpropagation, we can piece this code together to train a neural network:

```python
class NeuralNetwork:
    def __init__(self, features, labels, hidden_node_count):
        num_features = features.shape[1]
        num_samples = features.shape[0]
        num_output = labels.shape[1]

        self.input = features
        self.expected_output = labels
        self.hidden_node_count = hidden_node_count

        self.weights_input =
        np.random.randn(num_features, hidden_node_count) * 0.01
        self.weights_hidden =
        np.random.randn(hidden_node_count, num_output) * 0.01

        self.hidden = np.zeros((num_samples, hidden_node_count))
        self.output = np.zeros((num_samples, num_output))
```

measures how far off the network's guess was from the actual answer. If this is zero, no changes are needed

```python
def forward_propagation(self):
    self.hidden = sigmoid(np.dot(self.input, self.weights_input))
    self.output = sigmoid(np.dot(self.hidden, self.weights_hidden))

def back_propagation(self):
    error_output = self.expected_output - self.output

    d_output = 2 * error_output * \
    (self.output * (1 - self.output))

    d_weights_hidden = \
    self.hidden.T @ d_output

    error_hidden = \
    d_output @ self.weights_hidden.T * \
    (self.hidden * (1 - self.hidden))

    d_weights_input = self.input.T @ error_hidden

    self.weights_hidden += d_weights_hidden
    self.weights_input += d_weights_input
```

Uses matrix multiplication to find out how much each hidden node contributed to the final error

Calculate its error by looking at the output's error and the weights connecting them

Combines the error with the derivative of the sigmoid. This tells us how much to change the output weights and in what direction

Finally, we adjust the actual weights

Determines how much the original input features contributed to the errors found in the hidden layer

NOTE The symbol • means matrix multiplication.

In the next piece of code, we have a run_neural_network function that accepts epochs as an input. This function scales the data and creates a new neural network with the scaled data, labels, and number of hidden nodes. Then the function runs forward_propagation and back_propagation for the specified number of epochs:

Initializes the network architecture, creates
the random weight matrices, and allocates
memory for the hidden and output layers

Normalizes the input data
before it enters the network

```
def run_neural_network(epochs, feature_data, label_data, hidden_node_count):

    scaled_feature_data = scale_dataset(
        feature_data, FEATURE_COUNT, FEATURE_MIN, FEATURE_MAX
    )

    nn = NeuralNetwork(
        scaled_feature_data,
        label_data,
        hidden_node_count
    )

    for epoch in range(epochs):
        nn.forward_propagation()
        nn.back_propagation()

        if epoch % 100 == 0:
            loss = np.mean(np.square(nn.expected_output - nn.output))
            print(f"Epoch {epoch:03d}: Loss = {loss:.6f}")

    return nn
```

One "epoch" represents a
single full pass of the entire
dataset through the network

The network makes a guess
based on the current weights

Calculates the average squared
difference between the network's
guess and the actual target

The network calculates its mistake and
updates every weight in the system to be
slightly more accurate for the next round

You've learned the complete life cycle, from scaling input data and feeding it through
an ANN to training the ANN via backpropagation by calculating the loss of predictions
versus actual outcomes. This is the essence of how large neural networks operate and is
the fundamental concept for understanding more sophisticated applications of it, like
large language models (LLMs) and generative image models.

Options for activation functions

This section discusses the intuition of activation functions and their properties in
detail. In the examples of the Perceptron and ANN, we used a sigmoid function as
the activation function, which was satisfactory for the examples we were working
with. Activation functions introduce nonlinear properties to the ANN. If we don't use

an activation function, the neural network can behave similarly to linear regression (described in chapter 8). Figure 9.29 depicts some commonly used activation functions.

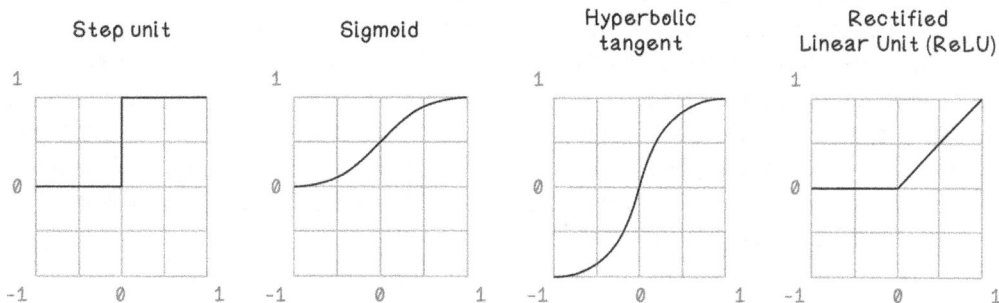

Figure 9.29 Common used activation functions

Activation functions are useful in different scenarios and have different benefits. Following are some of those benefits:

- *Step unit*—The step-unit function is used as a binary classifier. Given an input between -1 and 1, it outputs a result of exactly 0 or 1. A binary classifier isn't useful for learning from data in a hidden layer, but it can be used in the output layer for binary classification. If we want to know whether an animal is a cat or a dog, for example, 0 could indicate cat, and 1 could indicate dog.

- *Sigmoid*—The sigmoid function results in an S curve between 0 and 1, given an input between -1 and 1. Because the sigmoid function allows changes in x to result in small changes in y, it enables learning and solving nonlinear problems. A problem that sometimes occurs with the sigmoid function is that as values approach the extremes, derivative changes become tiny, resulting in poor learning. As mentioned earlier in this chapter, this problem is known as the vanishing gradient problem.

- *Hyperbolic tangent*—The hyperbolic-tangent function is similar to the sigmoid function, but it results in values between -1 and 1. The benefit is that the hyperbolic tangent has steeper derivatives, which allow faster learning. The vanishing-gradient problem is also a problem at the extremes for this function, as with the sigmoid function.

- *Rectified linear unit (ReLU)*—The ReLU function results in 0 for input values between -1 and 0 and results in linearly increasing values between 0 and 1. In a large ANN with many neurons using the sigmoid or hyperbolic-tangent function, all neurons activate all the time (except when they result in 0), resulting in lots of computation and many values being adjusted finely to find solutions. The ReLU function allows some neurons to not activate, which reduces computation and possibly finds solutions faster.

Designing ANNs

Designing ANNs can be experimental, depending on the problem being solved. The architecture and configuration of an ANN usually change through trial and error as we attempt to improve the performance of the predictions or on the basis of well-researched architectures that are proven to work. This section lists the parameters of the architecture we can change to improve performance or address various problems. Figure 9.30 illustrates an artificial neural network with a different configuration from the one used so far throughout this chapter. The most notable differences are the additions of a new hidden layer and two outputs in the network.

> **NOTE** As in most scientific or engineering problems, the answer to "What is the ideal ANN design?" is often "It depends." Configuring ANNs requires a deep understanding of the data and the problem being solved.

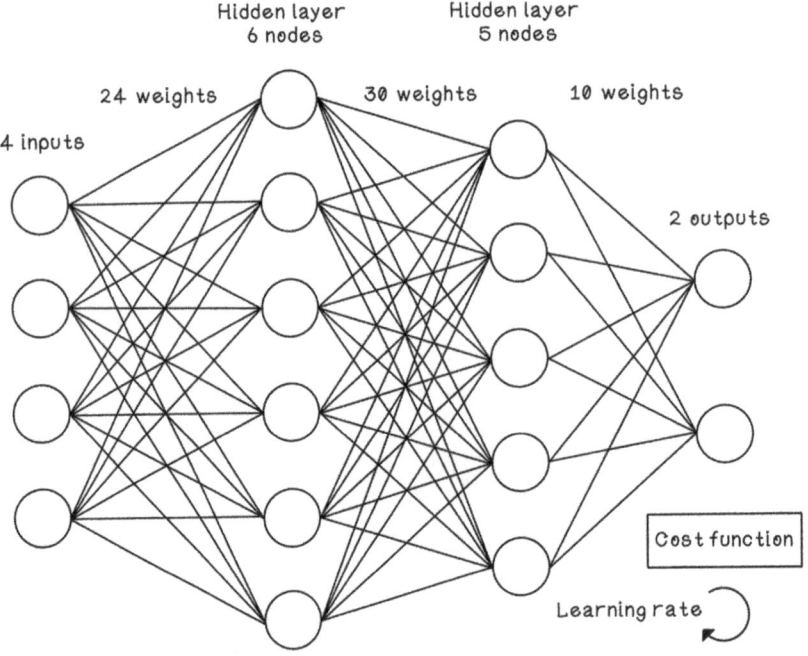

Figure 9.30 An example of a multilayer ANN with more than one output

Inputs and outputs

The inputs and outputs of an ANN are the fundamental parameters for use of the network. After an ANN model has been trained, the trained ANN model will potentially be used in different contexts and systems and by different people. The inputs and outputs define the interface of the network. Throughout this chapter, we've seen an example ANN with four inputs describing the features of a driving scenario and one output describing the likelihood of a collision. We may have a problem when the inputs and outputs mean different things, however. If we have a 16- by 16-pixel image that represents a handwritten digit, for example, we could use the pixel values as inputs and the digit they represent as the output. The input would consist of 256 nodes representing the pixel values, and the output would consist of 10 nodes representing 0 to 9, with each result indicating the probability that the image is the respective digit.

Hidden layers and nodes

An ANN can consist of multiple hidden layers with varying numbers of nodes in each layer. Adding more hidden layers allows us to solve problems with higher dimensions and more complexity in the classification discrimination line. Think of additional layers as finding more high-level abstractions of the relationships among the outputs of the layer before it.

In figure 9.8 earlier in this chapter, a simple straight line classifies data accurately. Sometimes, the line is nonlinear but fairly simple. But what happens when the line is a more-complex function with many curves potentially across many dimensions (which we can't even visualize)? Adding more layers allows us to find these complex classification functions. The selection of the number of layers and nodes in an ANN usually comes down to experimentation and iterative improvement. Over time, we may gain intuition about suitable configurations based on experiencing similar problems and solving them with similar configurations.

Although it's common to describe ANNs using nodes (representing neurons) and edges (representing connections), high-performing implementations are designed for computational efficiency and rely on tensors instead. A *tensor* is a flexible, multidimensional data structure that generalizes simpler mathematical objects. To understand tensors, consider the following:

- *Scalar*—A single numerical value (0D tensor), such as 5.
- *Vector*—A 1D array of numbers (1D tensor), such as [2.1, -0.3, 4.7].
- *Matrix*—A 2D grid of numbers (2D tensor), such as a table with rows and columns.
- *Tensor*—A generalization of all the above. A tensor can have three or more dimensions:

- ° A 3D tensor might represent a stack of matrices (e.g., color image with height × width × RGB channels).
- ° A 4D tensor might represent a batch of images (batch size × height × width × channels).

In deep learning frameworks such as TensorFlow and PyTorch, entire ANN layers are treated as tensor operations. Inputs, weights, and outputs are all represented as tensors, allowing for highly optimized parallel computation. Instead of simulating each node and edge individually, the network performs efficient bulk transformations on entire layers using tensor algebra, making large-scale training and inference practical by using the power of GPUs optimized for operations on tensors. We'll learn how this math works shortly. Figure 9.31 illustrates the difference in dimensions between scalars, vectors, matrices, and tensors.

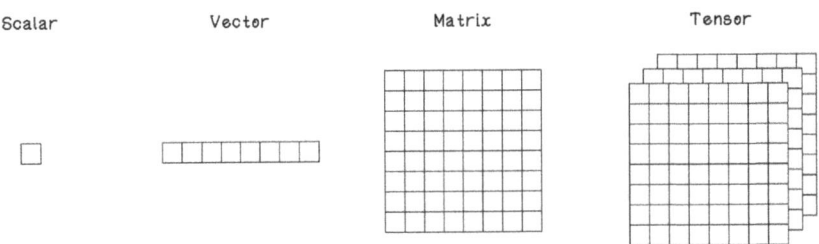

Figure 9.31 Comparison of tensor data structures

Weights

Weight initialization is important because it establishes a starting point from which the weight will be adjusted slightly over many iterations. Weights that are initialized to be too small lead to the vanishing-gradient problem. Weights that are initialized to be too large lead to another problem: the *exploding-gradient problem*, in which weights move erratically around the desired result.

Various weight-initialization schemes exist, each with its own pros and cons. A rule of thumb is to ensure that the mean of the activation results in a layer is 0—the mean of all results of the hidden nodes in a layer. Also, the variance of the activation results should be the same: the variability of the results from each hidden node should be consistent over several iterations.

The Goldilocks principle of initialization

Why do we care about the mean and variance? Imagine a game of Telephone played by 100 layers of neurons:

- *If the weights are too small*—The whisper gets quieter and quieter until the last person hears nothing. The network stops learning because the signal died. This problem is the vanishing gradient.
- *If the weights are too large*—The whisper turns into shouting. By the end, the signal is a distorted, screaming mess. This problem is the exploding gradient.

The solution is smart initialization. To fix this problem, we don't pick random numbers; we use smart formulas (such as Xavier/Glorot initialization) to pick weights that are just right. The goal is simple: ensure that the variance (the spread of the signal strength) remains the same from the first layer to the last. If the input signal has a strength of 1, we also want the output signal to have a rough strength of 1, preventing the signal from exploding or vanishing as it travels deep into the network.

Bias

We can use bias in an ANN by adding a value to the weighted sum of the input nodes or other layers of the network. A bias can shift the activation value of the activation function. It provides flexibility in an ANN and shifts the activation function left or right.

A simple way to understand bias is to imagine a line that always passes through 0,0 on a plane. We can influence this line to pass through a different intercept by adding +1 to a variable. This value is based on the problem to be solved.

Activation functions

Earlier, we covered the common activation functions used in ANNs. A key rule of thumb is to ensure that all nodes on the same layer use the same activation function. In multilayer ANNs, different layers may use different activation functions based on the problem to be solved. A network that determines whether loans should be granted, for example, might use the sigmoid function in the hidden layers to determine probabilities and a step function in the output to get a clear 0 or 1 decision.

Cost function

In our example, we used a simple cost function in which the predicted output is subtracted from the actual expected output, but many cost functions are available. Cost functions influence the ANN greatly. Using the correct function for the problem and dataset at hand is important because it describes the goal for the ANN. One of the most common cost functions is *mean square error*, which is similar to the function used in the machine learning chapter (chapter 8). But cost functions must be selected based on understanding of the training data, size of the training data, and desired precision and recall measurements. As we experiment more, we should look into the cost-function options.

Learning rate

Finally, the learning rate of the ANN describes how dramatically weights are adjusted during backpropagation. A slow learning rate may result in a long training process because weights are updated by tiny amounts each time, and a high learning rate might result in dramatic changes in the weights, making for a chaotic training process. One solution is to start with a fixed learning rate and adjust that rate if the training stagnates and doesn't improve the cost. This process, which would be repeated through the training cycle, requires some experimentation. Stochastic gradient descent is a useful tweak to the optimizer that combats these problems. It works similarly to gradient descent but allows weights to jump out of local minimums to explore better solutions.

Standard ANNs, such as the one described in this chapter, are useful for solving nonlinear classification problems. If we're trying to categorize examples based on many features, this ANN style is likely to be a good option.

That said, an ANN isn't a silver bullet and shouldn't be the go-to algorithm for anything. Simpler, traditional machine learning algorithms like those described in chapter 8 often perform better for many common use cases. Remember the machine learning life cycle. You may want to try several machine learning models during your iterations while seeking improvement.

Expressing ANNs mathematically

We've looked at ANNs as biological neurons, visualized as graphs and as code. But ANNs also speak another language: linear algebra.

When you read AI research papers, you usually don't see code or diagrams of neurons; you see mathematical equations. Let's translate what we've learned into this universal language.

The weighted sum as a dot product

Recall that a single neuron takes inputs, multiplies them by weights, sums them up, and adds a bias. Mathematically, if we have inputs x, weights w, and bias b, the weighted sum z is

$$z = x_1 w_1 + x_2 w_2 + x_3 w_3 \ldots + b$$

Writing this equation out for every neuron is tedious. In linear algebra, we treat the inputs as a *vector* (a list of numbers) and the weights as a vector. This approach allows us to use the dot product, which means multiplying pairwise and summing the results. Given the following,

- *Inputs (X)* —[0.542, 0.5, 0.5, 0.2]
- *Weights (W)* —[3.35, -5.82, 0.85, -4.35]

the dot product is $(0.542 \times 3.35) + (0.5 \times -5.82) + (0.5 \times 0.85) + (0.2 \times -4.35)$. The following single equation replaces the loop we'd otherwise have to write in code:

$$z = X \cdot W + b$$

The hidden layer as matrix multiplication

In our car-collision example, we didn't have a single neuron; we had a layer of five hidden nodes. We don't want to calculate five separate dot products. Instead, we bundle the weights of all five neurons into a *matrix* (a 2D grid):

- *Inputs (X)*—A vector of size 4 (Speed, Terrain, Vision, Experience)
- *Weights (W)*—A matrix of size 4×5 (four inputs connecting to five hidden nodes)

Now the entire layer's calculation happens in one operation. This matrix multiplication calculates the weighted sums for all five hidden neurons simultaneously:

$$Z_{hidden} = X \cdot W_{input}$$

Adding the activation function

After we have the weighted sums (Z), we apply the activation function (such as the sigmoid). We denote the activation function with σ (the Greek letter sigma). The output of the hidden layer (H) becomes

$$H = \sigma(X \cdot W_{input})$$

The output layer

The output of the hidden layer (H) becomes the input for the next layer. This is where the concept of composite functions (functions inside functions) appears.

To get the final prediction ($\hat{y}$, pronounced "y hat"), we multiply the hidden-layer results by the second set of weights and apply the activation function again:

$$\hat{y} = \sigma(H \cdot W_{hidden})$$

> **NOTE** You pronounce this equation as "y hat equals sigma of H dot W hidden."

The final neural network equation

If we substitute H for the equation from the activation function step, we can express the entire neural network in a single mathematical line. This "sentence" describes the architecture we built:

$$\hat{y} = \sigma\left(\sigma\left(X \cdot W_{input}\right) \cdot W_{hidden}\right)$$

This elegant equation tells the full story of forward propagation:

1. Take inputs X.
2. Multiply by first weights W_{hidden}.
3. Apply activation σ.
4. Multiply that result by second weights W_{hidden}.
5. Apply activation again to get the final prediction $\hat{y}$.

The cost function

Finally, how do we express the error? A common method is *mean squared error*, a type of cost function used to measure how well (or poorly) the neural network is performing. It calculates the average of the squares of the errors. The error is the difference between what the network predicted and the actual expected value (*Actual – Predicted*). The mathematical notation for the cost function (*J*) using mean squared error looks like this:

$$ J = \frac{1}{2}(y - \hat{y})^2 $$

- y—The actual value (whether the collision happened)
- $\hat{y}$—The predicted value (the probability of a collision)

Expressing backpropagation mathematically

If forward propagation is about composing functions (wrapping inputs inside layers), backpropagation is about decomposing them using the Chain Rule. Our goal is simple: we want to know how much to adjust a specific weight (W) to decrease the cost (J). In calculus terms, we're looking for the *partial derivative* (∂; the Greek letter del) of the cost with respect to the weight:

$$ \frac{\partial J}{\partial W} $$

If this value is positive, increasing the weight increases error, so we should decrease the weight. If it's negative, increasing the weight decreases error, so we should increase it.

The Chain Rule: Domino effect

We can't calculate $\frac{\partial J}{\partial W}$ directly because the weight (W) doesn't touch the cost (J) directly; it's buried deep inside the network. W affects the *hidden layer*, which affects the *predicted output*, which affects the *cost*. To find the relationship, we multiply the derivatives of these steps together. This is the Chain Rule:

$$ \frac{\partial J}{\partial W} = \frac{\partial J}{\partial Output} \cdot \frac{\partial Output}{\partial Hidden} \cdot \frac{\partial Hidden}{\partial W} $$

Calculating the gradients: Backward pass

We calculate the gradients starting from the end and moving backward:

1. *Calculate the output error* (δ_{output}, the Greek lowercase letter delta). First, we see how wrong our prediction was and how sensitive the activation function is at that point:

$$\delta_{output} = (\hat{y} - y) \cdot \sigma' \left(Z_{output} \right)$$

   a. $((\hat{y} - y))$—The difference between prediction and reality (the raw error)

   b. $\sigma'(Z_{output})$—The derivative (slope) of the activation function (e.g., Sigmoid derivative)

   The symbol σ' is pronounced "sigma prime." In calculus, the little tick mark (') indicates the derivative of a function. So whereas σ gives us the activation value (e.g., 0.7), σ' gives us the *slope* of the curve at that point (how steep it is).

2. *Calculate the output weights gradient* (∇W_{hidden}, the Greek letter nabla). Now we find how much the weights that connect the hidden layer to the output layer contributed to that error.

   A note on notation: In the Chain Rule earlier, we used $\frac{\partial J}{\partial W}$ to describe the change for a single weight. In the following steps below, we use the symbol ∇W. This symbol represents the gradient, which is a matrix containing the partial derivatives for every weight in the layer at the same time:

$$\nabla W_{hidden} = H^T \cdot \delta_{output}$$

   We multiply the transpose of the hidden layer values (H^T) by the output error. What does it mean to transpose? The *T* stands for *transpose*, a simple instruction to flip the matrix over its diagonal. Imagine turning a table on its side. The rows become columns, and the columns become rows. In matrix multiplication, the inner dimensions must match (e.g., a 1×5 matrix can't multiply a 1×1 matrix directly). Transposing the matrix flips its dimensions (becoming 5×1), allowing the multiplication operation to work.

3. *Propagate error to the hidden layer* (δ_{output}). This step is the relay-race moment. We pass the error backward through the weights to find out how much the hidden nodes were responsible for the error:

$$\delta_{hidden} = \left(\delta_{output} \cdot W^T{}_{hidden} \right) \cdot \sigma' \left(Z_{hidden} \right)$$

We take the error from the future (δ_{output}), pull it back through the weights (W^T), and multiply by the derivative of the hidden activation.

4. *Calculate the input weight gradient* (∇W_{input}). Finally, we calculate the gradient for the first set of weights:

$$\nabla W_{input} = X^T \cdot \delta_{hidden}$$

The weight update: Gradient descent

Now that we have the gradients (∇W), which represent the slope of the cost function, we simply move in the opposite direction:

$$\nabla W_{new} = W_{old} - \alpha \cdot \nabla W$$

- α (the Greek letter alpha)—The learning rate, which controls how big a step we take
- ∇W—The gradient we calculated in steps 2 and 4

With that, you've unlocked your ability to see ANNs not just as code or diagrams but also as mathematical equations. Don't worry if the notation seems dense at first; the more you look at these types of equations, the more familiar the symbols will become.

ANN types and use cases

ANNs are versatile and can be designed to address different problems. Specific architectural styles of ANNs are useful for solving certain problems. Think of an ANN architectural style as being the fundamental configuration of the network. The examples in this section highlight different configurations.

Recurrent neural networks

Whereas standard ANNs accept a fixed number of inputs, *recurrent neural networks (RNNs)* accept a sequence of inputs with no predetermined length. These inputs are like spoken sentences. RNNs have a concept of memory consisting of hidden layers that represent time; this concept allows the network to retain information about the relationships among the sequences of inputs. When we're training an RNN, the weights in the hidden layers throughout time are also influenced by backpropagation. Multiple weights represent the same weight at different points in time (figure 9.32).

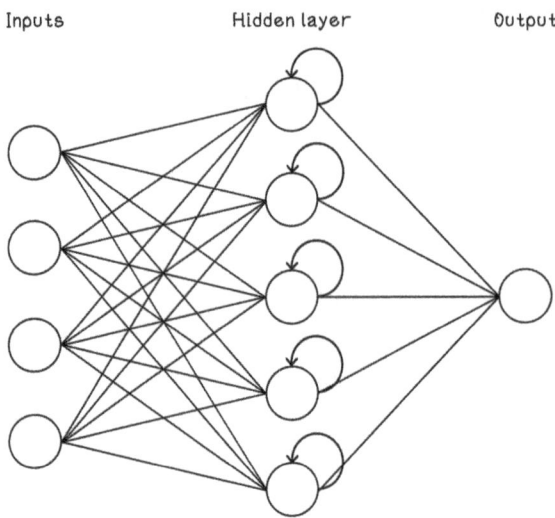

Figure 9.32 Simple example of a RNN

RNNs are useful in applications that pertain to speech and text recognition and prediction. Related use cases include autocompletion of sentences in messaging applications, translation of spoken language to text, and translation between spoken languages.

Although RNNs perform decently, the Transformer architecture has become the state-of-the-art option for tasks like text generation and LLMs. We'll explore this architecture further in chapter 11.

Convolutional neural networks

Convolutional neural networks (CNNs) were originally designed for image recognition. These networks can be used to find the relationships among different objects and unique areas within images. In *image recognition*, convolution operates on a single pixel and its neighbors within a certain radius. This technique is traditionally used for edge detection, image sharpening, and image blurring.

CNNs use convolution and pooling to find relationships among pixels in an image. *Convolution* finds features in images, and *pooling* downsamples the patterns by summarizing features, allowing unique signatures in images to be encoded concisely through learning from multiple images (figure 9.33).

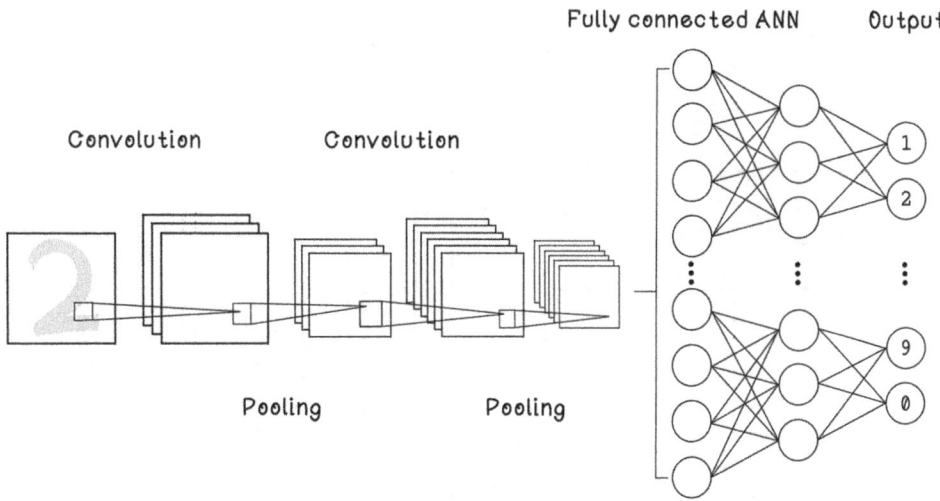

Figure 9.33 Simple example of a CNN

CNNs are used for image classification. If you've ever searched for an image online, you've likely interacted indirectly with a CNN. These networks are also useful for optical character recognition for extracting text data from an image. CNNs have been used in the medical industry for applications that detect anomalies and medical conditions via X-rays and other body scans.

Generative adversarial networks

A *generative adversarial network (GAN)* consists of a generator network and a discriminator network. The *generator* creates a potential solution such as an image or a landscape, for example, and a *discriminator* uses real images of landscapes to determine the realism or correctness of the generated landscape. The error or cost is fed back into the network to further improve its ability to generate convincing landscapes and determine their correctness.

The term *adversarial* is key, as we saw with game trees in chapter 3. These two components are competing to be better at what they do, and through that competition, they generate incrementally better solutions (figure 9.34).

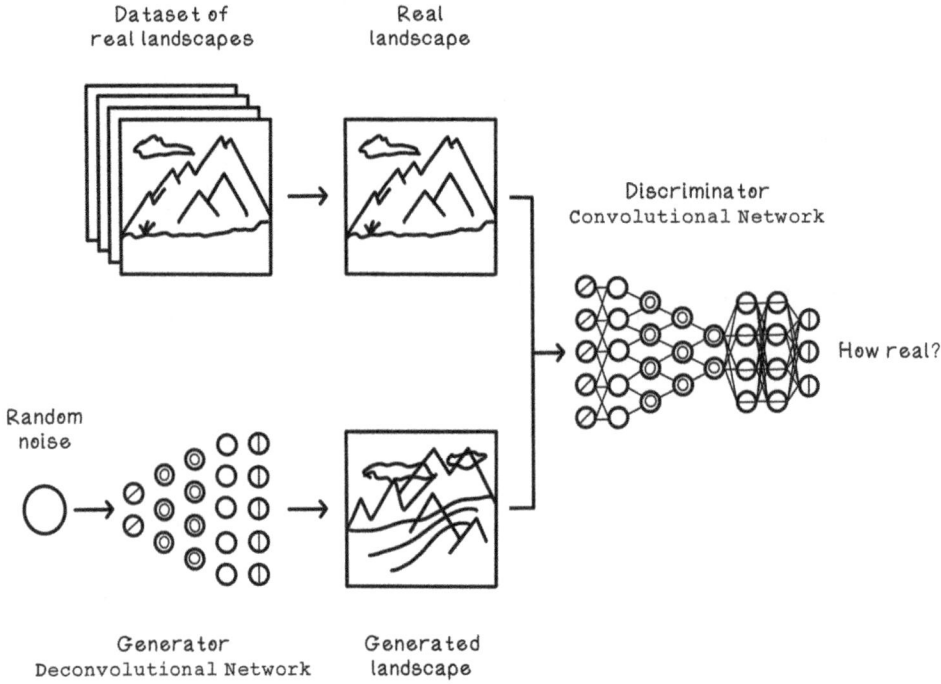

Figure 9.34 Simple example of a GAN

GANs are used to generate convincing fake videos (known as *deepfakes*) of famous people, which raises concern about the authenticity of information in the media. GANs also have useful applications such as overlaying hairstyles on people's faces.

GANs have been used to generate 3D objects from 2D images, such as generating a 3D chair from a 2D picture. This use case may seem unimportant, but the network is accurately estimating and creating information from an incomplete source—a huge step in the advancement of AI and technology in general. Although GANs have been useful, we'll explore how CNNs and the U-Net architecture have become the standard for modern image generation in chapter 12.

> **TIP** This chapter aimed to tie the concepts of machine learning with the somewhat-mysterious world of ANNs. For further information about ANNs and deep learning, try *Grokking Deep Learning*, by Andrew W. Trask (https://www.manning.com/books/grokking-deep-learning). For a practical guide to a framework for building ANNs, see *Deep Learning with Python, Third Edition*, by François Chollet and Matthew Watson (https://www.manning.com/books/deep-learning-with-python-third-edition).

SUMMARY OF ARTIFICIAL NEURAL NETWORKS

Artificial neural networks are inspired by the brain and can be seen as just another ML model

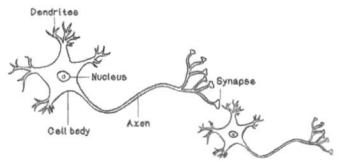

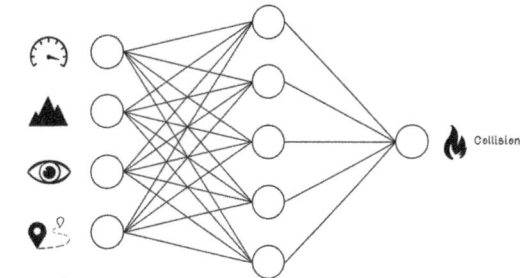

ANNs are based on the idea of a Perceptron (single neuron) at scale.

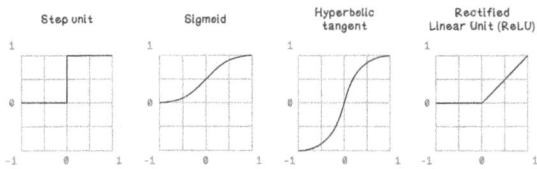

Activation functions help solve nonlinear problems.

Forward propagation is used to feed data into an ANN to make predictions.

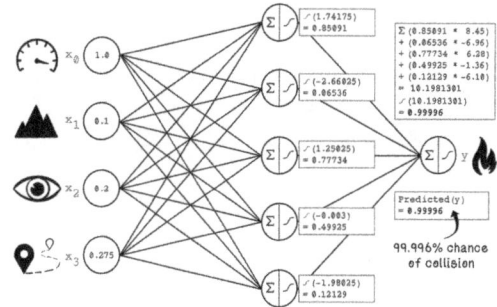

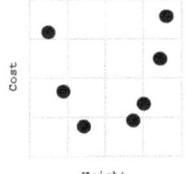 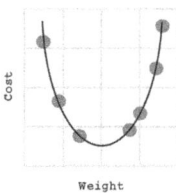

Gradient descent optimization is a popular way to train ANNs.

ANNs are flexible and can be adapted to solve many problems.

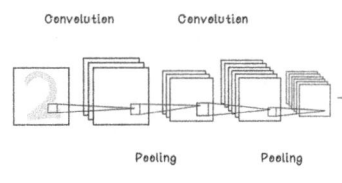 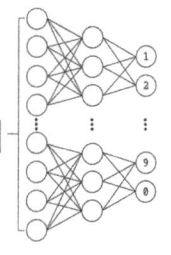

In this chapter

- Understanding the inspiration for reinforcement learning

- Identifying problems solved with reinforcement learning

- Designing and implementing a reinforcement learning algorithm

- Understanding reinforcement learning with ANNs

What is reinforcement learning?

Reinforcement learning is an area of machine learning inspired by behavioral psychology. The concept of reinforcement learning is based on cumulative rewards or penalties for the actions an agent takes in a dynamic environment. Think about a young dog growing up. The dog is the agent in an environment that is our home. When we want the dog to sit, we might simply say, "Sit." The dog doesn't understand English, so we might nudge it by lightly pushing down on its back. After the dog sits, we pet it or give it a treat—a welcome reward. We need to repeat this process many times, but eventually, we positively reinforce the idea of sitting for the dog. The trigger in the environment is saying "Sit"; the behavior learned is sitting; the reward is petting or treats.

Reinforcement learning is another approach to machine learning alongside supervised learning and unsupervised learning. Supervised learning uses labeled data to make predictions and classifications, and unsupervised learning uses unlabeled data to find clusters and trends, but reinforcement learning uses feedback from actions performed to learn what actions (or sequence of actions) are more beneficial in different scenarios. Reinforcement learning is useful when you know what the goal is but don't know what actions to achieve it are reasonable. Figure 10.1 shows a map of machine learning concepts and how reinforcement learning fits in.

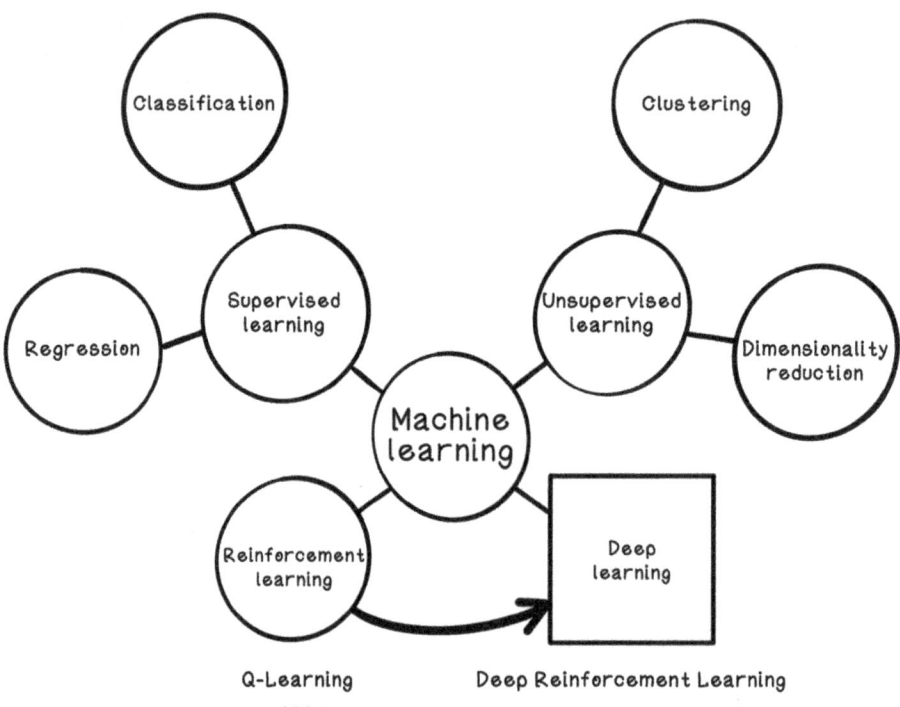

Figure 10.1 How reinforcement learning fits into machine learning

Reinforcement learning can be achieved through classical techniques or deep learning involving artificial neural networks. Either approach may work better depending on the problem being solved.

Figure 10.2 illustrates when different machine learning approaches may be used. We'll explore reinforcement learning through classical methods in this chapter.

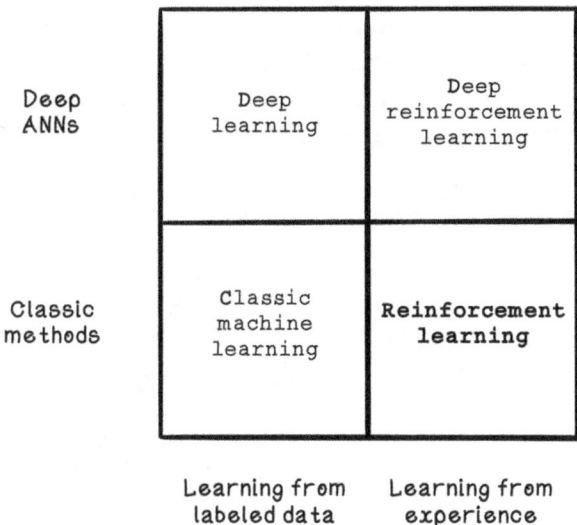

Figure 10.2 Categorization of machine learning, deep learning, and reinforcement learning

The inspiration for reinforcement learning

Reinforcement learning in machines is derived from behavioral psychology, a field that's interested in the behavior of humans and other animals. Behavioral psychology usually explains behavior through a reflex action or something learned in the individual's history. The latter includes exploring reinforcement through rewards or punishments as motivators for behaviors, as well as aspects of the individual's environment that contribute to the behavior.

Trial and error is one of the most common ways that most evolved animals learn what is and isn't beneficial to them. Trial and error involves trying something, potentially failing at it, and then trying something different until you succeed. This process may happen many times before a desired outcome is obtained, and it's largely driven by some reward.

We can observe this behavior in nature. Newborn chicks, for example, try to peck any small piece of material that they come across on the ground. Through trial and error, they learn to peck only food. As they grow, they peck less at random things and learn to identify seeds and grain. Another example involves chimpanzees learning through trial and error that using a stick to dig soil is more favorable than using their hands.

Goals, rewards, and penalties are important in reinforcement learning. The goal for a chimpanzee is to find food; a reward or penalty may be the number of times it has dug a hole or the time it's taken to dig a hole. The faster a chimp digs a hole, the faster it finds food. Figure 10.3 illustrates the terminology used in reinforcement learning with reference to the simple dog-training example.

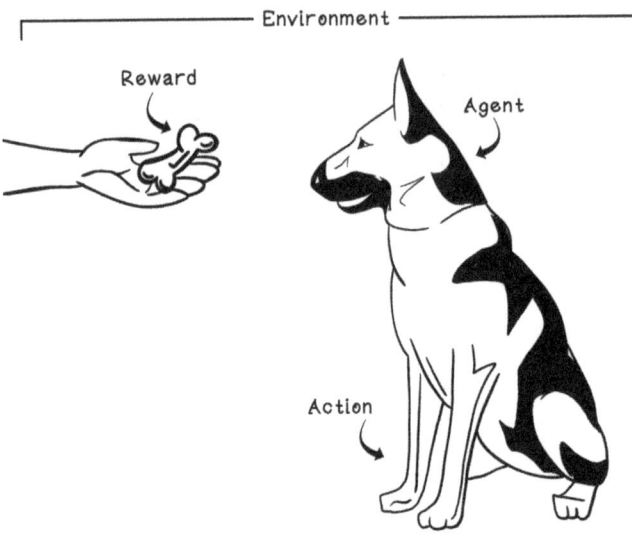

Figure 10.3 Example of reinforcement learning: teaching a dog to sit by using food as a reward

Reinforcement learning relies on a feedback loop of rewards and penalties (sometimes called *punishments*):

- *Positive reward*—Receiving value after performing a good action, such as a dog getting a treat after it sits. This reward encourages the behavior.
- *Negative reward (penalty)*—Receiving a negative value after performing a bad action, such as a dog being scolded after it tears up a carpet. This penalty discourages the behavior.

Positive reinforcement is meant to motivate desired behavior, and negative reinforcement is meant to discourage undesired behavior. Another concept in reinforcement learning is balancing instant gratification with long-term consequences. Eating a chocolate bar is great for getting a boost of sugar and energy; this is *instant gratification*. But eating a chocolate bar every 30 minutes will likely cause serious health problems over time; this is a *long-term consequence*. Reinforcement learning aims to maximize the long-term benefit over short-term benefit, although short-term benefit may contribute to long-term benefit in some scenarios because we want to exploit knowledge of current situations but also explore new things and discover new strategies.

Reinforcement learning is concerned with the long-term consequence of actions in an environment, so time and the sequence of actions are important. Suppose that we're stranded in the wilderness, and our goal is to survive as long as possible while traveling as far as possible in the hope of reaching safety. We're positioned next to a river and have two options: swim to travel downstream faster or walk alongside the river. Notice the boat in figure 10.4. If we swim, we'll travel faster but might miss the boat by being dragged down the wrong fork of the river. If we walk, we're guaranteed to find the boat, which will make the rest of the journey much easier, but we don't know that at the start.

Figure 10.4 An example of possible actions that have long-term consequences

This example shows the importance of the sequence of actions in reinforcement learning. It also shows that instant gratification may lead to long-term detriment. Furthermore, in a landscape that doesn't contain a boat, the consequence of swimming is that we'll travel faster but get our clothing soaked, which could be very problematic if the weather turns cold. The consequence of walking is that we'll travel slower but avoid getting our clothing wet. A specific action may work in one scenario but not in others. Learning from many simulation attempts is important for finding more-general approaches.

Problems that reinforcement learning can solve

To sum up, reinforcement learning aims to solve problems in which a goal and allowed actions are known but the best plan for using the available actions isn't known. These problems involve controlling an agent's actions in an environment. Individual actions may be rewarded more than others, but the main concern is the cumulative reward of all actions.

Reinforcement learning is most useful for problems in which individual actions build up toward a greater goal. Areas such as strategic planning, industrial-process automation, and robotics are good cases for the use of reinforcement learning. In these areas, individual actions may be suboptimal for gaining a favorable outcome. Imagine the strategic game of chess. Some moves may be suboptimal based on the current state of the board, but they help set the board up for a greater strategic win later in the game.

Reinforcement learning works well in domains in which chains of events are important for a good solution. To work through the steps in a reinforcement learning algorithm, we'll use the Car-Collision Problem from chapter 9 as inspiration. This time, however, we'll work with visual data about a self-driving car in a parking lot trying to navigate to its owner. Suppose that we have a map of a parking lot, including a self-driving car, other cars, and pedestrians. Our self-driving car can move north, south, east, and west. The other cars and pedestrians remain stationary.

The goal is for our car to navigate the road to its owner while colliding with as few cars and pedestrians as possible—ideally, not colliding with anything. Colliding with a car isn't good because it damages the vehicles, but colliding with a pedestrian is more severe. In this problem, we want to minimize collisions, but if we have a choice between colliding with a car and a pedestrian, we should choose the car.

Figure 10.5 depicts this scenario. We'll use this example problem to explore how reinforcement learning teaches us good actions to take in dynamic environments.

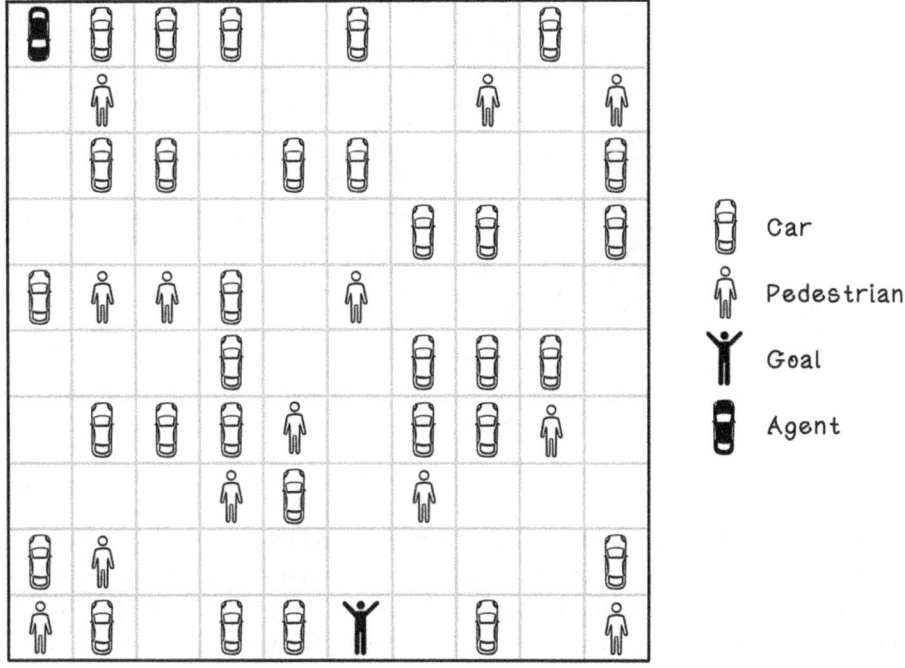

Figure 10.5 The self-driving car in the Parking-Lot Problem

The life cycle of reinforcement learning

Like other machine learning algorithms, a reinforcement learning model must be trained before it can be used. The training phase centers on exploring the environment and receiving feedback, given specific actions performed in specific circumstances or states. The life cycle of training a reinforcement learning model is based on the *Markov Decision Process*, which provides a mathematical framework for modeling decisions (figure 10.6). By quantifying decisions made and their outcomes, we can train a model to learn what actions toward a goal are most favorable.

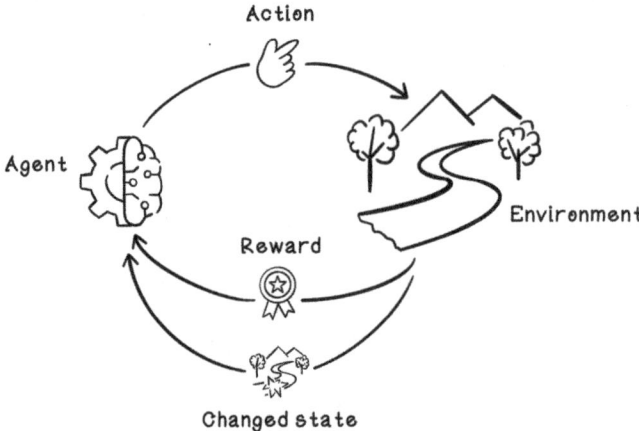

Figure 10.6 The Markov Decision Process for reinforcement learning

Before we start tackling the challenge of training a model by using reinforcement learning, we need an environment that simulates the problem space we're working in. Our Parking-Lot Problem entails a self-driving car trying to navigate a parking lot filled with obstacles to find its owner while avoiding collisions. We have to model this problem as a simulation so that actions in the environment can be measured toward the goal. This simulated environment is different from the model that will learn what actions to take.

> **NOTE** This example is intentionally simplified for clarity. In a real-world application, the environment would be far more dynamic and intricate, giving the agent a much broader array of possible actions and a more nuanced spectrum of consequences for each choice.

Simulation and data: The agent's environment

Figure 10.7 depicts a parking-lot scenario containing several other cars and pedestrians. The starting position of the self-driving car and the location of its owner are represented as black figures. In this example, the self-driving car that applies actions to the environment is known as the *agent*. The agent can take several actions: moving north, south, east, and west. Choosing an action results in the agent moving one block in that direction. The agent can't move diagonally. When actions are taken in the environment, rewards or penalties occur.

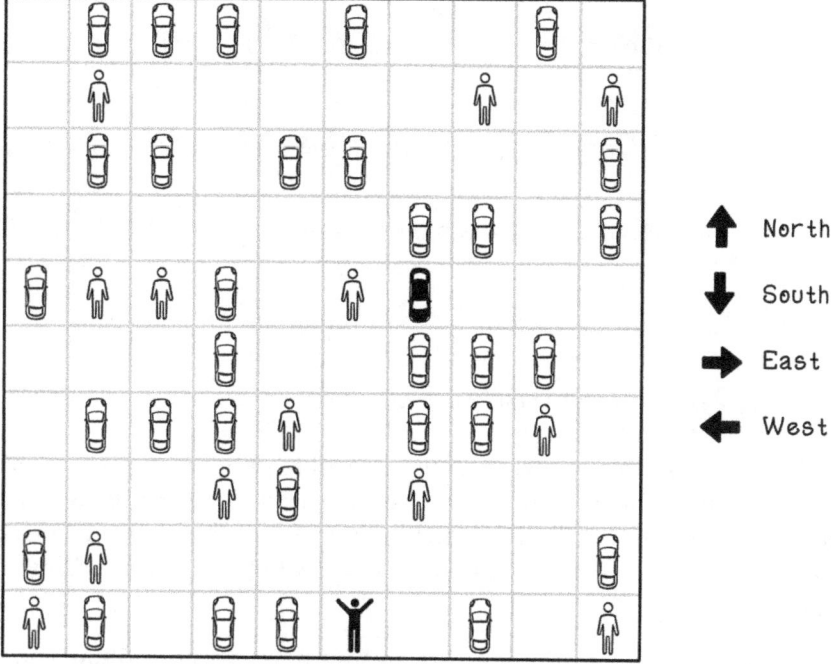

Figure 10.7 Agent actions in the Parking-Lot Problem

Figure 10.8 shows the reward points awarded to the agent based on the outcome in the environment. A collision with another car is bad; a collision with a pedestrian is terrible. A move to an empty space is good; finding the owner of the self-driving car is better. The specified rewards aim to discourage collisions with other cars and pedestrians and to encourage moving into empty spaces and reaching the owner. There could be a reward for out-of-bounds movements, but for simplicity, we'll disallow this possibility.

> **NOTE** An interesting outcome of the rewards and penalties is that the car may drive forward and backward on empty spaces indefinitely to accumulate rewards. We'll dismiss this action as a possibility in this example, but it highlights the importance of crafting good rewards.

Figure 10.8 Rewards for specific events in the environment (actions performed)

The simulator must model the environment, the actions of the agent, and the rewards received after each action. A reinforcement learning algorithm will use the simulator to learn through practice by taking actions in the simulated environment and measuring the outcome. The simulator should provide at least the following functionality and information:

1. *Initialize the environment.* This function involves resetting the environment, including the agent, to the starting state.
2. *Get the current state of the environment.* This function should provide the current state of the environment, which will change after each action is performed.
3. *Apply an action to the environment.* This function involves having the agent apply an action to the environment. The environment is affected by the action, which may result in a reward.
4. *Calculate the reward of the action.* This function is related to applying the action to the environment. The reward for the action and its effect on the environment must be calculated.
5. *Determine whether the goal is achieved.* This function determines whether the agent achieved the goal. Sometimes, the goal can be represented as completed. In an environment in which the goal can't be achieved, the simulator must signal completion when it deems it necessary to do so.

Figures 10.9 and 10.10 depict possible paths in the Parking-Lot Problem. In figure 10.9, the agent travels south until it reaches the boundary; then it travels east until it reaches the goal. Although the agent achieves its goal, it has five collisions with other cars and one collision with a pedestrian—not an ideal result.

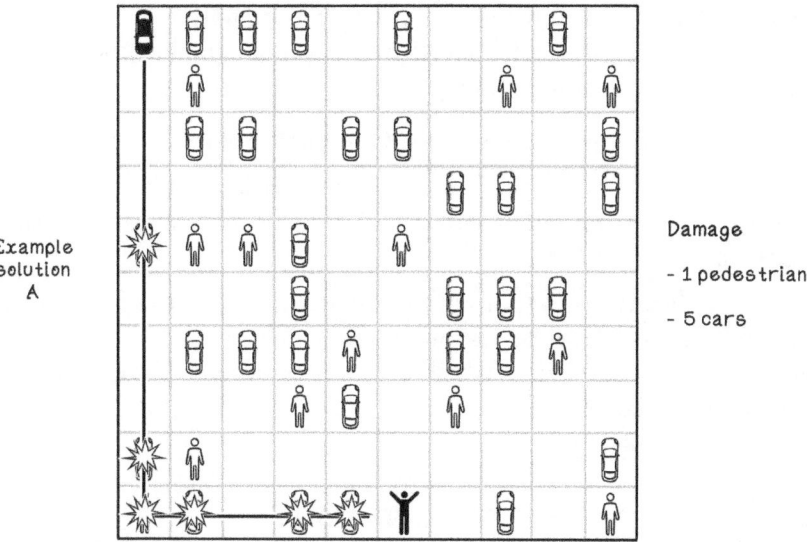

Figure 10.9 A bad solution to the Parking-Lot Problem

Figure 10.10 depicts the agent traveling along a more specific path toward the goal, resulting in no collisions, which is great. It's important to note that given the specified rewards, the agent isn't guaranteed to achieve the shortest path; because we heavily encourage avoiding obstacles, the agent may find any obstacle-free path.

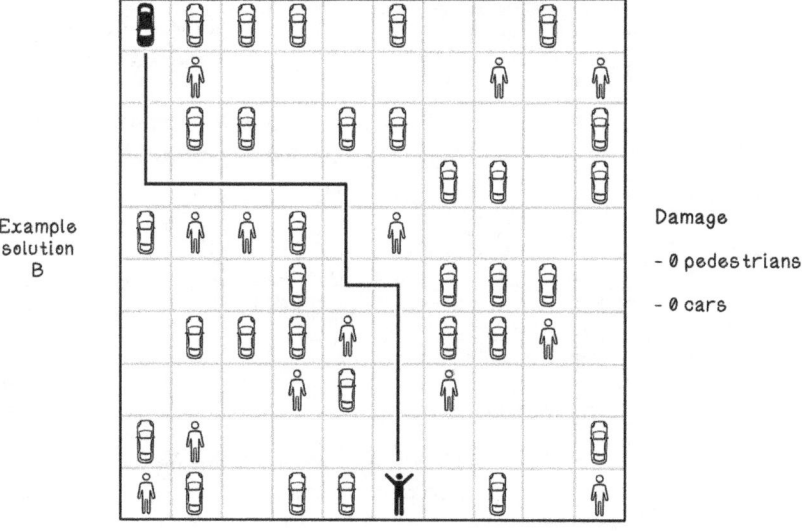

Figure 10.10 A good solution to the Parking-Lot Problem

At this moment, there's no automation in sending actions to the simulator. The scenario is like a game in which a human, not an AI system, provides input. The next section explores how to train an autonomous agent.

Python code sample for simulating the Parking-Lot Problem

The code for the simulator encompasses the functions discussed in this section. The simulator class would be initialized with the information relevant to the starting state of the environment.

The move_agent function is responsible for moving the agent north, south, east, or west based on the action. It determines whether the movement is within bounds, adjusts the agent's coordinates, determines whether a collision occurred, and returns a reward score based on the outcome:

```python
class Simulator:
    def __init__(self, road, road_size_x, road_size_y,
        agent_start_x, agent_start_y):
        self.road = road
        self.road_size_x = road_size_x          Sets up the dimensions and
        self.road_size_y = road_size_y          layout of the environment
        self.agent_x = agent_start_x
        self.agent_y = agent_start_y

    def move_agent(self, action):
        next_x, next_y = self.agent_x, self.agent_y

        if action == COMMAND_NORTH:             Defines how an abstract
            next_x -= 1                         command (like "North")
        elif action == COMMAND_SOUTH:           physically changes the
            next_x += 1                         agent's coordinates
        elif action == COMMAND_EAST:
            next_y += 1
        elif action == COMMAND_WEST:            Validates the move if the agent
            next_y -= 1                         tries to drive off the map

        reward_update = 0

        if self.is_within_bounds(next_x, next_y):
            reward_update = self.cost_movement(next_x, next_y)
            self.agent_x, self.agent_y = next_x, next_y
        else:
            reward_update = ROAD_OUT_OF_BOUNDS_REWARD    Calculates
                                                         the reward
        return reward_update                             for the move

                          Assigns a penalty if the agent
                          attempts an invalid move
```

Here are descriptions of the functions in the next code snippet:

- The `cost_movement` function determines the object in the target coordinate that the agent will move to and returns the relevant reward score.
- The `is_within_bounds` function is a utility function that ensures that the target coordinate is within the boundary of the road.
- The `is_goal_achieved` function determines whether the goal has been found, in which case the simulation can end.
- The `get_state` function uses the agent's position to determine a number that enumerates the current state. Each state must be unique. In other problem spaces, the state may be represented by the actual native state itself.

```python
class Simulator:
    def __init__(self, road, road_size_x, road_size_y,
     agent_start_x, agent_start_y):
        self.road = road
        self.road_size_x = road_size_x
        self.road_size_y = road_size_y
        self.agent_x = agent_start_x
        self.agent_y = agent_start_y

    def cost_movement(self, x, y):                    # Defines the reward and
        cell_content = self.road[x][y]                # penalty of the environment

        if cell_content == 'G':      # A large positive reward
            return 10
        if cell_content == 'C':      # A negative reward
            return -5
        return -1

    def is_within_bounds(self, x, y):
        return 0 <= x < self.road_size_x and
     0 <= y < self.road_size_y

    def is_goal_achieved(self):                       # Checks if the agent's
        return self.agent_x == self.goal_x and        # current coordinates
     self.agent_y == self.goal_y                       # overlap with the
                                                       # target coordinates
    def get_state(self):
        return (self.road_size_x * self.agent_x) + self.agent_y
```

Training with the simulation using Q-learning

Q-learning is an approach in reinforcement learning that uses the states and actions in an environment to model a table of information that describes favorable actions based on specific states. Q-learning is a model-free approach, meaning that it doesn't need to know the physics of the world beforehand. It learns to estimate the quality of taking actions in specific states. (For more information, see "Model-free and model-based learning" later in this chapter.)

Reinforcement learning with Q-learning employs a reward table called a *Q-table*. Think of a Q-table as a scorecard. The rows are the possible states, and the columns are the possible actions. Each cell contains a Q-value (quality value). The table doesn't explicitly store the best action; rather, it stores a score for every possible action. To find the best action, the agent looks at the row for its current state and picks the action with the highest Q-value.

The point of a Q-table is to describe which actions are most favorable for the agent as it seeks a goal. The values that represent favorable actions are learned through simulating the possible actions in the environment and learning from the outcome and change in state. It's worth noting that the agent has a chance of choosing a random action or an action from the Q-table, as shown later in this section. The Q represents the function that provides the reward, or quality, of an action in an environment.

Figure 10.11 depicts a trained Q-table and two possible states that might be represented by the action values for each state. These states are relevant to the problem we're solving; another problem might allow the agent to move diagonally as well. The number of states differs based on the environment, and new states can be added as they are discovered. In state 1, the agent is in the top-left corner, and in state 2, the agent is in the position below its previous state. The Q-table encodes the estimated value of taking an action in a state. When the table is fully trained (*converged*), the action with the largest number is considered most beneficial. At the start of training, these numbers are random guesses; they become accurate best actions only after many trials. Soon, we'll see how they're calculated.

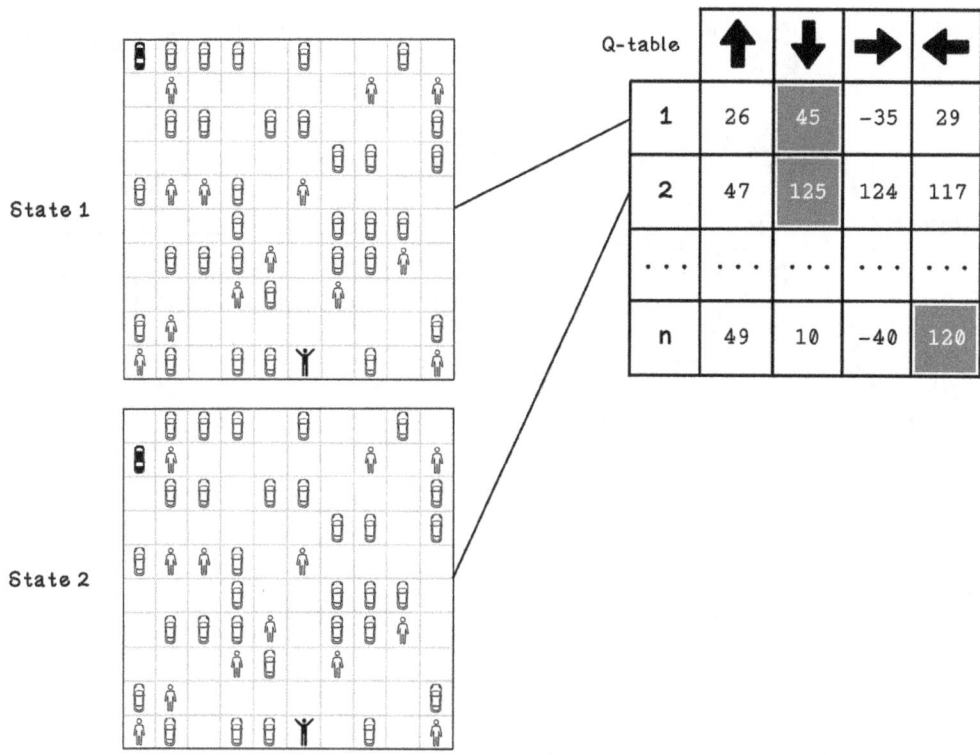

Figure 10.11 An example Q-table and states that it represents

The big problem with representing the state using the entire map is that the configuration of other cars and people is specific to this problem's configuration. The Q-table learns the best choices only for this map layout.

A better way to represent state in our example problem is to look at the objects adjacent to the agent. This approach allows the Q-table to adapt to other parking-lot configurations because the state is less specific to the example parking lot from which it's learning. This approach may seem trivial, but a block could contain another car or a pedestrian, or it could be empty or out of bounds, which works out to four possibilities per block, resulting in a massive 65,536 possible states. With this much variety, we'd have to train the agent in many parking-lot configurations many times for it to learn good short-term action choices (figure 10.12).

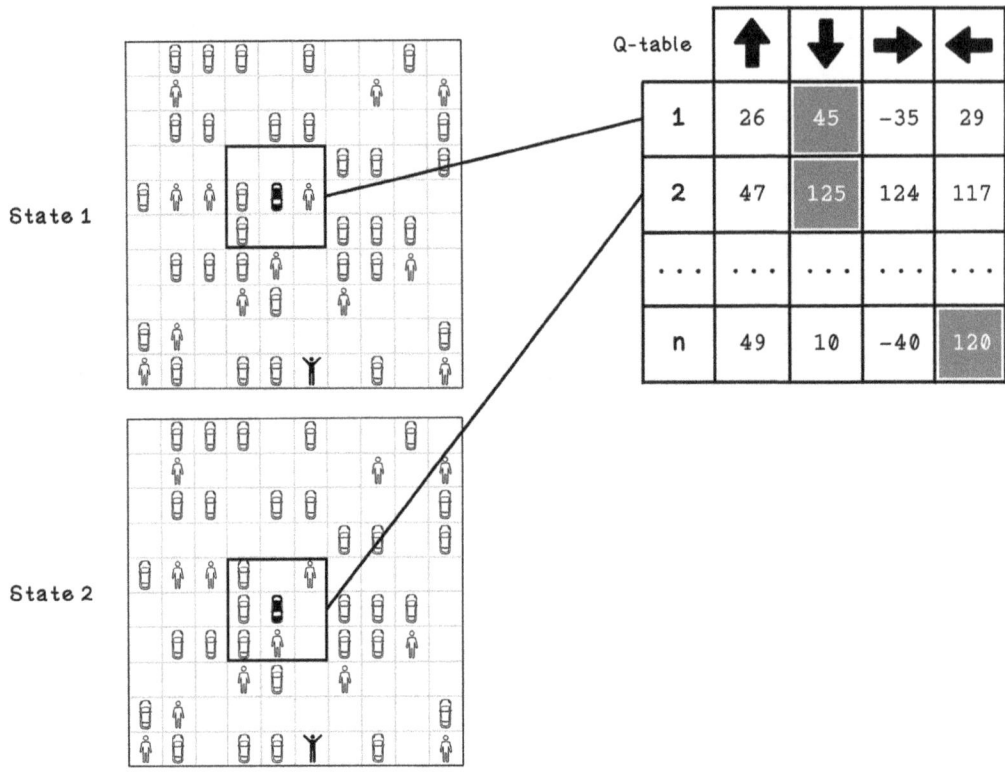

Figure 10.12 A better example of a Q-table and states that it represents

Keep the idea of a reward table in mind as we explore the life cycle of training a model using reinforcement learning with Q-learning. It represents the model for the actions the agent will take in the environment.

Let's take a look at the life cycle of a Q-learning algorithm, including the steps involved in training. We'll look at two phases: initialization and repetition over several iterations as the algorithm learns (figure 10.13).

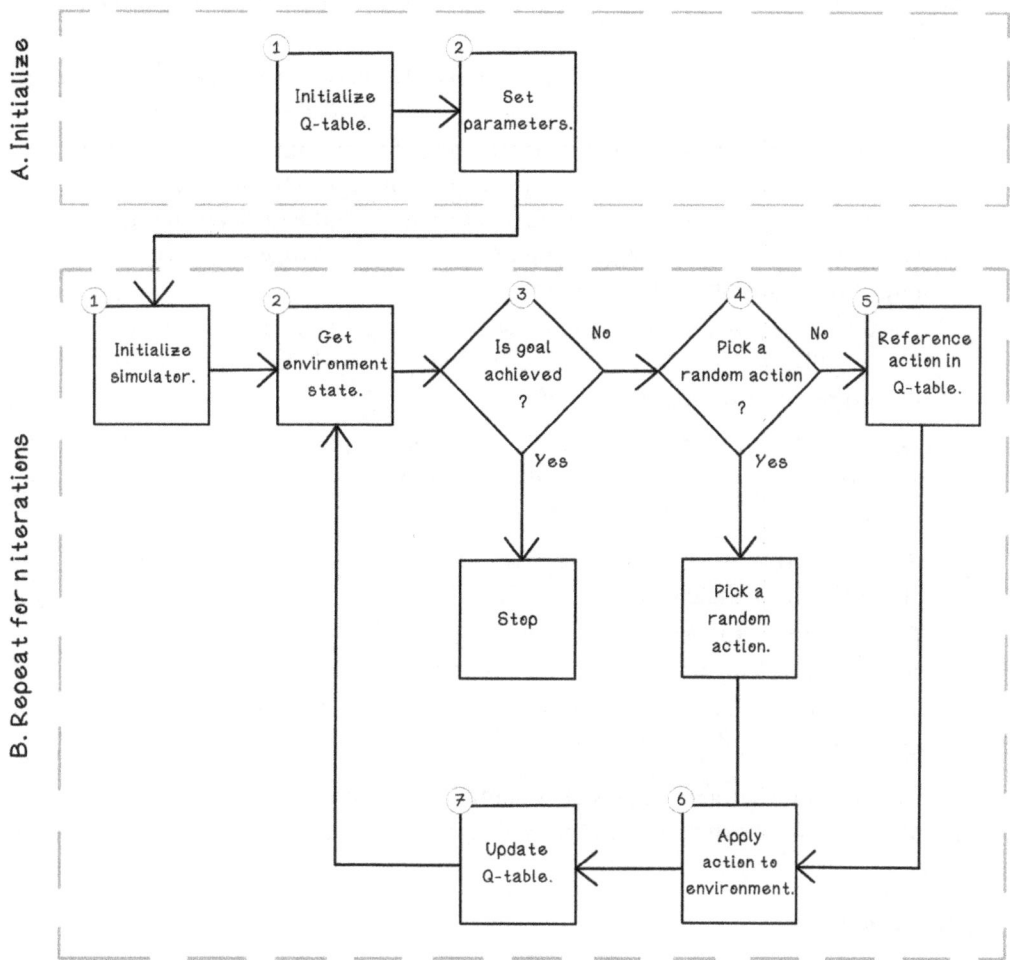

Figure 10.13 Life cycle of a Q-learning reinforcement learning algorithm

Initialize

The initialization step involves setting up the relevant parameters and initial values for the Q-table:

1. *Initialize the Q-table.* Initialize a Q-table in which each column is an action and each row represents a possible state after actions based on the current state. States can be added to the table as they're encountered because it can be difficult to know the number of states in the environment at the beginning. The initial action values for each state are initialized with 0s.

2. *Set parameters*. This step involves setting the parameters for various hyperparameters of the Q-learning algorithm, including the following:

    ° *Chance of choosing a random action*—This parameter is the value threshold for choosing a random action over choosing an action from the Q-table.

    ° *Learning rate*—The learning rate is similar to the learning rate in supervised learning. It describes how quickly the algorithm learns from rewards in different states. With a high learning rate, values in the Q-table change erratically, and with a low learning rate, the values change gradually, but it may take more iterations to find good values.

    ° *Discount factor*—This parameter determines the present value of future rewards. It works like inflation: a reward received today is worth more than the same reward received 10 steps from now.

    Think of the discount factor as being like the *Marshmallow Test* (a study of delayed gratification in which a child is offered one treat now or two treats if they wait for a short period).

    ° *0 = Impulsive*—"I want one marshmallow right now." The agent cares only about the immediate reward.

    ° *0.9 = Patient*—"I'll wait. One marshmallow now is less valuable than five marshmallows in 10 minutes." The agent plans for long-term rewards.

    ° *1 = Infinite patience*—"I'll wait forever if it means getting the highest score eventually."

    Mathematically, the value decays exponentially over time. This decay forces the agent to find the shortest path to the goal rather than wander around aimlessly, eventually gathering rewards.

Repeat for n iterations

To learn the optimal path, the agent must learn from experience through thousands of trial-and-error repetitions. Each full trial, from a starting point to a concluding state (such as reaching the goal or failing), is called an *episode*.

> **DEFINITION** One term that comes up in the process of learning more about reinforcement learning is *episodes*. An *episode* includes all the states between the initial state and the state when the goal is achieved. If it takes 14 actions to achieve a goal, we have 1 episode with 14 actions within it.

Within an episode, the agent takes a series of steps (e.g., the car makes a single move), receiving feedback and updating the Q-table after each one. Running many episodes is crucial because it allows the estimated value of future rewards to slowly propagate backward from the goal state. This is how the agent learns to make good short-term decisions that lead to the best possible long-term outcomes. The repetition process consists of these steps:

1. *Initialize the simulator.* This step involves resetting the environment to the starting state, with the agent in a neutral state.

2. *Get the environment state.* This function should provide the current state of the environment. The state of the environment changes after each action is performed.

3. *Is the goal achieved?* This step determines whether the goal is achieved (or the simulator deems the exploration to be complete). In our example, the goal is to pick up the owner of the self-driving car. If the goal is achieved, the episode ends.

4. *Pick a random action.* This step determines whether a random action should be selected. If so, a random action (move north, south, east, or west) is selected. Random actions are useful for exploring all the possibilities in the environment instead of learning a narrow subset of them.

5. *Reference the action in the Q-table.* If the decision to select a random action isn't selected, the current environment state is transposed to the Q-table, and the respective action is selected based on the values in the table.

6. *Apply the action to environment.* This step involves applying the selected action to the environment, whether that action is random or selected from the Q-table. An action has a consequence in the environment and yields a reward.

7. *Update the Q-table.* The following material describes the concepts involved in updating the Q-table and the steps that are carried out.

The key aspect of Q-learning is the equation used to update the values of the Q-table. This equation is based on the *Bellman equation*, which determines the value of a decision made at a certain point in time, given the reward or penalty for making that decision. In the Q-learning equation, the most important properties for updating Q-table values are the current state, the action, the next state given the action, and the reward outcome. The learning rate is similar to the learning rate in supervised learning, which determines the extent to which a Q-table value is updated. The discount is used to indicate the importance of possible future rewards, which balances favoring immediate rewards versus long-term rewards.

To clarify how the discount factor enables long-term planning, it's important to distinguish between the agent's final policy and its training process. Although a trained agent's policy may be simply to choose the action with the highest Q-value in a given state (which seems shortsighted), those Q-values themselves are inherently farsighted. During thousands of training episodes, the discount factor ensures that the value of distant rewards is propagated backward through every state–action pair that leads to them. As a result, a high Q-value represents not just a good immediate reward but also the start of a path that the agent has learned will lead to the highest total discounted future reward:

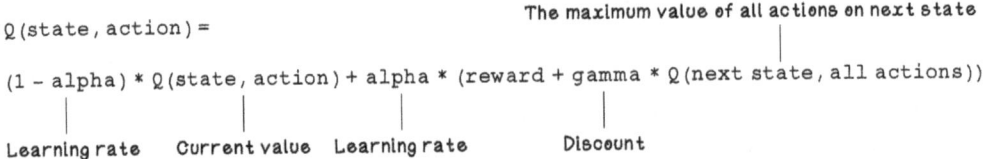

In this specific example, we initialize the Q-table with 0s (figure 10.14). Although this starting point is a common one, advanced implementations sometimes use *optimistic initialization*—filling the table with high numbers to trick the agent into exploring every state to verify those high rewards.

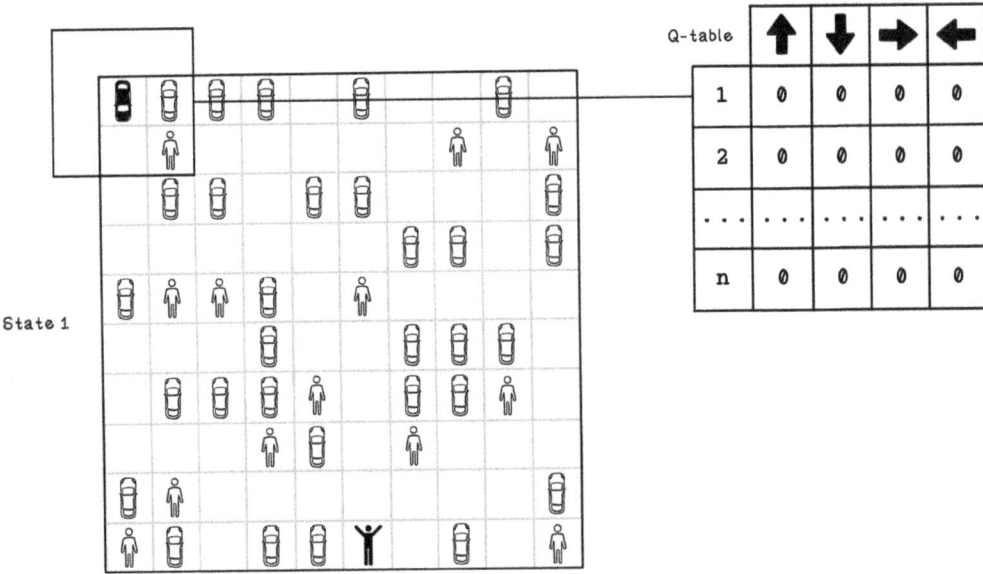

Figure 10.14 An example initialized Q-table

Next, we explore how to update the Q-table by using the Q-learning equation based on actions with different reward values. These values will be used for the learning rate (alpha) and discount (gamma):

- *Learning rate (alpha)—0.1*
- *Discount (gamma)—0.6*

Figure 10.15 illustrates how the Q-learning equation is used to update the Q-table if the agent selects the east action from the initial state in the first iteration. Remember that the initial Q-table consists of 0s. The learning rate (alpha), discount (gamma), current action value, reward, and next best state are plugged into the equation to determine the new value for the action that was taken. The action is east, which results in a collision with another car, yielding -100 as a reward. (A negative reward can be interpreted as a punishment.) After the new value is calculated, the value of east in state 1 is -10.

Action ➡   Reward 🚗 👤   -100

```
Q(1, east) =
(1 - alpha) * Q(1, east) + alpha * (reward + gamma * max of Q(2, all actions))

Q(1, east) = (1 - 0.1) * 0 + 0.1 * (-100 + 0.6 * 0)

Q(1, east) = -10
```

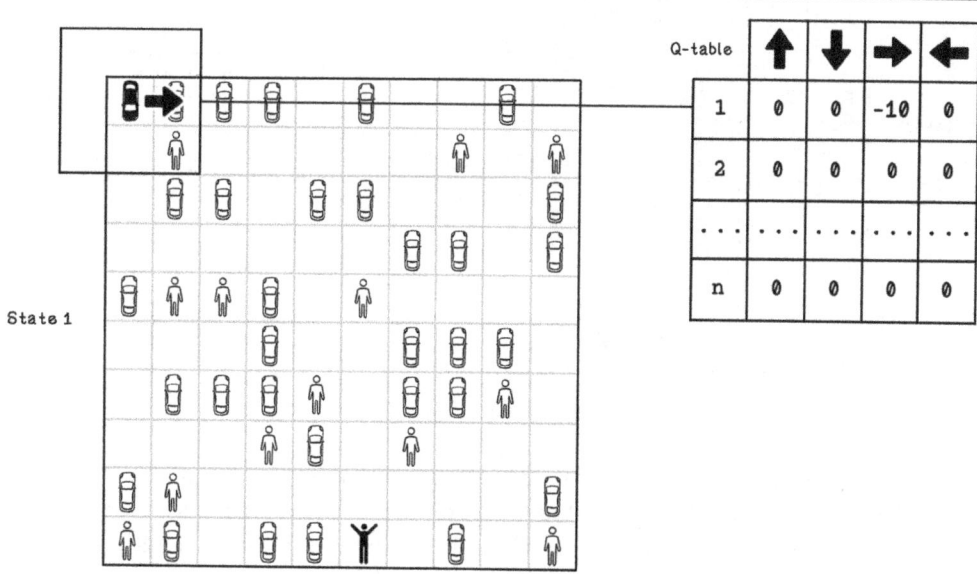

Figure 10.15 Example Q-table update calculation for state 1

The next calculation is for the next state in the environment following the action that was taken. The action taken, south, results in a collision with a pedestrian, which yields -1000 as the reward. After the new value is calculated, the value for the south action in state 2 is -100 (figure 10.16).

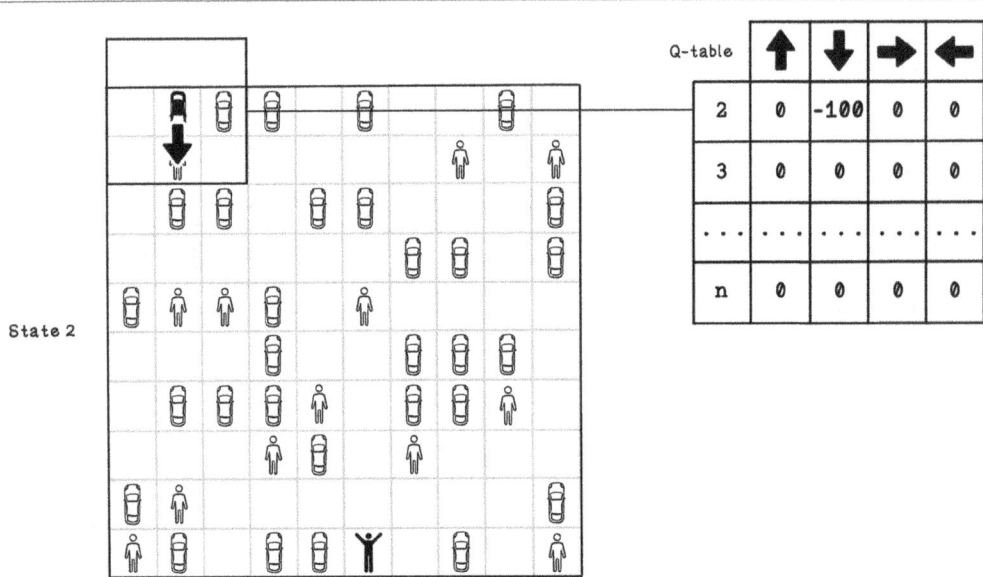

Figure 10.16 Example Q-table update calculation for state 2

Figure 10.17 illustrates how the calculated values differ in a Q-table with populated values because we worked on a Q-table initialized with 0s. The figure is an example of the Q-learning equation updated from the initial state after several iterations. The simulation can be run multiple times to learn from multiple attempts. So this iteration succeeds many before it in which the values of the table have been updated. The action for east results in a collision with another car and yields -100 as a reward. After the new value is calculated, the value for east in state 1 changes to -34.

Action ➡   Reward 🚗 🚶 -100

Q(1, east) =
(1 - alpha) * Q(1, east) + alpha * (reward + gamma * max of Q(2, all actions))

Q(1, east) = (1 - 0.1) * -35 + 0.1 * (-100 + 0.6 * 125)

Q(1, east) = -34

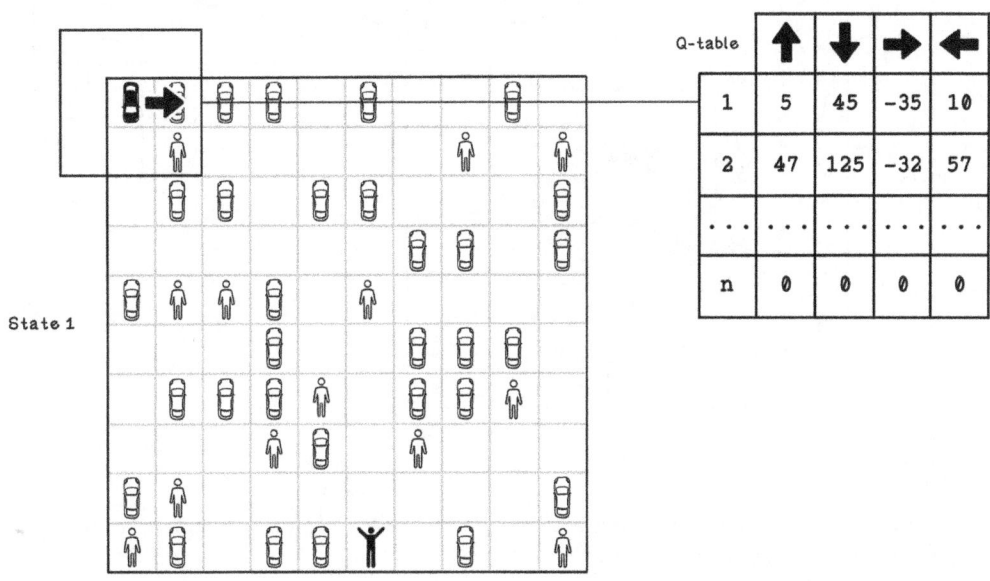

Figure 10.17 Example Q-table update calculation for state 1 after several iterations

Exercise: Calculate the change in values for the Q-table

Using the Q-learning update equation and the following scenario, calculate the new value for the action performed. Assume that the last move was east with a value of -67:

Q(state, action) =

                                                    The maximum value of all actions on next state
                                                                    |
(1 - alpha) * Q(state, action) + alpha * (reward + gamma * Q(next state, all actions))
        | | | |
Learning rate   Current value   Learning rate   Discount

(continued)

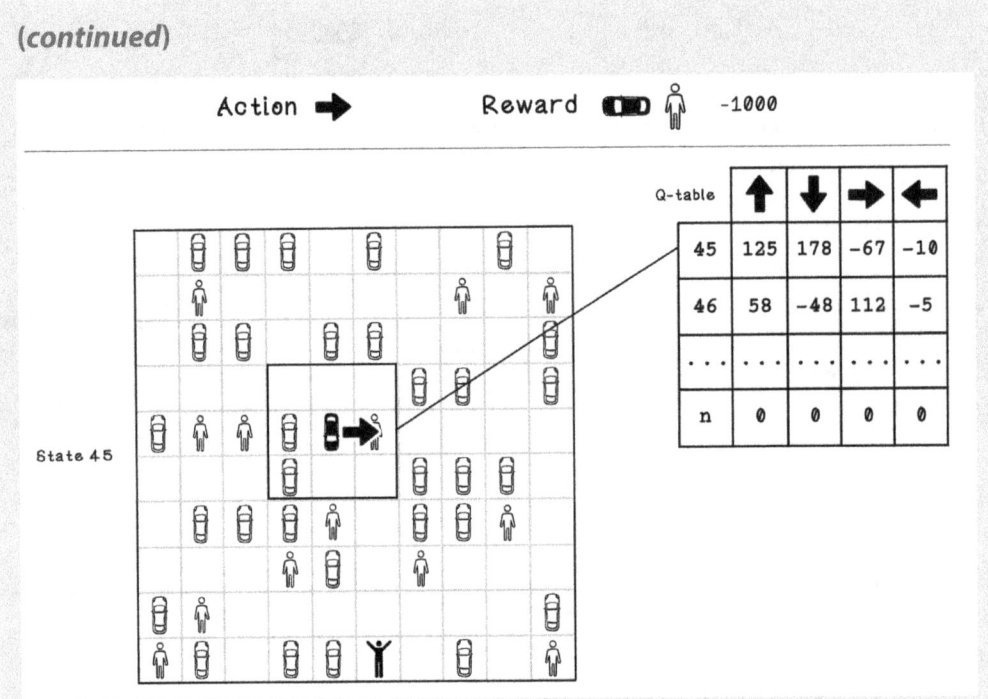

Solution:

The hyperparameter and state values are plugged into the Q-learning equation, resulting in the new value for Q(1, east):

- *Learning rate (alpha)—0.1*
- *Discount (gamma)—0.6*
- *Q(1, east)— -67*
- *Max of Q(2, all actions)—112*

```
Q(1,east) =
(1 - alpha) * Q(1,east) + alpha * (reward + gamma * max of Q(2,all actions))

Q(1,east) = (1 - 0.1) * -67 + 0.1 * (-100 + 0.6 * 112)

Q(1,east) = -64
```

Python code sample for training using a Q-table

This code describes a function that trains a Q-table by using Q-learning. It could be broken into simpler functions but is represented this way for readability. The function follows the steps described in this chapter.

The Q-table is initialized with 0s; then the learning logic is run for several iterations. Remember that an *iteration* is an attempt to achieve the goal. The next piece of logic runs while the goal has not been achieved:

1. *Decide whether a random action should be taken to explore possibilities in the environment.* If not, the highest-value action for the current state is selected from the Q-table.
2. *Proceed with the selected action, and apply it to the simulator.*
3. *Gather information from the simulator, including the reward, the next state given the action, and whether the goal is reached.*
4. *Update the Q-table based on the information gathered and hyperparameters.* In this code, the hyperparameters are passed through as arguments of this function.
5. *Set the current state to the state outcome of the action just performed.*

These steps continue until a goal is found. After the goal is found and the desired number of iterations is reached, the result is a trained Q-table that can be used to test in other environments. We look at testing the Q-table in the next section.

A matrix where rows are States (locations) and columns are Actions (North, South, East, West). It stores the expected quality (Q-value) of every possible move

```python
def train_with_q_learning(observation_space, action_space_size,
    number_of_iterations, learning_rate, discount, chance_of_random_move):

    q_table = np.zeros((observation_space, action_space_size))

    for i in range(number_of_iterations):

        simulator = Simulator(DEFAULT_ROAD,
            DEFAULT_ROAD_SIZE_X, DEFAULT_ROAD_SIZE_Y,
            DEFAULT_START_X, DEFAULT_START_Y,
            DEFAULT_GOAL_X, DEFAULT_GOAL_Y)

        state = simulator.get_state()
        done = False

        while not done:

            if random.uniform(0, 1) > chance_of_random_move:
```

The agent rolls the dice

```
            action_index =
            ➥get_action_index_from_max_q(q_table[state])
        else:
            action_index =
            ➥get_random_action_index(action_space_size)

        action_command = COMMANDS[action_index]

        reward = simulator.move_agent(action_command)
        next_state = simulator.get_state()
        done = simulator.is_goal_achieved()

        current_value = q_table[state, action_index]
        next_state_max_value = np.max(q_table[next_state])

        new_value = (1 - learning_rate) * current_value +
        ➥learning_rate * (reward + discount * next_state_max_value)

        q_table[state, action_index] = new_value
        state = next_state

    if i % 100 == 0:
        print(f"Episode {i:04d} complete.")

    return q_table
```

Determines how much the agent values future rewards compared to immediate ones

The heart of Q-learning where it updates current knowledge by looking at the immediate reward plus the discounted future potential of the next state

Testing with the simulation and Q-table

We know that in the case of Q-learning, the Q-table is the model that encompasses the learning. When presented with a new environment with different states, the algorithm references the respective state in the Q-table and chooses the highest-value action. Because the Q-table has already been trained, this process consists of getting the current state of the environment and referencing the respective state in the Q-table to find an action until a goal is achieved (figure 10.18).

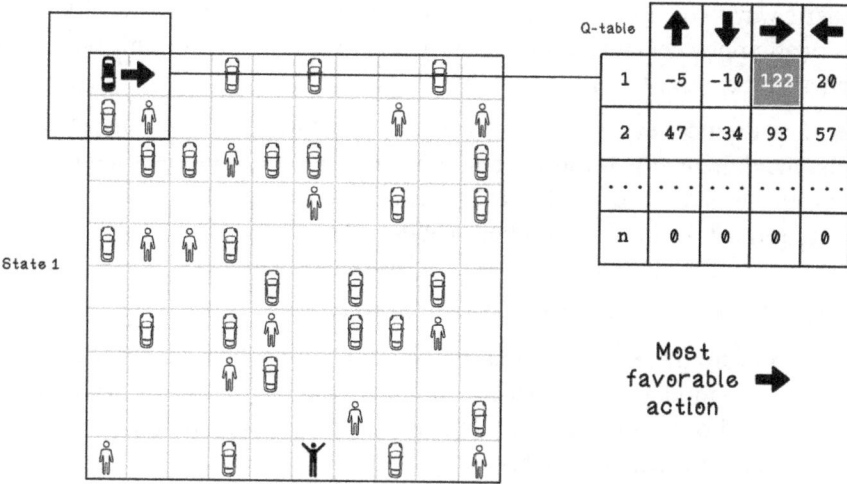

Figure 10.18 Referencing a Q-table to determine what action to take

This example, however, highlights a fundamental limitation of a Q-table: a basic Q-table can't generalize to new situations. If a state isn't in the table, the agent has no learned information and must resort to a default policy, such as picking a random action, which is rarely optimal. This inability to handle novel states is a key reason why, for complex problems, we often replace the rigid Q-table with models like neural networks that can estimate the best action even for situations they haven't seen before.

Because the state learned in the Q-table considers the objects directly next to the agent's current position, the Q-table has learned good and bad moves for short-term rewards, so the Q-table could be used in a different parking-lot configuration, such as the one shown in figure 10.18. The disadvantage is that the agent favors short-term rewards over long-term rewards because it doesn't have the context of the rest of the map when taking each action.

Measuring the performance of training

Reinforcement learning algorithms can be difficult to measure generically. Given a specific environment and goal, we may have different penalties and rewards, some of which have a greater effect on the problem context than others. In the Parking-Lot Problem, we heavily penalize collisions with pedestrians. In another example, we may have an agent that resembles a human and tries to learn what muscles to use to walk naturally as far as possible. In this scenario, penalties may be assigned for falling or doing something more specific, such as taking strides that are too long. To measure performance accurately, we need the context of the problem.

One generic way to measure performance is to count the number of penalties in a given number of attempts. Penalties could be events that we want to prevent from happening in the environment due to an action.

Another measurement of reinforcement learning performance is average reward per action. By maximizing the reward per action, we aim to prevent poor actions, whether or not the goal was reached. We can calculate this measurement by dividing the cumulative reward by the total number of actions.

Model-free and model-based learning

To support your future learning in reinforcement learning, be aware of two approaches: model-based and model-free, which are different from the machine learning models discussed in this book. Think of a model as being an agent's abstract representation of the environment in which it operates.

We may have a model in our heads of locations of landmarks, intuition of direction, and the general layout of the roads within a neighborhood. We've formed this model by exploring some roads, but we're able to simulate scenarios in our heads to make decisions without trying every option. To decide how we'll get to work, for example, we can use this model to make a decision; this approach is *model-based*. *Model-free* learning is similar to the Q-learning approach described earlier in this chapter; trial and error is used to explore many interactions with the environment to determine favorable actions in different scenarios.

Figure 10.19 depicts the two approaches in road navigation. We can employ different algorithms to build model-based reinforcement learning implementations.

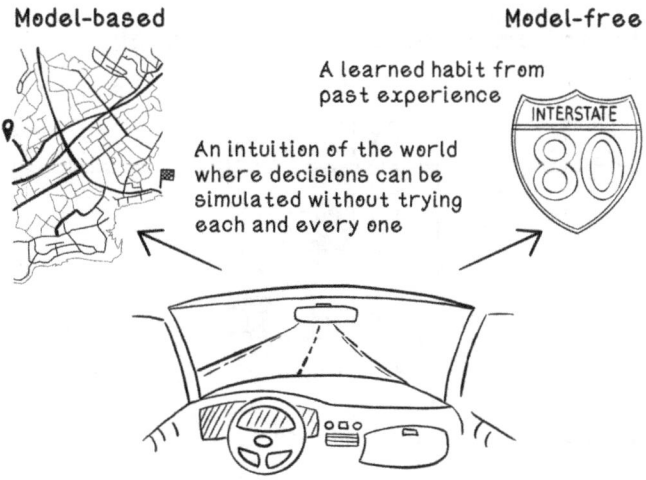

Figure 10.19 Examples of model-based and model-free reinforcement learning

Deep learning approaches to reinforcement learning

Q-learning is one approach to reinforcement learning. Having a good understanding of how it functions allows you to apply the same reasoning and general approach to other reinforcement learning algorithms. Several alternative approaches depend on the problem being solved. One popular alternative is *deep reinforcement learning*, which is useful for applications in robotics, video-game play, and problems involving images and video.

Deep reinforcement learning can use artificial neural networks (ANNs) to process the states of an environment and produce an action. The actions are learned by adjusting weights in the ANN, using the reward feedback and changes in the environment. Reinforcement learning can also use the capabilities of convolutional neural networks (CNNs) and other purpose-built ANN architectures to solve specific problems in different domains and use cases. Instead of having the learnings encoded into a table of actions, as in Q-learning, the learnings are encoded as weights in an ANN. Figure 10.20 illustrates this difference.

Q[state][action] = expected future reward

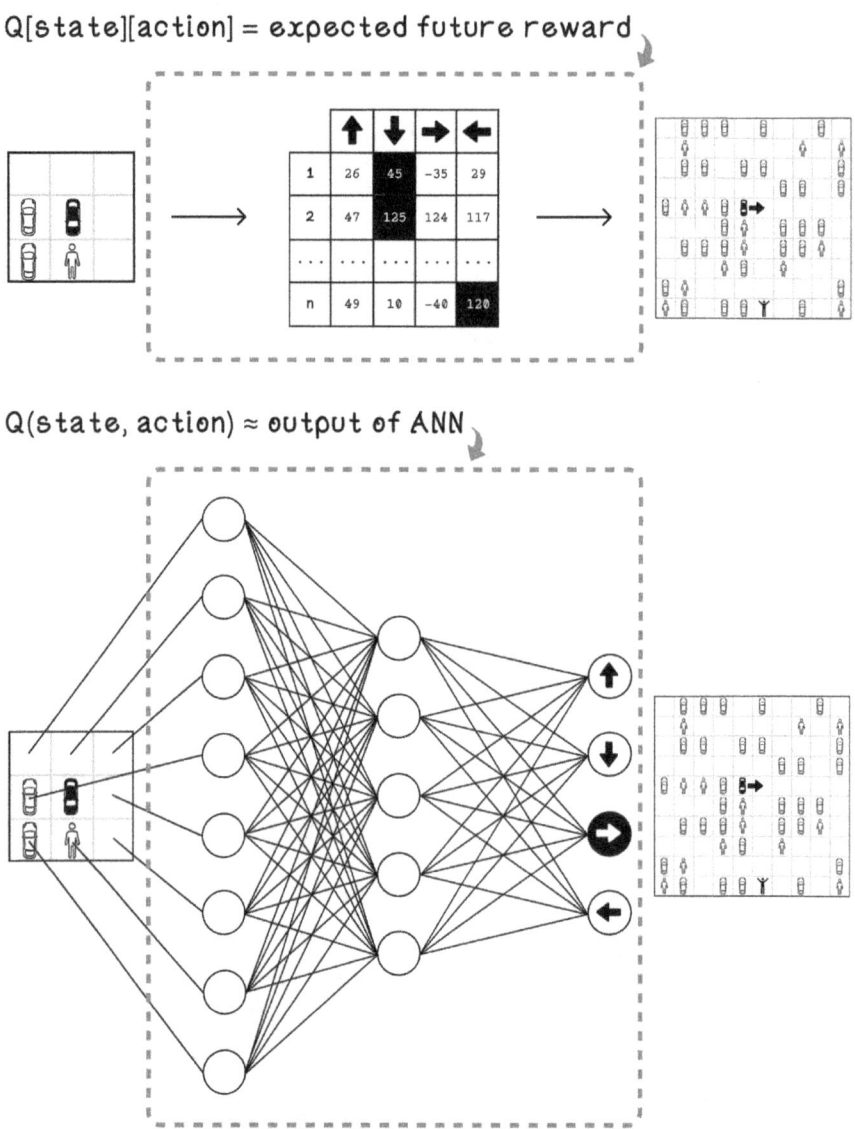

Q(state, action) ≈ output of ANN

Figure 10.20 The difference between using a Q-table and an ANN for the Parking-Lot Problem

In deep Q-learning, the neural network serves as a function approximator that learns to predict Q-values: the expected long-term reward of taking a particular action in a particular state. As you can probably tell, the primary change is how the actions for specific states are learned. As we know from chapter 9, neural networks are great at finding fine-grained relationships and then finding abstractions of those relationships learned from a loss function. In this case, the loss function is based on the reward or penalty for a specific action taken, given a specific state.

Training with an ANN

Let's revisit the Parking-Lot Problem, but instead of using a Q-table, we'll use a neural network as the model that will be trained to predict actions with a state of the car's surroundings as the input, and an action as the output.

As always when designing ANNs, we have to define the inputs, hidden layer configurations, and the output. Let's explore how these elements can look for the Parking-Lot Problem:

- *Input nodes*—The input nodes represent a specific state of the map. In chapter 9, we had four input nodes representing the speed, terrain quality, degree of vision, and total experience as scaled values between 0 and 1. In the Parking-Lot Problem, we must encode the state in a way that's conducive to effective learning by the neural network. The way the input is expressed also influences the design of the hidden layers and activation functions. We'll look at two options soon.

- *Hidden layers*—The hidden layers depend on the number of input nodes we have. If we have more nodes in the input, we'll likely need more nodes in the first layer to find patterns well from the inputs. Naturally, this additional complexity would affect the subsequent hidden layers in the network. The choice of two hidden layers is sensible for this use case. If we have too many hidden layers, we increase training time and risk overfitting to the training data.

- *Output node*—The output is four nodes representing one score for each respective action. This configuration isn't influenced by the input nodes and hidden nodes because we know we need an output that's an action, and the clearest way is to have four discrete values that represent the associated reward for each action. We'll use a linear activation function for the nodes in the output because the values can be positive or negative.

Training the network follows the same reinforcement learning loop; we simply replace the Q-table update with a backpropagation step. Let's take this opportunity to learn about the difference that input encoding makes on the design of the neural network.

Scalar encoding

Scalar encoding represents each category in a cell with a single numeric value that reflects its relative importance or impact. A goal might be encoded as 1, an empty space as 0, a vehicle as -0.5, and a pedestrian as -1. This compact representation reduces the number of input nodes and can help the model learn faster by embedding domain knowledge directly in the input. But it assumes a meaningful ordinal relationship between the categories, which may limit flexibility or mislead the model if the relationships aren't truly linear. In this case, the values hold meaning:

- 1 is as positive as can be and represents reaching the goal.
- 0 is neutral and represents an empty space.
- -0.5 represents colliding with another vehicle. It's bad but not as bad as -1.
- -1 is the worst and represents colliding with a pedestrian.

These values represent a risk/reward gradient within the network. It's more compact but less explicit and may lead the network to learn unrelated relationships. With scalar encoding, we use eight input nodes to represent all surrounding blocks (including diagonals). Why do we use inputs if we can move in only four directions? Even though the agent can't move diagonally, it needs full situational awareness. An obstacle in the northeast corner becomes an immediate danger if the agent decides to move north. By observing all eight surrounding cells, the network can anticipate future collisions and recognize complex environment shapes.

Given this input and the fact that we've decided to have two hidden layers in the network, let's look at a possible configuration. Using 32 nodes in the first hidden layer for the 8 input nodes gives the network enough capacity to learn complex feature interactions from a compact input. Each of the eight input nodes (representing the state of nearby cells) may carry nonlinear signals about obstacles, goals, or dangers. A 4x expansion to 32 hidden nodes allows the network to extract diverse patterns, such as recognizing dangerous obstacles or promising paths to the goal, without overfitting on such a small input space.

The 16 nodes in the second hidden layer act as a refinement stage. The nodes in the layer compress the features extracted by the first layer into a more abstract representation, suitable for selecting one of the four possible actions. This structure—8→32→16→4— encourages the network to distill the raw input into meaningful, generalizable decisions while avoiding complexity. Figure 10.21 depicts this network.

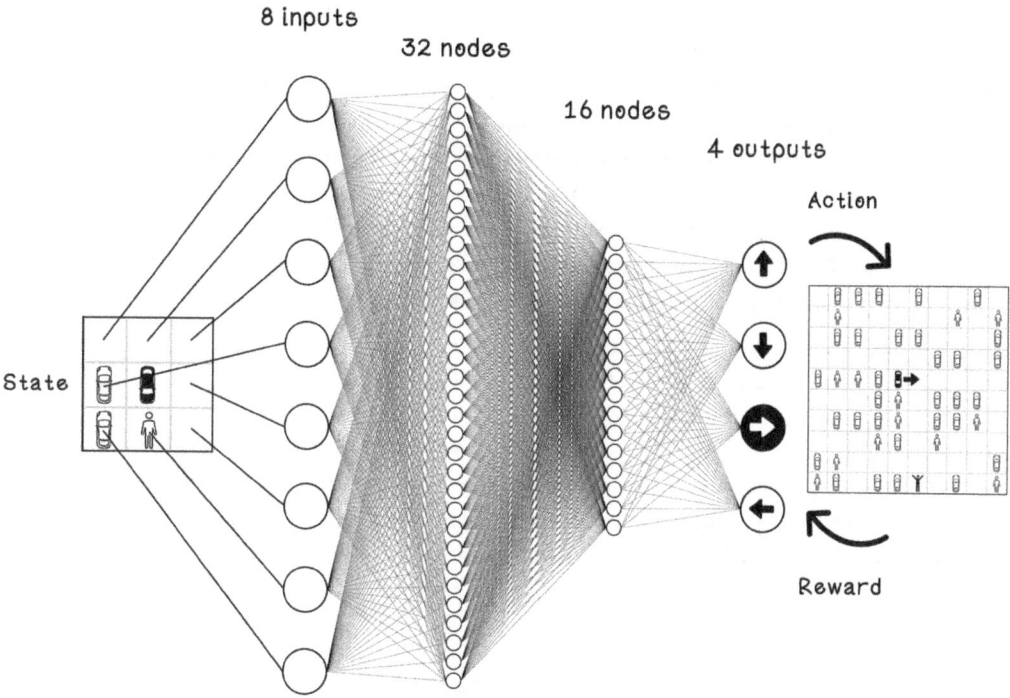

Figure 10.21 Example 8-input ANN for the Parking-Lot Problem

For scalar inputs, such as 8 input values ranging from -1 to 1, feeding into the 32 hidden nodes, the recommended activation function is ReLU (rectified linear unit), discussed in chapter 9. ReLU is computationally efficient and introduces nonlinearity while preserving the magnitude of positive values, making it ideal when inputs already carry semantic meaning, such as danger or reward. It activates only when useful patterns emerge, helping the network focus on relevant signals. If negative input values, such as -1 for pedestrians, are critical to the task, we can use *Leaky ReLU* instead to retain some gradient flow for negative signals.

One-hot encoding

One-hot encoding represents each possible category in a cell with a separate input node, activating only one node per block. A block could be encoded as [1, 0, 0, 0] for empty, [0, 1, 0, 0] for a vehicle, [0, 0, 1, 0] for a pedestrian, and [0, 0, 0, 1] for the goal. This approach creates a larger input vector of size 32 (because we have eight adjacent blocks with four possible states). Although it's large, it avoids implying any ordinal or linear relationship between categories because values are simply 0 or 1 for specific input nodes. One-hot encoding gives the model full flexibility to learn independent outcomes for each category, making it ideal when the categories (empty/vehicle/person/goal) are distinct and unordered, as in the Parking-Lot Problem.

Using 64 nodes in the first hidden layer for 32 one-hot-encoded input nodes allows the network to learn a rich set of patterns and interactions across the input features. Because each cell in the input grid is represented by multiple one-hot nodes, the model needs more capacity to combine and interpret these sparse inputs, enabling it to, say, recognize dangerous arrangements such as a pedestrian to the left and a vehicle ahead. Doubling the size of the input gives the network enough flexibility to capture nonlinear relationships and local spatial patterns without becoming overly complex.

The 32 nodes in the second hidden layer serve to refine and condense the higher-level features learned in the first layer. This gradual reduction helps the model generalize by forcing it to prioritize the most relevant information for decision-making, ultimately feeding into the output layer of four actions. This structure balances learning capacity with training efficiency, making it well-suited to one-hot-encoded grid inputs where categorical relationships must be learned independently. Figure 10.22 illustrates an example 32-input ANN for the Parking-Lot Problem.

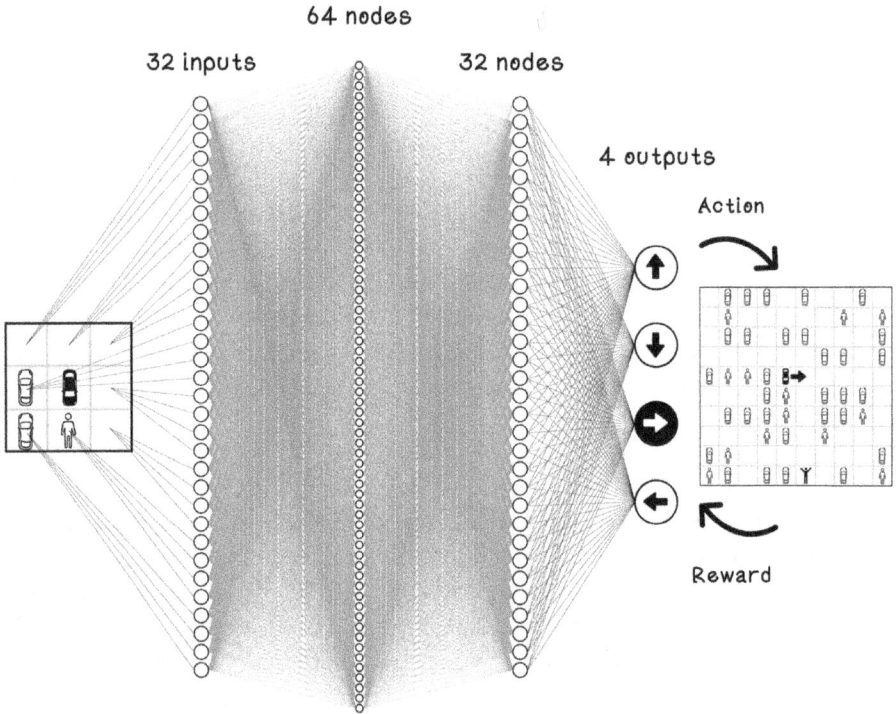

Figure 10.22 Example 32-input ANN for the Parking-Lot Problem

One-hot inputs are sparse by nature, and ReLU efficiently activates only when meaningful signals are present, ignoring inactive inputs. So ReLU is a good choice as the activation function for the nodes in the hidden layers for our one-hot-encoding scenario as well. Because one-hot vectors don't carry ordinal meaning, ReLU enables the network to learn useful patterns from scratch. Activation functions such as sigmoid and tanh are less suitable here because they can squash values unnecessarily and slow learning.

Calculating loss and backpropagation

The goal is to train the network to approximate the Q-function, which guides the agent toward actions that maximize cumulative rewards over time. Instead of learning from fixed labeled data, the network learns through interactions with the environment, using feedback from each action it takes.

After each action, the agent receives a reward and observes the next state. These four elements—current state, action taken, reward received, and resulting next state—form a training sample. The network uses this training sample to compute a target Q-value: the immediate reward plus the discounted maximum predicted Q-value for the next state. Then it compares this target with its own predicted Q-value for the action taken, and the squared difference becomes the loss.

Suppose that the algorithm has the current state (S) and chooses east as the action. The outcome is a new state (S') and a reward of +1 for performing that action. Let's assume that the rewards for S' look like the following:

- *North*—1.2
- *South*—0.5
- *East*—2.0
- *West*—0.3

Based on this, the network thinks the best possible move will be east and gives a reward of 2.0—the maximum reward among the options. This is good, but remember: we want the network to learn that moving right from the previous state should be worth today's reward plus future rewards.

The discount factor controls how much the agent values future rewards compared with immediate ones, and 0.9 is a typical default value used in many reinforcement learning problems. A high factor (e.g., 0.9 or 0.99) means that the agent values long-term rewards almost as much as immediate rewards. A low factor (e.g., 0.1 or 0.3) means that the agent is shortsighted: it cares more about immediate rewards and less about the future. Given these values, we calculate the target as follows:

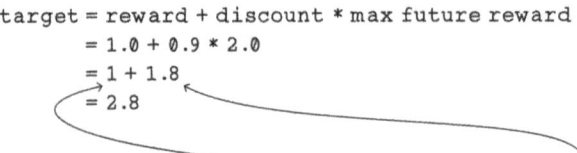

```
target = reward + discount * max future reward
       = 1.0 + 0.9 * 2.0
       = 1 + 1.8
       = 2.8
```

If I go right, I'll get 1 point immediately and likely 1.8 more points later

Now we look at what the network currently thinks is the value of going right from state S:

- *North—0.7*
- *South—1.1*
- *East—2.2*
- *West—0.5*

The network believes that moving east is 2.2, but we know from our target calculation that it should be 2.8. We compute the difference as the loss, and as usual, the network minimizes this loss for future epochs by using backpropagation and gradient descent. During backpropagation, the gradients of the loss are used to adjust the weights in the direction that reduces future error. Over time, this tunes the network to predict Q-values more accurate, enabling better decision-making.

Number of episodes

Learning occurs across many episodes. Each episode is a simulation run from the starting state to a goal state or a failure/timeout condition. Contrary to what we might have expected, the agent doesn't need to complete the episode for learning to happen. Even partial progress, such as a few steps before a failure, contributes useful training data, allowing the model to improve gradually.

Before starting the training loop, we must decide how each new episode begins. A key choice is the initial state. In some problems, such as chess, the agent always starts from a single fixed state. For many tasks, however, a more powerful approach is to begin each episode from a randomly chosen valid state. For our self-driving car, this approach means placing it in a different spot in the parking lot for each new trial run. This method forces the agent to learn a more robust and complete strategy because it must discover valuable paths from all over the environment, not just a single starting point.

As training progresses, the agent balances exploration and exploitation. Early on, it explores the environment by trying random actions to discover valuable paths. Over time, it exploits the best-known actions more frequently as the network's predictions improve, much like many algorithms we've learned about in this book.

Using reinforcement learning with ANNs is a powerful way to handle complex decision-making problems in which rules aren't explicitly known and the solution must be discovered through trial and error. By continually adjusting its predictions based on outcomes, the network learns not only to react but also to strategize, balancing short-term gains against long-term rewards. This approach opens new possibilities for intelligent agents in dynamic, unpredictable environments, from robotics to game AI and beyond.

Use cases for reinforcement learning

Reinforcement learning excels at solving complex problems in which an agent must make a sequence of decisions to achieve a goal. The key to applying reinforcement learning isn't simply the absence of a static dataset but the ability to learn through active trial and error. This approach is most powerful when we can both simulate a realistic environment at scale and define a clear reward function that provides feedback on the agent's actions. By interacting with this environment, taking actions, and receiving rewards or penalties, the agent learns the optimal strategy over time. The use cases for this approach are potentially endless; this section describes a few of the most popular ones.

Robotics

Robotics involves creating machines that interact with real-world environments to accomplish goals. Some robots are used to navigate difficult terrain with a variety of surfaces, obstacles, and inclines. Other robots are used as assistants in a laboratory, taking instructions from a scientist and passing the right tools or operating equipment. When it isn't possible to model every outcome of every action in a large, dynamic environment, reinforcement learning can be useful. By defining a greater goal in an environment and introducing rewards and penalties as heuristics, we can use reinforcement learning to train robots in dynamic environments. A terrain-navigating robot, for example, may learn which wheels to drive power to and how to adjust its suspension to traverse difficult terrain successfully. It achieves this goal after many attempts.

We can simulate these scenarios virtually if the key aspects of the environment can be modeled in a computer program. Computer games have been used in some projects as a baseline for training self-driving cars before they're trained on the road in the real world. The aim in training robots with reinforcement learning is to create more-general models that can adapt to new and different environments while learning more-general interactions, much the way that humans do.

Recommendation engines

Recommendation engines are used in many of the digital products we use. Video-streaming platforms, for example, use recommendation engines to learn an individual's likes and dislikes in video content and try to recommend something most suitable for the viewer. This approach has also been employed in music-streaming platforms and e-commerce stores.

Reinforcement learning models are trained by using the viewer's behavior when they face a decision about watching a recommended video. The premise is that if a viewer selected a recommended video and watched that video in its entirety, there's a strong reward for the reinforcement learning model because it assumed that the video was a good recommendation. Conversely, if the person never selects a video or watches little of its content, it's reasonable to assume that the video didn't appeal to the viewer. The result would be a weak reward or a penalty.

Financial trading

Financial trading is a classic example of a sequential decision-making problem, making it a prime candidate for reinforcement learning. Although vast amounts of historical market data are publicly available, why not simply use supervised learning?

The answer is that trading isn't about making a single isolated "correct" prediction. A supervised model might predict whether a stock will go up tomorrow, but it can't tell you whether buying today is part of a long-term winning strategy. The consequence of your action—owning the stock—changes your situation for all future decisions.

Reinforcement learning is designed for exactly this task. An agent's state includes not just market data but also its current portfolio (what it owns and its cash balance). The agent learns a policy by taking actions (buy, sell, or hold) and receiving rewards or penalties based on the change in its portfolio's value. To avoid the risk of real financial loss, the agent is trained in a simulated market environment—a sandbox—that uses historical data to let the agent practice and learn from the past without real-world consequences.

Although a reinforcement learning model could help generate a good return on investment, here's an interesting question. If all investors were automated and completely rational, with the human element removed from trading, what would the market look like?

Game playing

Popular strategy computer games have been pushing players' intellectual capabilities for years. These games typically involve managing many types of resources while planning short-term and long-term tactics to overcome an opponent. These games have filled arenas, and the smallest mistakes have cost top-notch players many matches.

Reinforcement learning has been used to play these games at the professional level. These reinforcement learning implementations usually involve an agent watching the screen the way a human player would, learning patterns, and taking actions. The rewards and penalties are directly associated with the game. After many iterations of playing the game in different scenarios with different opponents, a reinforcement learning agent learns what tactics work best toward the long-term goal of winning the game.

The goal of research in this space is related to the search for more-general models that can gain context from abstract states and environments and understand things that can't be mapped logically. As children, for example, we never had to be burned by multiple objects before learning that hot objects are potentially dangerous: we developed an intuition and tested it as we grew older. These tests reinforced our understanding of hot objects and their potential harm or benefit.

AI research and development strives to make computers learn to solve problems in ways that humans are already good at: in a general way, stringing abstract ideas and concepts together with a goal in mind and finding good solutions to problems.

SUMMARY OF REINFORCEMENT LEARNING

Reinforcement learning is useful when a goal is well
defined but robust examples to learn from are not

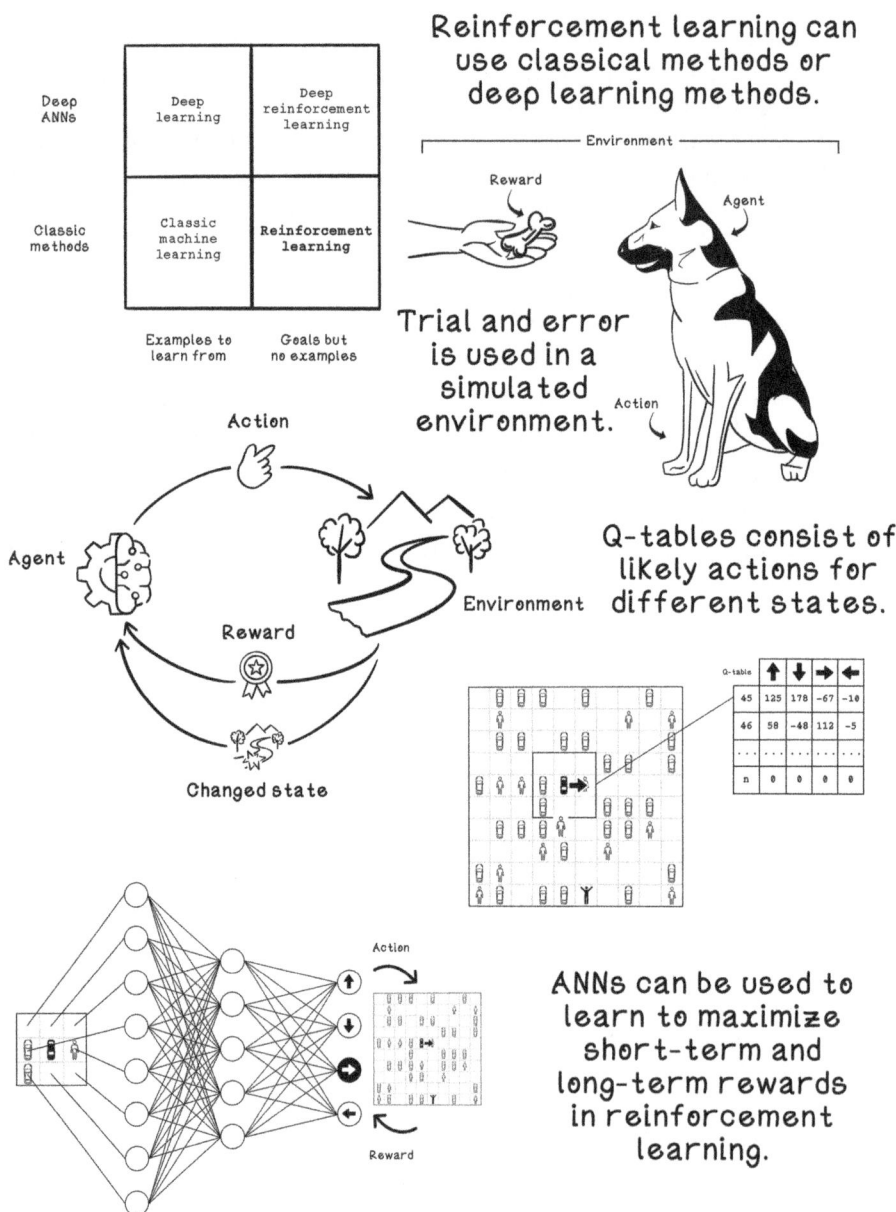

Reinforcement learning can
use classical methods or
deep learning methods.

	Examples to learn from	Goals but no examples
Deep ANNs	Deep learning	Deep reinforcement learning
Classic methods	Classic machine learning	**Reinforcement learning**

Trial and error
is used in a
simulated
environment.

Q-tables consist of
likely actions for
different states.

ANNs can be used to
learn to maximize
short-term and
long-term rewards
in reinforcement
learning.

In this chapter

- Understanding the intuition of large language models (LLMs)

- Identifying and preparing LLM training data

- Deeply understanding the operations in training an LLM

- Implementation details and LLM tuning approaches

What are LLMs?

LLMs are machine learning models specialized for natural language processing (NLP) problems such as language generation. Consider the autocomplete feature on your mobile device's keyboard (figure 11.1). When you type *Hey, what are*, the keyboard likely predicts that the next word is *you, we,* or *the* because those words are the most common ones after that phrase. It makes this choice by scanning a table of probabilities that was trained on commonly available pieces of content. This simple table is a language model.

Figure 11.1 Example of autocomplete as a language model

An LLM is exactly the same idea, with some fundamental upgrades to enable interesting capabilities that come with predicting more than one word at a time:

- *More capacity*—Instead of a table of thousands of probabilities, an LLM holds billions or trillions of parameters. Parameters behave like adjustable settings that represent subtle patterns in language, such as relationships between words, vocabulary, grammar, facts, and even writing styles.
- *More training data*—Instead of the most popular and commonly available texts, a typical LLM is trained on entire libraries of content—web pages, novels, research papers, forum posts, code repositories, and more—often reaching terabytes in size.
- *More complex architecture*—Modern LLMs are built on the Transformer framework. Although the original Transformer consisted of an Encoder (to read) and a Decoder (to write), modern LLMs often use one part. (GPT models, for example, are decoder-only.) Regardless of the configuration, the core magic lies in the Transformer Block, which combines Attention Mechanisms (to focus on context), Feed-Forward ANNs (to process information), and Normalization layers. The attention mechanism allows the model to decide which earlier words deserve focus when predicting the next ones. Imagine reading a book and highlighting important words or phrases as you go.

With these upgrades, LLMs are capable of performing tasks far beyond predicting single words. They're able to generate coherent paragraphs, translate languages, answer questions, and write code; and more possibilities are being unlocked every day.

The most popular architecture and approach for modern LLMs are Transformers; figure 11.2 shows how they fit into the mental model of machine learning algorithms. Notice that *generative models* use approaches from the other categories of machine learning algorithms that we've explored through this book, such as unsupervised learning (finding relationships between words), supervised learning (determining whether predicted words are correct), reinforcement learning (fine-tuning the model based on human preferences), and deep learning.

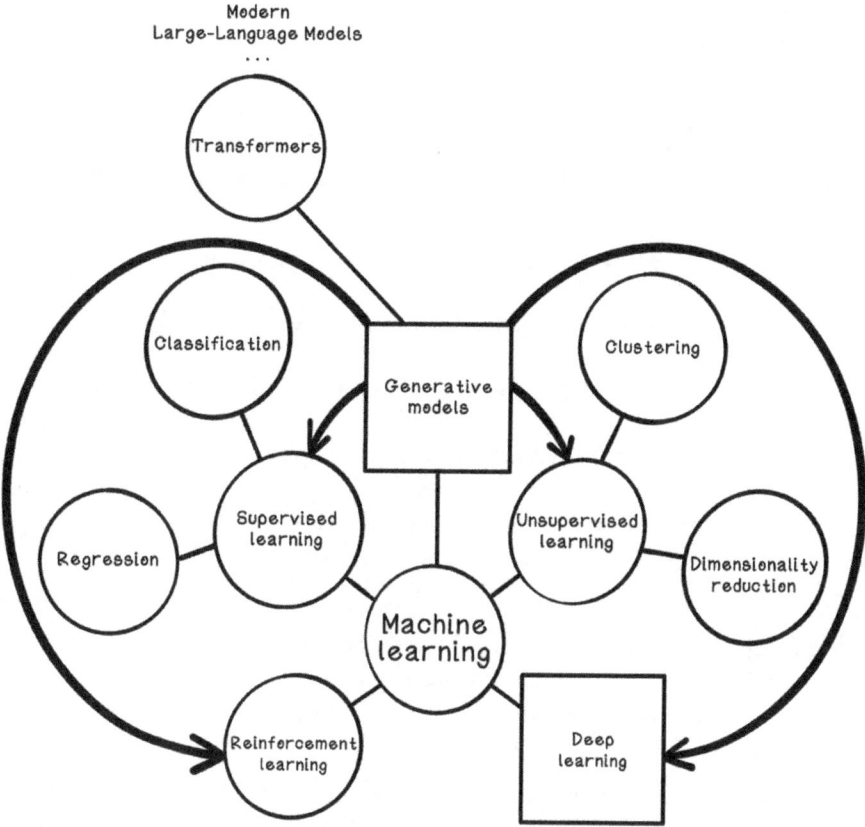

Figure 11.2 How generative models and Transformers fit into machine learning

The intuition behind language prediction

Before we explore the complete LLM training workflow, let's warm up with a practical problem that we can use basic calculations and our intuition to solve. Suppose that we have the following short sentences from the book *Alice's Adventures in Wonderland*:

1. Alice was beginning to get very tired.
2. Alice was getting very sleepy.
3. The White Rabbit was late.
4. The White Rabbit was very late.
5. Alice and the Rabbit were friends.

Simply by reading these sentences, we may recognize some patterns: *Alice* and the *White Rabbit* are always nouns, *was* normally comes after *Alice* and after the *White Rabbit*, and the adjective *very* is used often (figure 11.3). This recognition is normal for humans because our brains are pattern-matching machines. But let's quantify the words into something a computer can understand and find patterns by using calculations.

Alice was beginning to get very tired.

Alice was getting very sleepy.

The White Rabbit was late.

The White Rabbit was very late.

Alice and the Rabbit were friends.

Figure 11.3 How we subconsciously identify patterns in language

A simple concept in language models is bigrams. *Bigrams* are two-word sequences such as *Alice was* or *White Rabbit*. If the first word is the one we're making a prediction about and the next word is a possible prediction, we can build a table of probabilities based on the sentences that we have available to train on.

To calculate probabilities, we use the formula in figure 11.4. The count for a specific word is the total occurrences of a word (Next word) after the word (Previous word) divided by the sum of all occurrences of the word (Previous word). This *next* and *previous* pairing is a bigram.

Think of your phone's autocomplete feature. If you type *Alice*, the model looks at its training data to see what word usually comes next. If *was* appears 90 times after *Alice* and *ran* appears only 10 times, the model assigns a 90% probability to *was* and suggests it as the next word. Table 11.1 lists all bigrams in our dataset of five sentences and their respective probabilities.

$$P(Next|Previous) = \frac{\text{number of times } \textbf{Next} \text{ occurs after } \textbf{Previous}}{\text{total occurrences that start with } \textbf{Previous}}$$

Figure 11.4 Formula for probability of a word occurring after another word

Table 11.1 Bigram counts for the five sample sentences

	Previous word	Next word	Occurrence count	Probability calculation	Probability
1	Alice	was	2	2/3	**0.67**
2	Alice	and	1	1/3	**0.33**
	Alice occurrence count		3		
3	was	beginning	1	1/4	**0.25**
4	was	getting	1	1/4	**0.25**
5	was	late	1	1/4	**0.25**
6	was	very	1	1/4	**0.25**
	was occurrence count		4		
7	beginning	to	1	1/1	**1**
8	to	get	1	1/1	**1**
9	get	very	1	1/1	**1**
10	very	tired	1	1/3	**0.33**
11	very	sleepy	1	1/3	**0.33**
12	very	late	1	1/3	**0.33**
	very occurrence count		3		
13	getting	very	1	1/1	**1**
14	the	White	2	2/3	**0.67**
15	the	Rabbit	1	1/3	**0.33**
	the occurrence count		3		
16	White	Rabbit	2	2/2	**1**
17	Rabbit	was	2	2/3	**0.67**
18	Rabbit	were	1	1/3	**0.33**
	Rabbit occurrence count		3		
19	and	the	1	1/1	**1**
20	were	friends	1	1/1	**1**

Using this table of probabilities, we can make predictions. Given the word *Alice*, the model has two options for the next word: *was*, with a probability of 0.67, and *and*, with a probability of 0.33. This means that the next word predicted will be *was* with the probability of 67%, so the result is *Alice was* (figure 11.5). Given the word *the*, the options are *White*, with a probability of 0.67, and *Rabbit*, with a probability of 0.33. So the completion will be *the White*, with a probability of 67%. For the next word, *White* has only one option—*Rabbit*, with a probability of 100%— progressing to *White Rabbit*.

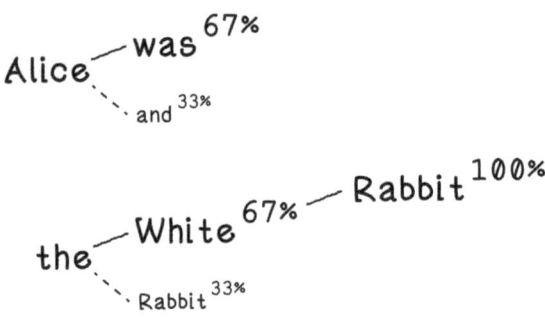

Figure 11.5 Example of the probability of words occurring

You can see how this tiny example of five sentences and 29 tokens can start producing a semblance of intelligent behavior that's expected from a language model. A *token* in this example is a single word in the five sentences. The example has 29 tokens (words). A token is the smallest unit of text the model processes. Although they're often whole words, tokens can also be parts of words (such as *ing*) or even punctuation, depending on the tokenizer used.

A simplified understanding of a parameter is each row in the table. The table has 20 parameters. In actual LLMs, parameters are weights in the Transformer used to train it.

On a conceptual level, LLMs use a similar counting and normalizing approach on billions of tokens, allowing them to model much larger contexts. In the following sections, we'll build on this idea, swapping the simple bigram count table for trainable embeddings and attention layers and explore how the same underlying principle scales up to modern LLMs.

Why the sizes of tokens and parameters matter

More tokens mean a larger training set to learn from. This means that we need more weights in the artificial neural network (ANN), giving the model capacity to store fine relationships among words and other combinations of words, not just pairs. As a result, the LLM can learn edge cases, rare words, and different writing styles, which powers the goal of generalization, in which a model can answer any prompt sensibly. In the example that we'll explore later in this chapter, we'll be working with 35 tokens to train the LLM. Modern production-grade LLMs, however, have been trained with more than 5 trillion tokens (figure 11.6).

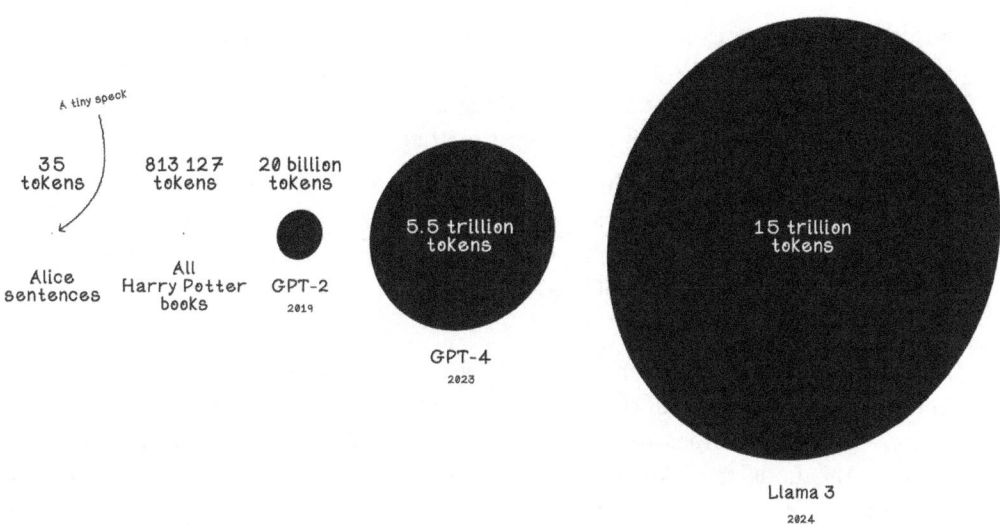

Figure 11.6 Comparison of size of training sets in popular language models

An LLM training workflow

Training an LLM is conceptually similar to any other machine learning endeavor. We need to collect and prepare the right data, architect the model toward the goal we're trying to achieve, and train a model using that data (figure 11.7).

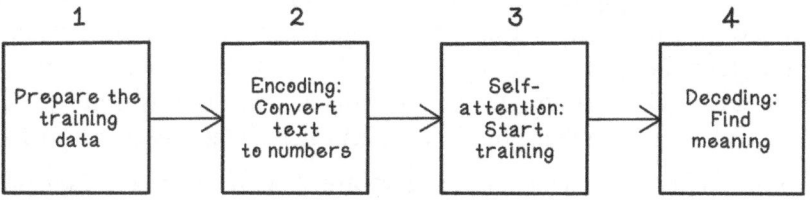

Figure 11.7 An overview of the LLM training workflow

Let's break down the training workflow into its core components:

1. *Prepare the training data.* Before we can teach a model anything, we must build its library. This first step involves gathering and cleaning a massive, diverse dataset of text (including books, research papers, web-forum discussions, and code), which will serve as the foundation for all the knowledge the model will eventually learn.

2. *Encoding: Convert text to numbers.* Computers don't understand words, so this step acts as a translator. We create a vocabulary of unique tokens (words or parts of words) and then convert the entire text dataset to a long sequence of corresponding numerical IDs that the model can process mathematically.

3. *Self-attention: Start training.* This step is where the core learning happens. The model repeatedly processes the numerical data using the self-attention mechanism, which allows it to look at all the tokens in a sequence and learn the complex relationships between them, figuring out which words are important to one another in different contexts.

4. *Decoding: Find meaning.* After the model learns these relationships, it holds its understanding in a series of complex vectors. The decoding step takes these internal numerical representations and projects them back to human-readable language, allowing the model to make predictions and generate new text based on the patterns it found.

As in any machine learning project, we have to understand what hyperparameters we can adjust, such as configuring the Transformer, stacking Transformers, and adjusting attention heads.

Prepare the training data

Before any training can happen, we must select and prepare the data that we want the LLM to train on and be knowledgeable about (figure 11.8). After reading chapter 8, you should understand the importance of preparing data and the various techniques for preparing discrete and continuous data. Preparing data for LLMs is similar, but requires a massive amount of data to make the model perform anywhere close to satisfactory.

The main steps in preparing data to train LLMs are selecting data, collecting data, cleaning the data, and preprocessing the data. From reading chapters 8 and 9, you probably understand the importance of selecting the right data given the question you're trying to answer. With LLMs, however, the challenge is immense: to understand an entire language and the domain-specific meanings and knowledge the language expresses. Cleaning the training data is as important as cleaning numeric data.

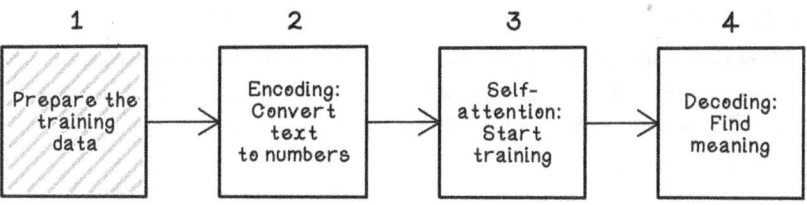

Figure 11.8 First step (preparing training data) in the LLM training workflow

Selecting and collecting data

The LLM will become as broad-minded or narrow-minded as the data it's trained on. The goal in selecting data to train with is to choose data that's broad enough to teach general language skills and relevant enough in the domain you specifically care about. Any LLM that performs well requires many general texts to understand a specific language, such as English. If you're interested in having an LLM perform well in a specific domain, such as rocket science, you have to train it on a wealth of texts about that discipline. Here are some sources of text that powerful modern LLMs are trained on:

- *Public-domain books*—Literary works for which the copyright has expired, making them free to use. Sources such as Project Gutenberg provide high-quality, well-edited texts that help LLMs learn grammar, vocabulary, and coherent long-form narrative structures.
- *Web crawlers*—Automated programs that download vast amounts of text from the public internet. Although this approach is the best way to achieve massive scale and capture a wide range of current topics, the resulting data is noisy, containing everything from high-quality articles to repetitive spam, and requires significant cleaning.
- *User-generated text*—Content from public forums, Q&A sites, and social media platforms. This type of data is invaluable for teaching the model how real people have conversations; how to answer questions; and what jargon is used in different communities, such as technical problem-solving or casual discussions.
- *Domain-specific text*—Large collections of text that focus on a single field, such as legal documents and medical textbooks. Including this type of data is crucial for training a model to be expert in a specific domain's concepts and jargon.

- *Code repositories*—Sources like GitHub that provide access to millions of public software projects. This data is essential for teaching a model how to understand, write, and debug code across a wide variety of programming languages, as well as common design patterns and likely implementations of common functions.

- *News archives*—Collections of public articles from news organizations, often spanning many decades. The archives are valuable sources of high-quality factual information about historical and current events, which helps ground the model's knowledge of the world.

Volume and quality of tokens

Different LLMs have different goals. You might want to make an LLM that can help scientists make a breakthrough in research. A good approach might be to include many academic papers from different specialty fields: medicine, mathematics, computer science, engineering, law, and so on. But the resulting model may come across as very formal because research papers are intended to be formal and clear. Also, although the dataset on the right in figure 11.9 has more sources, you may not know the quality of the data extracted from those sources. The pure size of the data doesn't matter as much as its quality. A small curated dataset could be better than a large uncurated dataset.

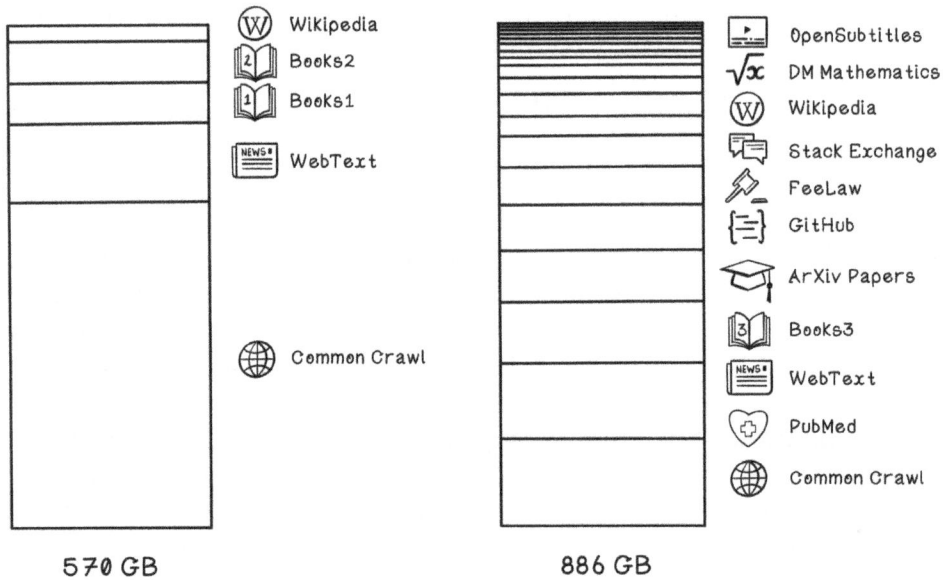

Figure 11.9 Sample training datasets and their domain compositions

Although accessing information on the internet is easy, there are complexities in using that information to train an LLM. With current intellectual-property laws, not everything you see is free to use as training data.

Licensing of content

Much of the text and media you find online is protected by copyright, which means you can't freely use it to train a model, especially for commercial purposes. To avoid legal issues, it's best to rely on data that's in the public domain, such as old books for which the copyright has expired; content with permissive licenses that allow this kind of use; and data that the owners have explicitly licensed for this use. Specialty content becomes more valuable as the LLM landscape evolves. If a model can be trained on special knowledge not available to competing models, it might have an edge.

Cleaning and preprocessing data

To work through the LLM training algorithm, we'll use the public-domain text *Alice's Adventures in Wonderland*. First, we have to clean the text data from the book. For the sake of brevity, we'll use only the first paragraph of the book, but these principles apply to the entire text of the book and all training data. Figure 11.10 shows an excerpt of the original text that we'll modify as we progress in data preparation.

```
*** START OF THE PROJECT GUTENBERG EBOOK ALICE'S ADVENTURES IN WONDERLAND ***
[Illustration]
Alice was beginning to get very tired of sitting by her sister on the
bank, and of having nothing to do: once or twice she had peeped into
the book her sister was reading, but it had no pictures or
conversations in it, "and what is the use of a book," thought Alice
"without pictures or conversations?"
```

Figure 11.10 Excerpt of training data from *Alice's Adventures in Wonderland*

Language filtering

If the training data contains multiple languages, the model has to juggle multiple vocabularies and grammars in the same weights of the Transformer. Less-common languages are drowned out, and common languages are trained poorly. Also, having multiple languages dramatically increases the vocabulary size; you'll see why this is important in the "Tokenization" section later in this chapter.

The book in our example is already in English, so we don't have to do any language filtering. In a real-world dataset, however, we have to filter out the languages we're not interested in.

Boilerplate stripping

Some data may contain boilerplate content, such as licensing declarations, HTML tags, cookie-banner code from websites, or navigation menu code from a website, among other noise. This content provides no semantic meaning in the context of the domain you're trying to train for. You can strip out this content, reducing the token size, and preventing the model from learning irrelevant patterns from repeated content.

In the original text, two boilerplate lines don't provide any context that's related to the meaning of the story. These lines should be stripped out, resulting in the text shown in figure 11.11.

↙ Boilerplate stripped

Alice was beginning to get very tired of sitting by her sister on the
bank, and of having nothing to do: once or twice she had peeped into
the book her sister was reading, but it had no pictures or
conversations in it, "and what is the use of a book," thought Alice "without pictures or
conversations?"

Figure 11.11 Training data with boilerplate stripped

Near-duplicate removal

Sometimes, the same content is mirrored in many places from which the training data was sourced. A quote, for example, might appear hundreds of times in forums and blogs. As a result, the model assigns an artificially high probability to that piece of text and starts to provide that text verbatim even when that response is incorrect. By removing duplicates, we encourage the network to learn how to generalize meaning instead of memorizing specific phrases. In our example, there are no duplicates.

Safety and compliance filters

Another task is removing profanity, slurs, toxicity (highly opinionated views that may be harmful), and personally identifiable information (PII). Normally, we don't want our model to use obscene words; this practice carries a reputational risk and could create a poor experience for users of the model. Also, training data could contain phone numbers, credit card numbers, and other PII that we wouldn't want our model to reproduce due to data-protection laws, so stripping out this data is important.

Normalization

Normalization involves standardizing the content of the text in terms of special characters, whitespace, and emojis. The words *cafe* and *CAFÉ* may look the same to humans, for example, but they're two different tokens, because the last letter isn't the same in both words and one word is all uppercase. Here are some common normalization operations:

- *Lowercase all the words.* This operation ensures that the model treats the same word, such as *The* at the start of a sentence and *the* in the middle, as a single token. It also reduces the size of the vocabulary the model has to learn and helps it generalize better. Lowercasing is common in traditional NLP pipelines to reduce vocabulary size. In modern NLP pipelines (especially LLMs), casing is preserved because capitalization carries meaning (as in *apple* versus *Apple* and *us* versus *U.S.*). For simplicity, we'll lowercase the training data in our example.
- *Strip smart quotes.* Word processors often create curly smart quotes, which are different characters from straight quotes. This step converts them all to the standard version to ensure consistency across the dataset.
- *Collapse whitespace.* Text from different sources may have extra spaces, tabs, or line breaks for formatting. This process replaces any sequence of these elements with a single space, creating clean, uniform separation between words.
- *Handle accented characters.* This step involves deciding how to handle characters with diacritics, as in *café*. You may want to convert them to their basic alphabetical equivalents, such as *cafe*, to simplify the vocabulary or keep them to retain their original meaning in other languages.

Figure 11.12 shows the normalized text of our example. All characters are lowercase, opening- and closing-quote characters are normalized, all whitespace is single whitespace characters, and special characters have whitespace around them to identify them as their own semantic symbol.

```
alice was beginning to get very tired of sitting by her sister on the bank,
and of having nothing to do : once or twice she had peeped into the book her
sister was reading , but it had no pictures or conversations in it , " and what
is the use of a book," thought alice "without pictures or conversations ? "
```

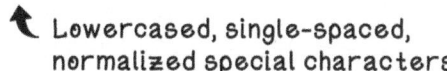 Lowercased, single-spaced,
normalized special characters

Figure 11.12 Training data normalized

Data-quality audit

When our data has been collected and normalized, we can perform a data-quality audit to ensure that the dataset is clean, balanced, and suitable for our goals. This process involves calculating key metrics to check for common issues such as repetitive text, toxic content, and formatting problems. By setting a target for each metric, we can systematically measure and improve the quality of our data before feeding it to the model. Table 11.2 is a checklist of areas that we can evaluate and goals for these areas.

> **NOTE** You can use reliable libraries for these tasks. To get to know some of them, see the Python repository for this book (https://github.com/rishal -hurbans/Grokking-Artificial-Intelligence-Algorithms).

Table 11.2 A summary of areas important for data quality

Metric	Why it matters	Goals
Duplicate rate	It prevents memorization and reduces dataset size.	< 5% exact-paragraph matches
Average sentence length	Very short sentences lack context, and very long sentences overflow the model window.	5–40 tokens per segmented sentence
Toxicity rate	It keeps generation safe and inoffensive.	< 0.3% words flagged for toxicity
Profanity ratio	It provides a more precise count than toxicity rate.	Depends on the use case; can be < 0.2% for general models but can be higher for "edgy" domains
Language purity	Mixed languages confuse the model and add unnecessary vocabulary.	> 98% of the content in the desired language
PII leaks	It reduces privacy and legal risks.	0 emails, 0 phone numbers, 0 ID numbers
Non-UTF8 character rate	Binary junk characters can cause the tokenizer (explored next) to crash.	0 control characters (realistically, < 0.01% is good enough)
Forbidden phrases	It prevents generation of phrases you don't want to see.	0 occurrences of forbidden phrases
Markup density	Markup like HTML and markdown noise wastes the context window and makes tokenizing less accurate.	< 2% lines containing code characters such as <, [, ^, >,], +, > and links

Table 11.2 A summary of areas important for data quality (*continued*)

Metric	Why it matters	Goals
Readability score	It makes the LLM generate text that's easy to read (written for a certain reading level).	The Flesch-Kincaid Grade-Level readability score (F-K score) is a formula to determine ease of readability. A score of 6 means 11-year-olds can read it easily; a score of 12 means 17-year-olds can read it easily.
Domain balance	If you curate multiple domains (medical, fiction, geography, and so on), you want to represent them as intended.	No more than 10% variance per domain. If you planned 20% medical content, for example, your actual data shouldn't be less than 10% or more than 30%.

Encoding: From text to numbers

Now that we have our clean training data, we face a fundamental challenge: Computers don't understand words. They understand numbers. For a model to learn from our text, we first have to convert the text to a numerical format it can work with (figure 11.13). The process of translating text into a list of numbers is known as *encoding*.

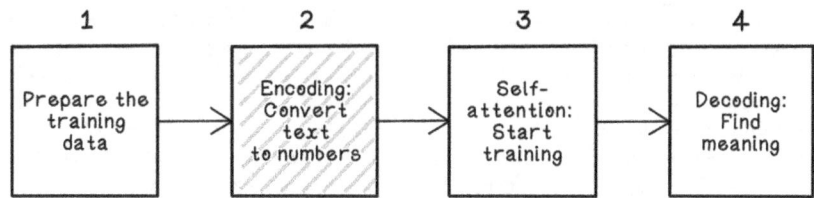

Figure 11.13 Encoding step in the LLM training workflow

Tokenization

As humans who understand English, our lowest building blocks for reading, writing, and processing the language are words, and punctuation. In "Alice was beginning to get very tired of sitting," we understand each word independently. Based on the rules of language, we understand nouns like *Alice*, verbs like *sitting*, and adjectives like *very* and *tired*. We also know the meanings of words. We know that *beginning* is different from *ending*, but we also know that the words are related (as opposites).

LLMs don't understand language in the same intuitive way that humans do. Instead, the input text undergoes a process called *tokenization*, which breaks the text into a sequence of these smaller units.

The sentence "Alice was beginning to get very tired of sitting," for example, might be tokenized as `Alice`, `was`, `beginning`, `to`, `get`, `very`, `tired`, `of`, `sitting`. In this simple case, each token is a word. But actual tokens end up looking quite different so that the model can learn the core semantics of a language. The word unbelievable, for example, could be broken down into the tokens `un`, `believ`, `able`. This allows the model to handle a vast vocabulary, with `un` having a similar meaning in `unrealistic` and `unforgettable`. Understanding that tokens aren't necessarily words is an important intuition in LLMs. Breaking words down in this way allows the model to handle a large vocabulary flexibly and efficiently.

Using characters as tokens

Let's explore how text training data can be tokenized and used to build a vocabulary. We'll work with a paragraph of training data.

First, we break each word in the sentence into individual characters. We also add a special end-of-word marker, `</w>`, after the last character of each original word (figure 11.14). This step is important because it allows the algorithm to distinguish between a sequence of characters that occurs inside a word (such as in in *spin*) and one that makes up a word itself (such as the word *in*).

```
alice</w> was</w> beginning</w> to</w> get</w> very</w> tired</w> of</w>
sitting</w> by</w> her</w> sister</w> on</w> the</w> bank</w> ,</w> and</w> of
</w> having</w> nothing</w> to</w> do</w> :</w> once</w> or</w> twice</w> she
</w> had</w> peeped</w> into</w> the</w> book</w> her</w> sister</w> was</w>
reading</w> ,</w> but</w> it</w> had</w> no</w> pictures</w> or</w>
conversations</w> in</w> it</w> ,</w> "</w> and</w> what</w> is</w> the</w> use
</w> of</w> a</w> book</w> ,</w> "</w> thought</w> alice</w> "</w> without</w>
pictures</w> or</w> conversations</w> ?</w> "</w>
```

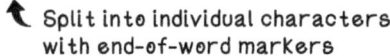
Split into individual characters
with end-of-word markers

Figure 11.14 Training data split into characters with end-of-word markers

Counting all bigrams

Remember that bigrams are two-word sequences. In this case, bigrams are pairs of tokens that appear next to each other. Table 11.3 is a partial bigram frequency table for our sentence. There are eight occurrences of `i` and `n`. Examples include `beginning`, with two occurrences, and `sitting`, with 1 occurrence. The token pairs with the fewest occurrences are s and ?, appearing only in conversations?, and ? and " , appearing at the end of ...conversations?".

Table 11.3 The initial bigram count for the training data

	Previous word	Next word	Occurrence count
0	i	n	8
1	e	r	7
2	t	h	7
3	t	i	6
4	h	e	6
5	o	n	6
6	i	c	5
7	n	g	5
8	c	e	4
	...		
24	a	t	3
25	a	l	2
	...		
125	s	?	1
126	?	"	1

Merging the most frequent pair

Counting the bigrams is the first step in byte-pair-encoding (BPE) the data. Now we can merge the most common pairs into a single token and repeat the process. In the output shown in figure 11.15, we've merged all occurrences of i and n because this pair has the most occurrences.

> **NOTE** The end-of-word (</w>) markers have been omitted for readability.

```
alicewasbeginningtogetverytiredofsittingbyhersisteronthebank,
andofhavingnothingtodo:
onceortwiceshehadpeepedintothebookhersisterwasreading,
butithadnopicturesorconversationsinit,
"andwhatistheuseofabook,"thoughtalice"
withoutpicturesorconversations?"
```

Figure 11.15 Training data after one iteration of merging with BPE

After repeating the process of counting bigrams with the new input, we have the bigram frequency table shown in table 11.4. The new most frequent pair is e and r. The pair t and i, which had six occurrences in the first iteration, now has only five occurrences. Our new token with the pair in and g has five occurrences.

Table 11.4 The bigram count after one iteration

	Previous word	Next word	Occurrence count
0	e	r	7
1	t	h	7
2	h	e	6
3	o	n	6
4	i	c	5
5	in	g	5
6	t	i	5
7	c	e	4
8	r	e	4
...			
129	?	"	1

After merging our most frequent bigram, which is e and r, we have tokens that look like the training paragraph in figure 11.16. This process is done until we reach the stopping point. The stopping point is usually defined based on a desired vocabulary size; it occurs when the most frequent bigram count falls below a minimum threshold. If we iterate until there are no bigrams with frequency more than 1, for example, we may end up with tokens that don't make sense.

```
alicewasbeginningtogetverytiredofsittingbyhersisteronthebank,
andofhavingnothingtodo:
onceortwiceshehadpeepedintothebookhersisterwasreading,
butithadnopicturesorconversationsinit,
"andwhatistheuseofabook,"thoughtalice"
withoutpicturesorconversations?"
```

Figure 11.16 Training data after two iterations of merging with BPE

In our example, going that route would result in one token being picturesorconversations, which isn't a word or phrase commonly found in languages.

When we stop the iterations at a maximum of three (figure 11.17), our final bigram count and result look like table 11.5.

```
alicewasbeginning togetvery tiredofsitting byhersister onthebank,
andofhavingnothing todo:
onceortwiceshehadpeepedinto thebookhersisterwasreading,
butithadnopicturesorconversationsinit,
"andwhatistheuseofabook,"thoughtalice"
withoutpicturesorconversations?"
```

Figure 11.17 Training data after three iterations of merging with BPE

Table 11.5 The bigram count after two iterations

	Previous word	Next word	Occurrence count
0	ic	e	3
1	t	o	3
2	d	o	3
3	o	f	3
4	th	e	3
...			
136	?	"	1

Python code sample for a BPE tokenizer

The following code implements a simplified version of BPE for tokenizing text. It starts by splitting words into characters and marking word boundaries. Then it iteratively finds and merges the most frequent adjacent character pairs (bigrams), forming longer tokens until a target vocabulary size is reached. Finally, it builds a vocabulary of unique tokens and assigns each a unique integer ID, which can be used to convert text to model-ready numerical inputs.

```python
def tokenize(text, vocabulary_size):
    words = text.split()
    current_tokens = []

    for word in words:
        current_tokens.extend(list(word) + ['</w>'])

    vocabulary = set(current_tokens)

    while len(vocabulary) < vocabulary_size:
```

Breaks every word down into its individual letters

```
bigram_counts = collections.defaultdict(int)
for i in range(len(current_tokens) - 1):
    pair = (current_tokens[i], current_tokens[i+1])
    bigram_counts[pair] += 1

if not bigram_counts:
    break

most_frequent_bigram = max(bigram_counts, key=bigram_counts.get)
count = bigram_counts[most_frequent_bigram]

if count <= 1:
    break

new_token = "".join(most_frequent_bigram)
next_tokens = []
i = 0

while i < len(current_tokens):
    is_match = (i < len(current_tokens) - 1 and
    current_tokens[i] == most_frequent_bigram[0] and
    current_tokens[i+1] == most_frequent_bigram[1])

    if is_match:
        next_tokens.append(new_token)
        i += 2
    else:
        next_tokens.append(current_tokens[i])
        i += 1

current_tokens = next_tokens
vocabulary.add(new_token)

final_vocabulary = sorted(list(vocabulary))
token_ids = {token: i for i, token in enumerate(final_vocabulary)}

return final_vocabulary, token_ids
```

Scans the current list of tokens to see which two characters (or sub-words) appear next to each other most often

Takes the most common pair and glues them together into a single, new token

When a match is found, the loop skips the next character because it has been swallowed up by the new, combined token

The new merged token is officially added to the vocabulary

Computers don't speak words, they speak numbers

Assigning IDs to the tokens

With our final set of bigrams, we can assign integer IDs to each token. Integer IDs are important because algorithms work with numeric representations of data so our text tokens can be interpreted correctly. Table 11.6 is a table of all tokens and their respective IDs. There are 34 unique tokens, so our vocabulary size is 34.

Table 11.6 The vocabulary based on the training data

ID	Token	ID	Token	ID	Token
0	a	12	o	24	th
1	l	13	v	25	k
2	ic	14	er	26	,
3	e	15	y	27	:
4	w	16	ti	28	c
5	s	17	re	29	r
6	b	18	d	30	p
7	g	19	f	31	u
8	in	20	i	32	"
9	n	21	h	33	?
10	ing	22	ers		
11	t	23	on		

Vectorization

After building our vocabulary through tokenization, the next step is using it to transform our entire training text into the numerical format that the model requires for learning. This process is often called *vectorization* because we're turning the text into a long vector (token stream). Each number in this sequence corresponds to a specific token from our learned vocabulary.

With our tokens represented as IDs, we can represent our input as a token stream of the token IDs. Our original input training data, shown in figure 11.18, becomes the token stream shown in figure 11.19.

```
alice was beginning to get very tired of sitting by her sister on the bank,
and of having nothing to do :
once or twice she had peeped into the book her sister was reading ,
but it had no pictures or conversations in it ,
" and what is the use of a book," thought alice
"without pictures or conversations ? "
```

Figure 11.18 Original training data

```
a l ic e ...
 \ \ | /
 0 1 2 3 4 0 5 6 3 7 8 9 10 11 12 7 3 11 13 14 15 16 17 18 12
 19 5 20 11 11 10 6 15 21 22 20 5 11 14 23 24 3 6 0 9 25 26 0 9 18
 12 19 21 0 13 10 9 12 24 10 11 12 18 12 27 23 28 3 12 29 11 4 2 3 5
 21 3 21 0 18 30 3 3 30 3 18 8 11 12 24 3 6 12 12 25 21 22 20 5 11
 14 4 0 5 17 0 18 10 26 6 31 16 24 0 18 9 12 30 2 11 31 17 5 12 29
 28 23 13 22 0 16 23 5 8 20 11 26 32 0 9 18 4 21 0 16 5 24 3 31 5
 3 12 19 0 6 12 12 25 26 32 24 12 31 7 21 11 0 1 2 3 32 4 20 24 12
 31 11 30 2 11 31 17 5 12 29 28 23 13 22 0 16 23 5 33 32
```

Figure 11.19 Tokenized training data as a token stream

Now our token stream is a complete numerical representation of the text, but it's far too long for us to work through in training our model all at once. LLMs have a fixed input size called a *context window*, which is the maximum number of tokens they can look at in a single pass. To prepare the data for training, we break this long stream into smaller, manageable chunks called *batches*. Each batch is a self-contained training example that fits within the model's context window. Then we can create training batches based on a context-window size. Our context-window size is 32, but modern LLMs have context windows of 1,024 to 30,000 tokens. Figure 11.20 illustrates the six batches of tokens we can use for training. We'll use only one batch at a time.

[a, l, ic, e, w, a, s, b, e, g, in, n, ing, t, o, g, e, t, v, er, y, ti, re, d, o, f, s, i, t, t, ing, b]

Batch 0
[0, 1, 2, 3, 4, 0, 5, 6, 3, 7, 8, 9, 10, 11, 12, 7, 3, 11, 13, 14, 15, 16, 17, 18, 12, 19, 5, 20, 11, 11, 10, 6]

32 tokens in size

Batch 1
[15, 21, 22, 20, 5, 11, 14, 23, 24, 3, 6, 0, 9, 25, 26, 0, 9, 18, 12, 19, 21, 0, 13, 10, 9, 12, 24, 10, 11, 12, 18, 12]

Batch 2
[27, 23, 28, 3, 12, 29, 11, 4, 2, 3, 5, 21, 3, 21, 0, 18, 30, 3, 3, 30, 3, 18, 8, 11, 12, 24, 3, 6, 12, 12, 25, 21]

Batch 3
[22, 20, 5, 11, 14, 4, 0, 5, 17, 0, 18, 10, 26, 6, 31, 16, 24, 0, 18, 9, 12, 30, 2, 11, 31, 17, 5, 12, 29, 28, 23, 13]

Batch 4
[22, 0, 16, 23, 5, 8, 20, 11, 26, 32, 0, 9, 18, 4, 21, 0, 16, 5, 24, 3, 31, 5, 3, 12, 19, 0, 6, 12, 12, 25, 26, 32]

Batch 5
[24, 12, 31, 7, 21, 11, 0, 1, 2, 3, 32, 4, 20, 24, 12, 31, 11, 30, 2, 11, 31, 17, 5, 12, 29, 28, 23, 13, 22, 0, 16, 23]

Batch 6
[5, 33, 32]

Figure 11.20 Tokenized training data as training batches

Exercise: What are the tokens for batch 1?

Determine the text tokens that map to the token IDs for batch 1.

Solution:

```
[15, 21, 22, 20, 5, 11, 14, 23, 24, 3, 6, 0, 9, 25, 26, 0, 9,
18, 12, 19, 21, 0, 13, 10, 9, 12, 24, 10, 11, 12, 18, 12]
[y, h, ers, i, s, t, er, on, th, e, b, a, n, k, ,, a, n, d, o,
f, h, a, v, ing, n, o, th, ing, t, o, d, o]
```

Python code sample for batching tokens

This code segments a continuous stream of token IDs into batches, based on a given `context_window_size`. It moves through the token stream in steps equal to the window size, slicing out sequences of tokens that fit within the model's attention span. These batches are returned as a list of token sequences, ready for input into the model during training or inference:

```python
def batch_tokens(token_stream, context_window_size):
    batches = []

    start_index = 0
    while True:
        end_index = start_index + context_window_size

        if end_index > len(token_stream):
            break

        batch = token_stream[start_index:end_index]
        batches.append(batch)

        start_index += 1

    return batches
```

Defines how many tokens the model can "see" at once

Prevents the loop from trying to grab data past the end of the text

Shifts the window forward by just one token

Extracts a specific segment of tokens

Designing the architecture

Now that we have our training data in a state that's understandable for computing and algorithms, the next step is choosing a training architecture (figure 11.21). In chapter 9, we explored how ANNs take input data, learn the relationships between the inputs, and provide predictions based on those relationships. If we didn't use ANNs to train the LLM, we'd have to come up with the rules and relationships between all the tokens in the vocabulary. Even in the simple example that we're using, this task would require immense effort.

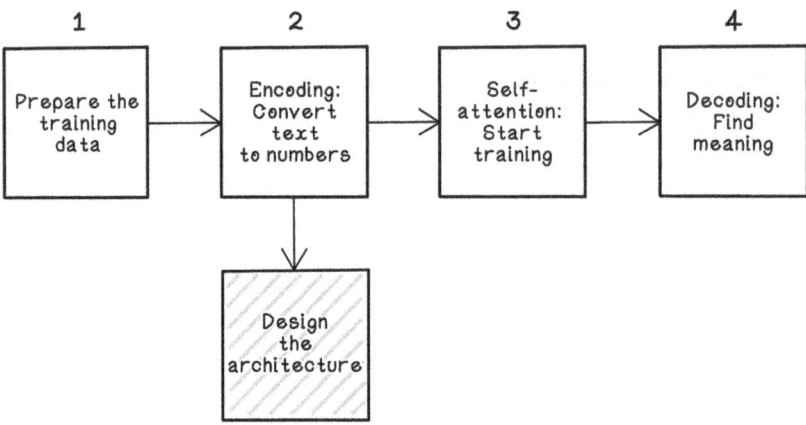

Figure 11.21 Designing the architecture in the LLM training workflow

A major decision in training the LLM is choosing the ANN architecture to use. Different architectures have different tradeoffs based on the problem you're solving. Following are three key concerns in choosing an architecture to train an LLM:

- *Memory capacity*—The amount of RAM or graphics processing unit (GPU) memory required to hold the model's parameters. Larger, more complex models can capture more nuance but demand more memory, which often requires more expensive and specialized hardware.
- *Compute cost*—The sheer amount of processing power and energy use required to train the model. Training massive architectures on huge datasets is an enormous, expensive effort, sometimes taking weeks or months on clusters of thousands of GPUs.
- *Latency*—The delay between giving the model an input and receiving its output. For applications such as chatbots, low latency is critical for a good user experience, but

larger, more capable models often take longer to generate a response, and the model's architecture dictates this latency.

Chapter 9 discussed the hyperparameters of ANNs and showed how to adjust them for different problem spaces. In the context of the car-collision example in chapter 9, a small ANN was good enough to understand relationships between inputs and use them to make fairly accurate predictions based on a small training dataset. You're probably gaining the intuition, however, that the input tokens in an LLM are massive. In our small paragraph, we have a vocabulary of 34 tokens to find relationships among. A usable smart LLM is trained with a vocabulary of 50,000 to more than 250,000 tokens. More tokens usually result in more generalization in language understanding and diverse knowledge in various domains. You can use three ANN architectures to train an LLM (figure 11.22).

- *Recurrent neural network (RNN)/long short-term memory (LSTM)*—This architecture processes text sequentially, one word at a time, while maintaining a memory of what it has seen so far. Basic RNNs, however, have short memories. A more advanced version is LSTM, which uses a sophisticated mechanism to remember context over much longer sequences, making it well-suited to language tasks. But it suffers from an information bottleneck. It has to summarize its entire understanding of the preceding text learned into its fixed-size memory vector, losing the rich context of early text learned.
- *Convolutional neural network (CNN)*—Though CNNs are famous for image processing, you can apply them to text by using sliding windows to detect local patterns of words. CNNs are effective for tasks such as text classification in which specific key phrases are important, but they're less suitable for capturing the complex, long-range meaning of a sentence.
- *Transformer*—The Transformer is the modern, state-of-the-art architecture that powers virtually all modern LLMs. Unlike an RNN, the Transformer architecture processes all words in a sequence at the same time. Its key innovation is the self-attention mechanism, which allows every word to look at and weigh the importance of all other words in the sentence, enabling the model to build a deep, contextual understanding of language.

Recurrent Neural Network

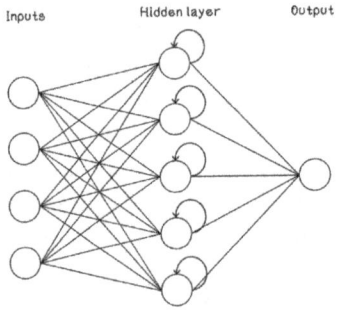

Convolutional Neural Network

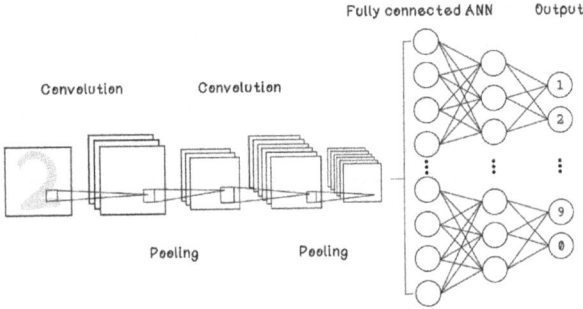

Transformer

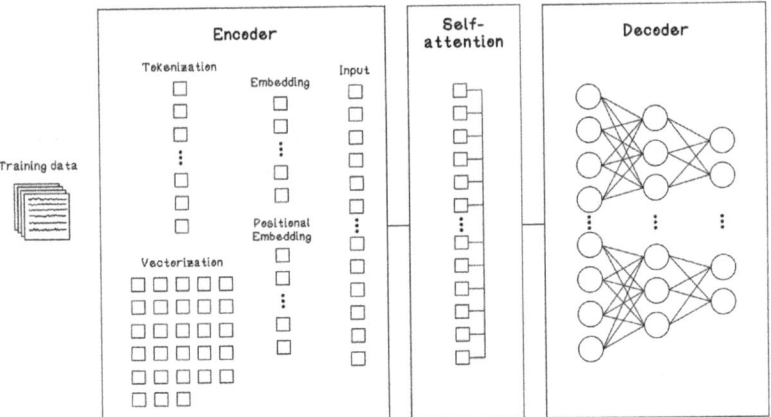

Figure 11.22 Comparison of different ANN architectures aimed at training LLMs

We'll be training our LLM with the Transformer framework. First, we must think about the following parameters of the Transformer components:

- *Vocabulary size*—The number of unique tokens after BPE merging. We've already performed this step and know the number of tokens for our example (34).
- *Context window*—The number of tokens a model can see at the same time. A larger window means more memory to work from. A 256-token window won't be able to write a novel, but it could write some sentences because it would have context of the last 256 tokens.
- *Width (embedding)*—How many floating-point numbers describe one token in each layer. Wider embeddings hold more details about the meaning of words in different contexts.
- *Depth (number of layers)*—Steps in a reasoning chain. One layer looks left and right one time, so 12 layers can think a dozen steps ahead.
- *Attention heads*—The number of unique patterns or concepts the model can notice at the same time.
- *Feed-forward size*—The number of layers and nodes in the feed-forward ANN.

As a refresher, figure 11.23 illustrates a typical ANN. These networks are great for learning from numeric inputs, finding deep relationships in the independent data, and taking further meaning from the correlations of that data until it can make an accurate prediction.

The Transformer architecture uses ANNs but performs several steps first to prepare text data for efficient processing while maintaining information about the original data, such as positions of tokens. Furthermore, Transformers have a step called *self-attention* that's extremely beneficial for helping tokens understand language semantics before further meaning can be found.

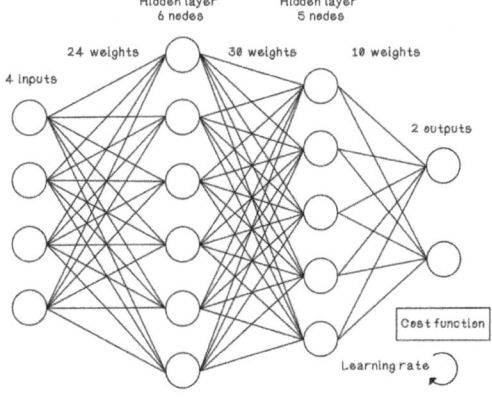

Figure 11.23 The fundamental composition of an ANN

Figure 11.24 illustrates the components of a Transformer:

- *Encoder*—Encompasses the tokenization and vectorization process, which we've already done. It also creates a data object that's suitable for self-attention and ANN processing by creating a numeric embedding of tokens and their positional data in relation to one another.

  > **NOTE** We're using *Encoder* here to refer to operations in the initial embedding step. Many modern LLMs are Decoder-only and don't use the classic, multilayer Encoder architecture.

- *Self-attention*—Lets all tokens figure out how they relate to all other tokens with a specific perspective in mind, such as how tokens relate to other tokens that are nouns.
- *Decoder*—Encompasses the ANN that intends to derive meaning after the self-attention step and decodes back to human-understandable outcomes, resulting in a probability distribution of predictions for the next token in the sequence.

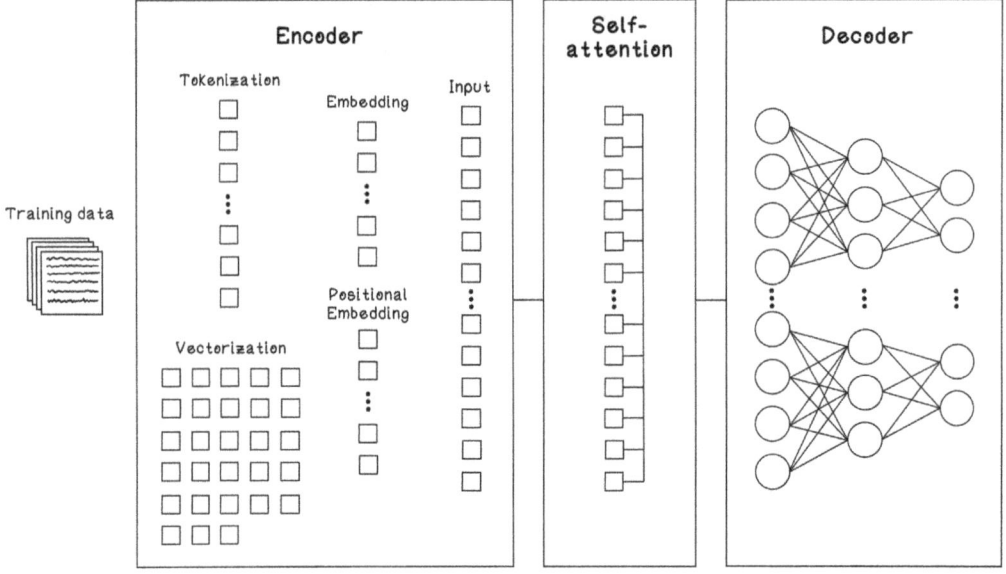

Figure 11.24 A simplistic overview of the Transformer framework

At this point in the chapter, we can work out the steps in the algorithm with small simple examples. But having it perform with some level of intelligence is difficult with only a single paragraph of training data. The power of LLMs comes from having massive language text datasets to learn from. This in turn affects the number of tokens to process, which affects the vocabulary size, which in turn influences the design of the Transformer and the complexity of the calculations that must be done. From now on, we'll use the single paragraph to explore the steps and logic in the algorithm, but the results of calculations move us only a tiny bit closer to intelligence, rather than make explicit progress like the operations we've seen thus far.

Table 11.7 and figure 11.25 show the details of the hyperparameters and how they differ in our example compared with real-world LLMs. Figure 11.25 is the Transformer diagram with the hyperparameter values for the components.

Table 11.7 The hyperparameters for the Transformer framework

Hyperparameter	Rule of thumb	Toy LLM example	Real-world LLM
Vocabulary size (V)	Based on training data	34 sentence pieces	50,000 (more than 250,000 sentence pieces
Context window (T)	Longest prompt you need, rounded to power of 2, that still fits batch on a GPU	32 tokens	1,024 (more than 32,000 tokens)
Width (d)	Start near $4\sqrt{\text{Vocabulary size}}$	4 channels	768 (more than 20,000 channels)
Depth (L)	1–2 layers per 100,000 characters of training text	2 layers	12 (more than 120 layers
Attention heads (h)	h = Width ÷ 64 (round to even)	1 head	12 (more than 128 heads
Feed-forward size (d_n)	$d_n = 4 \times$ Width is a safe default	Layer 1: 8 neurons Layer 2: 4 neurons	3,027 (more than 80,000 neurons)

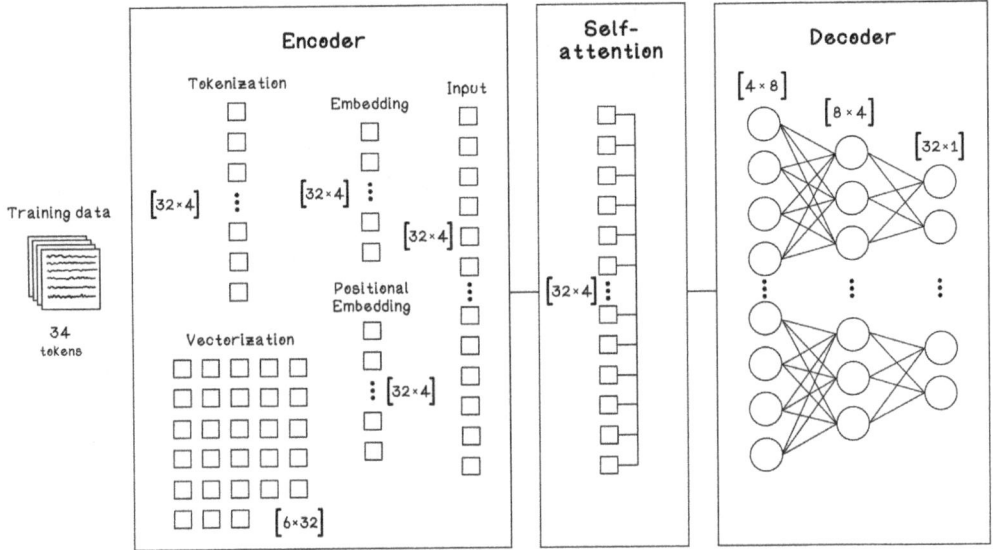

Figure 11.25 The data shapes for the components of our Transformer framework

Encoding: Creating trainable embeddings

With a basic understanding of the Transformer architecture bedded down, we'll jump back to the encoding step (figure 11.26). Because we designed our Transformer to be a width of 4, it influences how we further encode our training data. Let's dive into how our numeric token values become embeddings that can be used in the ANN.

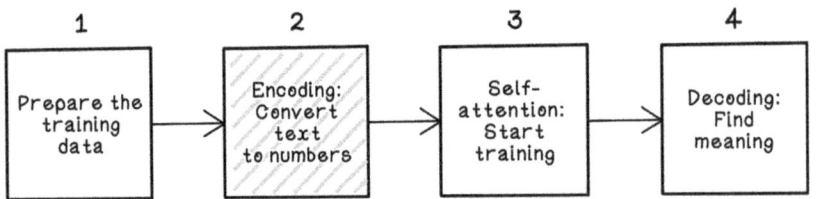

Figure 11.26 Continuation of the encoding step in the LLM training workflow

We've converted our text to a sequence of token IDs, but these numbers are arbitrary. ID 10 has no mathematical relationship to ID 11, so the model can't learn from them directly. To solve this problem, we map each unique token ID to a list of numbers called an *embedding vector*. This vector isn't arbitrary; its values represent the token's meaning in a high-dimensional space. Initially, these vectors start as random, but they're adjusted and improved during training. Think of embeddings as being like a grocery store:

- `apple` and `banana` are close together (fruit aisle).
- `apple` and `apple pie` are somewhat close. (The bakery is near the produce area.)
- `apple` and `laundry detergent` are on opposite sides of the store.

The vector is simply the GPS coordinate of the item in this massive store of meaning. The math calculates distance to see whether two concepts are related flavors or totally distinct.

Sampling a batch of tokens

To walk through the training process, we must select one of these batches to act as our sample input. Let's take the first one from our list of training data (figure 11.27). This single batch of 32 tokens will be the input we pass through all the layers of our Transformer model.

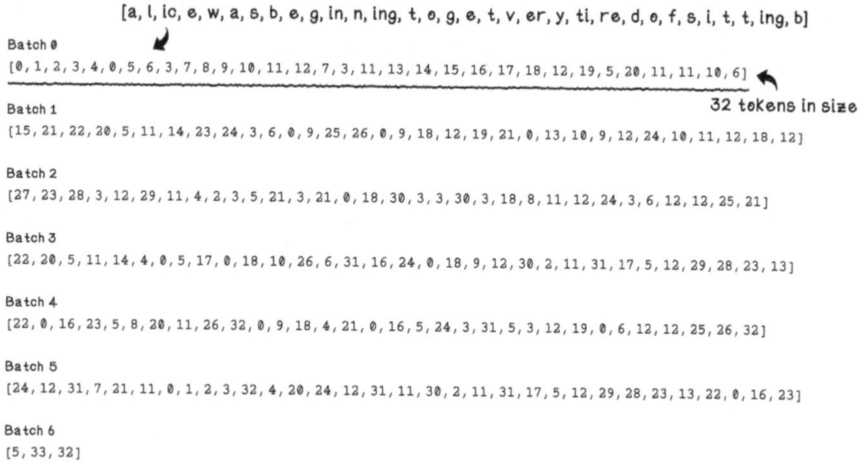

[a, l, ic, e, w, a, s, b, e, g, in, n, ing, t, o, g, e, t, v, er, y, ti, re, d, o, f, s, i, t, t, ing, b]

Batch 0
[0, 1, 2, 3, 4, 0, 5, 6, 3, 7, 8, 9, 10, 11, 12, 7, 3, 11, 13, 14, 15, 16, 17, 18, 12, 19, 5, 20, 11, 11, 10, 6]

32 tokens in size

Batch 1
[15, 21, 22, 20, 5, 11, 14, 23, 24, 3, 6, 0, 9, 25, 26, 0, 9, 18, 12, 19, 21, 0, 13, 10, 9, 12, 24, 10, 11, 12, 18, 12]

Batch 2
[27, 23, 28, 3, 12, 29, 11, 4, 2, 3, 5, 21, 3, 21, 0, 18, 30, 3, 3, 30, 3, 18, 8, 11, 12, 24, 3, 6, 12, 12, 25, 21]

Batch 3
[22, 20, 5, 11, 14, 4, 0, 5, 17, 0, 18, 10, 26, 6, 31, 16, 24, 0, 18, 9, 12, 30, 2, 11, 31, 17, 5, 12, 29, 28, 23, 13]

Batch 4
[22, 0, 16, 23, 5, 8, 20, 11, 26, 32, 0, 9, 18, 4, 21, 0, 16, 5, 24, 3, 31, 5, 3, 12, 19, 0, 6, 12, 12, 25, 26, 32]

Batch 5
[24, 12, 31, 7, 21, 11, 0, 1, 2, 3, 32, 4, 20, 24, 12, 31, 11, 30, 2, 11, 31, 17, 5, 12, 29, 28, 23, 13, 22, 0, 16, 23]

Batch 6
[5, 33, 32]

Figure 11.27 Sampling the first batch of tokens from the training data

We'll sample the first 32 tokens as a batch to work with:

[0, 1, 2, 3, 4, 0, 5, 6, 3, 7, 8, 9, 10, 11, 12, 7, 3, 11, 13, 14, 15, 16, 17, 18, 12, 19, 5, 20, 11, 11, 10, 6]

What happens to batch 6, which has only 3 tokens? Because working with uniform data is more efficient on GPUs and results in consistent operations, batch 6 may be a problem. There are three possible ways to handle it:

- *It gets dropped.* This approach is the simplest and most common one, especially for large datasets. The loss of a tiny fraction of the data from the last incomplete batch is considered negligible and won't affect the final trained model.
- *It gets padded.* The batch is filled with a special padding token until it reaches the required size of 32 tokens. It might become `[5, 22, 32, PAD, PAD, …, PAD]`. Then the model is specifically taught to ignore these padding tokens during its calculations.
- *It's used as is.* Some model architectures can handle input sequences of variable lengths. In this case, the model could be fed the smaller batch of three tokens directly, but this approach can be less computationally efficient than using fixed-size padded batches.

Creating a trainable embedding matrix

If you hand a Transformer the raw ID 17, it has no idea whether that ID is a verb, a comma, or something else. The network can only add and multiply real numbers, so every discrete ID must first be translated into a small vector of floating-point-numbers to represent its meaning. This vector is the *embedding*. That trainable lookup table is called the *embedding matrix* (E). We represent embeddings based on vocabulary size (V) and width (d). The expression in figure 11.28 describes the respective values as a matrix.

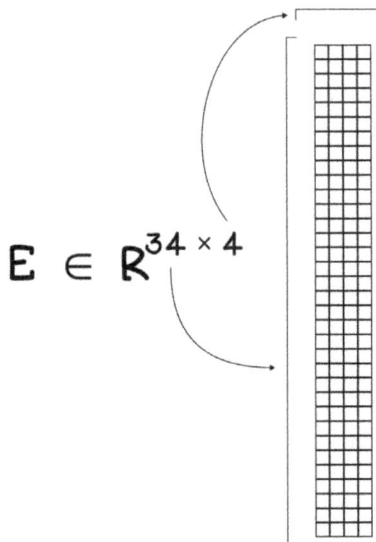

$$E \in R^{34 \times 4}$$

Figure 11.28 A view of how the vocabulary size and width dimensions shape the embedding

We're choosing a width of 4 (d = 4) for ease of understanding. We start with the values in the matrix being random numbers between -0.01 and 0.01 as long as each row starts with a different number. During training, these values will be nudged. If *a* often precedes *l*, for example, row 0 will shift closer to row 1 in the massive multidimensional space. Table 11.8 shows the first two tokens, the last token, and their respective random starting values.

> **NOTE** We're showing the values with a maximum four decimal places for the sake of simplicity in learning. In actual training, the model relies on high precision to work well, so numbers have many decimal places.

Table 11.8 A subset of tokens and their initial embedding values

Position	Token ID	Token	x0	x1	x2	x3
0	0	a	0.0030	-0.0070	0.0120	0.0010
1	1	l	-0.0080	0.0050	-0.0020	0.0090
			...			
31	6	b	0.7381	-0.2512	-0.6719	0.7938

Creating positional encodings

Positional encoding is a technique that gives the model information about the order of words in a sequence. It injects a positional signal into each token's embedding. Self-attention, which is the next step (and the core mechanism of the Transformer), processes all words in a sentence simultaneously. By itself, it has no idea of order. To the self-attention layer, the sentences "The dog bit the man" and "The man bit the dog" look like identical sequences of tokens.

To solve this problem, we add a unique positional vector to each token's embedding. This vector ensures that the model can distinguish between the same token at different positions and understand the overall grammar and meaning of the sentence. If the following is the first batch,

[0, 1, 2, 3, 4, 0, 5, 6, 3, 7, 8, 9, 10, 11, 12, 7, 3, 11, 13, 14, 15, 16, 17, 18, 12, 19, 5, 20, 11, 11, 10, 6]

we can create the position-encoding matrix. We have to calculate position values for the 32 tokens in our first batch. We'll find four values for each token because we have a width of 4.

Imagine a physical odometer on a car's dashboard (the display that shows how many miles the car has traveled). Each number rotates on a dial to tick over to the next number, which means there's a gear for each dial. If we have four dials, we can represent four individual numbers that are read as one number. We can store the rotation of each gear that lets the machine represent a chosen number. In figure 11.29, for example, the number 2,145 is represented as 42, 19, 22, 7 because those numbers represent the rotation of each gear to get the odometer to show the number 2,145.

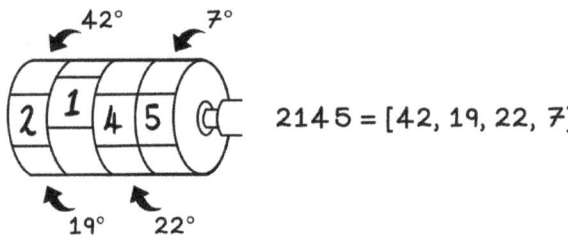

Figure 11.29 An odometer analogy showing how sinusoidal positional encoding works

This is the intuition for representing the token position within the four-width embedding we're working with, using the concept of *sinusoidal positional encoding*. To find the values, we use the formula in figure 11.30.

$$angle = \left(\frac{\rho}{1000^{\frac{2\lfloor i/2 \rfloor}{model\ dimensions}}} \right)$$

$2\lfloor i/2 \rfloor$ means $2 \times$ floor of $i/2$
and rounds down to the
nearest integer

So, because $d = 4$

$i = 0$ angle: $\rho\ /\ 1000^{(2\lfloor 0/2 \rfloor\ /\ 4)} = \rho\ /\ 1$

$i = 1$ angle: $\rho\ /\ 1000^{(2\lfloor 1/2 \rfloor\ /\ 4)} = \rho\ /\ 1$

$i = 2$ angle: $\rho\ /\ 1000^{(2\lfloor 2/2 \rfloor\ /\ 4)} = \rho\ /\ 100$

$i = 3$ angle: $\rho\ /\ 1000^{(2\lfloor 3/2 \rfloor\ /\ 4)} = \rho\ /\ 100$

$$PE(\rho, i) = \begin{cases} sin(angle) & \text{if } i \text{ is odd} \\ cos(angle) & \text{if } i \text{ is even} \end{cases}$$

Figure 11.30 A breakdown of the calculations involved in sinusoidal encoding

Table 11.9 shows the tokens and their respective calculations for finding their positional encoding. This method of positional encoding was introduced in 2017 for the first Transformer. The results provide uniqueness so that every position has a distinct value; nearby positions have similar values and can be adapted to different widths of embeddings. This method is nifty because we can reconstruct any position by knowing its width (d), position (p), and dimension inside the d-width embedding (i).

Table 11.9 A subset of tokens and their positional-encoding calculations

Position (p)	Token ID	Token	Index (i)	Angle formula	Formula	Positional encoding
0	0	a	0	0/1	sin(0/1)	0
			1	0/1	cos(0/1)	1
			2	0/100	sin(0/100)	0
			3	0/100	cos(0/100)	1
1	1	l	0	1/1	sin(1/1)	0.8415
			1	1/1	cos(1/1)	0.5403
			2	1/100	sin(1/100)	0.0100
			3	1/100	cos(1/100)	1.0000
			...			
31	6	b	0	31/1	sin(31/1)	-0.4040
			1	31/1	cos(31/1)	0.9147
			2	31/100	sin(31/100)	0.3051
			3	31/100	cos(31/100)	0.9523

Exercise: What are the positional encodings for token 2?

Calculate the positional encodings for token 2.

Solution:

2	2	ic	0	2/1	sin(2/1)	0.9093
			1	2/1	cos(2/1)	-0.4161
			2	2/100	sin(2/100)	0.0200
			3	2/100	cos(2/100)	0,9998

Combining the embedding matrix and positional encodings

For each token in our batch, we have two pieces of information: its embedding vector (what the token means) and its positional encoding vector (where the token is in the sequence). We must combine this data into a single, information-rich vector that we can feed into the main Transformer architecture. To do so, we add the two vectors together element by element. The two meanings are added to become one (figure 11.31).

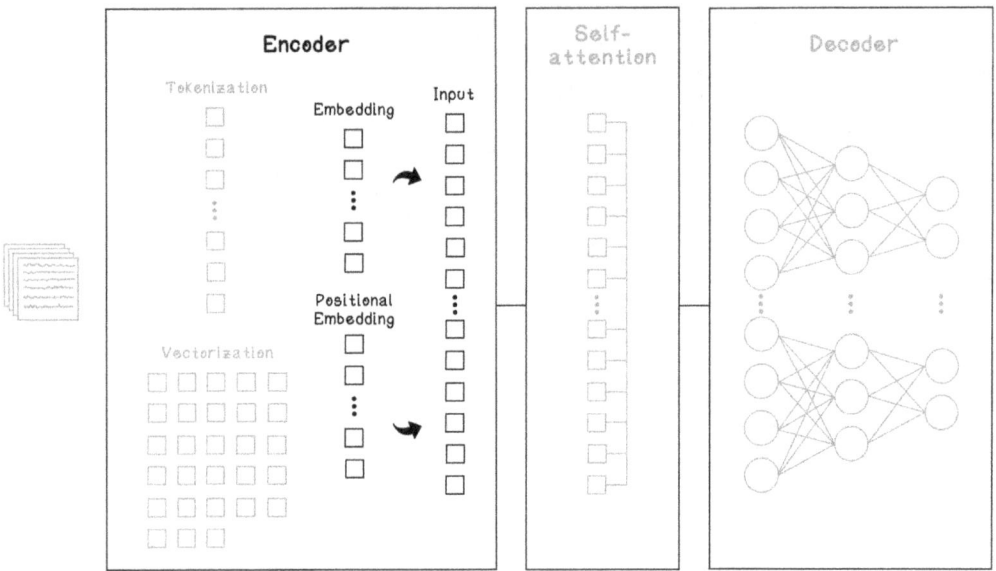

Figure 11.31 A view of the embedding-combination step in the encoding stage

With this training batch, we do addition with embedding and positional encoding:

[0, 1, 2, 3, 4, 0, 5, 6, 3, 7, 8, 9, 10, 11, 12, 7, 3, 11, 13, 14, 15, 16, 17, 18, 12, 19, 5, 20, 11, 11, 10, 6]

Table 11.10 shows the embedding values for each token, the positional values for each token, and the operation used to get the final result. The complete input data results in a 32×4 matrix (table 11.11).

Table 11.10 A subset of tokens and their embedding added to the positional encodings

Position	Token ID	Token	x0	x1	x2	x3
E for 0	0	a	0.003	-0.007	0.012	0.001
P for 0			0	1	0	1
X for 0			**0.0030**	**0.9930**	**0.0120**	**1.0010**
E for 1	1	l	-0.008	0.005	-0.002	0.009
P for 1			0.8415	0.5403	0.0100	1.0000
X for 1			**0.8335**	**0.5453**	**0.0080**	**1.0090**
			...			
E for 31	6	b	0.7381	-0.2512	-0.6719	0.7938
P for 31			-0.4040	0.9147	0.3051	0.9523
X for 31			**0.3341**	**0.6635**	**-0.3668**	**1.7461**

Table 11.11 A subset of tokens and their embedding results

ID	Token	x0	x1	x2	x3
X for 0	a	0.0030	0.9930	0.0120	1.0010
X for 1	l	0.8335	0.5453	0.008	1.009
		...			
X for 31	b	0.3341	0.6635	-0.3668	1.7461

Now our token embedding vector represents the "what" (the concept of Alice), and the positional encoding vector represents the "where" (position 0). When we added them, we created a new vector that holds both pieces of information simultaneously. In the high-dimensional space in which the model operates, there's plenty of room for both signals to coexist without corrupting each other. The model's subsequent layers (specifically, the linear weight matrices for Query, Key, and Value, explored in the next section) are trained from scratch to understand this combined format. They learn that certain directions in this new vector space correspond to meaning and other directions correspond to position.

Exercise: What is the final input vector for token 2?

Determine the final input vector for token 2.

Solution:

ID	Token	x0	x1	x2	x3
X for 2	ic	0.9093	-0.4161	0.0200	0.9998

Python code sample for creating embeddings

The following code generates embedding vectors for a batch of tokens by combining two components: token embeddings and positional encodings. First, each token ID is mapped to a vector using an `embedding_matrix`. To help the model understand the order of tokens, a sinusoidal `positional_encoding` is calculated for each position in the sequence. Then these two vectors are added together to form the `final_embedding`, a matrix representing the identity and position of each token, ready to be passed to the Transformer layers:

Uses a specific pattern of sine and cosine waves

Used to tell the model where a word is in the sentence

```python
def create_embedding(batch, embedding_width):
    vocab_size = VOCABULARY_SIZE
    context_window_size = CONTEXT_WINDOW_SIZE

    embedding_matrix = np.random.randn(vocab_size, embedding_width)

    positional_encoding =
        np.zeros((context_window_size, embedding_width))

    for position in range(context_window_size):
        for dimension in range(embedding_width):
            if dimension % 2 == 0:
                exp_term = dimension / embedding_width
                positional_encoding[position, dimension] = np.sin(
                    position / np.power(10000, exp_term)
                )
            else:
                exp_term_cos = (dimension - 1) / embedding_width
                positional_encoding[position, dimension] = np.cos(
                    position / np.power(10000, exp_term_cos)
                )
```

```
final_embedding = np.zeros((len(batch), embedding_width))

for token_position, token_id in enumerate(batch):
    token_embedding = embedding_matrix[token_id]
    position_embedding = positional_encoding[token_position]

    final_embedding[token_position] =
    token_embedding + position_embedding

return final_embedding
```

Retrieves the specific vector of numbers associated with the current word – the "meaning"

Adds the position signal directly to the meaning vector.

Self-attention: Start training the LLM

You're reading "Alice was beginning to get very tired" with a highlighter pen in your brain. When you get to the word *tired*, internally, your brain instantly goes back to *Alice* to know who is tired and *very* to know how tired. Self-attention gives the Transformer the same capability (figure 11.32). Every token peeks at other tokens in the current batch to decide how much each one should influence its new meaning.

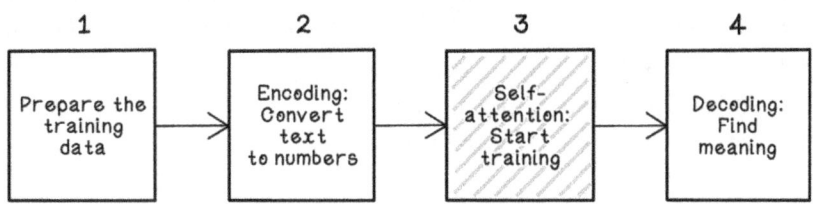

Figure 11.32 The self-attention step in the LLM training workflow

The math behind self-attention has a purpose. We follow the steps shown in figure 11.33 for a single attention head. Think of heads as unique perspectives while figuring out meaning between tokens. Trivially, one attention head may focus on the adjectives, and another may focus on the nouns. For simplicity, we're working through the operations for a single attention head.

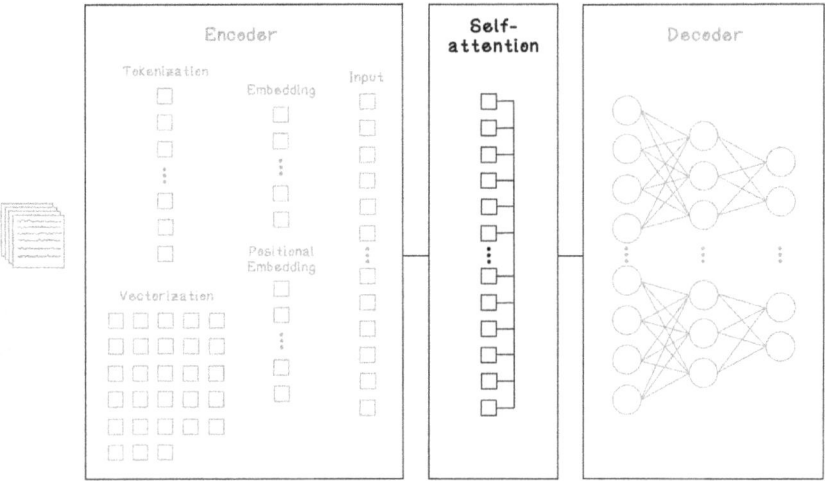

Figure 11.33 Where self-attention fits into the Transformer framework

Making linear weight matrix projections

The first step in self-attention is multiplying the embedding input by three matrices: Query (Q), Key (K), and Value (V). These are the self-attention weight matrices, starting off random and resulting in learned values determined during training. These matrices transform each token into three specialized roles, making the process of comparing them much more effective.

Think of each token as a core ingredient: pasta, tomato, basil, and so on (figure 11.34) The self-attention mechanism has three roles related to the ingredients:

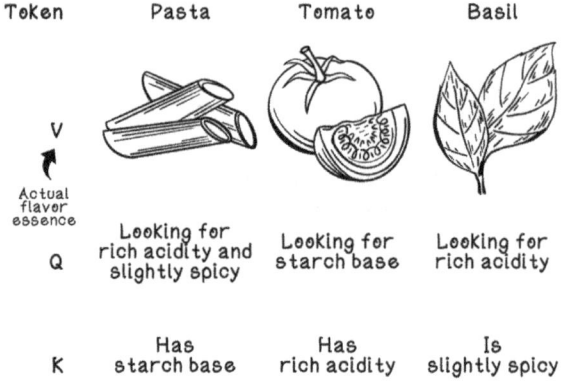

Figure 11.34 An analogy of the purposes of Query, Key, and Value

- *Query (Q) creates a shopping list.* This matrix looks at the ingredients and decides what it needs from other ingredients to maximize its potential. Perhaps the tomato is looking for something with a starch base.
- *Key (K) creates a flavor label.* This matrix labels ingredients according to flavor (starch base, rich acidity, or slightly spicy, for example).
- *Value (V) creates a flavor essence.* This matrix looks at the outcome of what ingredients would produce together—the actual contribution, not just the label, like K.

During self-attention, each ingredient (Query) checks other ingredients' flavor labels (Keys) to find complementary flavors. When compatible ingredients are identified through matching the Query and Keys, their actual flavor essence (Values) are combined in a balanced way to achieve the best overall taste.

Replace this analogy with the concept of language, and you can see how flavor labels are the individual meaning of tokens (Keys). The flavor essence is the actual meaning being applied together with other tokens (Value). Looking for matching flavor labels for one ingredient is akin to tokens looking for other related tokens (Query).

Q, K, and V start as tiny random numbers that allow for gradient descent to learn. For this example, we'll use random integers to illustrate how the calculations work (figure 11.35), but an actual self-attention operation would use random numbers between -1 and 1.

$$Q = [\, 2, 0, 1, 0 \qquad K = [\, 1, 0, 1, 0 \qquad V = [\, 1, 0, 0, 1$$
$$ 0, 2, 0, 1 \qquad 0, 2, 0, 1 \qquad 0, 1, 1, 0$$
$$ 1, 0, 2, 0 \qquad 1, 0, 2, 0 \qquad 1, 0, 1, 0$$
$$ 0, 1, 0, 2\,] \qquad 0, 1, 0, 2\,] \qquad 0, 1, 0, 1\,]$$

Figure 11.35 Initialization of the values for Queries, Keys, and Values

Given token 0's input value as shown in table 11.2, we add the random numbers so that Q, K, and V are initialized with to token 0's values. See tables 11.13, 11.14, and 11.15.

Table 11.12 The final embedding for token 0

ID	Token	x0	x1	x2	x3
X for 0	A	0.0030	0.9930	0.0120	1.0010

Table 11.13 The Query values for token 0

Q0=	$2 \times 0.0030 + 0 \times 0.9930 + 1 \times 0.0120 + 0 \times 1.0010$	0.0180
Q1=	$0 \times 0.0030 + 2 \times 0.9930 + 0 \times 0.0120 + 1 \times 1.0010$	2.9870
Q2=	$1 \times 0.0030 + 0 \times 0.9930 + 2 \times 0.0120 + 0 \times 1.0010$	0.0270
Q3=	$0 \times 0.0030 + 1 \times 0.9930 + 0 \times 0.0120 + 2 \times 1.0010$	2.9950

Table 11.14 The Key values for token 0

K0=	$1 \times 0.0030 + 0 \times 0.9930 + 1 \times 0.0120 + 0 \times 1.0010$	0.0150
K1=	$0 \times 0.0030 + 2 \times 0.9930 + 0 \times 0.0120 + 1 \times 1.0010$	2.9870
K2=	$1 \times 0.0030 + 0 \times 0.9930 + 2 \times 0.0120 + 0 \times 1.0010$	0.0270
K3=	$0 \times 0.0030 + 1 \times 0.9930 + 0 \times 0.0120 + 2 \times 1.0010$	2.9950

Table 11.15 The Value values for token 0

V0=	$1 \times 0.0030 + 0 \times 1.0070 + 0 \times 0.9930 + 1 \times 1.0010$	0.0150
V1=	$0 \times 0.0030 + 1 \times 1.0070 + 1 \times 0.9930 + 0 \times 1.0010$	1.9940
V2=	$1 \times 0.0030 + 0 \times 1.0070 + 1 \times 0.9930 + 0 \times 1.0010$	1.0050
V3=	$0 \times 0.0030 + 1 \times 1.0070 + 0 \times 0.9930 + 1 \times 1.0010$	1.0040

The result is three new matrices in which every token has a reference to its input value and to its Q, K, and V values. Table 11.16 represents how these values relate in one simple view for ease of reference.

Table 11.16 A subset of tokens and their Query, Key, and Value values

Position	ID	Token	x0	x1	x2	x3
0	0	a	0.0030	0.9930	0.0120	1.0010
1	1	l	0.8335	0.5453	0.008	1.009
...						
31	6	b	0.3341	0.6635	-0.3668	1.7461

Position	ID	Token	Q0	Q1	Q2	Q3
0	0	a	0.018	2.9870	0.0270	2.9950
1	1	l	1.6749	2.0996	0.8495	2.5632
...						
31	6	b	0.3013	3.0732	-0.3996	4.1558

Position	ID	Token	K0	K1	K2	K3
0	0	a	0.0150	2.9870	0.0270	2.9950
1	1	l	0.8415	2.0996	0.8495	2.5632
...						
31	6	b	-0.0328	3.0732	-0.3996	4.1558

Position	ID	Token	V0	V1	V2	V3
0	0	a	0.0150	1.9940	1.0050	1.0040
1	1	l	0.815	1.5543	0.5533	1.8424
...						
31	6	b	-0.0328	2.4097	0.2967	2.0802

Asking every other token

Now that we have initial values for Q, K, and V, we dot-product each Query with every other token's Key, resulting in a raw score value that determines "how relevant are you to me?" for this attention head. We take the Q values for each row and dot-product them with each set of Keys.

The dot product is useful for finding angles between vectors in multidimensional spaces. Think of the dot product as a mathematical operation that calculates an alignment score. If you're a chef for a Query vector, like Pasta, you're checking every other token's Key to see how well the values match. Suppose that the ingredients' flavor labels were written on all the walls of the kitchen in the order of relatedness. You point to the Pasta's flavor label. There's a chef for each token's Key pointing to its respective flavor labels. You want to find how close each chef is to pointing where you're pointing. If you and another chef are pointing to the same spot, high alignment exists, meaning that the Key is highly relevant to your Query (high score). If the other chef is pointing to the wall next to your wall, no alignment exists (0 score). If the other chef is pointing to the wall behind yours, the Key is maximally misaligned (negative score). In figure 11.36, we're concerned with Pasta, and we have good matches for both Tomato and Basil.

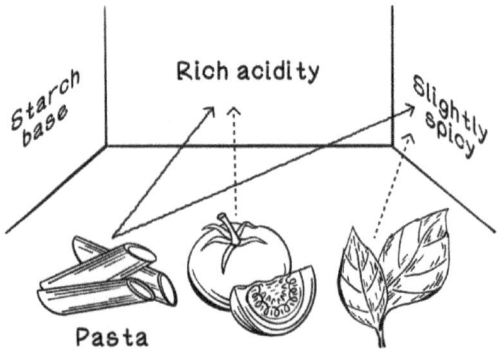

Figure 11.36 An analogy of how self-attention works

Because we want to find the relevance between vectors, this operation is ideal. The angle suggests something like "Do my needs match your content" and the length indicates "How confident am I?" As a bonus, GPUs compute dot products extremely efficiently, making training faster than on traditional CPUs.

So if we have Q = [0.018, 2.9870, 0.0270, 2.9950] for token 0, we dot-product it with each set of K keys. We have 32 results for token 0, as shown in table 11.17. This operation must be done for each token in the embedding matrix, resulting in a 32×32 overall matrix.

Table 11.17 A subset of tokens and their Q dot-product K results

0 (a)	Token ID	Token	Key vector (Kq)	Score
0	0	a	[0.0150, 2.9870, 0.0270, 2.9950]	17.8932
1	1	l	[0.8415, 2.0996, 0.8495, 2.5632]	13.9862
			...	
31	6	b	[-0.0328, 3.0732, -0.3996, 4.1558]	21.6150

Exercise: What is the score for token 2?

Determine the score for token 2.

Solution:

0 (a)	Token ID	Token	Key Vector (Kq)	Score
2	2	ic	[0.8415, 2.0996, 0.8495, 2.5632]	-8.2245

Calculating attention weights

The next step is scaling the scores and running the scaled scores through *softmax*—a way of scaling values to emphasize their relative differences. Then the values become attention weights; each value is between 0 and 1, and they sum to a total of 1. Think of a pie chart of relevance for all the tokens. When the dimensions are small, such as 4 in our example, the dot products stay modest. In larger dimensions (64, 128, and so on), these numbers explode. If we don't scale the numbers, softmax doesn't behave well.

To scale the values, we use the formula in figure 11.37. Remember that dimensions = 4. These calculations will result in the values shown in table 11.18 for token 0.

$$\text{Scaled score} = \frac{score}{\sqrt{\text{dimensions}}}$$

```
Scaled score = score / sqrt(dimensions) = score / sqrt(4)
Scaled score = score / 2
```

Figure 11.37 The formula for scaling scores given the score and dimensions

Table 11.18 A subset of tokens and their initial scaled scores

0 (a)	Token ID	Token	Score	Scaled score
0	0	a	17.8932	8.9466
1	1	1	13.9862	6.9931
		...		
31	6	b	21.6150	10.8075

Next is softmax. We exponentiate the scaled score with $e^{scaled\ score}$. Exponentials make every score positive, magnifying differences. A score two times larger becomes much larger, highlighting clear differences between scores (table 11.19).

Max value = 10.81

Table 11.19 A subset of tokens and their scaled scores

0 (a)	Token ID	Token	$e^{(Scaled\ score\ -\ Max\ for\ token\ 0)}$	Exponential
0	0	a	$e^{(8.9466\ -\ 10.81)}$	0.1555
1	1	1	$e^{(6.9931\ -\ 10.81)}$	0.0221
		...		
31	6	b	$e^{(10.8075\ -\ 10.81)}$	1.0000

To softmax so all weight values summed equal 1, we take the exponential value divided by the sum of all values for all tokens (figure 11.38). For token 0's Q in our example, the total is 2.46, as shown in table 11.20. (This was calculated by the accompanying Python code.) Now we have attention weights that have been scaled and normalized with softmax.

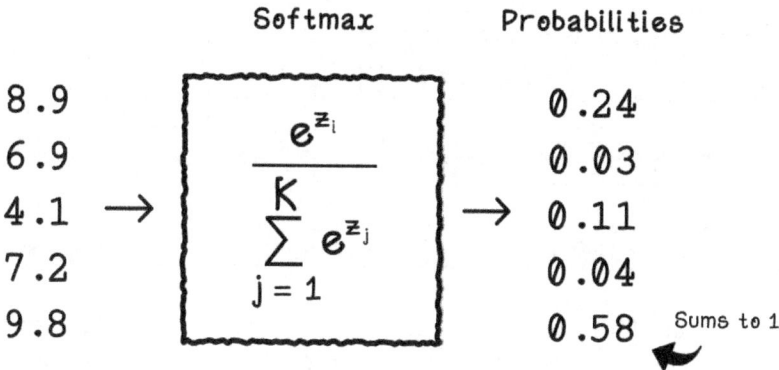

Figure 11.38 How softmax scales scores to probabilities

Table 11.20 A subset of tokens and their softmax scaled scores

0 (a)	Token ID	Token	Exponential/sum of all	Weight (after softmax)
0	0	a	0.1555 / 2.46	0.0632
1	1	1	0.0221 / 2.46	0.0090
			...	
31	6	b	1.0000 / 2.46	0.4064

Calculating the weighted sum

We have our attention weights, which act as a precise recipe for our token in question. The recipe tells us exactly how much influence every other token in the token sequence should have. We also have the Value vector (V) for each token, which represents its actual meaning or substance.

The next step is using this recipe to create a new blended representation. To do this, first we multiply each token's Value vector by its corresponding attention weight. This step scales each token's contribution, making the influential ones stronger and the irrelevant ones weaker. Finally, we add all the new weighted vectors to get our final, context-rich output vector.

Remember that we created linear projections for Q, K, and V and used Q and K to create the dot products for the original score. Now we use the values for V and multiply each by the attention weights we just calculated. Table 11.21 shows the tokens and their attention weights, original vectors, and results.

Table 11.21 A subset of tokens and their result values

q	Weight	V0	V1	V2	V3	V0 result	V1 result	V2 result	V3 result
0	0.0632	0.0150	1.9940	1.0050	1.0040	0.0009	0.1261	0.0635	0.0635
1	0.0090	0.8415	1.5543	0.5533	1.8424	0.0075	0.0139	0.0050	0.0165
					...				
31	0.4064	-0.0328	2.4097	0.2967	2.0802	-0.0133	0.9794	0.1206	0.8455

Finally, add all results for each V as the context vectors. We add all values for V0, V1, V2, and V3, respectively, to get the context vector for Q. Given the results for V for token 0 in table 11.22, we calculate the attention-context vectors as shown in figure 11.39.

Table 11.22 A subset of tokens and their final values

q	Weight	V0 result	V1 result	V2 result	V3 result
0	0.0632	0.0009	0.1261	0.0635	0.0635
1	0.0090	0.0075	0.0139	0.0050	0.0165
		...			
31	0.4064	-0.0133	0.9794	0.1206	0.8455

$$C0 = 0.0009 + 0.0075 + 0.0000 + \ldots + -0.0133 = 0.2283$$
$$C1 = 0.1261 + 0.0139 + 0.0000 + \ldots + 0.9794 = 2.1990$$
$$C2 = 0.0635 + 0.0050 + -0.0000 + \ldots + 0.1206 = 0.4526$$
$$C3 = 0.0635 + 0.0165 + 0.0001 + \ldots + 0.8455 = 1.9747$$

Figure 11.39 A subset of the context-vector calculations

Table 11.23 shows 0's final context. We'll do the same for the remaining 31 tokens, resulting in a 32×4 matrix (table 11.24).

Table 11.23 Token 0 and their attention context vectors

q	Token	C0	C1	C2	C3
0	a	0.2283	2.1990	0.4526	1.9747

Table 11.24 A subset of tokens and their attention-context vectors

q	token	C0	C1	C2	C3
0	a	0.2283	2.1990	0.4526	1.9747
1	l	0.4641	2.0770	0.4670	2.0741
		...			
31	b	0.2383	2.2812	0.3188	2.2007

You've learned how to complete the self-attention step in a LLM Transformer. Loads of math is involved, but these small steps combined create fascinating emergent intelligence in which tokens negotiate the importance of their relationships.

Python code sample for self-attention

This code implements scaled dot-product self-attention, a core operation in Transformers. It starts by projecting the input embeddings in three matrices—Query (Q), Key (K), and Value (V)—using learned weights. Then it computes a matrix of attention scores by taking the dot product of each Query with every Key and scaling by the square root of the dimensionality. After applying the softmax function to get attention weights, we use the weights to blend the value vectors, producing the final attention output. This mechanism allows the model to focus selectively on different parts of the input sequence:

Turns raw scores into percentages that add up to 1

```python
def softmax(x):
    e_x = np.exp(x - np.max(x, axis=-1, keepdims=True))
    return e_x / np.sum(e_x, axis=-1, keepdims=True)

def calculate_attention(embeddings, dimensions):
    query_weights = np.random.randn(dimensions, dimensions)
    key_weights = np.random.randn(dimensions, dimensions)
    value_weights = np.random.randn(dimensions, dimensions)

    Q = embeddings @ query_weights
    K = embeddings @ key_weights
    V = embeddings @ value_weights

    attention_scores = (Q @ K.T) / np.sqrt(dimensions)

    attention_weights = softmax(attention_scores)

    attention_output = attention_weights @ V

    return attention_output, attention_weights
```

Transforms each word into Q, K, and V vectors

multiplies Queries by Keys

Uses the attention percentages to create a weighted sum of the values

Using multiple attention heads

In our simple example, we have only one attention head. Remember that attention heads look at the relationships between tokens from a specific perspective; more heads learn more-distinct relations. To continue the cooking analogy, you can see attention heads as being different chefs who look at the ingredients from unique perspectives. Similar ingredients with varied preparation can be used to make different dishes, so a chef (attention head) may look at the ingredients from the perspective of making a Japanese dish, whereas another chef (attention head) is looking at them from the perspective of making an Italian dish (figure 11.40).

Figure 11.40 An analogy of the usefulness of multiple attention heads

Multiple attention heads are powerful concepts for LLMs. We might have an emergent grammar expert, pronoun expert, positional expert, and so on. Each expert (attention head) has its own independent set of Q, K, and V matrices, allowing it to specialize in finding one specific type of connection. Then the model combines the findings from all these experts to build a single, incredibly rich, layered understanding of each word. This approach enables the model to analyze a sentence from many perspectives at the same time, capturing a much deeper, more robust understanding of the language than a single head ever could.

If we have two heads, we repeat this entire self-attention process for each one. But the initial Q, K, V step would have two vectors, not four. This means that each of the two heads will be a 32×2 matrix, which will be concatenated into a 32×4 matrix, which matches our width. If we had a width of 8, for example, we could have

- 1 head that is 32×8, or
- 2 heads that are 32×4 each, or
- 4 heads that are 32×2 each

We've completed the self-attention step. In a large set of tokens, this entire process is massive in terms of computing and data calculated. Although we've been performing each operation independently, in practice, we use the power of specialized chips like GPUs that have built-in matrix manipulation operations to make these computationally heavy operations happen in an instant compared to running them on traditional CPUs.

Normalizing layers

Now we have to add the calculated attention to our original token embeddings. Layer normalization stabilizes training by keeping every token's vector roughly zero-mean so later layers in training aren't working with exploding or vanishing magnitudes. The model can always fall back on the original embedding representation if the attention heads are unhelpful; it can even learn to ignore the attention heads if necessary.

Given the original embedding for token 0, shown in table 11.25, we add the residual connection by means of the calculation shown in figure 11.41. Layer normalization is done with the equation in figure 11.42.

Table 11.25 Token 0's original weights and attention context

Original weights					
ID	Token	x0	x1	x2	x3
0	a	0.0030	0.9930	0.0120	1.0010
Attention context					
ID	Token	C0	C1	C2	C3
0	a	0.2283	2.1990	0.4526	1.9747

```
y = x + c
x = [0.0030, 0.9930, 0.0120, 1.0010]
c = [0.2283, 2.1990, 0.4526, 1.9747]
y = [0.0030, 0.9930, 0.0120, 1.0010] + [0.2283, 2.1990, 0.4526, 1.9747]
y = [0.2313, 3.1920, 0.4646, 2.9757]
```

Figure 11.41 Calculations for the residual connection

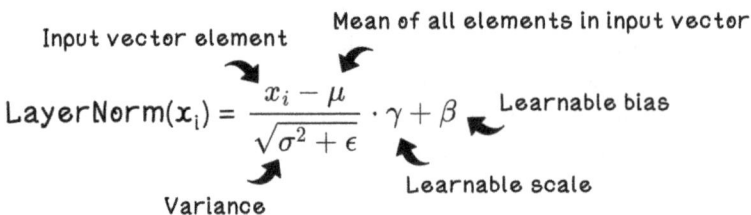

$$\text{LayerNorm}(\pmb{x}_i) = \frac{x_i - \mu}{\sqrt{\sigma^2 + \epsilon}} \cdot \gamma + \beta$$

Input vector element Mean of all elements in input vector Learnable bias Learnable scale Variance

Figure 11.42 The formula for layer normalization

To understand this complex-looking expression, let's take it step by step, given this input:

x = [0.2313, 3.1920, 0.4646, 2.9757]

- Calculate mean (μ)
  (0.2313 + 3.1920 + 0.4646 + 2.9757) / 4
  = 1.7159
- Calculate deviations (x−μ)
  [0.2313 - 1.7159, 3.1920 - 1.7159, 0.4646 - 1.7159, 2.9757 + 1.7159]
  = [-1.4846, 1.4761, -1.2513, 1.2598]
- Squared deviations (($x-\mu$)^2)
  [(-1.4846)^2, (1.4761)^2, (-1.2513)^2, (1.2598)^2]
  = [2.2040, 2.1789, 1.5657, 1.5871]
- Calculate variance (σ^2)
  (2.2040 + 2.1789 + 1.5657 + 1.5871) / 4
  = 1.8839
- Normalize
  Deviations / ($\sqrt{\text{Variance}}$)
  = [-1.0816, 1.0754, -0.9116, 0.9178]

For the sake of simplicity, we've omitted the learnable bias and learnable scale variables from this example:

z0 = [-1.0816, 1.0754, -0.9116, 0.9178]

We'll have to perform this operation for all 32 tokens in our example, which will result in a 32×4 matrix ready for the decoding components.

Exercise: What is the normalized vector for token 2?

Determine the normalized vector for token 2.

Solution:

Final output for z0 : [-1.0816, 1.0754, -0.9116, 0.9178]

Python code sample for layer normalization

This code performs layer normalization on the attention output. For each row (each token's vector), it computes the mean and variance; then it standardizes each value by subtracting the mean and dividing by the standard deviation (with a small epsilon added for numerical stability). This helps stabilize and accelerate training by ensuring that each token's vector has a consistent distribution, regardless of its raw values:

measures how much the values in the layer "scatter" around the mean

Calculates the average value of all features for a single token

```python
def normalize_layer(attention_output, epsilon=1e-5):
    mean = np.mean(attention_output, axis=1, keepdims=True)
    variance = np.var(attention_output, axis=1, keepdims=True)
    standard_deviation = np.sqrt(variance + epsilon)
    normalized_output = (attention_output - mean) / standard_deviation
    return normalized_output
```

Shifts the data so the mean is 0 and the standard deviation is 1 "centering" the data

This ensures that even if the variance is zero, the math doesn't break

Decoding: Finding meaning through neural networks

Now that we've found the relationships between tokens from different perspectives (attention heads), the feed-forward network works with that blended data and finds relationships between the features within it (figure 11.43). The self-attention step delivered a bundle of clues for a word. Now the feed-forward network decides which clues to amplify, suppress, or even merge into higher-level features. If the result of self-attention is ingredients, the result of the feed-forward network is the full course of dishes created from the ingredients. Table 11.26 is our normalized layer for all tokens.

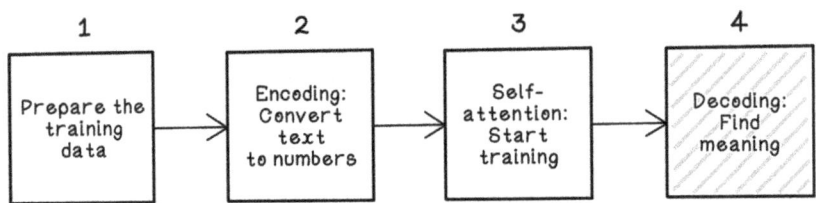

Figure 11.43 The decoding step in the LLM training workflow

Table 11.26 A subset of tokens and their normalized values

ID	Token	y0	y1	y2	y3
0	a	-1.0816	1.0754	-0.9116	0.9178
1	1	-0.5509	0.7252	-1.3432	1.1689
31	b	-0.7789	0.6629	-1.1559	1.2719

For the ANN example in chapter 9, we had four inputs: speed, terrain quality, degree of vision, and total experience. For the LLM, we have a much larger set of inputs describing the relationships between tokens, the positional relationship between tokens, and the outcomes of self-attention. Now we have to define the parameters for the feed-forward network.

- *Project up layer*—An eight-node layer with a width of 4 based on our initial width of 4. This layer is called W1. The bias will be four values that match our width, called b1.
- *Project down layer*—A four-node layer that takes eight vectors as inputs (8×4) called W2. The bias will be four values that match our width, called b2.

Figure 11.44 illustrates the architecture of our feed-forward network. This network will produce probabilities of what the next token will be given our current training batch.

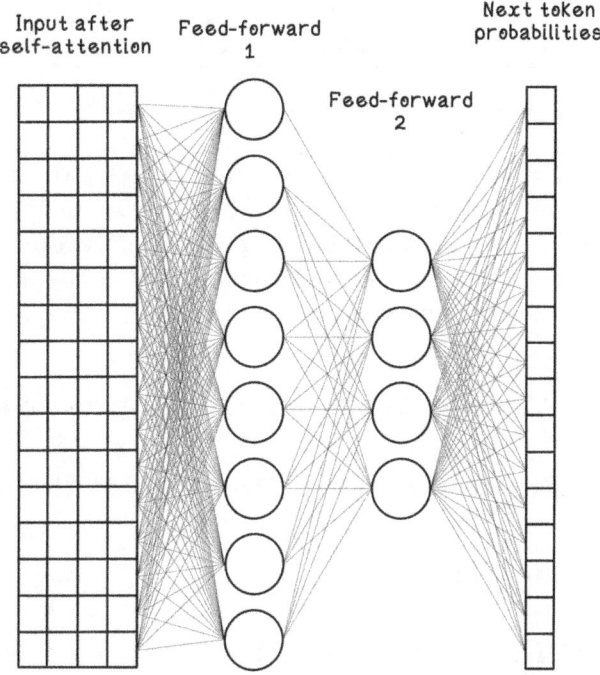

Figure 11.44 The architecture of the feed-forward network to output token probabilities

Project up layer

This is the first weight matrix, W1, in our feed-forward network. Its job is to project the 4D input vector from the previous layer into a larger 8D space. In a real scenario, these weights start as random numbers and are slowly adjusted during training. For our example, we'll define them with the following fixed values. We choose random numbers between -1 and 1 for the weights in our layer, as shown in table 11.27. Now we can take the input for token 0 and multiply it with the weights matrix.

Table 11.27 Random weights for the project up layer

0.1	-0.2	0.3	0.4	-0.5	0.6	0.7	-0.8
0.9	0.8	-0.7	0.6	0.5	-0.4	0.3	0.2
-0.3	0.2	0.1	-0.9	0.8	0.7	-0.6	0.5
0.5	-0.6	0.7	0.8	-0.9	0.1	0.2	-0.3

The process of multiplying the input vector with the weight matrix involves calculating each of the eight new output values one by one. To get the first output value, we multiply each element of our input vector with the corresponding element from the first column of the weights matrix and sum the results. We repeat this process for each of the eight columns in the weights matrix to get all eight final values. So given the input

[-1.0816, 1.0754, -0.9116, 0.9178]

for token 0, we can calculate the weights (figure 11.45). The result of weight multiplication is

[1.5921, 0.3436, -0.5260, 1.7674, -0.4769, -1.6255, 0.2961, 0.3492]

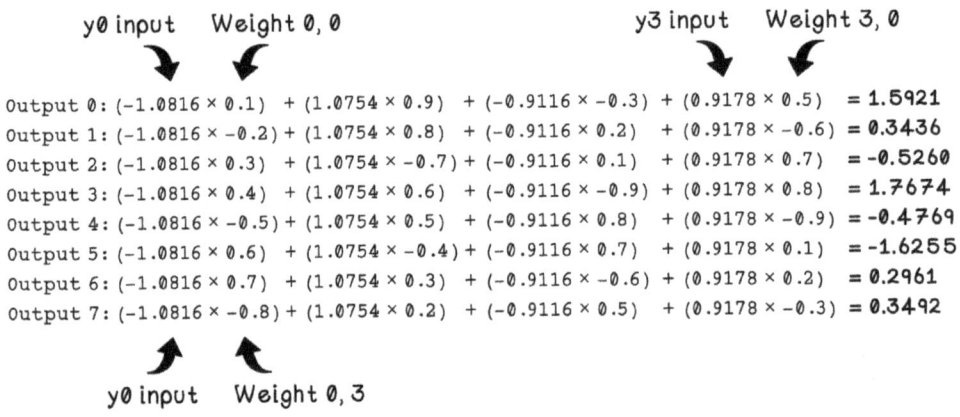

Figure 11.45 Calculations for feed-forward outputs

After the weight multiplication, the next step is adding a bias vector—another list of learnable numbers, one for each of our eight dimensions. Adding a bias gives the network more flexibility, allowing it to shift the output of each node up or down to better fit the data.

Let's assume that our bias is [0.1, -0.05, 0.2, -0.15, 0.0, 0.1, -0.2, 0.05]. Figure 11.46 shows the result.

[1.5921, 0.3436, −0.5260, 1.7674, −0.4769, −1.6255, 0.2961, 0.3492]
+ [0.1, −0.05, 0.2, −0.15, 0.0, 0.1, −0.2, 0.05]
= [1.6921, 0.2936, −0.3260, 1.6174, −0.4769, −1.5255, 0.0961, 0.3992]

Figure 11.46 Calculations for adding bias to the output

So far, all our operations have been linear. To give our network the capability to learn more-complex, nonlinear patterns, we must apply a nonlinear activation function. One of the most common and effective activation functions is ReLU (rectified linear unit). The rule is simple: it goes through each number in our vector and replaces any negative value with 0, leaving all positive values unchanged (figure 11.47).

Given the last result:
[1.6921, 0.2936, −0.3260, 1.6174, −0.4769, −1.5255, 0.0961, 0.3992]

after ReLU, we have:
[1.6921, 0.2936, 0, 1.6174, 0, 0, 0.0961, 0.3992]

Figure 11.47 Calculations for applying the ReLU activation function

Python code sample for a project up layer

This code applies a feed-forward projection layer that expands or transforms the normalized token representations. Each token vector is multiplied by a learned `projection_weights` matrix to produce a higher-dimensional representation (`projected_output`). This step allows the model to learn richer, more abstract features before continuing through the Transformer block. It's commonly referred to as the project up step in the feed-forward sublayer:

Identifies the current size of the word vectors

```
def project_up(normalized_output, output_dimensions):

    input_embedding_width = normalized_output.shape[1]

    projection_weights =
    np.random.randn(input_embedding_width, output_dimensions)

    projected_output = normalized_output @ projection_weights

    return projected_output
```

Creates a matrix that maps the input to a larger space

Uses matrix multiplication to create new, higher-level features

Project down layer

The second and final layer of our feed-forward network takes the 8D vector from the ReLU step and projects it back down to our original embedding size of 4 using the W2 weight matrix. This step ensures that the output of the feed-forward block has the same dimensions as its input, which is necessary for the final residual connection. Again, we choose random numbers between -1 and 1 for the weights in our layer, as shown in table 11.28.

Table 11.28 Random weights for the project down layer

0.5	-0.1	0.2	0.9
0.3	0.2	-0.4	-0.2
-0.7	0.8	0.1	0.6
0.2	-0.9	-0.3	0.5
0.4	0.3	0.7	-0.8
-0.5	0.6	-0.2	0.1
0.1	-0.8	0.4	-0.7
0.9	0.7	-0.1	-0.6

The calculation is the same as before. To get the first of our four new output values, we multiply each of the eight elements of our input vector with the corresponding element from the first column of the W2 matrix and then sum the results. We repeat this process for all four columns to produce our final 4D vector (figure 11.48). The input

[1.6921, 0.2936, 0, 1.6174, 0, 0, 0.0961, 0.3992]

gives us the result of weight multiplication:

[1.6265, -1.3635, -0.2657, 1.9661]

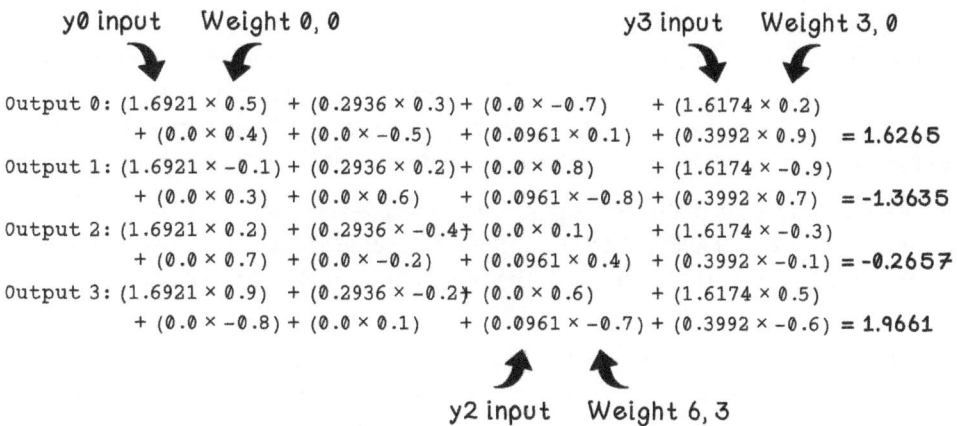

y0 input   Weight 0, 0   y3 input   Weight 3, 0

Output 0: (1.6921 × 0.5)   + (0.2936 × 0.3) + (0.0 × −0.7)   + (1.6174 × 0.2)
          + (0.0 × 0.4)   + (0.0 × −0.5)   + (0.0961 × 0.1) + (0.3992 × 0.9)   = 1.6265
Output 1: (1.6921 × −0.1) + (0.2936 × 0.2) + (0.0 × 0.8)   + (1.6174 × −0.9)
          + (0.0 × 0.3)   + (0.0 × 0.6)   + (0.0961 × −0.8) + (0.3992 × 0.7)   = −1.3635
Output 2: (1.6921 × 0.2)   + (0.2936 × −0.4) + (0.0 × 0.1)   + (1.6174 × −0.3)
          + (0.0 × 0.7)   + (0.0 × −0.2)   + (0.0961 × 0.4) + (0.3992 × −0.1) = −0.2657
Output 3: (1.6921 × 0.9)   + (0.2936 × −0.2) + (0.0 × 0.6)   + (1.6174 × 0.5)
          + (0.0 × −0.8)   + (0.0 × 0.1)   + (0.0961 × −0.7) + (0.3992 × −0.6) = 1.9661

y2 input   Weight 6, 3

Figure 11.48 Calculations for the project-down layer output

Adding bias

As with the first layer, a final bias vector, b2, is added to the output of the project down multiplication. Because this layer returns a 4D vector, the bias also contains four values, providing a final adjustment to the output. Let's assume that our bias is [0.05, -0.1, 0.15, -0.02]. Figure 11.49 shows the result.

$$[1.6265, -1.3635, -0.2657, 1.9661]$$
$$+ [0.05, -0.1, 0.15, -0.02]$$
$$= [1.6765, -1.4635, -0.1157, 1.9461]$$

Figure 11.49 Calculations for adding bias to the output of the project down layer

Adding the residual

We've reached the second residual connection in our Transformer block. As we did after the self-attention step, we add the input of the feed-forward network to its output. This shortcut helps stabilize training and allows the model to bypass the feed-forward layer if it determines that its calculations aren't needed for a particular token. We take the initial input after self-attention and add the result after bias is added (figure 11.50).

$$[-1.0816, 1.0754, -0.9116, 0.9178]$$
$$+ [1.6765, -1.4635, -0.1157, 1.9461]$$
$$= [0.5949, -0.3881, -1.0274, 2.8640]$$

Figure 11.50 Calculations for adding the residual

Layer normalization

The final step in our Transformer block is applying layer normalization one last time. We take the output from the second residual connection and normalize each vector independently. This ensures that the data we pass to the next Transformer block is clean and has a consistent scale, which helps stabilize the training of deep networks.

We follow the layer normalization operations described earlier, giving us the final result for token 0: [0.0569, -0.6089, -1.0419, 1.5939]. The same process happens for all 32 tokens in the batch. Table 11.29 shows the results for a subset of these tokens.

Table 11.29　A subset of tokens and their results after layer normalization

ID	Token	y0	y1	y2	y3
0	a	0.0569	-0.6089	-1.0419	1.5939
1	l	0.2189	-1.0396	-0.7153	1.5361
31	b	-0.0047	-0.9123	-0.7135	1.6305

Stacking Transformer blocks

Now that we've completed one full pass of a Transformer block, the process continues in one of two ways, depending on where we are in the model's architecture. The most common next step is repeating the entire process by feeding the output into an identical Transformer block. If this block were the final one, however, the model would move to predict the next token. In practice, when using the LLM after training, we can do this repeatedly to generate a complete sensible output.

The power of LLMs comes from stacking many Transformer blocks. The output from the block we just finished ([0.0569, -0.6089, -1.0419, 1.5939]) would become the input for the next block.

This new block would perform its own self-attention and feed-forward calculations using its own unique set of learned weights. This allows the model to refine the token's representation at progressively deeper and more abstract levels. A common production-scale LLM has dozens of these blocks stacked on top of one another (figure 11.51).

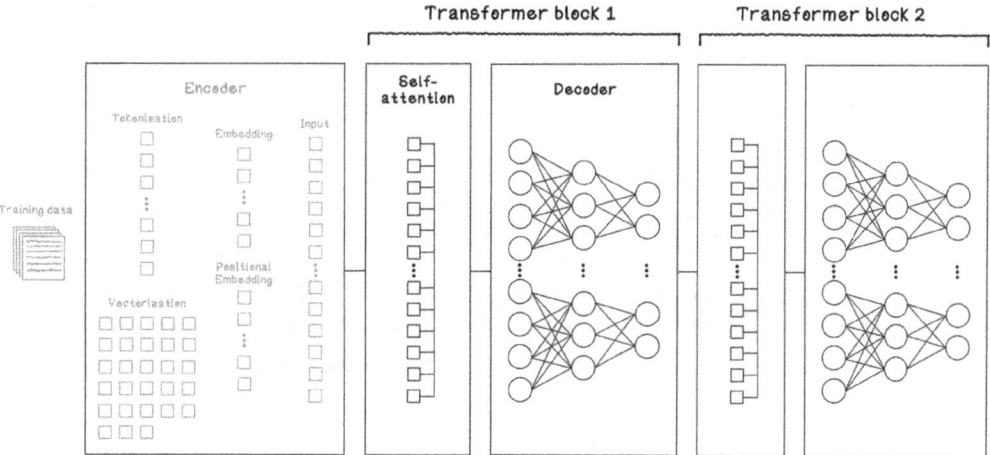

Figure 11.51 How multiple Transformer blocks are stacked

Let's examine how the model's understanding evolves as data moves up the stack:

- *Early layers (bottom of the stack)*—These layers tend to learn simpler, more local patterns. They might focus on basic syntax, word-level relationships, and ways to resolve ambiguity in specific sentences. In the sentence "Alice was beginning to get very tired of sitting," for example, an early layer might learn that `sitting` is a verb associated with `Alice`.
- *Middle layers (middle of the stack)*—These layers take the language's syntactically-aware representations from the early layers and start building a more semantic understanding. They connect concepts across sentences, recognizing pronoun relationships and understanding the overall structure of the text.
- *Late layers (top of the stack)*—The final layers receive a rich, contextually aware representation. They use this information to perform high-level inference, understand complex ideas such as sarcasm and metaphors, and synthesize all the previous data to make the best possible prediction.

Making a prediction

For simplicity, let's assume that the current output of this Transformer block is the final output for the neural network. The entire purpose of the Transformer block is to create a final, information-rich vector for each token in our input, making a matrix. Now we'll use this final matrix to perform the model's main purpose: predicting the next token in the sequence. The model does this by taking a specific output vector and transforming it into a list of scores, one for every token in our vocabulary. We enable it to do this by creating logits.

Creating logits

Logits are used as an intermediate step because they provide a numerically stable foundation for the final probability calculation. *Logits* are the raw, unnormalized scores that a model produces right before the final prediction step. They're not probabilities; they can be any real numbers.

Logits are calculated by taking the final output matrix from the last Transformer block and passing it through one final linear layer (sometimes called the *language model head*). We need another weighted matrix that is the width by vocabulary (4×35).

> **NOTE** We're no longer using only the first 32-token batch context window. We're working with the entire vocabulary.

Given the results in table 11.30, we'll use the last token to make a prediction because the model will attempt to predict what comes after the sequence of tokens in the context window that was trained. That will be token b (table 11.31).

Table 11.30 A subset of tokens and their vectors

ID	Token	y0	y1	y2	y3
0	a	0.0569	-0.6089	-1.0419	1.5939
1	1	0.2189	-1.0396	-0.7153	1.5361
31	b	-0.0047	-0.9123	-0.7135	1.6305

Table 11.31 Token b's vector

ID	Token	y0	y1	y2	y3
31	b	-0.0047	-0.9123	-0.7135	1.6305

Think of this process as being like reading a sentence. To predict the word that comes after "The cat sat on the", you use the context of the whole phrase. The original weight matrix that like table 11.32. Figure 11.52 shows the results.

Table 11.32 A subset of tokens and their vectors

Position	Token ID	Token	x0	x1	x2	x3
0	0	a	0.0030	-0.0070	0.0120	0.0010
1	1	l	-0.0080	0.0050	-0.0020	0.0090
		...				
31	6	b	0.7381	-0.2512	-0.6719	0.7938

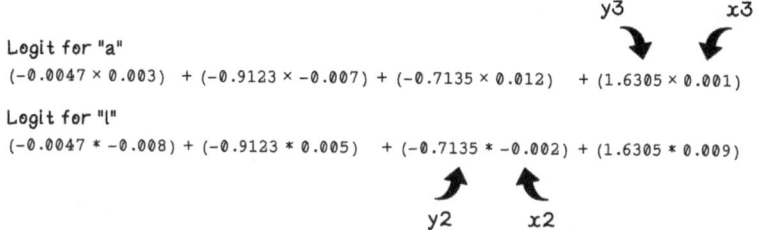

Logit for "a"
(-0.0047 × 0.003) + (-0.9123 × -0.007) + (-0.7135 × 0.012)   + (1.6305 × 0.001)

Logit for "l"
(-0.0047 * -0.008) + (-0.9123 * 0.005)   + (-0.7135 * -0.002) + (1.6305 * 0.009)

Figure 11.52 Calculations for logits for tokens

Exercise: What is the logit for token 31?

Determine the logit for token 31.

Solution:

$(-0.0047 \times 0.7381) + (-0.9123 \times -0.2512) + (-0.7135 \times -0.6719) + (1.6305 \times 0.7938) = 1.2$

Using softmax

Finally, you can use softmax to convert the raw logits to probabilities. If you're still unsure about the softmax calculation, refer to the third step in the self-attention section. This step results in a vector of 35 probabilities; we have a probability of each token in our vocabulary to appear after the batch in question (figure 11.53 and table 11.33).

Table 11.33 A subset of tokens and their probabilities of appearing after token 0

ID	Token	Probability
0	a	0.0243
1	l	0.0246
...		
6	b	0.1799
...		
34	?	0.0251

Final prediction: "b" with a probability of 17.99%

Figure 11.53 Final prediction for the next token after a

Let's see whether that makes any sense. Figure 11.54 shows our training batch.

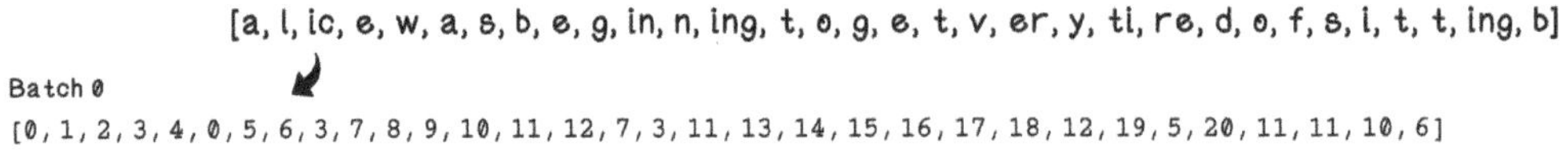

[a, l, ic, e, w, a, s, b, e, g, in, n, ing, t, o, g, e, t, v, er, y, ti, re, d, o, f, s, i, t, t, ing, b]

Batch 0

[0, 1, 2, 3, 4, 0, 5, 6, 3, 7, 8, 9, 10, 11, 12, 7, 3, 11, 13, 14, 15, 16, 17, 18, 12, 19, 5, 20, 11, 11, 10, 6]

Figure 11.54 Revisiting the first training batch of tokens

By using our intuition, we can tell that b is probably not the correct token to appear next. We may find it suspicious that b is predicted because it's the last token in the training batch we used, but that is pure coincidence.

We did all that work only to get an incorrect prediction. But remember that we used a single 32-token batch to train with, a single attention head, a tiny feed-forward network, and only one iteration of training. LLMs require masses of data, many attention heads, massive feed-forward networks, stacked Transformer blocks, and many iterations of training before they start showing signs of intelligence. This intensity in training is the key reason why GPUs are preferred from a performance perspective due to their blazing-fast matrix manipulation. Even so, LLMs are notorious for requiring immense computing resources.

Python code sample for a project down layer

This code projects the model's internal representations back down to the vocabulary space to generate predictions. It multiplies each token's high-dimensional vector by a `projection_down_weights` matrix, producing a score for every token in the vocabulary. The index of the highest score in each row is selected as the model's predicted next token:

> Creates a matrix that connects every "feature" the model has learned to every possible word in the dictionary

```
def project_down_and_predict(projected_output, vocabulary_size):

    input_width = projected_output.shape[1]

    projection_down_weights =
    np.random.randn(input_width, vocabulary_size)

    final_output_logits =
    projected_output @ projection_down_weights

    predictions = np.argmax(final_output_logits, axis=1)

    return predictions.tolist()
```

> Calculates a "score" for every word in the vocabulary for each position in the sentence

> Scans the thousands of scores and identifies the index of the single highest value

Backpropagation and calculating loss

The next step is calculating the loss, which measures how wrong the model's prediction was. This is a critical part of training. You compare the probability the model assigned to the actual correct next token with the ideal probability (1.0 or 100%). This comparison gives you a single number: the loss (how wrong the model was).

Chapter 9 covered computing loss/cost, but the essence of it is correcting weights given the predicted values. For the car-collision example in chapter 9, we calculated the loss/cost by comparing it with the training data reference. With LLMs, the actual next token is already known because it's the next token in the training data sequence that we feed the model. For that reason, the network understands the loss.

Calculating cross-entropy loss

To measure the model's error, we calculate the cross-entropy loss. For each token in the input sequence, we look at the probability the model assigned to the actual next token and then take its negative log. A perfect prediction has a probability of 1.

The negative logarithm function -log(p) has two properties that make it perfect for measuring error. When the model is correct, the probability it assigns to the correct token is high (close to 1). -log(1) is 0, so the loss is low, which is what we want. When the model is wrong, the probability p for the correct token is low (close to 0). As p approaches 0, -log(p) gets huge, approaching infinity. This heavily penalizes the model for being confident in the wrong answer.

Let's look at three examples of how the loss varies based on the model's confidence:

- *Confident and correct (p = 0.99)*—The model assigned a 99% probability to the right answer. The loss is tiny (about 0.01).
- *Uncertain (p = 0.50)*—The model was unsure. Loss is moderate (around 0.69).
- *Confident and wrong (p = 0.01)*—The model assigned only a 1% probability to the right answer. The loss is huge (about 4.60).

Using this method, we can calculate the loss for each token using the correct next ID and its probability (table 11.34). This is the expected result because our model is untrained; it has learned no patterns from the data. Its weights are fixed and random. For a vocabulary of 35 tokens, a random guess would have a loss of approximately -log(1/35), or about 3.55. Our model's performance is in that ballpark. Therefore, a probability of 11% for the token b doesn't mean that the model is quite confident and wrong; it means that the model's performance is only slightly better than a random guess. The high loss value correctly reflects this deep uncertainty.

Table 11.34 A subset of tokens and their loss values

ID	Token	Correct next ID	Correct next token	Probability	Loss
0	a	1	l	0.0243	3.7221
1	l	2	ic	0.0395	3.2304
...					
30	ing	6	b	0.1123	2.1869

Backpropagation

The loss score we just calculated is the starting signal for backpropagation. The algorithm works backward from the loss value through every layer of the network: the feed-forward layers, the attention mechanism, and the embedding matrices. It calculates how much each individual weight and bias contributed to the final error and then "nudge" every parameter in a direction that will make the loss smaller on the next attempt. This is how the network learns the relationships between words and refines its understanding of language based on the training data.

See chapter 9's discussion of backpropagation if you need a refresher. In short, backpropagation starts with the loss value and works backward through the network using the chain rule from calculus:

1. It calculates the gradient of the loss with respect to the output of the last layer (the logits).
2. It uses that result to find the gradient with respect to the parameters of that layer (the final weights and biases).
3. It continues this process backward, layer by layer, until it has a gradient for every single parameter all the way back to the initial embedding matrix.

When backpropagation has calculated the gradient for a specific weight, that weight is updated. Let's take a single weight from our final 4×35 weight matrix and assume that after the complex backpropagation process, its calculated gradient is -0.5:

- *Old weight*—Let's say the original value of this weight was 0.5.
- *Learning rate*—We need a small number to ensure that we don't update the weights too aggressively. A common value is 0.01.
- *Gradient*—The calculated gradient for this weight is -0.5.

Figure 11.55 shows the backpropagation update calculation. The weight is nudged from 0.5 to 0.5050. This tiny adjustment, applied to all parameters, makes the entire network slightly better at its task. Again, we have to do this for all predictions so that all weights are updated respectively.

```
New weight = Old weight - (Learning rate × gradient)
New weight = 0.5000 - (0.01 * -0.5)
New weight = 0.5000 - (-0.005)
New weight = 0.5050
```

Figure 11.55 Calculations for new weights given the learning rate and gradient

Python code sample for calculating training loss

This code computes the training loss using cross-entropy between the predicted tokens and the actual ground-truth tokens. Then it performs backpropagation, calculating gradients for all trainable weights in the model, including embedding and projection matrices, and updates them using the specified `learning_rate`. This step is essential for learning because it gradually adjusts the model's internal parameters to reduce future prediction errors:

Conceptual function representing
the backpropagation step

Provides a single number
representing the total error

```
def calculate_cross_entropy(predictions, actual_tokens):
    return np.mean(np.square(actual_tokens - predictions))

def compute_gradients_and_update_all_weights(weights_list, loss,
➥learning_rate):
    pass

def calculate_loss_and_backprop(predictions, actual_tokens,
➥learning_rate):

    loss = calculate_cross_entropy(predictions, actual_tokens)

    trainable_weights = [
        'embedding_matrix', 'query_weights', 'key_weights',
        'value_weights', 'projection_weights', 'projection_down_weights'
    ]

    compute_gradients_and_update_all_weights(trainable_weights, loss,
➥learning_rate)

    return loss
```

The specific matrices we've
built in previous steps

Calculates the gradient for every
weight and nudges them slightly

We've completed one full training cycle on a single batch of 32 tokens. The model is slightly better than it was before. The training flow continues by sampling a new batch of 32 tokens from the token stream. This cycle is repeated thousands or millions of times, iterating through the entire dataset until the model's performance is satisfactory.

Control the LLM

Well done. You've made it to the end of the core training cycle for an LLM. After digesting the steps, you may find it unbelievable that these operations can create amazing emergent intelligence in powerful LLMs, but it's difficult for humans to visualize and perceive the complexity of the huge datasets and high-dimensional spaces that these Transformers play in. That said, you can train, evaluate, tweak, and improve. Let's explore some concepts for controlling LLMs.

Training epochs

A key to Transformers is many cycles of learning on different data. To accomplish this, we have to process many batches of the token stream in different orders and run this entire process many times.

An *epoch* is one complete cycle through the entire training dataset. A *batch* is a small chunk of that dataset that you process at one time before updating the model's weights. One training cycle (figure 11.56) consists of the following steps:

1. *Pick a batch.* Get the next 32 tokens from the dataset.

2. *Forward pass.* The input goes through the entire model—including embeddings, self-attention, and the feed-forward network—to produce the final predictions.

3. *Calculate the loss.* Compare the model's predictions to the correct next tokens to get a single loss value for the batch.

4. *Backpropagate.* Use the loss to calculate the gradients for all of the model's weights.

5. *Update the weights.* Use gradients to nudge all the weights, making the model slightly better.

6. *Repeat the process.* Go back to step 1 and process the next batch with the newly updated weights.

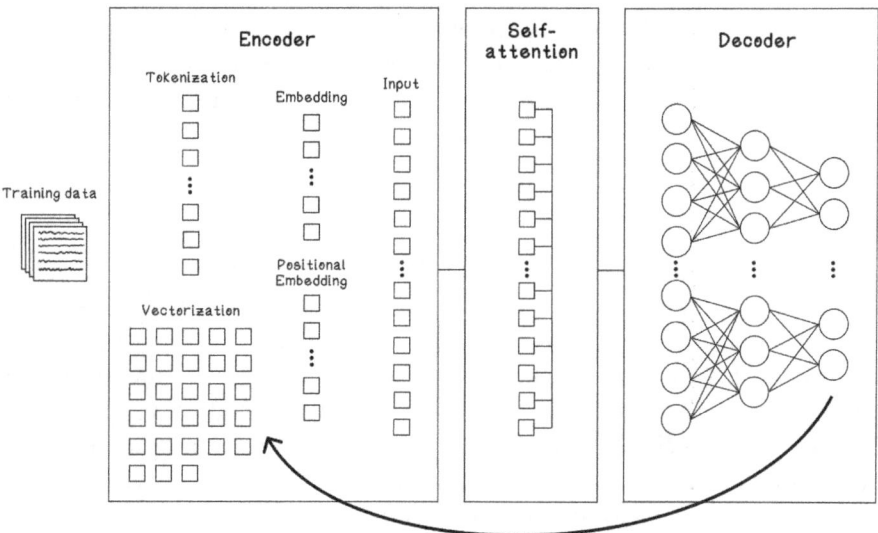

Figure 11.56 How epochs repeat in the Transformer framework

When all batches in the dataset have been processed, epoch 1 is complete. Then the training process continues by starting epoch 2, often after shuffling the data, and this cycle repeats for many epochs until the model's performance is satisfactory.

Surprisingly, some powerful modern LLMs were trained on less than one epoch. This means that the amount of data in their token stream was so massive that they were able to learn extremely well purely by sampling batches of tokens within a single epoch.

Saving checkpoints

During a long training process, you should periodically save the model's state to a file, including all its learned weights and parameters. This process is called *saving a checkpoint*. Training can take days, weeks, or months. If the process crashes for any reason, checkpoints allow you to resume where you left off instead of starting from scratch. They also let you preserve different versions of your model to evaluate later. We can employ different strategies for saving these checkpoints:

- *Periodic saving*—The most common strategy. The model's state (all weights and parameters) is saved at regular intervals. We can save every N training steps or every M minutes. We should always do this for fault tolerance. The frequency is a tradeoff. More frequent saves mean less lost work, but they also mean use of more disk space, and they can slow training slightly.

- *Best-model saving*—With this strategy, we save a checkpoint only when the model's performance improves on a validation set of data (i.e., when the loss reaches a new minimum for data that it hasn't seen before). We can overwrite the same file every time a new best is found. A common practice is to combine this process with periodic saving.

Stopping mechanisms

We need a way to measure whether the model is truly learning to generalize or just memorizing the training data (the problem of overfitting). We set aside a portion of the data as a validation set, which the model never trains on. Periodically, we pause training and calculate the loss on this validation set. If the training loss continues to go down but the validation loss starts to go up, that's a clear sign that the model is no longer learning useful patterns and is beginning to memorize. Early stopping is the practice of stopping the training process when validation loss stops improving, which saves significant time, computational resources, and costs and often results in a better-performing final model. Let's look at two common approaches for managing this process:

- *Validation-set evaluation*—The standard strategy is to run your model on a separate validation dataset that it never trains on.

- *Early stopping*—This strategy automatically stops the training process to save time and prevent overfitting. The main parameter is patience—the number of evaluation cycles you wait without seeing any improvement in validation loss before you stop training. A patience of 3, for example, would stop training if the validation loss fails to improve for three consecutive evaluations. This saves significant computational cost and prevents the model from getting worse by continuing to train past a known optimal state.

Hyperparameter tuning

Before training begins, you have to set several key parameters that define the model's architecture and how it learns. Finding the best values for these hyperparameters is a critical part of the process. Here are more details on hyperparameters for Transformer LLMs:

- *Learning rate*—How big a step the model takes when updating its weights during backpropagation
- *Batch size/context window*—The number of tokens the model processes at once—in our example, 32
- *Model architecture*—The dimensions of the model, such as its width (embedding size), depth (number of layers), and number of attention heads

Adjusting parameters can be tricky. The adjustments may be based on trial and error or on another algorithm. Trial and error in training LLMs can consume a great deal of time and resources. Using known well-performing hyperparameters is preferred. Here are the most common strategies for tuning these hyperparameters:

- *Manual tuning*—This process involves using your intuition and experience to choose parameters, running training cycles, observing the results, and then manually tweaking the parameters for the next run. This is practical when you have a deep understanding of the model or limited computational resources. It's often the starting point for any project.
- *Grid search*—You define a specific list of values to try for each hyperparameter (e.g., learning rate = [0.01, 0.001, 0.0001], batch size = [32, 64], and so on). Then the system exhaustively trains a model for every possible combination. This is useful for a small number of hyperparameters but becomes extremely slow and expensive as the number of options grows.
- *Random search*—Instead of trying every combination, you define a range for each hyperparameter and then test a fixed number of random combinations from within

those ranges. This is often more efficient than grid search. It can explore a wider range of values and frequently finds better models in less time.

- *Bayesian optimization*—In this advanced strategy, an algorithm builds a probabilistic model to predict which hyperparameter combinations are likely to perform best. (How meta!)

- *Machine learning for machine learning*—This approach uses the results from previous runs to decide intelligently which combination to try next.

Few-shot and zero-shot learning

In-context learning is the process of adapting a pretrained model to perform well on a specific task, such as summarization, question-answering, or classification. This process is often more efficient than training a model from scratch. It doesn't mean training or adjusting the weights in the architecture, but using prompting techniques in using an pretrained model. One of the most powerful aspects of LLMs is their ability to perform tasks they weren't explicitly trained for, which a key goal of generalization. Here are the two primary approaches to in-context learning:

- *Zero-shot learning*—You ask the model to perform a task without giving it any examples in the prompt, such as "Translate 'hello world' to French." The model understands the instruction and provides the answer based on the patterns it learned during its broad training.

- *Few-shot learning*—You provide a few examples of the task within the prompt itself to give the model context (figure 11.57).

```
Q: What is the capital of Japan?
A: Tokyo.

Q: What is the capital of USA?
A: Washington, D.C.

Q: What is the capital of Egypt?
A: The model follows the pattern and responds with "Cairo".
```

Figure 11.57 Example of use cases for few-shot learning

Refining LLMs with reinforcement learning

Although pretraining teaches an LLM to understand and generate humanlike text, it doesn't inherently teach it to be helpful or harmless or to follow instructions accurately. Reinforcement learning is a fine-tuning technique used to align the model's behavior with human-centric goals. It boosts the base model's capabilities by teaching it what makes a good response beyond the basic next-word prediction. The most common method for this purpose is *reinforcement learning with human feedback (RLHF)*. RLHF can even be used to teach LLMs how to solve problems correctly and can influence the intelligence of the model. RLHF is a multistep process that uses human preferences to guide the model's learning.

Collecting human-feedback data

First, a dataset of human preferences is created. For a given prompt, the pretrained LLM is used to generate several different responses.

Instead of always picking the single most probable next word, the model creates this variety by sampling from its list of likely options. This process is often controlled by a parameter called *temperature*. A higher temperature encourages more diverse and diverse responses. Think about temperature as a creativity lever. Here is how the model behaves at different temperature settings:

- *Low temperature*—The model acts like a strict accountant. It always picks the most likely, safest answer. It's accurate but can be boring or repetitive.
- *High temperature*—The model acts like a jazz musician. It takes risks, picking less likely words to be surprising, creative, or diverse.

Human labelers review the responses and rank them from best to worst. This process is repeated for thousands of prompts, creating a dataset that captures what humans consider to be high-quality and helpful answers.

Training a reward model

Next, a separate, smaller model called the *reward model* is trained on the human-feedback data. The goal of this model is to learn to predict which responses a human would prefer. It takes a prompt and a response as input and outputs a single score/reward that represents the response's quality. A higher score means a better response.

Fine-tuning the LLM with reinforcement learning

Finally, the original LLM is fine-tuned using the reward model as a guide. The process works as follows:

1. The LLM receives a prompt from the dataset and generates a response.
2. The response is shown to the reward model, which gives it a reward score.
3. This reward is used in a reinforcement learning algorithm to update the LLMs weights. Rewards and penalties are determined with a cost function.

The LLM learns to adjust its responses to maximize the reward score it receives from the reward model. By doing this, it learns to generate answers that are more aligned with human preferences with the goal of effectively boosting its own helpfulness and safety.

LLMs and Mixture of Experts

A Mixture of Experts (MoE) model is a type of Transformer architecture designed to make models much larger without a proportional increase in computational cost. Instead of having one massive feed-forward network that every token must pass through, an MoE model has many smaller, specialized feed-forward networks called *experts*. A small routine network examines each token and decides which one or two experts are best suited to process it. Then the token is sent only to those selected experts; the others remain inactive.

This approach means that for any given token, only a fraction of the model's total parameters are used. It allows us to build models with trillions of parameters, giving them a vast capacity for knowledge while keeping the computational cost for training and inference manageable.

LLMs and retrieval-augmented generation

Retrieval-augmented generation (RAG) is a technique that enhances an LLM by connecting it to an external knowledge source. This technique addresses two key weaknesses of LLMs: their knowledge is frozen at the time of training, and they sometimes hallucinate facts. RAG combines a pretrained LLM with a retrieval system that can pull information from a database, such as a collection of company documents or a recent snapshot of Wikipedia.

When a user asks a question, first the system searches the external database for relevant documents. Then the original prompt is combined with the retrieved information. This combined text is fed to the LLM, which uses both its internal knowledge and the provided external context to generate an accurate, up-to-date answer.

RAG reduces hallucinations, allows the model to cite its sources from the ones provided, and enables it to answer questions about information it was never trained on, making it highly valuable for enterprise and domain-specific applications. We could analyze libraries of proprietary documents, for example, without having to build a dedicated LLM for that purpose. We see RAG being incorporated into mainstream LLM platforms more and more often.

Use cases for LLMs

LLMs are a significant leap in AI's capability to understand, generate, and manipulate human language. Because the models are trained on vast, diverse datasets from the internet, books, code, and even user-generated content, they learn the intricate patterns, context, and nuances of communication. This deep understanding of patterns allows them to be applied beyond language, giving them the capability to find relationships between domain-specific contexts. Using an LLM is like querying a person who has almost the entire human knowledge pool in their head. This unlocks the potential of a wide variety of tasks that were previously difficult to automate.

Content generation

Creating original written content, whether it's an email or a fictional novel, can be a slow, difficult process. The initial step, getting ideas, is often the hardest one. An LLM can act as a powerful assistant in this process. By providing the model a simple prompt or an outline, a user can generate a complete first draft of an article, a marketing slogan, or a business report. The process becomes one of augmentation; the human guides the creative direction and refines the AI-generated output rather than spending hours on initial composition. This makes creating high-volume content, such as product descriptions for an e-commerce store with thousands of items, a much more manageable task. LLMs also have immensely useful domain-specific information that can enhance writing in ways that people might not have thought of alone. Here are a few examples of how specific industries use content generation:

- *Marketing and advertising*—Creative teams can use LLMs to rapidly produce multiple versions of ad copy for testing or generate a wide range of social media posts tailored to different platforms and then test which perform better. This allows them to focus more on strategy and campaign performance than on the time-consuming task of writing every piece of content from scratch.

- *E-commerce and retail*—For online stores with thousands of products, writing unique, engaging descriptions for each item is a major challenge. An LLM can be tasked with generating these descriptions based on a list of product specifications, ensuring that every item has a compelling standardized summary for potential buyers.

- *Education*—Teachers and instructional designers can generate customized learning materials, such as practice questions, lesson summaries, and case studies. This allows them to create a richer variety of content to suit different learning styles without being burdened by the creation of every document.

- *Legal services*—Although it's not a replacement for a qualified lawyer, an LLM can create a first draft of standard legal documents, such as lease agreements, based on a set of parameters. This allows legal professionals to speed their workflow by focusing their time on reviewing, customizing, and providing expert legal advice unique to the situation at hand.

LLMs can also be used to augment and enhance existing offerings in digital products. If you have a fitness tracker, for example, you can use LLMs to give users clear instructions on performing exercises. If you have a recreational-flight computer app, you could supplement and standardize takeoff-site information for a better user experience. The possibilities are endless.

Information synthesis

Many professions involve reading and understanding vast amounts of text. A lawyer may have to review hundreds of pages of legal precedents; a developer may have to stay current with dozens of newly published code frameworks and small packages, all of which have their own documentation. Reading all this material to find the key information is incredibly time-consuming.

LLMs can process large documents in seconds and generate concise summaries that highlight the most important information based on a unique context. The models don't replace expert analysis, but they dramatically speed the process by allowing users to determine quickly which documents or areas of information require a closer look. Here are a few examples of how professionals in various fields use information synthesis:

- *Legal services*—A paralegal or lawyer can use an LLM to get a high-level summary of hundreds of pages of discovery documents or case law. This helps them quickly identify which documents are most critical to their case, saving countless hours of manual review.

- *Financial services*—Financial analysts must digest quarterly earnings reports, market news, and complex filings to make timely investment decisions. An LLM can extract the key financial metrics and commentary from these documents, allowing analysts to react faster and make better-informed decisions.
- *Market research*—Companies often collect thousands of customer reviews, survey responses, and support tickets. Instead of having a team read them one by one, an LLM can analyze the entire dataset and produce a summary of the most common themes, complaints, and feature requests.

Coding assistants

Writing code requires precise syntax and logic, and even experienced programmers spend time looking up functions and debugging errors. Because LLMs have been trained on massive amounts of publicly available code from sources like GitHub, they've learned the patterns and structure of many programming languages. LLMs are very well-suited for programming languages because the languages are well-defined, and many established code design patterns exist, with examples available publicly in thousands of codebases. A developer can describe a desired function in plain English, and the model can generate the code to accomplish that task. This is also useful for learning and debugging. If you encounter a complex block of code written by someone else, you can ask the LLM to explain what it does. Let's look at some common coding tasks at which these assistants excel:

- *Translating between programming languages*—If a team needs to convert a utility script from Python to JavaScript to run in a different environment, an LLM can perform the translation. Although the model requires human review, it handles most of the syntactic and structural conversion automatically.
- *Code refactoring and optimization*—A developer can provide a working piece of code and ask the LLM to improve it. This could involve making the code run more efficiently, improving its readability, or rewriting it to conform to a specific coding style guide or best practice.
- *Debugging and error analysis*—Instead of spending hours trying to figure out a cryptic error message, a developer can paste both the problematic code and the error message into the LLM. Then the model can analyze the context and suggest the most likely cause of the error and how to fix it.

Enhancement of digital products

Many digital products and services are built around a core function but involve secondary tasks that require users to process, organize, or create information. These tasks are often a source of friction, delaying the user from achieving their main goal. A well-implemented LLM can remove this friction by acting as an intelligent assistant embedded directly in the product's workflow. This approach adds a layer of intelligence that makes the product more responsive, personalized, and powerful. Consider how these capabilities transform these common types of applications:

- *Collaboration and productivity tools*—An online brainstorming or whiteboarding application is designed to help teams capture ideas. Although the application is great at collecting raw input, making sense of a massive board filled with virtual sticky notes is often chaotic and time-consuming. An LLM can be integrated to solve this specific problem. With a single click, it can scan all the text contributed by the group members, identify the main themes, group similar ideas, and generate a structured summary with action items. This transforms a messy, creative brainstorm into clear, organized output, bridging the gap between ideation and execution.

- *Travel and hospitality apps*—Booking a flight and hotel are only the first steps in planning a trip. The next, more time-consuming part is figuring out what to do. A travel app can use an LLM to act as a concierge. After a user books a five-day trip to Cape Town, for example, the app could automatically generate a sample itinerary. Based on the user's interests (such as hiking, history, or wine tasting) and the location of their hotel, the LLM can suggest a logical sequence of activities, grouping them by location to minimize travel time and dramatically simplifying the user's planning process.

- *Personal finance and budgeting tools*—Most budgeting apps are good at categorizing spending, but they often leave the user to figure out the story behind the numbers. An LLM can analyze a user's transaction history and provide narrative insights. Instead of just showing a chart, the app could generate a weekly summary like this: "You did well on your dining-out budget this week, but your grocery spending was 15% higher than average, mostly from a large trip to Whole Foods on Tuesday." This turns raw financial data into a more understandable, actionable story.

We began this chapter with a simple intuition: the autocomplete feature on your phone. By peeling back the layers, we discovered that modern LLMs are essentially that same concept scaled to massive proportions --swapping simple probability tables for high-dimensional embeddings and self-attention mechanisms. While the emergent intelligence of these models can seem unbelievable, you now possess the blueprint to look past the hype. You understand that behind the generated poetry and code lies a deterministic process of dot products, matrix multiplications, and backpropagation, all striving to minimize the loss in predicting the next token. The magic isn't in the machine; it is in the math.

SUMMARY OF LARGE LANGUAGE MODELS

At their core, LLMs predict the probability of the next word. Chained together, this becomes powerful

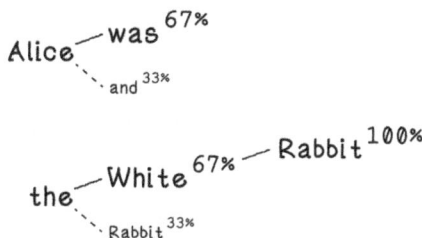

It's key to encode words/tokens as numbers, for LLMs to learn effectively.

[a, l, ic, e, w, a, s, b, e, g, in, n, ing, t, o, g, e, t, v, er, y, ti, re, d, o, f, s, i, t, t, ing, b]

[0, 1, 2, 3, 4, 0, 5, 6, 3, 7, 8, 9, 10, 11, 12, 7, 3, 11, 13, 14, 15, 16, 17, 18, 12, 19, 5, 20, 11, 11, 10, 6]

Token positions are a huge component for LLMs to learn the meanings of words and how they relate.

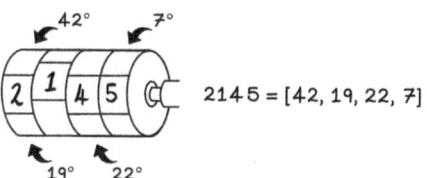

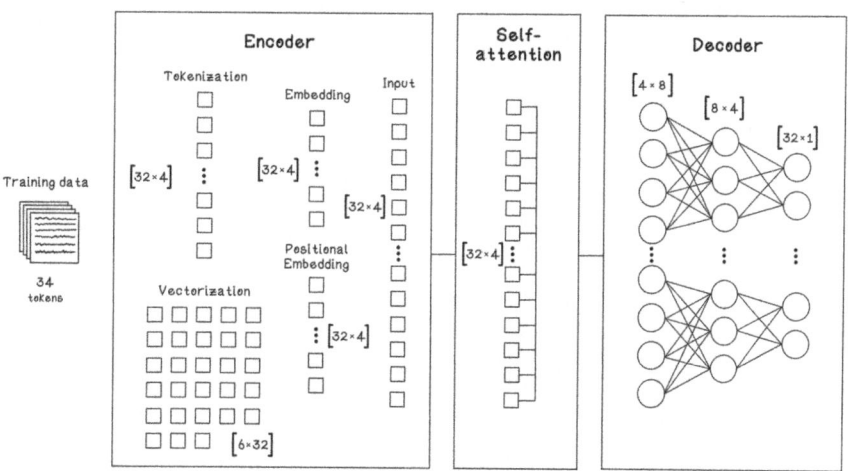

Attention is the superpower of the Transformer framework that lets words/tokens find meaning in words around them.

In this chapter

- Understanding the intuition of generative image models

- Cleaning and preparing image data for training

- Grasping and implementing the steps to train a diffusion model

- Implementing major components for a diffusion model and U-Net

What are generative image models?

Generative image models are a family of algorithms and artificial neural network (ANN) structures that specialize in generating accurate images based on human-language input. Imagine a sculptor who has spent his life observing people who are in deep thought. For years, he walked around town and thoroughly studied every aspect of every person he saw thinking deeply, observing their posture, expressions, and subtle details. Over time, he internalized what it means to look like someone thinking. He might have seen hundreds of thousands of people pass through the town over the years.

We blindfold the sculptor, give him a random block of marble, and say, "Make me a sculpture of a person thinking." The sculptor can't add new material to marble; instead, he feels the block of marble and chips away a small piece that he's confident does not look like a person thinking. He repeats this process thousands of times, each time feeling the edges of the marble and chipping away a little more noise. Slowly and methodically, a coherent image of a person thinking emerges from the random block of stone (figure 12.1).

Figure 12.1 An analogy showing that diffusion is about removing to create rather than adding

In the same way, a generative image model, trained on millions of images, begins with random noise and iteratively transforms it into a clear image, not by adding to a blank canvas but by learning how to remove what doesn't belong. Modern models that generate images with breathtaking complexity and realism are possible because of three core principles unlocked by the vast amounts of data available, using language models and harnessing powerful innovations in deep learning research:

- *A visual vocabulary*—Instead of learning the rules of language, an image model learns the visual grammar of images. It holds billions of adjustable parameters that store not just facts like "a cat has pointy ears" but also abstract visual concepts. It learns the interplay of light and shadow that makes a scene look dramatic, the specific textures that define rusted metal versus polished chrome, and the compositional rules that distinguish a portrait from a landscape. This allows the model to combine different concepts in novel ways, creating an image of "a snail surfing on a wave of lava in the style of Van Gogh because" it understands the core components of all those ideas.

- *Language models assist image generation*—Whereas a language model is trained on vast amounts of raw text, an image model is trained on two kinds of data: billions of images and their captions. It sees a picture of a futuristic city at night and reads the caption "a neon-lit cyberpunk cityscape." By processing millions of these pairs, it builds a powerful understanding between words and pixels. This is how it learns the specific aesthetic of cyberpunk or the subtle difference between a smirk and a smile.

- *The power of noise*—This innovation is the most important one, and it's counterintuitive. Instead of starting with a blank canvas and drawing shapes, the model starts with a canvas of pure random pixels, such as a scrambled TV screen with no signal. Then it carefully refines every pixel in the static step by step until the desired image emerges from the random noise. This process is called *diffusion*.

The most popular architectures and approaches for modern image generation are diffusion models and generative adversarial networks (GANs). Figure 12.2 shows how they fit into the mental model of machine learning algorithms that we've explored throughout this book. The broad generative models concept uses techniques from supervised learning, unsupervised learning, and reinforcement learning.

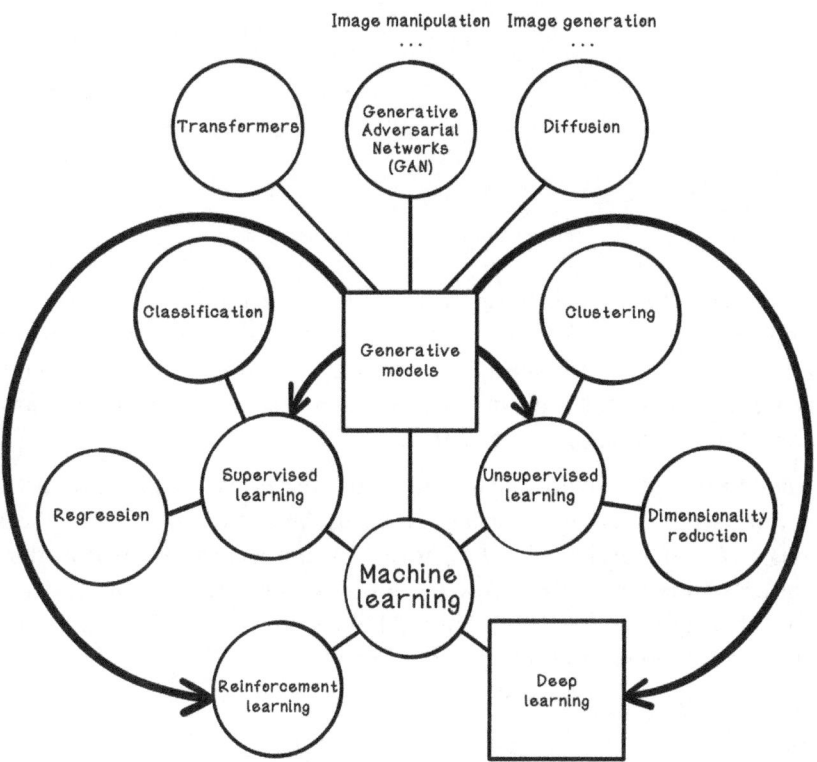

Figure 12.2 How diffusion models fit into machine learning

The intuition behind image generation

Before we explore the details of a generative image model, let's build some fundamental intuition using a simple practical example that illustrates what a diffusion model does. Suppose that we want to generate an image of a tree, starting with the random unclear image in figure 12.3.

Figure 12.3 An example of initial noise

What do you see? This image is the starting point for the model: a canvas of pure random noise. To your eyes, it's a meaningless, blurry blob. To the model, it's a field of potential, containing every possible image in a faint, ghostly form. At this stage, the model's job is to take its first look and decide which parts of this noise are least likely to belong in making the image look like a tree.

After several timesteps of denoising, a faint structure begins to emerge (figure 12.4). What do you see now? Perhaps a head of broccoli? An explosion? A tree? It's still ambiguous, but a general shape is taking form. The model has peeled away the most obvious layers of noise, revealing a low-resolution silhouette. It's beginning to commit to a general structure, but the details are still fluid. Can you identify which parts of the image need to be denoised to show the tree better?

Figure 12.4 An example of denoising

After many more refinement timesteps, the image becomes much clearer (figure 12.5). It's almost certainly a tree. The main trunk and the leafy canopy are well defined. The model has locked in the high-level concept. Its task is no longer about figuring out the overall structure but refining the details, carving out the smaller branches, and adding texture to the leaves.

Figure 12.5 An example of denoising after more timesteps

Finally, after hundreds of timesteps, we arrive at the final, crisp image (figure 12.6). We clearly see the tree, complete with detailed bark, individual leaf clusters, and a coherent structure. The model successfully removed all the noise that was inconsistent with its goal. The tree was hidden within the initial random noise. The journey from a noisy blob to a sharp final image is the essence of the diffusion process. This concept likely seems counterintuitive. When we think of image generation, we may think that it's about drawing and painting because those processes are how humans create images, but diffusion is the inverse: it starts with noise and iteratively removes the noise that shouldn't be there.

Figure 12.6 An example of denoising after all timesteps

A generative image model training workflow

The workflow for training a generative image model involves several key stages, from preparing a vast visual library to teaching the model how to reverse a noising process to create new images (figure 12.7).

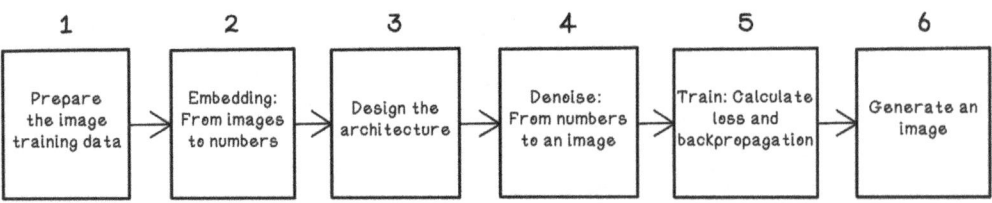

Figure 12.7 A workflow for training a diffusion model

These stages are

1. *Prepare the image training data.* Before the model can learn to create, it must study existing images. This step involves collecting a massive dataset of images and captions associated with each image and then cleaning and standardizing them so the model has high-quality examples to learn from.

2. *Embedding: From images to numbers.* Computers understand numbers, not pixels or text. This step converts images to numerical data and text captions to embeddings. Crucially, it includes forward diffusion, in which clean training images have noise added to them in stages to create the core training examples.

3. *Design the architecture.* This step involves choosing the model's structure. For modern image generation, the U-Net architecture is the standard choice because its design is perfect for image-to-image tasks such as denoising. U-Nets are discussed in detail later in this chapter.

4. *Denoise: From numbers to an image.* This is U-Net's main task during training. The model is given a noisy image and learns to predict the exact noise that was added to it, using the text caption as a guide.

5. *Train: Calculate loss and backpropagation.* To learn, the model has to know how wrong its predictions are. In this step, the model's predicted noise is compared with the noise that was added. The difference (*loss*) is used to update all the model's weights through backpropagation, making it a better noise predictor over time.

6. *Generate an image.* When it's trained, the model can generate new images—the reverse of the training process. The model starts with a canvas of pure random noise and, guided by a user's text prompt, iteratively subtracts the predicted noise until a clean final image is revealed.

Prepare the image training data

Before a model can learn to create art, it must go to a virtual art school. This first step is curating a massive library of images that the model will learn from (figure 12.8). The resolution quality, diversity, and (most important) description of each image will define everything the model is capable of. Unlike a large language model (LLM), which learns from text alone, a generative image model learns from the relationship between an image and its caption. If we want to build a generalized model, the dataset usually contains billions of image and text pairs of a huge variety of images: paintings, portrait photography, digital art, satellite photographs, and more.

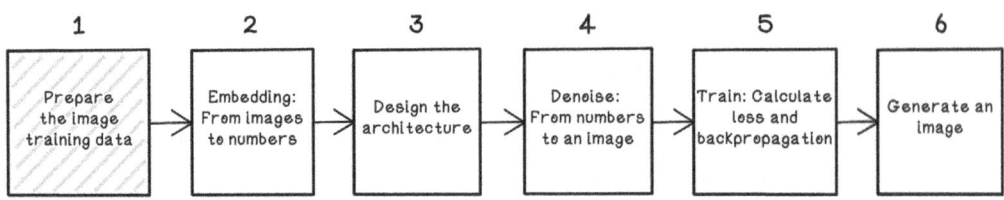

Figure 12.8 Preparing image data in the diffusion model training workflow

Selecting and collecting image data

As with most machine learning models, a diffusion model's ultimate ability is a direct reflection of the data it's trained on. A model trained only on paintings won't know how to create a photorealistic image. If we train using only photos of landscapes, the model can't create cartoons. The goal is to collect a dataset that's massive, diverse, and accurately captioned. Following are some common sources of image data:

- *Web-crawled data*—The largest datasets are created by crawling the public internet, gathering billions of images and their associated alt-text or summarizing the surrounding text. This approach provides immense scale and diversity but requires the greatest amount of cleaning and filtering to remove low-quality images and irrelevant captions. These images are often poorly captioned with varying aspect ratios and resolutions.

- *Public art and museum archives*—Collections from art museums provide access to high-resolution scans of classical and modern art. This data is good for teaching the model about different artistic styles, from Impressionism to Surrealism. This is how a model is able to understand the style of Vincent Van Gogh, for example.

- *Scientific archives*—Specialized datasets of biological diagrams, astronomical images from telescopes, or medical scans teach the model highly specific and technical visual information that usually isn't available in general web data.

- *Stock-photography databases*—Stock-photo sites contain millions of high-quality, professionally shot photographs. Crucially, these images come with detailed, descriptive captions written by the photographers, making them ideal for teaching the model about realism, object composition, and specific terminology.

- *Satellite and geospatial data*—To teach a model about geography, building layouts, or environmental patterns, we can use satellite imagery from sources such as NASA and the European Space Agency. This allows the model to generate realistic top-down views of cities, coastlines, and landscapes.

- *Synthetic data and 3D renders*—An increasingly popular source is purely computer-generated imagery. Training on synthetic data from 3D environments created with

3D modeling software gives the model access to perfectly labeled images with precise control of lighting, angle, and composition. This is also a powerful way to avoid many of the copyright and privacy issues inherent in web-scraped data, although it can be time-consuming and requires experts in design to create.

The crucial role of captions

An image without a good caption is useless for training a text-to-image model. The *caption* is the key that connects the visual data (pixels) to the linguistic concepts (words). The quality of the captions directly determine the model's ability to follow detailed prompts and generate an accurate image. Let's explore what good and bad captions look like:

- *Good caption*—"A photorealistic close-up of a red-tailed hawk perched on a pine branch, its feathers ruffled by the wind, with a soft-focus lush green forest background." This caption teaches the model about specific subjects such as "red-tailed hawk," actions such as "perched," and styles such as "photorealistic" and "soft-focus."
- *Bad caption*—"image1.jpg" or "bird." A model trained on millions of pairs like this would learn to associate the word *bird* with many species in many poses and situations, and it would struggle to generate a specific type of bird when prompted for one.

Licensing of content

The data collected for image models has even more complex legal and ethical challenges than the pure text data we use to train LLMs. Here are the primary legal and ethical concerns regarding image training data:

- *Copyright*—Most images online are copyrighted. Using an artist's work to train a commercial model without a license is a major legal and ethical issue. This is why many foundational models should be trained on datasets with permissive licenses or on large, licensed stock-photo archives.
- *Style mimicry*—Although image generation models create unique images each time, they can also create the recognizable styles of living artists. This raises profound ethical questions about originality, consent, and compensation. Without that artist's work, the model could not produce that style of image. Furthermore, mass generation of a specific art style could devalue it, making it a commodity.
- *Representation and bias*—If the training data disproportionately shows people of a certain demographic or people in certain stereotypical roles, such as "doctors are male" and "nurses are female," the model will learn and amplify these biases. Curating

a diverse, representative dataset is one of the most important and difficult challenges in responsible AI development.

- *Misuse of likeness*—Training a model on photographs scraped from the internet without consent can be a major privacy violation. When a model learns a person's face, it has effectively captured that person's visual likeness. This likeness can be used to generate new synthetic images of that person in situations they were never in, potentially for harassment, misinformation, or creating fake endorsements, going beyond privacy issues and entering the realm of identity appropriation.

Cleaning and preprocessing image data

Just as raw text from the internet is messy, image datasets are filled with visual noise that can confuse the model and degrade its performance. The goal of preprocessing is to create a clean, standardized, high-quality dataset before training begins. Suppose that we have a typical image scraped from a pet blog. It may be a high-resolution landscape aspect ratio JPG with a large watermark from the website and a nondescriptive filename like img_2207 as its only caption (figure 12.9).

img_2207	img_2207	a black and white line drawing of a playful tabby cat holding the end of a thread from a ball of yarn
2600 × 1800	1024 × 1024	1024 × 1024
Original image	Watermark removed and cropped	Labeled with rich caption

Figure 12.9 Cleaning image data for training

This single image-text pair must go through some cleaning steps:

- *Resolution and aspect ratio standardization*—Image models are most efficient when they train on images of the same size. This means resizing all images to a standard resolution, such as 512×512. Images that are too small are often discarded because they lack detail, whereas nonsquare images are usually cropped or padded to fit the target aspect ratio.

- *Watermark and overlay removal*—Watermarks, logos, timestamps, and social media borders are visual noise. If they're left in the image, the model will learn to replicate them, leading to generated images that are littered with nonsensical text and artifacts. If these artifacts are consistent in the training set, they'll be emphasized in the generated images because the model will learn that strong pattern from seeing it many times. Automated tools are used to detect and remove or paint over these overlays, ensuring that the model learns from the content of the image itself.

- *Duplicate removal*—The same image often appears many times across the web. Removing identical or similar images prevents the model from becoming overtrained on specific examples and encourages it to learn more general concepts.

- *Corrupted-file removal*—Large datasets often contain corrupted files that can't be opened or are incomplete. These files must be filtered to prevent errors during training.

- *Safety and content filtering*—This step is critical for responsible AI development. The dataset must be scanned to identify and remove harmful or inappropriate content, such as graphic violence or explicit material. This filtering helps ensure that the final model doesn't generate harmful or offensive images.

- *Caption cleaning and enhancement*—In our example, the initial caption "img_2207" isn't helpful. A significant amount of work can be done to generate a rich caption. Often, a separate, powerful captioning model is used to analyze the cleaned image and generate a new descriptive caption. For our cat example, it might generate "a black and white line drawing of a playful tabby cat holding the end of a thread from a ball of yarn." This transforms a low-quality data point into a high-quality one.

Embedding: From images to numbers

The next fundamental challenge is that computers don't see images or read text like people do; computers understand only numbers. The process of preparing data for the model involves converting the training images to numerical representations and preparing the text label for the image as a numerical representation (figure 12.10).

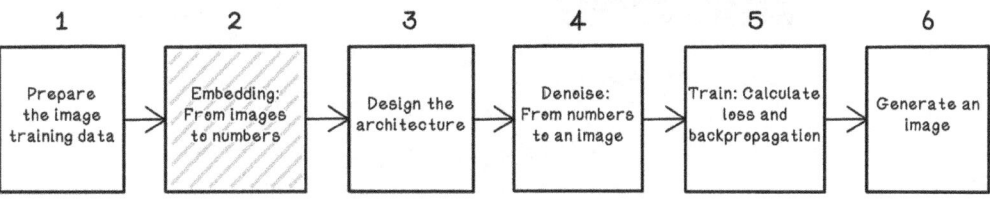

Figure 12.10 Embedding in the diffusion model training life cycle

For our working example, we'll train the model to learn how to generate a happy face, a sad face, and a neutral face. For the sake of simplicity, we'll use an 8x8 grayscale image as our training data (figure 12.11).

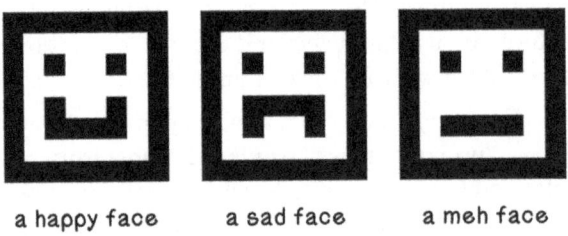

Figure 12.11 Example basic image training data

Image normalization

A computer can see an image as a grid of pixels. Each pixel has a value typically from 0 (black) to 255 (white) in a grayscale image, as in our examples. Although computers can work with these numbers and use them to render colors, deep learning networks train effectively when the input values are small and centered around 0 (to employ gradient descent, explored in chapter 9). So we must normalize the pixel values. A common practice is to scale the 0-to-255 range to a -1-to-1 range. This simple conversion makes the training process stable and efficient. In figure 12.12, the image data is an 8×8 matrix in which 1 indicates complete white, -1 indicates complete black, and all numbers between -1 and 1 are shades of gray.

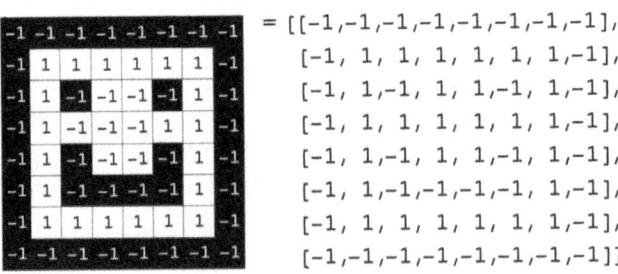

Figure 12.12 How images are represented as normalized numbers

Most training images are in full color and use the RGB (red, green, blue) color scheme. Instead of a single grid of pixels, a color image is composed of three separate grids (also called *channels*) stacked on top of one another. Each channel represents the intensity of red, green, or blue, with values for each pixel also ranging from 0 to 255.

To normalize a color image, we perform the same scaling operation on each channel separately. If we have the color pixel to normalize, we can scale it using the formula

$$(\text{original value} / 127.5) - 1$$

We divide by 127.5 to scale the result between 1 and -1. If we use 255, we'll scale to between 1 and 0, which isn't what we want. Red: 100, green: 150, blue: 250 results in

- *Scaled red*—-0.22
- *Scaled green*—0.18
- *Scaled glue*—0.96

We do this for all pixels in the image. The overall result is represented as three separate matrices, one for each color, all dimensions of the original image (figure 12.13).

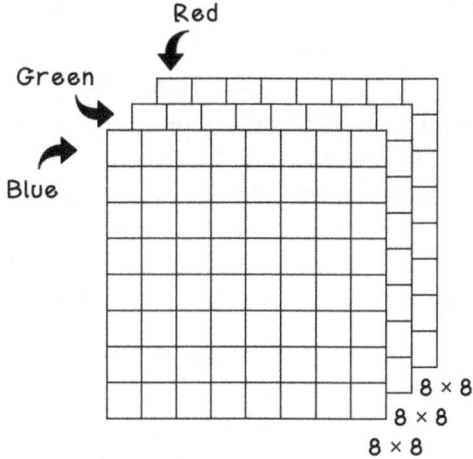

Figure 12.13 How RGB images are represented as matrices

Forward diffusion

The core of diffusion training is teaching the model to denoise an image. *Denoising* means iteratively removing noise in a way that makes sense for the goal of revealing the correct final image. To do this, we need a lot of noisy images to practice with. We use the *forward diffusion* process, in which we take a clean image from our dataset and deliberately destroy it by adding noise step by step.

Imagine taking a perfectly clear photograph and gradually adding layers of static. After one step, the image is slightly fuzzy. After 100 steps, the original image is barely visible. After 1,000 steps, the image is pure noise. Each time we add noise to the image, we save a snapshot that includes the noisy image at that step number and the noise pattern we added to get to that noisy image.

Keeping track of the noise pattern added at a specific timestep is critical for teaching the model how noise was added to an image and what the result was. This process is called a *noise schedule*. The algorithm creates different levels of noise at each timestep, derived from the original image each time. It's important to note that a new timestep doesn't add noise to the previous noisy image; it always adds noise to the original image. The following values control the noising schedule:

- *Beta*—We start by defining a noise schedule that gradually increases from a small number at timestep 1 to a larger number at the final timestep, T (the total number of timesteps to create). This controls how much noise is added at each individual step. We might start at 0.0001 and end at 0.02 over 100 steps. This means Beta will be 0.0001 at timestep 1 and 0.02 at timestep 1000 (If $T = 1000$).
- *Alpha*—Alpha is defined as 1 - Beta at a specific timestep. It represents the *signal rate*—how much of the original image information is preserved at each step.
- *Alpha-Bar (cumulative product)*—This value represents the total signal remaining after t steps. Even though we're jumping directly to a specific timestep, the math relies on the idea that the image decays sequentially. At step 1, we keep 99% of the signal. At step 2, we keep 99% of the remaining signal. To jump to step 100, we must calculate the cumulative product of the previous decay rates to determine how much original signal should remain and how much noise should replace it.

Given any timestep, we can calculate Beta, Alpha, and Alpha-Bar, as shown in table 12.1. Using a formula we can calculate the new value for each pixel given the original pixel value, the Alpha-Bar value, and a random number sampled from a standard distribution. In figure 12.14, we're calculating the random noise for the top-left pixel of the image (i.e. the pixel at 0,0 of the matrix).

Table 12.1 A subset of values for the noise schedule

Timestep (t)	Beta	Alpha calculation (1 - beta)	Alpha	Alpha-Bar calculation	Alpha-Bar
1	0.00010	1 - 0.00010	0.99990	0.99990	0.99990
2	0.00012	1 - 0.00012	0.99988	0.99990 × 0.99988	0.99978
3	0.00014	1 - 0.00014	0.99986	0.99990 × 0.99988 × 0.99986	0.99964
			...		
1000	0.02000	1 - 0.02000	0.98000		0.00004

noisy image   = original image * $\sqrt{\text{alpha-bar}}$ + $\sqrt{1 - \text{alpha-bar}}$ * random

noisy image[0][0] = 1   * $\sqrt{0.99990}$ + $\sqrt{1 - 0.99990}$ * 0.65

noisy image[0][0] = 1.00645

So, the top-left pixel is 1.00645.

Figure 12.14 Calculations for adding noise to an image

Exercise: What is the noise for pixel [1, 1] if the random number is 0.25?

Calculate the noise for pixel [1,1].

Solution:

0.9974499987

In figure 12.15, we see the forward diffusion results for a happy-face image. Here, t = 1000 isn't the result of adding noise to t = 999 but the result of adding a lot of noise to the original training image.

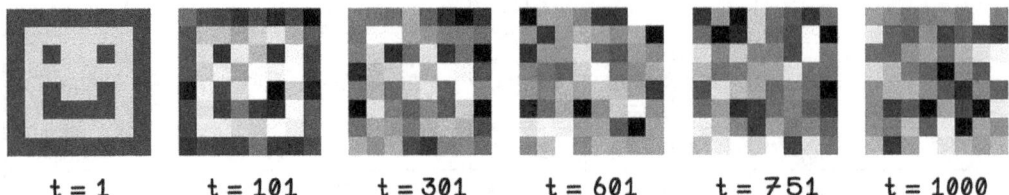

t = 1   **t = 101**   **t = 301**   **t = 601**   **t = 751**   **t = 1000**

Figure 12.15 A progression of adding noise to an image over 1,000 timesteps

This process creates our training pairs of noise and text labels. The model is given the noisy image, and its job is to predict the noise pattern that was added. By doing this millions of times with millions of images and noise levels, the model becomes an expert at seeing a noisy image and knowing precisely what noise needs to be removed to make it cleaner.

You may wonder why we sample a random number from a standard normal distribution. The reason is that the random number and resulting noise are statistically predictable because most numbers are centered around 0, with a lower likelihood that the number will be between -1 and 1 and an even lower likelihood of being between -2 and 2 (figure 12.16). This process is called *Gaussian noise*. Its unique mathematical properties make both the forward (noising) and reverse (denoising) processes analytically tractable and learnable.

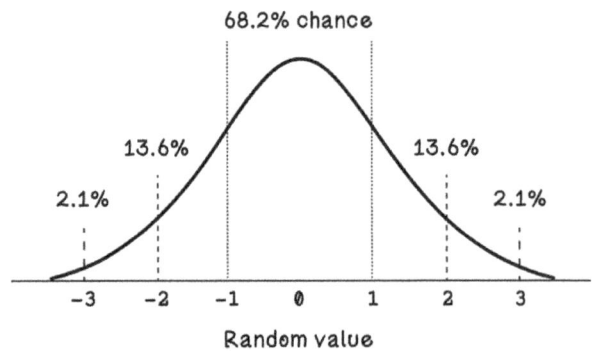

Figure 12.16 A view of probability of selection in a normal distribution

Python code sample for forward diffusion

This code describes the forward diffusion process, which gradually adds noise to a clean image over a series of timesteps to generate training data for a diffusion model. It begins by defining a noise schedule (`beta_schedule`) and computing the corresponding alpha and cumulative `alpha_bar` values. For each timestep, it samples Gaussian noise and mixes it with the original image using a weighted combination determined by `alpha_bar`. This produces a progressively noisier version of the image (`noisy_image`) and stores the exact noise used (`noise_patterns`) for each step, later used to train the model to reverse the process.

```
def define_schedules(timesteps):
    beta_min = 0.0001
    beta_max = 0.02

    beta_schedule = np.linspace(beta_min, beta_max, timesteps)

    alpha_schedule = 1.0 - beta_schedule

    alpha_bar_schedule = np.cumprod(alpha_schedule)

    return beta_schedule, alpha_bar_schedule

def forward_diffusion(image, timesteps):

    _, alpha_bar_schedule = define_schedules(timesteps)

    noisy_images = []
    noise_patterns = []

    for t in range(timesteps):
        alpha_bar = alpha_bar_schedule[t]

        random_noise = np.random.randn(*image.shape)

        sqrt_alpha_bar = np.sqrt(alpha_bar)
        sqrt_one_minus_alpha_bar = np.sqrt(1.0 - alpha_bar)

        noisy_image = (sqrt_alpha_bar * image) +
            (sqrt_one_minus_alpha_bar * random_noise)

        noisy_images.append(noisy_image)
        noise_patterns.append(random_noise)

    return noisy_images, noise_patterns, alpha_bar_schedule
```

Defines how much noise we add at each step

This tells us how much of the original image is still left at any given step

These constants ensure that the "energy" of the image stays consistent

This is the core formula

We save the exact noise we used

Timestep embedding

With an understanding of how timesteps and the noise schedule can dicate the amount of noise added, we need a way to give the model the timestep number of each noisy image we're training it with. This is important because an image that's only slightly noisy, such as timestep 10, needs a subtler denoising operation than an image that's almost pure static, such as timestep 900.

We give the model this information by creating a timestep embedding. Much like in positional encoding (chapter 11), we use a sinusoidal formula to convert the integer timestep, such as t = 22, to a unique vector. This vector gives the model a precise mathematical representation of the noise level, allowing it to adjust the strength of its denoising prediction accordingly. To find the values, we use the formula in figure 12.17. After calculating the values of all timesteps, we'll have something like table 12.2.

$$\text{angle} = \left(\frac{t}{1000^{\frac{i}{\text{half dimension}}}} \right)$$

embedding dimensions = 16,
so half dimensions = 8

So, given half dimensions = 8, and t = 22,

d = 0 angle: 22 / 1000 $^{(0\,/\,8)}$ = 22 / 1

d = 1 angle: 22 / 1000 $^{(1\,/\,8)}$ = 22 / 3.16

d = 2 angle: 22 / 1000 $^{(2\,/\,8)}$ = 22 / 10

d = 3 angle: 22 / 1000 $^{(3\,/\,8)}$ = 22 / 31.62

d = 4 angle: 22 / 1000 $^{(4\,/\,8)}$ = 22 / 100

d = 5 angle: 22 / 1000 $^{(5\,/\,8)}$ = 22 / 316.23

d = 6 angle: 22 / 1000 $^{(6\,/\,8)}$ = 22 / 1000

d = 7 angle: 22 / 1000 $^{(7\,/\,8)}$ = 22 / 3162.23

Figure 12.17 Calculations for timestep embeddings

Table 12.2 Calculations for creating timestep embeddings

Index (i)	angle calculation	angle	sin(angle)	cos(angle)
0	22 / 1	22	-0.0089	-0.9999
1	22 / 3.16	6.957	-0.6277	0.7784
2	22 / 10	2.2	0.8085	-0.5885
3	22 / 31.62	0.696	0.6411	0.7674
4	22 / 100	0.22	0.2182	0.9759
5	22 / 316.23	0.070	0.0699	0.9975
6	22 / 1000	0.022	0.0220	0.9997
7	22 / 3162.23	0.007	0.0070	0.9999

Finally, our timestep embedding for t = 22 will be all the sin(angle) values concatenated with all the cos(angle) values. The results is a vector of size 16 (figure 12.18):

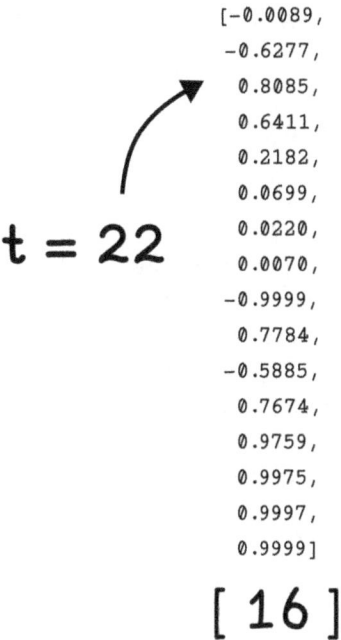

```
        [-0.0089,
         -0.6277,
          0.8085,
          0.6411,
          0.2182,
          0.0699,
          0.0220,
          0.0070,
         -0.9999,
          0.7784,
         -0.5885,
          0.7674,
          0.9759,
          0.9975,
          0.9997,
          0.9999]
```

t = 22

[16]

Figure 12.18 The embeddings for timestep 22

Python code sample for timestep embedding

This code generates a timestep embedding vector using a sinusoidal encoding scheme. For a given timestep and embedding size, it computes each element of the vector using alternating sine and cosine functions scaled by exponential factors of the timestep. This creates a unique, continuous representation of the timestep that captures both absolute and relative position information. The resulting embedding helps the model understand how much noise has been added and how aggressively it should denoise at each stage.

```python
def create_timestep_embedding(timestep, embedding_size):
    embedding_vector = np.zeros(embedding_size)

    for i in range(embedding_size):
        exponent = i / embedding_size

        div_term = np.power(10000, exponent)

        argument = timestep / div_term

        if i % 2 == 0:
            value = np.sin(argument)
        else:
            value = np.cos(argument)

        embedding_vector[i] = value

    return embedding_vector
```

Like the Transformer positional encodings, this uses a geometric progression of frequencies

Alternating sine and cosine waves, we create a unique signature for every single timestep

Text label embedding

The model understands images as numbers, but we still have the problem of the text labels. To guide the denoising process, we have to translate the text label (such as "a happy face") into a numerical representation. We don't have to train a text model (like a LLM) from scratch; instead, we can use a powerful pretrained text encoder. These models read the text label and output a single, information-rich vector: the embedding. This vector represents the semantic meaning of the label. After being processed by a text encoder, "a happy face" can be expressed as the following, resulting in an array of size 16 (figure 12.19).

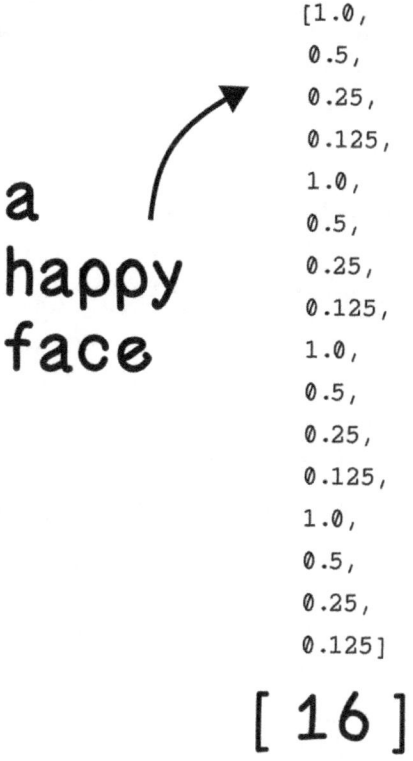

Figure 12.19 The embeddings for "a happy face"

When we have the initial text embedding, there's one more crucial step: processing it through a normal feed-forward network, such as a Multilayer Perceptron (MLP). An MLP is a small, linear feed-forward neural network that acts as a specialized translator. The text encoder provides a generic, all-purpose embedding. Think of it as a direct dictionary translation. The feed-forward network's task is to transform the generic embedding into a specialized guidance vector tailored to the unique language of our model. It converts the embedding, making it more expressive and useful for our model to work with. This network's weights will also be adjusted based on the loss during backpropagation. More-sophisticated architectures use actual multilayer ANNs instead of a simple MLP.

Python code sample for text embedding

This code describes how to create a text embedding vector for a given label to guide image generation. First, it uses a pretrained tokenizer and text encoder to convert the label to a series of token embeddings, which are averaged into a single vector.

This embedding is passed through a two-layer feed-forward network with sigmoid linear unit (SiLU) activation function, using learned projection weights to transform the generic embedding into a specialized vector (figure 12.20). The result is a refined representation of the text prompt that can be injected into the model to condition and guide the denoising process.

```python
def sigmoid(x):
    return 1 / (1 + np.exp(-x))

def silu(x):
    return x * sigmoid(x)

def create_text_embedding(text_label, embedding_size):

    token_count = 6
    mock_token_embeddings =
        np.random.randn(token_count, embedding_size)

    text_embedding = np.mean(mock_token_embeddings, axis=0)

    text_embedding = text_embedding.reshape(1, -1)

    projection_weights_1 =
        np.random.randn(embedding_size, embedding_size)

    sum_hidden = text_embedding @ projection_weights_1
    hidden_layer = silu(sum_hidden)

    projection_weights_2 =
        np.random.randn(embedding_size, embedding_size)

    sum_final = hidden_layer @ projection_weights_2
    final_embedding = silu(sum_final)

    return final_embedding.flatten()
```

Summarizes the token embeddings into a single vector by averaging them

These weights are essentially a translation layer

The model passes the summary through two fully-connected layers

Returns a single, flat array of numbers

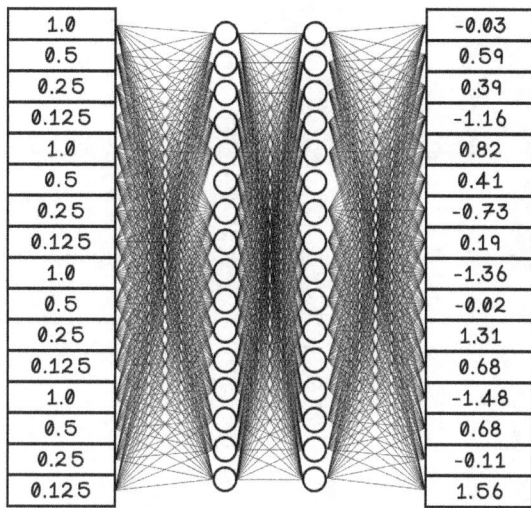

Figure 12.20 A view of a feed-forward ANN processing the text embedding

Similarly, the timestep embedding is passed through a feed-forward network, resulting in a vector of size 16. This is done for the same reason: to transform the generic timestep embedding vector into a vector tailored to our generative image model.

Here's an overview of the input data that we have available to feed into the model for training. We'll have T many of the following (figure 12.21):

- *Noise image*—Each is an 8×8 matrix.
- *Timestep embedding*—Each is a vector of size 16 after sinusoidal embedding and its feed-forward network.
- *Text label embedding*—Each is a vector of size 16 after being passed through a text encoder and its feed-forward network.

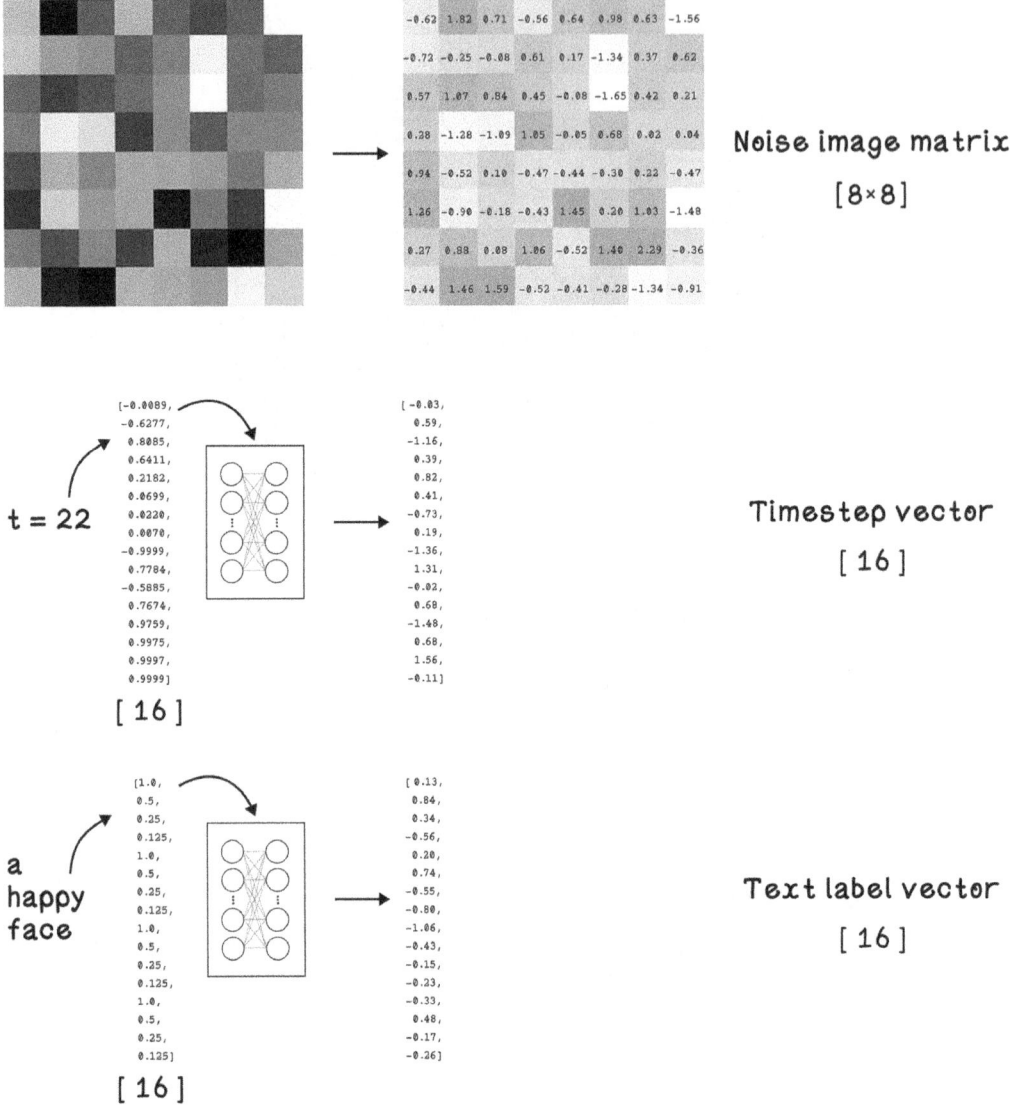

Figure 12.21 A complete representation of one training data input

Design the architecture

Now that we have our clean, normalized dataset of image–text pairs as numeric representations, the next step is choosing the training architecture (figure 12.22). This architecture is the brain of our operation and the specific type of deep learning architecture that will learn to perform the denoising task.

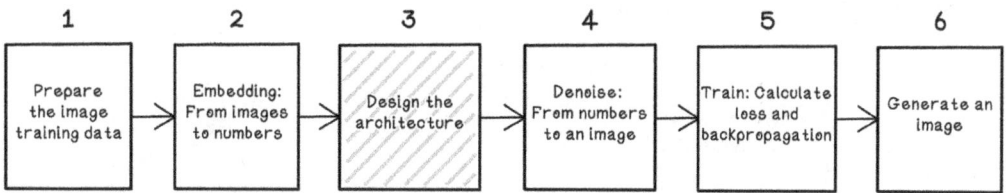

Figure 12.22 Designing the architecture in the diffusion model training workflow

As in chapter 11, a major decision in training specialized generative models is choosing the right architecture for the problem at hand. Different architectures have different tradeoffs, and for image generation, the key concerns are

- *Spatial awareness*—Can the model understand the 2D layout of an image? It must know that a pixel's neighbors are far more important than pixels on the other side of the image.
- *Multiscale processing*—Can the model see both the big picture (the overall composition) and the fine-grained details (textures and edges) at the same time?
- *Parameter efficiency*—Can the model learn complex visual patterns without requiring an unmanageable number of weights, which would make it too slow and expensive to train?

Convolutional neural networks

Famous for their power in image classification, convolutional neural networks (CNNs) are the foundation of modern computer vision. They use sliding filters to detect hierarchies of features and find anything from simple edges in early layers of the network to complex objects such as faces and cars in later layers. Although they're masters of analyzing images, CNNs aren't inherently designed to generate images from scratch. But CNNs are used extensively in the U-Net architecture, an innovation that makes generating images with diffusion possible. Let's explore how CNNs differ from the linear feed-forward networks that we've used thus far in the book.

Because we're working with image data, the positions of the pixels are of huge importance. The positions of the pixels are just as important as their color when the model is learning and generating coherent images. This is where CNNs are powerful.

Figure 12.23 illustrates the difference between an ordinary linear feed-forward layer and a convolutional layer. The node in the first one processes all the inputs provided linearly to learn relationships between them. But the convolutional layer analyzes different regions of the matrix independently to find relationships in a region. CNNs let learning happen with the spatial data intact.

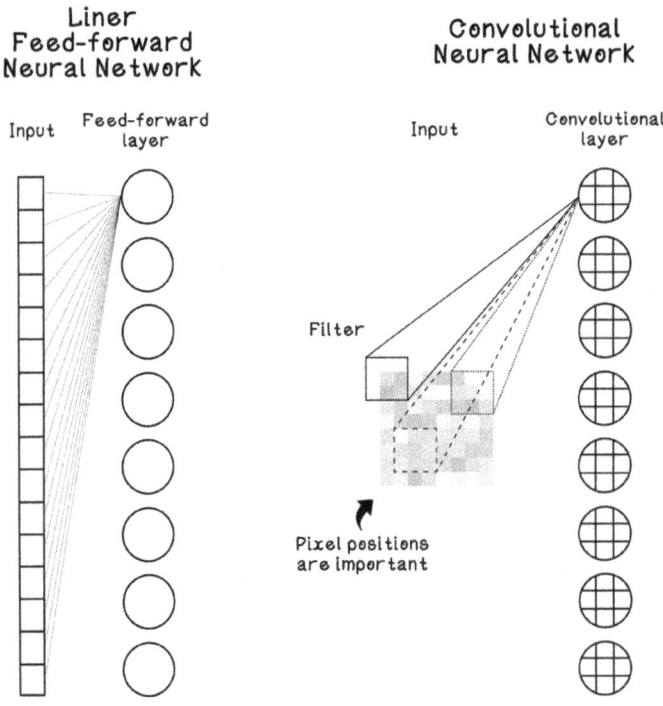

Figure 12.23 The difference between an ANN and a CNN

CNN input shape

Each node in a convolutional layer takes a matrix (2D grid shape) as input. In the case of our grayscale example, we have only one channel, so the input will be an 8×8 matrix. In a full-color image, we'd have three channels (red, green, and blue), in an 8×8×3 *tensor*. If we're training with Portable Network Graphics (PNG) images that can have transparency, we'd have four channels to include the alpha value for the pixels.

Filter (AKA kernel)

The core of a convolutional layer is a small filter, usually a 3×3 grid. The values in this grid are weights that act as a specialized feature detector. See one filter as a tiny magnifying glass that's trained to find one specific pattern. In the early layers of a network, these patterns are simple:

- One filter might learn to detect vertical edges. Its grid of weights might have positive numbers on the left, negative numbers on the right, and zeros in the middle.
- Another filter might learn to find horizontal edges.
- Other filters might learn to recognize simple textures or color gradients.

Crucially, the model isn't told what features to look for. These filter weights start as random numbers and are adjusted during the training process. If detecting corners is useful for the model's final goal, through backpropagation, some filters naturally evolve into corner detectors because doing so helps reduce overall loss.

Convolution operation

Each node in a convolutional layer slides a 3×3 filter over every possible position of the input image. At each position, it calculates the dot product between the filter's weights and the image pixels underneath it. Mathematically, the dot product pairs every number in the filter with the corresponding pixel in the image, multiplies them, and sums the total.

As a simplified example, let's look at a single row of the filter: If the filter row is [2, 7, 2], and the pixel row is [11, 2, 1], the dot product is $(2×11) + (7×2) + (2×1) = 38$.

The process starts at the top-left corner of the image. The filter lays over that patch, and the calculation is performed. Then the filter slides one pixel to the right and repeats the calculation. This process continues until the filter reaches the end of the row. Then it moves down one pixel and starts again from the left edge, continuing the scan until it has viewed every part of the image (figure 12.24).

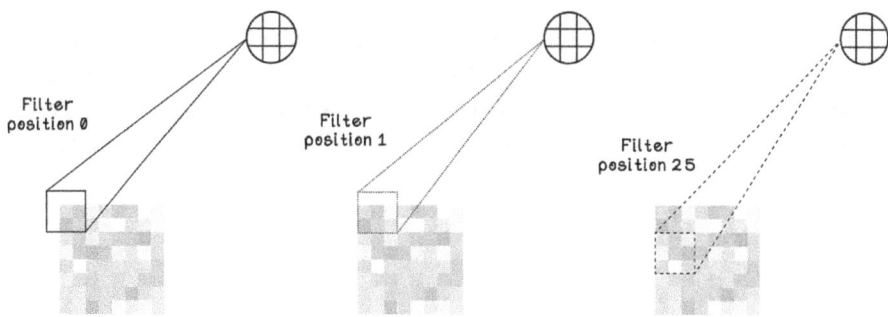

Figure 12.24 How a CNN filter scans an image

This approach preserves the spatial relationships of the input image. A feature detected in the top-left corner of the image results in an activation in the top-left corner of the output, maintaining the structure and features.

But what happens when the filter reaches the edge of the image? If a 3×3 filter tries to center on a border pixel, part of the filter will hang off the edge. To solve this problem and control the output size, we use a technique called padding. Padding involves adding a border of extra pixels, usually zeros, around the entire input image before convolution begins. This has two major benefits:

- *It preserves the image size.* With the right amount of padding, the output feature map can have exactly the same height and width as the input image—essential for building deep networks without image shrinking.
- *It processes edges properly.* Padding allows the filter to be centered over every pixel of the original image, including the corners and edges, ensuring that the information at the borders isn't lost or under-represented during training.

Feature map

The output of sliding one filter over the entire input is a 2D grid called a *feature map*—a new image that shows where the filter's specific feature was detected. The value of each pixel in this feature map is the result of a dot product. At each position, the numbers in the filter are multiplied by the corresponding pixel values in the patch of the image directly underneath it, and the results are summed to produce a single number. The value of this number indicates how well the filter matches the underlying image patch:

- If a filter is designed to find a vertical line and it's currently over a vertical line in the image, the dot product will result in a large positive number.
- If the filter is over a blank area, the result will be near zero.
- If the filter is over a feature that's the opposite of what it's looking for, such as a horizontal line, the result will be a large negative number.

The final feature map, therefore, is a new filtered image that highlights the presence and strength of a specific feature across the entire input image. A convolutional layer has many nodes with filters, each producing its own feature map. These feature maps are passed to the next layer. For more information, see the "Denoising: From numbers to an image" section later in this chapter.

Let's explore how the filter weights are initialized and how the filter produces a value by evaluating the pixel values. In figure 12.25, our 3×3 filter is initialized with a column of 1s, a column of 0s, and a column of -1s. This filter is a vertical line detector, designed to produce a high value when it detects a sharp change from dark to light. We're using this filter for convenience. Remember that the network would learn these weights through training.

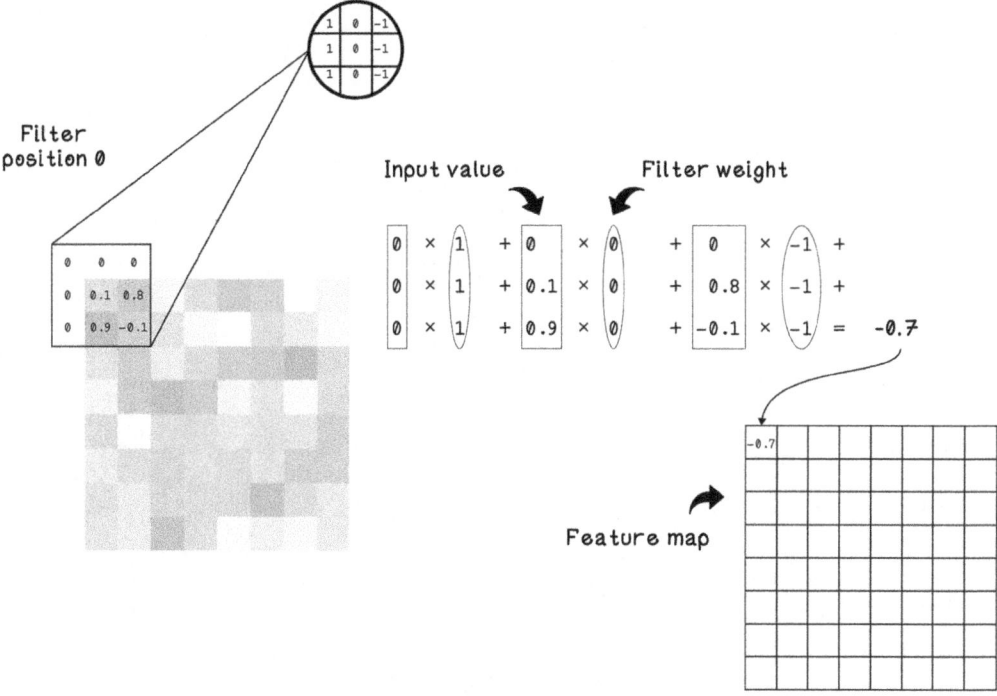

Figure 12.25 Calculations of a filter on an image for the first pixel

The result of the filter on the pixels is a dot product between the filter's weights and the pixel values underneath it. So each filter value is multiplied by the respective pixel value, and all resulting products are summed. In the preceding example, the filter produces the value -0.7 which becomes the first value in the feature map for the top-right value of a 8×8 matrix. Naturally, the entire process is repeated for every other position the filter scans, completing the feature map one pixel at a time.

Exercise: What is the outcome of the filter on the next pixel position?

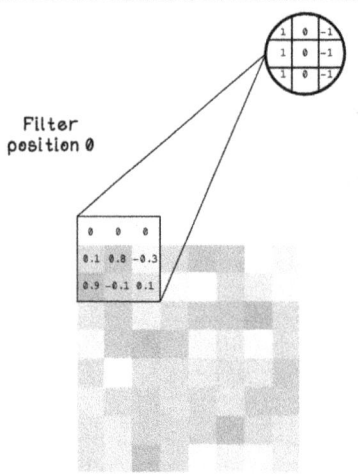

Solution:

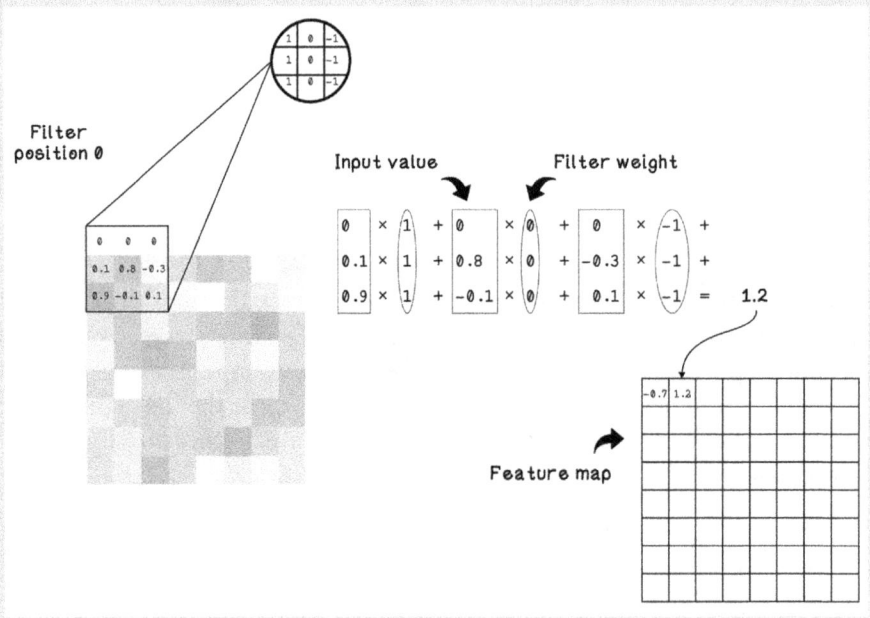

This process is applied to all the other nodes in the layer. We may have emergent nodes to detect vertical lines, horizontal lines, a certain rough texture, and much more. Each node has its own filter weights and results in a separate 8×8 feature map, as depicted in figure 12.26.

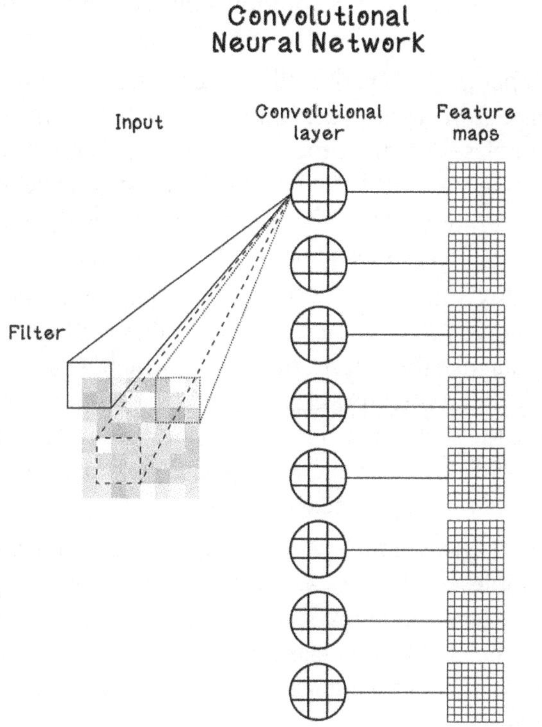

Figure 12.26 Feature maps produced by a convolutional layer

U-Net

Now that we have a fundamental understanding of CNNs, we're ready to explore the innovation that makes modern image generation possible: *U-Net*, the state-of-the-art architecture that powers virtually all modern diffusion models and the one that we will build in this chapter. The U-Net is a special type of CNN designed specifically for image-to-image tasks. Its key innovation is a U-shape design with three core components:

- *Encoder (downsample path)*—Think of this path as a summarizer. It progressively shrinks the image using convolutional layers, forcing the network to move beyond individual pixels to capture the high-level context and generalize better. As the image gets smaller, the network gets better at understanding what the image contains ("this is a face") but loses the precise information about where the fine details are located. This process creates a rich but low-resolution summary of the image's abstract meaning.

- *Decoder (upsample path)*—This path is like an artist tasked with reconstructing the full-resolution image from an abstract summary created by the downsample path. It progressively upsamples the feature maps using transposed convolutions, taking the high-level concepts ("a face") and attempting to add the fine details back in. By itself, it would struggle to position every edge and texture perfectly because much of the precise spatial information was lost during downsampling.

- *Skip connections*—This is the U-Net's superpower and the solution to the upsampling path's problem. A *skip connection* is a shortcut. It takes the high-resolution feature map from an early stage of the downsample path, which is rich in fine spatial details, and feeds it directly to the corresponding layer in the upsample path. This allows the decoder to combine the abstract "what" information from the deep layers with the precise "where" information from the early layers, making it exceptionally good at reconstructing images with high fidelity.

- *Bridge (aka bottleneck)*: This is the lowest point in the U-shape path, connecting the end of the downsample path to the start of the upsample path. It processes the most compressed, abstract representation of the image. In a diffusion model, this stage is the critical one in which the timestep and text embeddings are injected, combining the model's understanding of the image with the guidance of the text label before reconstruction begins.

Figure 12.27 illustrates the U-Net. The initial stage of preparing the training has already been covered in this chapter; now we have to feed that data into the U-Net itself.

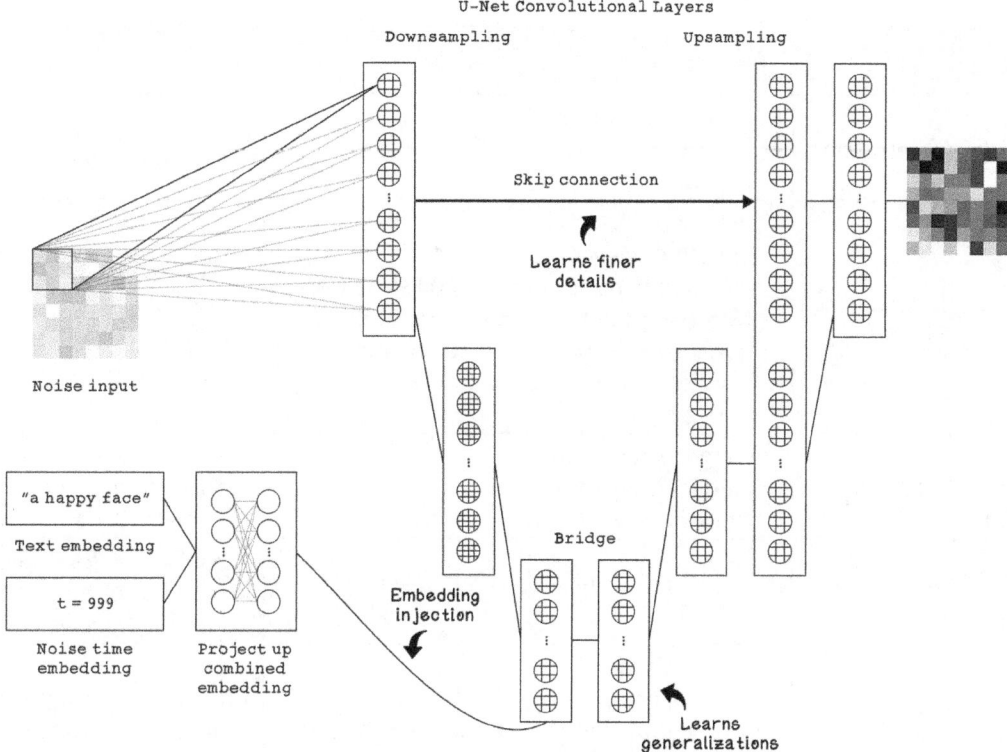

Figure 12.27 The U-Net architecture

The unique structure of the U-Net makes it the perfect tool for our diffusion model. It can look at a noisy image, understand the high-level context, and use the fine-grained skip connections to precisely predict the noise in every pixel.

Table 12.3 shows the concerns and hyperparameters for the diffusion model and U-Net. Use it as a reference as you work through each step in the denoising and learning process.

Table 12.3 The hyperparameters for the diffusion model

Hyperparameter	Rule of thumb	Toy diffusion example	Real-world diffusion model
Image resolution	Based on training data and available GPU memory	8×8	512×512 or 1,024×1024
Diffusion timesteps (T)	Large enough for a smooth transition from data to noise. More steps can improve quality but are slower to train and sample.	1,000 steps for training, 1,000 steps for inference	1,000 steps for training, 20 to 50 steps for inference
Batch size	As large as can fit on GPU memory for stable gradients	1	256 - 2,048+ (distributed over many GPUs)
Channels	Based on the training image format	1 (grayscale pixels only)	3 (for RGB), 4 (for RGB and alpha for transparency)
Attention mechanism	Essential for conditioning on text and capturing long-range spatial relationships	Not used (text embedding is added directly)	Cross-attention layers at multiple U-Net depths
Text embedding dimensions	Determined by the pretrained text encoder	16 dimensions	768 or 1,024 dimensions
Text embedding projection	Projects the generic text embedding into a space tailored for the U-Net	Multinode-Linear-Projection (MPL) 16 dimensions to 64 dimensions	Projects text embedding (e.g., 768 dimensions) to match U-Net's internal width (e.g., 4,096 dimensions)
Timestep embedding dimensions	A hyperparameter balancing expressiveness and efficiency	16 dimensions	Typically larger (e.g., 320 dimensions)
Timestep embedding projection	Projects the time signal into a space that can be added to image features	MLP 16 dimensions to 64 dimensions	Projects time embedding to match the U-Net

Table 12.3 The hyperparameters for the diffusion model (*continued*)

Hyperparameter	Rule of thumb	Toy diffusion example	Real-world diffusion model
U-Net base width	A core-capacity parameter. More channels allow for more complex features but increase model size.	32 nodes downsampled to 64 nodes	320 to 1,280+ nodes
U-Net depth	Deeper models capture more hierarchical features. Usually, there are 3 to 5 downsample/ upsample blocks.	1 downsample/ upsample block	4 to 5 downsample/ upsample blocks
Bridge size	The channel count at the deepest point of the U-Net	64 channels	1,280 channels

Figure 12.28 is a visualization of the entire diffusion architecture that we'll use in our example.

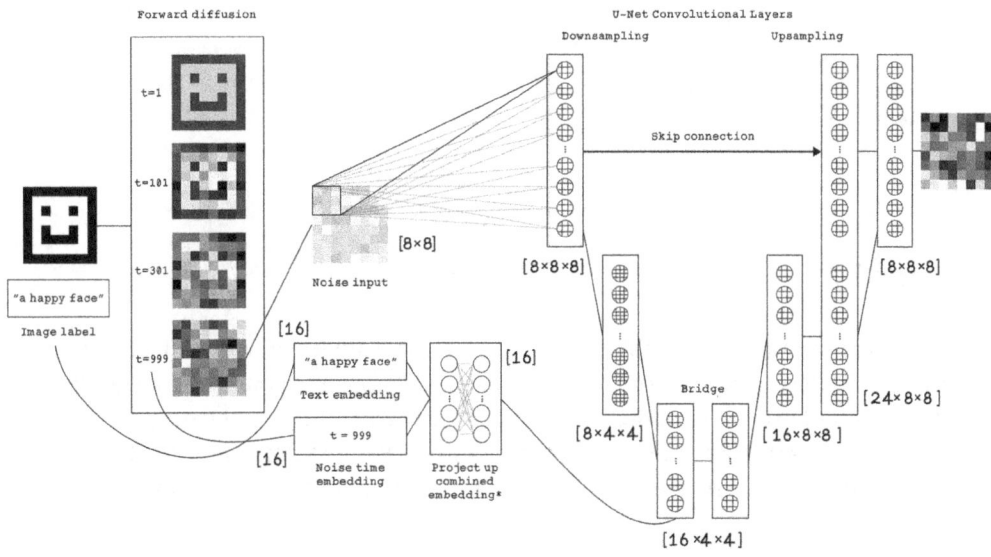

Figure 12.28 The U-Net architecture for our example

You'll see the following:

1. The original "a happy face" training image has noise added to it with forward diffusion to create our noisy training data.
2. A noisy image is fed into a convolutional layer to find initial specific features.
3. The results of that convolutional layer are fed into a downsample convolution layer, making the image dimensions go from 8×8 to 4×4 and compressing the information to find more general features.
4. The results of the downsample layer are fed into the bridge to find the most general features.
5. The text embedding and timestep embedding are fed through a feed-forward network.
6. The text embedding and timestep embedding are combined with the compressed image data in the bridge, essentially mixing the generalized understanding with the text label.
7. The results of those feature maps are upscaled from 4×4 back to 8×8 to smartly interpolate what the image could be from the generalized information.
8. The skip connection combines the results of the initial convolutional layer with the results of the upscale layer, resulting in both generalized information and information on finer details.
9. The convolutional layers compress those inputs in a single 8×8 matrix output to represent the predicted image at a timestep.

> **NOTE** Don't worry if this process looks daunting. We'll dive into the steps in the next section.

Denoise: From numbers to an image

Now that we've prepared the inputs and designed the deep learning architecture, we can explore the denoising process of U-Net (figure 12.29). U-Net's goal is to look at the 8×8 input matrix and predict the exact noise pattern that was added to the original clean image. It does this by summarizing the image into more abstracted representations to understand its essence and then skillfully reconstructing it by removing the noise.

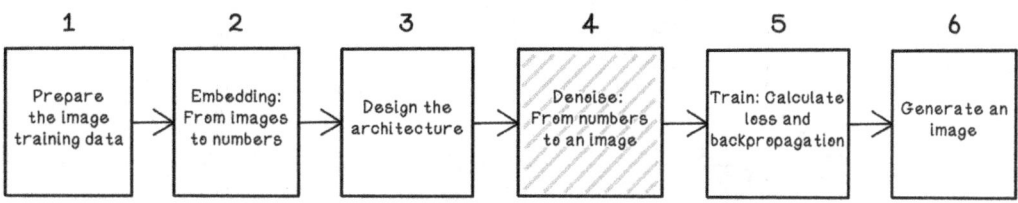

Figure 12.29 Denoising in the diffusion model training workflow

Encoder: Downsampling layers

The first half of U-Net is the encoder, or downsampling path. Its job is to act like a summarizer. It takes the high-resolution noisy image and progressively shrinks it, forcing the network to move beyond individual pixels and capture the abstract, high-level context of the image. It answers the question "What am I looking at?"

First convolutional layer

The 8×8 noisy image enters a convolutional layer with eight unique 3×3 filters. Each filter slides across the image, performing a dot product at every position. This operation, along with an added bias for each filter, produces an 8×8×8 tensor of feature maps because we have eight nodes in this convolutional layer. This tensor passes through a few more steps:

1. *Calculate the feature maps.* This step is the primary feature-extraction step. Each of the eight unique 3×3 filters slides across the entire 8×8 noisy input image. As discussed earlier, at every one of the 64 positions, each filter performs a dot-product calculation with the image patch underneath it. After the dot product is calculated, a single learnable number is added to the result. Because there are eight independent filters, this process creates eight unique feature maps, resulting in the 8×8×8 tensor. Figure 12.30 shows only the top-left value for each feature map.

Feature
maps

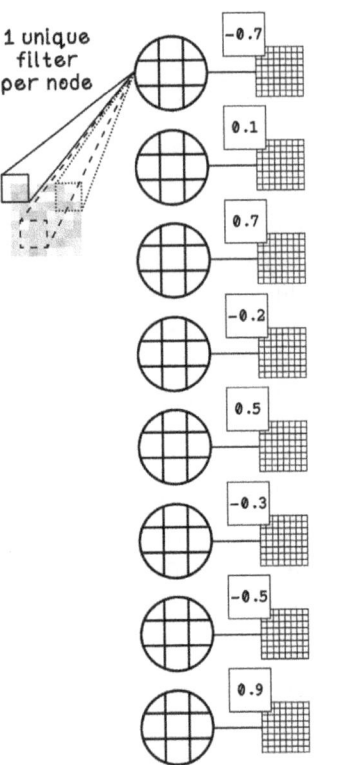

1 unique
filter
per node

-0.7

0.1

0.7

-0.2

0.5

-0.3

-0.5

0.9

Figure 12.30 The first pixel of all feature maps produced by the first convolutional layer

2. *Perform group normalization.* Before the feature maps are passed to the activation function, they go through a normalization step. As data flows through a deep network, the distribution of values in each layer can change wildly—a problem known as *internal covariate shift*. This makes it difficult for the network to learn effectively; it's like trying to hit a moving target.

    Group normalization solves this problem by recentering and rescaling the data. It takes the eight output feature maps and divides them into smaller, predefined groups. For each group, it calculates a single mean and standard deviation and then uses them to normalize the values only within that group.

    Think of it like this: if the eight feature maps are sketches by a team of artists, group normalization is like having four art directors, each of whom is responsible for a small team of two artists. Each director adjusts the overall brightness and contrast of their team's set of sketches to ensure that they're consistent before being passed on. This stabilization makes the training process much more robust and efficient.

For simplicity, we're using one group (art director) for all eight feature maps in our layer. In the example shown in figure 12.31, we're considering only the first pixel in each feature map. First, we calculate the group mean by adding all eight values and then dividing by 8. Next, we find the standard deviation for each value by subtracting the original value from the feature map from the mean and squaring it. Finally, we find the normalized values using the original value, mean, and standard deviation.

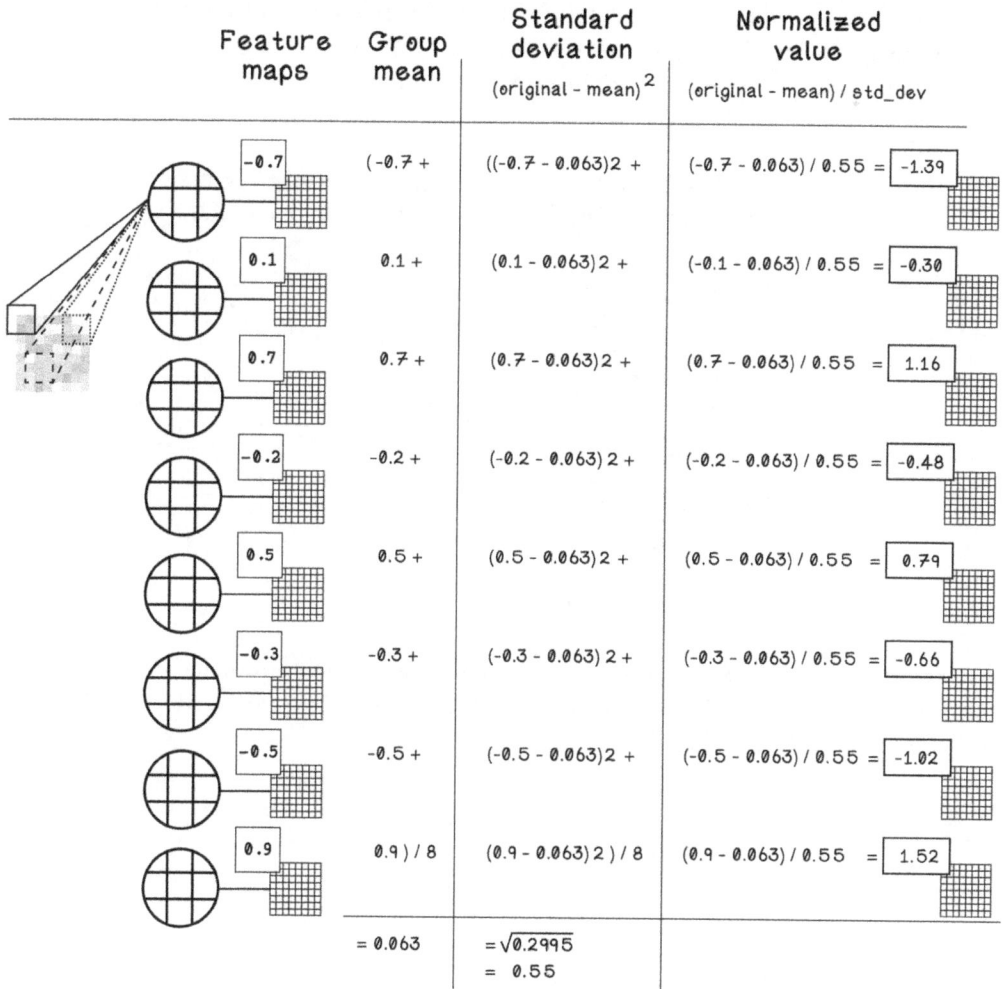

Figure 12.31 Normalized values for the first pixel in all feature maps produced from the first convolutional layer

3. *Apply the sigmoid-weighted Linear Unit (SiLU) activation function.* A nonlinear activation function is applied to every number in the 8×8×8 tensor. This crucial step allows the network to learn complex patterns beyond simple linear relationships.

   The SiLU function (also known as *Swish*) is calculated by multiplying the input value (x) by the output of a sigmoid function applied to that same input (x × sigmoid(x)). For positive input values, it behaves similarly to the ReLU function, resulting in a nearly linear output. The key difference is its handling of negative values. Instead of outputting a hard zero, as ReLU does, SiLU produces a smooth curve that dips slightly below zero before approaching zero (figure 12.32). This smoothness can prevent the "dying ReLU" problem and often leads to better performance by allowing a more complex response and better gradient flow during training. See chapter 9 for more information about activation functions.

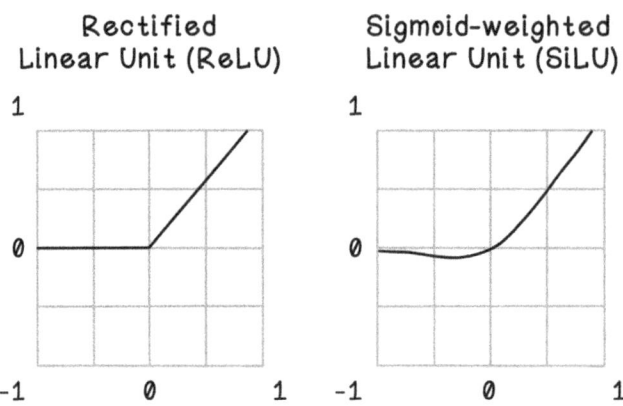

Figure 12.32 ReLU vs SiLU activation functions

The resulting 8×8×8 tensor, which we'll call h1, is rich with information about low-level features and saved in memory for the skip connection step that we'll work through later (figure 12.33).

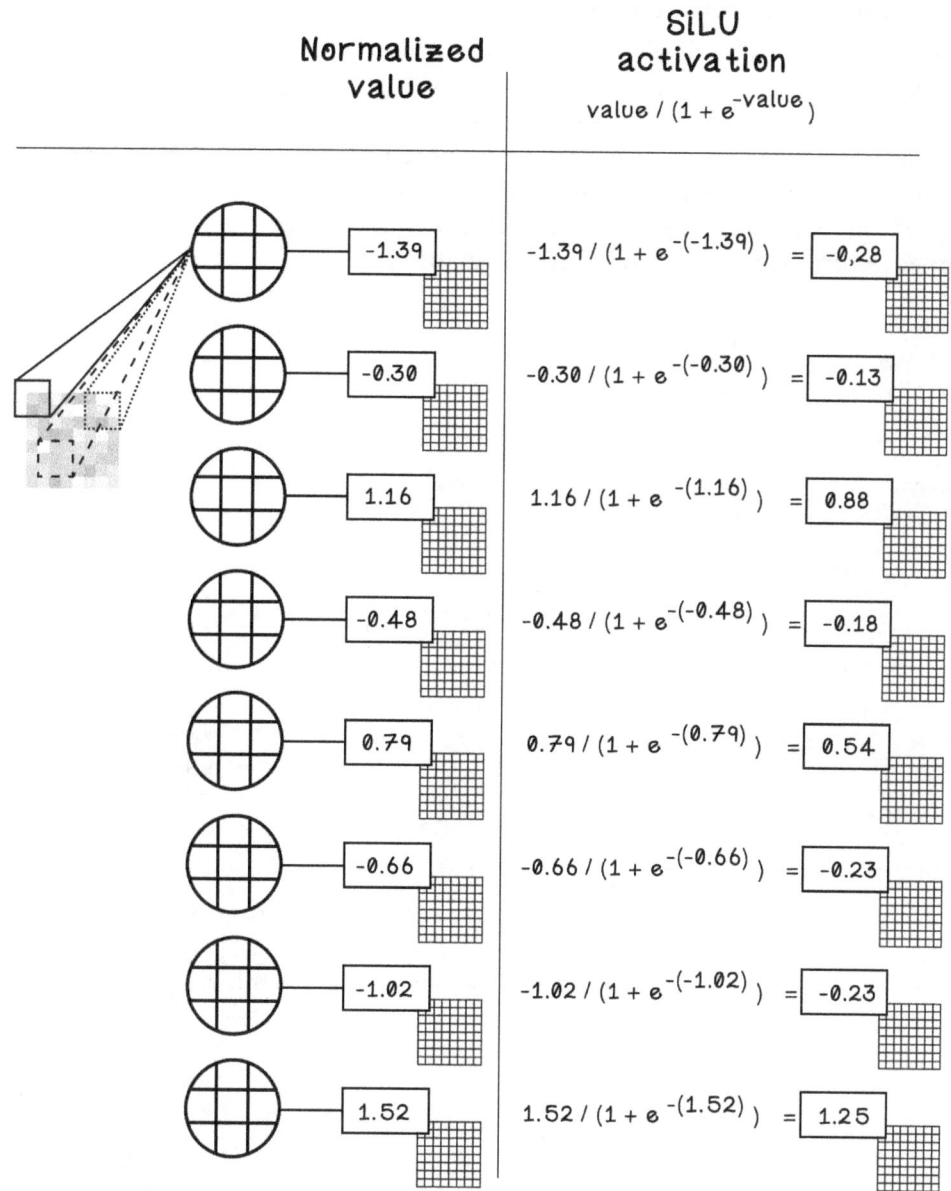

Figure 12.33 Calculations for the SiLU activation function

Python code sample for a convolutional layer

This code defines the first convolutional layer in the U-Net encoder, which extracts low-level features from a noisy input image. It begins by applying padding to preserve spatial dimensions; then it applies multiple learnable 3×3 filters across the image using a sliding window. At each position, it computes the dot product between the filter and the local region of the image, adds a bias term, and stores the result in the corresponding output map. The output of all filters is stacked into a 3D tensor (h1), representing the first set of learned feature maps for further processing in the network.

Adds a border of zeros around the image

```python
def apply_padding(image, padding):
    return np.pad(image, ((padding, padding),
    (padding, padding)), mode='constant', constant_values=0)

def first_convolution(noisy_image, num_filters):
    filter_size = 3
    stride = 1
    padding = 1

    padded_image = apply_padding(noisy_image, padding)

    H, W = noisy_image.shape

    filters = np.random.randn(num_filters,
    filter_size, filter_size) * 0.01
    bias = np.random.randn(num_filters) * 0.01

    feature_maps = []

    for filter_index in range(num_filters):
        current_filter = filters[filter_index]
        current_bias = bias[filter_index]
        output_map = np.zeros((H, W))

        for i in range(H):
            for j in range(W):
                region = padded_image[i : i + filter_size, j : j
                + filter_size]

                value = np.sum(region * current_filter)
                + current_bias

                output_map[i][j] = value

        feature_maps.append(output_map)
    h1 = np.stack(feature_maps, axis=0)
```

Collection of matrices that start as random noise, then learn to detect features

Iterates through every single pixel coordinate in the image

The filter only "looks" at a tiny 3×3 neighborhood

multiplies the image pixels by the filter weights

Combines all the individual feature maps into a single 3D tensor

Downsampling

The entire purpose of downsampling is to increase the network's high-level understanding of the areas in the original image that each respective node considers. Think of it like squinting when looking at a detailed painting. You lose your ability to see the fine brushstrokes, but you get a much better sense of the overall composition, shapes, and colors. This process forces the network to learn high-level, abstract concepts (such as "eye" or "mouth") instead of simple features (such as "vertical edge" or "corner"). It's a conglomeration of more specific features.

Next, the tensor from the first layer, h1, is passed to a second convolutional layer. This layer's primary job is to downsample (shrink) the feature maps, essentially lowering the resolution of the image.

In figure 12.34, each node in the downsample convolutional layer accepts every feature map from the first convolutional layer. This means each node will have eight unique filters corresponding to each input. Also, these filters are 4×4, not 3×3 as in the first convolutional layer. Furthermore, the output of these nodes results in a 4×4 feature map instead of an 8×8 feature map.

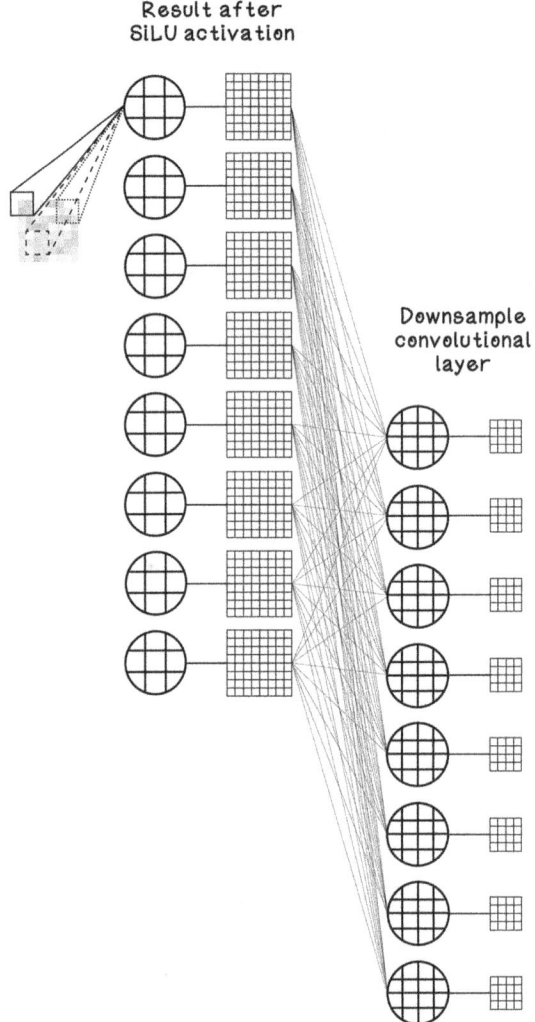

Figure 12.34 The downsampling convolutional layer in our U-Net

The model achieves a 4×4 feature map by using filters with a stride of 2, meaning that the filters jump 2 pixels at a time as they slide across the input instead of 1 pixel at a time. This approach is a good way to halve the height and width of the feature maps, producing a more compressed summary of the image's content. In our example, the 8×8 feature maps are shrunk to 4×4. Figure 12.35 illustrates how the different positions of the 4×4 filter with a stride of 2 correspond to the new pixel values. Note the additional border of blank values that has been added to the input feature map. This border is the padding that was mentioned in the CNN section. It helps preserve the image size and edge data during downsampling and upsampling.

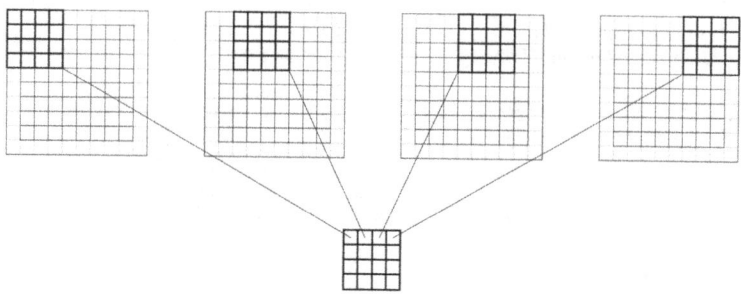

Figure 12.35 How filters scan an image with padding

Exercise: What is the next position of the filter?

Determine the filter position as it scans.

Solution:

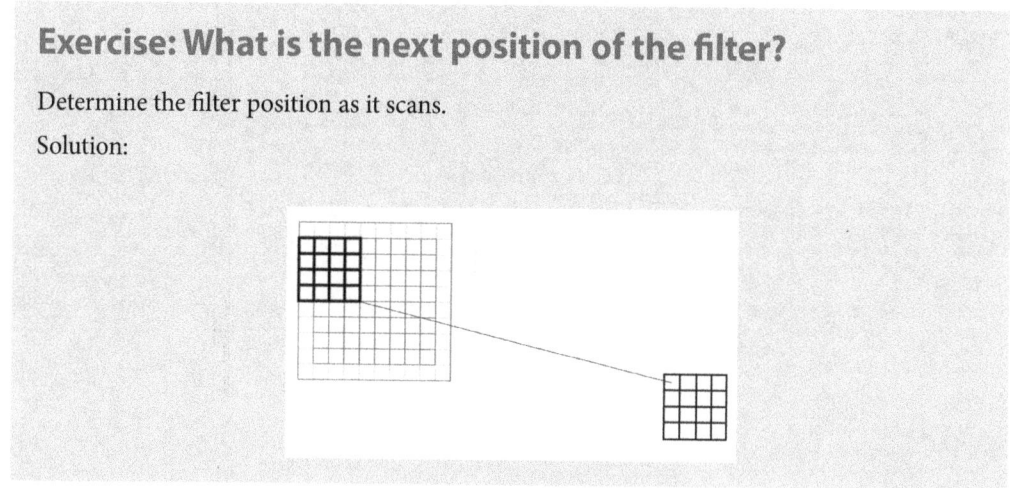

Because the input, `h1`, has multiple channels (in this case, eight feature maps from the first layer), the convolution process at this stage is more complex than in the first convolution layer. For our example, each filter in the downsampling layer is eight layers deep, designed to process all eight input channels simultaneously. To calculate a single pixel value in the new output feature map, the network performs eight separate convolutions (one for each input feature map) and then sums all the results. This step combines the simple features detected in the first layer into more complex and abstract representations.

In figure 12.36, all feature maps are being processed by the first node of the downsampling layer. It's important to note that each feature map will be associated with a unique filter of its own unique weights (these weights are adjusted separately during backpropagation) and that all filter slides will happen for each node.

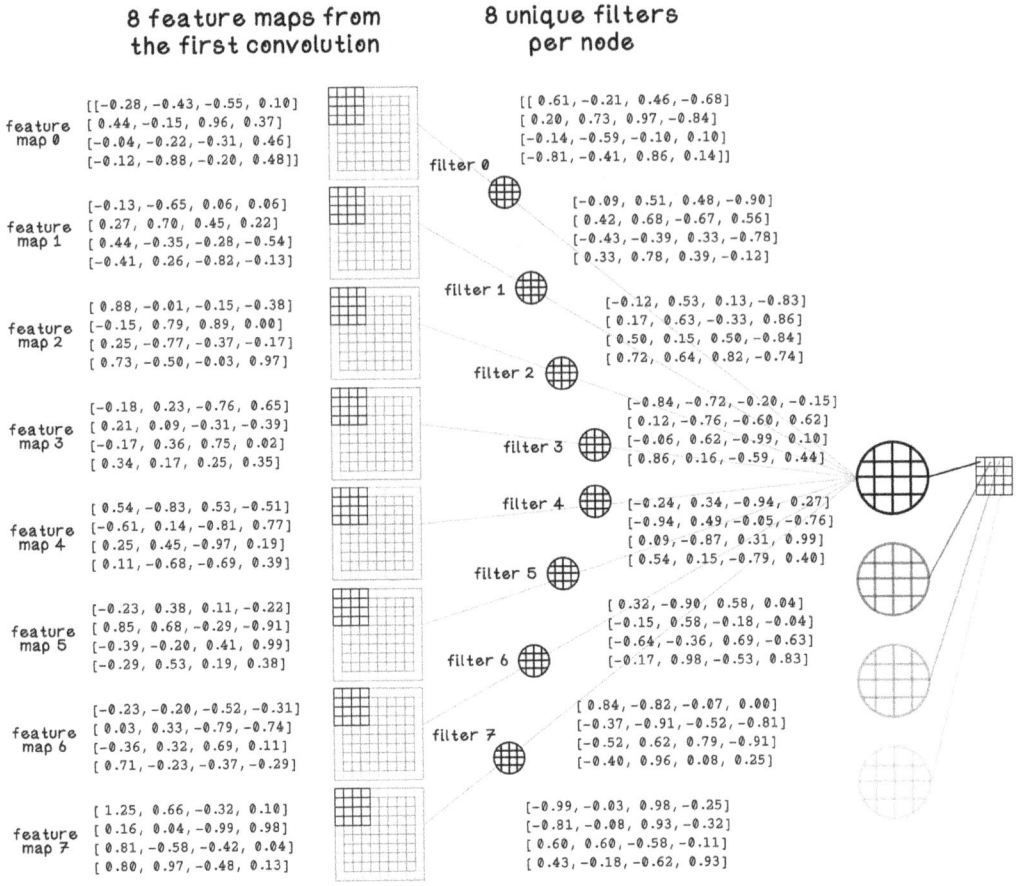

Figure 12.36 Calculations for the downsampling convolutional layer in our U-Net

Now that we have the foundational idea of how initial feature maps are processed by the downsampling layer, let's look at how to find the single value for a single pixel. Each feature map (8×8) is multiplied by its respective filter weights (4×4), resulting in a single scalar number, such as 0.75. This is done for every feature map and filter pair; then all results are summed to obtain the value for the pixel at that position. In figure 12.37, the top-left pixel in the 4×4 feature map is -0.646. As expected, this is done for all nodes in the layer, and in our case, because we have eight nodes in the downsampling layer, we have eight 4×4 feature maps.

```
convolution = sum(feature map * filter)

convolution 0 = 0.75
convolution 1 = 0.11
convolution 2 = -0.21
convolution 3 = -0.24
convolution 4 = -0.75
convolution 5 = 0.75
convolution 6 = 0.93
convolution 7 = -1.99

final pixel = sum(all convolutions)
```

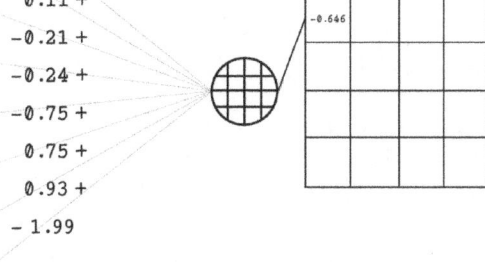

```
0.75 +
0.11 +
-0.21 +
-0.24 +
-0.75 +
0.75 +
0.93 +
- 1.99
```

Figure 12.37 Calculations for producing the final value for the first pixel in the feature map

Python code sample for downsampling

This code performs the downsampling convolutional step in the U-Net encoder. It takes a multichannel feature map and applies a set of learnable 4×4 filters with stride 2 and padding 1 to reduce the spatial resolution by half. Each output channel is computed by combining contributions from all input channels through weighted dot products over sliding patches, summing them, and adding a bias. The resulting output maps are stacked into a 3D tensor (h2), which captures increasingly abstract features while compressing the spatial size, preparing the data for deeper layers in the network.

Adds a border of zeros around the image

```python
def apply_padding_3d(tensor, padding):
    return np.pad(tensor, ((0, 0), (padding, padding),
      (padding, padding)), mode='constant', constant_values=0)

def downsample_convolution(feature_maps_in, num_output_channels):
    input_channels = feature_maps_in.shape[0]
    input_height = feature_maps_in.shape[1]
```

```
filter_size = 4
stride = 2
padding = 1

padded_maps = apply_padding_3d(feature_maps_in, padding)

output_height = (input_height + 2 * padding - filter_size)
 // stride + 1
output_width = output_height

filters = np.random.randn(num_output_channels,
 input_channels, filter_size, filter_size) * 0.01
biases = np.random.randn(num_output_channels) * 0.01

feature_maps_out = []

for k in range(num_output_channels):
    current_bias = biases[k]
    output_map = np.zeros((output_height, output_width))

    for i in range(output_height):
        for j in range(output_width):

            accumulation_sum = 0

            for c in range(input_channels):

                current_filter = filters[k, c]

                r_start, c_start = i * stride, j * stride
                region = padded_maps[c, r_start : r_start +
                 filter_size, c_start : c_start + filter_size]

                accumulation_sum += np.sum(region * current_filter)

            output_map[i, j] =
             accumulation_sum + current_bias

    feature_maps_out.append(output_map)

h2 = np.stack(feature_maps_out, axis=0)

return h2
```

Determines the size of the new image

These are the "eyes" of the model

Instead of moving one pixel at a time, the filter jumps 2 pixels

Adds a bias value to the sum, giving the model more flexibility

Bridge

The bridge is the lowest point of the U, connecting the encoder and the decoder. It receives the most compressed and abstract summary of the image. This is the critical point at which the image information meets the external guidance from our text prompt and timestep. The image information is as abstract and generalized as possible. In figure

12.38, we see that the initial convolutional layer produced eight feature maps of the original size; then the downsampling layer produced eight 4×4 feature maps, which are the inputs for the bridge convolutional layer.

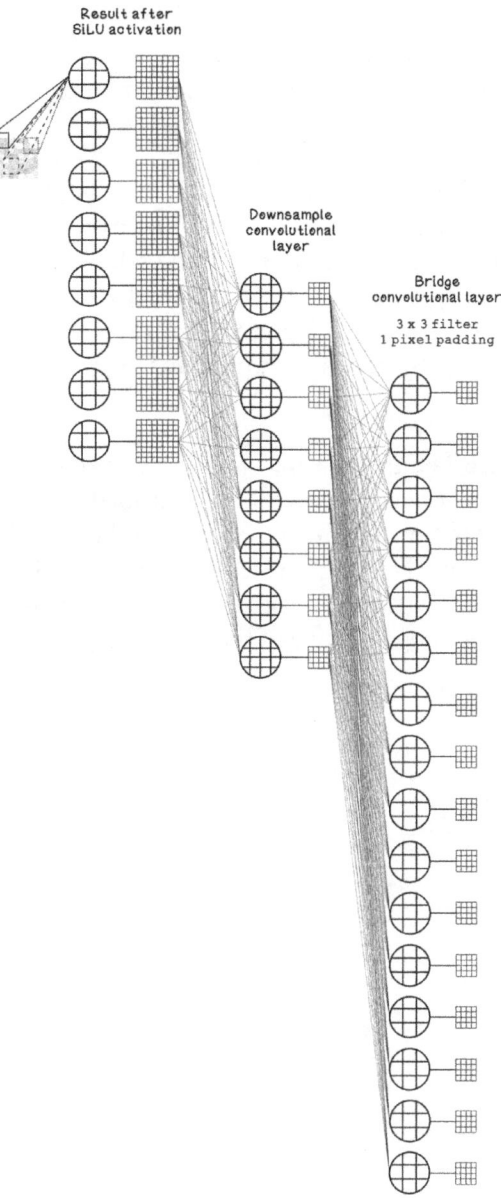

Figure 12.38 The bridge convolutional layer in our U-Net

Notice that the convolution layer in the bridge has 16 nodes instead of 8. Because the number of channels increases at this stage, the network has a greater capacity to create a rich, expressive summary of the image's core content. Think of it as giving the model a larger vocabulary to describe the "what" of the image before reconstructing the "where" in the upsampling path.

Increasing the number of nodes in the bridge layer enhances the model's ability to capture complex, abstract information and prepares it to integrate guidance from the text and time embeddings.

Bridge convolution

The convolution layer at this level works similarly to the previous convolution layer. The 8×4×4 tensor from the previous layer enters the bridge and passes through another convolutional layer. This layer increases the node depth from 8 to 16, resulting in a 16×4×4 tensor. This tensor, called h2, represents the most abstract understanding of the image content and serves as the integration point for the text-label embedding.

Embedding injection

Now the external text label guidance is injected. The text and time embeddings are added to form a single 16D vector. This vector is reshaped into a 16×1×1 tensor and added to the 16×4×4 h2 tensor. The first number from the embedding vector is added to every pixel in the first channel of h2, the second number is added to every pixel in the second channel, and so on. This step infuses the prompt and timestep information into the network's generalized understanding of the image (figure 12.39).

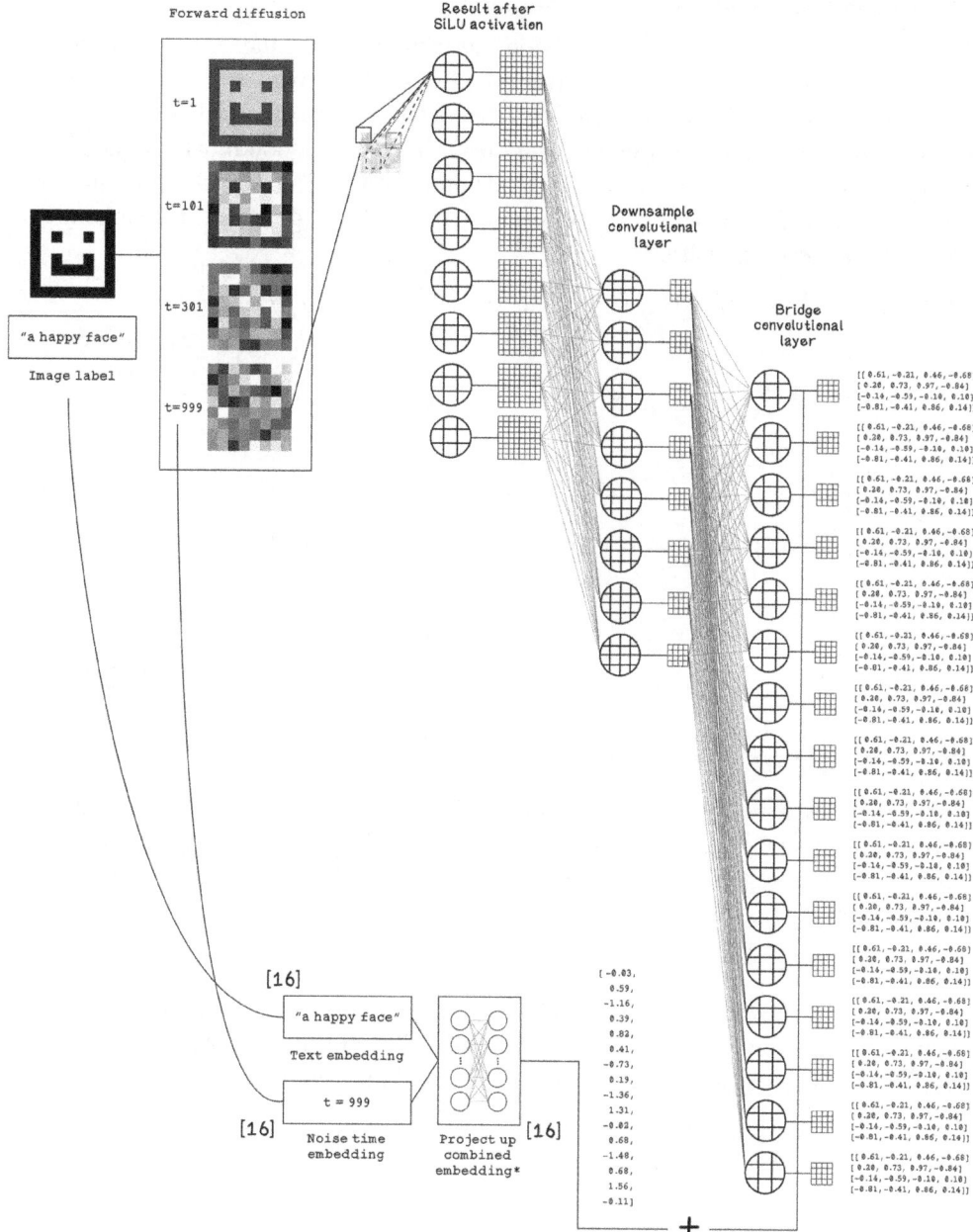

Figure 12.39 How the text embedding and timestep embedding are injected

Python code sample for injecting embeddings

This code injects text and timestep embeddings into the bridge tensor at the bottleneck of the U-Net. First, it combines the two embeddings elementwise; then it reshapes the result to match the spatial dimensions of each feature map channel. The reshaped embedding is broadcast and added to every pixel in the corresponding channel of the bridge tensor. This operation allows the model to condition its internal representation on the prompt and the current diffusion timestep, effectively guiding the denoising process in the decoding path.

```
def inject_embeddings(bridge_tensor,
    text_embedding, timestep_embedding):

    combined_embedding = text_embedding
    + timestep_embedding

    channels = combined_embedding.shape[0]
    reshaped_embedding = combined_embedding.reshape(channels, 1, 1)

    output_tensor = bridge_tensor + reshaped_embedding

    return output_tensor
```

Combines the "meaning" with the "schedule"

Every single pixel in every feature map receives the guidance signal

Decoder: Upsampling layers

At this point, we have 16 4×4 feature maps that include the generalized image data, the text-label embedding data, and the timestep embedding data. The first step of the decoder (upsampling process) is to take the compressed 4×4 feature maps from the bridge and enlarge them.

Upsampling

The simplest way to visualize this process is through an operation such as nearest-neighbor interpolation, as shown in figure 12.40. With this method, each pixel from the smaller feature map is duplicated to fill a 2×2 area of the new, larger feature map.

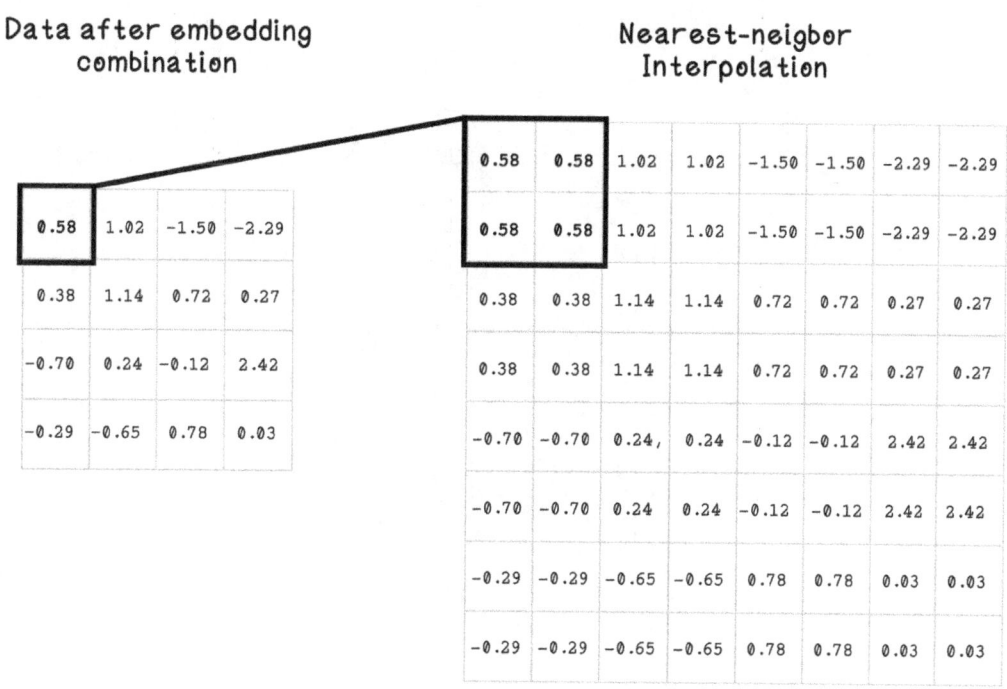

Figure 12.40 Simplistic upsampling with nearest neighbor interpolation

Although this approach is a fast, straightforward way to double the resolution to 8×8, it's basic. For a more sophisticated reconstruction, the U-Net uses a transposed convolution (figure 12.41). Unlike simple interpolation, a *transposed convolution* is a learnable layer similar to the other convolutional layers you've seen. It doesn't just copy pixels but also uses a set of trainable filters to intelligently project the data from the low-resolution feature map onto a larger feature map.

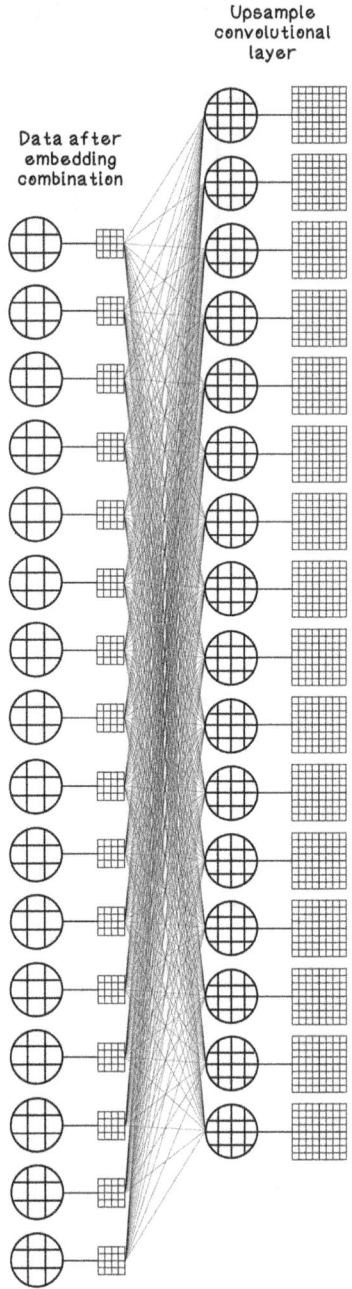

Figure 12.41 The upsampling layer in our U-Net

Imagine hiring a skilled artist. You give the artist the low-resolution feature map, and they use their learned skills to paint a large detailed version. They don't just copy the lines but also intelligently add the right brushstrokes and textures to create a high-quality result. Here's how the process works:

1. The network takes one pixel at a time from the small feature map.
2. Instead of reading a patch to produce one pixel (like a normal convolution), it uses a learnable filter to paint a larger patch of pixels on the bigger output map.
3. It repeats the preceding steps for every single pixel in the small map. Where the painted patches overlap, their values are added together.

The filter's weights are learned during the training process. The network figures out the best way to add detail when upsampling, allowing it to reconstruct a much cleaner and more coherent image.

After this upsampling convolution step, we have 16 8×8 feature maps. These maps have the generalized image data, text-label embedding, and timestep embedding and have been upscaled to the actual dimensions of the images we're working with.

Skipping connection

Up to this point, the network has been good at understanding the high-level context of the "what" an image contains, but it loses precise spatial information about the "where" of fine details. The skip-connection step is a U-Net superpower that solves this problem. It acts as a shortcut for feeding the decoder a direct copy of the high-resolution details that it needs to reconstruct the image accurately.

In figure 12.42, the skip connection takes the rich, detailed feature maps from the early stage of the encoder and sends them directly across to the corresponding layer in the decoder. Now this decoder layer has 8×8×8 tensor h1 and stacks it with the 16×8×8 upsampled tensor from the preceding step. This concatenation process creates a single 24×8×8 tensor.

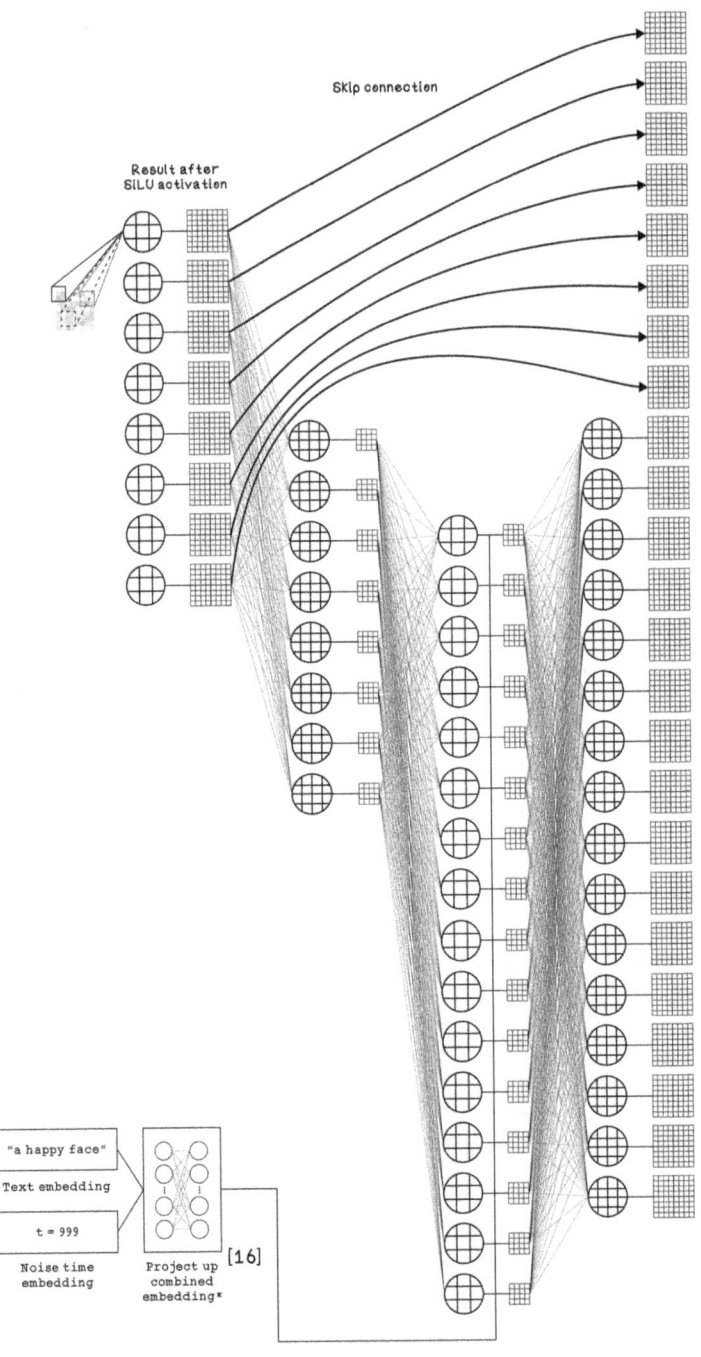

12.42 How skip-connection feature maps are combined with the upsampled feature maps

This combined tensor is the key to a high-quality reconstruction. It gives the decoder both the abstract information from the deep layers and bridge and the precise information from the early layers, allowing the model to generate a final image that's not only conceptually correct but also has well-defined details.

Python code sample for upsampling

This code performs transposed convolution for upsampling in the decoder path of the U-Net. It increases the spatial resolution of the input tensor by using learned 4×4 filters to project each input pixel into a larger output space. At each location, the pixel value is multiplied by a filter and the result is added to a larger output region, effectively painting detail back into the image. Overlapping contributions are summed, and a bias is added to each output channel. This operation enables the model to reconstruct higher-resolution images from compressed feature maps.

```python
def upsample_transposed_convolution(input_tensor, num_output_channels):
    input_channels = input_tensor.shape[0]
    input_height = input_tensor.shape[1]
    input_width = input_tensor.shape[2]

    filter_size = 4
    stride = 2
    padding = 1

    output_height = (input_height - 1) * stride
    + filter_size - 2 * padding
    output_width = (input_width - 1) * stride
    + filter_size - 2 * padding

    filters = np.random.randn(num_output_channels, input_channels,
    filter_size, filter_size) * 0.01
    biases = np.random.randn(num_output_channels) * 0.01

    output_tensor = np.zeros((num_output_channels,
    output_height, output_width))

    for oc in range(num_output_channels):
        for ic in range(input_channels):
            current_filter = filters[oc, ic]

            for i in range(input_height):
                for j in range(input_width):
                    value = input_tensor[ic, i, j]

                    for m in range(filter_size):
                        for n in range(filter_size):

                            out_y = i * stride + m - padding
                            out_x = j * stride + n - padding
```

Calculates the larger output size

Broadcasts a single input pixel's value back out

```
                    if 0 <= out_y < output_height and 0 <=
                ⇒out_x < output_width:
                        output_tensor[oc, out_y, out_x] +=
                    ⇒value * current_filter[m, n]

        output_tensor[oc] += biases[oc]

    return output_tensor
```

For every single pixel in the small input, the model multiplies it by a 4×4 filter and "paints" the result onto the output canvas

Final convolutions

Before we look at the final layers, it's important to remember the U-Net's single, specific job in this process. It receives three key inputs: a noisy image, the text prompt, and a timestep (which indicates how much noise the image contains). Its goal is to analyze this information and output a prediction of the exact noise pattern that was added to the image for that specific timestep.

The rich 24×8×8 tensor, which now contains both the high-level concepts from the decoder and the fine-grained details from the skip connection, is passed through a final set of convolutional layers (figure 12.43).

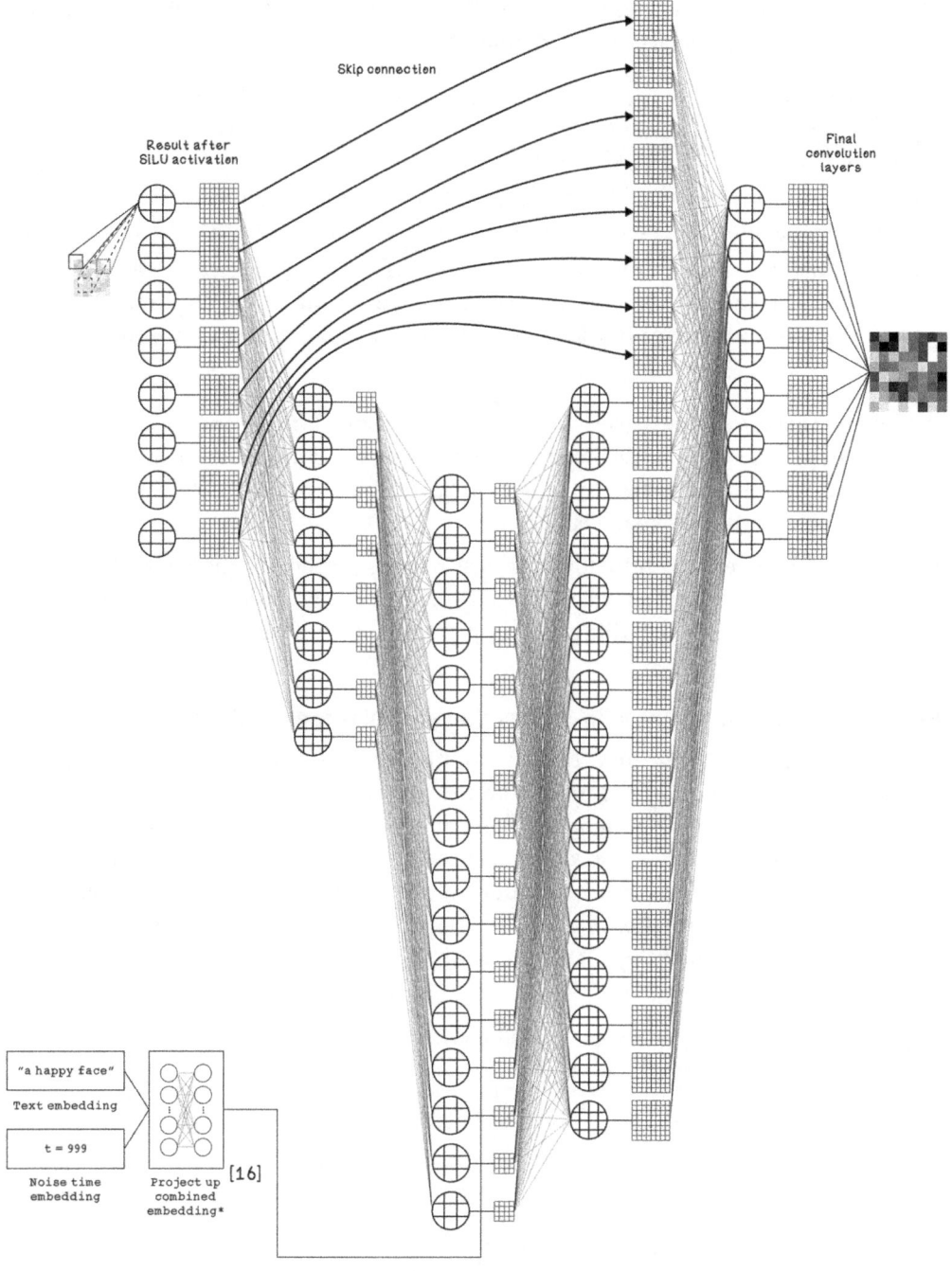

Skip connection

Result after
SiLU activation

Final
convolution
layers

"a happy face"

Text embedding

t = 999

Noise time
embedding

Project up
combined
embedding*

[16]

Figure 12.43 The final convolutions to produce a noise prediction

At this last stage, the model must distill all of this complex information into a single useful output. Here is how the final layers accomplish this task:

- *Blending and distilling*—The first of these final layers takes the 24-node tensor and performs a blending operation. It must learn to synthesize the two distinct types of information it received (the generalized and the detailed). This convolutional layer reduces the channels from 24 to 8 while keeping the resulting feature maps 8×8, effectively distilling the most important combined features into a manageable tensor.

- *Final prediction*—This layer is the last convolutional layer, and it has a single vital job: taking the 32 blended feature maps and collapsing them into a final 8×8 image. The final output is the model's pixel-by-pixel prediction of the noise that was added at the beginning of the process.

Remember that the entire U-Net architecture was trained for this one specific regression task: predicting the exact noise pattern for a given image at a given timestep, guided by a text prompt. This final matrix isn't the desired clean image, but it's the key that unlocks it as the model learns over many epochs.

We've now completed the entire forward-pass process for the diffusion model. After one epoch, the model would have processed a noise step and produced a prediction for the initial noise at timestep 0 (likely a wrong prediction because this epoch was the first one).

Python code sample for the skip-connection and final convolutions

This code defines the skip-connection convolution in the decoder stage of a U-Net. It merges the upsampled feature maps with the corresponding encoder feature maps (the skip connection) by concatenating them along the channel axis. Then a 3×3 convolution is applied across the combined tensor using multiple learnable filters. Each filter processes all input channels to produce refined output feature maps that blend high-level abstract information with fine spatial details. This operation enables precise reconstruction of the image by preserving both the "what" and the "where" from earlier layers.

```
def apply_padding_3d(tensor, padding):
    return np.pad(tensor, ((0, 0),
      (padding, padding), (padding, padding)),
      mode='constant', constant_values=0)

def skip_convolution(upsampled_tensor, skip_tensor,
    num_output_channels):

    input_tensor = np.concatenate
      ([upsampled_tensor, skip_tensor], axis=0)
```

Glues two different data sources together

```
input_channels = input_tensor.shape[0]
output_height = input_tensor.shape[1]
output_width = input_tensor.shape[2]

filter_size = 3
stride = 1
padding = 1

padded_input = apply_padding_3d(input_tensor, padding)

filters = np.random.randn(num_output_channels, input_channels,
    filter_size, filter_size) * 0.01
biases = np.random.randn(num_output_channels) * 0.01

output_tensor =
vnp.zeros((num_output_channels, output_height, output_width))

for oc in range(num_output_channels):
    current_bias = biases[oc]

    for i in range(output_height):
        for j in range(output_width):

            accumulation_sum = 0

            for ic in range(input_channels):
                current_filter = filters[oc, ic]

                region = padded_input[ic, i : i + filter_size, j :
                    + filter_size]

                accumulation_sum += np.sum(region * current_filter)

            output_tensor[oc, i, j] =
                accumulation_sum + current_bias

return output_tensor
```

The convolution scans across the combined stack

A new set of features that are significantly more accurate than the upsampled version alone

The following code performs the final output convolution in the U-Net, reducing a multichannel tensor to a single-channel image. It applies one 3×3 convolutional filter per input channel, computes the dot product over each patch, sums the results across channels, and adds a scalar bias. The resulting 2D matrix represents the model's prediction of the noise present in the original image. This output is used during training to calculate the loss or during inference to denoise the image step by step toward a clean result.

```
def final_output_convolution(input_tensor):
    input_channels = input_tensor.shape[0]
    height = input_tensor.shape[1]
    width = input_tensor.shape[2]

    filter_size = 3
    stride = 1
    padding = 1

    padded_input =
    apply_padding_3d(input_tensor, padding)

    filters = np.random.randn(input_channels,
    filter_size, filter_size) * 0.01

    bias = np.random.randn() * 0.01

    output_image = np.zeros((height, width))

    for i in range(height):
        for j in range(width):

            accumulation_sum = 0

            for c in range(input_channels):
                current_filter = filters[c]

                region = padded_input[c, i : i +
                filter_size, j : j + filter_size]

                value =
                np.sum(region * current_filter)
                accumulation_sum += value

            output_image[i, j] =
            accumulation_sum + bias

    return output_image
```

Apply padding to the input tensor to maintain spatial dimensions

Notice there is only one set of filters per input channel

A single bias value for the whole image

Unlike previous layers that returned 3D tensors, this layer returns a 2D grid

Looks through every single feature map the U-Net has generated

For every 3×3 area, the model calculates a single number

Train: Calculate loss and backpropagation

After the U-Net makes its prediction, learning begins. In this process, the model determines how wrong the prediction was and uses that information to improve itself (figure 12.44). This process is a critical two-step cycle: calculating a single loss score and then using that score to update every weight parameter in the network through backpropagation.

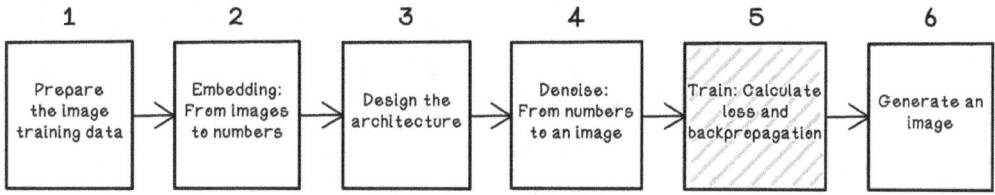

Figure 12.44 Learning in the diffusion model training life cycle

Calculating loss

The first step is getting a single number that measures exactly how wrong the model's prediction was. In our diffusion model, the U-Net predicts a noise pattern. Because we added the noise ourselves, we know precisely what the actual noise looks like at a specific timestep. Therefore, we can calculate the loss by comparing the predicted noise with the actual noise.

Because the U-Net performs a regression task (its goal is to predict the exact continuous values of the noise that was added to an image), mean squared error (MSE) is an ideal method for calculating loss because it measures the average difference between predicted and actual noise pixel by pixel.

MSE measures the average of the squares of the error—that is, the average squared difference between the predicted and actual values (figure 12.45).

Actual noise at timestep

```
[[ 0.25 -0.95  0.46  0.19 -0.69  0.78  0.94 -0.96 ]
 [-0.68 -0.88 -0.27  0.20 -0.84  0.78 -0.94 -0.56 ]
 [-0.57  0.71  0.61 -0.25  0.46 -0.91 -0.63 -0.88 ]
 [ 0.22 -0.67 -0.62  0.37 -0.13  0.39  0.71  0.88 ]
 [-0.32 -0.95  0.01 -0.90  0.54 -0.53  0.20  0.06 ]
 [ 0.97  0.47  0.73 -0.46  0.01 -0.92 -0.26 -0.81 ]
 [ 0.47 -0.96 -0.31  0.74  0.02  0.70  0.89 -0.45 ]
 [-0.46  0.58  0.11 -0.84 -0.68 -0.96  0.11 -0.91 ]]
```

Predicted noise at timestep

```
[[-0.20 -0.28  0.89 -0.58 -0.78 -0.36 -0.62  0.45 ]
 [-0.36  0.26 -0.13  0.62 -0.30  0.68  0.59  0.17 ]
 [-0.15 -0.41  0.12  0.64  0.84  0.87 -0.89  0.62 ]
 [ 0.99 -0.59  0.18 -0.96  0.33  0.47 -0.49 -0.42 ]
 [-0.63  0.34  0.33  0.69 -0.55 -0.51 -0.92 -0.26 ]
 [-0.38 -0.74 -0.69 -0.99  0.04 -0.40 -0.61  0.78 ]
 [ 0.53  0.40  0.69  0.97 -0.01  0.65  0.60  0.36 ]
 [-0.82 -0.83 -0.89 -0.64  0.10 -0.89 -0.83  0.15 ]]
```

Actual - Predicted

```
[[ 0.45 -0.67 -0.43  0.77  0.09  1.14  1.56 -1.42 ]
 [-0.32 -1.14 -0.14 -0.42 -0.55  0.10 -1.53 -0.73 ]
 [-0.41  1.12  0.49 -0.89 -0.38 -1.78  0.26 -1.49 ]
 [-0.77 -0.08 -0.80  1.33 -0.46 -0.08  1.20  1.30 ]
 [ 0.31 -1.29 -0.32 -1.59  1.09 -0.02  1.12  0.32 ]
 [ 1.34  1.21  1.42  0.52 -0.03 -0.52  0.35 -1.59 ]
 [-0.07 -1.36 -1.00 -0.22  0.03  0.06  0.29 -0.81 ]
 [ 0.36  1.41  1.00 -0.20 -0.78 -0.07  0.94 -1.06 ]]
```

Squared difference

```
[[0.21 0.45 0.18 0.59 0.01 1.30 2.43 2.01 ]
 [0.10 1.30 0.02 0.18 0.30 0.01 2.34 0.54 ]
 [0.17 1.26 0.24 0.79 0.14 3.17 0.07 2.21 ]
 [0.59 0.01 0.63 1.77 0.21 0.01 1.44 1.70 ]
 [0.10 1.67 0.10 2.52 1.19 0.00 1.25 0.10 ]
 [1.79 1.46 2.01 0.27 0.00 0.27 0.12 2.53 ]
 [0.00 1.85 1.00 0.05 0.00 0.00 0.08 0.65 ]
 [0.13 1.99 1.00 0.04 0.60 0.01 0.88 1.12 ]]
```

$$\text{Mean squared error} = \frac{\text{Sum of all squared difference}}{\text{Number of values}}$$

$$\text{Mean squared error} = \frac{44.86}{64} = 0.701$$

Figure 12.45 Calculations for finding the loss

When we use the MSE formula to calculate the loss, we have a loss of 0.701. We can interpret the loss as being quite large for the following reasons:

- *Loss = 0* is a perfect score. It means that the predicted noise matrix was identical to the actual noise matrix, with no error.
- *A low loss like 0.01* indicates that on average, the squared difference between the predicted and actual pixel values is tiny; the model is performing well, and its predictions are close to the truth.
- *A high loss like 2.0* indicates that on average, the predictions are far from the actual values; the model is performing poorly.

The absolute value of the loss at a specific time isn't as important as its trend over time. A primary use of the loss value during training is to see whether the value consistently decreases. A steadily decreasing loss means that the model is successfully learning from the training data with each backpropagation step. If the loss value increases, the model is getting worse over time. If the value stagnates over many epochs, the model is unlikely to improve by continuing for more epochs. Figure 12.46 illustrates a common ideal trend line for loss in diffusion models.

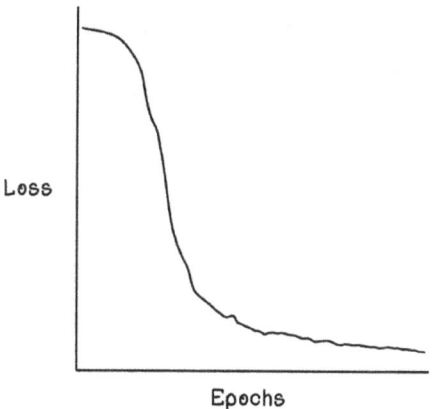

Figure 12.46 The ideal loss-over-time for a diffusion model

Backpropagation

The *loss score* is the signal that is used in backpropagation. In this step, the model learns from its mistakes. The algorithm works backward from the loss value through every layer of the network, including the feed-forward layers for embedding the text label and timesteps and the convolutional layers. It calculates how much each individual weight contributed to the final error and then nudges every weight in a direction that makes the loss smaller on the next attempt.

To accomplish this task, we use the Chain Rule (chapter 9) to calculate how much each weight contributes to the final error. The algorithm moves backward from the final layer of the network to the one before it, and so on, all the way to the beginning. At each layer, it calculates the gradient for each weight. The gradient tells the model which direction to nudge the weight to decrease the error. When the gradient for a specific weight is known, the model updates the weight. If a weight's original value is 0.5, learning rate is 0.01, and calculated gradient is -0.5, the update would be determined as shown in figure 12.47.

```
new weight = old weight - (learning rate × gradient)

new weight = 0.5000 - (0.01 * -0.5)
new weight = 0.5000 - (-0.005)
new weight = 0.5050
```

Figure 12.47 Adjusting weights based on loss

This adjustment, applied to all weights over thousands or millions of training steps, at allows the U-Net to refine its understanding and improve its ability to generate images. In figure 12.48, every arrow indicates the layers and their respective weights, which will be updated during backpropagation.

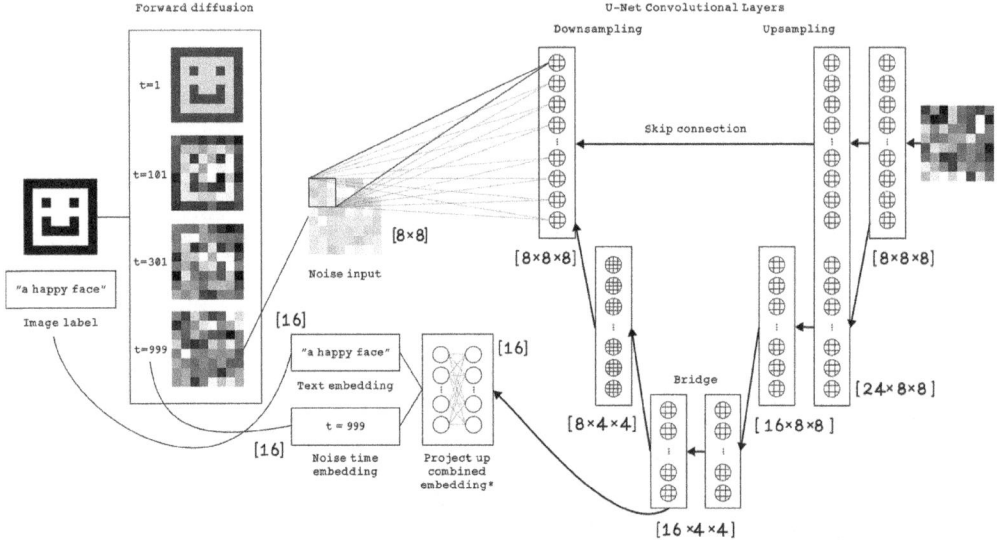

Figure 12.48 The components whose weights are updated with backpropagation

Generating an image

Now that the U-Net has been trained, we can use it for its main purpose: generating a new image from a text prompt (figure 12.49). This process, often called *inference,* and applies the diffusion process in reverse. We start with pure noise and use the trained model to denoise it step by step until a clean image emerges.

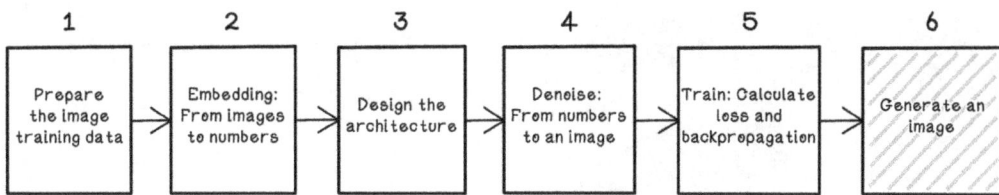

Figure 12.49 Generating an image in the diffusion model life cycle

Python code sample for backpropagation

This code shows how to calculate loss and perform backpropagation in a diffusion model. It begins by computing the MSE between predicted and actual noise across all pixels, producing a scalar loss value. Then it performs backpropagation, iterating backward through each model layer to compute gradients of the loss with respect to each weight using the Chain Rule. Each weight is updated using gradient descent, scaled by the learning rate. This process gradually tunes the model to predict noise more accurately over many training steps.

Calculates the pixel-by-pixel difference

```python
def calculate_loss_and_backprop(predicted_noise, actual_noise,
    learning_rate):

    error = predicted_noise - actual_noise

    loss = np.mean(np.square(error))

    dummy_weights = ['conv1_w', 'resblock_b_w',
        'attn_v_w', 'proj_up_w']

    backprop_and_update(dummy_weights, loss, learning_rate)

    return loss
```

Squashes the error into a single positive number

Lists the key components of the U-Net

Triggers the math that flows backward through the entire U-Net

Starting with a blank canvas (of pure noise)

Unlike the training process, the inference process doesn't start with an existing image. Instead, it begins with a blank canvas filled with random noise (figure 12.50). We create an 8×8 matrix of random numbers drawn from a standard normal distribution. Remember that drawing numbers from the standard normal distribution will result in statistically predictable random numbers.

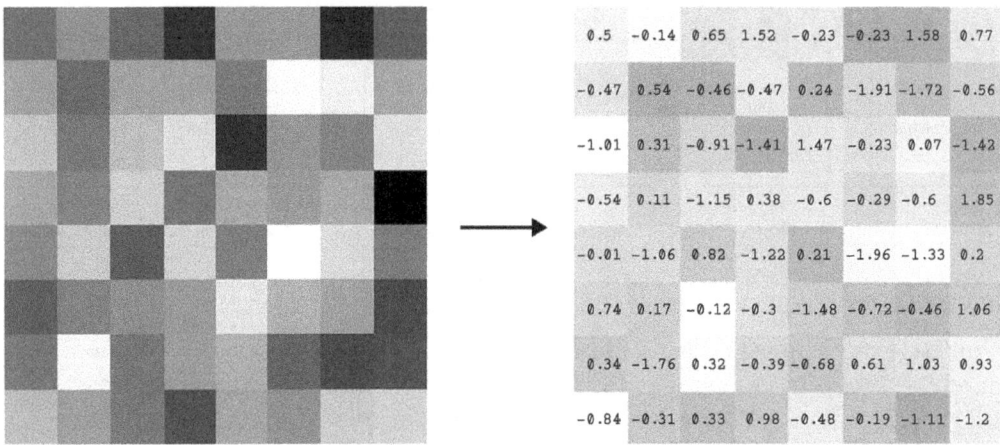

Figure 12.50 Starting with pure noise for making a prediction

This noisy canvas is what an image looks like at the final timestep (t = 1000) of the forward-diffusion process. Think of this noisy image as a block of marble. The final, coherent image is already hidden inside. The U-Net's job is to act as a sculptor, carefully chiseling away the noise to reveal a masterpiece within.

Denoising the data

The model works backward from timestep 1000 (or the total timesteps in forward diffusion) to timestep 0. This happens inside a loop that iteratively cleans the image, with each step making the image slightly less noisy and over time making the image more true to its predicted form. At each step in the loop, several things happen (figure 12.51).

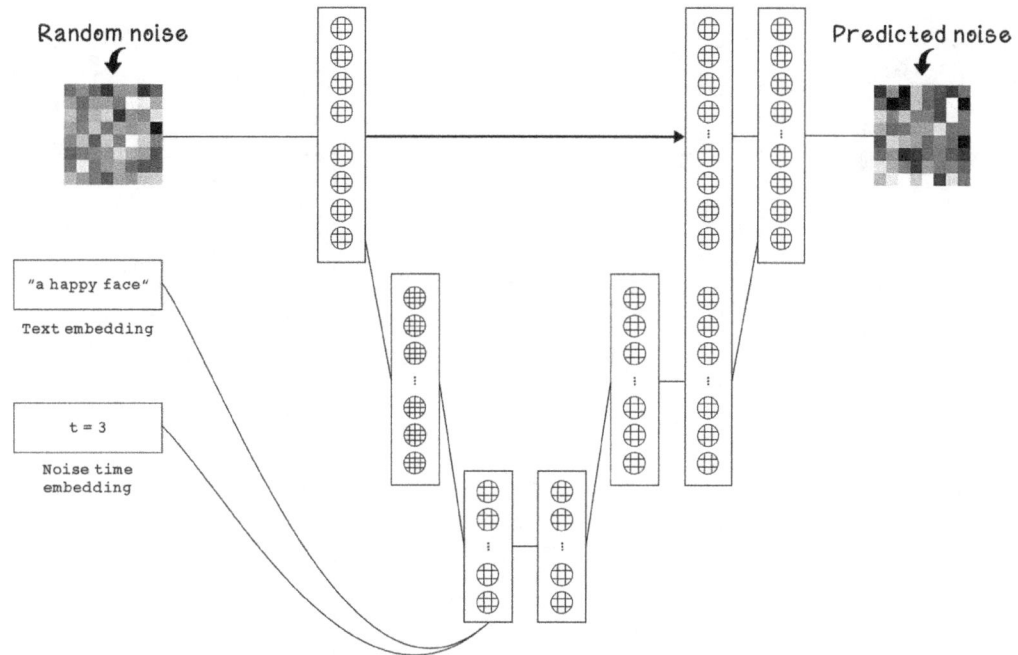

Figure 12.51 How a denoised image is predicted

Predict the noise

The U-Net is given three inputs: the current noisy image, the current timestep (t), and the text prompt embedding (such as "a happy face"). With this information, the U-Net predicts the noise pattern that it thinks is present in the image at that specific timestep.

Subtract the noise

We use this prediction to take one small step toward a cleaner image. Remember during the forward-diffusion process, we calculated a noise schedule. We use the same schedule constants (alphas and betas) to calculate exactly how much of the predicted noise to subtract from the current image. We have to use the same alphas and betas because the denoising (reverse) process is designed to be the mathematical mirror of the noising (forward) process. The schedule of alphas and betas acts as a precise, shared recipe for both adding and removing noise. Figure 12.51 conceptually illustrates the end-to-end process of predicting a denoised image.

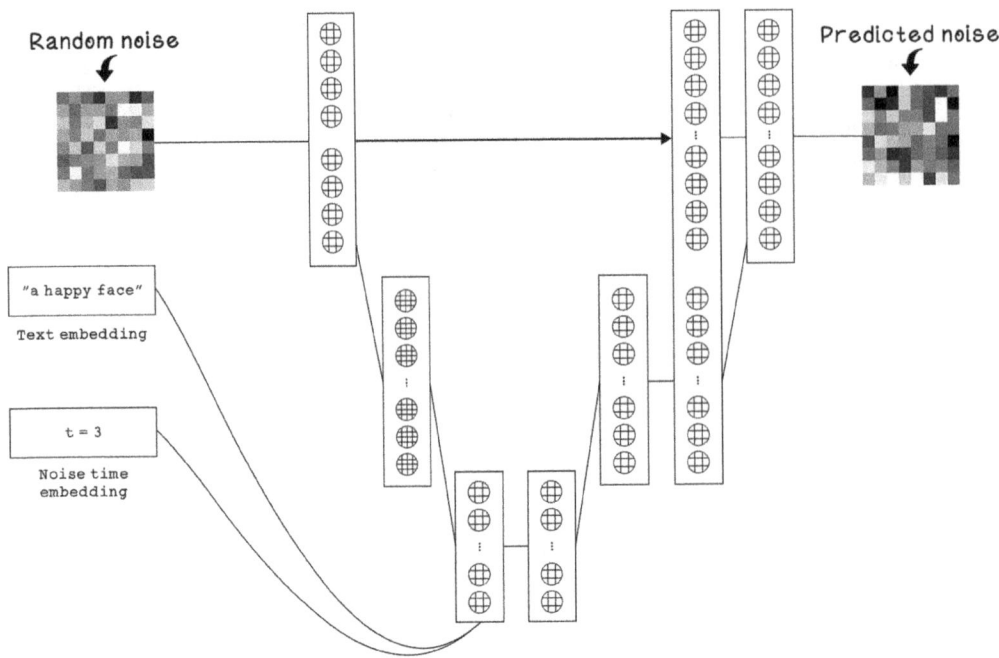

Figure 12.51 How a denoised image is predicted

Table 12.4 shows the alphas and betas that were previously calculated. Figure 12.52 is the denoising calculation for timestep 1000. First, we calculate the timestep scale, which determines how much of the predicted noise we must subtract from the current image in question.

Table 12.4 A subset of values for the noise schedule

Timestep (t)	Beta	Alpha calculation (1 - beta)	Alpha	Alpha-Bar calculation	Alpha-Bar
1	0.00010	1 - 0.00010	0.99990	0.99990	0.99990
2	0.00012	1 - 0.00012	0.99988	0.99990 × 0.99988	0.99978
3	0.00014	1 - 0.00014	0.99986	0.99990 × 0.99988 × 0.99986	0.99964
			...		
1000	0.02000	1 - 0.02000	0.98000		0.00004

Timestep scale for t = 1000

$$\text{timestep scale} = \frac{1 - \text{alpha}}{\sqrt{1 - \text{alpha-bar}}}$$

$$\text{timestep scale} = \frac{1 - 0.98}{\sqrt{1 - 0.00004}}$$

$$\text{timestep scale} = 0.01998$$

Figure 12.52 Calculations for finding timestep scale for timestep 1000

Typically, the scale is larger closer to the initial noise timestep and smaller closer to the final image generated step. This means the model takes a bigger, more aggressive step, subtracting a significant portion of the predicted noise at the beginning. Then, taking tiny, cautious steps, it subtracts only a minuscule amount of the predicted noise, like a sculptor chiseling out fine details.

Exercise: What is the timestep scale for t = 3?

Calculate the timestep scale for timestep 3.

Solution:

Timestep scale for t = 3

$$\text{timestep scale} = \frac{1 - \text{alpha}}{\sqrt{1 - \text{alpha-bar}}}$$

$$\text{timestep scale} = \frac{1 - 0.99986}{\sqrt{1 - 0.99964}}$$

$$\text{timestep scale} = 0.00738$$

(continued)

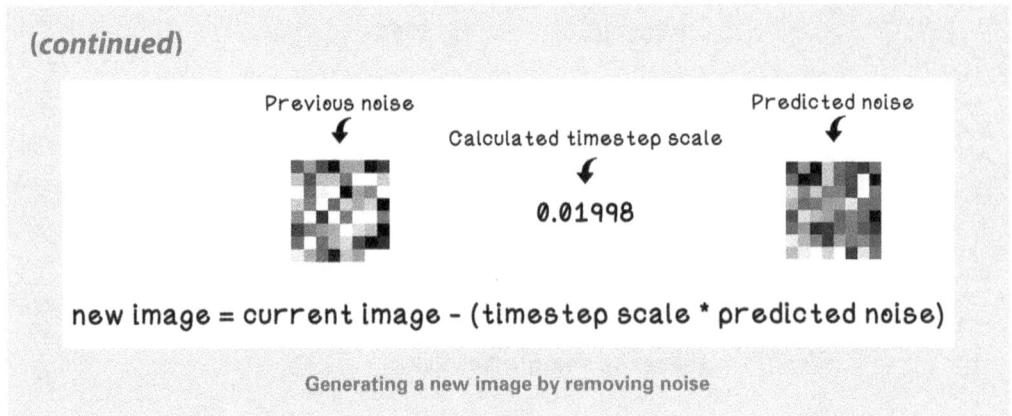

Generating a new image by removing noise

The calculated timestep scale is used with the current input matrix and predicted noise to produce the new image from the network. To do this, subtract the predicted noise at the respective scale, as shown in the following figure.

Repeat

This cycle of predicting and subtracting a small amount of noise is repeated hundreds of times. With each iteration, the image becomes less noisy and more defined, gradually revealing the final result guided by the text prompt.

Figure 12.53 shows the chaotic nature of the denoising process at the start. Notice that the noise changes dramatically but still doesn't resemble a happy face.

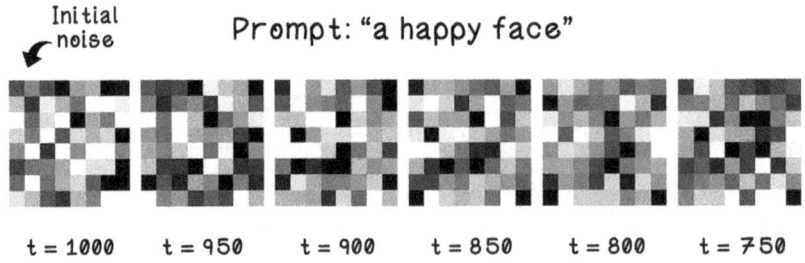

Figure 12.53 The denoised images from timestep 1000 to timestep 750

In the timesteps closer to the final timestep, however, a resemblance to a happy face starts appearing as soon as timestep 100 and gradually denoises to an almost perfect image at timestep 1 (figure 12.54).

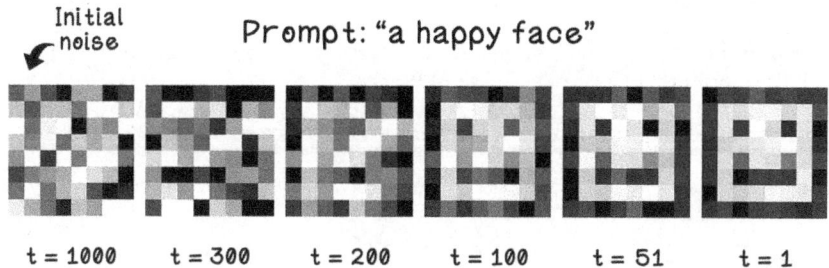

Figure 12.54 The denoised images from timestep 1000 to timestep 1

As an interesting experiment, we can tinker with the timesteps in the inference stage. In figure 12.55, we're cycling through only 50 timesteps. We have fewer opportunities to remove noise, and because diffusion models excel at removing small amounts of noise at a time, the final image is poorer than it was when we ran it over 1,000 timesteps.

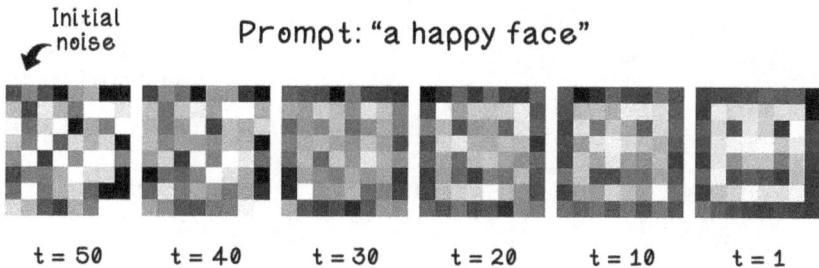

Figure 12.55 The denoised images when we generate with only 50 timesteps instead of 1,000

Python code sample for generating an image

This code describes the inference process for generating an image from a text prompt using a trained diffusion model. It starts with pure Gaussian noise and iteratively denoises it over a defined number of timesteps. At each step, it generates a timestep embedding, combines it with the text embedding, and passes the embeddings through the U-Net to predict the noise present in the image. Then it uses the learned noise schedule (alphas and betas) to subtract the predicted noise, gradually refining the image. After all timesteps, the result is a fully generated image guided by the input prompt.

```
def generate_image_with_prompt(prompt, total_timesteps):

    alpha_schedule, beta_schedule, alpha_bar_schedule =
    ➡define_schedules(total_timesteps)

    text_embedding = create_text_embedding(prompt, EMBEDDING_SIZE)

    current_image = np.random.randn(IMAGE_H, IMAGE_W)

    for t in range(total_timesteps, 0, -1):

        idx = t - 1

        timestep_embedding =
        ➡create_timestep_embedding(t, EMBEDDING_SIZE)
        combined_embedding = inject_embeddings_into_bridge(None,
        ➡text_embedding, timestep_embedding)

        predicted_noise = run_unet_forward_pass(current_image,
        ➡combined_embedding, t)

        alpha_t = alpha_schedule[idx]
        alpha_bar_t = alpha_bar_schedule[idx]
        beta_t = beta_schedule[idx]

        noise_scale = 1.0 / np.sqrt(alpha_t)
        residual_scale = (1.0 - alpha_t) / np.sqrt(1.0 - alpha_bar_t)

        denoised_image = noise_scale *
        ➡(current_image - residual_scale * predicted_noise)

        if t > 1:
            z = np.random.randn(*current_image.shape)
            sigma_t = np.sqrt(beta_t)
            denoised_image += sigma_t * z

        current_image = denoised_image

    return current_image
```

We start with pure, 100% Gaussian noise

move backward from T

We show the U-Net the current messy image and the text prompt

This is the core subtraction

The slightly cleaner image becomes the starting point for the next

Controlling the diffusion model

Congratulations—you've completed the entire training and inference cycle for a generative image model using diffusion. It's amazing and interesting that something as counterintuitive as learning how noise can be removed can produce the fantastical images that modern image generation models create. Large-scale models are trained with billions of images, have more channels to support color images, have thousands of nodes in their U-Net layers, and perform many more matrix-manipulation operations than we used in this small example. Even so, the core principles are the same, just scaled up. Now let's explore ways to control the effectiveness of training and the quality of the images generated by a model.

Training data composition and diversity

Before a diffusion model touches a pixel, we need to decide what kind of visual world it should learn from. The quality, diversity, and structure of an image dataset are crucial to how flexible, creative, and useful the model will be. Just as an LLM trained on narrow legal text might struggle with poetry, an image model trained solely on X-rays won't know how to paint a dog in a sunflower field—not because it's unintelligent but because it's never seen that image. The dataset defines the model's visual vocabulary, which includes the following:

- *What kinds of objects exist*
- *What relationships those objects have*
- *What textures, styles, lighting, and colors appear*
- *What prompts those images were paired with*

In essence, the dataset sets the imaginative boundaries of your model. If your dataset is filled with architectural blueprints, don't expect it to generate whimsical landscapes. But if you feed it a variety of paintings, photos, doodles, and diagrams, you're giving it the essence for creativity. Consider the effect of training on a narrow dataset versus a broad one:

- *A narrow dataset* (such as chest X-rays, satellite images, or architecture diagrams) trains the model to be expert-level in one thing. This is great for niche tasks but not for general-purpose image generation.
- *A broad dataset* teaches the model about the messy, diverse real world: cities, people, animals, art, memes, and so on. These models generalize much better.

Timesteps and noise schedule

Diffusion models are trained to do one main thing: recover a clean image from a noisy one. But how that noise is added, how much, how fast, and over how many steps plays an important role in how well the model learns to denoise and generate sharp, coherent images. This process is controlled by the *noise schedule*, the crafted plan that determines how much noise is added at each timestep during training. There are a few popular choices for the noise schedule:

- *Linear*—Noise is added at a steady, constant rate. This option is simple but not always ideal. Early steps may be too subtle and later ones too aggressive.
- *Cosine*—This schedule starts gently and accelerates over time, resulting in smoother degradation, especially in the early timesteps, giving the model a more consistent training signal. Many modern models prefer this option.
- *Sigmoid or custom*—The exotic schedules try to tailor the noise curve to the dataset. They can offer improvements but are harder to tune manually.

The core idea is that how you destroy the image determines how easy it is to learn to reverse that destruction. If your noise schedule is too harsh in the early stages, the model may struggle to learn. If the noise schedule is too gentle, the later steps become computationally expensive, with diminishing returns.

Attention layers and cross-attention injection

In our example, we've manually translated the prompt "a happy face" into a vector of numbers that we used to train the U-Net at the level of the bridge. But in a large-scale model, the words and their relationships to the vast model space are much more complex and interconnected. This is where the powerful tool of attention plays a role. As in LLMs, where self-attention helps tokens find semantic relationships, in U-Nets, the text-label embedding is applied through cross-attention with the noise pixels and becomes associated with the patterns found. The image features act as the Queries (Q). The text embedding acts as Keys (K) and Values (V). See chapter 11 for more on Queries, Keys, and Values for attention.

Remember our earlier prompt "a snail surfing on a wave of lava in the style of Van Gogh." The model learns to attend to relevant words while refining each region of the image. This lets the model decide things like these:

- Which parts of the text label/text prompt apply to this layer
- Which word is relevant to this spatial feature
- Whether this patch should be yellow because of the word *sunlight*
- Whether that patch should be rounded because it's a snail

Figure 12.56 illustrates how cross-attention can be applied in the model architecture we've explored in this chapter. Cross-attention is an additional layer of abstraction between the downsampling and upsampling layers.

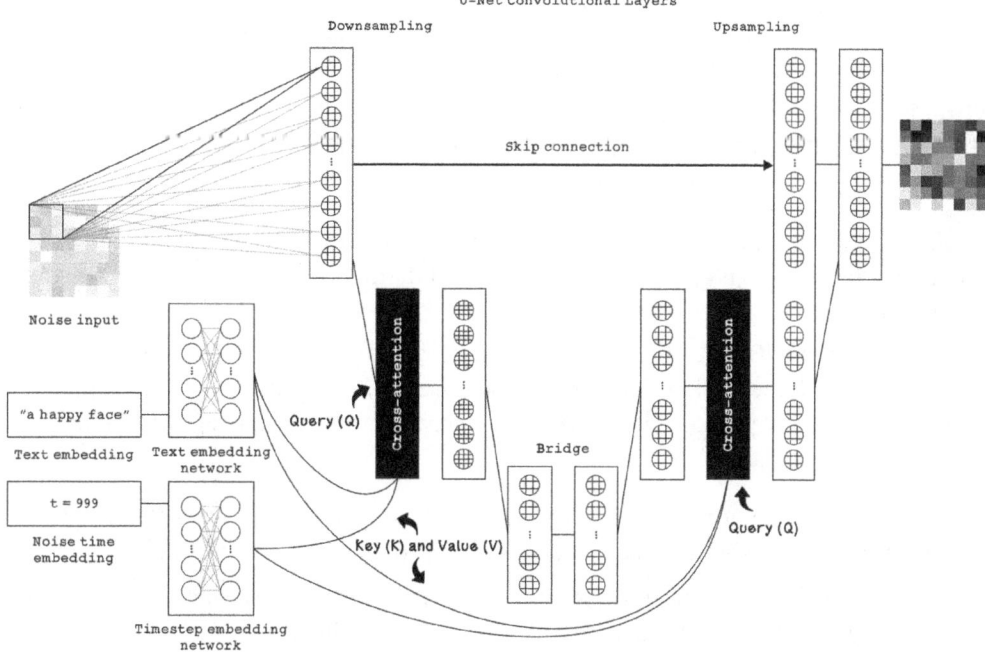

Figure 12.56 How cross-attention fits into the U-Net architecture

In large-scale models that have many of these layers, cross-attention is applied at each stage:

- *Deeper layers* (low-resolution layers at the bottom of the diagram) focus on layout and composition, such as where the snail is and where the lava is.
- *Shallower layers* (high-resolution layers at the top of the diagram) refine details such as what the snail's shell looks like and how many brush strokes to simulate for Vincent Van Gogh's style.

Cross-attention is the bridge between language and vision. By injecting attention at each stage, the model builds a coherent scene that aligns with the text prompt.

Training epochs

Diffusion models are powerful, but they're also computationally expensive and sensitive to overtraining. Let a diffusion model run too long, and it may memorize the training set instead of learning how to generalize. If you let it stop too early, the images it generates may look noisy, dull, or half-baked.

Finding the balanced moment to stop training is a key part of controlling the overall quality. We want to find where the model has learned enough to generate high-quality images without slipping into overfitting.

With LLMs, we measure the next-token prediction loss. Diffusion models require alternative signals to tell us when training is going well. Here are the most common metrics used to guide training duration:

- *Validation loss*—Measures how well the model predicts the noise on a validation set of image–noise pairs it's never seen before. If validation loss stops improving or starts increasing, the model is overfitting.
- *Fréchet inception distance (FID) score*—A statistical comparison between the generated images and real ones. A low FID means that your model is producing images that look more like real photos. This metric is slower to compute but provides a strong perceptual quality signal.

The trick is not to wait for training to collapse. Instead, you want to track these signals as early indicators of whether the model is still improving or starting to stall.

As in other deep learning models that are computationally expensive and time intensive, it's always a good idea to save checkpoints. This means saving the model's state, including weights, and points in the training process. With a diffusion model, monitor the validation loss or FID score, and save a new best model only when performance improves. This gives you a single golden checkpoint without using massive storage space.

Inpainting and outpainting

Beyond creating images from scratch, diffusion models are powerful tools for editing existing images. These techniques allow a user to selectively add, remove, or change parts of an image:

- *Inpainting* is like using a magical erase-and-redraw tool. A user can mask (erase) an unwanted object or area in a picture and then provide a new text prompt describing what should be in its place. The diffusion model performs its denoising process only within the masked region. It uses the surrounding pixels as context to ensure that the newly generated content blends seamlessly with the rest of the image.
- *Outpainting* (often called *uncropping*) is like infinitely expanding the canvas. A user takes an existing image and extends its borders, creating a blank area around it. This blank area acts as the mask. Then the model looks at the original image and the text prompt and hallucinates what should exist beyond the original borders, creating a wider, panoramic scene that makes sense given the starting picture.

To support these features, the U-Net must be aware of which parts of the image to change (the mask) and which parts to use as context. During the denoising process, after each step in which the U-Net predicts noise, the model uses the mask to paste back the original known pixels from the unmasked region. This ensures that only the area you want to change is progressively denoised while the context from the original image remains locked in place, resulting in a seamless blend.

Low-rank adaptation

Fine-tuning a massive, multigigabyte diffusion model for a specific art style or character, for example, is computationally expensive and would result in a new, equally massive file for every concept that we want to focus on. Low-rank adaptation (LoRA) is an efficient technique that solves this problem.

Think of the main diffusion model as a master artist with a vast library of skills. A LoRA is a tiny set of instruction notes (often 10–100 MB) that you give the artist. These notes don't teach the artist how to paint; they provide the small, specific adjustments required to draw in a new style or capture a particular character's likeness.

Technically, LoRA works by freezing the model's original, massive weight matrices and training two much smaller, low-rank matrices that capture the changes required for the new style. During generation, the outputs from these small matrices are added to the outputs of the original model, effectively adapting its style on the fly. This allows users to have a single base model and thousands of small LoRA files to switch rapidly among countless art styles, characters, and concepts.

High-resolution fixes and upscalers

Diffusion models are typically trained on images of a fixed size (such as 512×512). Generating directly at high resolutions can cause strange artifacts, such as repeated heads or distorted composition. To create large, detailed images, we often use a two-stage process:

- *High-resolution fix*—This technique is used during the initial text-to-image generation. First, the model generates a smaller, coherent image (such as 512×512) to get the overall composition right. Then it upscales this image slightly and runs a few final diffusion steps to add detail at the higher resolution without breaking the underlying structure.
- *Dedicated upscalers*—After a good image has been generated, a separate, specialized AI model called an *upscaler* can be used. Upscalers are trained for one task: taking a low-resolution image and intelligently adding new pixels to increase the image size (2x or 4x, for example) while preserving and often enhancing the clarity and detail of the image.

ControlNets and Image Prompt Adapters

A text prompt provides general guidance. But ControlNets and Image Prompt Adapters (IP-Adapters) offer much more direct and fine-grained control of the final image's composition and style.

ControlNets act as structural guides. They're auxiliary neural networks that run alongside the main U-Net. A user provides a control map, such as a human pose skeleton, a Canny edge map (a simple line-art outline of an image), or a depth map along with the text prompt. Think of this input image as the blueprint. The ControlNet reads this blueprint and injects guidance signals directly into the layers of the main diffusion model, forcing the generated image to conform strictly to the structure of your blueprint (the lines or pose) while using the text prompt to fill in the colors, lighting, and textures.

IP-Adapters function as style and character reference sheets. An IP-Adapter is a small module that allows you to provide a reference image along with your text prompt. The adapter extracts the core stylistic elements or character features from the reference image and injects this information into the U-Net's attention layers. This allows you to generate new compositions based on your text prompt that mimic the style or feature of the character from your reference image.

Refining aesthetics with human feedback

A diffusion model can learn to create an image accurately from a prompt, but it doesn't inherently know what makes an image beautiful, aesthetically pleasing, or even as accurate as it could be. This is where a process similar to reinforcement learning with human feedback (RLHF), which is used to align LLMs, comes into play.

Think of it as sending the model to art school. Here is how this training curriculum is structured:

1. *Collect human feedback.* First, the model generates several images for the same prompt, varying the initial noisy image fed into the model. Thousands of human labelers review these images and rank them from best to worst based on aesthetic appeal.

2. *Train a reward model.* A separate aesthetics predictor model is trained on this dataset of human preferences. Its only job is to learn to predict which images a human would find most visually appealing, outputting a single aesthetics score.

3. *Fine-tune with reinforcement learning.* Finally, the main diffusion model is fine-tuned. It generates an image, the aesthetics predictor gives it a score, and this score is used as a reward to update the diffusion model's weights. Over time, the model learns to generate images that not only match the prompt but are also consistently scored higher for aesthetic quality.

Use cases for image generation

Image generation models are a significant leap in AI's ability to create, modify, and conceptualize visual content. Because they're trained on vast, diverse datasets of images and their corresponding text descriptions, they learn the intricate relationships between concepts and visual aesthetics. This deep understanding allows them to act as powerful visual synthesizers, translating complex text prompts into unique, high-quality images. Using one of these models is like having a world-class artist and photographer on call, ready to create any scene imaginable. They unlock the potential for a wide variety of tasks that were previously expensive or time-consuming or that required specialized skills.

Creative ideation and concept art

For artists, designers, and creators, the most difficult step can be overcoming the blank canvas. An image generation model can act as a powerful brainstorming partner, rapidly generating a wide range of visual ideas based on a simple prompt. The process becomes one of augmentation, in which the human guides the creative direction and refines the AI-generated concepts rather than starting from scratch. Here is how this capability serves some creative industries:

- *Entertainment industry (film and gaming)*—Concept artists can generate dozens of variations for characters, environments, creatures, and props in minutes instead of days. This allows directors and creative leads to visualize and approve a direction much earlier in the production pipeline.
- *Graphic design and illustration*—Designers can use these models to create initial drafts for logos, posters, book covers, and other illustrations. This provides a rich starting point that can be professionally refined and customized.

Commercial design and advertising

Creating high-quality visual assets for commercial use often requires expensive and logistically complex photoshoots. Image generation models offer a fast and cost-effective alternative for creating unique, on-brand imagery. Here are a few examples of how businesses use image generation:

- *Marketing and advertising*—Creative teams can produce multiple versions of ad visuals for A/B testing, generate social media content tailored to different platforms, or create entire campaign aesthetics without a single photographer, model, or location.
- *Product visualization*—Companies can generate realistic mockups of products in

various lifestyle settings. A new brand of handbag can be shown in a city, at the beach, or in a cafe, allowing marketing teams to create compelling visuals before the product is manufactured.

- *Architectural and interior design*—Architects and designers can turn blueprints or simple descriptions into photorealistic renders of buildings and interior spaces, helping clients visualize the final result long before construction begins.

Content creation and media

Image generation models can create perfectly tailored visual assets on demand, freeing content creators from the limitations of generic stock-photo libraries. Consider how this flexibility benefits different types of visual creators:

- *Custom stock photography*—Bloggers, journalists, and corporate presenters can generate a specific image that perfectly matches their content—for example, "a scientist in a lab looking at a blue liquid in a beaker with a concerned expression"— instead of spending hours searching for a suitable-but-not-perfect stock photo.
- *Fashion design*—Designers can visualize entire clothing collections on a diverse range of virtual models, experimenting with fabrics, colors, and styles instantly, dramatically speeding the design and prototyping phase.

Personalization and photo editing

These tools empower individuals to become creators and editors, regardless of their technical skill. Here are two ways people can use these capabilities for their own projects:

- *Personalized content*—Users can create custom avatars for their social media profiles or unique banners for their channels, or simply generate art for personal projects and enjoyment.
- *Intelligent photo editing*—Using inpainting, a user can easily remove an unwanted person or object from a personal photograph by masking it out and letting AI fill in the background. With outpainting, they can take a favorite photo and expand its borders, allowing AI to creatively extend the scene.

SUMMARY OF GENERATIVE IMAGE MODELS

Counterintuitively, Diffusion starts with noise and learns how to remove tiny bits to reveal a clear image

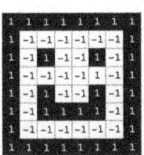 = [[1, 1, 1, 1, 1, 1, 1,1],
[1,-1,-1,-1,-1,-1,-1, 1],
[1,-1, 1,-1,-1, 1,-1, 1],
[1,-1,-1,-1,-1,-1,-1, 1],
[1,-1, 1,-1,-1, 1,-1, 1],
[1,-1, 1, 1, 1, 1,-1, 1],
[1,-1,-1,-1,-1,-1,-1, 1],
[1, 1, 1, 1, 1, 1, 1,1]]

a happy face

Images are nothing but numbers represented as matrices.

CNNs are crucial for learning shapes, colors, textures, subjects, and more.

Downsampling, embedding injection, upsampling, and skip connections are the core superpowers of the U-Net.

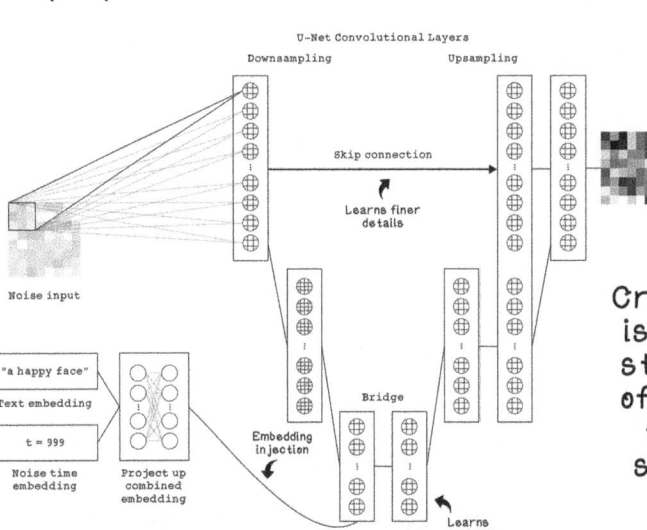

Cross-attention is powerful for strong learning of rich prompts to generate sophisticated images.

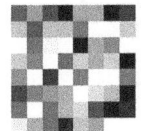     

index

RELATED MANNING TITLES

Deep Learning with Python, Third Edition
by François Chollet, Matthew Watson

ISBN 9781633436589
648 pages, $79.99
September 2025

Timeless Algorithms: The Seminal Papers
by Gary Sutton

ISBN 9781633434462
375 pages (estimated), $69.99
August 2026 (estimated)

Deep Learning with R, Third Edition
by François Chollet, Tomasz Kalinowski

ISBN 9781633435186
700 pages (estimated), $79.99
March 2026 (estimated)

For ordering information, go to www.manning.com

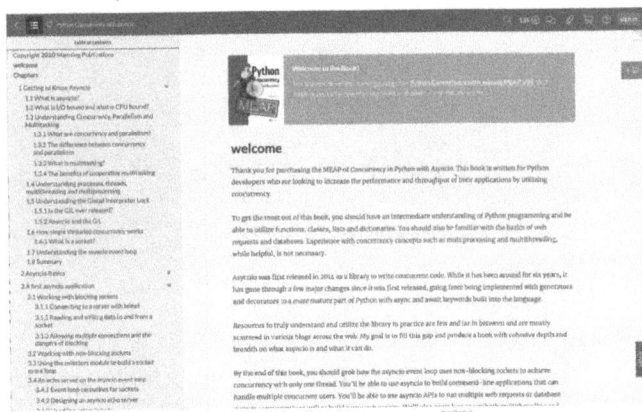

A new online reading experience

liveBook, our online reading platform, adds a new dimension to your Manning books, with features that make reading, learning, and sharing easier than ever. A liveBook version of your book is included FREE with every Manning book.

This next generation book platform is more than an online reader. It's packed with unique features to upgrade and enhance your learning experience.

- Add your own notes and bookmarks
- One-click code copy
- Learn from other readers in the discussion forum
- Audio recordings and interactive exercises
- Read all your purchased Manning content in any browser, anytime, anywhere

As an added bonus, you can search every Manning book and video in liveBook—even ones you don't yet own. Open any liveBook, and you'll be able to browse the content and read anything you like.*

Find out more at www.manning.com/livebook-program.

*Open reading is limited to 10 minutes per book daily